Sleeping price codes

LL	over CUC$200
L	CUC$151-200
AL	CUC$101-150
A	CUC$66-100
B	CUC$46-65
C	CUC$31-45
D	CUC$21-30
E	CUC$12-20

Prices refer to the cost of a double room in the high season, excluding taxes.

Eating price codes

₸₸₸	over CUC$12
₸₸	CUC$6-12
₸	under CUC$6

Prices refer to the cost of a two-course meal for one person.

Cuba
Handbook

Sarah Cameron

**with contributions from
Claire Boobbyer**

Footprint story

It was 1921

Ireland had just been partitioned, the British miners were striking for more pay and the federation of British industry had an idea. Exports were booming in South America – how about a handbook for businessmen trading in that far away continent? The Anglo-South American Handbook was born that year, written by W Koebel, the most prolific writer on Latin America of his day.

1924

Two editions later the book was 'privatized' and in 1924, in the hands of Royal Mail, the steamship company for South America, it became The South American Handbook, subtitled 'South America in a nutshell'. This annual publication became the 'bible' for generations of travellers to South America and remains so to this day. In the early days travel was by sea and the Handbook gave all the details needed for the long voyage from Europe. What to wear for dinner; how to arrange a cricket match with the Cable & Wireless staff on the Cape Verde Islands and a full account of the journey from Liverpool up the Amazon to Manaus: 5898 miles without changing cabin!

1939

As the continent opened up, The South American Handbook reported the new Pan Am flying boat services, and the fortnightly airship service from Rio to Europe on the Graf Zeppelin. For reasons still unclear but with extraordinary determination, the annual editions continued through the Second World War.

1970s

Many more people discovered South America and the backpacking trail started to develop. All the while the Handbook was gathering fans, including literary vagabonds such as Paul Theroux and Graham Greene (who once sent some updates addressed to "The publishers of the best travel guide in the world, Bath, England").

1990s

During the 1990s the company set about developing a new travel guide series using this legendary title as the flagship. By 1997 there were over a dozen guides in the series and the Footprint imprint was launched.

2000s

The series grew quickly and there were soon Footprint travel guides covering more than 150 countries. In 2004, Footprint launched its first thematic guide: *Surfing Europe*, packed with colour photographs, maps and charts. This was followed by further thematic guides such as *Diving the World*, *Snowboarding the World*, *Body and Soul escapes*, *Travel with Kids* and *European City Breaks*.

2010

Today we continue the traditions of the last 89 years that have served legions of travellers so well. We believe that these help to make Footprint guides different. Our policy is to use authors who are genuine experts who write for independent travellers; people possessing a spirit of adventure, looking to get off the beaten track.

Title page: Old Havana.
Above: Traditional transport is of the four-legged and four-wheeled variety in provincial towns.

Cuba is a tropical paradise for foreign holidaymakers where residents play the lottery to get an exit visa. In city centres, from Havana to Santiago, ramshackle streets are lined with decaying colonial mansions and art deco towers, while rectangular Soviet apartment blocks dominate the suburbs. 1950s Cadillacs chug alongside horse-drawn carriages, arthritic rickshaws and sleek diplomats' saloons, swiftly overtaken by bright yellow eggshells on motorbike chassis. Out in the countryside, from the tobacco fields to the Sierra Maestra, the high-ways are lined with billboards extolling the virtues of the Revolution.

Initially a cash cow for Spanish colonial masters, Cuba became a pleasure zone for US neocolonialists in the 20th century. A heady cocktail of gambling, rum and sex lured Americans during Prohibition, when movie stars and mobsters came to sample the wares of celebrity bartenders. Yet life is hard for the average Cuban. The welfare state is unsurpassed but material pleasures are few and far between. Antique Russian fridges and American cars are held together with rubber bands and sticking plaster, and houses crumble into rubble-strewn alleyways. Residents still dust off their ornaments, polish their antiques and surgically scrub their floors and, when it comes to music and dance, their rhythm, skill and innovation make Cubans world leaders.

HAVANA
PINAR DEL RIO
MATANZAS
CENTRE
WEST
THE ISLANDS
CENTRE
EAST
HOLGUIN
& GRANMA
SANTIAGO &
GUANTANAMO

Contents

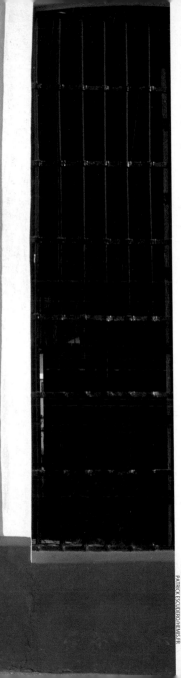

Planning your trip

PATRICK ESCUDERO/HEMIS.FR

Colonial houses in Trinidad, a
UNESCO World Heritage Site, are
painted in a variety of pastel
colours to soften bright sunlight.

• 7

Where to go

Most visitors spend some time in Havana, and the capital city is always a good place to start and gain insight into the culture of the island. The old town, Habana Vieja, is being painstakingly renovated and many of the colonial palaces have been converted into desirable boutique hotels. Others are museums and art galleries containing unrivalled treasures or Revolutionary memorabilia. Theatres, churches, fortresses, a cigar factory, bars, restaurants and a magnificent seafront drive provide plenty to see and do. Further west is the university and the new city, Vedado, where much of the nightlife and cultural activities take place. The enormous Plaza de la Revolución is famed for May Day gatherings and Fidel Castro's interminable speeches as well as for the iconic image of Che Guevara attached to the front of the Ministry of the Interior.

The west end of the island is the major tobacco-growing area, where the rich soil produces crops for some of the best cigars in the world. The beautiful mountain landscape of the Sierra del Rosario, containing a Biosphere Reserve at Las Terrazas, tapers down to the fascinating and evocative limestone *mogotes* around Viñales. When the mists swirl around their sheer cliffs the view is reminiscent of a Chinese painting. There are some good beaches along the north coast and western tip of Pinar del Río province and some excellent diving at María la Gorda and Cayo Levisa.

East of Havana is Varadero, a mega-resort on a thin peninsula, with huge hotels dotted all along the white-sand beach stretching 20 km along the north shore. Like other resort areas along the north coast, such as Cayo Coco or Cayo Santa María, it is a remote enclave, devoted entirely to beach tourism.

Historians and fans of Che Guevara should head east to Santa Clara, a pleasant university city famous for being the site of the last and decisive battle of the Revolution in December 1958. It is also the last resting

REGIEN PAASSEN/SHUTTERSTOCK

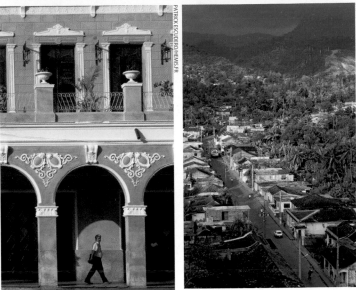

Opposite page: Iconic image of Che on the outside of the Ministry of the Interior in Havana: *Hasta la Victoria Siempre*. **Above left**: Ornate colonnades and balustrades in colonial Camagüey, a UNESCO World Heritage Site since 2008. **Above right**: The fishing town of Baracoa nestles at the foot of mountains covered in lush rainforest.

place of Che and his comrades who were killed in Bolivia. On the south coast, Trinidad is one of the best-preserved towns in the Americas and is a UNESCO World Heritage Site. It remains in a time warp from the Spanish colony of the 19th century, with its cobbled streets, tiled roofs, wrought-iron railings, churches, palaces and humble dwellings.

A journey east through the cattle lands and sugar plantations of central Cuba offers several historical cities convenient for stopovers and detours to north coast beaches. Sancti Spíritus, Ciego de Avila, Camagüey, Las Tunas, Holguín and Bayamo are all benefitting from renovation and beautification projects. Camagüey is also a UNESCO World Heritage Site, with a maze of streets to confuse potential invaders in colonial times. These cities lie along the route to the Sierra Maestra, the eastern

mountain range from where Fidel Castro and his comrades launched their attacks on the dictatorship in the 1950s and which surrounds and protects the second city, Santiago de Cuba.

Sheltered by the mountains, Santiago is hot and steamy, with a culture to match. More Afro-Caribbean than Havana, it also has strong French influences on music, dance and art because of past immigration from Haiti. Carnival in July is a particular highlight, a noisy, colourful, energetic event.

Baracoa, almost as far east as you can get, is an attractive, restful seaside town where travellers come to get away from it all. Backed by mountains and tropical forests intersected by rivers, you can go hiking, river bathing, explore pre-Columbian archaeological sites or just kick off your shoes and relax on a beautiful, unspoiled beach.

Itineraries

Cuba, the largest island in the Caribbean, is nearly as big as England. If your time is restricted you should decide which end of the island you would prefer to see in detail. If you have got all the time in the world, then start at one end and work your way to the other. An excellent road runs all the way from Havana to Santiago down the centre of the island, passing through many of the important cities, with side roads off to other interesting places.

major sites in the suburbs as well as take in some of the nightlife in music-mad Vedado. Use the capital as a base for day trips out to the countryside or the beaches along the coast. Places within striking distance of Havana include the lush green valley of Viñales and the fields of top-class tobacco in the Province of Pinar del Río, or the beaches to the east of the capital, Playas del Este, Jibacoa and the resort of Varadero.

One week

The old colonial city of Havana is unmissable. You need a day to see the old city with its palaces, mansions, museums and plazas and a couple of days to get round some of the

Two weeks

With two weeks you could spend more time in the western province of Pinar del Río and divers would particularly appreciate a few days at the isolated María la Gorda in the far west.

FEDOR KONDRATENKO/SHUTTERSTOCK

Above: Skilfully rolling the world's best cigars.
Opposite page: Pristine white sand at the beach resort of Varadero.

You could stay a night at the eco-lodge at Las Terrazas where you can go walking in the rainforest and visit the colourful orchid gardens at Soroa. With two weeks, you could explore the UNESCO World Cultural Landscape of the Viñales valley with excursions to the *mogotes* (steep-sided, limestone mountains) and caves before heading up to the north coast beaches. Alternatively head east into the sugar-growing farmlands and forested mountains in the centre of the island. Allow yourself a couple of nights in Santa Clara, last resting place of Che Guevara; visit the Che memorial and the cays off the north coast via the charming old town of Remedios. Trinidad, the UNESCO World Heritage Site with its single-storey 18th- and 19th-century houses and cobbled streets, is a must-see on anyone's itinerary. Allow plenty of time to explore the town and surrounding areas, including the Valley of the Sugar Mills, the Escambray mountains and the beach at Ancón as well as enjoy the nightlife. The return trip to Havana could take in Cienfuegos for its colonial architecture and fortress, the Bay of Pigs and the Zapata Peninsula if you have your own car. The route Havana–Santa Clara–Trinidad–Cienfuegos–Havana can be done by bus.

Four weeks

A month will give you more time to get to know both ends of the island and some places in between. The central towns are often missed because travellers concentrate on one end of the island or the other and skip the bits in between. Nevertheless, colonial Camagüey is well worth a day's exploration. If taking the bus or train the length of the island, make sure you break your journey in this city, preferably on a Saturday, when the streets come alive at night for an open-air fiesta: Noche Camagüeya. From here you can take in a day trip to the beach at Playa Santa Lucía. Another recommended break in the journey is at Bayamo, the jumping-off point for hiking in the Sierra Maestra and a visit to Castro's atmospheric mountain headquarters during the Revolution. Lively Santiago de Cuba,

Cuba's second city, is an infectious contrast to the capital, with an Afro-Caribbean culture laced with French influences, and where the climate is hotter and drier. You need up to two weeks to do justice to these eastern parts of the island: as well as experiencing Santiago de Cuba, there are excellent day excursions to La Gran Piedra, a tremendous viewpoint from where it is claimed that you can see Haiti and Jamaica on a clear day, and El Cobre, where the shrine of Cuba's patron saint is built over a working copper mine. An easterly round trip will take in Guantánamo (see the US Naval base through binoculars), Baracoa (currently one of the most popular destinations for its beaches and laid-back lifestyle), Holguín and the beaches of Guardalavaca, before returning to Santiago through the mountains or back to Havana. The main towns can be reached by bus or train, but places off the beaten track are difficult to get to on public transport and it is advisable to rent a car unless you like negotiating travel by truck.

Cuba highlights

See colour maps at back of book

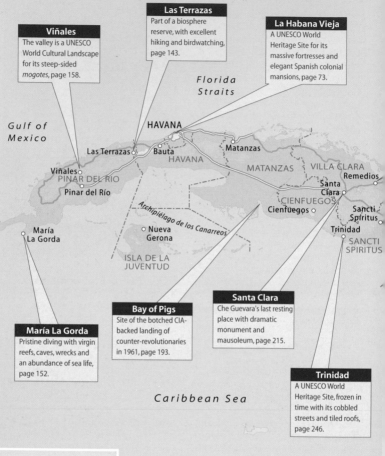

Viñales
The valley is a UNESCO World Cultural Landscape for its steep-sided *mogotes*, page 158.

Las Terrazas
Part of a biosphere reserve, with excellent hiking and birdwatching, page 143.

La Habana Vieja
A UNESCO World Heritage Site for its massive fortresses and elegant Spanish colonial mansions, page 73.

Florida Straits

Gulf of Mexico

HAVANA

Las Terrazas ○   ○ Bauta   HAVANA   ○ Matanzas

MATANZAS   VILLA CLARA

Viñales ○
PINAR DEL RÍO
○ Pinar del Río

Santa Clara
CIENFUEGOS
Cienfuegos ○

Remedios ○

Sancti Spíritus

Trinidad

Archipiélago de los Canarreos

○ María La Gorda

○ Nueva Gerona

SANCTI SPIRITUS

ISLA DE LA JUVENTUD

María La Gorda
Pristine diving with virgin reefs, caves, wrecks and an abundance of sea life, page 152.

Bay of Pigs
Site of the botched CIA-backed landing of counter-revolutionaries in 1961, page 193.

Santa Clara
Che Guevara's last resting place with dramatic monument and mausoleum, page 215.

Trinidad
A UNESCO World Heritage Site, frozen in time with its cobbled streets and tiled roofs, page 246.

Caribbean Sea

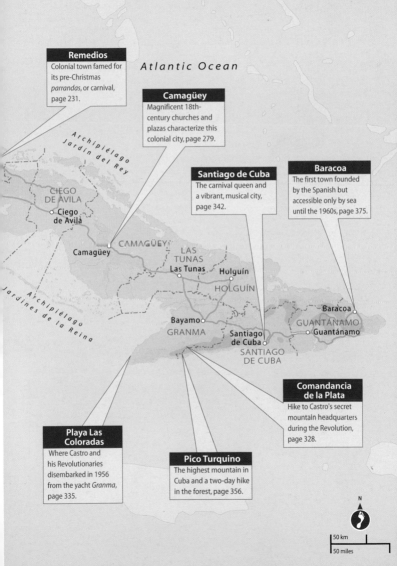

Remedios
Colonial town famed for its pre-Christmas *parrandas*, or carnival, page 231.

Atlantic Ocean

Camagüey
Magnificent 18th-century churches and plazas characterize this colonial city, page 279.

Santiago de Cuba
The carnival queen and a vibrant, musical city, page 342.

Baracoa
The first town founded by the Spanish but accessible only by sea until the 1960s, page 375.

Archipiélago Jardín del Rey

CIEGO DE AVILA
○ Ciego de Avila

Archipiélago Jardines de la Reina

CAMAGÜEY

● Camagüey

LAS TUNAS
○ Las Tunas

○ Holguín
HOLGUÍN

● Baracoa
GUANTÁNAMO
○ Guantánamo

Bayamo ○
GRANMA
Santiago de Cuba ○
SANTIAGO DE CUBA

Comandancia de la Plata
Hike to Castro's secret mountain headquarters during the Revolution, page 328.

Playa Las Coloradas
Where Castro and his Revolutionaries disembarked in 1956 from the yacht *Granma*, page 335.

Pico Turquino
The highest mountain in Cuba and a two-day hike in the forest, page 356.

N

50 km
50 miles

Music and dance

Tradition and roots

Cuban music, famously vibrant, is a marriage of African rhythms, expressed in percussion instruments and the Spanish guitar, accompanied by an equally strong tradition of dance. There are four basic elements out of which all others grow: The **rumba** is one of the original black dance forms, which transferred from the plantations to the slums around the end of the 19th century. Originating in eastern Cuba, **son** is the music out of which salsa was born. **Danzón** was originally ballroom dance music but was the root for the cha-cha-cha, invented in 1948. The fourth tradition is **trova**, the itinerant troubadour singing ballads, which has been transformed, post-Revolution, into the Nueva Trova, made famous by singers such as Pablo Milanés and Silvio Rodríguez. The new tradition adds politics and everyday concerns to the romantic themes. There are many other styles, such as the *guajira* (the most famous example of which is the song, *Guantanamera*), *tumba francesa* drumming and dancing, and Afro-Cuban jazz, performed by internationally renowned artists like Irakere and Arturo Sandoval.

Rhythm and ritual

From traditional son to Cuban rap via jazz and salsa, Cuba throbs to drums beating out the rhythm of the island's Afro-Cuban heritage. The sacred *cueros batá* (the three drums used in Santería rites) have been incorporated into mainstream bands, while performances of Yoruba and Congo devotional and profane song and dance are colourful spectacles, with Cubans fervidly chorusing the Santero chants and swaying to the infectious *guaguancó*. Carnival festivities are exuberant and colourful; the best is in Santiago in July when rum-fuelled revellers take to the streets to dance in the conga to ear-splitting drum music.

JULIO MUÑOZ

Above: Carnival comes to the beach, the Semana de la Cultura festival at Playa Ancón, near Trinidad.

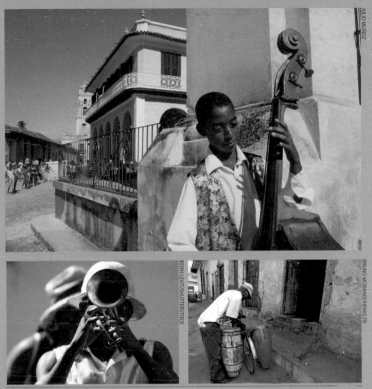

Above: Music pervades daily life throughout Cuba, with a huge variety of styles and instruments reflecting the cultural and ethnic diversity of the people.

Venues

In every town there is a Casa de la Trova, where you can find old-timers crooning the traditional songs, and a club or disco where the local youth party until the small hours. Bars are patrolled by trios, or other small groups, playing all the old favourites and tunes on request while trying to sell their CDs. Check locally for concerts and other events (the Casa de Cultura is always a good place to start in any town), which are often held in the open air, even in the atmospheric shell of a ruined building awaiting funds for restoration.

On the street

Reggaeton, a fusion of reggae, rap, Latin and electronic rhythms, is taking the dance floors by storm, despite official reservations about its 'neoliberal' influence. It is street music with raunchy lyrics and a sensual beat, hugely popular with young Cubans. Cuban reggaeton can't be found in shops, nor on the radio; it is recorded independently, at makeshift studios in people's homes and is distributed via home-made CDs and flash memory sticks. However, it is not a subversive political movement and one artist, Yoandys 'Baby' Lores, has even composed a song, *Creo* (I believe), dedicated to Fidel Castro.

When to go

The high season is from mid-December to mid-April, when there are more dry days, more sunshine and less humidity. The season for hurricanes and tropical storms begins in August and can go on until the end of November. A serious hurricane does not come every year by any means, but in the last few years there have been several storms that have caused flooding and damage to houses and crops. There are also variations in climate on the island: it is hotter and drier in Santiago than in Havana, and wetter and cooler in the mountains than in the lowlands.

Northeast trade winds temper the heat, but summer shade temperatures can rise to 33°C (91.4°F) in Havana, and higher elsewhere, particularly Santiago where it can be unbearably hot in July and August. In winter, day temperatures drop to 20°C (68°F) and there are a few cold days, 8-10°C (45° -50°F), with a north wind. Average rainfall is from 860 mm in Oriente, the east, to 1730 mm in Havana; it falls mostly in the summer and autumn, but there can be torrential rains at any time. Walking is uncomfortable in summer but most offices, hotels, leading restaurants and cinemas are air conditioned.

Special events

Despite the heat, July is a good time to visit Santiago if you want to catch the carnival, although New Year is also lively with parades and street parties. New Year is celebrated everywhere as the anniversary of the 1959 Revolution, so you can expect speeches as well as parties. In Havana, carnival used to be held at weekends between July and August but in 2003 it was moved to November and it is likely to remain a movable feast. If you are staying on the Malecón you won't get much sleep.

Havana	Average temperature in °C max-min	Average rainfall in mm
Jan	26 - 18	71
Feb	26 - 18	46
Mar	27 - 19	46
Apr	29 - 21	58
May	30 - 22	119
Jun	31 - 23	165
Jul	32 - 24	125
Aug	32 - 24	135
Sep	31 - 24	150
Oct	29 - 23	173
Nov	27 - 21	79
Dec	26 - 19	58

Santiago de Cuba	Average temperature in °C max-min	Average rainfall in mm
Jan	30 - 20	15
Feb	30 - 20	13
Mar	30 - 22	17
Apr	31 - 23	17
May	32 - 24	44
Jun	32 - 25	18
Jul	33 - 25	25
Aug	33 - 25	29
Sep	33 - 25	52
Oct	32 - 24	65
Nov	32 - 23	32
Dec	30 - 22	11

Opposite page: Stress relief; El Saltón waterfalls in the Sierra Maestra where you can relax, have a massage, bathe and soak away your cares. **Above:** The tiled roofs of Trinidad.

Sport and activities

Caving

ⓘ Sociedad Espeleológica de Cuba (SEC) www.sec1940.galeon.com.

There are huge cave systems in Cuba, some of which are developed tourist attractions. The Santo Tomás and Cueva del Indio caves in Viñales are visited by thousands of people every year, but many others are almost unknown. Amerindian pictographs can be found in some, for example the Los Generales, Las Mercedes, Indio and Pichardo caves in the Sierra de Cubitas, Camagüey, El Paraíso, Perla de Agua and other caves around Baracoa and the Cuevas del Punta del Este on the Isla de la Juventud. The largest stalagmite in Cuba can be found in the Cueva Martín Infierno near Trinidad, 67 m high and 40 m at its base. In the Zapata peninsula there are flooded caves, which can be dived, as can Tanques Azules, at Caletones. An adventure park at the Silla de Gibara offers rock climbing, caving, potholing and cave diving,

or you can get in touch with the local espeleologists to explore underground rivers and caves in the area. In Matanzas province there are some 350 caves, of which about 20 can be visited. The Bellamar caves receive hundreds of visitors daily, while the Saturno caverns have underwater tunnels suitable for trained cave divers.

Climbing

ⓘ For more information on routes and hazards, see www.cubaclimbing.com.

Climbing is still in its infancy in Cuba and has not, so far, been hijacked by state tour companies with organized excursions. However, you can't go off and climb wherever you want, as access to national parks is restricted. This means that climbing in the Sierra Maestra is effectively out of bounds. The best place for rock climbing is Viñales, where the *mogotes* are a magnet for climbers. There's a local climbing group who are equipped mostly with gear left behind by foreign climbers. Possible contacts include Josué Millo Gómez, Calle Rafael Trejo 108A, and Oscar Jaime Rodríguez, Calle Adela Azcuy 43, T48-793381, who has a *casa particular* often used as a base camp.

Fishing

ⓘ Fly fishing off Isla de la Juventud, Cayo Largo and Jardines de la Reina with **Avalon Cuban Fishing Centers**, www.cubanfishingcenters.com.

Freshwater fishing Cuba has been a fisherman's dream for decades, not only for its deep-sea fishing, popularized by Ernest Hemingway, but also for its freshwater fishing in the many lakes and reservoirs spread around the island. Freshwater fishing is mostly for the

MARC PAGANI PHOTOGRAPHY/SHUTTERSTOCK

Climbing in Cueva Larga, Viñales.

Cycling

Take off on a bike where and when you please. Cruise the cycle lane along the Malecón with the salt spray in your face and a bright yellow cocotaxi at your side. Outside Havana, quiet roads wind through flat or rolling countryside, where the majestic Royal palm towers over farmers' thatched cottages (*bohíos*), oxen are still used to work the fields and horses and bicycles are the main forms of transport.

With millions of bicycles on the roads, all transport moves at the speed of the cyclist.

To get out to the beaches east of Havana, ride with your bike on the *ciclobus* through the tunnel under the harbour before picking up the Vía Blanca. For a multi-day trip to the Western Sierras, head out along Salvador Allende and Avenida Rancho Boyeros past the airport to San Antonio de los Baños and the next day to Viñales. Side trips can be made in the Sierra del Rosario, with some demanding hill climbs. If you do not have the time to cycle the length and breadth of the island, you can always put your bike on the train (if it is running) or on a domestic flight.

From Santa Clara you can cycle to Trinidad (88 km) via Manicaragua and Condado, head west along the coast road to Guajimico (44 km), Cienfuegos (43 km) and inland to Hanabanilla (51 km) via Cumanajagua. There is a steep 7-km climb to the Hanabanilla lake. Return to Santa Clara (47 km) via La Moza and Manicaragua, giving you some steep hills.

Test yourself and your bike in the mountains of the Sierra Maestra. Leave Santiago, heading west along Avenida las Américas, and cycle to El Saltón (87 km) via El Cobre. Then to Bayamo (67 km), Manzanillo (93 km), Punta Piedra (99 km), Chivirico (100 km) and return to Santiago (68 km). This takes in the mountains and the outstanding coast road squeezed between the mountains and the Caribbean.

If you don't want to go it alone there are many organized group tours. You need to bring your own bike. You may also be able to join a group of Cuban bikers (mostly English speaking) through the **Club Nacional de Cicloturismo Gran Caribe** (National Bike Club), or one of the regional clubs, such as the **Club de Cicloturismo Comandante Che Guevara**, in the west, desmonteguira@enet.cu. They run tours of one to 28 days in all parts of the country, some with political themes. Most tours offer a fully supported programme and have a dedicated back-up team including tour leader, mechanic and support vehicle. Even better, luggage is carried for you while you cycle. Cuba has become a popular destination for UK charities' cycle challenge events. These are large-scale events with up to 60 participants cycling over 385 km in seven days, support vehicles and support teams, including doctors and mechanics. The **Cuba Solidarity Campaign**, T020-72636452, www.cuba-solidarity.org.uk, runs an annual sponsored bike ride in Western Cuba and delivers consignments of medical aid to a Havana Policlínico (local medical centre). See Friendship Associations, page 64, for possible contacts in other countries.

large-mouth bass (*trucha*), which grow to a great size in the Cuban lakes. The main places are Maspotón, in Pinar del Río, where you can fish in La Juventud reservoir or in the mouth of the Río Los Palacios or Río Carraguao; Laguna del Tesoro in the Ciénaga de Zapata, where there is a wide variety of fish; Presa Alacranes in Villa Clara province, which is the second largest reservoir in the country; Presa Zaza, in Sancti Spíritus, the largest artificial lake in Cuba, where the record catch of *trucha* is 16.5 lbs; Lago La Redonda, near Morón in Ciego de Avila province, and in the province of Camagüey on the Porvenir, Muñoz and Mañana de Santa Ana dams. Equipment can be hired, but serious fishermen will prefer to bring their own and a large quantity of insect repellent. Freshwater fishing is allowed all year round.

Deep-sea fishing This can be organized at marinas around the island, although most of the tournaments and the best facilities are at the Marina Hemingway, just west of Havana. Marlin, swordfish, tarpon, sawfish, yellowfin tuna, dorado, wahoo, shark and a host of others are all caught here. Varadero is a good point from which to go fishing and take advantage of the Gulf Stream which flows between Key West in Florida and Cuba, but records have been broken all along the northern coast in the cays of the Archipiélago de Sabana and the Archipiélago de Camagüey. There is also good fishing off the south coast around the Isla de la Juventud and Cayo Largo.

Bonefishing This is excellent off the south coast in the Archipiélago de los Jardines de la Reina, or off Cayo Largo. It is also increasingly popular at Las Salinas, the salt flats on the Zapata peninsula, previously a protected area, but recently opened to fly fishermen. Still tightly controlled, with only six anglers allowed into the national park at any one time, you have your own personal guide and a flat-bottomed skiff to take you through the many channels to the shallow lagoons, where you can wade or fish from the boat. Flats species include bonefish, permit, jack crevalle and barracuda.

Hiking

ⓘ The Ramblers Association take guided groups to Cuba, www.Ramblersholidays.co.uk.

The highest peaks are in the Sierra Maestra in the east, where there are also many historical landmarks associated with the Wars of Independence and the Revolution. A three-day walk will take you from Alto del Naranjo up the island's highest peak, Pico Turquino, and down to the Caribbean coast at Las Cuevas, giving you fantastic views of the mountains and the coastline. The Sierra del Escambray, in the centre of the island, is conveniently located just north of Trinidad, and there are some lovely walks in the hills, along trails beside rivers, waterfalls and caves. The mountains of the west of the island, the Sierra del Rosario and the Sierra de los Organos, have some of the most unusual geological features, as well as a wide variety of flora and very rewarding birdwatching.

The first months of the year are the best for walking, as they are drier, less humid and not so hot. However, temperature varies with the altitude and the higher you get in the Sierra Maestra, the cooler it will become, so take appropriate clothing. Also remember that in the rainforest there are few days when it does not rain, so expect to get wet. The months from August to November are the wettest, when the risk of hurricanes or tropical storms increases, but you can still encounter days when there is plenty of sunshine. It is best to start early, before it gets too hot. Always carry plenty of drinking water, some food, a hat and suntan lotion. Good footwear is essential and a walking stick is extremely useful on hilly forest trails. Good large-scale maps are non-existent and you are advised to take a guide when embarking on long walks. Not only will this prevent you getting lost, but you will learn a lot more about your surroundings, as many of the guides are professional botanists or ornithologists. If you are walking in national parks a guide is compulsory.

Scuba-diving

ⓘ Listings of dive sites and operators at www.netssa.com/scuba_diving_cuba.html.

The majority of Cuba's coral reefs are alive and healthy and teeming with assorted marine life. Much marine life is protected around the entire island, including turtles, the manatee and coral. There are three main marine platforms, the Archipiélago del Rey, the Archipiélago de la Reina and the Archipiélago de los Canarreos. There are believed to be some 900 species of fish, 1400 species of mollusc, 60 species of coral, 1100 species of crustacean, 67 species of shark and ray and four types of sea turtle around the island, as well as the manatee.

The main dive areas are Isla de la Juventud, Varadero, Faro de Luna, María La Gorda, Cayo Levisa, Santa Lucía and close to Santiago de Cuba. Most offer a variety of diving, including reefs and walls and an assortment of wrecks, from the remains of ancient Spanish ships to many modern wrecks sunk as dive sites.

All dive shops are government owned. Most staff speak Spanish, English and often German, Italian or French. Diving is usually done as part of all-inclusive packages, although dives can be booked direct with dive shops for around CUC$35-40, including all equipment. Most companies use European dive gear. Good-quality, basic rental gear is available, but if you use your own you should be prepared with all spares needed for diving and photography (batteries, replacement parts such as a regulator mouthpiece, etc), as these are usually not available. In the summer months, on the south of the island, tiny jelly fish may abound and can cause stings on areas not covered by a wet suit, particularly when entering or leaving the water. A tropical hood is a good idea to protect the neck and face in jelly fish season, often referred to as *agua mala*, or 'bad water'. Dives can sometimes be delayed for a variety of reasons, including limited available fuel, Coast Guard clearance to depart port, etc, so patience is needed. The authorities are very concerned about security as boats have been 'borrowed' for a quick getaway to Florida.

SCUBA IMAGE/SHUTTERSTOCK

Porcupinefish.

How big is your footprint?

Travel to the furthest corners of the globe is now commonplace and the mass movement of people for leisure and business is a major source of foreign exchange and economic development in Cuba. The benefits of international travel are self-evident for both hosts and travellers: employment; increased understanding of different cultures; business and leisure opportunities. At the same time there is clearly a downside to the industry. Where visitor pressure is high and/or poorly regulated, adverse impacts to society and the natural environment may be apparent.

The travel industry is growing rapidly and its impact is becoming increasingly apparent. Air travel is clearly implicated in global warming and damage to the ozone layer, while resort location and construction can destroy natural habitats. Individual choice and awareness can make a difference and, collectively, travellers are having a significant effect in shaping a more responsible and sustainable industry.

Of course travel can have beneficial impacts. Travellers can promote patronage and protection of important heritage sites through their interest and entrance and performance fees. In Cuba, they can also support small-scale enterprises by staying in privately run *casas particulares*, eating at private *paladares* and by purchasing local goods, arts and crafts. They can also support animal welfare. As in many countries where the local population struggle to make a living, animals are low down on many Cubans' priorities. While Cubans enjoy one of the best health services in the world, there is no equivalent for animals, whether pets or working beasts; veterinarians are desperately lacking in supplies. All donations are welcome. Check your horse's health before setting out on a ride (see box, page 253). Think also about the plight of the dolphins before you go swimming with them.

Above: Waves crash against the seafront Malecón, Havana, where salt-eroded buildings are under restoration.

Cuba captures dolphins from the wild, separates them from their pods (families) and sells them to dolphinariums to perform tricks for tourists in return for dead fish and antibiotics.

The following organizations are developing and/or promoting ecotourism projects and destinations and their websites are an excellent source of information:

▸▸ Conservation International, T001-703-341 2400, www.conservation.org.
▸▸ International Ecotourism Society, T001-202-506 5033, www.ecotourism.org.
▸▸ Tourism Concern, T44-(0)20-7133 3800, www.tourismconcern.org.uk.
▸▸ The Travel Foundation, T44-(0)117-927 3049, www.thetravelfoundation.co.uk.
▸▸ The Whale and Dolphin Conservation Society, T44-(0)1249-449500, www.wdcs.org, monitors Cuba's activities with marine mammals.

Responsible travel

»» Spend money on locally produced (rather than imported) goods and services and use common sense when bargaining; your few dollars saved may be a month's salary to someone else.

»» Use water and electricity carefully, travellers may receive preferential supply while the local communities are rationed.

»» Learn about local etiquette and culture, consider local norms of behaviour and dress appropriately for local cultures and situations.

»» Protect wildlife and other natural resources: don't buy souvenirs or goods made from wildlife unless they are clearly sustainably produced and are not protected under CITES legislation (CITES controls trade in endangered species and Cuba is a party to CITES).

»» Always ask before taking photographs or videos of people.

»» Consider staying in local accommodation rather than hotels; the economic benefits for host communities are greater – and there are far greater opportunities for you to learn about the local culture. In the same vein, consider eating at *paladares*, which are privately run rather than at state-run restaurants.

»» Miminize waste; take used batteries home with you and anything that can be recycled, such as empty shampoo bottles. Waste disposal is a sensitive issue on an island.

Above: Fuel shortages have forced Cubans to rely on traditional methods of farming, cutting sugar cane by hand with an ox and cart for transport. **Next page**:The Capitolio, Havana.

Contents

Footprint features

Essentials

Getting there

Air

The frequency of scheduled and charter flights depends on the season, with twice-weekly flights in the winter being reduced to once a week in the summer. Some of the longer haul flights, such as from Buenos Aires, are cut from once a week in winter to once a month in summer. Most international flights come in to Havana, but the international airports of Varadero, Holguín (for Guardalavaca beaches), Santiago de Cuba, Ciego de Avila, Cayo Coco, Cayo Largo, Santa Clara (for Cayo Santa María), Las Tunas, Manzanillo and Camagüey (for Santa Lucía beaches) also receive flights.

Buying a ticket

A **specialist travel agency**, such as **Journey Latin America** will be able to get you better deals than anything you can find on the internet. The state airline, **Cubana de Aviación**, flies to Europe, Canada, Central and South America and to many islands in the Caribbean. It is cheaper than competitors on the same routes but the service is worse, seats are cramped, and some travel agents do not recommend it. Charter flights with accommodation packages can be good deals even if you ditch the hotel and tour Cuba independently. Early booking is essential as agents need at least 14 days' notice to get confirmations from Havana. **High seasons** cover the Easter period, the July to August European summer and the last three weeks of December. Prices quoted below include all taxes except for Cuban departure tax, CUC$25.

Flights from the UK

Direct flights are about nine hours. **Virgin Atlantic** flies from London direct, while **Air France**, **Iberia** and **Martinair** operate connecting services via Paris, Madrid and Amsterdam respectively. **Virgin Atlantic**'s low-season prices start at about £600, including all taxes and fees, its high season prices go up to over £900 at Christmas. Indirect flights can be cheaper by £100 or so, but are more time consuming and not so comfortable. **Cubana** uses aircraft leased from **Air Europa** and flies direct from London to Havana via Holguín for £445-551 (£829 at Christmas), allowing a two-centre holiday.

Flights from the rest of Europe

Direct flights are available from Amsterdam, Berlin, Dusseldorf, Frankfurt, Madrid, Milan, Munich, Paris, Rome and Shannon depending on the season and the Cuban airport. **Air Europa** and **Iberia** fares from Madrid to Havana are from €635 return. **Martinair**'s flights to Havana from Amsterdam start at €599. **Cubana** starts at €532. Other airlines offering scheduled flights to various Cuban cities include **LTU/Air Berlin**, **Condor** and **Aeroflot**. All flights from Europe arrive in Havana around 2000-2130, returning overnight.

Flights from North America

Since 1962, US citizens have only been permitted to visit Cuba providing they can prove they are travelling for journalistic, cultural, sporting or scientific purposes. However, despite the risk of hefty fines, US travellers are increasingly travelling via a gateway city, such as Nassau, Mexico City, Cancún, or Grand Cayman. For advice on ticketing, see www.cubalinda.com. Nassau is not particularly recommended because you have to clear

US customs and immigration at Nassau airport and officials may become suspicious if a flight from Cuba has just landed. Try overnighting in the Bahamas on your return as a way of covering your tracks. Cuban Americans are now allowed to visit relatives regularly and in 2009 direct flights were available from Los Angeles to Havana and from Miami to Havana or Cienfuegos (**Cuba Travel Services**, www.ctscharters.com). A bill pending in Congress would allow all Americans to visit Cuba.

Cubana offers good deals from neighbouring gateways (US$270 round trip from Cancún) including from Santo Domingo to Havana, while **AeroCaribbean** flies from Santo Domingo to Santiago de Cuba. **Air Jamaica** flies from Montego Bay or Kingston. From Canada there are direct flights from Montréal and Toronto with high, low and shoulder seasons. There are flights to Havana from lots of Mexican cities, with connections to other Cuban airports, and also from many Central American cities with local airlines (www.grupotaca.com).

Flights from Australia and New Zealand
There are no direct flights and you have to connect in a European, Canadian or Latin American city. Even if you fly Virgin all the way, you will have to change airports in London (Heathrow–Gatwick). Get a round-the-world ticket for the best deals and tack Cuba on to a South or Central American itinerary.

Airlines and agents
Aeroflot, T020-7355 2233 (UK), T+7 (495) 223 5555 or T8 800 333 5555 (Russia), www.aeroflot.ru.
Air Canada, T1-888-247 2262 (Canada) www.aircanada.com.
Air Europa, T0871-222 9122 (UK), T034-902 401501 (Spain), www.aireuropa.com.
Air France, T0871-663 3777 (UK), T33-820 820820 (France), www.airfrance.com.
Air Jamaica, T020 7590 3600 (UK), T876-922 3460 (Jamaica), T1-800-523 5585 in the USA and the Caribbean, www.airjamaica.com.
Condor, T +49 (0) 180 5 707202 (Germany), www.condor.de, www.flythomascook.com.

Cubaism, UK Toll-free T0800 298 9555, www.havanaflights.com.
Cubalinda, www.cubalinda.com.
Cubana de Aviación, T020-7538 5933 (UK), T537-834 4446, www.cubana.cu.
Iberia, T0870-6090500 (UK), T34-902 400500 (Spain), www.iberia.com.
LTU/Air Berlin, T0871 500 0737 (UK), T01805 737800 (Germany), www.ltu.com, www.airberlin.com.
Martinair, T31-2060 11767 (Netherlands), www.martinair.com.
Mexicana, T0808-101 7600 (UK), T 1-800-531 35850 (USA/Canada), T52-55 2881 000, www.mexicana.com.

Airport information
Cuba has several airports classified as international, but only Havana is of any size. Havana now has three terminals, the third and newest one being for international flights, with **exchange** facilities open during normal banking hours, snack bars, shops, car rental and a 24-hour tourist information bureau (**Infotur**, limited information). The airport is safe at night, which is when the European flights come in, and taxi services are efficient. See page 68 for transport from Havana airport into the city. **Immigration** can be very slow with long queues. Coming into one of the other airports (see Getting there, Air, page 26) is a more relaxed and speedy affair with less traffic.

There are a couple of *casas particulares* in the Altahabana district, Boyeros, quite close to Havana airport, see page 106, but there is no airport hotel and you will need to take a taxi to any accommodation.

Packing for Cuba

Bring all medicines you might need as they can be difficult to find and a simple first-aid kit (see page 53). You might not be offered even a painkiller if you have an accident, as they are in very short supply. Many other things are scarce or unobtainable in Cuba, so take in everything you are likely to need other than food: razor blades; medicines and pills; antacid tablets for indigestion; sachets of rehydration salts plus anti-diarrhoea preparations; insect repellent; sun protection; sunglasses for intense sunlight; toilet paper; tampons; condoms and other contraceptives; disposable nappies if you are travelling with children; reading and writing materials; photographic supplies; torch and batteries; an adaptor for any electrical items, phone charger, etc.

The seating everywhere at Havana airport is uncomfortable. The **restaurant** upstairs, before you go through passport control, is OK for sandwiches or full meals, welcome after a long check-in and this will be your last chance to hear a live Cuban band while eating. The food on offer in the departure lounge is awful, with a choice between a microwaved hot dog or a soggy pizza. As most European flights leave late at night this can be a problem if you have a long wait for a (delayed) **Air France** or **Iberia** flight, but you can savour your last *mojito* in this vast, uncomfortable shed. At least the toilets are free and there is unlimited toilet paper. The selection of shops is limited but there is lots of rum, coffee, biscuits, a few books, postcards and magazines on sale. The selection of cigars is poor; if you know which brand you particularly want, get it in a specialist shop before you get to the airport. Rum costs much the same as elsewhere. The *Cubita* coffee, on the other hand, is marginally cheaper than in town.

Sea

Ports of entry

Before arriving in **Cuban territorial waters** (12 nautical miles from the island's platform), you should communicate with port authorities on channel HF (SSB) 2760 or VHF 68 and 16 (National Coastal Network) and 2790 or VHF 19A (Tourist Network). There are lots of rules and regulations and you must expect paperwork to take hours while the many bureaucrats board your boat and check you out. Not many 'yachties' visit the island because of the political difficulties between Cuba and the USA. The US administration forbids any vessel, such as a cruise ship, cargo ship or humble yacht from calling at a US port if it has stopped in Cuba. This effectively prohibits anyone sailing from the US eastern seaboard calling in at a Cuban port on their way south through the Caribbean islands, or vice versa. However, it does not seem to prevent regattas being held between Florida and Cuban marinas. It is better to rent a bareboat or crewed yacht from a Cuban marina and sail around the island, rather than include it in a Caribbean itinerary. From Cienfuegos marina you can sail west to the Archipiélago de los Canarreos, visiting Cayo Largo, Isla de la Juventud and the many cays in between, or east to the Jardines de la Reina, stopping at Trinidad (Ancón) and the many cays south of Júcaro. It would be worthwhile to invest in *The Cruising Guide to Cuba*, by Simon Charles (Cruising Guide Publications, 2nd edition 1997) before embarking.

Havana, Cienfuegos and Santiago receive **tourist cruise** vessels. There are now some 20 marinas and nautical centres all around the island and the only prohibited area is the Bay of Pigs. The largest marina is the Hemingway in Havana, but there are three in Varadero and others in Cienfuegos, Cayo Largo, Santiago and several along the north coast. See the noticeboards for crewing opportunities on boats to Mexico, Florida, etc. There are no ferries linking Cuba with neighbouring islands.

Getting around

Shortages of fuel and spare parts in Cuba still cause difficulties in the supply of transport. The Government has segregated tourists from Cubans and encourages them to hire cars or travel on dedicated buses to maximize foreign exchange income. Many cheap forms of transport are reserved for Cubans and are prohibited for foreigners.

Internal flights are frequent and efficient but generally only link Havana with other towns, so you can not criss-cross the island by air. **Roads** are good and there is little traffic, except in Havana, which is a bit of a nightmare if you have just arrived. Out of the city, however, roads are fairly empty and you can often travel for miles without seeing another vehicle. **Buses** operated by **Víazul** and paid for in CUC$ run on long-distance routes between cities commonly visited by foreigners, while the more extensive **Astro** bus network is now reserved only for Cubans. All long-distance travel by foreigners is paid for in CUC$. **Tour buses** are flexible, allowing you to stay a night or two in, say, Pinar del Río, before rejoining the tour for the return to Havana, and **Transtur** now runs some of its tour buses as a scheduled service, for example between Havana and Trinidad. **Car hire** is available, although you may not get the car you want unless you arrange it in advance from abroad. The disadvantage of car hire is that it is expensive and petrol stations are not always conveniently located, but you will have the freedom of going where you want, when you want and you will have the roads almost to yourself. A good way of getting around and meeting the people is to hire a **private car** with driver to take you out for a day. He will want to be paid in CUC$, and he runs a considerable risk because it is illegal, but enforcement of the law varies between regions and if there are two or three of you it can work out cheaper and more enjoyable than taking an organized excursion on a tour bus. Most **rail** journeys are fraught with difficulties and generally are subject to breakdowns and long delays. There have also been some fatal accidents. Repairs and new rolling stock from China are awaited.

Air

There are **Cubana de Aviación** services between most of the main towns, see Transport sections in each chapter for details. Tourists must pay air fares in CUC$; it is advisable to prebook flights at home as demand is very heavy, although you can get interprovincial flights from hotel tour desks if you are on a package deal. It is difficult to book flights from one city to another when you are not at the point of departure, except from Havana; the computers are not able to cope. Airports are usually a long way from the towns, so extra transport costs will be necessary. Delays are common. **Cubana** and **AeroCaribbean** flights are very cold, take warm clothes and possibly some food for a long flight. Although theoretically possible to get a scheduled flight as listed above, it is often only possible for tourists to travel on excursions: day trips or packages with flights, accommodation, meals and sightseeing.

Aerogaviota is a charter airline owned by the armed forces, with a growing list of national and international flights to Central America and the Caribbean from its own terminal. Head office is at Avenida 47 2814 entre 28 y 34, Rpto Kohly, Havana, T7-203 0668, www.aerogaviota.com.

Rail

Train journeys are recommended for the adventurous traveller, although long delays and breakdowns must be expected. Be at the station at least one hour before the scheduled departure time. Fares are reasonable but have to be paid for in CUC$, which will usually entitle you to a waiting area, seat reservation and to board the train before the big rush starts. There is a CUC$ ticket office in every station. The tourist desks in some of the larger hotels may sell you train tickets, but many tour agencies have ceased that service as trains are too unreliable. Long-distance trains allow only seated passengers, they are extremely cold unless the air conditioning is broken, so take warm clothes and a torch (needed for the toilets). All carriages are smoking areas. **Bicycles** can be carried but often cost more than the fare for a person (see Cycling, page 36). Sometimes there is food available, but it is advisable to take food with you. Cold fried meat with rice and black beans is sometimes sold in a cardboard box for 15 pesos cubanos. You have to tear off a piece of the box to use as an eating tool. This is sold soon after leaving Havana and there will be nothing else for the rest of what may be a 30-hour trip unless you can get something at station stops. Make sure you have pesos cubanos with you. Also take toilet paper.

Road

Bus (guagua)
Local The local word for a bus is *guagua*. Urban transport is varied; buses can be motorized or horse drawn (*coches*). Horses made a comeback during the crisis of the 1980s when fuel shortages limited services and are still common in provincial towns, where buses are only used between towns rather than within them. The huge double-jointed buses pulled by a truck, called *camellos* (camels) because of their shape, also irreverently known as 'Saturday night at the cinema' because they are full of 'sex, crime and alcohol' have been withdrawn from the streets of Havana and are now found only in the provinces. There are also regular buses in Havana and other major towns. The urban bus fare throughout Cuba is 20 centavos for *camellos* and 40 centavos for all others; it helps to have the exact fare. Urban tickets can only be bought in pesos cubanos. Foreigners are not encouraged to use buses. The Government prefers tourists to use taxis.

Long distance For bus transport to other provinces from Havana there are two companies: **Víazul** and **Astro**, but foreigners can travel on only **Víazul** (*Viajes Azul*), at Avenida 26 entre Avenida Zoológico y Ulloa, Nuevo Vedado, T7-8811413, www.viazul.cu, 0900-2300. The buses are reasonably comfortable, are air conditioned, and films are shown on the longer journeys. Tickets can be bought online, but you pay 8% more than in the ticket offices. See box, page 32, for routes, schedules and fares. Children aged 0-4 travel free, those aged 5-11 are half price when the fare is over CUC$10, CUC$5 when it is less than CUC$10.

It is essential to book in advance during peak season and August, which can be very busy with an increased number of Cuban tourists. Even booking up to two or three days in advance may not be sufficient to guarantee a seat, especially if you are a family with children or travelling in a group. If you are picking up a **Víazul** bus en route between Havana and Santiago, for example, it's worth bearing in mind that a minimal number of seats will be allocated.

Baggage handlers in Havana, Trinidad and some other tourist towns have an irritating habit of demanding a tip even though they hardly touch your bag. Any small coin will satisfy them. **Astro** is based at the Terminal de Omnibus Nacional, Boyeros y 19 de Mayo, T7-8703397, daily 0700-2100. Cubans often have to book tickets (in pesos) months in advance at busy times of the year. Away from the capital and off the beaten track, it is not so controversial to travel on Astro to minor towns and pay in pesos, in fact you may have no option. The **Víazul** terminal in Havana is a long way from the centre and you will have to get a taxi. In other cities **Víazul** and **Astro** use the same bus terminal. There is a weight limit for luggage of 20 kg on all long-distance bus journeys and the bus-ferry to Isla de la Juventud. (See page 389).

Car

Hiring a car is recommended, in view of the difficulties of getting public transport to out-of-the-way places and you can save a considerable amount of time, but it is the most expensive form of travel. Breakdowns are not unknown, in which case you may be stuck with your rented car many kilometres from the nearest place that will help you. Be careful about picking up hitchhikers, although it can be an interesting way of meeting Cubans, as well as being a useful talking road map.

Petrol stations are not self-service. Petrol and diesel is available in **Servi Cupet** stations and must be paid for in CUC$ at around CUC$1 per litre for Regular and diesel and CUC1.10 for Especial. If possible, get the rental company to fill the car with fuel, otherwise your first day will be spent looking for petrol. A number of hire cars use diesel, which can be more difficult to get hold of than petrol. Only the main fuel stations sell diesel.

Autopistas were incredibly empty of traffic during the 1980s and 1990s, but as the economy picked up, traffic increased. Cubans often use the hard surface for other purposes, such as drying rice on the roadside. Oxen, horses, donkeys, bicycles and tractors will be sharing the fast lane with you. A military band was seen practising as though the soldiers were on a parade ground. The dogs on the side of the road are often not dead, just asleep. Watch out for low-flying vultures preying on any animals that really are dead. Cubans slow right down and give them a wide berth; they can do enormous damage to your car if you do hit one. Main roads can be good places to shop for fresh fruit and vegetables, vendors stand by the roadside (or in the road) or sell from broken down trucks. Most ordinary roads are in reasonable condition, but minor roads can be very badly maintained and signposting is uniformly atrocious or non-existent. Even when there are road signs they are usually so bleached by the sun that they are illegible until you draw level with them. Finding your way across a large city like Havana can present problems, in spite of the courteous assistance of police and pedestrians. Your best bet is to get the *Guía de Carreteras* (Road Guide) and follow the distances marked between junctions. Getting into towns is usually easy, finding a road out again has been described as a nightmare. There are numerous police checks on the roads. They will sometimes stop hired cars and try to impose a fine of CUC$30 for a traffic violation you may or may not have committed. If you can speak Spanish, try and discuss the matter with them and ask for evidence of the violation. They will usually not be able to produce any and will let you go.

Driving at night can be extremely hazardous and is not recommended. Even in major cities many streets are not lit. You are likely to encounter horses, cattle, pigs, goats and

Víazul routes, fares and daily schedules
www.viazul.cu. Online reservations are 8% more expensive than those quoted here.

Route	Fare	Departure times			
Havana to Santiago de Cuba	CUC$51	0930	1500	1815	2200
Santa Clara	CUC$18	1400	1930		0150
Sancti Spíritus	CUC$23	1520	2050		0310
Ciego de Avila	CUC$27	1635	2210		0425
Camagüey	CUC$33	1825	0000	0125	0615
Las Tunas	CUC$39	2105	0200		0830
Holguín	CUC$44		0315		
Bayamo	CUC$44	2225	0435		0950
Santiago de Cuba	**Arrives**	0030	0640	0635	1200
Santiago de Cuba to Havana	CUC$51	0900	1515	1800	2200
Bayamo	CUC$7	1110	1725		0010
Holguín	CUC$11	1230	1845		
Las Tunas	CUC$11	1345	2000		0130
Camagüey	CUC$18	1630	2245	2320	0335
Ciego de Avila	CUC$24	1820	0035		0525
Sancti Spíritus	CUC$28	2025	0155		0645
Santa Clara	CUC$33		0315		0820
Havana	**Arrives**	0115	0655	0630	1205
Havana to Holguín	CUC$44	0840	2030		
Santa Clara	CUC$18	1255			
Sancti Spíritus	CUC$23	1415	0105		
Ciego de Avila	CUC$27	1535	0220		
Camagüey	CUC$33	1725	0400		
Las Tunas	CUC$39	1925	0555		
Holguín	**Arrives**	2035	0705		
Holguín to Havana	CUC$44	0920	2100		
Las Tunas	CUC$6	1035	2215		
Camagüey	CUC$11	1235	0010		
Ciego de Avila	CUC$17	1510	0155		
Sancti Spíritus	CUC$21	1630	0305		
Santa Clara	CUC$27	1750			
Havana	**Arrives**	2125	0725		
Havana to Trinidad	CUC$25	0815	1300		
Entronque de Jagüey	CUC$12	1035	1525		
Girón	N/A	1135			
Cienfuegos	CUC$20	1320	1710		
Trinidad	**Arrives**	1445	1845		

Route	Fare	Departure times			
Trinidad to Havana	CUC$25	0730	1500		
Cienfuegos	CUC$6	0910	1630		
Girón	N/A		1820		
Entronque de Jagüey	CUC$15	1055	1920		
Havana	**Arrives**	1310	2120		
Havana to Viñales	CUC$12	0900			
Pinar del Río	CUC$11	1205			
Viñales	**Arrives**	1250			
Viñales to Havana	CUC$12	0800			
Pinar del Río	CUC$6	0850			
Havana	**Arrives**	1110			
Havana to Varadero	CUC$10	0800	1000	1200	1800
Infotur de Guanabo	N/A	0850			
Matanzas	CUC$7	1015	1210	1410	2020
Varadero Airport	CUC$10	1045	1240	1440	
Varadero	**Arrives**	1110	1305	1505	2105
Varadero to Havana	CUC$10	0800	1125	1530	1800
Varadero Airport	CUC$6	0830	1145	1600	1830
Matanzas	CUC$6	0900	1215	1630	1900
Infotur de Guanabo	N/A				2025
Havana	**Arrives**	1055	1415	1825	2105
Varadero to Trinidad	CUC$20	0800	1400		
Cárdenas	CUC$6	0820	1420		
Coliseo	CUC$7	0840	1440		
Jovellanos	CUC$8	0855	1455		
Jagüey Grande	CUC$9	0930	1530		
Santa Clara	CUC$11	1115			
Cienfuegos	CUC$16	1235	1710		
Trinidad	**Arrives**	1415	1950		
Trinidad to Varadero	CUC$20	0900	1530		
Cienfuegos	CUC$6	1030	1700		
Santa Clara	CUC$8		1820		
Jagüey Grande	CUC$15	1210	2005		
Jovellanos	CUC$16	1245	2040		
Coliseo	CUC$17	1300	2055		
Cárdenas	CUC$19	1320	2115		
Varadero	**Arrives**	1340	2135		

Route	Fare	Departure times
Trinidad to Santiago	CUC$33	0800
Sancti Spíritus	CUC$6	0925
Ciego de Avila	CUC$9	1045
Camagüey	CUC$15	1320
Las Tunas	CUC$22	1520
Holguín	CUC$26	1635
Bayamo	CUC$26	1755
Santiago	**Arrives**	2000
Santiago to Trinidad	CUC$33	1930
Bayamo	CUC$7	2140
Holguín	CUC$11	2300
Las Tunas	CUC$11	0015
Camagüey	CUC$18	0215
Ciego de Avila	CUC$24	0405
Sancti Spíritus	CUC$28	0525
Trinidad	**Arrives**	0645
Santiago to Baracoa	CUC$15	0745
Guantánamo	CUC$6	0930
Baracoa	**Arrives**	1235
Baracoa to Santiago	CUC$15	1415
Guantánamo	CUC$10	1715
Santiago	**Arrives**	1905
Varadero to Santiago de Cuba	CUC$49	2125
Cárdenas	CUC$6	2150
Colón	CUC$6	2300
Santa Clara	CUC$11	0050
Sancti Spíritus	CUC$17	0225
Ciego de Avila	CUC$19	0345
Camagüey	CUC$25	0535
Las Tunas	CUC$32	0750
Holguín	CUC$38	0905
Bayamo	CUC$42	1025
Santiago	**Arrives**	1230
Santiago de Cuba to Varadero	CUC$49	2015
Bayamo	CUC$7	2225
Holguín	CUC$11	2340
Las Tunas	CUC$11	0055
Camagüey	CUC$18	0250
Ciego de Avila	CUC$24	0440
Sancti Spíritus	CUC$28	0555
Santa Clara	CUC$33	0740
Colón	CUC$43	0930
Cárdenas	CUC$48	1040
Varadero	**Arrives**	1100

sheep monopolizing the road without any semblance of lighting. In addition, cyclists, bullock carts and other vehicles without lights are common. It is best to travel early in the day and reach your destination before nightfall. During the winter months, November to March, sunrise is at 0700 and sunset at 1830 (2000 in summer months). Cubans drive on the right-hand side.

Car hire

There are state rental companies at international airports and most large hotels, or try the companies direct. During July and August it is extremely difficult to hire a car without booking well in advance. It is advisable to arrange car hire from home before you travel. Drivers need to be minimum of 21 years of age, although for some vehicles the age limit goes up to 25 years. You must present your passport and home driving licence.

All car rental agencies are state owned and operated by one or other of the four state corporations (**Cimex**, **Cubalse**, **Cubanacán** and **Gaviota**), so there is no real competition on prices. **Cubacar**: www.transtur.cu. **Havanautos**: www.havanautos.cu. **Rex**: www.rexcarrental.com. **Transtur**: www.transtur.cu. **Vía Rent-a-Car**: www.gaviota-grupo.com. Try also www.havanacarhire.com or www.carrentalcuba.com. Minimum CUC$40 a day (or CUC$50 for air conditioning) with limited mileage of 100 km a day, and CUC$10-20 a day optional insurance, or CUC$50-88 per day unlimited mileage; cheaper rates over seven days. Non-US credit cards accepted for the rental. If you pay cash it will have to be in advance and they will still need a credit card for a deposit, which may be debited for the whole rental even if you have paid up front. Credit cards will be debited in CUC$, converted immediately to US$ plus tax – even if your bank is non-US – and then convert the charge to euro, sterling, yen, or whatever. In practice, you may find car hire rates prohibitively expensive when small cars are 'unavailable' and a four-door sedan at CUC$93, unlimited kilometres, insurance included, is your only option. Staff have been reported as 'unhelpful' in finding what you want. However, it pays to shop around, even between offices of the same company. If you want to drive from Havana to Santiago and return by air, try **Havanautos**. They will charge at least CUC$100 to return the car to Havana, but most companies will not even consider it. **Vía Rent-a-Car** (Gaviota) charges CUC$160, calculated at CUC$0.18 per km on a distance of 884 km from Santiago to Havana, but this is reduced to CUC$0.09 if the car is hired for more than 15 days. If you hire in Havana and want to drop off the car at the airport, companies will charge you extra, around CUC$10, although this is sometimes waived if you bargain hard. Check what is required concerning fuel, you don't always have to leave the tank full, but make sure the tank is really full when you start. Fly and drive packages can be booked from abroad through **Cubacar**, part of the **Grupo Cubanacán**, who have a wide range of jeeps and cars all over the country and can even arrange a driver. Or you can do it through **Cubanacán** in the UK, who can organize rentals of Suzuki Samurai jeeps (or equivalent). Most vehicles are Japanese or Korean makes, Suzuki jeeps can be hired for six to 12 hours in beach areas. Watch out for theft of the radio and spare tyre; you will have to pay about CUC$350 if stolen unless you take out the costly extra insurance. **Campervans** are also available, see www.vacacionartravel.com or www.cubamarviajes.cu. A suggested tour of the whole island covers 2550 km with demarcated stops for overnight and refueling. **Moped rental** (moto) is around US$24 per day, cheaper for longer.

Cycling

For people who really want to explore the country in depth and independently, cycling around is excellent. A good-quality bicycle is essential if you are going to spend many hours in the saddle, although that does not mean it has to be very sophisticated. We have heard from cyclists who have toured Cuba without gears, although they did have plenty of muscle. ⟩⟩ *See also page 19.*

Warnings Look out for potholes. Cuba has an extensive network of tarmac and concrete roads, which are in good condition in areas of heaviest tourist use, but rural roads suffer from lack of funds for maintenance and from storm damage. The old cars, buses and trucks on the roads may be fascinating to see, but they belch obnoxious fumes from their exhausts, which are difficult to avoid in towns. Watch out for railway crossings that have no barriers or warning lights. They often look unused, but it is absolutely essential that you stop and look for approaching trains, particularly in sugar-growing areas. Plan to finish each journey in daylight, as cycling in the dark is dangerous. Street lighting can be subject to power cuts. Other vehicles on the road often do not dip their headlights for bikes. Book your accommodation in advance to check they can safely store bikes.

Useful vocabulary A puncture is a *ponche*; to mend a puncture is *coger un ponche*; the man who mends your puncture is a *ponchero* and his workshop is a *ponchera*. Other useful words include: *la cadena* – chain, *el freno* – brake, *el cuadro* – frame, *los rayos* – spokes, *la goma* – tyre, *la cámara* – inner tube, *el sillín* – seat.

Hitchhiking

With the shortage of fuel and decline in public transport since 1991, Cubans have taken to organized hitchhiking to get about. At every major junction outside towns throughout Cuba you will find the *Azules*, traffic wardens who organize a queue, stop traffic to find out where the trucks or vans are going, and load them with passengers. Foreigners are no longer allowed to use this service, nor to travel on trucks. Cubans also hitchhike (*a botella*) unofficially and get rides in ancient cars without floors, trucks and other makeshift vehicles. Cubans are not allowed to carry paying foreigners in their vehicles, so if stopped it is the Cuban's problem not yours, but you should be aware that you could cause him/her trouble.

Taxis

There are three types of taxi: **tourist taxis**, **Cuban taxis** (*colectivos*) and **private taxis** (*particulares*). See also Transport, Havana, page 126. **Tourist taxis**, paid for in CUC$, can be hired for driving around; you pay for the distance, not for waiting time. On short routes, fares are metered. **Cuban taxis**, or *colectivos*, also operate on fixed routes and pick you up only if you know where to stand for certain destinations. The flat rate fare is 10 pesos. Travelling on them is an adventure and a complicated cultural experience. If you are lucky enough to get into a *colectivo*, sit at the back and keep quiet. Tourists are not supposed to use this service. Cubans are not allowed to carry foreigners in their vehicles, but they do. **Private taxis**, *particulares*, are cheaper than other taxis. A *particular* who pays his tax will usually display a 'taxi' sign, which can be a hand-written piece of board, but have a private registration plate. Some have meters, in others you have to negotiate a price in CUC$.

For long distances you can negotiate with official taxis as well as *particulares*, and the price should be around CUC$10 per hour. Taxis can work out cheaper than going on organized tours, if you are in a group and are prepared to bargain. As a general rule, the cost will depend on the quality of your Spanish and how well you know the area. One family paid CUC$80 to travel from Havana to Viñales by taxi, although someone else was quoted CUC$50 for the return journey.

Sea

There is currently only one journey you can do by public transport across the sea, and that is the ferry to the Isla de la Juventud (see page 389). It leaves from Surgidero de Batabanó on the coast due south of Havana, from where there are bus links.

Maps

Mapa Geográfico (Ediciones GEO) is one of the best maps, with a large map of Cuba, accompanied by several smaller maps of towns, regions and routes. It is one of the more accurate and up to date. The best map for drivers is the *Guía de Carreteras* (Road Guide), Directorio Turístico de Cuba, which has proved remarkably accurate. It grades all the roads, gives distances and marks fuel stations. *Cuba, Mapa de Carreteras* (Road Map), Ediciones GEO (1999), is a good general purpose map as well as being moderately useful for drivers. Its inset map of La Habana includes details of all the major road junctions around the capital. Ediciones GEO's *Mapa Turístico* of La Habana (with Cuba, Varadero, Trinidad, Santiago, Guardalavaca, Cayo Largo and Cayo Coco on the reverse) is good in that it includes a lot of the city. For individual states and areas there are very good provincial maps going under the name of *Mapa Turístico* (Ediciones GEO), usually including the provincial capital and sometimes other places of interest, but you will probably only find them in the relevant province. **Infotur** is worth trying, see page 69.

Stanfords ① *12-14 Long Acre, London, WC2E 9LP, T020-7836 1321, www.stanfords. co.uk (also at 29 Corn St, Bristol, BS1),* with over 80 well-travelled staff and 40,000 titles in stock, is the world's largest map and travel bookshop. In Cuba, one shop to try for maps of all kinds including nautical maps is the **El Navegante** ① *Mercaderes entre Obispo y Obrapía, Habana Vieja.*

Sleeping

All hotels are state owned. The best are those with foreign investment or foreign management contracts, which are found in the resort areas. However, there are hotels to suit most budgets, even if at the lower end they are basic. Peso hotels are reserved for Cubans and are rarely available to foreigners, although Cubans are now permitted to stay in resort hotels as well if they have sufficient CUC$. It is legal to stay with a Cuban family and rent a room as long as the family is registered and pays taxes. These places are known as *casas particulares*. There are also *casas particulares* reserved for the Cuban market, identifiable by the different coloured logo above the door. Cubans on holiday stay in campsites (*campismo*), which are cabins, not tents, a few of which accept foreigners.

Hotels

The **Gran Caribe** chain owns the four- and five-star grand old hotels such as the **Nacional** and the **Riviera** in Havana. **Cubanacán** has upmarket, modern resort hotels, with an international standard of accommodation and facilities, as does **Gaviota**, owned by the military, which has most of the strategic beach areas. The Cubanacán group comprises all the Brisas, Club Amigo, Cubanacán, Horizontes and Hoteles E (Encanto) labels. Hoteles E are renovations of colonial mansions into boutique hotels in provincial towns and are some of the nicest places to stay at very reasonable prices. **Islazul** owns the two- and three-star, older hotels, often in the countryside. **Habaguanex** is in charge of the renovations of colonial mansions in La Habana Vieja and their conversion to hotels, restaurants, bars, etc.

Most three-star hotels were built in the 1940s and 1950s and are showing their age, but some have been refurbished and are now considered four star. In remote beach resorts the hotels are usually all-inclusive and classify themselves as four or five star. At the cheaper end of the market you can expect old bed linen, ill-fitting sheets, intermittent water and electricity, peeling paintwork, crumbling tiles and indifferent service.

Accommodation for your first day in a hotel should be booked in advance of travelling. You have to fill in an address (any hotel will do) on your **tourist card** and if you leave it blank you will be directed to the reservations desk at the airport, which is time consuming. A voucher from your travel agent to confirm arrangements is usual and hotels expect it as confirmation of your reservation. This can be done abroad through travel agencies, accredited government agencies, or through **Turismo Buró** desks in main hotels. It's a good idea to book hotel rooms generally before noon. In the peak seasons, December to February and August, it is essential to book in advance. Lack of sufficient rooms has sometimes forced tourists to sleep in their cars in Trinidad in December and in the plaza in Viñales in August.

At other times it is possible to book at the hotel reception. Prices given in the text are for a double room in high season (15 December-15 March); low-season prices are about 20% lower. Shop around for prices, travel agencies can get you a better deal than the hotel, which will usually offer you the rack rate. **Cubaism** offers real-time hotel availability and online reservations for a number of hotel groups, www.cubahotelbookings.com.

Casas particulares/private accommodation

Cuba is geared more to package tourism than to independent visitors, but self-employment has opened up opportunities that can prove rewarding for the visitor. Lodging with a family is possible at CUC$15-35 per room depending on the season, the length of stay and the location, with the highest rates charged in Havana and Trinidad. Cubans are allowed to rent out only two rooms sleeping two people plus one child in each, subject to health and hygiene regulations and incorporation into the tax system. Hustlers on the street will offer accommodation, but it is safer to arrange rooms through our recommendations or other contacts if you can. A guide or hustler (*jinetero*) taking you to a private home will expect CUC$5 commission per night, which goes on your room rate. Less obvious, but still an insidious form of touting is the networking of the *casa particular* owners. Most have an address book full of owners in other towns. If you ask whether they know someone in the next town you are going to, they will happily ring up a 'friend' and book a room for you. This may be a useful service, but you will be charged CUC$5 extra a night for the favour, a sum which will be sent to the first owner as his commission. Some owners take this so seriously that they travel around the country in low season, inspecting the properties they recommend and getting to know the families.

Private homes vary considerably and can be extremely comfortable or very basic. Houses in the town centre can be very noisy if your room is on the street and traffic starts at 0530. Colonial houses have no soundproofing and even a door shutting can be heard all over the

Sleeping price codes and facilities

LL over CUC$200	**L** CUC$151-200
AL CUC$101-150	**A** CUC$66-100
B CUC$46-65	**C** CUC$31-45
D CUC$21-30	**E** CUC$12-20

LL-AL These hotels will be of an international standard, probably with a foreign partner in management. On the beach they will mostly be all-inclusive and the price will be per person with all the day and nighttime entertainment you could possibly need and a high quality of fixtures and fittings. In cities they are a mixture of brand-new, foreign-run hotels in which you may forget you are in Cuba, and delightful renovated colonial mansions with lots of charm and character.

A These will be very good hotels with newish furnishings, a pool, tour desk and good facilities. In Havana and other city centres many of them are in the old city and are 'boutique' hotels, small and intimate, colonial and newly renovated. On the beach they will be older properties, not as luxurious as the mega-resorts but they may have the best bits of beach.

B-C The lower end of the state hotel sector, older properties often in need of upgrading, less attactive areas of town or just off the beach, but bargains can be had and in the countryside are often delightful rural retreats. The best *casas particulares* in Havana and Trinidad have now crept up into this price bracket and you can expect good furnishings and facilities for any house charging over CUC$30.

D-E You wouldn't want to stay in many of the hotels in this range, but this is where the private sector comes in. *Casas particulares* cost more in Havana than in the provinces. Quality is variable; check availability of water, electricity and food, test the beds. Most are spotlessly clean and friendly.

house at 0600. Because of shortages things often don't work, there may be water and power cuts. Take a torch, there may not be good street lighting in the area, let alone power in your house. The sheets don't always fit the bed, the pillows can be often old and lumpy, bathrooms are often shared between the two rooms but they should be exclusive to tourists' use. Towels are usually very small so take your own to complement theirs. Soap will probably be provided, but don't rely on it. However, over the last few years casa owners have invested large amounts of money, time and effort into improving their visitors' accommodation. Nearly all the houses we list are in a good state of repair, newly painted and offer a private bathroom with new fixtures and fittings (although the water may still be tepid and the pressure poor), air conditioning and either a ceiling or free-standing fan and often a fridge.

All *casas* now have to pay a 'gastronomic' tax whether they want to provide food or not, so they usually do. Food is nearly always better at a *casa particular* than in a state restaurant or private *paladar*. The family eats at a different time and the food is prepared in stages, but it will still be fresher and made from better ingredients than in a restaurant. Remember that what Cubans can buy with ration coupons is not enough to feed a visitor and any extra food has to be bought in CUC$. Theft is not a problem, as the licence would be revoked if there was a serious complaint against the owner but you should always be careful with your belongings.

It is best to check that the *casa particular* you stay in is legally registered and pays taxes. All *casas particulares* should have a sticker on their front door of two blue chevrons on a white background with *Arrendador Inscripto* written across, if they are legal. Those with red triangles rent in pesos to Cubans and it is illegal for them to rent to foreigners. If you stay at an illegal residence and it is discovered, the Cuban family will have to pay a huge fine. Illegal homestays are usually reported to the police by neighbours. All clients must sign and complete address and passport details in a Registration Book within 24 hours of arrival. This book must be made available to municipal inspectors.

If you have made a phone booking in advance and are arriving by Víazul, your host will probably come to the bus station with a taxi to collect you. This is not just for your benefit. A common scam is to steal guests, sometimes from the bus terminal and sometimes from outside the front door. If you are told by someone in the street that the owners no longer rent, or are full, or have asked this person to take you to another casa, do not go with them until you have rung the bell and checked the story with someone inside the house. *Jineteros* are very skilled at diverting you from your intended path. Some even change the numbers above the door to take you to another house where they will receive a commission.

Camping

There are 84 Campismo Popular sites all over the island, although only 79 were in operation in 2009; they are usually in nice surroundings and are good value. They consist of basic cabins rather than tents and are designed for Cubans on holiday rather than foreigners. Many of them have been renovated and upgraded with games and sports equipment as well as improved food services. Camping out on the beach or in a field is forbidden. **Cubamar Viajes**, T7-833 2523, www.cubamarviajes.cu, will arrange bookings and transport to villa or cabin-style accommodation in most provinces. They have several campsites for tourists using camper vans, with water, power and waste disposal. Every year over two million Cubans and 15,000 foreigners stay in Campismo resorts.

Eating

Food is not Cuba's strong point, although the supply of fresh food has improved. In Havana the peso food situation is improving but there are still shortages. It is not unusual to be told '*no hay*' (there isn't any) at restaurants where you would expect the full menu to be available (eg an Italian restaurant had no tomatoes, let alone the mozzarella and parma ham that were on the menu). The Ministry of Agriculture has set up many *organopónicos* in the city to provide the capital with fresh vegetables, grown under organic conditions and to avoid transport costs.

Outside Havana shortages are not so bad, having recovered from the hurricane damage of 2008, but the island is not self-sufficient. Farmers' markets are good places to buy fruit and vegetables. Shops sell mostly imported supplies in CUC$ such as tins of food from Spain, packets of biscuits, cookies and crackers. Tourists do not have access to local stores, or *bodegas*, as these are based on the national ration card system. Bread, rice, beans, sugar and coffee are rationed to Cuban families but they are not given enough to live on and have to purchase the balance at market prices. Milk is rationed only for children up to the age of seven. You can buy almost anything in CUC$.

Eating price codes

††† over CUC$12   †† CUC$6-12   † under CUC$6

Prices refer to the cost of a two-course meal for one person.

Food

The national dish is *congrís* (rice mixed with black beans), roast pork and yuca (*cassava*) or fried plantain. Rice with kidney (red) beans is known as *moros y cristianos*. Pork is traditionally eaten for the New Year celebrations, so before then all the pigs that have been fattened up on people's balconies or smallholdings are on the move in the backs of trucks, cars and bicycles, to be sold privately or at the markets. Pork and chicken are the most common meats available and the cheapest. Despite government investment in fisheries, seafood such as lobster and shrimp is reserved for the export and tourist markets. There is a story that the government tried to improve the diet of the Cuban people by reducing the price of fish, but all that happened was that the cats got fat. Not even price manipulation could wean Cubans off their habitual diet of pork, rice and beans. Most food is fried and can often be greasy and bland. Spices and herbs are not commonly used and Cubans limit their flavourings to onions and garlic. Salads in restaurants are mixed vegetables which are slightly pickled and not to everyone's taste. Shredded pickled cabbage and sliced cucumber are a common garnish to the main dish. Take advantage of whatever is in season as Cuba's range of tropical fruit and vegetables is magnificent. At the right time of year there will be a glut of avocados, mangoes, guavas, zapote or papaya.

Some *casa particular* owners freeze things in times of plenty so that you can have mango or papaya juice at any time of the year. They spend a lot of time scouring the various food supply outlets every day to make sure they have a wide range of provisions for their guests. Breakfast is usually coffee, fruit and/or fruit juice, bread, honey and eggs or a cheese and ham sandwich. Many Cubans have no more than a cup of coffee for breakfast and eat their main meal at lunch time, but they expect foreigners to eat at night. Cubans are particularly hooked on ice cream, although it usually only comes in vanilla, strawberry or chocolate flavours. The ice cream parlour, **Coppelia**, can be found in every town of any size and is quite an experience, with long queues because of its popularity. There are other ice cream parlours for a change.

Drink

Rum is the national drink and all cocktails are rum based. There are several brand names and each has a variety of ages, so you have plenty of choice (see box, page 190). Do not buy cheap firewater, or cane spirit, as it is unlikely to agree with you and you may be ill for a while. The good stuff is cheap enough. Beer is good and there are regional varieties, which come in bottles or cans. The locally grown coffee is good, although hotels often manage to make it undrinkable in the mornings. Some of the best coffee comes from back gardens, home grown and home roasted.

The most widely available **beer** throughout the island is *Cristal*, made by **Cervecería Mayabe**, in Holguín. Found in bottles or cans at 4.9% alcohol content, it costs CUC$1-1.15

A thirst for freedom

The first Cuban resistance fighter we know of was an Amerindian chief called Hatuey, who has now become a symbol of rebellion. He lived at the time of the Spanish invasion and when he discovered what the Spanish really wanted from his island he travelled from the island of Hispaniola to Cuba to warn the Cuban Taínos of the Conquistadores' plans and mobilize his people. However, he was no match for the better-armed Spaniards, who chased him into the mountains, captured him and burnt him alive. The story goes that when approached by a priest and asked whether he would like to make a last request, confess and make his peace with God, he asked whether there would be Spanish people in heaven. When told that there would, he declined the offer, saying he certainly didn't want to go there. Nowadays, Hatuey has the dubious honour of having a beer named after him.

in supermarkets and CUC$1.50-2.50 in bars. From the same brewery is *Mayabe*, with Ordinary at 3.5% and Extra at 5%, both costing the same as Cristal and also popular with more flavour. Sometimes you can find *Mayabe* beer in pesos cubanos, at 18 pesos. *Hatuey*, made in Havana, is reckoned by some to be the best of Cuba's many beers, named after an Amerindian chief ruling when the Spanish arrived, but it is very hard to find. *Bucanero*, from Holguín, is easily bought in the east of the island, 5.4% in bottles or cans. *Tínimo* (from Camagüey, good with more flavour than Cristal) is also difficult to find. Cuba now also produces **wines** under the *Soroa* label, grown and produced in Pinar del Río and sold for about CUC$4 in shops. It is not to be recommended except to marinate tough meat, but it is improving. There is also a more expensive range sold for about CUC$9-10, including Cabernet Sauvignon, Chardonnay, Tempranillo and other grapes, produced with the help of a Spanish company in a joint venture. If you want wine you are better off buying something imported.

Eating out

State restaurants/hotels

State-owned 'dollar' restaurants are recognizable by the credit card stickers on the door, where meals are about CUC$10-40, paid only in CUC$. Some can be quite good and there are variations in menus, so you can find Italian, Spanish or French restaurants. Be warned that the Cuban idea of Chinese food is unlike anything you might find in your home country and very sweet. You get what you pay for, and at the cheap end of the market you can expect poor quality, limited availability of ingredients and disinterested staff. Generally, although restaurants have improved in the last few years, the food in Cuba is not very exciting. Restaurants are more innovative in Havana than elsewhere and some of the *paladares* are eccentric in their tastes. Always check restaurant prices in advance and then your bill. Discrepancies occur in both the state and private sector.

Resort **hotels** tend to serve buffet meals, which can get tedious after a while, but breakfast here, and in large, urban hotels where buffets are served, is usually good and plentiful and you can stock up for the day. Breakfast in other hotels can be particularly slow. If not eating at a buffet, service, no matter what standard of restaurant or hotel, can be very slow (even if you are the only customers).

Paladares/casas particulares

Paladares are privately owned restaurants, licensed and taxed and limited to 12 chairs, as well as having employment restrictions. Some very good family-run businesses have been set up, offering a three-course meal in Havana for CUC$10-20 per person, less than that outside the capital. Things like olives and coffee are usually charged as extras, be sure to check what the meal includes. They are not allowed to have lobster or shrimp on the menu as these are reserved for hotels and the export market. However, if you ask, there are often items available which are not on the menu. Remember that if someone guides you to a *paladar* he will expect a commission, so you end up paying more for your food. There are also illegal *paladares*, which will serve meals with meat for CUC$3-5 per person. We do not list them. The cheapest, legal, way of getting a decent meal is by eating in a *casa particular*. This is generally of excellent quality in plentiful, even vast, proportions, with the advantage that they will cook whatever you want. Vegetarians can be catered for. They usually charge CUC$6-10 for a meal, chicken and pork is cheaper than fish, while some *casa* owners seem to have access to all sorts of delicacies (illegal of course). Breakfast is usually CUC$3-5 and far better value than in a state hotel. You can negotiate a package of dinner, bed and breakfast which can give good value. While quality and style of cooking naturally varies, as a general rule you will get fresher food in a *casa particular* than you will in a restaurant or *paladar*, both of which now have the reputation of recycling meals and reheating leftovers.

Fast food/peso stalls

For a cheap meal you are better off trying the Cuban version of **fast-food** restaurants, such as **El Rápido**, or **Burgui**, or try a *cafetería*, of which there are many all round the island. As well as chicken and chips or burgers, they offer a 'wide' range of sandwiches: cheese, ham, or cheese and ham, but they do come in different sizes. A sandwich in a restaurant or bar in Havana costs about CUC$4, a coffee costs CUC$1. In a provincial town you can pay as little as CUC$2 for a sandwich and beer for lunch. Breakfast and one other meal may be sufficient if you fill in with street or 'dollar shop' snacks. All towns and cities have **peso street stalls** for sandwiches, pizza and snacks; change about CUC$10 for a two-week stay if planning to avoid restaurants. In out-of-the-way places, you will be able to pay for food in pesos, but generally you will be charged in CUC$.

Vegetarians

For vegetarians the choice is very limited, normally only cheese sandwiches, spaghetti, pizzas, salads, bananas and omelettes. Even beans (and *congris*) are often cooked with meat or in meat fat. If you are staying at a *casa particular* or eating in a *paladar*, they will usually prepare meatless meals for you with advance warning. Always ask for beans to be cooked in vegetable oil. Some vegetarians even recommend taking your own oil and lending it to the cook so that you can be absolutely sure that lard has not been used. Hotels usually have quite extravagant all-you-can-eat buffet spreads you can choose from.

Entertainment

Of all the islands in the Caribbean, Cuba has the best and most varied nightlife with a great music scene including Latin, jazz, folk music and rock. There are theatres for drama and ballet, concert halls for classical music or touring bands, discos, nightclubs, bars, cinemas showing Cuban and foreign movies, and indoor and outdoor music venues around the country. Most of the action is concentrated in Havana, but every town has a *Casa de la Trova* for traditional music and a *Casa de la Cultura* for cultural events, art exhibitions and concerts, as well as a theatre and cinema in the larger towns. There is usually an open-air bar called the *Patio de Artex*, where you can find more contemporary music and arts with a variety of entertainment in the evenings. Santiago is no poor relation and has its own regional variations in music and culture.

Every visitor will experience the vibrant rhythms of Cuban music and dance, it is inescapable. Bands patrol the bars and restaurants to serenade you at every opportunity, even up to the airport departure lounge before you leave. Hotels offer constant night time entertainment, with cabaret, concerts, discos and comedy. No one wastes the chance to get up and salsa, from toddlers to grandmas, Cubans have the sexiest hip-swaying movements and are not shy about demonstrating and sharing their technique. There are even daytime events for those unable to keep going until dawn in the clubs, perfect for families. Several provincial towns, such as Bayamo, have a weekly street party when stalls sell food and drink from the region, bars and restaurants spill out onto the street and there is music and dancing until late. All of this is washed down with rum of varying degrees of excellence. At many places you take the bottle of rum and they provide the ice and mixers in the price for entrance. It is easy to get a party started.

Cartelera, www.cartelera.com is a free magazine in English and Spanish where you can find out what's on in Havana. Other towns have leaflets or pin up flyers in strategic places, for example Casas de la Cultura, but your hotel or *casa particular* will be able to tell you what is happening, where and when.

Festivals and events

In contrast with other Latin American countries, there are no national religious festivals, although you will find some patron saints' days celebrated in churches (often linked to *Santería*) and Easter is an important time. Processions are usually limited to taking place within the church itself and not all round the streets of the town. **Christmas Day** was reintroduced as a public holiday in 1997 (having been banned after the Revolution) prior to a visit from the Pope and has become a regular event with Christmas trees and tinsel, but a whole generation missed out on celebrating it and there is little awareness of what it signifies. Public holidays are political and historical events and are marked by speeches, rallies and other gatherings, often in each town's Plaza de la Revolución. **Carnival** takes place in the heat of July in Santiago. Havana's Carnival is moved around a lot, sometimes August, sometimes October or November; you can't rely on the date. While operating with limited budgets, these events are colourful, energetic and have a raw vibrancy. Parades are accompanied by music, drumming, dancing and competitions involving children and adults and requiring lots of stamina. There are lots of cultural and sporting festivals and events held throughout the year, see below.

Spectator sports

Baseball

Cuba is a baseball-mad nation and vies with the USA for poll position in the world. During international matches every television set in the island is tuned to the match. The Serie Nacional baseball season runs from November to May, culminating in the national play-offs, followed a couple of weeks later by the Liga Superior, which lasts a month. In August, 'Que Siempre Brille el Sol' is a popular tournament, see page 46, for contact details. Baseball games have a fanatical following and can last up to three hours. Later that night and the following day you can see groups of fans in plazas around the country heatedly discussing the recent match with wild gestures and raised voices. See Havana, page 124, for information on matches there.

Basketball

Young Cuban men can be seen playing basketball in every town and village. This is the second most popular sport in the country and visitors are welcome to join in. The main stadium is the Ramón Fonst stadium near the Plaza de la Revolución in Havana and the season runs from September to November.

Boxing

Cuban boxers can always be expected to come out of the Olympic Games with a clutch of medals in all boxing weights and Cubans enthusiastically support their athletes. The best place to catch a tournament or just watch some training matches for international team events is the Sala Kid Chocolate in Havana.

Cycling

There is keen interest in cycling as a sport and Cuba is a respected competitor in the Americas. Havana's professional racetrack is at the Velódromo Reinaldo Paseiro, part of the Estadio Panamericano, built in 1991 for the Pan-American Games. It is located on the southern side of the Vía Blanca, next to the swimming facilities. Cuba hosts several international competitions including Vuelta a Cuba (February), a staged road race from Baracoa to Pinar del Río. See Festivals and events for contact details.

Festivals

January

New Year is celebrated around the country with great fanfare, largely because it coincides with **Liberation Day**, marking the end of the Batista dictatorship, on 1 Jan. There is lots of music and dancing, outdoor discos and general merriment, washed down with copious quantities of rum.

Cubadanza is a twice-yearly dance festival. Contact **Danza Contemporánea de Cuba**, Eddy Veitía or Leonor Rumayor, T7-8796410, danzacontcuba@ cubarte.cult.cu.

Festival de la Trova 'Longina' in Santa Clara, celebrating the life of the great trovador, Manuel Corona, with a pilgrimage to Caibarién, his birth place on 9 Jan.

February

International Jazz Plaza Festival is held every other year at theatres and the Casa de la Cultura de Plaza. It is one of the world's major jazz festivals with the best of Cuban and international jazz. There are masterclasses and workshops available and the event is organized by Grammy winner Jesús 'Chucho' Valdés. CUC$20 entrance per concert or CUC$120 unlimited access to all the events, workshops etc, www.festival jazzplaza.icm.cu.

Havana International Book Fair is held at La Cabaña; a commercial fair in the castle, immensely popular with book-hungry families, who come for a day out. Look out for new book launches. Also held in many cities around the island, www.cubaliteraria.com.

Vuelta a Cuba de Ciclismo is a cycle through every province. Contact Alberto Puig de la Barca, T7-2040945, agencia@cubadeportes.cu.

Cigar Festival, www.festivaldelhabano.com, introduced in the last few years, is for true aficionados of *Habanos*. Held at the Palacio de las Convenciones, you can learn about the history of cigars and there are opportunities for visits to tobacco plantations and cigar factories.

March

Bienal de la Habana is held over a month and takes place every 2 years (next in 2011), gathering over 200 artists from 40 countries in the Centro de Arte Contemporáneo Wifredo Lam, Centro de Arte La Casona, Parque Morro-Cabaña, Pabellón Cuba and other venues, www.bienalhabana.cult.cu.

Festival Danzón Habana, held at the Teatro América, Centro Hispanoamericano de Cultura y Unión Fraternal, at the end of the month and into April, musicians and dancers celebrate danzón, contact José Loyola, eventos@paradis.artex.cu.

International Electrical Acoustic Music Festival takes place every other year (next in 2010) in Havana, with workshops and performances. Contact Emmanuel de Juan Blanco Hernández of the **Laboratorio Nacional Música Electroacústica** (LNME), T7-8303983, lnme@cubarte.cult.cu.

Festival Internacional de la Trova 'Pepe Sánchez' is held at the Casa de la Trova and the Sala de Concierto Dolores in Santiago with concerts, roving musicians, conferences and other events. Contact Leydis Torres, cpmusica@cultstgo.cult.cu.

April

Festival Internacional de Cine Pobre de Humberto Solás in Gibara, a film festival to showcase low-budget movies, contact Sergio Benvenuto, festivalcinepobre@icaic.cu. A very popular event is the **Copa Cuba Ciclismo** track cycle racing competitions. Contact Jackeline, T7-204 0945, agenciaco@cubadeportes.cu.

May

Romerías de Mayo, Holguín. A cultural festival with young and old artists, musicians and intellectuals from Cuba and overseas, events take place all over the city. Contact Alexis Triana Hernández, eventos@paradis.artex.cu.

Festival Internacional de Poesía de La Habana at the Basílica Menor de San Francisco de Asís and other locations. The Unión Nacional de Escritores y Artistas de Cuba (UNEAC) gathers poets from all corners for a celebration of poetry. Contact Alex Pausides, eventos@paradis.artex.cu.

June

International Ernest Hemingway White Marlin Fishing Tournament is one of the major events at the Marina Hemingway. Contact José Miguel Díaz Escrich, T7-204 6653, yachtclub@cnih.mh.cyt.cu.

Cuculambeana Festival, Las Tunas. Celebration of traditional folk music of the area. Contact Lourdes Medina Pérez, eventos@paradis.artex.cu.

July

Cuballet de Verano is a summer dance festival. Contact Lourdes Bermejo, T7-265 0848, prodanza@cubarte.cult.cu.

Festival del Caribe 'Fiesta del Fuego' is held in the 1st week of Jul in Santiago with theatre, dancing and conferences, continuing later in the month to coincide with the Moncada celebrations on 26 Jul.

Carnival in Santiago (18-27 Jul) is a week-long musical extravaganza taking in the city's patron saint's day, 25 Jul, but it traditionally stops for a day on 26 Jul for a day of more serious political celebrations. Contact Orlando Vergés Martínez, caribe@cultstgo.cult.cu.

August

Que Siempre Brille el Sol baseball tournament is always a popular event. Contact Higinio Vélez Carrión T7-879 7980, or Cubadeportes, T7-2040945, agencia@cubadeportes.cu.

Cubadanza, the 2nd of the year, with workshops and courses, see Jan for details.

September
International Blue Marlin Fishing Tournament at Marina Hemingway. The marina fills up with mostly US fishermen eager to pit their strength against marlin and their fellow competitors, with lots of après-fishing social events. Contact José Miguel Díaz Escrich, T7-204 6653, yachtclub@cnih.mh.cyt.cu.

October
Havana Contemporary Music Festival held at UNEAC and theatres at the end of the month. Contact Guido López Gavilán, T7-832 0194, promoven@uneac.co.cu.
Festival Internacional del Son 'Matamoros Son' at Teatro Heredia, Santiago. Music and dancing to celebrate *son* and famous *soneros*.
Havana International Ballet Festival held every other year in the 2nd half of the month at the Gran Teatro, Teatro Nacional and Teatro Mella. Run by Alicia Alonso, head of the Cuban National Ballet, bnc@cubarte.cult.cu.
Fiesta de la Cubanía, Bayamo, with celebrations in the plazas of traditional folklore, music, dance and other cultural activities.
Fiesta de la Cultura Iberoamericana, in Holguín, celebrating all things Spanish and Latin American at the Casa de Iberoamérica. Contact Alexis Triana Hernández, eventos@paradis.artex.cu.
Havana Theatre Festival, at theatres and plazas all over the city at the end of Oct and into Nov, contemporary international and Cuban drama, workshops and seminars, contact Bárbara Rivero, eventos@paradis.artex.cu.

November
International Tournament of Wahoo Fishing at the Marina Hemingway. Contact José Miguel Díaz Escrich, T7-204 6653, yachtclub@cnih.mh.cyt.cu.
Marabana, Havana's marathon, T7-204 0945/8, agencia@cubadeportes.cu, or for more information contact the Federación Cubana de Maratones, marabana@inder.cu.

Festival Internacional de Coros held at the Sala de Concierto Dolores in Santiago. Contact Raúl Fernández Campanioni, eventos@paradis.artex.cu.

December
International Festival of New Latin American Cinema shows prize-winning films (no subtitles) at cinemas around Havana. This is the foremost film festival in Latin America with the best of Cuban and Latin American films along with documentaries and independent cinema from Europe and the USA. See the stars as well as the films, as the festival attracts big-name actors and directors, festival@festival.icaic.cu, www.habanafilmfestival.com.
Happy End of Year Regatta at the Marina Hemingway for 3 days with social events that always accompany the racing fraternity. Contact José Miguel Díaz Escrich, T7-204 6653, yachtclub@cnih.mh.cyt.cu.

Public holidays

1 Jan Liberation Day.
1 May Labour Day.
25, 26, 27 Jul Revolution Day.
10 Oct Beginning of War of Independence.
25 Dec Christmas Day.
Other festive days which are not public holidays are **28 Jan** (birth of José Martí, 1853), **24 Feb** (anniversary of renewal of War of Independence, 1895), **8 Mar** (International Women's Day), **13 Mar** (anniversary of 1957 attack on presidential palace in Havana by a group of young revolutionaries), **19 Apr** (anniversary of defeat of mercenaries at Bay of Pigs, 1961), **30 Jul** (martyrs of the Revolution day), **8 Oct** (death of Che Guevara, 1967), **28 Oct** (death of Camilo Cienfuegos, 1959), **27 Nov** (death by firing squad of 8 medical students by Spanish colonial government, 1871), **7 Dec** (death of Antonio Maceo in battle in 1896). These public holidays are often marked by speeches and displays by school children.

Shopping

Where to shop

Compared with much of Latin America, Cuba is expensive for the tourist, but compared with many Caribbean islands it is not. Whereas in the 1990s most towns would have one or two dollar shops, there are now lots of supermarkets and smaller shops selling imported items in CUC$. Some of these may actually have been made in Cuba in the free-trade zones (see Economy, page 419), where they are allowed to sell 25% of their produce on the domestic market in CUC$. Shopping centres are springing up and the materialist culture is creeping in. It is not unusual for a *casa particular* to have two or three fridge freezers and a microwave, yet the woman will be doing the laundry in cold water in an outside sink as she has done all her life, and the family will travel on a bicycle.

There is very little you can buy in pesos cubanos apart from some food in some areas. Shoes, clothing, cosmetics, toiletries, camera film, imported food and drink are all available in CUC$. Throughout the country, stores are surprisingly busy, despite the small proportion of the population having direct access to CUC$, or *divisa*, as hard currency is known. All bags and receipts are checked on leaving a store.

What to buy

The main souvenirs to take home with you have to be **rum, cigars** and **coffee**. The street price of a bottle of rum ranges from CUC$2-10 depending on its age and quality. Cigars can cost whatever you are prepared to pay, but they are still the best in the world (see box, page 150). Remember that all the best tobacco leaves go into cigar making rather than cigarettes. Make sure you buy the best to take home and don't get tricked into buying fakes, you may not get them through customs. You are only allowed to take 23 cigars out of the country without a receipt. If you are buying any souvenirs to take home, remember to keep the official receipt in case you have to show it at customs on departure. If you are after a specific cigar brand, go to a specialist shop, where the cigars are stored at the correct temperature and the staff are knowledgeable. While there is a fairly large stock at the airport you can't rely on finding what you want.

Handicrafts are now being developed for the tourist market and there are *artesanía* markets in Havana, Trinidad and Varadero, which hold an overwhelming amount of stock. Wooden carvings, inlaid wooden boxes for cigars, jewellery, key rings, baseball bats, model sailing ships, cotton crochet garments, ceramics, Che Guevara berets and innumerable T-shirts will be offered to you. There is a considerable amount of **artwork** of varying degrees of worth, but you may pick up a bargain. If you are a serious collector, skip the markets and go straight to the galleries in Havana. Taking art out of the country requires a special licence.

Essentials A-Z

Accident and emergency

Fire T105. **Police** T106. **Ambulance** T104 (in Cienfuegos, Villa Clara, Camagüey, Holguín and Guantánamo, but it varies in other towns). There are international clinics (Clínicas del Sol) and pharmacies (Farmacias Internacionales) in beach resort areas and many large towns for tourists' use, see main text for details, www.servimedcuba.

It is a serious crime to do anything to harm tourism and the penalties are extremely severe with long prison sentences. The police are usually (but not always) helpful and thorough when investigating theft. Ask for a stamped statement for insurance purposes, although this is reported to be like getting blood out of a stone from some police stations. In the event of a crime, make a note of where it happened. Visitors should remember that some of the local population will often do anything to get hard currency, from simply asking for money or foreign-bought goods, to mugging. Foreigners will be offered almost anything on the street – from cigars to cocaine to *chicas* (girls). Buying cigars on the street is not illegal, but they are often not genuine and may be confiscated at customs if you have more than 23 and cannot produce an official receipt of purchase.

Take extra passport photos with you and keep them separate from your passport. If you have to get more photos while you are in Cuba, there is a place in Havana next to the **International Press Centre** at Calle 21 esquina O, which produces them with a wait of about 1 hr.

Children

Cubans love children and the experience of travelling with children in Cuba can be rewarding for both parents and offspring.

The children will love the beaches and the sea of course, but inland there are lots of opportunities for entertaining them, with trips to amusement parks, caves, rivers, farms and animals everywhere. Cuba is also tremendously educational; how many children living in Europe or North America have seen sugar cane, tobacco or coffee growing? Who wouldn't enjoy seeing a *bicitaxi* or a horse-drawn *coche* and watching the oxen ploughing the fields? Trinidad is recommended for families, combining sightseeing for the adults with the proximity of a beach for the kids and a relaxed atmosphere. Sightseeing can be a very hot activity for small children, but the promise of the beach in the afternoon can smooth many a path. Many of Cuba's best beach resorts are remote from places of interest for sightseeing trips, which means several hours of sitting in a bus or car to get to where the grown-ups want to go. If travelling in high season (Dec-Feb) or the Cuban holiday season (Aug) hiring a car or buying enough Víazul bus tickets, see page 30, can be very difficult, so advance reservations are essential. For younger teenagers interested in music, many of the best venues in Havana offer afternoon *peñas* and discos popular with Cuban youth. Apart from the sun and the need to drink plenty of water, there are no particular health problems to watch out for. Diarrhoea and vomiting are the most common problems, so take the usual precautions, but more intensively (see Health, page 52, for further advice). Breastfeeding is best and most convenient for babies, but powdered milk is generally available and so are baby foods. Papaya, bananas and avocados are all nutritious and can be cleanly prepared. The treatment of diarrhoea is the same as for adults, except that it should start earlier and be continued with more persistence. Children get dehydrated very quickly and can become drowsy and uncooperative unless cajoled to drink water or juice plus salts. Upper respiratory infections, such as colds, catarrh and middle-ear infections are also common and if your child suffers from these normally, take some antibiotics against the possibility. Outer-ear infections after swimming are also common and antibiotic eardrops will help.

'Wet wipes' are always useful and sometimes difficult to find, as are disposable nappies. State-run restaurants have toilets for customers' use, but not all private restaurants have them; public toilets can be found in the centre of some towns, but you cannot rely on it. There are unlikely to be any facilities for changing babies' nappies/diapers, and remember to take a good supply of toilet paper as it is not usually supplied.

Clothing

This is generally informal and summer calls for the very lightest clothing. Sunglasses, a high-factor sun lotion and some kind of head cover are recommended. A jersey and light raincoat or umbrella are needed in the cooler months; a jersey or fleece is also needed if you plan to travel on a/c internal flights, buses (particularly overnight on Víazul bus) or trains, which are very cold. You should be appropriately dressed to go into a church or temple. Cubans dress up to go out at night.

Customs and duty free

Personal baggage and articles for personal use are allowed in **duty free**; as are 1 carton of cigarettes and 2 bottles of alcoholic drinks. You may take in up to 10 kg of medicine, so long as it is in its original packaging. It is prohibited to bring in fresh fruit and vegetables, which will be confiscated if found. On departure you may take out 50 cigarettes without a receipt, tobacco worth US$2000 with a receipt, but only 23 cigars without a receipt, up to 6 bottles of rum and personal jewellery. To take out works of art you must have permission from the Registro Nacional de Bienes Culturales de

la Dirección de Patrimonio del Ministerio de Cultura. Books that are more than 50 years old may not be taken out of the country, nor those belonging to Ediciones R. For further details on customs regulations, see www.aduana.co.cu.

Disabled travellers

There are few facilities for disabled people. In the resort areas new hotels have been built with a few rooms adapted for people using wheelchairs, but the older, state-run, 3-star hotels usually have no facilities and neither do casas particulares. Cuba is not easy to get around in a wheelchair and a certain amount of determination is required. Pavements are usually built up much higher than the roads, because of rain and flash flooding, which makes crossing the road hazardous. Potholes and loose paving stones compound the difficulties. If you are travelling independently it is not impossible to get around and stay in private accommodation, but you will have to do plenty of research first to make sure you can have a ground-floor room and that passages and doorways are negotiable with wheels. You can use the bus company Víazul if you have someone to help you, or you can hire your own vehicle. Don't be discouraged, you will not be the first disabled person to travel around Cuba and Cubans are tremendously helpful and supportive.

Electricity

110 volts, 3 phase 60 cycles, AC. Plugs and sockets are usually of the American flat 2-pin type, so bring an adaptor from home if necessary. In some new tourist hotels however, European plugs are used, with 220 volts, check in advance if it is important to you. Some casas particulares now have both 110v and 220v, which is better for charging laptops, phones, etc. In 2009 severe economic difficulties meant that the Government had to ration electricity to the

general population and to industry. Do not be surprised if there are power cuts.

Embassies and consulates

→ www.cubminrex.cu.

Argentina Virrey del Pino No 1810, Belgrado (1426), Capital Federal, Buenos Aires, T5411-4782 9049, argoficemb@ ecuargentina. minrex.gov.cu.

Australia Ground Floor, 128 Chalmers St, Surry Hills NSW 2010, PO BOX 2382, Strawberry Hills, NSW 2012, Sydney, T02-9698 9797, http://embacuba.cuba minrex.cu/australiaing.

Austria Himmelhofgasse 40 A-C, A-1130, Vienna, T43-1-8778198, embajador@ ecuaustria.jet2web.at.

Belgium rue Roberts Jones 77, 1180 Bruxelles, T32(0)2-343 7146, www.embacuba.be.

Brazil SHIS Q1-5, conjunto 18, Casa No 1, Lago Sul, Brasilia, T55-61-248 4710/248 4130, http://embacu.cubaminrex.cu/brasil.

Canada 388 Main St, Ottawa, Ontario, K1S 1E3, T1-613-563 0141, embacuba@embacuba.ca.

Colombia Carrera 9 No 92-54, Santa Fe de Bogotá, T57-12-621 7054, embacuba@cable.net.co.

Denmark Carolinevej 12, st.tv, DK-2900, Hellerup, Copenhagen, T45-394 01506, www.cubaembassy.dk.

France 16 rue de Presles 75015, Paris, T33-1-456 75535, embacu@ambacuba.fr.

Germany Stavanger Str 20, 10439 Berlin, T030-916 11811, www.botschaft-kuba.de.

Italy Via Licinia No 7, 00153, Rome, T39-06-571 724299, www.ambasciatacuba.com.

Mexico Presidente Mazaryk No 554, Colonia Polanco, Delegación Miguel Hidalgo, 11560, México DF, T52-5-280 8039, www.embacuba.com.mx.

Netherlands Scheveningseweg 9, 517 KS, The Hague, T31-70-360 6061, www.embacuba.nl.

Norway Oscars Gate 78B, 3rd floor, 0244 Oslo, T47-2-308 3260, www.embacuba.no.

Portugal Rua Pero Da Covilha No 14, Restelo, 1400-297, Lisbon, T351-21-304 1860, ambaixada.cuba@netcabo.pt.

South Africa 45 Mackenzie St, Brooklyn 0181, Pretoria, T27-12-346 2215, http://emba.cubaminrex.cu/sudafrica.

Spain Paseo de La Habana No 194, CP 28036, Madrid, T34-91-359 2500, http://emba.cubaminrex.cu/espana.

Sweden Sturevagen9, 18273 Stocksund, T46-8-545 83277, primero.enero59@swipnet.se.

Switzerland Gesellsschaftsstrasse 8, CP 5275, 30112, Berne, T41-0-31 302 2111, http://emba.cubaminrex.cu/suiza.

UK 167 High Holborn, London WC1 6PA, T44-(0)207-240 2488, embacuba@cubaldn.com.

Venezuela Calle Roraima entre Río de Janeiro y Choroni, Chuao, Caracas, T058-0212-0991 6661, embajador@ embajadacuba.com.ve.

Gay and lesbian travellers

Cuba has in the past been notoriously homophobic and after the Revolution many homosexuals were sent to hard labour camps to be 'rehabilitated'. The Mariel exodus was characterized as being the flight of criminals and homosexuals, who could no longer stand their human rights being flouted. However, attitudes gradually changed, and although Cuba is still a macho society, there is more tolerance of gays just as there is more religious freedom. The film, *Fresa y Chocolate* (see Cuban cinema, page 439), has done much to stimulate debate and acceptance. For an excellent account of Cuban attitudes to homosexuals, before and after the Revolution and up to the present, read Ian Lumsden's *Machos, Maricones and Gays, Cuba and Homosexuality*, published by the Temple University Press, Philadelphia and Latin American Bureau, London. Gay travellers will not generally encounter any problems in Cuba, there are no laws against homosexuality and physical assaults are rare. However, in practice, there can be difficulties with accommodation if you want to stay in *casas particulares* as some owners prefer not to rent rooms to same-sex partners, particularly if one of them is Cuban.

Gifts

If you are planning to stay with Cubans, whether with friends or in private rented accommodation, there are some items in short supply in Cuba which they may appreciate: T-shirts (preferably with something written on them), household medicines such as paracetamol or aspirin, cosmetics, cotton wool, tampons, washing-up or kitchen cloths, soap, neutral shoe polish, pens, pencils, notebooks and writing paper. The list of items in short supply changes according to whether foreign exchange is available to pay for imports.

Health

Cuba has a high-quality national health service and is one of the healthiest countries in Latin America and the Caribbean. Travel in Cuba poses no health risk to the average visitor provided sensible precautions are taken. It is important to see your GP or travel clinic at least 6 weeks before departure for general advice on any travel risks and necessary vaccinations. Try phoning a specialist travel clinic if your own doctor is unfamiliar with health conditions in Cuba. Check with your national health service or health insurance on coverage in Cuba and take a copy of your insurance policy with you. Also get a dental check, know your own blood group and if you suffer a long-term condition such as diabetes or epilepsy, obtain a Medic Alert bracelet/necklace (www.medicalert.co.uk). If you wear glasses, take a copy of your prescription.

Vaccinations
It is important to confirm your primary courses and boosters are up to date. It is also advisable to vaccinate against **tetanus**, **typhoid** and **hepatitis A**. Vaccines

sometimes advised are **hepatitis B**, **rabies** and **diphtheria**. **Yellow fever** vaccination is not required unless you are coming directly from an infected country in Africa or South America. Although **cholera** vaccination is largely ineffective, immigration officers may ask for proof of such vaccination if coming from a country where an epidemic has occurred. Check www.who.int for updates. **Malaria** is not normally a danger in Cuba.

Health risks
The most common affliction of travellers to any country is probably diarrhoea and the same is true of Cuba. Tap water is good in most areas of the country, but bottled water is widely available and recommended. Swimming in sea or river water that has been contaminated by sewage can be a cause of diarrhoea; ask locally if it is safe. Diarrhoea may also be caused by viruses, bacteria (such as E-coli), protozoal (such as giardia), salmonella and cholera. It may be accompanied by vomiting or by severe abdominal pain. Any kind of diarrhoea responds well to the replacement of water and salts. Sachets of rehydration salts can be bought in most chemists and can be dissolved in boiled water. If the symptoms persist, consult a doctor.

There is no malaria in Cuba but dengue fever has been reported and there are lots of mosquitoes in the wetlands, so take insect repellent and avoid being bitten as much as possible. Sleep off the ground and use a mosquito net and some kind of insecticide. Remember that DEET (Di-ethyltoluamide) is the gold standard. Apply the repellent every 4-6 hrs but more often if you are sweating heavily. If a non-DEET product is used, check who tested it. Validated products (tested at the London School of Hygiene and Tropical Medicine) include Mosiguard, Non-DEET Jungle formula and non-DEET Autan. If you want to use citronella remember that it must be applied very frequently (ie hourly) to be effective.

The climate is hot; Cuba is a tropical country and protection against the sun will be

First aid

A well-stocked first-aid kit is recommended for, although the medical profession is well trained, supplies are limited. Always carry toilet paper with you, it is not always available in public toilets and even some hotels do not have it. Things you might like to take for precautionary purposes include antibiotics for possible ear or sinus infections, nasal sprays, ear drops, antihistamine cream, diarrhoea remedies and seasickness pills.

Be particularly careful to avoid infection from any lesions and make sure you are up to date with your anti-tetanus injections. If diving, you should avoid touching any coral (which will die if you do anyway) and not go poking about in holes and overhangs, where you might get stung or bitten by something you can't see. There are five hyperbaric chambers around the country, staffed by well-qualified medical professionals.

needed. To reduce the risk of sunburn and skin cancer, make sure you pack high-factor sun cream, light-coloured loose clothing and a hat.

If you get sick

Medical service is no longer free for foreign visitors in areas where there are international clinics that charge in CUC$ (credit cards accepted). Visitors requiring medical attention will be sent to them. Emergencies are handled on an ad hoc basis. Make sure you have adequate insurance (see below). Remember you cannot dial any toll-free numbers abroad so make sure you have a contact number. Charges are generally lower than those in Western countries. According to latest reports, visitors are still treated free of charge in parts of the country away from Havana, with the exception of tourist enclaves with on-site medical services.

Doctors and health facilities in major cities are listed in the Directory sections of this book.

Useful websites

www.btha.org British Travel Health Association.
www.cdc.gov US government site that gives excellent advice on travel health and details of disease outbreaks.
www.fco.gov.uk British Foreign and Commonwealth Office travel site has useful information on each country, people, climate and a list of UK embassies/consulates.

www.fitfortravel.scot.nhs.uk A-Z of vaccine/health advice for each country.
www.numberonehealth.co.uk Travel screening services, vaccine and travel health advice, email/SMS text vaccine reminders and screens returned travellers for tropical diseases.

Insurance

We strongly recommend that you invest in a good insurance policy that covers you for theft or loss of possessions and money, the cost of medical and dental treatment, cancellation of flights, delays in travel arrangement, accidents, missed departures, lost baggage, lost passport and personal liability and legal expenses. Also check on inclusion of 'dangerous activities'. These generally include climbing, diving, horse riding, parachuting, even trekking. Always read the small print carefully. Not all policies cover ambulance, helicopter rescue or emergency flights home.

There are a variety of policies to choose from, so it's best to shop around. Your travel agent can advise on the best deals available. Reputable student travel organizations often offer good-value policies. Some companies will not cover those over 65. The best policies for older travellers are through **Age Concern**, T0800-009966, www.ageconcern.org.uk.

All loss must be reported to the police and/or hotel authorities within 24 hrs of discovery and a written report obtained. This is notoriously difficult to obtain in Cuba. **Asistur** is linked to overseas insurance companies and can help with emergency hospital treatment, robbery, direct transfer of funds to Cuba, etc. Main office Prado 208, entre Colón y Trocadero, Habana Vieja, for 24-hr service T7-866 8339/866 8920, www.asistur.cu.

Internet

Cubans' access to the internet is tightly controlled and limited to those who can afford to pay in CUC$. The only Cubans who are permitted to use the internet at home are civil servants, doctors and party representatives, on a regular phone line paid for in pesos; others have to pay in CUC$.

Foreign tourists using the internet will invariably be asked to show their passport. The large, international hotels of 4 or 5 stars, such as the **Nacional**, **Habana Libre**, Parque Central and **Meliá Cohiba**in Havana and the **Meliá Santiago de Cuba** in Santiago, have business centres with computers for internet access for guests and others, but this is the most expensive way of checking emails, at anything up to CUC$15 for 1 hr. Nearly every hotel for foreigners now has internet access for its guests in some form or other and this is always worth trying even if you are not staying there. The telephone company, **Etecsa**, sells prepaid cards that give you an access code and a password code for when you log in and these cost CUC$6 for 1 hr, useful if you are in the country for a few weeks. The main telephone office in each town usually has internet access, but if not, look for **Telepunto** offices, or **Etecsa** cabins (large blue telephone boxes) with international and national phone services and a computer for internet access. **Telecorreos** sells a different prepaid card for use in post offices but this is of little use to

foreigners; you can send emails but you cannot surf the internet, which means that if you use Hotmail or any other system that uses the internet, you will not be able to access your inbox and you will have to set up a new account. There are very few places that could be termed internet cafés, eg in the Capitolio in Havana and in a couple of cafés in Trinidad, where you can pay in cash for the time used, but at the same rate as at **Etecsa**. Connection can be terribly slow and keyboards hammered.

Language

Spanish is the official language, spoken fast with some consonants dropped. In the main tourist areas you will find staff often speak several languages, but off the beaten track you will need Spanish or very efficient sign language. **English** is becoming more commonly used; it is a university entrance requirement and encouraged by the influx of Canadian and now American tourists. **German**, **Italian** and **French** are now spoken by people working in the tourist industry and tour guides are usually multilingual. Many older people also speak **Russian**.

For a list of Spanish words and phrases, see Footnotes, pages 460. For details of Spanish language and other courses, see page 59.

Money

CUC$1=US$1.04 (before tax), CAN$1.11, euro 0.70, £0.63 (Nov 2009).
Cuba operates a dual currency system with a domestic peso and a convertible peso. The **peso cubano** (CP$ or CUP$), also referred to as moneda nacional (MN) has notes for 1, 3, 5, 10, 20, 50 and 100 pesos, and coins for 5, 20 and 40 centavos and 1 peso. You must have a supply of coins if you want to use the local town buses (20 or 40 centavos). The 20 centavo coin is called a *peseta*. Cubans are paid in *pesos cubanos* and pay for most of

their goods in the same currency. The **peso convertible** (CUC$, pronounced 'cook') has a different set of notes and coins. It is fully exchangeable with authorized hard currencies such as euro, sterling and Canadian dollars. Foreigners are expected to pay for their accommodation, meals, transport and other items with the *peso convertible*. In some tourist enclaves, such as Varadero, Guadalavaca or the cays, the euro is accepted as well. Remember to spend or exchange any *pesos convertibles* before you leave as they are worthless outside Cuba. The exchange rate fluctuates around 24 *pesos cubanos* (CP$) to the *peso convertible* (CUC$). There is no black market. Food in the markets (*agromercados*), at street stalls and on trains, as well as books and popular cigarettes (but not in every shop), can be bought in *pesos cubanos*. You will need *pesos cubanos* for the toilet, rural trains, food at roadside *cafeterías* during a journey and drinks and snacks for a bus or train journey. Away from tourist hotels, in smaller towns such as Manzanillo, you will need *pesos cubanos* for everything. Visitors on pre-paid package tours do not need *pesos cubanos*.

Exchange

In 2004 Cuba introduced a 10% tax on exchange transactions involving the US dollar and in Apr 2005 an 8% revaluation/tax was introduced for all currencies such as the euro, sterling, US dollar or the Canadian dollar. While the peso convertible was formerly fixed at US$1 = CUC$1, you now get 18% less when you exchange dollars and 8% less when you exchange euro, etc. It is best to bring lots of cash, but take care not to bring any notes with writing or extraneous stamps on them as they will not be accepted. There are **banks** and CADECAS (*casas de cambio*) for changing money. The latter have longer opening hours and are usually open at weekends. If arriving at Havana airport, change what you need for a couple of days at the exchange desk there, then go to a Cadeca in town for larger amounts. Wear a money belt to store your cash safely.

Plastic/TCs/Banks (ATMs)

Traveller's cheques (TCs) and credit cards issued in the USA will not be accepted. Most British banks will not issue TCs for use in Cuba. A British credit card issued by a US bank (eg **MBNA**) is not valid. Visa or MasterCard credit cards are acceptable in most places. American Express, no matter where issued, is unacceptable. You can obtain cash advances with a credit card at banks and Cadecas, but it is best to bring plenty of cash to avoid hefty fees and commissions. ATMs (dispensing CUC$ only) have been installed in most banks, but it is often quicker and easier to queue at the counter. All credit card transactions are converted from CUC$ into US dollars at point of use, and your bank or credit card company will then convert that into your own currency. This means that you pay the US dollar conversion tax as well as bank fees and commissions, making all credit card transactions very costly. There are no toll-free numbers for you to call if your credit card is lost or stolen. You will have to phone home to the financial institution that issued you the card in order to put a stop on its use. Make a note of this number before you leave home, together with your credit card account number and keep them separate from your card. If you get really stuck and need money sent urgently to Cuba, you can get money transferred from any major commercial bank abroad direct to a Cuban bank, to **Asistur** (see Insurance, page 54) immediately for a 10% commission, or to **Western Union** (see Directory sections of the main text for contact information) which is used largely by Cubans abroad to send money home to relatives.

Cost of living/travelling

Raúl Castro has increased wages and removed the cap on salaries to allow bonuses to be paid but still most state employees earn no more than 300-500 pesos cubanos a month, whatever their profession. Housing, education and medical care is provided at no cost and some basic foodstuffs are still rationed and heavily subsidized (see Eating, page 40), but making ends meet is extremely hard. Most consumer goods are priced in pesos convertibles, and families have to have access to CUC$ to buy nice things for their home and family. It is therefore not surprising that Cubans will do almost anything to earn *divisa* and many families make sure that at least 1 member works in the dollar economy, eg tourism. The entire peso economy is subsidized, and although there are opportunities for travellers to use pesos cubanos, it is understandable that you will be expected to pay your way in CUC$. You earn hard currency, so you pay in hard currency.

It is important to remember that Cuba is competing in the Caribbean, rather than the Latin American, market and its neighbours are selling themselves as luxury destinations. Compared with islands like the Bahamas or the Virgin Islands, it is cheap, but if you have just come from a backpacking trip through Latin America and want a stop-off on an island before you go home, you will find your last few dollars don't go very far. However, by Caribbean standards, Cuba has it all. You can stay at luxury hotels (over CUC$100 a night for a double room), dine in elegant restaurants (up to CUC$50 per person) and frequent world-famous nightclubs (CUC$70 at **Tropicana**), or for those on a mid-range budget you can stay in pleasant colonial hotels (CUC$60-80 for a double room), eat reasonably well (CUC$15-20 for a decent dinner) and find plenty to do in the evenings in the clubs, theatres and cinemas (CUC$2-10). Anyone with a more restricted budget should consider staying with Cuban families in the *casa particular* system (CUC$15-35 per room), which is the equivalent of a bed and breakfast place in Europe. You can eat at private restaurants (CUC$7-15) or on the street, changing a few dollars into pesos to make resources stretch further, and head for the **Casa de la Trova** (CUC$1-5) for entertainment. At the bottom end of the scale you could get by on CUC$40 a day, including transport, but few treats. It

depends what you want to do, after all, sitting on the beach is free if you don't want a sunbed. A beer can cost CUC$1-3 depending on where you go and a *mojito* can vary from CUC$2 in a local bar to CUC$6 in the touristy **Bodeguita del Medio**, a Hemingway haunt. Based on 2 people sharing, this budget would include a simple *casa particular* of CUC$20 per room (CUC$10 each), CUC$3 for breakfast and CUC$7 for dinner in the *casa particular*, CUC$10 for transport or an excursion and CUC$10 for snacks, entry fees and entertainment, assuming you manage to buy some of your food with pesos cubanos. Increasing that budget by 50% would give you flexibility to take advantage of opportunities when they arise, stay in a more comfortable casa and have the freedom to explore a bit more.

Newspapers

All newpapers are state owned. *Granma*, mornings except Sun and Mon; *Trabajadores*, Trade Union weekly; *Tribuna* and *Juventud Rebelde*, also only weekly. *Opciones* is a weekly national and international trade paper. *Granma* has a weekly edition, *Granma International*, published in Spanish, English, French and Portuguese, and a monthly selected German edition; all have versions on the internet, www.granma.cu. Foreign magazines and newspapers are sometimes on sale at the telex centre in the **Habana Libre** hotel and in the **Riviera** hotel (also telex centre, open 0800-2000). The previous day's paper is available during the week. Weekend editions on sale Tue.

Opening hours

Government offices: Mon-Fri 0830-1230 and 1330-1730. Some offices open on Sat morning. **Banks**: Mon-Fri 0830-1700. **Cadecas**: Mon-Sat 0800-1700, Sun 0800-1200. **Shops**: Mon-Sat 0830-1800,

Sun 0900-1400. **Hotel tourist shops:** generally open 1000-1800 or 1900.

Post

When possible, correspondence to Cuba should be addressed to post office boxes (*Apartados*), where delivery is more certain. Stamps can be bought in pesos cubanos at post offices, or at **Telecorreos** in certain hotels. Hotels will charge you in CUC$, making the stamps very expensive, but they should be CP$0.45 for a postcard to Europe and CP$0.75 for a letter to Europe. Some postcards are now sold with postage included, look for the ones with the airmail stripe on the side. All postal services, national and international, have been described as appalling. We have had reports of postcards getting from Havana to Austria in 10 days and to Sweden in 2 weeks but that seems to be the exception rather than the rule, with others from Trinidad to the UK taking 5 weeks. Cubans will stop you in the street and ask you to take letters out of Cuba for them. Courier services are available, with DHL Express in big hotels, *correos* or *telecorreos* in Havana and many towns, www.dhl.com. They will take packages of up to 250 kg, important documents (not passports) for export or import, and also provide a national service in Cuba. They will send up to 3 postcards to anywhere in the world for CUC$10. Documents of 0.5 kg cost CUC$39 to North America, CUC$45 to Spain, CUC$49 to the rest of the world, packets of 0.5 kg cost CUC$45 to Mexico and Canada, CUC$50 to Spain and CUC$55 to the rest of the world.

Prohibitions

It is illegal to photograph military or police installations or personnel, port, rail or airport facilities. A fee is charged for photographs in some museums and national monuments. Cubans face more prohibitions than foreigners, particularly in the realm of politics and freedom of speech, but are usually happy to discuss their government, Cuba, their past and their future with you in private.

Safety

In general the Cuban people are very hospitable. The island is generally safer than many of its Caribbean and Latin neighbours, but certain precautions should be taken. See also page 64 for Women travellers. Visitors should never lose sight of their luggage or leave valuables in hotel rooms (most hotels and some *casas particulares* have safes). Do not leave your things on the beach when going swimming. Guard your camera closely. Pickpocketing and purse-snatching on buses is quite common in Havana and Santiago. Also beware of bag-snatching by passing cyclists. Street lighting is poor so care is needed when walking or cycling in any city at night. Some people recommend walking in the middle of the street. Dark and crowded bars can also be a haven for thieves; in 1 bar in Pinar del Río, 9 thefts from tourists were reported in 1 month.

Single travellers

Whether you are a man or a woman travelling on your own, and whatever your age and physique, you will be approached by hustlers, known as *jineteros/as* looking to make a quick buck out of you. Be careful who you allow to become attached to you, for obvious reasons, and if you choose to have a companion make sure that the terms and conditions are fully understood by both parties. Single men and women are targeted by Cubans of the opposite sex, not only for their dollars, but also as a way out of the country if they can find a marriage partner. Single women will encounter the usual macho attitudes found in all Latin American countries and can expect to receive stares, hissing and comments on their attributes. Rape is not common, but the usual precautions should be taken to avoid getting into a

Sex tourism

Cuba had a reputation for prostitution before the Revolution and after a gap of some decades it has resurfaced. Despite government crackdowns and increased penalties, everything is available for both sexes if you know where to look. The age of consent is 18 in Cuba, so if you are introduced to a young girl you are in danger of being led into a blackmail trap. Be warned, however, foreigners on the lookout for a sexual partner are seen as fair game. Sexual encounters often take place in *casas particulares*, private homes where there is little security and lots of risk. Cubans must have their *carnets de identidad*, which are registered in the book alongside the foreigner's passport details. This protects the owner and the

tourist from robbery, but if the girl/boy is found to be staying in different places with different foreigners, she/he will be assumed to be a prostitute and will be re-educated or put in prison. A foreign man on his own will probably not be given the key to the house in case he brings a friend back in the early hours when the family is asleep. If you go to an illegal *casa*, you have no protection and will probably be robbed. The *casa* owners face 15-year prison sentences for running brothels if too many *chicas* stay there. If you are a man out alone at night in Havana you will find the market very active and you will be tugged at frequently, mostly by females, but around Coppelia ice cream parlour in Vedado the prostitutes are mostly male.

compromising situation, trust your intuition, as always. See also sex tourism, above.

Smoking

Cubans are heavy smokers (48% of men and 26% of women, compared with about 25% of the population in the UK and USA) and every year about 6000 people die of smoking-related diseases. Fidel Castro gave up his trademark cigars in the 1980s and efforts are now being made to reduce smoking in the rest of the population. It is now banned in most workplaces and it is illegal to sell cigarettes near schools. It is more common now to find 'no smoking' notices, although whether people take any notice is another matter. Cigarettes remain among the cheapest in the world and people born before 1955 can even get the poorest quality cigarettes with their ration card.

Student travellers

Cuba is not geared up to offering student discounts unless you are part of a group that has been invited for a specific project. If you are travelling around Latin America as well as Cuba get an **International Student Identity Card** (ISIC), which is distributed by student travel offices and travel agencies in 77 countries. ISIC gives you special prices on all forms of transport (air, sea, rail, etc, but not in Cuba), and access to a variety of other concessions and services. The head office is in the Netherlands: **International Student Travel Confederation**, T31-20-4212800, www.istc.org. Student cards must carry a photograph if they are to be of any use for discounts in Latin America. Agencies that specialize in student travel can be found on university campuses, eg **STA Travel**, www.statravel.com, www.statravel.co.uk.

Studying in Cuba

There are no private schools but **language courses** are available at the universities of Havana and Santiago. They generally start on the 1st Mon of the month and you study 20 sessions of 45 mins a week, Mon-Fri 0900-1320. There are different levels of study and **Cuban cultural courses** are also available. At the Faculty of Modern Languages at the University of Havana, latest prices for beginners, intermediate and advanced are 1 week CUC$100, 2 weeks CUC$200, 3 weeks CUC$240, 4 weeks CUC$300. A 4-week upgrade course is CUC$360. A Cuban culture course, held every other month is CUC$360 for 3 weeks, or you can do a joint Spanish and Cuban culture course of 320 sessions for CUC$960, 480 sessions CUC$1392. Commercial Spanish and Intensive courses in Spanish are also available. Contact **Damaris Valdés**, Of de Postgrado, Calle J 556, entre 25 y 27, Vedado, T7-832 2445, damarys@rect.uh.cu.

2-week courses in **Spanish language with Cuban dance** and a cultural programme are offered in Havana and Santiago all year round by **Caledonia**, The Clockhouse, Bonnington Mill, 72 New Haven Rd, Edinburgh, EH6 5QG, I0131-621 7721, www.caledonialanguages. com. They also do round-the- island cultural tours of 10 days or more, a 10-day Revolutionary Trail trip in Feb and Oct, visiting all the main sites associated with the Revolution as well as trekking tours, music and dance trips for individuals and groups all year round. **Julio César Muñoz Cocina**, José Martí 401 entre Fidel Claro y Santiago Escobar, Trinidad, T/F41-993673, www.trinidadphoto.com, runs photography workshops. **Cubaism**, Unit 30, DRCA Business Centre, Charlotte Despard Av, Battersea Park, London, W11 5HD, toll free T0800-298 9555, T44 20-7498 7671, www.cubasalsa holidays.com, offers **dance holidays** in Cuba.

Taxes

There is a departure tax of CUC$25 paid at airports after you have checked in at the airline counter. A tax of 10% is charged when you change US dollars but not on other currencies. Only the private sector (*casas particulares, paladares*) pays taxes. There is no sales tax.

Telephone

→ *Country code +53.*

To make a call to another province, dial 0 then the code and then the number. If you need the operator's help, dial 0, pause, then dial 0 again. Many public phones now take prepaid cards (*tarjetas*) which are easier to use than coins. If you do use a phone which takes coins, they only accept 20-centavo or 1-peso coins. For domestic, long-distance calls try and get hold of a peso phone card, eg 10 pesos, which works out much cheaper than the CUC$ cards, but which are not technically available to foreigners. There are 2 sorts of cards: '*chip*' and '*propria*', but only the latter has cheaper rates at night, otherwise they cost the same. The *propria* cards can be used to make calls from a private phone or from a cabin, dialling the personal code on the upper part of the card.

To phone abroad on a phone with **international dialling** facility, dial 119 followed by the country and regional codes and number. Many hotels and airports have offices where international calls can be made at high prices or you may be able to direct dial from your room. Look for the **Telecorreos, Telepunto** or **Etecsa** (www.etecsa.cu) signs. Collect (reverse charge) calls are possible to Argentina, Brazil, Canada, Colombia, Costa Rica, France, Italy, Mexico, Nicaragua, Panama, Puerto Rico, Spain, UK and USA. Dial 012, choose option 0 and follow instructions. **Phonecards** (*tarjetas propias*) are green if used for international calls as well as domestic calls. They come in CUC$5, CUC$10, CUC$15, CUC$25 denominations and are valid for 6 months. CUC$1.95 per min (CUC$1.40 1800-0600) to USA and Canada, US$2.60 per min (US$2.20) to Mexico, Central America and the Caribbean, CUC$2.35 (CUC$1.65) to South America, CUC$3.05 (CUC$2.10) to the rest of the world CUC$3.65 (CUC$2.55).

Most hotels have facilities for international calls and **faxes** which you can use even if you are not staying there. Faxes can also be sent from Telecorreos and Etecsa offices.

Mobile/cell phones are commonly used in Cuba. If you want to rent a cell phone you can do so from **Cubacel**, at Telepunto, Habana 406 entre Obispo y Obrapía, Havana, or other Telepunto or Etecsa offices nationwide, T5264 2266, www.cubacel.com. In Cuba, all cell phone numbers begin with 5. Add a 0 when calling from fixed to cell phones in Havana and 01 for the rest of the country. To make a call from cell to fixed phones, dial 0 + area code + phone number. To call a Cuban cell phone from abroad, dial 53 + the phone number. Cubacel operates on GSM (900 MHz) and TDMA (800 MHz) with national coverage and on GSM (850 MHz) to cover Havana City, Varadero, Cayo Coco and Cayo Guillermo.

Television and radio

There are 5 state-owned national channels: *Cubavisión*, *Tele Rebelde*, *Canal Educativo*, *Multivisión* and *Canal Educativo 2*. The *Sun Channel* can be seen at hotels and broadcasts a special programme for tourists 24 hrs a day. Some of the upmarket hotels also have satellite TV so you can catch up with *CNN* in Spanish or English.

There are 6 state-owned national radio stations and each province has its own provincial station (*Radio Ciudad de la Habana* is on 820MW/98.7FM), although you will not be able to tune in to all of them all over the country as the strength of the signal varies. *Radio Enciclopedia*, 1260MW/ 94.1FM, for instrumental music. *Radio*

Habana Cuba, 106.9FM, multilingual, news and information. *Radio Musical Nacional*, 590MW/99.1FM, classical music. *Radio Progreso*, 640MW/90.3FM, music and drama. *Radio Rebelde*, 670 and 710MW/96.7FM, current affairs, sport, music. *Radio Reloj*, 950MW/101.5FM, 24-hr news station. *Radio Taíno*, 1290MW/93.2-93.4FM, Cuban music with items of tourist interest.

Time

Eastern Standard Time, 5 hrs behind GMT; Daylight Saving Time, 4 hrs behind GMT. However, Cuba does not always change its clocks the same day as the USA or the Bahamas. On Sun, 5 Oct 1997, Cuba moved its clocks back 1 hr, which appeared to take everybody by surprise in the travel industry, including Cubans, and all flight times for the following week were changed on minimal notice. Best to check in the spring and autumn so that you are not caught out with missed flights and buses, etc.

Tipping

Tipping customs have changed after a period when visitors were not allowed to tip in hotels and restaurants. It is now definitely recommended. Tip a small amount (not a percentage). At times taxi drivers will expect (or demand) a tip. **Víazul** porters ask for tips in some bus stations (eg Trinidad) just for putting your luggage in the hold, but in others (eg Camagüey) they will do almost anything for you in return for a friendly chat. There is no service charge or tip for food or lodging at *casas particulares*. The attendants in toilets expect a tip in return for a sheet or 2 of toilet paper, pesos cubanos are useful for this. Musicians in bars and restaurants depend on your tips. Leaving basic items in your room, like toothpaste, deodorant, paper, pens, is recommended. Tourism workers pool all their tips so that behind-the-scenes staff also benefit, and regularly donate a percentage of their tips to the national health service for the purchase of equipment for cancer treatment in children, etc. However, any evidence of malpractice should be reported to the management.

Tour operators

UK and Ireland
Càlédöñiâ, T0131-621 7721, www.caledonialanguages.com.
Captivating Cuba, T08444 129916, www.captivatingcuba.com.
Cubanacán UK Ltd, T020-7537 7909, www.cubanacan.cu.
Cuba Welcome, T020-7584 6092, www.cubawelcome.com.
Havanatour UK Ltd, T01707-646463, www.havanatour.co.uk.
The Holiday Place, T020-7431 0670, www.holidayplace.co.uk.
Interchange, T020-8681 3612, www.interchangeworldwide.com.
Journey Latin America, T020-8622 8464, www.journeylatinamerica.co.uk.
Regent Holidays, T0117-9211711, www.regent-holidays.co.uk.
South American Experience Ltd, T0845 277 3366, www.southamericanexperience.co.uk.
Steppes Latin America, T01285-885333, www.steppeslatinamerica.co.uk.
Trips Worldwide, T0800 840 0850, www.tripsworldwide.co.uk.

Rest of Europe
STA Travel Worldwide, T01805-456422, www.statravel.de.
Nouvelles Frontières, T0825-000747, www.nouvelles-frontieres.fr.
Sol Meliá, T 902 144440, http://es.solmelia.com.

North America
Air Transat Holidays, T1-866-322 6649, www.transatholidays.com.

Cuba Travel Services, T800-963 2822, www.cubatravelservices.com.
Global Exchange, T415-255 7296, www.globalexchange.org.
Marazul Charters, T800-223 5334, www.marazulcharters.com.
Signature Vacations, T1-866-324 2883 www.signaturevacations.com.
Viñales Tours, T01-800 202 2937, www.vinalestours.com.

Australia and New Zealand
Adventure World, T1300 363055, www.adventureworld.com.au.

Cuba
Amistur, T7-834 4544/830 1220, www.cubasolidarity.net/amistur.
Cuba Deportes, T7-204 0945-7, www.cubadeportes.cu.
Cuba Linda, www.cubalinda.com.
Cubamar Viajes, T7-833 2523, www.cubamarviajes.cu.

Cubanacán, T7-204 1658, www.cubanacan.cu.
Cubatur, T7-833 3569, www.cubatur.cu.
Ecotur, T7-649 1055, www.ecoturcuba.co.cu.
Gaviota Tours, T7-204 7683, www.gaviota-grupo.com.
Havanatur, T7-830 8227, www.havanatur.cu.
Paradiso, T7-832 9538, www.paradiso.cu.
Sol y Son, T7-833 3271, www.solysonviajes.com.
Vacacionar Travel, T7-204 6457, www.vacacionartravel.com.

Tourist information

Various colourful, glossy brochures are produced by the tourist authorities, available in tourist offices worldwide, but for hard information you are better looking on the internet: www.dtcuba.com has lots of details and addresses of hotels, tour companies, car hire, etc. Infotur, www.infotur.cu, has background information and maps as well as details of events and excursions. The

Canadian tourist office site, www.gocuba.ca, is better than most.

Another website is www.cubaweb.cu, which has sections on news, travel, politics, business, internet and technology, health, science, art and culture, festivals and events. Many companies are linked to this website.

Cuban travel agencies on the net are www.vacacionartravel.com, www.travelnet.cu, and www.cubalinda.com, run by former CIA agent, Philip Agee, particularly helpful for travellers from the USA. You can book tickets and excursions online.

Some of the best unofficial websites for travel information and news are www.cubajunky.com, www.cubacasas.net and http://havanajournal.com.

Get your **maps** in Cuba, if you can wait, as they are generally more reliable and up to date than any of the foreign maps we have seen, although, even then, not perfect. The **Freytag** and **Berndt** map of Cuba has street plans of the principal towns. See page 37.

Vaccinations

There are no vaccinations demanded by immigration officials in Cuba. For further details, see Health, page 52.

Visas and immigration

Visitors from the majority of countries need only a passport, return ticket and **30-day tourist card** to enter Cuba, as long as they are going solely for tourist purposes. Tourist cards may be obtained from Cuban embassies, consulates, airlines or approved travel agents, which is a hassle-free way of obtaining a card. UK residents and EU citizens can also get their tourist cards online at www.visacuba.co.uk. Price in the UK, £15 from the consulate, or from travel agents (administration fee may be charged), some other countries US$15, Can$15, up to AU$60-140 in Australia depending on how

quickly you want it. To get a tourist card at a consulate you have to fill in an application form, photocopy the main pages of your passport (valid for more than 6 months after departure from Cuba), submit confirmation of your accommodation booking (or at least the name of any hotel or *casa particular*) and your return or onward flight ticket. Immigration in Havana airport will only give you 30 days on your tourist card, but for CUC$25 you can get it extended for a further 30 days only at Immigration in Nuevo Vedado, Factor esq Final, open 0830-1200 (go early, it gets busy and there are queues) and some other towns, eg Santiago de Cuba.

Nationals of countries without visa-free agreement with Cuba, journalists, students and those visiting on other business must check what visa requirements pertain and, if relevant, apply for an **official/business visa**.

Travelling from the USA

The **US Government** does not normally permit its citizens to visit Cuba. US citizens should have a US licence to engage in any transactions related to travel to Cuba, but tourist or business travel is not licensable, even through a 3rd country such as Mexico or Canada. For further information on entry to Cuba from the US and customs requirements, US travellers should contact the **Cuban Interests Section**, an office of the Cuban Government, at 2630 16th St NW, Washington DC 20009, T202-797 8518. They could also contact one of the travel agencies listed above for the latest information on how to sidestep the regulations. US citizens on business in Cuba should contact **Foreign Assets Control**, Federal Reserve Bank of New York, 33 Liberty St, NY 10045.

Many US travellers conceal their tracks by going via Mexico, the Bahamas, or Canada, where the tourist card is stamped, but not the passport. On your return, make sure that you have destroyed all tickets and other evidence of having been in Cuba. US travellers returning through Canada are stopped at the border and threatened with massive fines. If you are stopped by an immigration official and asked whether you have been to Cuba, do not lie, as that is an offence. If they want to take it further, expect a letter from the **Office of Foreign Assets Control** (OFAC; Department of the Treasury). This will either ask for information on your suspected unlicensed travel, in which case you should refuse to incriminate yourself, or it will be a pre-penalty notice assessing a civil fine, often US$7500, based on the money OFAC believes you would have spent in Cuba without a licence. The latter gives you 30 days to pay the fine or request an official hearing. The **National Lawyers' Guild** has drafted specimen letters you can use to reply to OFAC in either case; for further information see www.cubalinda.com. It is hoped that the Obama administration will overturn the travel restrictions at some stage, as restrictions have already been eased for Cuban Americans returning to visit relatives, but Congress had not voted to change anything when we went to press.

Women travellers

Whether single or in pairs, all women will be hassled in the street by men offering places to stay, eat, party or their services as guides. They can be persistent and annoying, although rarely threatening or violent. You can try ignoring them, saying 'no', or politely chatting and declining their offer. It doesn't make much difference. Your size and age is no problem to potential *jineteros* and the sex tourism industry is as active for women as it is for men. Men report similar approaches from Cubanas when they are on their own. It is simply a method of relieving you of your dollars. If you wear clothes which are too revealing or provocative, you will be considered fair game. Going to a club on your own at night is also an open invitation to the very macho Cuban men. Do not go to remote beaches on your own, choose a well-populated beach instead where there are Cuban families or a hotel for foreigners.

Working in the country

Foreign workers are brought in to Cuba for specific skilled jobs, but you cannot just turn up and hope to find work. If you want to stay in Cuba for a few months on a temporary basis, it is best to contact one of the Friendship Associations listed below for volunteering opportunities. Work brigades go to Cuba for a couple of weeks or a few months, helping in farming, construction or other activities and can be a great way to get to know the country and its people at a grass roots level, while also being taken to sites of interest and being entertained with music and dance on the brigade. For details of business visas, see page 63.

Friendship associations

There are over 1600 solidarity organizations in some 120 countries. Many organize work brigades, charity tours and donations of medical supplies and equipment to beat the US trade embargo, and produce newsletters and magazines. Their support for the government is usually uncritical. The link organization in Cuba is the **Cuban Institute for Friendship with the Peoples** (ICAP), in Havana, T7-838 2388. **Australia**: Australia Cuba Friendship Society, in Canberra, www.geocities.com/australiacubafriendship; in Brisbane, www.acfs-brisbane.org.au; in Sydney, www.sydney-acfs.org. **Canada**: Canadian Cuban Friendship Association (CCFA), T416-410 8254, www.ccfatoronto.ca. **UK**: Cuba Solidarity Campaign, T020-8800 0155, www.cuba-solidarity.org.uk. **USA**: National Network on Cuba, www.cubasolidarity.com; Pastors for Peace, T212-926 5757; www.ifconews.org; Center for Cuban Studies, T212-242 0559, www.cubaupdate.org; Global Exchange, Cuba Project, T415-255 7296, www.globalexchange.org.

Contents

Footprint features

At a glance

◎ **Getting around** On foot, by
bicycle, taxi and HabanaBusTour.

◉ **Time required** 2 days to a week.

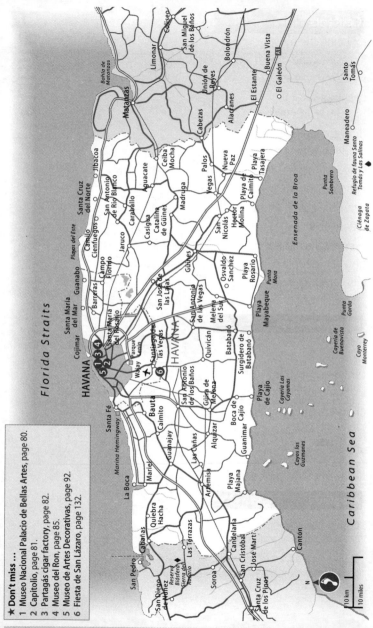

★ Don't miss ...
1 Museo Nacional Palacio de Bellas Artes, page 80.
2 Capitolio, page 81.
3 Partagás cigar factory, page 82.
4 Museo del Ron, page 85.
5 Museo de Artes Decorativas, page 92.
6 Fiesta de San Lázaro, page 132.

Florida Straits

Caribbean Sea

N

10 km
10 miles

Of all the capital cities in the Caribbean, Havana has the reputation for being the most splendid and sumptuous. Before the Revolution, its casinos and nightlife attracted the megastars of the day in much the same way as Beirut and Shanghai, and remarkably little has changed since then. There may be no casinos now, but Havana's bars and clubs with their thriving music scene are still a major draw for foreigners and Cubans alike. There have been no tacky modernizations, partly because of lack of finance and materials. Low-level street lighting, relatively few cars (and many of those antiques), no (real) estate agents or Wendyburgers, no neon and very little advertizing (except for political slogans), all give the city plenty of scope for nostalgia.

Havana is not a modern city in the materialist sense and is no good for people for whom shopping and eating well are the central leisure activities, although the privately run *paladares* offer a varied and eccentric dining experience. It is, however, probably the finest example of a Spanish colonial city in the Americas. Many of its palaces were converted into museums after the Revolution and more work has been done since La Habana Vieja (the old city) was declared a UNESCO World Heritage Site in 1982. There is also some stunning architecture from the first half of the 20th century, although much of the city is fighting a losing battle against the sea air – many of the finest buildings along the sea front are crumbling and emergency work is under way to save some of them.

Getting there

Air The José Martí international airport is 18 km from Havana and all flights from abroad use Terminal 3, the newest terminal, with the exception of flights from Cancún which arrive at Terminal 2. As many transatlantic flights arrive late at night it can be sensible to arrange the transfer from the airport to your hotel in advance with your travel agent. However, it is cheaper to get a taxi when you arrive; fares range from CUC$15-25, but CUC$25 is commonly asked to the old city. On the way back to the airport it is possible to arrange a private taxi, which may work out cheaper, if you negotiate with the driver. However, their cars are not as reliable as the state taxis and if they break down on the long drive out, you will be stuck. A metered taxi from the Parque Central to Terminal 3 cost CUC$19.75 in 2009. Travelling by bus is not practical. The P12 bus from Parque Fraternidad, or the P16 from Vedado go along Avenida Rancho Boyeros, relatively close to the domestic terminals, but still a long walk, it is difficult with luggage and it will take forever. Terminal 3 is a long way from the other two (although just five minutes in a taxi) there are no connecting public buses either between the terminals or from Terminal 3 into Havana.

Bus The **Víazul** bus service for foreigners is based quite far away from the old city and from Vedado and a taxi will be needed to get you to your destination. **Cubataxis** wait outside the terminal and will cost around CUC$5-6 to La Habana Vieja or Centro.

Train The train station is at the southern end of the old city, within walking distance of any of the hotels there or in Centro Habana, although if you arrive at night it would be better to take a taxi to your destination. ▶▶ *For further details see Transport, page 126.*

Getting around

Havana is very spread out along the coast. La Habana Vieja to Miramar along the Malecón (the seafront boulevard) is more than 8 km. **Bus** Tricky for the uninitiated, involving complicated queuing procedures and a lot of pushing and shoving. In 2009 the Government cut back on the number of buses in service to save fuel, increasing the difficulties of getting on them. There is, however, a hop-on, hop-off tour bus service for foreigners, the **HabanaBusTour**, CUC$5 per day, leaving from the Parque Central with one route to the Plaza de la Revolución and the other out to the Playas del Este. **Bicitaxi** More leisurely than taking the bus is to hire a *bicitaxi* (bicycle taxi) for short journeys. However, it is now illegal for *bicitaxis* to take foreigners and they risk a large fine if caught, so they are likely to charge you over the odds to make it worthwhile. **Cocotaxi** These overpriced, bright yellow motorcycle taxis are called *cocotaxis* because of their shape. **Taxi** You can opt for the traditional taxi, although those too come in lots of different styles. **Walking** Much of the city can be covered on foot, but the average visitor will be content with one district at a time and still feel well-exercised. It is also possible to hire **scooters** and **cars**. ▶▶ *For further details see Transport, page 126.*

Best time to visit

The driest and least humid time of the year is between December and March, when you can have completely cloudless days. From July to August is the hottest time but most public buildings have air conditioning and there is usually a breeze along the Malecón. Rain falls mainly in May and June and then from September to October, but there are wet days all year round. In recent years, the worst storms have hit between September and November, destroying many of the decrepit houses in the city, but Havana is exceptionally well prepared for hurricanes and loss of life is rare. Carnival is a movable feast. For some years it was held along the Malecón at the end of July and the beginning of August, then it was moved to November and it could be any time, check in advance. There are many cultural festivals (jazz, ballet, film, etc) and sporting events (baseball, cycling, boxing, fishing, sailing, etc) all through the year that are worth catching. There are many festive days which are not national holidays, for example José Martí's birthday (28 January 1853), which are very important, particularly in Havana. New Year celebrations are a major event, coinciding with the anniversary of the triumph of the Revolution on 1 January 1959.

Tourist information

In Havana are the headquarters of the **Oficina Nacional de Información Turística (Infotur)** ① *Calle 28 303 entre 3 y 5, Miramar, T7-204 6635 and Guanabo, Av 5 entre 468 y 470, T7-796 6868, www.infotur.cu*. There is a network of kiosks run by **Infotur**, which can provide you with information and maps: at the **airport**, Terminal 3, T7-266 4094/642 6101, open 24 hours; in **Habana Vieja**, Obispo entre Bernaza y Villegas, T7-866 3333; Obispo y San Ignacio, T7-863 6884; in **Playa**, at Avenida 5 y Calle 112, T7-204 7036, daily 0815-1615. At the **Santa María del Mar** office, Avenida Las Terrazas entre 11 y 12, Playas del Este, T7-797 1261/796 1111, you will find maps, excursions, internet, booking for hotels, souvenirs, but with no map of the area and with limited bus information, it remains to be seen how useful they're going to be.

If you want to book tours, do so before 1800 the day before. The state tour agencies, such as **Cubatur** and **Havanatur**, are found in hotels and other locations. Their main task is to sell tours, but they can also make hotel reservations, sell tickets for buses, trains and planes and organize pick-ups and transfers. If you are staying in a *casa particular* you will probably find your host is a mine of useful information who can fill you in on all the gossip and background detail to enrich a stay in the capital.

History

The colonial period

Havana, the capital, founded in 1519 on the present site, is situated at the mouth of a deep bay; in the colonial period, this natural harbour was the assembly point for ships of the annual silver convoy to Spain. Its strategic and commercial importance is reflected in the extensive fortifications, particularly on the east side of the entrance to the bay where there are two large fortresses, El Castillo de los Tres Reyes del Morro, built in 1589-1630 and San Carlos de la Cabaña, built in 1763-1774. On the west side of the canal are the smaller, 16th-century Castillo de la Punta and the Castillo de la Real Fuerza.

The city was prey to pirate attacks as well as being a pawn in European wars. In the 18th century, the British attacked Havana and held it from 1762-1763, but exchanged it for Florida. From that point, the city's importance as the gathering place for the silver convoy was superseded by trade. The local planters and merchants had briefly discovered the value of trading their crops with Britain and North America. From the second half of the 18th century to the end of the 19th century, ships came in to Havana carrying slaves, while exports of coffee, tobacco and, most importantly, sugar were the mainstay of the local economy.

19th century

From the beginning of the 19th century, the local sugar plantocracy began to move out of the city guarded by defensive walls and build neocolonial villas or country estates in what are now the municipalities of Cerro, 10 de Octubre and the high part of Marianao. One example of this architecture is Quinta del Conde Santo Venia, built in 1841, now a home for the elderly, just behind the Estadio Latino Americano. By the 1850s, the city walls had more or less collapsed and the Prado was absorbed into the old city instead of running outside the walls. A fine neoclassical example here is the Palacio de Aldama, opposite the Parque de la Fraternidad. Competition began to come from the west in the 1870s, with the rise of Vedado, which reached its high point in the 1920s, where neoclassical, romantic and art nouveau small palaces with internal courtyards vied with each other for luxury and originality. The Casa de la Amistad, on Paseo, is an example, and the Colón cemetery also reflects this bourgeois competitiveness.

20th century

By 1918, Miramar, on the western outskirts across the Río Almendares, now Playa municipality, began to take over, in another new style: that of beach resorts, exclusive seaside clubs and, of course, casinos. It was the salon of the city, American-style. In the

▣ Havana orientation

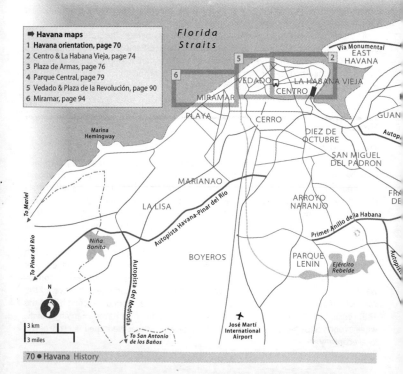

➡ **Havana maps**
1 Havana orientation, page 70
2 Centro & La Habana Vieja, page 74
3 Plaza de Armas, page 76
4 Parque Central, page 79
5 Vedado & Plaza de la Revolución, page 90
6 Miramar, page 94

1950s, the development had reached as far west as the present districts of Siboney and Cubanacán (now given Amerindian names in place of their former ones of Biltmore and the Country Club) in Playa, housing some 300 wealthy families. The houses where the wealthy lived in Miramar before the Revolution are today occupied by embassies and government buildings, but there are also many abandoned villas. Major building operations took place after the two World Wars in Miramar and after the Korean war in the far western suburbs, both of which were boom periods in terms of sugar and also nickel sales for armaments. This was also the moment for the extension of Nuevo Vedado, tower buildings like the Focsa, and the Hotel Nacional. The sea was regarded as a threat during most of Havana's history and only became an asset in the 20th century. The Malecón seafront drive was built in 1901, the tunnel to Miramar (replacing a bridge) in 1950, and the tunnel leading to Playas del Este, on the other side of the bay, in 1958.

The wealthy middle class also built property for rent (80% of Havana was rented to other nationals and foreigners). Landlords lived in houses built on the *manzana* (block), architectural style. Those that were built for rent were on a smaller scale, with fewer green areas and small apartments off passageways. Working- class areas within these suburbs or municipalities were also developed, such as Pogolotti (early 1900s in Marianao), and parts of San Miguel del Padrón, in 1948. Buena Vista, in Nuevo Vedado, was also a poorer

area. After the Revolution, construction was concentrated on the rest of the country, which had been largely forgotten. Havana was seen as relatively well-developed in comparison. Exceptions were service buildings, such as the Almeijeras hospital on the Malecón, and educational institutions. A whole section of the bay was also developed for the fishing industry. The municipality of Havana del Este is post-Revolution. The Camilo Cienfuegos housing estate was built in 1959-1961 and Alamar in 1970. There is also the scientific complex near Siboney in the far west of Miramar, housing a state-of-the-art genetic biology centre and a neurological hospital, among other facilities.

Contemporary Havana

Before the Revolution, Havana was the largest, the most beautiful and the most sumptuous city in the Caribbean. Today, it is rather run down and the weather has wreaked havoc on both pre- and post-Revolution buildings. Thanks to the government's policy of developing the countryside, it's not ringed with shanty towns like so many other Latin American capitals, although some reappeared in the 1990s. Nevertheless, the city is shabby and visitors are often taken by surprise by living conditions. Half the people live in housing officially regarded as sub-standard. Many buildings are shored up by wooden planks. Some of it is very old, but the ancient palaces, colonnades, churches and monasteries have undergone so much renovation that they are in considerably better shape than the newer housing.

The old city has been declared a World Heritage Site by the United Nations. Priorities include the restoration of the historic centre, under the auspices of UNESCO and the City Historian's Office, whose brief is also to rebuild communities in the widest sense of the word, with income from cultural tourism, and aid from European NGOs. Restoration will encompass the Malecón, starting from the historic centre, where housing has been badly affected by salination and sea damage, and the Bosque de la Habana, crossed by the Río Almendares, now suffering from pollution and contamination, which is a potentially rich green belt, extending over several kilometres.

Orientation

The city of Havana has 200 districts in 15 municipalities, including 14,000 *manzanas* (blocks). These municipalities are: **Playa**, **Marianao** and **La Lisa** in the west; **Boyeros** in the southwest; **Plaza de la Revolución**, **Centro Habana**, **La Habana Vieja**, **Cerro** and **Diez de Octubre** in the centre; south-central **Arroyo Naranjo**; **Regla**, **San Miguel del Padrón** going eastwards; **Cotorro** in the southeast; and in the east, **Playas del Este** and **Guanabacoa**. The centre is divided into five sections, three of which are of most interest to visitors, **La Habana Vieja** (Old Havana), **Centro Habana** (Central Havana) and **Vedado**, linked by the Malecón, a picturesque thoroughfare along the coast.

Most of the museums, palaces and churches of interest are in La Habana Vieja. Centro is largely residential and Vedado has most of the action, with clubs, bars, theatres, cinemas and hotels with murky pre-Revolution tales to tell. Beyond Vedado, west of the Río Almendares, is **Miramar** once an upper-class suburb, where embassies and hotels for businesspeople are located. Streets have names in La Habana Vieja and Centro, but numbers or letters in Vedado and numbers in Miramar, although some of the main roads in Vedado are still referred to by names.

An **address** is given as the street (*Calle* or *Avenida*), the building number, followed by the two streets between which it is located, eg **Hotel Inglaterra**, Prado 416 entre San Rafael y San Miguel. However, sometimes this is shortened to showing merely which corner it is on, eg **Hotel Florida**, Obispo 252 esquina Cuba. A large building will not bother with the number, eg **Hotel Nacional**, Calle O esquina 21. Cubans usually abbreviate *entre* (between) to e/ while *esquina* (corner) becomes esq.

The oldest part of the city, around the **Plaza de Armas**, is quite near the docks where you can see cargo ships from all over the world being unloaded. Here are the former **Palacio de los Capitanes Generales**, **El Templete**, and **Castillo de La Real Fuerza**, the oldest of all the forts. From Plaza de Armas run two narrow and picturesque streets, Calles Obispo and O'Reilly. These two streets go west to the heart of the city to **Parque Central**, with its laurels, poincianas, almonds, palms, shrubs and gorgeous flowers. To the southwest rises the white dome of the **Capitolio** (Capitol). From the northwest corner of Parque Central, a wide, tree-shaded avenue with a central walkway, the **Paseo del Prado**, runs to the fortress of **La Punta**. The Prado technically divides the old city from Centro, having once been the edge of the city, although architecturally there is little distinction. At its north sea-side end is Havana's beguiling oceanfront highway, the **Malecón**, which snakes westward from La Punta to the residential district of Vedado.

Further west Calle San Lázaro leads directly from the monument to **General Antonio Maceo** on the Malecón to the **Universidad de La Habana** (Havana University). Further inland, past **El Príncipe** castle, is **Plaza de la Revolución**, with the impressive monument to **José Martí** at its centre and the much-photographed, huge outline of Che Guevara on one wall.

From near the fortress of **La Punta** in the old city, a tunnel built in 1958 by the French runs east under the mouth of the harbour; it emerges in the rocky ground between the **Castillo del Morro** and the fort of **La Cabaña**, some 550 m away, and a 5-km highway connects with the Havana–Matanzas road. This is an area of post-Revolution housing, designed to improve the living conditions of the average citizen. Both the **Camilo Cienfuegos** *barrio*, dating from 1961, and **Alamar**, from 1970, were built by microbrigades, with citizens helping to build their own apartments, schools and clinics. There are also vast sporting facilities, built for the Panamerican Games, which include athletics tracks, a bicycle track, swimming pool and tennis courts, as well as a hotel. The three or four decades since construction started have taken their toll, however, and the tropical climate and sea winds have eaten into the concrete and metal structures, leaving the district looking run down and depressed.

Sights

La Habana Vieja (Old Havana)

The old city is the area with the greatest concentration of sites of interest and where most work is being done to restore buildings to their former glory. New museums, art galleries, hotels, restaurants and shops are opening all the time in renovated mansions or merchants' houses. Several days can be spent strolling around the narrow streets or along the waterfront, stopping in bars and open air cafés to take in the atmosphere, although the nightlife is better in Vedado. Don't forget to look up to the balconies; Habaneros live life in the open-air and balcony life is as full and intricate as street life. ▸▸ *For listings, see pages 99-130.*

Plaza de Armas

This is Havana's oldest square and it has been restored to very much what it once was. The statue in the centre is of the 'Father of the Nation', the revolutionary 19th-century landowner, Carlos Manuel de Céspedes. In the northeast corner of the square is the church of **El Templete** ① *Baratillo 1 entre O'Reilly y Narciso López*, a small neoclassical building finished in 1828 (renovated 1997). A column in front of it marks the spot where the first Mass was said in 1519 under a ceiba tree and, under its branches, the supposed bones of Columbus reposed in state before being taken to the cathedral. A sapling of the same tree, blown down by a hurricane in 1753, was planted on the same spot. This tree was cut down in 1828, the present tree planted, and the Doric temple opened. Habaneros celebrate here, every 16 November, the anniversary of the first Mass and the first town council of San Cristóbal de la Habana, the city's official name. It is also the starting point for all guided tours of La Habana Vieja. Inside El Templete there are paintings by the Frenchman, Juan Bautiste Vermay, a pupil of the Master David and the first director of the Academia Nacional de Bellas Artes, founded in 1818. His main artistic work was the creation of the paintings in El Templete. These represent the first Mass celebrated on that spot, the first *Cabildo* (local council) and the consecration of the small temple.

2 Centro & La Habana Vieja

➡ Havana maps
1 Havana orientation, page 70
2 Centro & La Habana Vieja, page 74
3 Plaza de Armas, page 76
4 Parque Central, page 79
5 Vedado & Plaza de la Revolución, page 90
6 Miramar, page 94

Sleeping
Ana María Rodríguez López cp **1** *B4*
Caribbean **2** *B4*
Carlos Luis Valderrama
    Moré cp **4** *C3*
Cary y Nilo cp **9** *C2*
Casa Marta **5** *C3*
Casa Mary cp **10** *B5*
Deauville **7** *B4*
Dr Alejandro Oses cp **8** *B4*
El Parador Numantino cp **6** *C4*
Eugenio y Fabio cp **3** *E6*
Evora Rodríguez **11** *B4*
Federico y Yamelis Llanes cp **17** *B4*
Jesús Deiro Rana cp **19** *C3*
Jesús y María cp **12** *D5*
Julio y Elsa cp **26** *B4*
Lido **14** *C4*
Marilys Herrera González cp **16** *B1*
Melba y Alberto cp **13** *B3*

Mercure Sevilla **24** *C4*
Nacional de Cuba **18** *A1*
Orlando y Lissett cp **20** *D5*
Villa Colonial Tomy cp **21** *C2*
Xiomara cp **25** *C4*

Eating
Bellomar Paladar **1** *C4*
Doña Blanquita Paladar **5** *B4*
Don Lorenzo Paladar **6** *D5*
Flor de Lotto **2** *D2*
La Dichosa **7** *C5*
La Divina Pastora **8** *A6*
La Guarida Paladar **9** *C2*
La Tasquita Paladar **10** *B1*
Los Tres Chinitos **21** *C3*
Los Vitrales **3** *B4*
Los XII Apóstoles **12** *A5*
Panadería Dulcería
    El Sol de Cuba **4** *D5*

Puerto de Sagua **20** *D5*

Bars
Bar Dos Hermanos **13** *D5*
Café Neruda **19** *B3*
Lluvia de Oro **18** *C5*

Entertainment
Callejón de Hamel **22** *B1*
Casa de la Cultura del
    Centro Habana **11** *D1*
Casa de la Cultura Julián
    del Casals **23** *E4*
Casa de la Música Galiano **14** *C3*
Casa de la Trova **15** *B2*
Casa del Tango Edmundo
    Daubar **16** *C3*
La Madriguera **17** *D1*
Palermo **24** *C4*

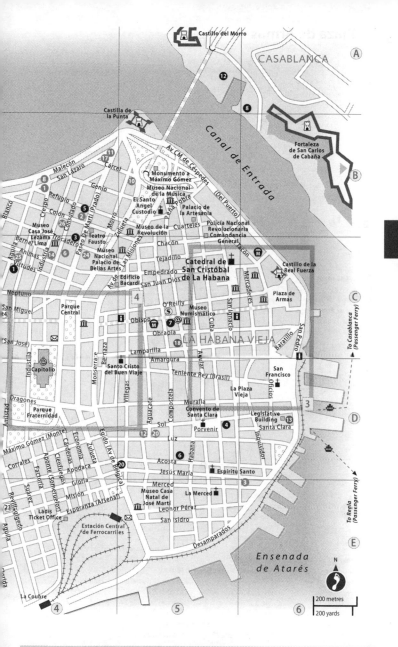

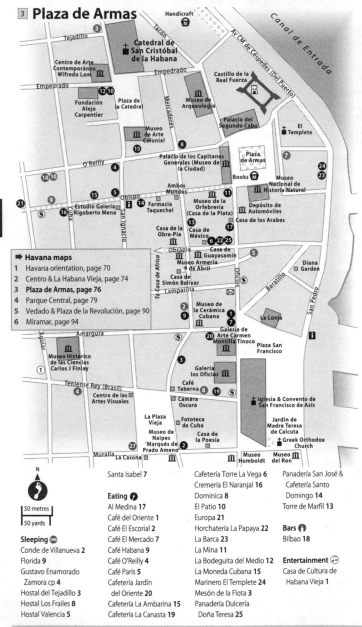

3 Plaza de Armas

Handicraft

Canal de Entrada

Tejadillo

Catedral de San Cristóbal de la Habana

Av CM de Céspedes (Del Puerto)

Centro de Arte Contemporáneo Wifredo Lam

Empedrado

Castillo de la Real Fuerza

Empedrado

Plaza de la Catedral

Museo de Arqueología

Fundación Alejo Carpentier

Palacio del Segundo Cabo

El Templete

Museo de Arte Colonial

Mercaderes

Plaza de Armas

O'Reilly

Palacio de los Capitanes Generales (Museo de la Ciudad)

Books

Museo Nacional de Historia Natural

Ambos Mundos

Obispo

Farmacia Taquechel

Museo de la Orfebrería (Casa de la Plata)

Depósito de Automóviles

Estudio Galería Rigoberto Mena

San Ignacio

Casa de los Arabes

Cuba

Casa de la Obra-Pía

Casa de México

Obrapía

Casa de Guayasamín

Diana Garden

Museo Armería 9 de Abril

Ta Casa de Africa

Casa de Simón Bolívar

Oficios

Barrillo

Lamparilla

San Pedro

➡ Havana maps

1 Havana orientation, page 70
2 Centro & La Habana Vieja, page 74
3 Plaza de Armas, page 76
4 Parque Central, page 79
5 Vedado & Plaza de la Revolución, page 90
6 Miramar, page 94

Museo de la Cerámica Cubana

La Lonja

Amargura

Galería de Arte Carmen Montilla Tinoco

Plaza San Francisco

Aguiar

Museo Histórico de las Ciencias Carlos J Finlay

Galería los Oficios

Teniente Rey (Brasil)

Café Taberna

Centro de las Artes Visuales

Cámara Oscura

Iglesia & Convento de San Francisco de Asís

La Plaza Vieja

Fototeca de Cuba

Jardín de Madre Teresa de Calcuta

Greek Orthodox Church

Museo de Naipes 'Marqués de Prado Ameno'

Casa de la Poesía

Muralla

La Casona

Museo Humboldt

Museo del Ron

N

50 metres
50 yards

Sleeping
Conde de Villanueva 2
Florida 9
Gustavo Enamorado Zamora cp 4
Hostal del Tejadillo 3
Hostal Los Frailes 8
Hostal Valencia 5

Santa Isabel 7

Eating
Al Medina 17
Café del Oriente 1
Café El Escorial 2
Café El Mercado 7
Café Habana 9
Café O'Reilly 4
Café París 5
Cafetería Jardín del Oriente 20
Cafetería La Ambarina 15
Cafetería La Canasta 19

Cafetería Torre La Vega 6
Cremería El Naranjal 16
Dominica 8
El Patio 10
Europa 21
Horchatería La Papaya 22
La Barca 23
La Mina 11
La Bodeguita del Medio 12
La Moneda Cubana 15
Marinero El Templete 24
Mesón de la Flota 3
Panadería Dulcería Doña Teresa 25

Panadería San José & Cafetería Santo Domingo 14
Torre de Marfil 13

Bars
Bilbao 18

Entertainment
Casa de Cultura de Habana Vieja 1

On the north side of the Plaza is the **Palacio del Segundo Cabo** ① *Mon-Sat 1000-1730*, the former private residence of the Captains General, now housing the **Instituto Cubano del Libro** and three bookshops. Its patio is worth a look. On the east side is the small luxury hotel, the **Santa Isabel**, and on the south side the modern **Museo Nacional de Historia Natural** ① *Obispo 61, entre Baratillo y Oficios, Plaza de Armas, T7-863 2687, museo@mnhc.inf.cu, Tue-Fri 0930-1730, Sat and Sun 0930-1630, CUC$3, guide CUC$1*, where you will find lots of stuffed animals, information (in Spanish) on Cuban bats, butterflies and endemic species. This is not the most exciting museum unless you take time to read, for example, that a flock of 50,000 bats eats 200 kg a night; there are 87 species of cockroach, two thirds of which are endemic, etc. Outside in the Plaza de Armas there is a small, second-hand **book market** ① *Wed-Sat 1000-1800*.

On the west side of Plaza de Armas is the former **Palacio de los Capitanes Generales**, built in 1780, a charming example of colonial architecture. The Spanish Governors and the Presidents lived here until 1917, when it became the City Hall. It is now the **Museo de la Ciudad** ① *Tacón 1 entre Obispo y O'Reilly, T7-861 5779, museologia@patrimonio.ohch.cu, daily 0900-1930, CUC$3, guided visit CUC$4, last tour 1700, charge for photos CUC$2, video CUC$10*, the Historical Museum of the city of Havana. The museum houses a large collection of 19th-century furnishings that illustrate the wealth of the Spanish colonial community, including 'his and her' large marble, shell-shaped baths. There are portraits of patriots, flags, military memorabilia and a grandly laid-out dining room. The building was the site of the signing of the 1899 treaty between Spain and the USA. The nation's first flag is here, together with a beautiful sword encrusted with diamonds belonging to Máximo Gómez. There is a curious portrait of Calixto García featuring his unusual wound: he was shot through the neck and the bullet emerged through his forehead. Also on display is the original slave freedom charter signed by Céspedes. The courtyard contains Royal palms, the Cuban national tree. Outside is a statue of Ferdinand VII of Spain, with a singularly uncomplimentary plaque. No Spanish king or queen ever came to Cuba in colonial times. In front of the museum is a collection of church bells. The former **Supreme Court** on the north side of the Plaza is another colonial building, with a large patio. North of the plaza, the **Castillo de la Real Fuerza** is Cuba's oldest building and the second oldest fort in the New World. It was first built in 1558 after the city had been sacked by buccaneers and was rebuilt in 1582. It is a low, long building with a picturesque tower from which there is a grand view. ① *O'Reilly entre Av del Puerto y Tacón, daily 0900-1830, CUC$1*. Just off Plaza de Armas, the **Museo de la Orfebrería (Casa de la Plata)** ① *Obispo 113 entre Mercaderes y Oficios, T7-8639861, plata@cultural.ohch.cu, Tue-Sat 0900-1730, Sun 0900-1300, free, guide CUC$1, photos CUC$2, video CUC$10*, has a silverware collection of fine pieces, jewellery and old frescoes on the upper floor.

La Catedral de San Cristóbal de La Habana
① *Empedrado esq San Ignacio, T7-861 7771. Open Mon-Fri 1000-1500, Sat 1100-1400, Mass Mon-Fri 1800 in chapel (entrance on San Ignacio), Sat 1500 in chapel, Sun Mass 0930-1200 in main Cathedral. Cathedral tower CUC$1.*

Heading northwest from Plaza de Armas, along Calle Oficios, brings you to one of Havana's most iconic and beautiful monuments, the Catedral de San Cristóbal de la Habana. Construction of a church on this site was begun by Jesuit missionaries at the beginning of the 18th century. After the Jesuits were expelled in 1767, the church was converted into a cathedral. On either side of the Spanish colonial baroque façade are bell towers, the left one (west) being half as wide as the right (east), which has a grand view.

The church is officially dedicated to the Virgin of the Immaculate Conception, but is better known as the church of Havana's patron saint, San Cristóbal de la Habana or the Columbus cathedral. The bones of Christopher Columbus were sent to this cathedral when Santo Domingo was ceded by Spain to France in 1795; they now lie in Santo Domingo (Dominican Republic). There is much speculation over whether they were indeed the bones of Columbus. They could have been those of his brother or son, but the Dominican Republic is convinced of their authenticity.

Plaza de la Catedral and around
In the former Palacio de los Condes de Casa Bayona is the **Museo de Arte Colonial** ① *San Ignacio 61, Plaza de la Catedral, T7-862 6440, colonial@cultural.ohch.cu, daily 0930-1700, CUC$2, guide CUC$1, camera CUC$2, video CUC$10*, with exhibits of colonial furniture and other items, plus a section on stained glass. Exquisite.

The work of Cuba's most famous painter can be seen at the **Centro de Arte Contemporáneo Wifredo Lam** ① *San Ignacio 22, esquina Empedrado, just next to the cathedral, T7-861 2096, rinterlam@wlam.cult.cu, free.* The changing exhibition programmes feature mostly Cuban artists but also world masters. Lam directed most of his work to a non-Latin American audience. The building was renovated in 2009 and is a fine exhibition centre.

Displays on colonial archaeology uncovered during excavation works in La Habana Vieja and the bay can be seen at the **Museo de Arqueología** ① *Tacón 12 entre O'Reilly y Empedrado, T7-861 4469, tony@arq.patrimonio.ohch.cu, Tue-Sat 0900-1700, Sun 0930-1300, CUC$1, CUC$2 with guide, CUC$15 to use video camera, permission for photos or videos must be obtained from Tacón 20, T7-863 9981.* Exhibits feature Cuban and Peruvian aboriginal artefacts. The house was built in the 17th century but redesigned in 1725 by Juana Carvajal, a freed slave who inherited the building from her owner, Lorenza Carvajal. It was further expanded by the Calvo de la Puerta family, who acquired it in 1748. It was restored in 1988 and converted into a museum. Just outside the museum on the corner of Tacón and Oficios, there is an archaeological excavation dug in 2006 on show, with photos of the artefacts discovered there. Part of the Muralla del Mar, a wall constructed in 1733, it includes the discovery of a site named El Boquete, Boquete de Pimientas from the 17th century, or Boquete de la Pescadería, a fish market built here in 1835.

Alejo Carpentier is revered throughout Latin America as the founder of Magical Realism. The **Fundación Alejo Carpentier** ① *Empedrado 215 entre Cuba y San Ignacio, closed for repairs in 2009, due to reopen end-year,* was the setting for his novel *El Siglo de las Luces.* The foundation runs literary courses and there is a small museum of the writer's letters and books.

Castillo de la Punta and around
Built at the end of the 16th century at the northernmost part of the old city to protect the entrance to the harbour, the **Castillo del la Punta** ① *Av del Puerto y Paseo del Prado, T7-860 3196, Wed-Sun 1000-1730, CUC$5, camera CUC$2,* is a squat building with 2.5-m-thick walls. There are three permanent exhibition rooms covering the history of the castle, naval design and construction and marine archaeology. On the seafront plaza in front of La Punta are metal floor plans of the local fortresses with numbers and a key showing what everything is. Opposite the fortress, across the Malecón, is the **monument to Máximo Gómez**, the independence leader.

The **Policía Nacional Revolucionario Comandancia General** is in another fortress in the block bounded by Cuba, Chacón, Cuarteles and San Ignacio. It is not open to the public but if you want to visit you can go to the offices of the **Centro Provincial de Selección PNR** ① *Tulipán y Boyeros, Mon-Fri 0830-1700,* to get permission. There are two other old forts in Havana: **Atarés**, finished in 1763, on a hill overlooking the southwest end of the harbour; and **El Príncipe**, on a hill at the far end of Avenida Independencia (Avenida Rancho Boyeros), built 1774-1794, now the city jail. The finest view in Havana is from this hill.

A small and beautiful old mansion houses the **Museo Nacional de la Música** ① *Capdevila (Cárcel) 1, entre Habana y Aguiar,* with an interesting collection of African drums and other instruments from all around the world, showing development of Cuban *son* and *danzón* and other musical styles between the 16th and 21st centuries. However, it has been closed for some time and no one knows when it will reopen.

The **Church of El Santo Angel Custodio** ① *Compostela 2 esq Cuarteles, T7-8610469, Tue-Sat 1000-1800, Mass 1700, Sun 0830-1200, Mass 0900,* was built by the Jesuits in 1689 on the slight elevation of **Peña Pobre** hill, with the tower added in 1704. The original church was largely destroyed by a hurricane in 1846, but in 1852 it became the parish church and in 1853 José Martí was baptized here. It was rebuilt and enlarged in its present neo-Gothic style in 1868-1870. It has white, laced Gothic towers and 10 tiny chapels, no more than kneeling places, the best of which is behind the high altar. There is some interesting stained glass depicting *conquistadores.* During the Christmas period some impressive figures around a manger are placed at the entrance. Other famous people baptized here include Amelia Goire (La Milagrosa), Alicia Alonso and Julián del Casal, while it is also the setting for the last chapter of the novel *Cecilia Valdés,* see Literature, page 427.

Museo de la Revolución
① *Refugio entre Monserrate y Zulueta, facing Av de las Misiones, T7-8624091/6, daily 1000-1700, CUC$5, guide CUC$2, cameras and video CUC$5. Allow several hours, explanations are mostly in Spanish.*
This huge, ornate building, topped by a dome, was once the Presidential Palace, but now contains the Museo de la Revolución. The history of Cuban political development is charted, from the slave uprisings to joint space missions with the

➡ **Havana maps**
1 Havana orientation, page 70
2 Centro & La Habana Vieja, page 74
3 Plaza de Armas, page 76
4 **Parque Central, page 79**
5 Vedado & Plaza de la Revolución, page 90
6 Miramar, page 94

4 **Parque Central**

N
400 metres
400 yards

Sleeping 💤
Inglaterra 2
NH Parque Central 1
Plaza 3
Telégrafo 4

Eating 🍴
A Prado y Neptuno 1
El Castillo de Farnés 2
El Floridita 4

Gentiluomo 6
Hanoi 3
La Zaragozana 5
La Julia 7
Los Nardos 8
Pastelería Francés 9
Soda Obispo 12

Bars & clubs 🍸
Casa del Escabeche 11
Monserrate 10

Entertainment 😀
Cine Payret 1
Gran Teatro de
 la Habana 2

ex-Soviet Union. The liveliest section displays the final battles against Batista's troops, with excellent photographs and some bizarre personal mementoes. The yacht *Granma*, from which Fidel Castro disembarked with his companions in 1956 to launch the Revolution, has been installed in the park facing the south entrance, surrounded by planes, tanks and other vehicles involved, as well as a Soviet-built tank used against the Bay of Pigs invasion and a fragment from a US spy plane shot down in the 1970s. Allow several hours to see it all.

Parque Central

A very pleasant park with a monument to **José Martí** in the centre. The north side of the Parque is entirely occupied by the **NH Parque Central**, while the **Hotel Plaza** is in the northeast corner. On its west side are the **Hotel Telégrafo**, the historic **Hotel Inglaterra**, which celebrated its 125th anniversary in 2000) and the **Gran Teatro de la Habana**, a beautiful building with tours of the inside. The theatre is a neo-baroque monument dating from 1838. It is used by the National Opera and National Ballet and also houses the Teatro García Lorca. Sarah Bernhardt once performed there when the Teatro García Lorca was called the Teatro Tacón. José Martí wrote of her performance, "Sarah is flexible, delicate, svelte. When she is not shaken by the demon of tragedy, her body is full of grace and abandon, when the demon takes her over, she is full of power and nobility... Where does she come from? From poverty! Where is she going? To glory!"

Museo Nacional Palacio de Bellas Artes

ⓘ *The Arte Cubano is at Trocadero entre Zulueta y Monserrate, and the Arte Universal is at San Rafael entre Zulueta y Monserrate, for both T7-861 5777/863 9484, www.museo nacional.cult.cu. Tue-Sat 1000-1800, Sun 1000-1400, both museums cost CUC$5 for foreigners, but a same-day entrance to both sites is CUC$8, 5 pesos cubanos for Cubans, reduced rates for children and students, guide CUC$2, no photography permitted. Both museum sites have shops selling books, art and souvenirs.*

On the east side of Parque Central, restoration of the **Centro Asturiano** site of the Museum and National Palace of Fine Arts, was completed after a five-year closure and extensive refurbishment estimated at CUC$14.5 million. Fidel Castro inaugurated this fantastic museum in 2001. The art collection (Arte Universal) is valued at more than CUC$500 million and consists of 47,628 works of art, from an ancient Egyptian sarcophagus to contemporary Cuban paintings. The impressively extended museum has two separate buildings. The exhibits are divided between the original museum in Trocadero, the 1954 Fine Arts Palace, housing the Cuban art collection (Arte Cubano) from colonial times to the 1990s including a section on the post-Revolution Art Schools, and the former Centro Asturiano, two blocks away on the east side of Parque Central on Zulueta, housing European and ancient art.

Cuban paintings in the modern building include the 20th-century painter Victor Manuel's *Gitana Tropical*, considered an important symbol of the Cuban vanguard. There are masterpieces of José Nicolás de la Escalera and Victor Patricio Landaluze from the colonial period and representations of modern-era Cuban paintings from Wifredo Lam and René Portocarrero. Exhibited works of more recent Cuban artists include those of Roberto Fabelo and Zaida del Río and some artists who have left the country. Start on the third floor with the colonial art and work your way down to the present day. This is a truly spectacular museum and well worth a look even if you are not keen on modern art. On the ground floor there are also temporary exhibitions, a small shop and toilets.

The older building designed by the Spanish architect Manuel del Busto in the early 20th century has been fabulously renovated with huge marble staircases giving access to five floors. The large collection of European paintings, from the 16th century to the present, contains works by Gainsborough, Van Dyck, Velázquez, Tintoretto, Degas et al. One painting by Canaletto, in the Italian room on the fifth floor, is in fact only half a painting; the other half of the 18th-century painting *Chelsea from the Thames* is owned by the National Trust in Britain and hangs in Blickling Hall, Norfolk. It is believed to have been commissioned in 1746-1748 by the Chelsea Hospital, which is featured in the Cuban half, but the artist was unable to sell it and cut it in two just before he died in 1768. The left half was sold to the 11th Marquis of Lothian, whose family owned Blickling Hall, where it has stayed ever since. The right half was bought and sold several times until it ended up with a Cuban collector, Oscar Cinetas, who donated it to the museum before the Revolution. A full-size photograph of the Blickling section of the panorama is now on display next to the Cuban section and a complete digital image of the two pieces has been shown at Blickling Hall. The museum also has Greek, Roman, Egyptian and Etruscan sculpture and artefacts, many very impressive. The unharmed Greek amphora from the fifth century BC is considered remarkable.

The museum has also included paintings from private collections left behind by rich Cuban families (including the Bacardí and Gómez Mena families) and members of the former dictator Fulgencio Batista's government who fled Cuba soon after the 1959 Revolution. The origin of these works, including Spanish artists Sorolla and Zurbarán, has been included in the catalogues. It had been rumoured that some of these collections had been sold by the Cuban government during the economic crisis of the Special Period. Additionally, there are rooms dedicated to Latin American art and 18th- and 19th-century paintings from the United States.

Between the two galleries on Avenida de las Misiones entre Empedrado y San Juan Dios, is the wonderful art deco former Bacardí building, topped by its signature bat. A great view of it can also be appreciated from the roof terrace of the Hotel Plaza.

Capitolio
① *Paseo de Martí entre San Martín y Dragones, T7-861 0261, www.capitolio.cu. Daily 0900-1800 but often shuts early, CUC$3 to go in the halls, tours available (T7-8615519, Departamento de Eventos, to arrange pre-planned tours), guide CUC$1, camera and video charge CUC$2. Entry to just the Salón de los Pasos Perdidos is CUC$1 including photos and video. Entrance for visitors is to the left of the stairway. Internet café (see below). All bags have to be left at kiosk on the left as you go up the stairs.*

The Capitolio was built in the style of the US Capitol in Washington DC in 1929-1932 by the dictator Machado in an attempt to impress his US paymasters with his loyalty. The white dome over a rotunda is 62 m high and inside there is a 17-m statue of Jupiter, representing the state. This is the tallest interior statue in Latin America and the third largest in the world. At the centre of the floor of the entrance hall is set a 24-carat diamond (or is it a fake?), which pinpoints zero for all distance measurements in Cuba. The interior has large halls and stately staircases, all most sumptuously decorated. It was initially used as the seat of parliament with the Senate and the House of Representatives meeting there, but they were dissolved after the Revolution. Now it houses the Cuban Academy of Sciences and the National Library of Science and Technology. Outside the Capitolio there are lots of old American cars waiting to offer taxi rides, as well as conventional taxis, *cocotaxis*, *bicitaxis*, etc.

Partagás cigar factory

ⓘ *Industria 520 entre Dragones y Barcelona, behind the Capitolio, T7-862 4604/863 5766. 40-min tours every 15 mins Tue-Sat 0930-1100 and 1200-1400, CUC$10, tickets must be bought in advance in hotel lobbies, English, Spanish or French-speaking guides available.*
The tour is very interesting but pricey. You are taken through the factory and shown the whole production process from storage and sorting of leaves, to packaging and labelling. Four different brand names are made here: *Partagás, Cubana, Ramón Allones* and *Bolívar*. These and other famous cigars can be bought at their shop here: open daily 0900-1700, as can rum (credit cards accepted). Cigars are also made at many tourist locations (for example Palacio de la Artesanía, the airport, some hotels). Also see box, page 150.

Parque Fraternidad and around

The park was originally called Parque de Colón, but was renamed to mark the VI Panamerican Conference in 1892. It has been landscaped to show off the Capitolio, north of it, to the best effect. At its centre is a ceiba tree growing in soil provided by each of the American republics. Also in the park is a famous statue of the Amerindian woman who first welcomed the Spaniards: La Noble Habana, sculpted in 1837. From the southwest corner the handsome Avenida Allende runs due west to the high hill, on which stands **El Príncipe Castle** (now the city jail). The **Quinta de los Molinos**, on this avenue, at the foot of the hill, once housed the School of Agronomy of Havana University. The main house now contains the **Máximo Gómez Museum** (Dominican-born fighter for Cuban Independence). Also here is the headquarters of the association of young writers and artists (Asociación Hermanos Saiz). The gardens are a lovely place to stroll.

Heading south along Egido, opposite the central railway station, the **Museo Casa Natal de José Martí** ⓘ *Leonor Pérez 314 entre Picota y Egido, T7-861 3778, nataljmarti@cultural.ohch.cu, Tue-Sat 0930-1700, Sun 0930-1300, CUC$1, CUC$2 for camera, CUC$10 for video,* is the birthplace of the country's great hero (see box, page 430), with his full life story documented with photos, mementoes, furniture and papers. A tiny house which has been devoted to his memory since a plaque was first put on the wall in 1899, a museum since 1925 and restored in 1952-1953.

Calle Obispo and Calle Obrapía

From the Parque Central you can walk back to the Plaza de Armas along Calle Obispo, now closed to traffic and one of the streets of La Habana Vieja which has seen most restoration, with many shops lovingly restored to their former splendour. There is a small handicrafts market on Obispo entre Aguacate y Compostela, where they sell leather goods, clothes, ceramics and jewellery. Avoid buying coral, which is protected internationally. Sundays are particularly busy. Calle Obrapía, which runs parallel, has some magnificent colonial buildings and many of them are now museums and galleries.

The **Museo Numismático** ⓘ *Obispo 305 entre Aguiar y Habana, T7-861 5811, numismatica@cultural.ohch.cu, Tue-Sat 0915-1645, Sun 0915-1300, CUC$1, no cameras allowed,* is a coin museum which exhibits and sells coins, medals and documentation. The extensive collection of more than 1000 pieces, including rare notes and valuable cold coins, dates from the colonial period up to the Revolution.

Farmacia Taquechel ⓘ *Obispo 155 entre Mercaderes y San Ignacio, T7-862 9286,* displays all manner of herbs, remedies and concoctions stored in porcelain jars, glazed and gilded with herbal motifs and meticulously arranged on floor to ceiling polished mahogany shelves. The original 1896 building was the workplace of Francisco Taquechel Mirabal.

Rigoberto Mena is one of Cuba's most respected contemporary artists and his studio, **Estudio Galería Rigoberto Mena** ① *San Ignacio 154 entre Obispo y Obrapía, T7-867 5884*, houses a fantastic collection of abstract art. His style is deceptively simple, a meticulous composition of brilliant colours radiating from dark backgrounds.

The vintage car museum, **Depósito de Automóviles** ① *Oficios 13 y Jústiz, just off Plaza de Armas, T7-863 9942, automovil@cultural.ohch.cu, Tue-Sun 0900-1900, CUC$1, photos CUC$2, video CUC$10*, lovingly presents vehicles from the 19th and 20th centuries. There are a great many museum pieces including pre-Revolution US models, which are still on the road especially outside Havana, in among the Ladas, VWs and Nissans.

Casa de los Arabes ① *Oficios 16 entre Obispo and Obrapía, T7-861 5868, arabes@cultural.ohch.cu, Tue-Sat 0900-1700, Sun 0900-1300, free, donations welcome*, is a lovely building built in Mudéjar style with vines trained over the courtyard for shade. The collection includes the only mosque in Havana, jewels, Saharan robes, gold- and silver-painted weapons and rugs. Bar and restaurant, **Al Medina**, see page 107, is a relaxing place to eat.

Casa de la Obra-Pía ① *Obrapía 158 entre Mercaderes y San Ignacio, T7-861 3097, obrapia@cultural.ohch.cu, Tue-Sat 0930-1630, Sun 0930-1230, no entry fee but donations welcome, photos free*, is a furniture museum, with examples from the 18th and 19th centuries, housed in a yellow building. It was built in 1665, then remodelled in 1793 by the Marqués de Cárdenas de Monte Hermoso, whose shield is over the door. The portico was made in Cádiz in 1793, but finished off in Havana. The building was restored in 1983.

The **Casa de Africa** ① *Obrapía 157 entre San Ignacio y Mercaderes, T7-861 5798, africa@cultural.ohch.cu, Tue-Sat 0900-1700, Sun 0900-1300, free*, is a small gallery of carved wooden artefacts and handmade costumes. Sculpture, furniture, paintings and ceramics from sub-Saharan Africa, including gifts given to Fidel by visiting African Presidents. There is also an exhibit of elements of African-Cuban religions.

Casa de México ① *Obrapía 116 entre Mercaderes y Oficios, T7-861 8166, mexico@cultural.ohch.cu, Tue-Sat 0930-1645, Sun 0930-1245*, also called **La Casa de Benemérito de las Américas Benito Juárez**, is more of a cultural centre than a museum, housed in a pink building draped with the Mexican flag. Exhibits include pre-Columbian artefacts and popular arts and crafts including ceramics from Jalisco.

Works donated to Cuba by the late Ecuadorean artist Oswaldo Guayasamín are displayed at the **Casa de Guayasamín** ① *Obrapía 111 entre Mercaderes y Oficios T7-861 3843, guayasamin@cultural.ohch.cu, Tue-Sat 0900-1645, Sun 0900-1300, donations welcome*. Exhibits are, generally, paintings, sculpture and silkscreens, but there are occasionally other exhibitions. Guayasamín painted a famous portrait of Fidel Castro.

On 9 April 1958 a group of revolutionaries of the Movimiento 26 de Julio attacked the business of Compañía Armera de Cuba. They were unsuccessful and four members of the group were killed. After the Revolution, the site was declared a National Monument in their honour and on 9 April 1971 a museum, the **Museo Armería 9 de Abril** ① *Mercaderes entre Obrapía y Lamparilla, T7-861 8080, armeria@cultural.ohch.cu, Tue-Sat 0900-1700, Sun 0900-1300*, was opened. At the front the original business is recreated, with some contemporary pieces, hunting and fishing accessories, including the collection of arms that Castro donated in the 1990s. At the back there is an exhibition on the events that took place there in 1958.

The **Casa de Simón Bolívar** ① *Mercaderes 158 entre Obrapía y Lamparilla, T7-861 3998, bolivar@cultural.ohch.cu, Tue-Sat 0930-1700, Sun 0930-1300, free, donations welcome*, contains exhibits about the life of the South American liberator and some Venezuelan art.

Plaza San Francisco and around

The **Iglesia y Convento de San Francisco de Asís** ⓘ *Oficios entre Amargura y Churruca, T7-862 9683, sanfrancisco@cultural.ohch.cu, daily 0900-1800, CUC$2 for museum and campanario (bell tower), photos CUC$2, video CUC$10, guide CUC$1,* built in 1608 and reconstructed in 1730, is a massive, sombre edifice suggesting defence, rather than worship. The three-storey bell tower was both a landmark for returning voyagers and a look out for pirates and has stunning views of the city and port. The **Basílica Menor de San Francisco de Asís** is now a concert hall (tickets for concerts are sold three days in advance) and the convent is a museum containing religious pieces. Restoration work continues. Most of the treasures were removed by the government and some are in museums. The sculpture outside the church is of the eccentric *El Caballero de París* (French Wanderer). The legendary Galician vagrant with a deluded sense of grandeur was notorious throughout the city and affectionately embraced by Habaneros. He died in 1985 in Havana's psychiatric hospital. The sculpture was the work of José Villa who was also responsible for the John Lennon monument in Vedado, see page 93. Behind San Francisco is the **Jardín de Madre Teresa de Calcuta** (Mother Teresa's Garden), and at the end of the garden is the Greek Orthodox Church.

The Corinthian white marble building on Calle Oficios, south of the post office was once the **legislative building** where the House of Representatives met before the Capitolio was built. The newly restored Cuban Stock Exchange building, **La Lonja**, Oficios and Plaza San Francisco de Asís, is worth a look, as is the new cruise ship terminal opposite.

The British Embassy financed the construction of the **Diana Garden** ⓘ *Baratillo, near Plaza San Francisco, daily 0700-1900,* in memory of Diana, Princess of Wales. It is dominated by a concrete tube covered in ceramics in the shape of liquorice all-sorts which don't reach to the top, symbolizing a life cut short. There is also a sculpture of the sun, representing the happiness in her life, but one triangle is missing, her heart. Around the base of the pole are rings for sadness.

Nelson Domínguez, one of Cuba's most respected and prolific of Cuba's contemporary artists, has his own studio/gallery at the **Galería Los Oficios** ⓘ *Oficios 166 entre Amargura y Teniente Rey, T7-863 0497, Tue-Sat 0900-1700, Sun 0900-1300.* Working in various mediums, he is primarily influenced by the natural environment and draws heavily on indigenous and spiritual symbolism. There are several other artists' galleries on Obispo, Oficios and Obrapía, such as **Galería de Arte Carmen Montilla Tinoco** ⓘ *Oficios 162 entre Amagura y Teniente Rey, T7-866 8768, Tue-Sat 0900-1700, Sun 0900-1300,* housed in an early 18th-century building. It was originally used as a shop below and dwelling above, then briefly as the Consulate of Paraguay at the beginning of the 20th century, but it was ruined by fire in the 1980s. The **Oficina del Historiador**, with the help of the Venezuelan artist, restored it and opened it as an art gallery in her name in 1994. Nearby is the **Museo de la Cerámica Cubana** ⓘ *Amargura y Mercaderes, T7-861 6130, ceramica@cultural.ohch.cu, daily 0900-1830, CUC$1, free for under 12s, no charge for cameras,* displaying Cuban ceramic art dating from the 1940s onwards, some of which is for sale.

The great explorer and botanist Federico Enrique Alejandro von Humboldt, 1769-1857, lived at Oficios 254 esquina Muralla, at the beginning of 1801 when he completed his calculations of the meridian of the city. His home is now the **Museo Humboldt** ⓘ *T7-863 9850, Humboldt@cultural.ohch.cu, Tue-Sat 0900-1700, Sun 0900-1300, free.* Humboldt travelled extensively in Central and South America, paving the way for Darwin, who called him the greatest naturalist of his time. His scientific works were not confined merely to plants. His name has been given to the cold current that flows northwards off the coast of Chile and Peru, which he discovered and measured. He also made important contributions to world meteorology, to the study of vulcanism and the earth's crust and the connection between climate and flora. In the process he discovered that mountain sickness is caused by a lack of oxygen at high altitudes. The last years of his life were spent writing *Kosmos*, an account of his scientific findings, which was soon translated into many languages. Nearby, is the **Casa de la Poesía** ① *Muralla 63 entre Oficios e Inquisidor, T7-862 1801, poeta@cultural.ohch.cu, Mon-Fri 0900-1700, 1st and 3rd Sat of every month 0900-1700.*

Museo del Ron
① *Av del Puerto 262 entre Sol y Muralla, T7-861 8051, www.havanaclubfoundation.com. Mon-Thu 0900-1700, Fri-Sun 0900-1600, CUC$7, includes a drink, under 15s free. Multilingual guides included.*
The **Fundación Destilería Havana Club** has a museum offering displays of the production of rum from the sugar cane plantation to the processing and bottling, with machinery dating from the early 20th century. The museum is well laid out but too dark and atmospheric to read the notices. There is a wonderful model railway which runs round a model sugar mill and distillery, designed and made by prize-winning Lázaro Eduardo García Driggs in 1993-1994 and restored in 1999-2000. At the end of the tour you get a tasting of a six-year old **Havana Club** rum in a bar that is a mock up of the once-famous *Sloppy Joe's*. There is also a restaurant (excellent shrimp kebab) and bar (see page 114), a shop and an art gallery where present-day Cuban artists exhibit their work.

La Plaza Vieja and around
An 18th-century plaza, restored as part of a joint project by UNESCO and **Habaguanex**, a state company responsible for the restoration and revival of La Habana Vieja. Many of the buildings around the plaza boast elegant balconies overlooking the large square with a fountain in the middle. The former house of the Spanish Captain General, Conde de Ricla, who retook Havana from the English and restored power to Spain in 1763, can be seen on the corner of San Ignacio and Muralla. Known as **La Casona** ① *Centro de Arte La Casona, Muralla 107 esq San Ignacio, T7-861 8544, www.galeriascubanas.com. Tue-Sat 1000-1730,* modern art exhibitions are held upstairs in the beautiful blue and white building. Note the friezes up the staircase and along the walls. There is a great view of the plaza from the balcony and trailing plants in the courtyard enhance the atmosphere. There is a museum of playing cards, **Museo de Naipes 'Marqués de Prado Ameno'** ① *Muralla 101 esq Inquisidor, T7-860 1534, naipes@cultural.ohch.cu, Mon-Sat 0930-1730, Sun 0900-1300.* On the west side of the Plaza is the hugely popular microbrewery, **Cervecería La Muralla** ① *San Ignacio esq Muralla, T7-866 4433, daily 1200-2400,* which is a great place for a midday brunch or a sundowner during or after your walk round the city. Their own beer is CUC$2. You can eat here too. Also on the west side is the **Centro de las Artes Visuales** ① *San Ignacio 352 entre Teniente Rey y Muralla, T7-862 9295, Tue-Sat 1000-1700,* which has a variety of art exhibitions. There are two galleries, Siglo XXI and Escuela de Plata. On the north side of the square, on Teniente Rey, is a posh and expensive restaurant, **Santo Angel**, which has tables outside and is a pleasant place for an evening cocktail.

In the northeast corner, Mercaderes y Teniente Rey, is the **Café Taberna**, T7-861 1637. After the English took Havana in 1762, the first coffee houses were established, and this one, the first, was called *Café de Taberna* because its owner was Juan Bautista de Taberna. It remained in operation until the 1940s and was known as a place where merchant traders congregated. It was reopened in 1999 as a restaurant with the theme of the musician, Benny Moré. Unfortunately the food is nothing special, rather greasy, and the service poor. On the top floor of the Gómez Vila building is the **Cámara Oscura** ① *Teniente Rey esq Mercaderes, Plaza Vieja, T7-866 4461, daily 0900-1720, CUC$1, free for under 12s,* where lenses and mirrors provide you with a panoramic view of the city. Donated by Cádiz, this camera obscura is the first in the Americas and one of the few in the world: two in England, two in Spain and one in Portugal. In one of the converted mansions on the east side, the **Fototeca de Cuba** ① *Mercaderes 307 entre Teniente Rey y Muralla, T7-862 2530, Tue-Sat 0900-1700,* showcases international photography exhibitions. The old post office, also on the east side, dates from 1909.

Carlos J Finlay was an eminent Cuban doctor who discovered that the mosquito was the vector of yellow fever in the late 19th century and helped to eradicate the disease in Cuba. The **Museo Histórico de las Ciencias Carlos J Finlay** ① *Cuba 460 entre Amargura y Brasil, T7-863 4824, closed for repairs in 2009,* housed in a strikingly ornate building, contains displays about science in Cuba, the history of the Royal Academy of Sciences (Academia Real de Ciencias) and exhibits on the role of the medical profession during the wars of independence.

Convento de Santa Clara
① *Cuba 610 entre Luz y Sol, closed for repairs in 2009.*
The convent of Santa Clara was founded in 1644 by nuns from Cartagena in Colombia. It was in use as a convent until 1919, when the nuns sold the building. In a shady business deal it was later acquired by the government and, after radical alterations, it became offices for the Ministry of Public Works until the decision was made to restore the building to its former glory. Work began in 1982, with the creation of the **Centro Nacional de Conservación, Restauración y Museología** (CENCREM), and is still continuing. The convent occupies four small blocks in La Habana Vieja, bounded by Calles Habana, Sol, Cuba and Luz, and originally there were three cloisters and an orchard.

Casablanca

Ins and outs
To cross the bay to Casablanca, take the left-hand ferry queue for Casablanca next to the Customs House, opposite Calle Santa Clara, 10 centavos. Security is very tight here since a ferry was hijacked in 2003 for an abortive attempt to get to Miami. Everybody is searched and there are metal detectors. Access to the Castillo del Morro is from any bus going through the tunnel (40 centavos or 1 peso), board at San Lázaro and Av del Puerto and get off at the stop after the tunnel, cross the road and climb following the path to the left. Alternatively take the **HabanaBusTour**, a taxi, or a 20-minute walk from the Fortaleza de San Carlos de la Cabaña.

Castillo del Morro
① *Casablanca, T7-863 7941, daily 0800-2000. CUC$5 includes CUC$1 for the parque, CUC$2 for the lighthouse and CUC$2 for the castle. No charge for photos.*
The Castillo del Morro (El Castillo de los Tres Reyes) was built between 1589 and 1630, with a 20-m moat, but has been much altered. It stands on a bold headland, with the best view of Havana and is illuminated at night. It was one of the major fortifications built to protect the natural harbour and the assembly of Spain's silver fleets from pirate attack.

The flash of its lighthouse, built in 1844, is visible 30 km out to sea. It now serves as a museum with a good exhibition of Cuban history since the arrival of Columbus.

On the harbour side, down by the water, is the **Battery of the 12 Apostles**, each gun being named after an Apostle. Every Saturday at around 1000-1100 there is a display of Afro-Cuban dancing and music. There is also a rather touristy disco, playing taped music; but it's worth a visit for the views of the harbour and the whole of Havana.

Fortaleza de San Carlos de Cabaña
ⓘ *T7-862 0617, daily 0900-1800, CUC$5, 1800-2200, CUC$8 (increased charge for the cannon firing ceremony). No charge for camera or video. Access as for Castillo del Morro, see above.*
It is believed that around 1590, the military engineer, Juan Bautista Antonelli, who built La Punta and El Morro, walked up the hill called La Cabaña one day and declared that 'he who is master of this hill will be master of Havana'. His prophecy was proved correct two centuries later when the English attacked Havana, conquering La Cabaña and thereby gaining control of the port. In 1763, after the English withdrew, another military engineer, Silvestre Abarca, arrived with a plan to build a fortress there. Construction lasted until 1774, when the fortress (the largest the Spanish had built until then in the Americas) was named San Carlos de la Cabaña, in honour of the king of Spain. It has a solid vertical wall of about 700 m with a deep moat connected to that of El Morro. The ditch is 12 m deep on the landward side and there is a drawbridge to the main entrance. From its position on the hill it dominates the city, the bay and the entrance to the harbour. In its heyday it had 120 cannon.

Inside are **Los Fosos de los Laureles**, where political prisoners were shot during the Cuban fight for independence. On 3 January 1959, Che Guevara took possession of the fortress on his triumphant arrival in Havana after the flight of the dictator, Batista. Every night the cannon are fired in an historical ceremony recalling the closure of the city walls to protect the city from attack by pirates. This used to happen at various times and originally in the 17th century the shot was fired from a naval ship in the harbour. Now, however, it is fired from La Cabaña at 2100 on the dot by soldiers in 18th-century uniforms, with the ceremony starting at 2045. There are two museums here, one about Che Guevara and another about fortresses with pictures and models, some old weapons and a replica of a large catapult and battering ram from the 16th to 18th centuries.

Parque El Cristo
ⓘ *You can walk from the statue to the Fortaleza (10 mins) and then, from there, on to the Castillo del Morro.*
Casablanca is also the site of a statue of a very human Jesus Christ, erected in white marble overlooking Havana harbour during the Batista dictatorship as a pacifying exercise. You can get a good view of Havana's skyline from Parque El Cristo, particularly at night, but be careful not to miss the last ferry back. Go up a steep, twisting flight of stone steps, starting on the other side of the plaza in front of the landing stage. Also across the river in the charming town of Casablanca, you will find the **National Observatory** and the old railway station for the (**Hershey line**) trains to Matanzas.

Centro

The state of the buildings in Centro Habana is inclined to shock the first-time visitor, appearing to be a war zone with piles of rubble and holes like craters on the streets and pavements. Centro is not a tourist attraction, although many visitors end up staying here in one of the many *casas particulares*, conveniently placed between the architectural and historical attractions of La Habana Vieja and the nightlife of Vedado. It is separated from La Habana Vieja by the Prado, although all those buildings on the west side of the avenue are still included in the old city.

Centro is bounded on the north side by the seafront drive, the Malecón, which is in a dire state of repair because of buffeting by sea winds, although renovation is under way in parts. Centro's main artery is Calle San Rafael, with runs west from the Parque Central and is initially closed to traffic. This was Havana's 19th-century retail playground, but today is spliced by ramshackle streets strewn with rubble and lined with decrepit houses. At the cross-section of Amistad and Dragones stands the gateway to **Barrio Chino**, a Cuban-Chinese hybrid. In its pre-Revolutionary heyday, this 10-block zone, pivoting around the Cuchillo de Zanja, was full of sordid porn theatres and steamy brothels. Now, a handful of restaurants strewn with lanterns, a colourful food market and a smattering of Chinese associations are all that remains of what was the largest Chinatown in Latin America.

The **Museo Casa José Lezama Lima** ① *Trocadero 162 entre Industria y Consulado, T7-863 4161, mlezama@cubarte.cult.cu Tue-Sat 0900-1700, Sun 0900-1300, CUC$2, CUC$3 with guide*, is the house where José Lezama Lima (1910-76) lived, one of the most important Cuban writers. There is a collection of his personal belongings and art by Cuban painters of the vanguard movement (La Vanguardia). ▸▸ *For listings, see pages 99-130.*

Malecón

The Malecón is Havana's oceanfront esplanade, which links Habana Vieja to the west residential district of Vedado. The sea crashing along the seawall here is a spectacular sight when the wind blows from the north. On calmer days, fishermen lean over the parapet, lovers sit in the shade of the small pillars and joggers sweat along the pavement. On the other side of the six-lane highway, buildings which from a distance look stout and grand, with arcaded pavements, balconies, mouldings and large entrances, are salt-eroded, faded and sadly decrepit inside. Restoration is progressing slowly, but the sea is destroying old and new alike and creating a mammoth renovation task. Parts of the wall are also being rebuilt and there is always construction work somewhere along the Malecón.

Vedado

The largely residential district of Vedado was built in the mid 19th century, funded by the massive wealth generated by the sugar industry. According to Cuban historian Hugh Thomas, between 1917 and 1925 money flooded into the capital as Cuba supplied the United States with its entire sugar needs following the First World War. Prosperity and decadence went hand in hand as opportunistic officials grew rich on non-existent projects and gambling was allowed. The sumptous houses of Vedado reflected the opulence of life under the dictatorship. However, imagination is now required with many of these beautiful residences, with crumbling but magnificent staircases, twisted wrought-iron work and patched or broken stained-glass windows. Most government offices are in Vedado or around Plaza de la Revolución, which is the place to be for any demonstration, political rally or festive occasion, the scene of most of Castro's marathon speeches in the days when they lasted for hours. With the University straddling the divide between Vedado and Centro, the area is full of students, helping to make it a lively and happening part of town. The hotels here harbour many secrets and legends from the past. Some, such as the **Nacional**, were built with Mafia money and were frequented by the mob, but the **Hilton** had barely opened in 1958 before it was taken over by the victorious revolutionaries in 1959 and renamed the **Habana Libre**. Some things don't change: Vedado is still the place to come for nightlife. This is where you'll find all the hottest clubs and discos, bars and floor shows. If you are a night owl, find yourself a hotel or *casa particular* here so that you can walk home in the early hours, after enjoying salsa, jazz, *son*, boleros, cabaret, a show, theatre, cinema, ballet or a classical concert, whatever turns you on.➤ *For listings, see pages 99-130.*

Plaza de la Revolución

This vast open space looks more like a car park than the venue for some of the most rousing speeches and memorable gatherings including the May Day parade. Surrounded by imposing 1950s buildings housing most of the more important ministries, it is a focal point for anyone wanting to understand the charisma of Fidel and his marathon speeches. Suspended on the outside of the Ministry of the Interior is the 30-m steel sculpture of Che Guevara seen in all photos of Havana, a replica of the iconic image, originally shot in 1960, by the celebrated photographer Alberto Korda. Also overlooking the Plaza is the 17-m statue of the national hero, José Martí, carved from white marble extracted from La Isla de la Juventud. The base of the monument is where Castro stood to address the people. The long grey building behind the monument is the former Justice Ministry (1958), now the headquarters of the Central Committee of the Communist Party. The plaza was completely transformed for an open-air mass held by the Pope in January 1998 with huge religious paintings suspended over the surrounding buildings.

The **Memorial José Martí** ① *Plaza de la Revolución, T7-859 2347, Mon-Sat 0900-1700, CUC$3, children under 12 free, lookout CUC$2 extra*, is a beautifully restored and most impressive museum, located in the base of the memorial. Don't miss the lookout accessed by mirrored lift. This is the highest point in the city with good panoramic views of Havana. You should receive a certificate from the lift attendant on your descent. The history of the Cuban postal service is revealed at the **Museo Postal Cubano** ① *Ministry of Communications, Plaza de la Revolución, T7-881 5551, Mon-Fri 0900-1630, CUC$1, guide CUC$3 with prior reservation*, where you will also find a collection of stamps and the story books of José Antonio de Armona (1765).

La Rampa

Calle 23, familiarly known as La Rampa, runs through Vedado from the Malecón at its eastern end, to the Cementerio Colón and the Río Almendares in the west. The eastern end is full of activity, overlooked as it is by the grand **Hotel Nacional de Cuba**, and the infamous **Hotel Habana Libre**. There are airline offices and the International Press Centre clustered together alongside restaurants and nightclubs and the ice cream parlour, **Coppelia**, which found movie fame in *Strawberry and Chocolate*. The parlour, which occupies a whole block, is a good example of the architectural creativity of the post-Revolution years. It was built by Mario Girona in 1966, based on an idea by Celia Sánchez Manduley, a heroine of the Sierra Maestra. Just to the south is the **Universidad de La Habana** (Havana University). A monument to **Julio Antonio Mella**, founder of the Cuban Communist Party, stands across from the university's magnificent stairway.

Sleeping

Adita cp **1** A5
Alicia Horta cp **16** B6
Apartments 18
 & 19 **10** C6
Armando Gutiérrez cp **3** B6
Colina **7** C6
Daysie Recio cp **8** B4
Eduardo cp **11** C5
Gisela Ibarra y Daniel
 Riviero cp **12** A4
Habana Libre **26** C6
Habana Riviera **13** A3
Hostal Paraíso cp **30** A3
Jorge Coalla Potts cp **15** B5
Martha Vitorte cp **17** B5
Meliá Cohiba **18** A3
Mercedes González cp **33** B5
Nacional de Cuba **20** B6
Natalia Rodés León cp **21** C5
Pedro Mesa López cp **22** C5
Presidente **23** A4
Ramón y Tamasita cp **24** D6
St John's **9** C6
Vedado **27** C6
Victoria **29** B5

Eating

Adela **7** C4
Coppelia **4** B5
El Conejito **6** B5
Gringo Viejo **9** B4
La Casona de 17 **5** B6
La Roca **2** B5
La Tasquita **20** C6
La Torre Focsa
 & Sherezada **11** B6, C4
Los Amigos **12** B6
Pekín **8** C2
Trattoria Marakas **17** B6
Unión Francesa **18** B3

Entertainment

Acapulco **3** D1
Amadeo Roldán **16** A4
Cabaret Las Vegas **1** C6
Café El Gato Tuerto **12** B6
Centro de Música
 Ignacio Piñeiro **2** B5
Chaplin **4** C2
Club Atelier **8** B3
El Gran Palenque Bar **9** A3
Habana Café **13** A3
Imágenes **11** A4
La Rampa **5** B6
Riviera **6** C5
Sala Hubert de
 Blanck **15** A3
Teatro El Sótano **17** C5
Teatro Mella **18** B3
Teatro Nacional, Café Cantante
 & El Delirio Habanero **19** D4
Teatro Trianón **20** C6
Tikoa **21** B3
Yara **7** B5

Havana maps

1 Havana orientation, page 70
2 Centro & La Habana Vieja, page 74
3 Plaza de Armas, page 76
4 Parque Central, page 79
5 **Vedado & Plaza de la Revolución, page 90**
6 Miramar, page 94

Feria de Malecón

Monumento a Calixto García

Casa de las Américas
Galería Haydée Santamaría

CVD José Martí

Swiss Embassy (US Interests Section)

Tribuna Anti-Imperialista José Martí

Sagrado Corazón de Jesús

Museo de la Danza

Templo Bet Shalome

Banco Financiero Internacional

Museo de Artes Decorativas

International Press Centre

Airline Offices

Pabellón Cuba

To Old Havana

VEDADO

Monumento a Salvador Allende

Presidentes

Monumento a Julio Antonio Mella

Universidad de La Habana

Universitario Valdés Danzá Stadium

Museo Napoleónico

Iglesia del Carmen

Círculo Filatélico

Castillo del Príncipe

Universidad

Zapata

Ramón Fonst Stadium

Av Salvador Allende (Carlos III)

Terminal de Omnibus Interprovinciales

Bruzón

Museo Postal Cubano

Plaza de la Revolución

Memorial José Martí

Paseo

Almendares

Calzada de Infanta

Enrique Barnet (Estrella)

Maloja

Sitios

Peñalva

Desagüe

Benjumeda

Santo Tomás

Clavell

Santa Marta

To Train Station

CERRO

Vapor
Jovellar
Hamel
Concordia
Neptuno
San Miguel
San Rafael
España
Hospital
Ramburu
Soledad
Salud
Zanja
Jesús Peregrino
Sitios

San Francisco
San Martín

To Capitol & Parque Fraternidad

N

200 metres
200 yards

The **Cuban pavilion** (Pabellón Cuba) ① *Calle 23 entre N y M, closed Mon, music and dancing from 2100 Wed (reggae), Thu (son), Fri-Sun (disco),* is a combination of a tropical glade and a museum of social history. It tells the nation's story through a brilliant combination of objects, photos and the architectural manipulation of space. It also hosts the annual *Feria del Libro* in February (the main site is at La Cabaña), the *Cubadisco* music convention in May, a showcase for the latest Cuban music, and *Arte en la Rampa* in July and August, with handicrafts and souvenirs for sale, music and dancing.

Near the university the **Museo Napoleónico** ① *San Miguel 1159 esquina Ronda, T7-879 1460, closed for alterations in 2009,* houses 7000 pieces from the private collection of sugar baron, Julio Lobo: paintings and other works of art, a specialized library and a collection of weaponry. Check out the tiled fencing gallery.

Avenida de los Presidentes

The Avenida de los Presidentes, or Avenida G, joins the Plaza de la Revolución in the south to the Malecón in the north, bisecting La Rampa on its way through to the sea. It is a magnificent, wide boulevard with grand houses and blocks of apartments. A very desirable place to live. Just north of the intersection with La Rampa is a statue of Salvador Allende, the murdered President of Chile. At the Malecón the avenue is blocked by a monument to Calixto García. The **Museo de la Danza** ① *entrance on Línea esq G (Av de los Presidentes), T7-831 2198, musdanza@cubarte.cult.cu, Tue-Sat 1000-1800, Sun 0900-1300, CUC$2, guided tour CUC$1, CUC$5 to take photos,* presents an engaging collection of items from the dancer Alicia Alonso's personal collection and from the Ballet Nacional de Cuba. See box, page 432.

Close to the **Hotel Nacional**, the **Monumento al Maine** is a tribute to the 265 men who were killed when the *USS Maine* warship exploded in the bay in 1898. Close by, the **Tribuna Anti-Imperialista José Martí** built during the Elián González affair shows a statue of Martí holding his son Ismaelillo and pointing towards the US Interests Section fronted by a veil of mirrored glass windows and patrolled by Cuban military personnel. The famous billboard, with a fanatical Uncle Sam towering menacingly over a young Cuban patriot, has been relocated behind the Interests Section.

Casa de las Américas ① *Calle 3 52 esq G, T7-838 2706, www.casa.cult.cu, Mon-Fri 0800-1700,* was founded in 1959 by Haydée Santamaría (1923-1980) for pan-American cultural promotion and interchange. This active and welcoming centre hosts a varied programme of seminars workshops and investigative studies in addition to running its own publishing house. Exhibitions of art from all corners of Latin America are held in the Galería Latinoamericana, while contemporary Cuban art is shown in the Sala Contemporánea. On the ground floor is the **Librería Rayuela** book and music shop and a small peso bookstall. Next door is the **Galería Haydée Santamaría** ① *Calle G entre 3 y 5, alongside Casa de las Américas, T7-838 2706, Mon-Fri 0800-1700, Sat 1000-1500, CUC$2,* which displays the work of Latin American artists. There is a good representation of mostly 20th-century styles with over 6000 works of art including sculptures, engravings and photography.

The **José Martí sports ground**, on the Malecón entre Avenida de los Presidentes y J, is a good example of post-Revolutionary architecture; built in 1961 opposite the Casa de las Américas, it shows a highly imaginative use of concrete, painted in primary colours.

European and Oriental art from the 16th-20th centuries is displayed at the **Museo de Artes Decorativas** ① *Calle 17 502 esq E, T7-830 8037, artdeco@cubarte.cult.cu, Tue-Sat 1100-1800, CUC$2, or if you want a guide 1100-1630, CUC$3, CUC$5 to take photos,* housed in a French Renaissance-style mansion since 1964, which was originally designed by Alberto Camacho (1924-1927) for José Gómez Mena's daughter, who belonged to one of

Cuba's wealthiest families. Most of the building materials were imported from France. In the 1930s the mansion was occupied by Gómez' sister, María Luisa, Condesa de Revilla de Camargo, who was a fervent collector of fine art and held elegant society dinners and receptions for guests including the Duke of Windsor and Wallace Simpson. Her valuable collections were found in the basement after the family fled Cuba following the Revolution in 1959. The interior decoration was by House of Jansen and her furniture included a desk that had belonged to Marie Antoinette. There are 10 permanent exhibition halls with works from the 16th to 20th centuries including ceramics, porcelain (Sévres, Chantilly and Wedgewood), furniture (Boudin, Simoneau and Chippendale) and paintings. The Regency-inspired dining room is recommended viewing and includes a sumptuous dinner service that belonged to the dictator Batista. The attendants are very knowledgeable and informative about the exhibits, but only in Spanish.

Paseo

This is another of Vedado's grand thoroughfares, to the west of the district, running down from the Mafia-built **Hotel Riviera** on the Malecón to the Plaza de la Revolución. Many of the elegant mansions either side of the street have been converted into offices or embassies.

Casa de la Amistad ① *Paseo 406 entre 17 y 19, T7-830 3114*, is a former mansion dating from 1926. A beautiful dusky, coral pink building with gardens, it is now operated by **ICAP** (Cuban Institute for Friendship among the Peoples) and housing the **Amistur** travel agency (see Tour operators), which has a reasonably priced bar and cafeteria (open Monday-Friday 1000-1700, Sunday 1100-1800). You can eat on the balcony overlooking the garden, serenaded by the resident quartet, the food is consistently good with large portions; there are two menus: one has lobster and shrimp, the other is a house menu. Indoors is the **Primavera** restaurant, to the right of the entrance, which has elegant furniture and is expensive (open Monday Friday 0030-1700).

The recently re-landscaped and renamed **John Lennon Park** at Calle 17 entre 6 y 8, features a bronze statue of the Beatles legend sitting on a bench, sculpted by José Villa, who also sculpted the Che Guevara monument at the Palacio de los Pioneros in Tarará, in the Playas del Este area. Evocative words from Lennon's song *Imagine* have been translated into Spanish, "*dirás que soy un soñador, pero no soy el único*" (*You may say I'm a dreamer, but I'm not the only one*), and etched on the ground. It was inaugurated in December 2000, attended by Fidel Castro and Silvio Rodríguez (singer/songwriter and founder of the movement of *La Nueva Trova*). Theft of the statue's glasses has meant there is a 24-hour security guard and the replacement glasses have been permanently fixed in place. Classical guitar concerts are sometimes held here.

Cementerio Colón

① *Entrance on Zapata y 12, T7-830 4517, daily 0800-1700. CUC$1 entrance and CUC$1 for good map, CUC$1 to take photos.*

The Colón cemetery should be visited to see the wealth of funerary sculpture, including Carrara Marbles; Cubans visit the sculpture of Amelia La Milagrosa (Amelia Goire) at Calle 3 entre F y G and pray for miracles. Constructed in 1871, the 56-ha city of the dead is the second largest cemetery in the world. It was designed by the Spanish architect, Calixto de Lloira y Cardosa, who was also the first person to be buried there. The Chinese cemetery is at Avenida 26 y 31.

Miramar

Miramar is some 16 km west of the old city on the west side of the Río Almendares, and easily reached by bus. Access is via two road tunnels or bridges. Although there are many beautiful art nouveau and other houses from the early 20th century, the area is now being developed into a modern city with glossy new hotels for business people with state-of-the-art fitness and business centres. Most of the embassies are here, which

⑥ Miramar

Gulf of Mexico

Maqueta de la Ciudad

French Embassy

MIRAMAR

Museo del Ministerio del Interior

Santa Rita

Mexican Embassy

Canadian Embassy

La Maison

Av 5A

Clínica Central Ciro García

N

300 metres
300 yards

Eating 🍴
1830 **8** *B6*
El Aljibe **2** *B3*
El Palio **3** *A3*
El Tocororo **4** *B4*

La Cecilia **8** *B1*
La Cocina de Liliam **5** *D2*
La Esperanza **6** *A4*
La Fontana **7** *B1*

Entertainment ☺
Casa de la Música
Egrem **5** *C4*
Club Almendares **1** *D5*
Dos Gardenias **2** *B3*

always implies a certain status and level of comfort. It has the appearance of a wealthy suburb with broad avenues and neatly aligned rectangular blocks.

Avenida Primera (first) runs closest to the sea, which is rocky and not recommended for bathing (use the hotel pool instead), Avenidas Tercera (third), Quinta (fifth) and Séptima (seventh) run parallel, with the tunnels to Vedado at the end of Avenidas 5 and 7. Some of the best restaurants are in Miramar and there are good places to go at night, including the internationally famous *Tropicana* cabaret show to the south and some great places to go to listen to music and dance the night away.

To get a good idea of the layout of the city and its suburbs, visit the **Maqueta de la Ciudad** (scale model of Havana) ① *Calle 28 113 entre 1 y 3. T7-2027322, Mon-Fri 0930-1700, Sat 0930-1630, CUC$3, children, pensioners and students CUC$1, to use camera CUC$2, video CUC$5.* Opened in 1995, this is now a great attraction. The 88-sq-m model covers Havana and its suburbs as far out as Cojímar and the airport. Every building is represented. Colonial buildings are in red, post-colonial pre-Revolution buildings in yellow and post-Revolution buildings in white. Some of the model is difficult to see, especially in the middle, but there is an upper viewing gallery with two telescopes where it is a little easier to see.

Well worth a visit if you can read Spanish is the **Museo del Ministerio del Interior** ① *Av 5 y 14, T7-2034432, Tue-Fri 0900-1700, Sat 0900-1600, CUC$2, guided tour CUC$1, to take photos CUC$2* which details the history of the police force, canine work, drugs work and fire brigade as well as all the counter-revolutionary activity in Cuba since 1959 and plots to kill Fidel through a series of photographs and lengthy explanations (all in Spanish). Curious cases such as false money production, killer shampoo and airline terrorism through to the bombings of tourist hotels are all documented.
➤➤ *For listings, see pages 99-130.*

El Río Club
 (Johnnie's Club) **3** *B6*
Salón Rosado Benny
 Moré, La Tropical **4** *E3*
Tropicana **6** *E3*

Cayo Hueso

Cayo Hueso is a run-down *barrio* lying in a triangle between Infanta, San Lázaro and the Malecón in Centro Habana. It was named by cigar factory workers returning from Key West and has nothing to do with bones (*huesos* in Spanish), although it was once the site of the Espada cemetery and the San Lázaro quarry. There are about 12,000 homes in the *barrio*, mostly tenements, which have been earmarked for restoration. As in La Habana Vieja, the project also involves educating the community in its own particular culture and history.

In 1924, the cigar factory workers built a social club on San Lázaro, which became the site of the José Martí People's University. San Lázaro, with the University of Havana's wide stairway at its top, was the site of fierce and determined student movement demonstrations from the late 1920s onwards. By the mid-1950s, Infanta was the Maginot line where the students faced Batista's troops. On 25 Jul 1956, Fidel Castro departed from Calle Jovellar 107 for the attack on the Moncada Garrison in Santiago de Cuba. There is a memorial plaque there now.

Cayo Hueso has lots of little alleyways, one of which, **Calle Hamel**, an extension of Calle Animas, between Aramburu and Espada, unites two art forms: music and visual arts. It is home to Salvador González Escalona's art studio (Hamel 1054 entre Aramburu y Hospital, T7-781661, www.afrocubaweb.com, www.havana-cultura.com). Salvador is a self-taught painter and sculptor, inspired by the history of the neighbourhood and its *Santería* traditions. He has painted large bright Afro-Cuban murals on the walls of Calle Hamel, combining a mixture of abstract and surrealist design with phrases giving advice and warnings about danger, death and life. The project is affectionately called *Callejón de Hamel* and is recognized as the first open-air mural in Cuba dedicated to *Santería* and reflecting Afro-Cuban scenes. Salvador himself describes it as a community-based project, "from el barrio, to el barrio and with el barrio". As well as murals there are other surprises such as a typewriter pinned to the door of the gallery, painted drums and sculptures of corrugated iron and bike wheels.

Every Sunday 1200-1500 a free *Peña Cultural Alto Cubana*, known as **la Rumba de Cayo Hueso**, is held to honour the different *Orishas*. This is a very popular event, attracting large enthusiastic crowds (see box, page 446). Other community activities at Callejón de Hamel include **Té Con** on the last Friday of the month at 2030, featuring poetry, theatre, painting and music and **Callejón de Colores** on the first Saturday of the month at 1000, a children's event in which one child is chosen to represent Callejón de Hamel. **Peña de los Abuelos**, on the second Sunday at 1000, is an event for grandparents, although all join in the fun and music. A small bar in the street sells a strong drink of rum and honey, CUC$2, and a stall sells herbs, representing spiritual and curative roles within Santería.

This is a neighbourhood of *filín* (from 'feeling'), rumba and tango. Hamel 1108 is the home of singer-songwriter Angel Díaz and the birthplace of the musical genre known as *filín*, while Calle Horno was the site of the first cultural circle dedicated to Carlos Gardel (the Argentine maestro of tango) and is another centre for cultural activities.

Marina Hemingway

Off Avenida 5, 20 minutes by taxi (CUC$10-15) from Havana, is the Marina Hemingway tourist complex, in the fishing village of **Santa Fé**. Fishing and scuba-diving trips can be arranged here as well as other watersports and land-based sports. The Offshore Class 1 World Championship and the Great Island speedboat Grand Prix races have become an annual event in Havana, usually held during the last week in April, attracting power boat enthusiasts from all over the world. In May and June the marina hosts the annual Ernest Hemingway International White Marlin Fishing Tournament and in August and September the Blue Marlin Tournament. There are 140 slips with electricity and water and space for docking 400 recreational boats. The resort includes the hotel **El Viejo y El Mar**, restaurants, bungalows and villas for rent, shopping, watersports, facilities for yachts, sports and a tourist bureau. The Hemingway International Nautical Club is here, a social club for foreign executives based in Cuba. Founded in 1992, it currently has 730 members from 37 countries. The notice board is a good place to find crewing opportunities. The club organizes regattas, sailing schools and excursions, as well as the Hemingway Tournament. Another club in this area is the **Club Habana** (Sol Meliá) ① *Av 5 entre 188 y 192, Playa, T7-204 5700, 204 3301*. The main house dates back to 1928 and was the Havana Biltmore Yacht and Country Club. It is very posh but has lots of facilities on land and in the water.

Cubanacán

① *Escuela Superior de Arte, Calle 120 1110 esq 9, T7-208 8075, Relaciones Internacionales, T7-208 9771 to arrange visits, promocion@isa.cult.cu daily 0800-1700, CUC$3. Visits are usually arranged by tour agencies and a specialist guide is provided. Independent visitors should phone or email at least two days in advance.*

Three architects, Ricardo Porro, Roberto Gottardi and Vittorio Garati, were involved in designing a Revolutionary national school of art, begun in 1959. The complex was to combine schools of modern dance, plastic arts, dramatic arts, music and ballet, using domestic rather than imported materials. The **Escuela Superior de Arte** is located in the grounds of the former Havana Country Club in Cubanacán, southwest of Miramar. Architects will be interested in this 'new spatial sensation', which was an ambitious project of the early 1960s. Some parts were not completed and others have been abandoned (they were not entirely practical schemes), but you can still visit the **Escuela Superior de Artes Plásticas**, a series of interlinked pavilions, courtyards and sinuous walkways designed by Porro (which most people describe as laid out in the form of a woman's body, although some see it more as the womb itself, with a cervix-like fountain in the centre).

There is also the **Escuela Superior de Artes Escénicas**, built by Gottardi, in the form of a miniature Italian hill-top town, rather claustrophobic and quite unlike Porro's sprawling, 'permeable' designs, which are full of fresh air and tropical vegetation. Porro's Dance School, although part of the same complex, is not accessible via the Country Club (now the Music School, the 1960s Music School by Garati being now in ruins). Lack of maintenance, water leaks, a faulty drainage system, structural defects, vegetation and vandalism have led to deterioration of both the finished and unfinished buildings and there is a lack of funds for drawing up a master plan as well as carrying out repairs.

Hemingway's Havana

Marlin fishing, gambling, beautiful prostitutes: these were the things that attracted Ernest Hemingway to Cuba in 1932. At first he stayed at the Hotel Ambos Mundos in Havana, but his visits became so frequent that he decided to buy a property. In 1940 he bought Finca Vigía, a 14-acre farm outside Havana. The staff included three gardeners, a Chinese cook and a man who tended to the fighting cocks Hemingway bred.

During the Second World War, Hemingway set up his own counter-intelligence unit at the Finca, calling it 'the Crook Factory'; his plan was to root out Nazi spies in Havana. He also armed his fishing boat, the *Pilar*, with bazookas and hand grenades. With a crew made up of Cuban friends and Spanish exiles from the Civil War, the *Pilar* cruised the waters around Havana in search of German U-Boats. The project surprisingly had the blessing of the US Embassy, who even assigned a radio operator to the *Pilar*. With no U-Boats in sight for several months, the mission turned into drunken fishing trips for Hemingway, his two sons and his friends.

When Hemingway returned to Cuba after more heroic contributions to the War effort in France, he wrote the book that was to have the biggest impact on the reading public, *The Old Man and the Sea*, which won him the Pulitzer Prize in 1953. This was a period of particularly heavy drinking for Hemingway: early-morning scotches were followed by numerous *Papa Dobles* (2½ jiggers of white rum, the juice of half a grapefruit, six drops of maraschino, mixed until foaming) at the **Floridita**, absinthe in the evening, two bottles of wine with dinner, and scotch and soda till the early hours in the casinos of Havana.

When the political situation under Batista began to grow tense in 1958, a government patrol shot one of Hemingway's dogs at the Finca. By then he was older and wearier than he had been during the Spanish Civil War, and he quietly went back to his home in Idaho, from where he heard the news of Fidel Castro's victory. Hemingway made a public show of his support for the Revolution on his return to Cuba. He met Castro during the marlin fishing tournament, which the new president won.

Hemingway's last days at the Finca were taken up with work on *The Dangerous Summer*, a long essay about bullfighting, but his thoughts frequently turned to suicide, and he left for Florida in 1960. After the Bay of Pigs US-backed attempted invasion in 1961, the government appropriated the Finca. Hemingway committed suicide in the USA in 1961.

Bibliography: *Hemingway*, Kenneth S Lynn (Simon & Schuster, 1987).

Boyeros

Southwest of Havana in the district of Boyeros is **Expocuba** ① *T7-697 4252, Wed-Sun 0900-1700 (times subject to change), special trains leave from the main terminal in La Habana Vieja*, which was completed in January 1989. A sprawling facility, past Lenin Park, near the botanical gardens, it features a score of pavilions showing Cuba's achievements in industry, science, agriculture and the arts and entertainment. It also hosts various visiting art and cultural exhibitions, sometimes including live bands. Telephone to confirm listings. Information on times (and special buses) are available from hotels in Havana.

Parque Lenin

① *Northwest of Boyeros and the airport, T7-644 2721, Wed-Sun 0900-1700.*
Parque Lenin is a huge green space on the edge of Havana, which is very popular as a weekend escape for Cuban families. There are lakes for boating, you can hire horses for riding, there is an amusement park (very popular, with a circus show), an aquarium and an upmarket restaurant. To the south is the botanical garden and Expocuba. Hiring bikes has been recommended as a good way to visit; alternatively try getting on a *bus* (see page 68).

Jardín Botánico Nacional de Cuba

① *Km 3.5, Carretera Rocío, Calabazar, south of Havana in Arroyo Naranjo, beyond Parque Lenin. Many hotel tour desks offer day trips with lunch for CUC$25. Taxi from Habana Vieja CUC$15-18 one way, good for groups. T7-697 9170, www.uh.cu/centros/jbn/index.html, open daily for foreign tourists, Wed-Sun for Cubans, 0900-1600, but in practice you may not be allowed in after 1530, CUC$1, children CUC$0.50, CUC$3 if you take the 'train' with guide, children half price.*
The 600-ha botanical garden is well maintained with excellent collections of Cuban and other tropical plants, including a Japanese area with tropical adaptations. It is part of the University of Havana and much scientific research takes place here. A multilingual guide will meet you at the gate, no charge. You can take a 'train' tour along the 35 km of roads around the 60-ha site. This is an open-sided, wheeled carriage towed by a tractor, which enables you to see the whole garden in about two hours. There are few signs, so it is not as informative as it might be, and a guide is helpful, describing unusual plants in the various zones. Several interconnected glass houses are filled with desert, tropical and sub-tropical plants, well worth walking through. There is a good **organic vegetarian restaurant** (the only one in Cuba) using solar energy for cooking. There is only one sitting for lunch, but you can eat as much as you like from a selection of hot and cold vegetarian dishes and drinks for CUC$12. Water and waste food is recycled and the restaurant grows most of its own food. There are also other restaurants and snack bars serving criollo food in pesos cubanos or CUC$.

⊕ Havana listings

Hotel and guesthouse prices

LL over CUC$200	**L** CUC$151-200
AL CUC$101-150	**A** CUC $66-100
B CUC$46-65	**C** CUC$31-45
D CUC$21-30	**E** CUC$12-20

Restaurant prices

¶¶¶ over CUC$12 ¶¶ CUC$6-12 ¶ under CUC$6
See pages 37-43 for further information.

⊖ Sleeping

Payment for hotels used by tourists is in CUC$. Always tell the hotel each morning if you intend to stay on another day. Do not lose your 'guest card', which shows your name, meal plan and room number. Tourist hotels are a/c, with 'tourist' TV (US films, tourism promotion), restaurants with reasonable food, but standards are not comparable with Europe and plumbing is often faulty or affected by water shortages. Several important hotel renovation projects have been completed by **Habaguanex** in La Habana Vieja and these are now elegant places to stay, becoming known as 'boutique' hotels. Hotels in Vedado are some distance away from the colonial sites but are in a better district for nightlife. Miramar is further away still, hotels are designed for business travellers and package tourists but there are good restaurants, *paladares*, bars, clubs and Teatro Karl Marx.

La Habana Vieja *p73, maps p74, p76 and p79*

Hotels

LL-AL NH Parque Central (Cubanacán), Neptuno entre Prado y Zulueta, on north side of Parque Central, T7-860 6627/9, www.hotel nhparquecentral.com. 281 rooms of international standard, excellent bathrooms, separate shower and bathtub, business centre, WiFi internet access in lobby, 2 restaurants, 2 bars, great view of Havana from pool on 9th floor, fitness centre, charming and helpful multilingual staff, efficient Dutch management, good breakfast but expensive. A new section, the Torre, connected by a tunnel, was due to open in 2009.

LL-AL Santa Isabel , Baratillo 9 entre Obispo y Narciso López, Plaza de Armas, T7-860 8201, www.hotelsantaisabel.com. 5 star, only 27 rooms, 10 of them suites, busy with groups, height of luxury, very well-equipped bathrooms, rooms on 3rd floor have balcony overlooking plaza – great for people-watching, restaurant serving Cuban and international cuisine, central patio with fountain and greenery and lobby bar. Relax with a cocktail and watch the view from El Mirador, the cafeteria also has a good view of the Palacio de los Capitanes Generales, El Templete and other local sights.

LL-A Conde de Villanueva, Hostal del Habano, Mercaderes 202 esq Lamparilla, T7-862 9293/4, www.habaguanexhotels.com. Named after Claudio Martínez del Pinillo, Conde de Villanueva (1789-1853), a notable personality who promoted tobacco abroad and helped to bring the railway to Cuba. Just 9 rooms and suites around peaceful courtyard, attractive red and green colour scheme, cigar theme with cigar shop, café, bar, good restaurant, highly regarded, friendly staff.

L-A Florida, Obispo 252 esq Cuba, T7-862 4127, www.habaguanexhotels.com. Restored building dates from 1885, cool oasis, elegant restaurant, bar just off the street, serves great *daiquirís*, marble floors and pillars in courtyard, beautiful rooms with high ceilings, quiet a/c, TV, clean bathrooms, some balconies, some

singles, good cappuccino but overpriced and poor buffet breakfast, piano bar, parking. Has 16 more rooms in an adjacent building on O'Reilly esq Cuba, **Marqués de Prado Ameno**, same prices, breakfast included. Charming renovation, pictures of the archaeological excavations on the walls and some findings in display cabinets. Internet café on 3rd floor, 1000-2000 Mon-Sat, or a computer in reception for 24-hr access.

AL-A Hostal del Tejadillo, Tejadillo 12 esq San Ignacio, T7-863 7283, www.habaguanex hotels.com. Great location, comfortable rooms, high ceilings, tall wooden shuttered windows, fridge, good breakfast inside or in the courtyard, lively bar with entertaining barmen and music in the afternoon/evening.

AL-A Hostal Los Frailes, Teniente Rey 8 entre Mercaderes y Oficios, T7-862 9383, www.habaguanexhotels.com. In restored house of Marqués Pedro Pablo Duquesne IV, a captain in the French navy who came to Havana in 1793 and joined the Spanish marines while remaining loyal to the deposed French crown. The family continued to reside in Havana after his death there in 1834, and epitomized Franco-Cuban society. Recently converted to a small hotel with a monasterial theme; the bellboys are dressed in pseudo monks' habits. Rooms overlook the central courtyard. Pleasant, classical music (clarinets and saxophones) in the bar, 22 rooms, including 4 suites with balconies onto the street, the others don't have windows, a/c, phone, satellite TV, minibar, all meals at **La Marina** restaurant, 10 m from hotel, T7-862 5527, Mon-Sun 0700-2000, breakfast CUC$6, the only place in Old Havana where you can get *guarapo* (sugar cane juice) with rum.

AL-A Inglaterra, Prado 416 entre San Rafael y San Miguel, T7-860 8595/7, www.hotelinglaterra-cuba.com. Built in 1875 and now a National Monument next to the Teatro Nacional, famous former foreign guests included Sarah Bernhardt in 1887, General Antonio Maceo (one of the heroes of the Cuban Wars of Independence) in 1890, and the authors Federico García Lorca and

The Habana Libre

The **Havana Hilton** was inaugurated on 19 March 1958, a huge tower that symbolized everything that was luxurious and decadent in the capital and attracted a high-flying and wealthy clientele. However, after the fall of the dictatorship, Fidel Castro and some of his comrades settled temporarily into the hotel. The Continental Suite, room 2324, was used as the Revolution Headquarters for the first three months of 1959 and press conferences for foreign journalists were given here. Later, the first Soviet embassy in Havana occupied two floors. In the 1960s it was used for international meetings. Castro stayed in La Castellana Suite, room 2224, for the Tricontinental conference in December 1961.

The hotel is now under the wing of *Tryp*, part of the *Sol Meliá* group (see page 104). Even if you don't want to stay there, have a walk around the lobby area. There are fascinating photos of the Revolutionaries lounging around after their success in the war, and an account of the literacy campaign in 1961.

Rubén Darío in 1910. 86 rooms, colonial style, regal atmosphere, but a bit drab and rooms don't always get cleaned every day, balconies overlook Parque Central, some single rooms have no windows but at least you won't get woken by the traffic, reasonable breakfast, lovely old mosaic tiled dining room, 1 of 4 cafés or restaurants with a variety of services and cuisines. Delightful glazed tile pictures by famous and not-so-famous artists have been set into the pavement in front.
AL-A Mercure Sevilla, Trocadero 55 y Prado, T7 860 8560, www.accorhotels.com. First opened in 1908, the Sevilla's heyday was the 1930s when it was linked to the Italian-American mafia. 178 rooms of 1937 vintage on edge of La Habana Vieja, room sizes vary, most have no view, better bathrooms and equipment than at the **Plaza** but both have noisy a/c and are in need of redecoration, inviting pool (open to non-guests), shops, sauna and massage, tourism bureau, elegant restaurant and bar on top floor with great night time views over Centro and the Malecón, huge windows are flung open to let in the breeze. Expensive buffet breakfast. The spacious lobby is worth visiting for a peaceful and hassle-free *mojito* listening to live music.
AL-A Telégrafo, Prado 408 esq Neptuno, T7-861 1010, www.habaguanexhotels.com. Dating from 1860, the Telégrafo reopened in 2001 with the addition of a 3rd floor. Sleek 21st-century design is fused with the remaining 19th-century architecture. 63 spacious, stylish rooms with high ceilings, elaborate bathrooms and soundproofing. Great location on Parque Central. Internet access.
A-B Hostal Valencia, Oficios 53 esq Obrapía, T7-867 1037, www.habaguanexhotels.com. Joint Spanish/Cuban venture modelled on the Spanish *paradores*. 10 suites and rooms – some rather past their best – are named after Valencian towns. Tastefully restored building, nicely furnished, pleasant courtyard with vines, music, good restaurant (see Eating, below). The sister hotel, **El Comendador**, next door at Obrapía 55 esq Baratillo, is a discreet, well-appointed hotel with 14 rooms on 2 floors, using the facilities of the **Valencia** and with the same prices. The restaurant and bar on the corner is open from 1200 and serves pizza, *tortillas*, *empanadas*, etc for lunch.
A-C Plaza, Zulueta 267 esq Neptuno, or Ignacio Agramonte 267, T7-860 8583/9, www.hotel plazacuba.com. 186 rooms, generally shabby, high ceilings, reasonable bathrooms, don't rely on toilet paper being provided, street-front rooms very noisy, ask for one in the inner courtyard, breakfast on 5th floor with fine view, poor dinner, service generally poor.
B-C Caribbean, Paseo Martí (Prado) 164 esq Colón, T7-860 8210, reserva@lidocaribbean.

hor.tur.cu. Remodelled, good security, convenient for the old town, 36 rooms, many with no windows, try and get one on 5th floor, fan and TV, popular with budget travellers, but avoid noisy rooms at front and lower floors at back over deafening water pump, internet access, **Café del Prado** at street level for pasta, pizza, snacks, daily 0700-2300.

Casas particulares
C Casa Mary, Cárcel (Capdévila) 59 (2nd floor) entre Morro y Zulueta, T7-861 5911, mariange2850@yahoo.com. 2 rooms, a/c, with bath, breakfast CUC$4-5, evening meal available, next to the Spanish embassy, good views, convenient, roof terrace, spotless, Mary speaks some English and is most hospitable.
C Evora Rodríguez, Paseo del Prado 20 entre San Lázaro y Cárcel, 9th floor penthouse, T7-861 7932, evorahabana@yahoo.com. This huge apartment once belonged to a former president of Cuba and you can feel the style and opulence of a bygone age. Balconies and windows all round give fantastic views over Havana to Castillo del Morro (watch the boats going in and out of the harbour over breakfast, CUC$5) and down the Prado, Spacious bedrooms with TV, phone, sofa, fitted wardrobe, large, good bathrooms and enormous living area full of plants make this casa more comfortable than many hotel rooms and with better service too.
C Jesús y María, Aguacate 518 entre Sol y Muralla, T7-861 1378, jesusmaria2003@yahoo.com. Upstairs above the family and very private, 2 a/c bedrooms with twin beds, bathroom, living room and kitchenette with fan, fridge, also small outside sitting area, comfortable, clean.
D Eugenio y Fabio, San Ignacio 656 entre Jesús María y Merced, T7-862 9877, fabio.quintana@infomed.sld.cu. Rooms are well equipped and spacious but dark, overlooking interior courtyard, noisy a/c. House is stuffed with antiques and bric-a-brac and meals are served in an ornate baroque dining room.

D Federico y Yamelis Llanes, Cárcel 156 entre San Lázaro y Prado, T7-861 7817, fllanes@gmail.com. Excellent location just off the Prado and a stone's throw from the Malecón, technically in Centro but only just. You have to climb 64 stairs up to the apartment on the 3rd floor but Federico is strong and helpful with luggage. Large, light room with tiled floor and heavy dark furniture, double bed, extra bed on request, en suite bathroom, hot water in shower, a/c, CD player, phone, desk, safe box, run by pleasant young couple, formerly lawyers, some English spoken, good breakfast with lots of fruit and juice.
D Gustavo Enamorado Zamora – Chez Nous, Teniente Rey (Brasil) 115 entre Cuba y San Ignacio, T7-862 6287, cheznous@ceniai.inf.cu. 2 spacious double rooms, shared bathroom, hot water, fan, TV, safe box, balcony overlooking street, street noise, nice patio, parking, warm atmosphere, Gustavo and Kathy are kind and helpful, French spoken.
D Orlando y Lissett, Aguacate 509 Apto 301 entre Sol y Muralla, T7-867 5768, lisettesobrino@yahoo.es. 2 rooms in a lovely clean apartment, great view over La Habana Vieja from the terrace, garage, elevator, help with arranging buses, taxis or accommodation in other towns.

Centro p87, map p74
Hotels
B-C Deauville, Galiano y Malecón, T7-866 8813, reserva@hdeauville.gca.tur.cu. 148 basic rooms, some with no hot water, temperamental lifts, noise from Malecón but great view, balconies overlooking sea and fortress, breakfast included, under renovation 2009 but still open, helpful *buró de turismo*. Restaurant **Costa Norte** offers dinner 1900-2130 for CUC$10 with open bar, followed by a cabaret 2200-0230, daily Tue-Sun. The pool is open to non-guests for CUC$5 including a cocktail, or CUC$2.50 for children under 12, snack bar.
C Lido, Consulado 216 entre Animas y Trocadero, T7-871 102, mayda@lido

caribbean.hor.tur.cu. 65 basic rooms, inefficient a/c, TV, not bad for the price, but looking a bit forlorn and don't expect hot water in the shower, laundry expensive, done by hand and charged per item, central, 1 block from Prado, friendly reception with internet access, restaurant downstairs, food bland and overpriced, bar and café on roof terrace much better, excellent views but slow breakfast service.

Casas particulares

D Carlos Luis Valderrama Moré, Neptuno 404 entre San Nicolás y Manrique, 2nd floor, T7-867 9842. Carlos and Vivian are former teachers, he speaks English, 1940s apartment above a shop, 2 rooms, noisy front room has balcony overlooking street, good bathrooms, hot water, but very small beds.

D Cary y Nilo, Gervasio 216 entre Concordia y Virtudes, T7-862 7109, orixl@yahoo.es. Beautiful house, quiet, spotlessly clean, Nilo has decades of experience of hotel work and knows how to treat his guests. 2 rooms with bathrooms, antique furnishings, colonial style, good food.

D Casa Marta, Manrique 362 bajos, entre San Miguel y San Rafael, T7-863 3078. Warm and inviting with a family atmosphere with many long-term guests. Ex-revolutionary fighter Nelsón is an excellent host. Rooms have a/c, hot water and shared bathrooms.

D Dr Alejandro Oses, Malecón 163, 1st floor, entre Aguila y Crespo, T7-863 7359, alejandroses@cubacaribemail.com. Best view in city from balcony, of entire Malecón, from El Morro to Hotel Nacional, under renovation in 2009, make advance reservation.

D El Parador Numantino, Consulado 223 entre Animas y Trocadero, T7-864 1359. Argentine theme to these modern rooms only 5 mins' walk from Parque Central at the top of this price range. Private bathrooms, minibar, fans, a/c, TV, guests' reception room, breakfast CUC5.

D Jesús Deiro Rana, San Rafael 312 entre Galiano y San Nicolás, T7-863 8452. An Aladdin's cave of treasures with spacious rooms, high ceilings, leafy tiled courtyard, antique clocks and furnishings, including a haughty 1870s bed to sleep in. 2 rooms with shared bathroom, all well equipped.

D Marilys Herrera González, Concordia 714 altos entre Soledad y Aramburu, T7-870 0608, http://casaparticular.tripod.com/. Bathroom with warm water, fridge, a/c, TV, all modern, clean and comfortable, laundry offered, Marylis is very kind and caring, family atmosphere.

D Melba y Alberto, Galiano 115 Apto 81 entre Animas y Trocadero, T7-863 5178, T05-264 8262 (mob), barracuda1752@ yahoo.es. Unprepossessing entrance on street but once you've gone up the elevator to the 8th floor you're in another world with views of sea and city. 2 bedrooms, 1 with balcony, 1 or 2 beds, use of kitchenette and living room, good for families, charming hosts, excellent food, breakfast served on balcony, very comfortable and pleasant.

D-E Ana María Rodríguez López, San Lázaro 160 Apto 1 entre Aguila y Crespo, T7-863 7478, ismael.aguirre84@yahoo.com. 1st-floor apartment, 2 rooms, a/c, TV, fridge, hot water, 50 m from Malecón and short walk to old city.

D-E Julio y Elsa, Consulado 162 apto 2 entre Colón y Trocadero, T7 861 8027, julioroq@ yahoo.com 2 rooms, 1 with 2 beds, 1 with double bed, fridge, a/c, private bath, hot water and independent entrance for both. English spoken and the owners are friendly. Good and filling breakfast CUC4, supper CUC5-7, vegetarian suppers CUC6-7.

E Villa Colonial Tomy, Gervasio 218 entre Virtudes y Concordia, T7-860 6764. Ballet teacher Tomy is as colourful as his home, which is full of antiques and memorabilia including English tea cups, Spanish thrones, Italian Harlequin masks, Japanese screens and photos of his former pupil Carlos Acosta, now with the Royal Ballet in London. Bathroom is shared. Great rooftop terrace with murals dedicated to Oscar Wilde.

E Xiomara, Virtudes 216 entre Aguila y Amistad, piso 1, T7-861 0656, xiomara virtudes@yahoo.es. Run by Xiomara, her husband and brother-in-law, generous and friendly and you feel part of the family. Rooms simple but cheap for Havana, excellent food. Dining room, kitchen and lounge are on the top floor, great views of Habana Vieja from terrace.

Vedado *p88, map p90*
Hotels

The better hotels in Vedado are used by package tour operators and business travellers and are of a reasonable international standard. The cheaper hotels are basic, with intermittent electricity and water, poor water pressure, variable levels of cleanliness and security. For safety and comfort you might prefer to forego the facilities of a hotel and opt for a *casa particular*.

LL-AL Meliá Cohiba (Cubanacán), Paseo entre 1 y 3, T7-833 3636, www.solmelia cuba.com. International grand luxury, high rise and dominating the neighbourhood, 342 rooms, 120 suites, shops, gym, healthclub, pool, gourmet restaurant, piano bar.

LL-AL Nacional de Cuba, O esq 21, T7-873 3564, www.hotelnacionaldecuba.com. 467 rooms, some renovated, some not, some package tours use it at bargain rates, generally friendly and efficient service, faded grandeur, dates from 1930, superb reception hall, note the vintage Otis high-speed lifts, steam room, 2 pools, restaurants, bars, shops, business centre on lobby for emails, faxes, etc, exchange bureau, gardens with old cannons on hilltop overlooking the Malecón and harbour entrance, great place to watch people and vehicles, the hotel's tourist bureau is also efficient and friendly.

LL-AL Sol Meliá Tryp Habana Libre (Gran Caribe), L y 23, T7-838 4011, www.solmeliacuba.com. 606 rooms and suites in huge block, 25 floors, prices depend on the floor number, remodelled 1997, most facilities are here, eg hotel reservations, excursions, Polynesian restaurant, 24-hr coffee shop, Cabaret Turquino daily 2230-0300, shopping mall, includes liquor store, cigar shop, jewellery, perfume, handicrafts, shoe shop, hairdresser, Photoservice, Banco Financiero Internacional, postal service, swimming pool. See also page 101.

AL-A Presidente, Calzada y G (Presidentes), T7-838 1801, reserva@htpte.gca.tur.cu. Oldest hotel in Havana with a distinctly Mafia vibe, refurbishment taking place in 2009, 162 rooms, 10 suites, ask for a room on the 10th floor (Colonial Floor), which has sumptuous antiques, 2 restaurants, small pool. Popular with Italian tour groups.

AL-B Victoria (Gran Caribe), 19 y M, T7- 833 3510, www.hotelvictoriacuba.com. 4-star hotel with an elegant feel. 31 rooms, intimate and tasteful if conservative, good bathrooms, small pool, parking, good cooking.

B St John's O 206 entre 23 y 25, T7-833 3740, www.gran-caribe.com. Convenient location steps away from Vedado nightlife. Get a room on floors 9-12 for great views over either Habana Vieja or Vedado and Miramar. However, rooms are basic, hot water intermittent, a/c can be noisy, security not guaranteed. 24-hr internet access in lobby. Rooftop pool and nightclub daily 2230-0200.

B Vedado, O 244 entre 23 (Humboldt) y 25, T7-836 4072, www.gran-caribe.com. Great location, 203 basic rooms with dodgy bathrooms, a/c, TV, pool, gym and health centre with massages, restaurant, nightclub daily 2230-0200, admission CUC$10 then open bar.

C Colina, L y 27, T7-836 4071, reserva@ colina.gca.tur.cu. 79 rooms, street noise, small rooms, excellent buffet breakfast, open to non-residents CUC$3, popular with airport Cubatur desk, often used by students learning Spanish at the university opposite.

Casas particulares

C Martha Vitorte, G 301 Apto 14, 14th floor, entre 13 y 15, T7-832 6475, martavitorte@ hotmail.com. High-rise building near corner with Línea, 1 apartment on each floor, referred to as 'horizontals', beautiful modern building, very spacious, 2 rooms, en suite bathroom, a/c, security safe in each room, balcony on 2 sides for panoramic views of Havana, sea and sunsets, Martha is a retired civil servant and speaks some English and French.

C-D Jorge Coalla Potts, I 456 apto 11 entre 21 y 23, T7-832 9032, 52831237 (mob), www.havanaroomrental.com. The large room is very comfortable, bed with orthopaedic mattress, telephone in room. Excellent location close to the bars and restaurants of Vedado. Generous and fascinating hosts Jorge and Marisel have useful contacts throughout the island. English spoken.

D Adita, 9 257 entre J y I, T7-832 0643, edycaribe@gmail.com. 2 spacious, comfortable double rooms with private bathrooms in a warm, family home full of antiques. The building is dilapidated but the eclectic apartment is clean and a great place to stay.

D Alicia Horta, Línea 53 entre M y N, Apto 9, T7-832 8439, aorta@infomed.sld.cu. Alicia is a doctor, she and her daughter María are friendly but Spanish-speaking only, rooms cleaned daily, long stays possible, good view from 9th floor, popular so call in advance.

D Apartments 18 and 19, L 454 entre 25 y 27, close to the Habana Libre. Apto 18, T7-832 4214, is run by actress María and is a light and spacious apartment. 2 comfortable double rooms with private bathrooms, a/c, and great views over Vedado. Price negotiable for long stays. Apto 19, T7-8326471, run by animated Lisette, has 1 large bedroom with the biggest bathroom in Havana. The communal rooftop terrace has great views and is a peaceful retreat.

D Armando Gutiérrez, 21 62 entre M y N, Apto 7, 4th (top) floor, T/F7-832 1876. Large a/c rooms with 2 beds, bathroom, separate entrance, clean, hot water, Armando and his wife, Betty, and mother, Teresa, speak a little English and French and are knowledgeable on history and culture.

D Daysie Recio, B 403 entre 17 y 19, T7-830 5609. Spacious, light and clean. 2 airy rooms with interconnecting bathroom, 1 has a terrace overlooking the backyard, a/c, hot water, English spoken. Daysie is a vivacious hostess and this is a good option for families.

D Gisela Ibarra y Daniel Riviero, F104 altos entre 5 y Calzada, T7-832 3238, latinhouse@enet.cu. Straight out of the 1950s, marble staircase, balconies, very high quality, wonderful old rooms with original furnishings, a/c, fan, fridge, TV and safety box. Gisela is an excellent hostess, running a very proper, quiet and traditional home in a residential neighbourhood. Huge, filling breakfast for CUC$5, laundry service offered. If she is full, her daughter Marta Díaz runs another casa just round the corner on Calzada 452 Apto 5, same price but rooms are smaller, darker and hotter.

D Hostal Paraíso, Paseo 126 Apto 4B entre 5 y 7, T7-830 5160, crisjo@infomed.sld.cu. Large bedroom with double bed plus wardrobe, couch, dressing table, bedside lamps, a/c, fan, phone, TV, radio, ensuite bathroom, hot water, shower, kitchenette with 4 chairs, fridge/freezer. Excellent security, own entrance and keys. Bed linen and towels changed daily, laundry on request. Very cheerful and helpful family (hosts Eugenia y Rudel), some English spoken.

D Mercedes González, 21 360 Apto 2A, entre G y H, T7 832 5846, mccylupe@hotmail.com. 2 rooms, a/c, fan, good bathroom, hot water, airy rooms, 1 room has a balcony, smart, helpful and friendly, good location, near park.

D Ramón y Tamasita, Valle 174 entre Infanta y Basarrate, T/F7-879 4953. Large house, 2 rooms with bathroom, 1 with terrace, use of fridge, TV, a/c or fan, charming couple, English spoken.

Miramar *p94, map p94*
Hotels

There is a string of 4-star hotels west along the coast that are used by package tour operators; guests are often here for the first and last nights of their stay in Cuba before being whisked off round the island. They are not particularly convenient for visiting the old city, but you do get a sea view. Miramar is also popular with business people; hotels are of an international standard and the area is quiet at night.

Casas particulares
D Nieves y Marlen, 3 9401 entre 94 y 96, Apto 2, T7-203 5284. Clean, spacious and modern apartment, a/c, fridge in room, hot water, balcony.

Marina Hemingway *p97*
Hotels
AL-B El Viejo y El Mar, 248 y Av 5, Santa Fé, T7-204 6336. Pleasant enough hotel on seafront but out of the way and nothing to do unless you are busy at the marina, package tourists come here before going off on excursions, small pool, restaurant with buffet meals, lobby bar, clean, bath tub, tricky shower.

Boyeros *p98*
This quiet neighbourhood is convenient for the airport.
C-D Magalys y Lesme, Av Vento 9920 entre 10 y A, Altahabana, T7-644 1832. Large 1960s house on 2 floors with garden, garage, spacious, 2 rooms, ensuite bathroom, a/c, hot water, family atmosphere, English spoken, kitchen facilities.
C-D Manuela y Manolito Sosa, Parque 17010 entre A y B, T7-644 2437. 1960s house, 2nd floor, antiques and chandeliers, good security, garden, garage, a/c, hot water. Both houses are close to the **C** Hotel Altahabana, 7 entre A y B, Reparto Altahabana, T7-643 8758, which has a restaurant and snack bar.

🍴 Eating

In addition to the excellent and varied *paladares* and more predictable state restaurants, listed below, there are many street stalls and places where you can pick up cheap snacks, pizza, etc. Note that their prices are listed in pesos cubanos even though there is a $ sign as a price indicator. These are good for filling a hole at lunchtime, but don't expect a culinary masterpiece. Make sure you eat pizza fresh from the oven. They usually cost over 10 pesos cubanos in private cafeterias but 3-5 pesos cubanos in state

snack bars, depending on the size; can be very greasy, take plenty of napkins. Very sweet juice drinks 2 pesos per glass.

For **vegetarians** there is little choice and we have received many reports that a vegetarian travelling in Cuba is bound to lose weight. Havana restaurants and *paladares* are more enlightened than those in the rest of the country. Your best bet is the restaurant in the Jardín Botánico, **El Bambú**, see page 99, where lunch is served at around 1400. Many of the hotels, including the **Nacional**, see page 104, serve good all-you-can-eat lunchtime buffets. Italian restaurants offer the usual meatless pizza and pasta. Some *paladares* will serve meatless meals with advance notice, and all offer eggs on the menu, but always ask for the *congris* to be cooked in vegetable oil.

There are many **fast-food** outlets throughout the city: **El Rápido** (red logo) are clean with fast service and numerous locations; **Burgui**, serves hamburgers with cheese CUC$1.30 and fried chicken CUC$1.25, beer CUC$1. Branches of **DiTú** are springing up all over the city, open 24 hrs, selling pieces of chicken by weight. **Pain de París**, Línea entre Paseo y A, also Plaza de la Revolución, has 24-hr service, good coffee, *café cortadito* or *café con leche* CUC$0.65, croissants CUC$0.55 and *señoritas de chocolate* (custard slices).

La Habana Vieja *p73, maps p74, p76 and p79*
Restaurants
🍴 **A Prado y Neptuno**, address of the same name, opposite Hotel Parque Central, T7-860 9636. Daily 1200-2400. Trendy, good views over Parque Central, excellent tiramisu and good pizza, Italian chef.
🍴 **Dominica**, O' Reilly esq Mercaderes, T7-860 2918. Daily 1200-2400. Italian, very smart, set menus CUC$25-30, pasta from CUC$6, pizza CUC$4.50-12 depending on size, vegetarian options, outdoor seating nice for lunch, poor service, credit cards.

ᵀᵀᵀ El Castillo de Farnés, Monserrate 361 esq Obrapía, T7-867 1030. Restaurant daily 1200-2400, bar open 24 hrs. Tasty Spanish food, reasonable prices, good for *garbanzos* and shrimp, also Uruguayan beef and chateaubriand. Castro came here at 0445, 9 Jan 1959, with Che and Raúl.

ᵀᵀᵀ El Floridita, Obispo esq Monserrate, next to the Parque Central, T7-866 8856. Open 1200-2400. A favourite haunt of Hemingway. It has had a recent face-lift and is now a very elegant bar and restaurant reflected in the prices (CUC$6 for a *daiquirí*), but well worth a visit if only to see the sumptuous decor and 'Bogart atmosphere'. In the corner of the bar is a life-size bronze statue of Hemingway and on the bar, also in bronze, are his glasses resting on a open book. Live music.

ᵀᵀᵀ El Patio, San Ignacio 54 esq Empedrado, Plaza Catedral, T7-867 1034. Restaurant and snack bar daily 1200-2400. Expensive, small portions, slow service, but has selection of national dishes, tables outside take up most of the square, lovely location, worth stopping here for a coffee when visiting the cathedral.

ᵀᵀᵀ La Barca, Av del Puerto esq Obispo, T7 866 8807, habaguanex@temple.co.cu. Open daily 1200-2400. Just down from El Templete but cheaper, overlooking the road and the harbour opposite the old yacht club with outdoor seating. Good variety on the menu with some Spanish dishes, seafood and steaks, live music.

ᵀᵀᵀ La Bodeguita del Medio, Empedrado 207 entre Cuba y San Ignacio, near the cathedral, T7-867 1374. Restaurant 1200-2400, bar 0900-2400. Made famous by Hemingway and should be visited if only for a drink (*mojito* – rum, crushed ice, mint, sugar, lime juice and carbonated water – is a must, CUC$6), food poor, expensive, but very popular. It is here that Hemingway allegedly inscribed the now famous line "*Mi mojito en La Bodeguita, mi daiquirí en El Floridita*". It has been claimed that one of Hemingway's drinking buddies Fernando Campoamor and the owner of *La Bodeguita* hired a calligrapher to write the line as a lucrative tourist con.

ᵀᵀᵀ La Mina, on Obispo esquina Oficios, Plaza de Armas, T7-862 0216. Daily 1000-1900. Very much on the tourist trail, expensive, traditional Cuban food, sandwiches, pasta, lots of liqueur coffees, outdoor seating with live Cuban music.

ᵀᵀᵀ La Zaragozana, Monserrate 351 entre Obispo y Obrapía, T7-867 1040. Open 1200-2400. Oldest restaurant in Havana, international cuisine, good seafood and wine, good service but generally food nothing special.

ᵀᵀᵀ Marinero El Templete, Av del Puerto 12-14 esq Narciso López, T7-866 8807, habaguanex@templete.co.cu. Open daily 1200-2200. Eat inside or outside with view over the road to the harbour, pleasant, understated elegance. Good food, international with Cuban flavours, meat, fish or lobster.

ᵀᵀᵀ-ᵀᵀ Al Medina, Oficios 10 entre Obrapía y Obispo, T7-867 1041, 1200-2300. Open 1200-2300. Arab food in lovely colonial mansion, try Tangine chicken with olives, sesamo chicken and a huge vegetarian combo, appetisers include houmous and falafel, lovely fresh fruit juices, good coffee, some seating on large cushions, trios play during opening hours, also Mosque and Arab cultural centre off beautiful courtyard.

ᵀᵀᵀ-ᵀᵀ Europa, Obispo esquina Aguiar. Daily 1200-2200. International food, the most expensive dish is *solomillo de res* at CUC$10.

ᵀᵀᵀ-ᵀᵀ Mesón de la Flota, Mercaderes 257 entre Amargura y Teniente Rey, T7-862 9281. Restaurant-cum-tapas bar with wooden tables and impassioned flamenco *tablaos* after 2100 each evening. Reasonably priced menu with wide selection of dishes and plenty of fish and seafood, but the tapas choices are better value than the main dishes. Try the feisty *patatas bravas*.

ᵀᵀᵀ-ᵀᵀ Torre de Marfil, Mercaderes 115 entre Obispo y Obrapía, T7-867 1038. Open 1200-2200. Generally good-value Oriental cuisine with food surpassing anything that Chinatown has to offer in terms of authenticity, decked out with colourful lanterns and Chinese paraphernalia.

♥♥ **Café del Oriente**, Oficios y Amargura, T7-860 6686, daily 1200-2400. High-class food with a reasonably priced set menu and elegant surroundings.

♥♥ **Café El Mercado**, next to to Café del Oriente. Open 24 hrs. Informal, pleasant terrace.

♥♥ **Gentiluomo**, Bernaza esq Obispo, T7-867 1300 ext 134. Daily 1200-2400. Pasta, pizza, reasonable food but don't expect them to have everything on the menu, eg sometimes no fruit, no tomatoes except in season, no mozzarella, or no parmesan, but the chef produces a passable pizza, friendly service, pleasant environment, a/c.

♥♥ **Los Nardos** (Sociedad Juventud Asturiana), Paseo del Prado 563 entre Dragones y Teniente Rey, opposite the Capitolio, T7-863 2985. Open 1200-2400. Not obvious from the street but look out for the waiters at the entrance. Dining room upstairs lined with cabinets containing old football trophies, cups from 1936, while the heavy wooden furniture is reminiscent of a rancho. At one end are chefs in white hats busy in the kitchen while at the other you are overlooked by the stained glass windows of a pool room. Not an option for vegetarians, plenty of meat, pork, lamb or Uruguayan steak, although there is also fish and cocktails are CUC$2.50. Popular with Cubans and foreigners, large, filling portions, background music is limited to golden oldies played 2-3 times during the meal. In the same building: **El Trofeo**, 2nd floor, Cuban and international food, big portions, a little cheaper than Los Nardos, good *mojito* CUC$2, and **El Asturianito**, Cuban and Italian, good pizzas CUC$3.50-5.50. If you find a queue outside for Los Nardos, explain that you are going to El Asturianito and they will let you through.

♥♥ **Los Vitrales**, Prado 212 esq Trocadero. Open 0700-2200 for breakfast, lunch and dinner. Dining room has a cream and taupe baroque ceiling with a frieze of angels, marble floor and grand piano. Climb a beautiful staircase to the dining room, half way up look up for a skylight: a riot of coloured stained glass with chandeliers like buttons. American breakfast CUC$4. Also

soups, salads and sandwiches CUC$2-4, fried chicken CUC$6-7. Tables on the balcony overlooking the Prado. Food is average but the location is spectacular.

♥♥ **Puerto de Sagua**, Bélgica (Egido) 603 esq Acosta, T7-867 1026. Nautical theme, a cafetería serving dishes such as *arroz Puerto de Sagua* for CUC$6, and a more upscale restaurant specializing in seafood.

♥ **Hanoi**, Brasil (Teniente Rey) 507 y Bernaza, T7-867 1029. Open daily 1200-2400, Cuban food, 3 courses for CUC$6, *combinados* for CUC$2-3, *mojito* for CUC$2. Plenty of food although the meat tends to be reheated and the chicken dry, but the rice and beans are good and the garlic on the potatoes will keep away vampires, live music, nice atmosphere.

Paladares

♥♥♥ **Don Lorenzo**, Acosta 260A, entre Habana y Compostela, T7-861 6733. Daily 1200-2400. Not a cheap option with fish and meat dishes at CUC$15-30 and vegetarian options for CUC$12, but one of the most extensive menus, with over 50 dishes offered, all types of meat and fish with a huge variety of sauces, Basque-style, French-style, cider, fruity, almond, etc, an entertaining night when its full.

♥♥ **Doña Blanquita**, Prado 158 entre Colón y Refugio, T7-867 4958. Run by English-speaking lawyer, simple food done to a formula, pork, chicken or eggs, CUC$7-9, upstairs, inside with fan or on balcony if dry, neon sign. Good location but food nothing special.

♥♥ **La Julia**, O'Reilly 506A, T7-862 7438. Daily 1200-2400. Traditional, popular *paladar* with meals CUC$10, large portions, *creole* food, great rice and beans. Just a few tables so reserve or arrive early.

♥♥ **La Moneda Cubana**, San Ignacio 77 entre O'Reilly y Empedrado, T7-867 3852. 1200-2300. Limited choice, good fish with salad, beans and rice with fried banana, and usually good salads prepared for vegetarians. Menus for around CUC$8-10. More notable for the decor of wall-to-wall currency and business cards from all over the world.

Cafés and bakeries

Café El Escorial, Mercaderes 317 esq Muralla, escorial@enet.cu. Daily 0900-2100, coffees CUC$0.75-3.50, also coffee beans at CUC$2.25 for 250 g. Ice cream, juices, soft drinks and sweets.

Café Habana, Mercaderes 210 A entre Amargura y Lamparilla, T7-861 0071. Café charges in pesos cubanos, dirt cheap, 8 pesos cubanos for fried egg and chips, 1-2 pesos cubanos for coffee.

Café O' Reilly, O'Reilly 203 entre Cuba y San Ignacio. Coffee, snacks, pizza, spaghetti, sandwiches or the usual chicken and pork. Pleasant 2nd floor, with balcony, where there is often live music.

Café París, Obispo y San Ignacio. Serves good and reasonably priced chicken for CUC$3.50, beer CUC$1.50, snacks and pizza around the clock, live music, lively in evenings, pity about the hassling from harmless but irritating *jineteros*.

Cafetería Jardín del Oriente, Amargura entre Mercaderes y Oficios. Daily 1100-2200, for cheap beer and tuna sandwiches.

Cafetería La Ambarina, Obispo entre San Ignacio y Cuba. Daily 1000-2200, ice cream, juices, soft drinks, burgers, sandwiches, tea and candies.

Cafetería La Canasta, Teniente Rey 16 entre Oficios y Mercaderes. Mon-Sun 0900-2200, for soft drinks, ice cream, juices, beers and a 'special' of burger and soft drink at CUC$1.40.

Cafetería Torre La Vega, Obrapía 114, next to the Casa de México. Open 1000-2200. Cheap breakfast, bland chicken and chips, better value spaghetti, sandwiches, eggs, vegetables, juice, milkshakes and soft drinks, *Cristal* beer CUC$1.

Horchatería La Papaya, Obrapía entre Mercaderes y Oficios, next to Cafetería Torre La Vega. Juices and milkshakes. Daily 1000-2200.

La Dichosa, Obispo esq Compostela. Good place for breakfast or a snack, CUC$2-4. Open daily 1000-2200.

Panadería Dulcería Doña Teresa, Obrapía entre Mercaderes y Oficios. Daily 1000-1800, next to Horchatería la Papaya. Cakes and other bakery items.

Panadería Dulcería El Sol de Cuba, Cuba esquina Sol. Daily 0800-2000. Bread and pastries.

Panadería San José y Cafetería Santo Domingo, Obispo 161 entre San Ignacio y Mercaderes, T7-860 9326. Open daily 0900-2400. Bakery and café.

Pastelería Francés, between the Hotels Telégrafo and Inglaterra on the Prado. Smorgasbord of pastries and cakes in a peach-coloured dining room. Popular and some of the better cakes have gone by lunchtime. The hot *pan au chocolat* and *pan con pasas* (raisins) are particularly good.

Ice cream parlours

Cremería El Naranjal, Obispo esq Aguiar, Habana Vieja, T7-863 2430. Daily 0900-2100. Various flavours, including natural fruits.

Soda Obispo, Obispo esq Villegas, Habana Vieja, T7-862 0466. Daily 0900-2100. Natural and artificial flavoured ice cream, also fruit cocktails, accepts only pesos cubanos.

Casablanca *p86*
Restaurants

La Divina Pastora, Fortaleza de la Cabaña, T7-860 8341. Daily 1200-2300. Expensive, fish restaurant, food praised.

Los XII Apóstoles, in the Morro-Cabaña complex, T7-863 8295. Daily 1230-2300. Fish and good *criollo* food, good views of the Malecón.

Centro *p87, map p74*
Restaurants

Los Tres Chinitos, Dragones 355 y 357 entre Manrique y San Nicolás, T7-863 3388. Combination Chinese restaurant open 1200-0100 and pizzeria open 1200-2400.

Paladares

Bellomar, Virtudes 169A entre Industria y Amistad, T7-861 0023. Daily 1200-2300. Good fish and chicken dishes, generous salads, rice and beans, served in a fun, kitsch setting with friendly and obliging hosts.

YYY La Guarida, Concordia 418 entre Gervasio y Escobar, T7-866 9047, www.laguarida.com. Lunch daily 1200-1600, dinner 1900-2400 with reservation. Film location for *Fresa y Chocolate*, good food, fish a speciality, seafood and vegetarian paellas delicious, slow service, always busy, popular with US tourists, 'street guides' may not take you here because the owners do not pay commission to them.

YY-Y La Tasquita, Jovellar (27 de Noviembre) 160 entre Espada y San Francisco, T7-873 4916. Daily 1200-0200. Wonderful food and great atmosphere. House special for CUC$6.50 is a pork steak stuffed with ham, cheese and chorizo, served with a sweet and sour sauce and all the trimmings, including a drink, dessert and coffee. Other dishes of chicken, fish, pasta, pork, etc for CUC$2.50-4.50. Good for vegetarians with delicious sweet potato and Cuban fried eggs, served on mountains of rice and beans, plus good salads, run by Santiagüera Aralicia. Potent *mojitos*. No smoking.

Barrio Chino *p88*

At Zanja y Rayo, 1 block west of Galiano, there are several restaurants in a small street. Tables inside or outside, menus on view, you will be pestered for your custom. Do not expect authentic Chinese cuisine or you will be disappointed. Chop suey or chow mein is about the most Oriental you can get, 'sweet and sour' not recommended as it is very sweet and fruity. Spring rolls bear no relation to anything you might find in China. Meals around CUC$5-10. Food can be very good if there is water, if there is cooking gas and if there is any food – problems that affect all the restaurants around here. Lots of flies during the daytime. All prices in pesos cubanos or CUC$.

Restaurants

YYY-Y Flor de Lotto, Salud 313 entre Gervasio y Escobar, T7-860 8501. Daily 1200-2400. Chinese and Cuban food.

YYY-Y Tien Tan (Templo del Cielo), Cuchillo 17, entre Zanja y San Nicolás, T7-861 5478, taoqi@enet.cu. Daily 1100-2400. Always full, 2 chefs from Shanghai, pesos or CUC$ accepted, cheapest dish CUC$1, most expensive around CUC$25.

YY El Flamboyán, Cuchillo de Zanja entre Zanja y San Nicolás, T7-862 1490. Daily 1200-2400. Soup, main course, fried rice, dessert, drink and coffee for under CUC$10 (can pay in CUC$ or pesos cubanos).

YY Sociedad Chang Weng Chung Tong, San Nicolás 517 entre Zanja y Dragones, T7-862 1490. Bar, café and restaurant, daily 1200-2400. Part of the **Sociedad China de Cuba**, Chinese and *criollo* food.

YY Tong Po Laug, Cuchillo 10. Daily 1200-2400. Cheap, pesos cubanos accepted. The most expensive dish is CUC$8 or peso equivalent, or you can have chop suey, fried rice, vegetables and salad for CUC$2, Cuban beer CUC$1, imported beer CUC$1.50.

YY Viejo Amigo, Dragones 356 entre Manrique y San Nicolás. Daily 1200-2400. Combination Chinese restaurant and pizzeria.

Vedado *p88, map p90*
Restaurants

YYY La Torre, 17 y M, at top of Edif Fosca, T7-832 7306. Daily 1200-2400, best French food in Havana, about CUC$40 per person but worth it, great views over Havana, a/c.

YYY Polinesio, in the Habana Libre Hotel, with access from the street, T7-838 4011. Daily 1200-2400. Smart, dark and cool, a mix of Chinese and Indonesian dishes, CUC$12-20, and the **Bar Turquino** on the 25th floor (spectacular views of Havana which makes the food acceptable, service bad). Cabaret 2230-0430. Bar daily 1030-0430.

YYY-YY El Conejito, M esq 17, T7-832 4671. Daily 1200-2400. Specializes in rabbit in several different styles and sauces, with alternatives of chicken, pork or fish if you prefer, bar attached which closes at 0200.

YYY-YY Unión Francesa, 17 esq 6. Attractive colonial building, rooftop restaurant has good views, relaxed, nice atmosphere, photos of Fidel and Chirac, excellent wide menu, under CUC$25 per person including a beer. Live music.

ⓦ Casa de la Amistad, Paseo entre 17 y 19 (see page 93), 1100-2300. Serves chicken, snacks and pizza. Inside the main building is **Restaurant Primavera**, daily 1200-2400, is more elegant and expensive with antique furniture and good table service.

ⓦ La Casona de 17, 17 60 entre M y N, T7-838 3136. Daily 1200-2400. Elegant peach mansion with colonial terrace, once home to Castro's grandparents. House dish is *arroz con pollo a la chorrera*. Also good is *paella Casona*, or there is always a half roast chicken (a bit greasy) with bacon, rice'n'beans, chips and salad. Adjoining Argentine *parillada* serves up mixed grills. Nice for a relaxing lunch.

ⓦ-ⓨ La Roca, 21 102 esq M, T7-834 4501. 1200-0200. Restored 1950s building with stained-glass windows dating from when it was a guest house. Sleek but stark dining room, international menu for a range of budgets, *croquetas de pollo* CUC$1.50, onion soup CUC$1.50, spaghetti carbonara CUC$2.50, plus more expensive dishes. Set menu for CUC$3.25-3.75 with drink main course and dessert, excellent value but very popular so best to get there before 1900. Piano music while you eat. From 2230 there is a comedy show, CUC$3 including a cocktail, but this might change.

ⓨ Dinos Pizza, 23 y L in the same building as Cine Yara, open 24 hrs. Small and family-sized pizzas. Also beer, soft drinks, juices and ice cream.

ⓨ Pekín, 23 1221 esq 12, close to Cementerio Colón, T7-833 4020. Daily 1200-2200. Chinese food with options for vegetarians, charges in pesos cubanos. Unfortunately there are usually huge queues and slow service, the food is cold, tepid at best and the selection usually shrinks by closing time. The best branch is on Calzada entre D y E, in the loveliest area of Vedado, with pleasant outdoor seating, great views of Teatro Amadeo Roldán, and smaller queues.

Paladares

ⓦⓦ Adela, Calle F 503 entre 21 y 23, T7-832 3776. Call ahead for opening hours. Adela is an artist and this *paladar*, though legal, is primarily an art gallery. Clients come to buy art and stay to eat. Appetisers include cinnamon-baked bananas, fried *malanga*, corn and chorizo stew and others, although the choice of main course is limited. Prices around CUC$20-25 per person.

ⓦ Gringo Viejo, 21 454 entre E y F, T7- 831 1946. Daily 1200-2300. Nice atmosphere with wall-to-wall cinema memorabilia, good portions, main course of fish, chicken and pork with fruity or spicy sauces accompanied by rice, beans and salad.

ⓦ Los Amigos, M entre 19 y 21, opposite Victoria, T7-830 0880. Daily 1200-2400. Good, but check your bill. Convenient location for après-dining entertainment, popular with locals and ex-pats, dining among Christmas decorations, religious artefacts and wind chimes.

ⓦ Nerei, 19 110 esq L, T7-832 7860. Daily 1300-2400. Good food, main courses include lamb with pepper, chicken and beer, turkey with wine and grilled squid with salad and rice, tables outside on the veranda, English spoken.

Ice cream parlours

Coppelia, 23 y L, Vedado, T7-832 6184/ 832 7821. Tue-Sun 1100-2200. A visit to the most famous ice cream parlour in Cuba is recommended, see also page 89. With a capacity for 707 seated ice cream lovers, there are several separate outdoor areas to eat in, each with their own entrance and queue in the surrounding streets, or inside in La Torre. Extremely popular with Cuban families. If you pay in pesos cubanos, you will almost certainly have to queue for an hour or so, particularly at weekends, not unpleasant as the design is integral with the characteristic *copey* trees, which provide plenty of shade. A dedicated attendant (brown uniform) controls the queue and directs you into the seating area as tables become free. Alternatively, pay in CUC$, in the *Fuente de*

Soda kiosks outside (said to be open 24 hrs but often closed after midnight), but this can work out extremely expensive. Bring your own plastic spoons for the tubs as they invariably run out. CUC$2 for small portion, many different flavours, depending on availability (chocolate is still the top flavour), and styles (all come with a glass of water): *ensalada* (mixture of flavours), *jimaguas* (twins), *tres gracias*. After devouring your 1st choice you can stay and order a 2nd portion without queuing. Alternatively, sample the **Coppelia** ice cream in the tourist hotels and restaurants and some dollar food stores. Another ice cream shop is **Bim Bom**, 23 y Calzada de Infanta, Vedado.

Miramar *p94, map p94*
Restaurants

🍴 **1830**, 7 1252 entre 20 y 22, T7-838 3090. Daily 1200-2400. High-class dining with cabaret shows from 2200 and local bands in a wonderful setting at the mouth of the Río Almendares. International and Cuban cuisine, from CUC$12 for a local dish, to CUC$16.25 for tenderloin with blue cheese sauce and lobster at CUC$30.

🍴 **El Aljibe**, 7 entre 24 y 26, T7-204 1583. Daily 1200-2400. Originally opened in 1947 as *Rancho Luna*, drawing 50s movie stars like Eva Gardner and Errol Flynn with its secret recipe for roast chicken. Following the Revolution the restaurant closed in 1961, but reopened again as El Aljibe by state-run **Cubanacán** in 1993 and the original owner Sergio García Maciás began to bring his famed *pollo al Aljibe* to a new generation of movie stars, including Jack Nicholson, Steven Spielberg and Danny Glover. Open, breezy, framework design and friendly atmosphere. Generous portions of delicious black beans, rice, fried potatoes and salad, with more if you want, CUC$12 per person.

🍴 **El Tocororo** (national bird of Cuba), 18 302 esq Av 3, T7-204 2209. Daily 1200-2400, bar 1800-0200. Excellent food at CUC$30 a head, old colonial mansion with nice terrace, great

house band, no menu, ostrich steak, prices fluctuate widely but one of the best restaurants in town.

🍴 **La Cecilia**, 5 entre 110 y 112, T7-202 6700, daily 1200-2400. Good international food, mostly in an open-air setting. Thu-Sun features live bolero and salsa bands 2200-0300 with dancing outside, CUC$5-20 cover charge, depending on who is performing.

🍴 **La Ferminia**, 5 18207 entre 182 y 184, T727 36555. Daily 1200-2400. A beautiful neoclassical residence with an elegant atmosphere. Training school for chefs and the catering profession with varied cuisine, good for vegetarians or carnivores, vegetable pies, pasta and buffet, or *churrasquería* with skewers of Uruguayan beef.

Paladares

🍴 **La Cocina de Liliam**, 48 1311, entre 13 y 15, T7-209 6514. Sun-Fri 1200-1500, 1900-2200, closed 2 weeks in Aug, 2 weeks in Dec. Very good, imaginative Cuban food with tables outside in a lovely garden. Great appetizers and fresh fish. Popular with locals, reservations recommended, main course plus beer CUC$25-30, excellent service.

🍴 **La Fontana**, 3-A 305 esq 46, T7-202 8337. Daily 1200-2400. Good Cuban food, extremely popular with Cubans, tourists and diplomats, ask for the *menu de la casa* for non-inflated prices, about CUC$25 per person, arrive early or make a reservation, essential at night.

🍴-🍴 **El Palio**, Av 1 entre 24 y 26. Open air, Italian, fresh fish with choice of creative sauces, although portions can be rather small and atmosphere lacking.

🍴-🍴 **La Esperanza**, 16 105 entre 1 y 3, T7-202 4361, 1900-2330. Closed Sun. Small sign, very popular with Cubans and foreigners, traditional food, meal and drinks CUC$10-15 per person, plus 10% service, reservations advisable, run by Hubert and Manolo in their inviting living room surrounded by their paintings and antiques.

Cubanacán p97

Restaurants

El Rancho Palco, Av 19 y 140, Playa, T7-208 9346. Daily 1200-2300. Set in lovely jungle garden near the Palacio de las Convenciones, very popular with ex-pats for its Argentine steaks, good barbecued chicken, meats, typical *criollo* cuisine and international food, good live music provided by a quartet.

Boyeros p98

Restaurants

La Casa del Dragón, Cortina de la Presa y 100, off the main road to the right soon after entrance from Arroyo Naranjo, look for the sign, T7-443 026 ext 176. Tue-Sun 1200-2000. Chinese, only 4 tables, bamboo furniture, good food, reasonable prices, spring roll, sweet and sour pork, rice and salad CUC$6, beer CUC$0.85, nice walks nearby.

Palenque, beside Expocuba pavillions 17 y 190, Siboney. Cheap, good food, speciality suckling pig, open air, popular with locals and ex-pats. At Marianao beach there are also some cheaper bars and restaurants.

Fast-food outlets

El Rodeo, roundabout opposite Ciudad Deportiva, Rancho Boyeros y Vía Blanca. Open 1300-2245. Large, loud, popular snack bar, good place to head after a sports match.

Parque Lenin p99

Restaurants

Las Ruinas, 100 esq Cortina de la Presa in Parque Lenin, T7-643 1274. Daily 1200-2400. One of the best restaurants in Havana, the ruined plantation house has been incorporated into a modern structure. There's a great resident pianist, but watch out for mosquitoes at dusk. Tours of Parque Lenin often include a meal at Las Ruinas, otherwise you'll have to take a taxi, CUC$15, but try to persuade the driver to come back and fetch you, as it is difficult to get back into town.

Bars

Ordinary bars not on the tourist circuit will charge you in CUC$, if they let foreigners in at all. If it is a local bar and the Cubans are all paying in pesos, you will have to pay in CUC$. Even so, the prices in most places are not high by Caribbean standards: national brands of beer usually cost CUC$1-1.50, imported beers CUC$2-3. If you can pay in moneda nacional, beer is usually 10-18 pesos cubanos, according to quality, Tínima being the most expensive. You will find musicians in most bars. Have a ready supply of small change. Many play only 3 or 4 songs, then come round with the collecting bowl trying to sell their CDs, and move on, to be replaced by another band who do the same thing, adding quite a premium to your evening beer or cocktail.

La Habana Vieja p73, maps p74, p76 and p79

Bar Dos Hermanos, Av del Puerto esq Sol, opposite the ferry terminals, T7-8613514. Daily 0800-2400. Due to reopen end-2009 after renovation. It used to be a good, down-to-earth bar, bohemian atmosphere, popular with Cubans, just off the tourist circuit so lower prices, local late-night *son* band.

Bar El Louvre, Hotel Inglaterra, Prado 416, Parque Central, T7-860 8595. Daily 1200-2400. A pleasant place for an outdoor evening drink, where you can watch the sun going down catching the cream stone of the Museo de Bellas Artes through the Royal palms. Roving live musicians don't stay long and expect a generous tip, making your excellent CUC$2 daiquirí rather pricey. Very slow service.

Bar Monserrate, Monserrate y Obrapía, T7-860 9751. Daily 1100-2400. Beer CUC$1.50, *mojito* CUC$2.50, plenty of flavour but not very generous shots of rum, hot dogs, filling meal featuring unidentifiable meat in breadcrumbs, interesting to sit and watch comings and goings, high level of prostitutes/ *jineteras*, although bar staff seem to have unwritten agreement whereby girls are allowed in with a foreigner, or if they buy a drink, but if girl to punters ratio gets too high, some of the girls have to leave, hustling is not excessive though.

Bilbao, O'Reilly esq Aguiar. A shrine to Atlético Bilbao. An earthy bar off the main drag. You pay in pesos cubanos. Go for the experience.

Café de París, Obispo 202 esq San Ignacio. Daily 1200-2400. Predominantly tourist clientele but good location for people watching as long as you can fend off the *jineteros*. Cocktails from CUC$3 and barmen often bring you another even if you haven't ordered one. Live music 1200-1500, 2000-2400 except Thu.

Café O'Reilly, O'Reilly 203 entre Cuba y San Ignacio. Daily 1000-2400. Tour groups are often taken here for a *mojito*, pleasant, leafy, upstairs with balcony.

Casa del Escabeche, Obispo esq Villegas, T7-863 2660. Daily 0800-2400. Tiny bar but popular and welcoming, as well as very cheap, house quartet from 1200, cocktails CUC$2.50, *Cristal* and *Bucanero* CUC$1.50.

El Castillo de Farnés, Monserrate 361 esq Obrapía, T7-867 1030, see Eating, above. Restaurant at the back, lively bar 1200-2400, serves snacks.

El Floridita, see Eating, above. A favourite with tour groups for a mid-morning daiquirí.

La Bodeguita del Medio, see Eating above. The bar not to miss in the old town for Hemingway fans.

Lluvia de Oro, Obispo esq Habana. Open 24 hrs in winter, 1000-2400 in summer when there is no music. Good place to drink rum and listen to loud rock music or salsa, food is also served.

Museo del Ron, Av del Puerto 262 entre Sol y Muralla, T7-861 8051. As well as the Rum Museum, daily 0900-1730, there is also a shop selling Havana Club souvenirs, an art gallery 0900-1730, a courtyard restaurant and 2 bars, 1 with nightly music, 0900-2400. Serves good *Cuba Libre* and sometimes showcases quality live bands.

Centro *p87, map p74*

Café Neruda, Malecón entre Galiano y Aguila. Habaguanex has used the shell of an old building for this modern, open air bar with artistic flair. Very popular with young Habaneros, often queues at weekend when they're taking a break from a stroll along the waterfront. Reasonable prices, *mojitos* and daiquiris CUC$2. Meals and snacks available.

Vedado *p88, map p90*

Casa de la Amistad, Paseo 406 (see page 93). Bar with a beautiful garden extension, tasty cheap light meals optional, very peaceful surroundings.

Casa de las Infusiones, 23 y G, Vedado, open 24 hrs. Very cosy, lots of plants, an ideal place to read or talk.

❻ Entertainment

Cabaret

La Habana Vieja *p73, maps p74, p76 and p79*

Cabaret Nacional, San Rafael y Prado, entrance to the side of Gran Teatro, T7-863 0736. A cheap version of the **Tropicana**, see below, daily matinée 1600-2000, CUC$1-2, cabaret shows of salsa, reggaeton or disco 2200-0300, CUC$5 entry but expensive drinks. Lots of prostitutes. Also traditional music *peñas* Wed, Fri, Sat 1500-1930, CUC$3, and rock *peña* on Sun.

Vedado *p88, map p90*

Cabaret Las Vegas, Calzada de Infanta 104, T7-836 7939. Daily matinée 1600-2000, CUC$2, show with disco at 2200-0300, CUC$5. Minor salsa bands, hot and raw.

Copa Room, at the Habana Riviera, Paseo y Malecón, T7-834 4228 for reservation. Thu-Sun 2030-0300. Recently refurbished and has gone back to its pre-Revolution name (formerly *Palacio de la Salsa*). Traditional music including the boleros of Benny Moré. Glitzy Cuban cabaret *A lo Riviera*, skimpy outfits and sequins. Mon, Wed and Thu 2030-2430, show followed by recorded music; Fri, Sat, Sun, 2030-0300, show followed by salsa band, CUC$25 including cocktail, meal from CUC$50 per person.

Parisien, at Hotel Nacional, T7-873 3564. Daily 2100-0230. Excellent show for CUC$35, lasts longer than Tropicana and of equivalent standard, make a reservation.

Salón Rojo, Hotel Caprí, 21 entre N y O, T7-833 3747. The country's best musical groups play here, 2200-0400, CUC$10-35 depending on who is playing, drinks extra. The *Caprí* was Meyer Lansky and Lucky Luciano's turf in the days of the Mafia wheeling and dealing in the 1950s (the hotel was closed for refurbishment in 2009). Scenes from the *Godfather II* were filmed here.

Turquino, at Hotel Habana Libre, 25th floor, T7-834 6100. Daily 2230-0300, CUC$15, cabarets start at 2300 and 0100. Great setting with amazing views. The roof opens and you can dance under the stars. Expensive drinks at CUC$6. Unaccompanied males are likely to be fleeced as soon as they walk through the door.

The suburbs *p97*

Tropicana, 72 4504 entre 43 y 45, Marianao, 17-267 0110, reserves@tropicana.gca.tur.cu. Daily 2030 until some time after midnight. Reservations 1200-1600. Internationally famous and open air (entry refunded if it rains). Prices vary and there are good deals around. Best to take a tour, which will include transport, as a taxi from La Habana Vieja costs CUC$12; 3 prices: CUC$70, CUC$80 and CUC$90, depending on location of seat and whether you drink 3-, 5- or 7-year-old *Havana Club*. Transport, a snack or dinner can be added. If you fancy a cheap drink or snack go to **Rodneys**, daily 1200-0100, a 1950s bar and restaurant designed by Cuban painter, Nelson Domínguez, just beyond the entrance.

Cinemas

Comprehensive weekly listings of all films from Thu-Wed posted in cinema windows. Most have a/c. **Annual Film Festival** in Dec in all cinemas. International films, no translations into English. Information in **Hotel Nacional**.

La Habana Vieja *p73, maps p74, p76 and p79*

Payret, Prado 513, esquina San José, T7-863 3163. Films continuously from 1230.

Vedado *p88, map p90*

Acapulco, 26 entre 35 y 37, Nuevo Vedado, T7-833 9573, from 1830.

Chaplin, 23 1155 entre 10 y 12, T7-831 1101. Arty films at 1400, 1700 and 2000, shop good for film memorabilia.

La Rampa, 23 111 esq O, T7-878 6146. 2 films from 1630, dodgy toilets.

Riviera, 23 507 entre Av de los Presidentes y H, Vedado, T7-830 9564. Films Mon-Fri, 1800, 2100, Sat 1500, also has activities for children.

Yara, L 363, opposite Habana Libre hotel, T7-832 9430. From 1230, late weekend showings, 2 video lounges show recent US releases, but sound quality is sometimes poor in Salon B. Often sold out at weekends.

Dance

La Habana Vieja *p73, maps p74, p76 and p79*

Gran Teatro de la Habana, Prado y San José, Parque Central, T7-861 3078, dir.gth@cubarte.cult.cu CUC$10. Opened in 1838, this wonderful baroque building, which seats 1500 with 2 galleries, has seen countless famous performers on its stage. The Cuban National Ballet and Opera companies perform here in the Sala García Lorca. The Conjunto Folklórico Nacional and Danza Contemporánea dance companies sometimes perform here. It also hosts the International Ballet Festival.

Dancing lessons

Casa del Tango, Tango Academy Edmundo Daubar, Neptuno 309 entre Galiano y Aguila, T7-863 0097. Tango dance classes Mon-Fri 1900-2000, ask for Hanei and Rubén. The Escuela Danzamor also operates out of here. Ask for Adelaída and Wilki.

There are several people who give salsa and other dancing lessons.

Jazz

See also Live music venues, below, which often feature jazz sessions.

Vedado *p88, map p90*

All jazz venues are in Vedado. During the annual Jazz Festival in Feb you can hear international as well as Cuban stars, free or CUC$5-10 per show, but in the 2 weeks before there are also events at the **Nacional** and the **Habana Libre**. Information from the **Instituto de la Música**, 15 452 entre E y F, T7-832 3503-06, ask for schedule from Rita Rosa.

Jazz Café, Galerías del Paseo esq 1, T7-838 3556. 1200-0200. CUC$10 *consumo mínimo*. Sleek and savvy venue with class acts, a laid-back welcoming ambience and a highly appreciative audience. Star-studded line-up includes legendary pianist Chucho Valdés. Excellent for jazz lovers.

La Zorra y el Cuervo, 23 y O, T7-662402. Daily 2200-0200, CUC$10 (including 2 cocktails). The fox and the crow is one of the best nights in Havana for jazz enthusiasts. The small cellar space on La Rampa is entered through a fine reproduction red British telephone box. High-calibre jazz musicians playing to an appreciative crowd. Get there before 2300 if you want a table with an unobscured view of the stage. Cuban bands often feature visiting US musicians.

Live music and dance venues

See also Jazz, above. Havana clubs are late night/early morning affairs with most Cubans arriving around midnight and staying late. Expect queues at the weekends. Cubans dress up for club nights and most clubs have a smart dress code, strictly enforced by the door staff. This includes no shorts or sleeveless T-shirts for men. No one under 18 is admitted. The emphasis is on dancing, be it salsa and Latin dance styles, R&B, hip hop or rock. Many places are frequented by *jineteros/as* and lone travellers have reported feeling uncomfortable with the unwelcome attention. Several venues now feature earlier shows, aimed at young Cubans, with entrance in pesos.

Radio Taíno FM 93.3, English- and Spanish-language tourist station, gives regular details of a wide range of venues and Cuban bands playing, particularly in the programme *El Exitazo Musical del Caribe*, daily 1500-1800 presented by Alexis Nargona. Also **Radio Ciudad de la Habana**, 94.9 FM, 820 AM, in Spanish. Up-to-the-minute salsa programmes, *Disco Fiesta 98*, Mon-Sat 1100-1300, provides accurate information about musical events in Havana, *Rapsodia Latina*, Mon-Fri 1630-1730. The newspaper, **Opciones**, also has a listing of what's on and **Cartelera**, available free of charge every Thu, is found at most hotel reception desks.

La Habana Vieja *p73, maps p74, p76 and p79*

Casa de Cultura de Habana Vieja, Aguiar entre Amargura y Teniente Rey, T7-863 4860. Vibrant and welcoming cultural centre with varied programme. Rumba by *Tambor Llévame Contigo* on the 2nd and 4th Sat of the month 1800-2000, free, *Sonora Habana* every Wed 2000-2300, 40 pesos, *Descarga en Casa* 1st and 3rd Sun 1700-2000 free, *Con Té Teatro* last Sun 1900-2100, free, *Peña Chapotín y sus Estrellas* (son), every Fri 2100-2400, 40 pesos.

Centro *p87, map p74*

Callejón de Hamel, Hamel entre Aramburu y Hospital, Centro Habana. A fast, kicking *rumba* show with invited guests and community artists every Sun 1200-1600, a responsive audience and electric jam sessions make this a hot venue, recommended (see box, page 117). Take lots of sun screen and water. Rum and honey for sale CUC$2.

Casa de la Cultura del Centro Habana, Av Salvador Allende 720 entre Soledad y Castillejo, T7-878 4727. Phone for details as events vary considerably. Extensive programme from blasting rock to sedate *peñas campesinas*, frenetic rap to hip hop.

Casa de la Cultura Julián del Casals, Revillagigedo entre Gloria y Misión. Sun 1400-2000 show *Del Son al Son* (free); 1st Sat of month 1600, *Grupo Musical Aceituna sin*

Music in Havana

Havana is buzzing with musical activity. Rumba, conga, *son*, danzón, charanga, salsa – you'll hear it all, as Cuba's greatest musicians converge on the capital. This is the place to be if you want to hear Cuba's established artists – *Los Van Van, Sierra Maestra, NG La Banda, La Charanga Habanera, Isaac Delgado, Buena Vista stars* – all regularly liven up the theatres, hotels and parks. You might even get to wave a flag at Silvio, Sara or Pablito if the UJC are holding a rally in the Plaza de la Revolución.

Havana offers more than star quality, however. Fancy a conga? The revived carnival parade is in November. Many of the *comparsa congas* parade regularly throughout the year down Paseo Martí and through La Habana Vieja, and a newly established Christmas Day parade gives you another chance to go wild with the *farolas* and *tambores*. A rumba? The unmissable **Conjunto Folklórico Nacional de Cuba** performs Saturdays 1500-1700 in the **Patio de La Rumba** outside the **Gran Palenque Bar**, at Calle 4 entre Calzada y 5 in Vedado, where you can *guaguancó* with some of the best drummers and dancers in the land. There is also an outdoor rumba venue at **Callejón de Hamel**, where the action takes place around 1200-1500 on Sundays.

You might want to practise your *son* – there are plenty of willing partners at the **Casa 10 de Octubre** (Calzada de Luyanó entre Reforma y Guasabacoa, Santos Suárez, south of Cerro), where the *septetos* turn back the clock to the Havana of the 1920s. More up to date sounds can be heard at the annual Jazz Plaza festival in December, where Cuba's finest join forces with international stars for a world-class event. For a real history lesson, don't miss the ancient *Orquesta Típica* playing old *Danzones* with gusto in the Plaza de la Catedral. None of the band looks a day over 80.

Hueso; every Sat at 2000 live show *Vivo por mi Música*; 2nd Sat of each month at 1400 *Tarde del Creol*; 4th Sat at 1600 *Peña de Anais Abreu*. Every other Fri at 2000, comedy show *Llegó la Risa*. Every Thu at 2000 *Un Jueves Diferente*, live show with invited artists.

Casa de la Música Galiano, Galiano 255 esq Neptuno, T7-862 4165, cmh-eco@egrem. cult.cu. Music shop, restaurant and dance floor with popular bands. Daily matinée 1600-2000, CUC$5, beer CUC$1.50, *mojito* CUC$2.50, evening performances 2200-0300, CUC$10-25, beer CUC$2.50, *mojito* CUC$3.50.

Casa del Tango Edmundo Daubar, Neptuno 309 entre Aguila y Italia, T7-863 0097. Musical venue/museum with fascinating collection of tango memorabilia dating back to the 1940s, from record sleeves to all manner of Carlos Gardel idolatry.

La Madriguera, Quinta de los Molinos entre Av Infanta y Salvador, entrance on Jesús Peregrino (Final), after crossing over Infanta. T7-879 8175. This is the **Casa del Joven Creador de Ciudad Habana** and the headquarters of the **Asociación Hermanos Saíz** in Centro, with arts, crafts and musical workshops for all ages and talents. Hip hop, rap and traditional Cuban rhythms are all here; fascinating glimpse into Cuban youth culture. Mon-Sat 1800-2400, although best Thu-Sat. On the 3rd and last Wed of the month, *'Audiovisual Coffee'* with cinema express, documentary of young producers and videoclips, from 2000. Last Thu of the month *'Theater Coffee – A Red Drop'* from 2000. On the 2nd Fri *'Obsesión por el hip-hop'* (*Peña de Rap*), from 2000, 5 pesos. On the 3rd Fri from 2000, *'La Partidera'*, hip hop. On the last Fri from 1800, *'La Costurera'* performance, various art exhibitions and concert. There is also a gallery with various art exhibitions, daily 0800-1700, and when there are events and fiestas throughout the year.

Palermo, San Miguel y Amistad, T7-861 9745, Sun-Fri 2100-0300, Sat 2100-0400, CUC$2. Cabaret show from 2400 every night with weekend showcase feature of *Odelquis Revé y su Changüí*, followed by salsa disco. Also a bar-cafetería serving chicken, sandwiches, steak and pork. Beers CUC$1.50, entry CUC$5 includes one *mojito. Recorded music and TV with video; on Fri Disco Temba, on Sat an orchestra plays.*

Vedado *p88, map p90*

Café Cantante, Teatro Nacional, Plaza de la Revolución, Paseo y 39, T7-878 4275. Daily matinée 1700-2100, CUC$5, 2300-0300, price depends on who is performing, could be an *orquesta bailable*, or a disco. Highly regarded venue, top bands play here, popular with local musicians and others in the business. Start your night in *El Delirio*, see below, then head down to the basement for the last hour of *Café Cantante* (the doorman may let you in with no charge at this late hour). Matinées are particularly popular with Cuban youth.

Café El Gato Tuerto (the one-eyed cat), O entre 17 y 19, T7-838 2696. *Consumo mínimo* CUC$5, *Son, trova* and boleros performed 2400-0300. Bohemian people and post-modern decor, funky bordering on pretentious, local legends often perform here, *filín* and boleros, intimate stage with audience participation encouraged.

Centro de Música Ignacio Piñeiro, H esq 9, Vedado, T7-831 6898. The last Fri of every month, showcases new bands, young and very energetic crowd.

Cine Riviera, 23 entre G y H, Vedado, T7-830 9564. 1900-2300. 3rd Fri of each month the cinema is given over to a live music event with an ecological theme, Cuban reggae and jazz bands, young, friendly and relaxed, mostly Cuban crowd. On Sat at 2400, music and *trova*.

Club Atelier, 17 esq 6, corner of Parque John Lennon. Every night 2200-0400. Small L-shaped dance floor, pool table, beer CUC$1.50, various house styles from salsa to rap, CUC$5.

El Delirio Habanero, Teatro Nacional, Plaza de la Revolución, Paseo y 39, T7-878 4275. Piano bar upstairs on the 5th floor (lift sometimes not working) where you can hear quality music, *nueva trova*, bolero, etc, cover price depends on the act, could be an *orquesta bailable*, or a disco, daily 2300-0600, matinées on Sun 1600-2000. Resident band *Los Tres Habaneros* Thu and Sat for salsa. Rumba *peña* Sun 1600-2000. Great views of floodlit José Martí monument and Plaza de la Revolución. Take the big red sofa seats under the windows. Busy at weekends with a mostly Cuban crowd, phone to reserve the best tables. Delicious cocktails, good-value snacks, attentive service. Recommended, energetic clubbers leave here and head for the sweaty **Café Cantante** (see above) in the basement for the last hour. Downstairs in the theatre there are live concerts such as a *Nueva Trova* show.

El Gran Palenque Bar, 4 entre Calzada y 5, T7-830 3939/830 3060. On Sat at 1500-1700 the courtyard of this open-air café/bar is taken over by the acclaimed **Conjunto Folklórico Nacional de Cuba** for an upbeat rumba show: *Patio de la Rumba*. CUC$5.

El Pico Blanco, Hotel St John, O 206 entre 23 y 25, T7-833 3740. Daily 2200-0300, Tue, Thu CUC$5 and drinks CUC$5, Fri-Sun CUC$10 and drinks CUC$10. Spectacular rooftop setting but predictable variety show of comedy followed by salsa disco. At the weekend there is a show in the Restaurant La Plaza called *Café Concierto* 2230-0200, CUC$5 (CUC$3 *consumo mínimo*), with karaoke, comedy and recorded music.

Habana Café, in the Meliá Cohiba, Paseo entre 1 y 3, T7-833 3636. Very touristy and largely frequented by Meliá guests. A 1950s American pastiche, which has replaced the bombed-out disco. Old cars, small Cubana plane hanging from the ceiling, memorabilia on the walls, Benny Moré music and large screen showing brilliant film of old Cuban musicians and artistes. Food expensive and meals not recommended, overpriced cocktails CUC$6. CUC$10 minimum entry fee for show at 2100, Thu-Sat live bands, CUC$15.

Hurón Azul, 17 351 entre Av de los Presidentes y H, T7-832 4571. The headquarters of UNEAC (artists' and writers' union) in a majestic, colonial mansion. An inviting intelligentsia hang-out, the lovely, welcoming bar hosts regular upbeat afternoon *peñas*. Wed alternate between *Trova sin Traba* and *Peña del Ambia* 1700-2000. Sat bolero 2000-0100.

Imágenes, Calzada 602 esq C, T7-833 3606, matinée on weekdays 1530-2000, CUC$2 including 1 drink, weekend matinées CUC$3, plus CUC$1 for drink, daily 2130-0300 with musical comedy show at 2400 Tue-Sun. CUC$5 plus CUC$3 for drink. Intimate, classy piano bar, great for low-key evening. Local pianist Mario Romeu, also karaoke, salsa disco and *nuevo imagen*, a showcase for new talent.

Sherezada, Edificio Focsa, M y 19, next to Teatro Guiñol, T7-832 3042. Open 2200-0200. Disco and show, cover 50 pesos cubanos.

Tikoa, 23 entre N y O, T7-830 9973, 2200-0200. Disco, CUC$3, Mon-Thu live singer, Fri, Sat *Salsa Mi Son*, weekend matinées 1600-2000, cover 25 pesos cubanos for disco. Popular with travellers and locals, this small and sweaty basement club swings with a strong Afro Cuban vibe.

Miramar p94, map p94

Casa de la Música Egrem, Sala Té Quedarás, 20 3308 esq 35, T7-204 0447. CD shop daily 1030-2400. One of the top venues to listen to the cream of Havana's musical talent. The programme changes a lot so it's best to phone in advance to see who is on, CUC$10-25. Upstairs at the *Diablo Tun Tun* traditional music is played by small groups daily 2300-0600, CUC$10. Matinées Mon 1600-2100, Tue-Sun 1600-2000, CUC$5. Food service from the *parrilla* daily 1200-2400.

Club Almendares, Márgenes del Río Almendares, 49 y Av 28, Kohly, Miramar, T7-204 4990. The Salón Chévere (*Disco Temba*), daily 2200-0300, CUC$10 with open bar, all types of music. At the swimming pool Fri, Sat, Sun 2300-0300, there is a live show called a *Noche Cubana*, CUC$5, mosquitoes can be troublesome as you are in the Bosque de la Habana.

El Río Club, A entre 3 y 5, T7-208 3752. Locals still refer to it as *Johnnie's Club*, its previous name before the Revolution. Salsa disco CUC$5, hot and sweaty dance floor, current favourite with Havana's dance crowd, 2300-0300.

La Macumba, 222 esq 37, La Coronela in La Giraldilla tourist complex, T7-273 0568. Variable programme, recorded and live music, 2200-0400, CUC$5-20. Top Havana nightspot, open-air disco with 2 large dance floors for Latin and R&B, popular with Cubans and foreigners.

Salón Boleros en Dos Gardenias, 7 esq 26, Miramar, T7-204 2353. Daily 2200-0300, CUC$5. Upmarket *bolero* venue, 4-5 live shows every night, elegant, well-dressed crowd with popular Chinese restaurant and bar.

Salón Rosado Benny Moré, La Tropical, 41 y 46, T7-206 1282. Wed cabaret 2000-0200, Thu peña with the group Bamboleo, Fri recorded music, 5-20 pesos cubanos for Cubans. Sat an Sun 2300-0200, top-class *orquestas* play here and the price depends on the band. Sun matinée for dancing 1500-1900. Raunchy, popular dance venue with some of the best salsa in town.

Theatres

All productions are performed in Spanish. Tourists pay in CUC$; 1 peso cubano = CUC$1.

Vedado p88, map p90

Amadeo Roldán, Calzada y D, T7-832 1168. The fabulously renovated concert hall, Sala Caturla, is where you can hear the **Orquesta Sinfónica Nacional** as well as visiting international symphony orchestras, including several from the USA.

Sala Hubert de Blanck, Calzada 654 entre A y B, T7-833 5962. Specializes in classical and contemporary music concerts but has also staged major works by García Lorca and Cuban playwright Abelardo Estorino, and contemporary dance companies, Danzabierta and Danza Contemporánea.

Teatro El Sótano, K 514 entre 25 y 27, T7-832 0630. Shows contemporary drama, somewhere to find fringe theatre and home of the **Rita Montaner Company**.

Teatro Guiñol, M entre 17 y 19, T7-832 6262. A children's theatre that specializes in marionette shows.

Teatro Mella, Línea 657 entre A y B, T7- 833 5651. Specializes in modern dance but stages lots of other drama performances as well. **Galería Tina Modotti** bar, daily 1800- 2200, also a garden where you can eat, daily 1000-2200.

Teatro Nacional de Cuba, Paseo y 39, T7-879 3558. There's always lots going on here: concerts in the theatre downstairs, a piano bar, **El Delirio Habanero** and in the basement is the **Café Cantante**, see above.

Teatro Trianón, Línea entre Paseo y A, Vedado, T7-830 9648. Small theatre in good condition, headquarters of **Teatro El Público**. The seats have quirky pull-out extensions for you to rest your thighs on.

Miramar *p94, map p94*

Teatro Karl Marx, Av 1 1010 entre 8 y 10, T7-203 0801, T7-209 1991. Renovated in 2000 and now famous for hosting the 1st rock concert by a Western band, **Manic Street Preachers**, who played here in 2001 in the presence of Fidel Castro.

❀ Festivals and events

Havana *p73, maps p70, p74, p76, p79, p90 and p94*

The year in Havana is crammed with festivals of one sort or another. The most popular cultural events are the **cinema** and **jazz** festivals, but there are also several **ballet** and **contemporary dance** festivals as well as **folk** and **classical** music events. There are **book fairs**, many **sporting events** and even a **cigar festival**, while at the Marina Hemingway there always seem to be **regattas** and **fishing tournaments** in progress. For further details, see Festivals and events, page 44.

○ Shopping

Havana *p73, maps p70, p74, p76, p79, p90 and p94*

Art

Feria de Artesanías, between Tacón and Av del Puerto by Castillo de la Real Fuerza. A platform for many talented young artists to show off their skills, you may pick up a bargain, or you may be asked to pay Miami-type prices. You need documentation to take works of art out of the country or you may have them confiscated at the airport; galleries will provide the necessary paperwork and even vendors in the market can give you the required stamp.

Galería del Grabado, at the back of the Taller Experimental de Gráfica de la Habana, Callejón del Chorro 62, Plaza de la Catedral, T7-862 0979. Open all day, closed Sun. Original lithographs and other works of art can be purchased or commissioned directly from the artists. You can watch the prints and engravings being made and specialist courses are available for those who want to learn the skill for themselves, for 1 month, CUC$250, or 3 months, CUC$500.

Galería Forma, Obispo 255 entre Aguiar y Cuba, T7-862 0123. Daily 1000-2000. Formerly the bookshop, **Exlibris Swan** from 1927-60, now an art gallery belonging to the **Fondo Cubano de Bienes Culturales**, selling paintings, artesanías, ceramics, jewellery and sculpture.

La Victoria, Obispo 366 entre Compostela y Habana, T7-862 7914. Daily 1000-1900. An art gallery with a large choice of paintings at good prices, and books, owned by artist Natividad Scull Marchena.

Taller de Papel Artesanal, Mercaderes entre Obispo y Obrapía, T7-861 3356. Sells postcards and other items made from recycled paper.

Taller Serigrafía René Portocarrero, Cuba 513. Another big workshop, making screen prints; again, you can watch them being made and buy things.

Bookshops

There are second-hand bookstalls outside on the Plaza de Armas where you may be able to

Cuban all stars

Celebrities have always had a fascination for Cuba and there has always been a steady stream of rich and famous visitors to the 'Pearl of the Antilles'. In 1898 the young Winston Churchill narrowly missed being hit by a bullet on his 21st birthday when he visited to see what the Spanish-American War was all about. He returned, older and wiser, to paint and to smoke cigars, creating the ever-popular image of the wartime British leader puffing on a great fat *Habano*.

The US Prohibition Act of 1919 gave tourism in Cuba an unexpected boost, when drinking customers and whole bars moved to the island. The Irish-owned Donovan's Bar was relocated, lock, stock and barrel to a building opposite the Capitolio in Havana, and Cuban bartenders became world famous for their cocktails. Constante Ribalaigua, at the **Floridita**, was already an established expert before Hemingway discovered his *Daiquirís* (he allegedly regularly drank 11 double, sugarless daiquirís before 1100), but the author gave him the crowning touch by writing about his cocktails in the novel *Islands in the Stream*. He also invited his friend Marlene Dietrich to sample them and she became a regular visitor to Havana. Another actress visitor, Mary Pickford, had a cocktail created for her in the **Hotel Sevilla Biltmore**.

George Gershwin was so taken with the music and rhythms of Cuba that he composed the *Cuban Overture*, first performed in 1932. Frank Sinatra was a regular visitor and even had a modernist house in the former Country Club district. Many others came down in their yachts to sail around the cays and drink in the bars. Photos of Errol Flynn, Gary Cooper, Spencer Tracy, Ava Gardner, Carmen Miranda and other glamorous figures still grace the walls of the **Bodeguita del Medio** bar.

There were also, of course, the less salubrious visitors – gangsters like Al Capone, Lucky Luciano, Meyer Lansky and George Raft – who were attracted by the money to be made in the casinos and by bootlegging alcohol. George Raft had a penthouse apartment (now a restaurant) on top of the **Capri** casino hotel. The **Hotel Nacional** and the **Riviera** were also linked to mafia money. The bar of the **Nacional** has a rogues' gallery of photos of its famous guests.

Today, celebrities continue to flock to this last bastion of Communism in the Western world. Famous names have recently included Sir Paul McCartney, Francis Ford Coppola, Naomi Campbell, Kate Moss, Leonardo di Caprio (whose entourage was so large he took over whole hotels), while the annual Latin American Film Festival attracts a clutch of actors and directors, notably Robert de Niro, Arnold Schwarzenegger, Ken Loach, Jack Nicholson, Helen Mirren and Kevin Costner.

---

pick up a treasure if you know what you are looking for.

El Navegante, Mercaderes 115 entre Obrapía y Obispo, T7-861 3625. Mon-Fri 0830-1700, Sat 0830-1200. Maps and charts, both national and regional, also prepaid phone cards.

Fernando Ortíz, L 460 esq 27, T7-832 9653. Quite a wide selection, mostly in Spanish, and some beautiful postcards.

Instituto Cubano del Libro, Palacio del Segundo Cabo, O'Reilly 4 y Tacón. The institute has 3 bookshops: **Librería Grijalba Mondadori**, which has an excellent selection of novels, dictionaries, art books, children's books from around the world, all in Spanish; **Librería Bella Habana**, T7-863 2244, which has Cuban and international publications, and **Librería UNESCO Cultura**, which stocks

UNESCO publications, books on Cuba, a few thrillers in English and postcards.
La Moderna Poesía, Obispo 527 esq Bernaza, T7-861 6640, libreria@lamodernapoesia. ohch.cu. Daily 1000-2000. Biggest in Cuba, modern design, literature, sciences, art materials, CDs, posters, cards, café.

Food

For food shopping, there is the **Focsa Supermarket** on 17 entre M y N (at the base of the big tower block – closed for redesign in 2009) or the **Amistad**, on San Lázaro, just below Infanta. The **Isla de Cuba** supermarket on Máximo Gómez entre Factoría y Suárez has the best selection of food in La Habana Vieja, with prices stamped on the goods to prevent overcharging. Opposite the Plaza Hotel inside the small shopping centre is **El Cristal**, which also marks the prices on goods.

There are tourist mini-stores in most hotels, but they do not sell fresh food. **International Press Centre** (open to the public) on La Rampa sells items like chocolate in a shop to the right of the entrance. Bread is available at the **French bakery** on 42 y 19 and in the **Focsa** supermarket, see above.
Museo del Chocolate, Mercaderes entre Teniente Rey y Amargura, T7-866 4431. Sells chocolate candy made on the premises, also offers hot and cold chocolate, daily 1000-1700.

Food markets

Farmers are allowed to sell their produce (root and green vegetables, fruit, grains and meat) in free-priced city *agromercados*. You should pay for food in pesos cubanos. There are markets in Vedado at 19 y B and a smaller one at 21 esq J; in Nuevo Vedado, Tulipán opposite Hidalgo; in the Cerro district at the Monte and Belascoaín crossroads; and in Centro, the **Chinese market** at the junction of Zanja and Av Italia where you can eat at street food stalls (avoid Mon, not a good day). **Cadeca** exchange bureaux at the first and last listed. There are busy markets on the last Sun of every month in other Havana neighbourhoods. New state market Plaza del Cerro, Vía Blanca y Boyeros opposite Ciudad Deportiva entrance, Tue-Fri 0800-1800, Sat 0700-1700 and Sun 0700-1200. **Cadeca** exchange bureau, car and bike park. **Jardín Wagner**, Mercaderes 113 entre Obispo y Obrapía, Habana Vieja, T7-866 9017. Mon-Sat 0900-1700, Sun 0900-1300. Flowers for sale, including artificial flowers and pot plants.

Handicrafts

Asociación Cubana Artesanos y Artistas (ACAA), Obispo 411 entre Compostela y Aguacate, T7-866 6345. Mon-Sat 1000-1800. Handicrafts, clothing, humidors, glassware and musical instruments.
Casa del Abanico, Obrapía 107 entre Oficios y Mercaderes, La Habana Vieja, T7-863 4452. Mon-Fri 0900-1700, Sat 0900-1200. Beautifully decorated fans for sale from luxury silk to everyday cotton. Lots of historical details. You can have one customized to your own design, just as the *criollo* ladies used to.
Palacio de la Artesanía, Palacio Pedroso (built 1780) at Cuba 64 entre Peña Pobre y Cuarteles (opposite Parque Anfiteatro). A mansion converted into boutiques on 3 floors with musicians in the courtyard. A large selection of Cuban handicrafts is available. It also has things not available elsewhere, such as American trainers, as well as clothing, jewelry, perfume, souvenirs, music, cigars, restaurant, bar and ice cream. Visa and MasterCard accepted, passport required.

Handicraft markets

Many open-air markets, handicraft and tourist souvenir markets and *ferias de artesanías*, have sprung up.
Feria del Malecón, Malecón, entre D y E, Vedado. Including shoes, jewellery, lamps and the ubiquitous booksellers. Che Guevara and religious *Santería* items lead the sales charts. Illegal cigar sellers operate here.
Feria del Tacón, Av Tacón entre Chacón y Empedrado, La Habana Vieja, Plaza de la Catedral end. Daily, Wed-Mon 0800-1900. Havana's largest craft market, a multitude of products and if they don't have what you

want someone will know someone who does. Tourist souvenirs, clothing, paintings, the list is endless. Also sold here are carvings, crochet, ceramics, boxes, jewellery, T-shirts and baseball bats. The black coral is illegal to bring in to many countries, so avoid.
Feria del 23, 23 entre M y N, Vedado. Mon-Sat 0900-1800. Not a great selection, carvings and beads predominate.

Music, cigars and souvenirs
Artex, L esq 23, T7-832 0632. Mon-Sat 1000-2100, Sun 1000-1900. Excellent music section and tasteful T-shirts and postcards.
Caracol chain, in tourist hotels (eg Habana Libre) and elsewhere. Tourists' requisites and other luxury items such as chocolates, biscuits, wine, clothes, require payment in CUC$ (or credit cards: MasterCard, Visa).
Casa Cubana del Perfume, Teniente Rey 13 entre Oficios y Mercaderes. Mon-Sat 0930-1900, perfumes mixed on the premises, Suchel perfume. On the mezzanine is a little cafetería.
Casa de la Música Galiano, Galiano 255 esq Neptuno, Centro, T7-860 9640, cmh-eco@ egrem.cult.cu. Daily from 1000 until events finish. Shop specializes in music, extensive list of titles, past and contemporary.
Casa del Habano , 7 y 26, Miramar, T7-204 2353. Mon-Sat 1030-1830. Full range of cigars, one of many branches of state cigar shops. See box, page 150.
Casa del Tabaco, y Ron Obispo esq Monserrate, La Habana Vieja. Daily 1000-1900. Wide range of rums of all ages and tobacco.
EGREM, Casa de la Música, see Live music and dancing venues, above. A good selection of CDs and music.
El Siglo de las Luces, Neptuno esq Aguila, T7-860 6166, near Capitolio. Good place to buy *son, trova* and jazz (rock) records.
La Maison Calle 16, 701 esq 7 in Miramar. Luxurious mansion with dollar shops selling cigars, alcohol, handicrafts, jewellery and perfume. There is live music in the evening 2030-2450, in a lovely open-air patio, and fashion shows displaying imported clothes sold in their own boutique, CUC$10. However,

as with all shops depending on imports, the quantity and quality of stock is variable and can be disappointing. The Piano Bar is open daily 2200-0300, karaoke and comedy show as well as live music, CUC$5. The swimming pool has a bar and café daily 1000-1800, CUC$3.
Longina Música, Obispo 360 entre Habana y Compostela, La Habana Vieja, T7-862 8371. Mon-Sat 1000-1900, Sun 1000-1300. You can buy drums and other insturments here as well as CDs and stereos.
Perfumería Mercaderes, 156 entre Obrapía y Lamparilla, T7-861 3525. Daily 1000-1800. Manufacture and sale of perfumes and colognes from natural essential oils.

Shopping centres/department stores
Shopping centres tend to get very busy at weekends. Taxis and *bicitaxis* wait outside. Bags must be left outside shops in designated storage areas called *guardabolsas*; you should receive a numbered badge to identify your bag. Items purchased will be checked against receipt by security when you leave each shop. The large department stores are along Galiano (Av Italia) near San Rafael and Neptuno.
Galerías de Paseo, 1 entre Paseo y A, Vedado, opposite Meliá Cohiba, T7-833 9888. Mon-Sat 1000-1800, Sun 0900-1300. 3 levels, car showroom (for foreigners), supermarket, sports and clothes shop, café, Mon-Sat 1000-2100, Sun 0900-1300. Jazz café on 3rd floor.
Harris Brothers, Av de Bélgica 305, entre O'Reilly y Progreso, La Habana Vieja, T7-861 1615. Daily 0900-2100. 4 floors, supermarket, fashion stores, children's clothes, snack bars and café.
La Epoca, Av de Italia (Galiano) y Neptuno, Centro Habana, T7-862 5065. Mon-Sat 0900-1900, Sun 0930-1330. 5 floors, including clothes shops and supermarket.
La Plaza Carlos Tercera, Av Salvador Allende (Carlos III), entre Arbol Seco y Retiro, Centro Habana. Mon-Sat 1000-1900 and Sun 1000-1500, 3 levels, Western Union money transfer service, Mon-Fri 1000-1700 and Sat 1000-1200. ATM gives pesos convertibles. Wide range of shops including clothing,

cigars, photography, sports, supermarket and household appliances. Bank, Mon-Fri 0800-1500, last working day of the month 0800-1200. Selection of cafés and snack bars.

▲ Activities and tours

Havana p73, maps p70, p74, p76, p79, p90 and p94

Baseball
Estadio Latinoamericano, Pedro Pérez 302, Cerro, T7-870 6576. South of the centre, in Cerro district, this is the best place to see baseball (the major league level). Opened in the 1950s, it has a capacity for 55,000 spectators and is home to the 2 Havana teams, **Industriales** (Los Azules) and **Metropolitanos**. The *Serie Nacional* baseball season runs Nov-May, culminating in the national play-offs, followed a couple of weeks later by the *Liga Superior*, which lasts a month. Baseball games have a fanatical following and can last up to 3 hrs. Follow the evening's game by visiting the Parque Central in La Habana Vieja the next day, the traditional venue for groups of passionate fans to congregate and discuss match details using frantic hand gestures to illustrate their opinions. Games at 2000 Tue-Sat, 1400 Sun, CUC\$3 for the best seats and CUC\$1 for the regular stand.

Basketball
Ramón Fonst stadium, Av Independencia y Bruzón, Plaza de la Revolución, T7-881 4196. Local team is **Capitalinos**. No fixed match dates.

Boxing
Sala Kid Chocolate, Paseo de Martí y Brasil, La Habana Vieja, T7-861 1547. Sports centre hosts regular matches during boxing season. Also here are judo, weightlifting, chess and handball and for international events it hosts tennis, boxing and badminton, when tickets are CUC\$1. A monthly programme of events is on the notice board.

Cycling
Cycling is a good way to see Havana, especially the suburbs, you can reach the Playas del Este beaches and surrounding countryside quickly and easily; some roads in the Embassy area are closed to cyclists. The tunnel underneath the harbour mouth has a bus designed specifically to carry bicycles and their riders, from Parque El Curita, Aguila y Dragones, to Reparto Camilo Cienfuegos after the tunnel. Take care at night as there are few street lights and bikes are not fitted with lamps. **Poncheros**, small private businesses that crudely fix punctures, are everywhere.

Golf
Club de Golf, Calzada de Varona, Km 8, Capdevila, Boyeros, towards the airport, T7-649 8918, cgolf@continental.cubalse.cu. The course is par 70 for men and par 72 for women. CUC\$30 for 18 holes (caddy charges CUC\$6), CUC\$20 for 9 (caddy CUC\$3), CUC\$10 for a 30-min lesson, club rental CUC\$10. Non-members are welcome. For foreign residents or frequent visitors, club membership is CUC\$45 a month after an initial fee of CUC\$70, which gives you unlimited golf. There is also a 2-lane bowling alley, billiards (3 tables), tennis (5 courts, bring your own rackets, instruction available), squash and swimming pool, CUC\$5 (CUC\$8 in summer) including a drink, a bar (**Hoyo 19**, reserved for golfers and members) and a poor restaurant/snack bar, **La Estancia**.

Gyms
Some of the hotels have facilities that can be used by anyone. At the **Hotel Nacional** there is a small range of machines and free weights, sauna and massage available. Lockers provided, CUC\$5 including towel and shower (free to guests). The Hotel **Meliá Cohiba** has better facilities and range of machines, CUC\$10 including sauna, massage from CUC\$15. There is also a gym in the Barrio Chino, run by the **Sociedad Chang Weng Chung Tong**, San Nicolás 517 altos entre Zanja y Dragones, T7-862 1490, Mon-Sat for aerobics, Taibo,

apparatus, CUC$25 for monthly membership. Restaurant attached, see Eating, page 110.

Horseriding
You can go riding at **El Rodeo** near Las Ruinas in Parque Lenin, T7-644 1476, for CUC$15 per hr, including a guide. It is mostly for Cubans and you may be able to pay in pesos cubanos. Horses well cared for.

Running
Havana's marathon, Marabana, is held in Nov annually, CUC$10, including a marathon jersey, see Festivals and events for details. Another race is **Terry Fox** on 2 Feb each year to raise money for cancer treatments.

Sports centres
Ciudad Deportiva, at the roundabout on Avenida Boyeros y Vía Blanca, T7-881 6979. P2 bus passes outside. The 'Sports City' is a large circular sports stadium seating 18,000 spectators, enclosed by a dome with a roof diameter of 88 m. The architects were Nicolás Arroyo and Gabriela Menéndez; the complex was inaugurated on 26 Feb 1958. At the time it was considered one of the world's best indoor sports facilities. Entrance 2 pesos for seats and 1 peso for concrete benches in upper tiers. Buy tickets in advance at venue. International matches are usually a sellout. Volleyball (very popular), basketball, martial arts, table tennis. Great atmosphere, crowded, limited food and drink facilities. Large neon sign outside '*listos para vencer*' (ready to win).

Tour operators
Guides Many Cubans in Havana tout their services in their desperate quest for CUC$, they are a considerable nuisance and nearly all tourists complain of being hassled. If you feel you trust someone as a guide, make sure you state exactly what you want, eg private car, *paladar*, accommodation, and fix a price in advance to avoid shocks when it is too late. *Casas particulares* can often be a good source of information on reputable guides. You may find, however, that the police will assume

your guide is a prostitute and prohibit him or her from accompanying you into a hotel.

State-owned travel agencies There are lots of state-owned travel agencies, which cooperate fully with each other and have bureaux in all the major hotels.

As well as local trips to factories, schools, hospitals, etc, tours can be arranged all over Cuba by bus or air, with participants picked up from any hotel in Havana at no extra charge. Examples include a tour of the city's colonial sites (CUC$15, 4 hrs); a trip to the **Tropicana** cabaret; Cayo Largo for the day by air with boat trip, snorkelling, optional diving, lunch; Cayo Coco for the day with flight, all-inclusive package and changing room; Cayo Levisa day trip by bus and boat with snorkelling and lunch; Guamá and the Península de Zapata with a stop en route at the Finca Fiesta Campesina, tour of crocodile farm, lunch; Viñales and Pinar del Río, visiting *mogotes*, caves and tobacco factory, lunch; a day on the beach at Varadero with lunch, 10 hrs, and you get a changing room with shower and towel, Trinidad and Cienfuegos overnight, visiting the colonial city and the Valle de los Ingenios; ecological tour of Las Terrazas with walking and river bathing, lunch. Prices vary slightly between agencies and you can negotiate a reduction without meals.

Watersports
Club Habana (Sol Meliá), Av 5 entre 188 y 192, Reparto Flores, Playa, T7-204 5700. A club for permanent residents with annual membership of CUC$1500. Tennis, squash, pool, diving (with certification), windsurfing, training golf course, child care, shops, meetings facilities, sauna and massage, bar and restaurant, expensive. All motorized watersports were withdrawn in 2003 following a security clampdown.
Club Náutico Internacional 'Hemingway' (Hemingway International Yacht Club), Residencial Turístico 'Marina Hemingway', Av 5 y 248, Playa, T7-204 6653, yachtclub@cnih. mh.cyt.cu. Help and advice to visiting yachties.

Cubanacán Náutica (Marina Hemingway), same address, T7-209 7270, VHF 16, 68 and 72, direccion@prto.mh.cyt.cu. Office open Mon-Fri 0800-1700, but activities 24 hrs. Boat trips, sport fishing, CUC$450 half day, catamarans, sailing lessons in dinghies, diving and snorkelling. The dive centre, Centro de Buceo La Aguja, takes up to 8 divers on the boat.

Atlantic, 3 y 76, Centro de Negocios Miramar, T7-204 0747. If your luggage gets lost when flying to Havana, you should contact Violeta del Risco Martínez at Terminal 1 Jose Martí Airport, T7-275 1499. She is the lawyer in charge of helping travellers who have to cope with this sort of ordeal. She is incredibly helpful, demanding and determined to find the suitcase.

⊕ Transport

Air
Airlines
Most are at the seaward end of Calle 23 (La Rampa), Vedado. In 1 block on 23 entre P y Infanta, you can find Cubana, LTU, Aerocaribbean and Aeroflot. Another group can be found on the ground floor of the Hotel Habana Libre further up the same street: Grupo Taca (Aviateca, Lacsa, Nica, Taca), Air Europa, Aeropostal. Cubana, www.cubana.cu. For international sales, C 23 64, esq Infanta, T7-838 1039, or T834 4446 for reservations, ventas_online@cubana. avianet.cu, Mon-Fri 0830-1600, Sat 0830-1200. Aerocaribbean, T7-879 7524, www.cubajet. com/airlines/aerocaribbean.asp, or at the airport, T7-649 7648. Aeroflot, T7-204 3200. Aeropostal, 23 y P, T7-838 4000, Mon-Fri 0900-1200, Sat 0900-1300. Air Europa, Edif Santiago de Cuba, Av 5 esq 78, Miramar, T7-204 6904, ofic.cuba@air- europa.com, Mon-Fri 0800-1630, Sat 0900-1300. Air France, C 23 64, T7-833 2642, www.airfrance.cu. Mon-Fri 0830-1600, Sat 0830-1230; luggage service at the airport, T7-649 9708. Air Jamaica, C 23 64, T7-833 2447, havanaventas@ airjamaica.com, Mon-Fri 0830-1630, and at airport, Terminal 3, T7-649 7374. Iberia, Av 5 y 76, Centro de Negocios Miramar, Edif Santiago de Cuba, Planta Baja, T7-204 3444, Mon-Fri 0900-1600. Martinair Holland, T7-266 4900 at the airport. Mexicana de Aviación, 23 64 esq P, T7-833 3532, geventashav@mexicana.com.mx, Mon-Fri 0830-1630, Sat 0830-1200. TACA, L y 23, T7-833 3114, irodriguez@taca.com, at the airport T7-642 6042, www.taca.com. Virgin

Bus
Local
Town buses have been in crisis since 1993 and although there was a slight recovery in 2008 when new buses arrived, there were cutbacks in the service in 2009 because of fuel shortages. Buses are very crowded and foreigners are not expected to use them. They are hot and sweaty and uncomfortably crowded at all times. *Habaneros* insist they carry more people than a Boeing 747 and refer to them as *La Película del sábado* (Saturday Night Movie), since like the content advice prior to the film starting, they contain bad language, violence and sex scenes. Maybe a slight exaggeration, but be aware of pickpockets. The HabanaBus (see page 68) and taxis are the preferred method of transport for tourists, who pay in CUC$.

Metrobuses cover the main suburbs (40 centavos): P3, P11 and P15 (yellow) come in from Alamar, P11 being the most direct route to Vedado, P3 goes to Playa; P6 and P8 (pink) go south to Reparto Eléctrico from Vedado, while PC (also pink) goes all the way round the south of the city from Playa to the Hospital Naval via Cubanacán, Parque Lenin and Reparto Eléctrico; P1 (maroon) runs from Playa along the coast to Vedado then southeast to La Rosita, while P2 and P7 (also maroon) run from Vedado and Parque Fraternidad (respectively) to Alberro via La Rosita; P9 (red) runs from Vibora in the south up to Vedado and then west to the Hospital Militar, while P10 (red) skirts the southwest from Vibora to Playa; P12, P13 and P16 (blue) head southwest out to Santiago from Parque Fraternidad, Vibora and Vedado, with P12 and P16 passing through Boyeros, Vento and the airport terminals 3 and 1; P4 (green) heads west from the train station via Vedado and Playa to San Agustín; P5 (green) goes in the same direction via Centro and Vedado; P14 (green) takes a more southerly route from Parque Fraternidad out to San Agustín. Ask for the right queue. The queue may look disorganized but it is actually highly functional. Discover who is last (*el último*, you have to shout loudly) for the bus you want ; when identified, ask him/her who they are behind (*detrás de quién*), as people mark their places and then wander off until the bus comes. When the bus comes everyone reforms in an orderly queue. That's the theory. However, things may deteriorate at night, particularly if there has been a long wait, when the elbow becomes the preferred mode of queuing.

Long distance

Some ticket sellers refuse to sell tickets until the bus arrives. Passengers in the waiting lounge are not told when it does arrive and it leaves without them. The 'helpful' ticket seller then tries to sell them a seat in a private taxi, for which he/she no doubt receives a commission.

The tourist service, **Víazul**, leaves from Av 26 entre Av Zoológico y Ulloa, Nuevo Vedado, T7-881 1413/881 1108/881 5652/ 881 5657, www.viazul.cu, with a/c buses to most cities, with lots of intermediate stops. Víazul's terminal is small, and there is a poor snack bar upstairs, toilets, and outside there are taxis and an **Etecsa** cabin for local and long-distance calls. See Essentials, page 30, for advance booking addresses, and individual destinations for times and fares. **Astro** buses leave from the Terminal de Omnibus Interprovinciales, Av Rancho Boyeros (Independencia) 101 entre 19 de Mayo y Bruzón, by the Plaza de la Revolución, T7-870 9401/870 3397. However, foreigners are not allowed to use this service any more. **Víazul** buses often call in here after leaving their own terminal but you can't rely on seats being available.

Car

Hiring a car is not recommended for getting around Havana, roads are badly signed and there have been many accidents with tourists driving rental cars, see Essentials, page 35. Most of the hotels have car hire agencies in the reception area. Many streets around tourist locations have unofficial 'supervisors' who monitor car parking spaces and expect a CUC$1 payment on your return. If you want the real experience, **Gran Car**, T7-648 7338, rent classic cars (including Oldsmobiles, Mercury '54, Buicks and Chevvy '55) with driver, maximum 4 passengers, CUC$18 per hr or CUC$25 per hr for cars without roofs (go for the Oldsmobile '52). *Motos* (scooters) can be hired from **Palmares**, Av 3 entre 28 y 30, Miramar, T7-204 0646, 1 day CUC$24, 2-4 days CUC$23 daily, 5-12 days CUC$21 daily, 13-20 days CUC$18 daily, 21-29 days CUC$15 daily, 30 days CUC$13 daily.

Petrol stations Most widespread petrol chain is **Cupet-Cimex** (green logo) at Av Independencia y 271, Boyeros (near Terminal 2), Av Independencia esq Calzada de Cerro, Plaza (near Plaza de la Revolución), Paseo y Malecón (near Hotel Riviera), L y 17 and Línea y Malecón all in Vedado, 112 y 5, Miramar and Vento y Santa Catalina, Cerro. All open 24 hrs. Attached shops sell drinks, snacks and food. Second chain is **Oro Negro**, at 86 y 13, Miramar, and 7, entre 2 y 4, Miramar. Also open 24 hrs.

Ferry

There are ferries from La Habana Vieja to **Casablanca** and **Regla**, 10 centavos, which depart from Muelle de Luz, San Pedro opposite Bar Dos Hermanos. If you are facing the water, the Casablanca ferry docks on the left side of the pier and goes out in a left curve towards that headland, and the Regla ferry docks on the right side and goes out in a right curve. There are lots of security checks with X-ray machines and body searches following the 2003 hijacking of a ferry.

Taxi

Taxis are plentiful. It is a safe and easy way to travel around Havana, but relatively expensive. **Cubataxi**, T7-855 5555, is now the only company. They wait outside most hotels and at the airport, or ask your hotel to call one. Cubataxi also have minibuses, or big taxis, T7-204 2525, which take 7 people, useful if you are a group with lots of luggage. From Centro to the airport costs CUC$25.

Cuban peso taxis

Licensed Cuban peso taxis are reserved for Cubans and there is a hefty fine if the police catch a driver with a foreigner on board. Taxi *colectivos* ply their trade up and down main thoroughfares, usually stopping at bus stops to pick up passengers. They are large old American gas guzzlers in variable condition, usually poor, and everyone is squeezed in. Fixed 10 pesos cubanos fare.

Bicitaxi/cocotaxi

In La Habana Vieja and Vedado, bicycle or tricycle taxis are cheap and a pleasant way to travel, but they are currently prohibited for foreigners. A short journey will cost at least CUC$2, as the cyclist risks being fined if caught carrying you.

There is also the *coctaxi/cocomóvil*. If you can handle being driven around in a bright yellow vehicle shaped like a coconut shell on a 125cc motor bike, then these are quick and readily available. They take 2 passengers, no safety belts, plenty of pollution in your face. The fare is fixed in CUC$, but agree the fare before the journey. A typical fare from the Hotel Nacional to La Habana Vieja is CUC$3. Less conspicuous are the **Rentar una fantasía** vehicles, using the same 125cc engine but the vehicle is designed as a pre-1920s motor car.

Train

Trains leave from the Estación Central on Egido (Av de Bélgica) y Arsenal, Havana, T7-862 1920, to the larger cities. The Estación Central has what is claimed to be the oldest engine in Latin America, *La Junta*, built in Baltimore in 1842. Get your tickets in advance as destinations vary, the departure time is very approximate. Tickets are easily purchased from **LADIS** (Ferrocuba) office on Arsenal y Aponte, daily 0800-2000, T7-862 4971, pay in CUC$, passport needed, spacious, food and drink on board. The train to **Santiago de Cuba** leaves every other day at 1515, about 14-15 hrs on a good day, returning 2025, CUC$30. The trains are very uncomfortable, they stop at every town along the way and have to give way to a goods train, so there are always delays. The *especial* train operates summer only, Havana–Santiago CUC$30, T7-860 3161 at the Terminal de la Coubre next to the Estación Central for reservations.

There are also daily trains to **Pinar del Río** (No 21), 2235 arrives 0420, CUC$7 and **Matanzas**, several from 0940, CUC$3. A long-distance bus or dollar taxi may well do the same journey in a fraction of the time, eg **Havana–Pinar del Río**, 2 hrs or less by taxi, 7-8 hrs by train. It is not unusual for the trains to break down, in fact Cubans refer to this as 'normal service'. It will be mended and carry on, but be prepared to spend a serious amount of time travelling. The **Hershey** electric train with services to **Matanzas** starts from Casablanca 0445, 0835, 1235, 1720 daily, buy tickets at Casablanca booking office an hour before departure, CUC$2.80 1 way to Matanzas, CUC$1.40 to Hershey, but call first, T7-862 4888, because the service is 'informal'.

❶ Directory

Havana *p73, maps p70, p74, p76, p79, p90 and p94*

Accident and emergency

Ambulance: T7-838 1185/838 2185. Fire: T105. Police: Policía Nacional Revolucionaria (PNR) T106. Main police station is at Dragones entre Lealtad y Escobar, Centro, T7-863 2441.

Banks

For credit-card withdrawals, TCs and currency exchange, open Mon-Fri 0800-1500, last day of the month until 1200, **Banco Financiero Internacional**. In Vedado: Línea 1 esquina O, T7-833 3423, in Habana Libre complex, T7-838 4429; in La Habana Vieja: Oficios y Brasil, T7-860 9369; in Centro: Centro Comercial Carlos III, T7-873 6496; in Miramar: 18 111 entre 1 y 3, T7-204 2058, Av 5 esq 92, T7-267 5000, Edif Sierra Maestra, Av 1 y O, T7-203 9764. **Banco Internacional de Comercio**, 20 de Mayo y Ayestarán, Plaza de la Revolución, T7-855 5482, Mon-Fri 0830-1400. Branches at Empedrado y Aguiar, La Habana Vieja, T7-866 6410, Av 3 y 78, Playa, T7-204 3607, both open Mon-Fri 0830-1500. **Banco Metropolitano**, Av 5 y 112, Playa, T7-204 9189, Línea 63 esq M, Vedado, T7-838 3116, Mon-Sat 0830-1500.

Cadecas (exchange houses): Obispo 358 entre Compostela y Habana, T7-861 8501, daily 0800-2200; Neptuno 161 entre Consulado e Industria, T7-863 6853, Mon-Sat 0800-1800, Sun 0800-1300; in Hotel Sevilla daily, 0900-1900, in Hotel Nacional, 0800-1200 and 1230-1930, credit card cash advances.

ATMs Most banks and Cadecas now have ATMs for cash CUC$ withdrawal. An ATM outside the business centre of the NH Parque Central is a safe place to get money out. There is also an ATM in the Plaza Carlos III shopping centre, Av Carlos III.

Embassies and consulates

All in Miramar, unless stated otherwise: **Argentina**, 36 511 entre 5 y 7, T7-204297. **Austria**, Av 5 A 6617, T7-204 2825, Mon-Fri 0900-1200. **Belgium**, 8 309 entre 3 y 5, T7-204 2410. **Brazil**, Lamparilla 2, La Habana Vieja, T7-866 2912. **Canada**, 30 518 esq 7, Playa, T7-204 2516, Mon-Thu 0830-1700, Fri 0830-1400 (Consular section). **France**, 14 312 entre 3 y 5, T7-2013131, Consulate T7-201 3121, Mon-Thu 0830-1230. **Germany**, 13 652 esq B, Vedado, T7-833 2569. **Greece**, Av 5 7802, esq 78, Playa, T7-204 2995. **Italy**,

Av 5 402 esq 4, T7-2045615, Mon-Fri 0900-1230 (Consular section). **Japan**, Av 3 esq 80, Centro de Negocios, 5th floor, Playa, T7-204 3355, Mon-Fri 0900-1700. **Mexico**, 12 No 518 entre 5 y 7, T7-204 2583, daily 0900-1200, Mon-Fri. **Netherlands**, 8 307 entre 3 y 5, Playa, T7-2042511, Mon-Fri 0830-1130. **Peru**, 30 y Av 1, T7-204 2477. **Portugal**, 7 2207 esq 24, T7-204 0149, Mon-Fri 0900-1230. **South Africa**, 5 4203 esq 42, T7-204 1058, Mon-Fri 0900-1200. **Spain**, Cárcel 51 esq Zulueta, La Habana Vieja, T7-868 6868, Mon-Fri 0900-1300. **Sweden**, 34 510 entre 5 y 7, Playa, T7-2042831, ambassaden.havanna@foreign.ministry.se, Mon-Fri 0930-1130. **Switzerland**, Av 5 2005 entre 20 y 22, Playa, T7-204 2611, Mon-Fri 0900-1200, swissem@enet.cu. **UK**, 34 702 y 704 entre 7 y 17, T7-204 1771, embrit@ceniai.inf.cu (Consular Section), Mon-Fri 0800-1200. **US Interests Section of the Swiss Embassy**, Calzada entre L y M, Vedado, T7-833 3551, Mon-Fri 0830- 1700. **Venezuela**, 5 1601, Playa, T7-204 2662.

Insurance

Asistur is linked to overseas insurance companies and can help with emergency hospital treatment, repatriations, robbery, direct transfer of funds to Cuba, financial and legal problems, travel insurance claims, etc. For (24-hr) emergencies go to Prado 208 entre Trocadero y Colón, La Habana Vieja, T7-866 8339/8920/8527, F7-866 8087, www.asistur.cu.

Internet

Access is available at a limited number of places. Most hotels now have 1 or 2 terminals in the lobby, which are not reserved for guests but they will be more expensive than Etecsa, which charges CUC$6 per hr throughout the island. The large hotels of 4 or 5 stars, such as the **Habana Libre, Nacional, Parque Central** (business centre on 1st floor, ext 1911, 1833, daily 0800-2000), **Meliá Cohiba**, all have business centres with computers for internet access, as well as printing, photocopying, telephone, fax and telex facilities, but they charge a lot more.

The best place in La Habana Vieja is Etecsa's **Telepunto**, Habana 406 entre Obispo y Obrapía, T7-866 0547, daily 0830-2030, which has a communications centre with phones and fax service as well as 8 new terminals for internet access; **Lonja del Comercio**, Lamparilla 2, Plaza San Francisco de Asís, T7-866 2824, Mon-Fri 0830-1700, 4 terminals; Aguila y Dragones, Centro, T7-866 4641. There is a cybercafé in the **Capitolio**. Go in the main entrance and follow the signs to the left and through the building. There are 6 old terminals, very slow and appalling keyboards, open 0830-1800 (although 2000 is advertized but the Capitolio is shut by then). You may have to wait up to 45 mins for 1 to be free.

Medical services

Clínica Central Cira García, 20 4101 esq 41, Playa, T7-204 2811, www.cirag.cu. Payment in CUC$, emergency health care, also the place to go for emergency dental treatment. There are other branches at the Hotel Comodoro, Sevilla, Habana Libre, Marina Hemingway, Terminal 3 at the airport and at Clínica Playas del Este, Villa Tarará, and Villa Panamericana to the east. **Hotel La Pradera Pharmacy and Treatment Centre**, 230 entre 15A y 17, Reparto Siboney, T7-273 7467-76, comercia@pradera.cha.cyt.cu, water therapy, yoga, sauna, physiotherapy, Mon-Sat 0800-1700. **Servimed Biotop**, Av 41 2206 esq 22, T7-204 2377, F7-204 2378. Body and facial aesthetics, stress management, revitalizers, innovative techniques for psychological and physical evaluations, alternative non-invasory techniques.

Opticians Optica Miramar, 11 14614 esq 146A, Siboney, Playa, T7-208 6257, also branches at 7 y 22, Playa, T7-204 2269. **Optica Miramar Arrinda**, Neptuno 411 entre Manrique y San Nicolás, Centro, T7-863 2161, arrinda@opticam.cha.cyt.cu, Mon-Fri 1000-1800, Sat 1000-1300; **Optica El Almendares**, Obispo 364 entre Habana y Compostela, La Habana Vieja, T7-860 8262, Mon-Sat 1000-1800; and other locations,

Ophthalmology consultants, contact lenses, photochromic brown and grey lenses, lightweight glasses, plastic and metal frames.

Pharmacies The pharmacy at the Clínica Central Cira García (see above, open 24 hrs) T7-204 2880, sells prescription and patent drugs and medical supplies that are often unavailable in other pharmacies, as does the **Farmacia Internacional**, Av 41, esq 20, Playa, T7-204 2051, daily 0900-2100, and at the Habana Libre, L y 23, Vedado, T7-838 4593. **Camilo Cienfuegos Pharmacy**, L y 13, Vedado, T7-833 3599, daily 0800-2000.

Post/courier services

Post offices sell stamps in pesos, but hotels will charge in CUC$, making them very expensive.

Línea y Paseo, T7-830 5138, open 24 hrs, incredibly busy, long queues. Oficios 104 entre Amargura y Lamparilla, opposite the Lonja, open 24 hrs, T7-862 0103, and postal facilities in the **Hotel Nacional**. Also on Ejido esq Arsenal, next to central railway station, T7-862 2174, 24 hrs, and in the same building as Gran Teatro de La Habana.

Couriers Cubanacán Express, Av 5A 6223 esq 66, Miramar, T7-204 7848, www.cubanacan-express.cu, national and international courier service. DHL in Miramar on Av 1 102 esq 26, T7-204 1578, commercial@dhl.cutisa.cu, and at Calzada 818 entre 2 y 4, Vedado, T7-832 2112.

Telephones

Empresa Telecomunicaciones de Cuba (Etecsa) is on 18 3303 entre 33 y 31, Miramar, T7-204 1828, with offices listed above (Internet), also called Telepunto. There are also Minipunto cabins dotted around the city for phone services, internet, fax and pre-paid phone cards. There are phone boxes all over the city, taking coins or phone cards; it is written on the side whether they are for local, national or international calls. **Cubacel**, which operates mobile phone service, is part of Etecsa.

Around Havana

Several places of interest on the outskirts of Havana and in the Province of Havana can easily be reached as a day trip from the capital, with the option of staying a night or two if you wish. Readers of Ernest Hemingway novels will be fascinated to see his former home, now a museum dedicated to his memory, just as he left it, or Cojímar, the setting for his novel The Old Man and the Sea. *Alternatively you can base yourself on the beach and come in to Havana for sightseeing. The best beaches are east of Havana, at Playas del Este, an easy cycle ride or taxi from the city, or further afield at Jibacoa where you can explore the countryside as well as the sea. ▶▶ For listings, see pages 135-138.*

West of Havana

Playa Baracoa and El Salado

Heading out of the city west along the north coast, on the *autopista* La Habana–Mariel, you come to Playa Baracoa, a nice place to go for some relaxation on the beach. **El Salado**, 25 km west of Havana, is another beach, although some parts are rocky, but there is good snorkelling as a result. The water is slightly polluted and locals bring their pigs here for a bath. Further along the coast there is a completely abandoned holiday village with empty swimming pool and then the remains of a military coastal defence system, also deserted. There is a hotel here, described by one reader as a bungalow park, **Villa Cocomar**, see Sleeping, below. Parties of day-trippers come to use the swimming pool and there are lots of watersports on offer in season, including rowing boat hire and scuba-diving. The **Centro de Buceo Blue Reef** is based here, taking up to eight divers to 30 dive sites ranging from 5-35 m. In addition to the dive shop and other watersports this is now a centre for karting and international championships are held here at the kartódromo, http://cubakarting.org.

Mariel

Don't expect a beach at **Mariel**, further west from El Salado along the coast and scene of the mass exodus in 1980 known as the Mariel boatlift. This is a major industrial town, with the largest cement plant on the island, a shipyard, a thermal electricity plant and a duty-free industrial zone. If you continue along the coastal road, you enter the province of Pinar del Río on the way to Viñales.

San Antonio de los Baños

The capital of Havana Province is **Bauta**, near the beginning of the Carretera Central, the old route to Pinar del Río. South of Bauta is San Antonio de los Baños, a pleasant country town of some 30,000 people, set in an agricultural area where citrus and tobacco are grown. The Río Ariguanabo flows through the town, going underground by a large ceiba tree near the railway station. The town has an intriguing museum: the **Museo del Humor** ① *Calle 60 y Av 45, Tue-Sun 1000-1900, CUC$2*, which has an unusual collection of cartoons, drawings and other humorous items including political satire, worth visiting if you are in the area. The **Galería Provincial Eduardo Abela** ① *Calle 58 3708 entre 37 y 39, closed Mon, CUC$1*, is an art gallery displaying the work of local artists with changing exhibitions.

Outside the town, in the middle of a grapefruit plantation off the Nuera Vereda road, is the Cuban film school, **the International Film and Television School of San Antonio de** los Baños (EICTV), www.eictv.org, approached down an avenue of magnificent palm trees. It is not, unfortunately, open to the public unless you obtain prior authorization to visit with 24 hours' notice. This is one of the best film schools in the world, founded in 1986 by the triumvirate of Colombian novelist and journalist, Gabriel García Márquez, Argentine poet and film-maker, Fernando Pirri, and Cuban film-maker Julio García Espinosa. Their aim was to create a school for the developing as well as the developed world and since its creation, thousands of students and professionals from over 50 countries have studied there. The reason most tourists come here, though, is because of the hotel **Las Yagrumas**, see Sleeping and Activities and tours, below.

El Rincón

Northeast of San Antonio de los Baños, on the way back to Havana, is El Rincón, another country town that comes alive once a year for a fiesta. The day of **San Lázaro**, 17 December, is marked by the arrival of pilgrims on their knees, making their way to a very smart, brilliantly white church. Festivities start on 16 December and last until early 18 December, with many pilgrims asking Lazarus to cure them of illnesses. Behind the church is a leper hospital, with a good reputation for curing people. The Lazarus worshipped here is a mixture of the Lazarus of Bethany, who Jesus summoned to get up and walk, and Lazarus the beggar with leprosy. Additionally, African slaves merged the image with one of their Orishas, producing Babalú Ayé.

East of Havana

Cojímar

The former seaside village, now a concrete jungle, featured in Hemingway's *The Old Man and the Sea*, is an easy excursion (15 minutes by taxi) from central Havana. He celebrated his Nobel prize here in 1954 and there is a bust of him opposite a small fort built in 1645. Unfortunately the wharf where he kept the *Pilar* was smashed by the hurricanes in 2008 and has not been repaired. The coastline (no beach) is covered in sharp rocks and is dirty because of effluent from tankers. **La Terraza**, founded in 1926, is a restaurant with a pleasant view, where Hemingway used to sit and pass time with the local fishermen upon whom he modelled his 'Old Man', see page 98.

Regla

Regla is to the east of La Habana Vieja, across the harbour. You can take a ferry from near the Customs House, opposite Calle Santa Clara in La Habana Vieja (or the Ruta 6 bus from Zulueta entre Genios y Refugio inland). It has a largely black population and a long, rich and still active cultural history of the Yoruba and *Santería* (see page 447). The main street, Martí, runs north from the landing stage up to the church on your left. In the church is the Santísima Virgen de Regla, the spirit (Orisha) who looks after sailors. Next to the church, the **Museo Municipal de Regla** ① *Martí 158 entre Facciolo y La Piedra, T7-797 6989, www.cnpc.cult.cu, Tue-Fri 0900-1800, Sat 0900-1900, Sun 0900-1300, CUC$2,* has a room with information and objects of Yoruba culture. Three blocks further on is the **Casa de la Cultura** ① *Martí 212, T7-979905,* which has very occasional cultural activities.

Guanabacoa

① *5 km to the east of Havana and reached by a road turning off the Central Highway. Take a 40-centavo bus Ruta 195 (1 hr) from Calle 23 esq J, Vedado, Ruta 5 (1 hr) from 19 de Mayo,*

Ruta 3 from Parque de la Fraternidad, or launch from Muelle Luz (at the end of Calle Santa Clara, La Habana Vieja) to Regla, then by bus direct to Guanabacoa.

Guanabacoa is a small colonial town. Sights include the old parish church which has a splendid altar; the monastery of San Francisco; the Carral theatre; the Jewish cemetery; and some attractive mansions. The **Museo Histórico de Guanabacoa** ① *Martí 108 entre Versalles y San Antonio, T7-8979117, www.cnpc.cult.cu, Tue-Sat 1000-1800, Sun 1000-1300, CUC$2, CUC$3 with guide, CUC$5 photos, if you ask, you can have a 45-min guided tour in Spanish of the town with transport,* is a former estate mansion, with slave quarters at the back of the building. The *Festival de Raíces Africanas Wemilere* is held here in the last week of November, each year dedicated to a different African country. The **Cementerio de Judíos** (Jewish Cemetery) was founded in 1906-10 and is set back behind an impressive gated entrance on the left on the road to Santa Fé. There is a monument to the victims of the Holocaust and bars of soap are buried as a symbolic gesture. Saúl Yelín (1935-1977), one of the founding members of Cuban cinema, is buried under a large flamboyant tree and you can also see the graves of the *Mártires del Partido Communista*, victims of the Machado dictatorship.

Museo Ernest Hemingway

① *San Francisco de Paula, San Miguel del Padrón, 12.5 km from the centre of Havana, T7-910809, Wed-Mon 0900-1630, closed Tue and rainy days. CUC$2 without guide, CUC$3 with guide, camera CUC$5, video CUC$25. Hemingway tours are offered by hotel tour desks for CUC$35. No toilets. Bus P7 from Parque Fraternidad and P2 from Línea y G, Vedado. The signpost is opposite the post office, leading up a short driveway.*

Hemingway fans may wish to visit **Finca La Vigía**, where he lived from 1939 to 1961, now the Ernest Hemingway Museum. Visitors are not allowed inside the plain whitewashed house, which has been lovingly preserved with all Hemingway's furniture, books and hunting collections, just as he left it. But you can walk all around the outside and look in through the windows and open doors. There is a small annex building with one room used for temporary exhibitions and from the upper floors there are fine views over Havana. The garden is beautiful and tropical, with many shady palms. Next to the swimming pool (empty) are the gravestones of Hemingway's pets, shaded by a shrub. For details of the extraordinary joint US-Cuban project to restore the house and preserve Hemingway's papers, see the website of the Finca Vigía Foundation, http://fincafoundation.org/.

Playas del Este

This is the all-encompassing name for a truly tropical string of beaches within easy reach of Havana, which arguably surpasses Varadero's brand of beach heaven. The only blot on the picture postcard landscape is the ugly concrete mass of hotels, which erupt sporadically along the coastline. Travelling east, the first stretch is the pleasant little horseshoe beach of **Bacuranao**, 15 km from Havana and popular with locals. At the far end of the beach is a villa complex with restaurant and bar. Then comes **Tarará**, famous for its hospital where Chernobyl victims have been treated, and which also has a marina and vast hotel complex, and **El Mégano**.

Santa María del Mar is the most tourist-oriented stretch of beach. A swathe of golden sand shelves gently to vivid crystal blue waters, lined with palm trees, and dotted with tiki bars, sun loungers and an array of watersports facilities; the hip spot to chill out, flirt and play. For more undistracted sun worship, continue further eastwards to the pretty, dune-backed **Boca Ciega**, a pleasant, non-touristy beach 27 km from Havana. At the weekend, cars roll in, line up and deposit their cargo of sun worshippers at the sea's edge transforming the beach into a seething mass of baking flesh. For a more authentic seaside ambience, head to the pleasant, if rather more rough-hewn (avoid the sewage canals), beach of **Guanabo**. Most facilities here are geared towards Cubans and it can get very busy during the national holiday season of July and August. The small town of Guanabo is very laid-back, there is no hassle and it also enjoys a lush, green park between Avenida 474 y 476 and a children's playground. Generally, it is cheaper than Santa María del Mar and it's where a cluster of *casas particulares* are located, although there is little to do in the evening. The quietest spot is **Brisas del Mar**, at the east end.

Tourism bureaux offer day excursions (minimum six people) for about CUC$15 per person to Playas del Este, but for small groups of people it's worth hiring a private car for the day or just taking a taxi. There is also the **HabanaBusTour**, CUC$5, a hop-on-hop-off tour bus which runs 0900-2100 from the Parque Central in Havana past the Fortaleza Cabaña, the Villa Panamericana and Alamar with further stops at Villa Bacuranao, Villa Tarará, Villa Mégano, Hotel Tropicoco, Hotel Atlántico and Hotel Arenal. Cheap packages and all-inclusive holidays can be booked here from Canada and Europe, which can be good if you want to combine a beach holiday with excursions to Havana. However, most people report getting fed up after a few days of sitting on the beach here and the food is monotonous, so if you are the sort of person who likes to get out and about, avoid the all-inclusive deals. ▶▶ *For details of watersports, see Activities and tours, page 137.*

Vía Blanca

The main road along the coast towards Matanzas and Varadero is called the **Vía Blanca**. There are some scenic parts, but you also drive through quite a lot of industry, such as the rum and cardboard factories at **Santa Cruz del Norte**, a thermal electricity station and many smelly oil wells. The **Hershey Railway** runs inland from Havana, more or less parallel to the Vía Blanca, and is an interesting way to get to Matanzas. This electric line was built by the Hershey chocolate family in 1917 to service their sugar mill, at what became the Central Camilo Cienfuegos after the Revolution, now dismantled with the decline of the sugar industry. From Santa Cruz del Norte, you can drive inland via the former Central Camilo Cienfuegos to **Jaruco**, and 6 km to the west, the **Parque Escaleras de Jaruco**. The *escaleras*, or stairs, are geological formations in the limestone and there are caves, forests and other rocks to see, set in a very picturesque landscape. There is a hotel in the park, but it is for Cubans only. The restaurant at the entrance is only open at weekends for lunch, but there is a nice coastal view from the terrace.

Jibacoa

Continuing east from Santa Cruz del Norte, some 60 km east of Havana is Jibacoa beach, which is good for snorkelling as the reefs are close to the beach and it is also a nice area for walking. It is pretty, with hills coming down to the sea, and is a pleasant place to go for a weekend away from Havana. You can be served freshly caught lobster for lunch on the beach, by a man who spreads a white tablecloth on a table laid especially for you. Some 14 km east of Jibacoa is the **Puerto Escondido marina**, at Vía Blanca Km 80, which has boat trips, fishing, snorkelling, scuba-diving and a cafetería.

The south coast

The southern coast is mostly swamp and wetlands, but there is access by sea to the Isla de la Juventud. There is no coastal road, as along the north coast, which means that although there are several nice beaches within striking distance of Havana, they are difficult to get to and beach hopping is tricky. The easiest to get to from Havana is probably **Playa Majana**, in the west of the province, access to which is off the Carretera Central, the old road to Pinar del Río. From here, northwards is the **Bahía de Mariel**, is the island's narrowest point. The main town on the south coast is **Batabanó**, 51 km from Havana. There has been a settlement here since the 16th century, but most travellers are only passing through on their way to **Surgidero de Batabanó**, to catch the ferry to Isla de la Juventud. The latter is a ramshackle fishing town of wooden houses. There are several small restaurants selling fried fish, which makes a change from fried chicken, but they are poor quality and not worth making a detour for. There is only peso accommodation, which may not accept foreigners. The beach, 2 km east of the port, is dirty and muddy with the outflow from several rivers and there are mangroves.

⦿ Around Havana listings

For Sleeping and Eating price codes and other relevant information, see Essentials pages 37-43.

⦾ Sleeping

Playa Baracoa and El Salado *p131*
Hotels
C Villa Cocomar, Carretera Panamericana Km 23.5, Caimito, T47-378293. Small, single-storey hotel on the beach with a good reef for snorkelling and diving, fridge, a/c, TV, clean towels daily, in pretty setting, lots of coconut palms, pool, reasonably priced restaurant, tours offered, nightclub on Fri and Sat.

San Antonio de los Baños *p131*
Hotels
C Las Yagrumas, Calle 40 y Final Autopista, T7-335238, www.islazul.cu. Popular with tour parties, convenient for the airport, on the banks of the Río Ariguanabo 5 km outside the town, 22 km from Havana and 19 km from the airport, in a lovely setting. It is a low-key hotel in a 2-storey building, the rooms overlooking the river are quieter than those looking over the pool, which can be full of Cubans partying at weekends. The place is filthy afterwards and needs a lot of cleaning. You can take boat trips on the river, CUC$2 per hr, and there is tennis and an indoor games room, see Activities and tours, below.

Cojímar *p132*
Casas particulares
D-E Casa Ferrero, E entre 29 y 30, T7-765 0876. Alejandro Ferrero offers a large house with lots of space for guests including 2 bedrooms, bathroom, a living and dining room and a large terrace.
D-E Villa Estrella, Martí 460 entre 32 y 33, T7-652975, addyany64@yahoo.es. Independent, 2 rooms, a/c, 2 bathrooms, fridge, central heating, kitchen, small swimming pool.
D-E Yohana Ferra Veloso, 30 96 entre E y F, T7-933907. 2 rooms, 2 bathrooms, a/c, hot water, kitchen and living room for guests use only, interior garden.

Playas del Este *p133*
Hotels
LL-AL Villa Los Pinos, Av de las Terrazas 21 entre 4 y 5, Santa María del Mar, T7-797 1361, www.gran-caribe.com. 2- and 3-bedroomed houses, most with pools or near the beach, grill restaurant, café and pizzeria, popular with Italians, Spanish and French in that order, lots of repeat guests, comfortable, private, good for entertaining friends or for families, very flexible, friendly management, multilingual staff.
AL Club Atlántico, Av Las Terrazas entre 11 y 12, Santa María del Mar, T7-797 1085. 92 rooms, all-inclusive with all mod cons and it's right on the beach. Friendly service, food average in buffet but the à la carte restaurants

and beach barbecue that you have to book are better. Free shuttle bus 3 times a day to Havana, a taxi costs CUC$18-25 depending on where you go.

A-D Aparthotel Las Terrazas, Av de las Terrazas entre 10 y Rotonda, Santa María del Mar, T7-797 1315, www.islazul.cu. 62, 1-3 bedroomed apartments, a/c, each with extremely well-equipped cooking facilities (if only there was such variety of food in Cuba to merit), in a rather unattractive block opposite the beach, 2-tier swimming pool, restaurant, bar, tourist bureau, car rental, great location but rather run down. Not the best of what's on offer around here but service with a smile which can't be said for everyone in these parts.

B Aparthotel Atlántico, Av Las Terrazas entre 11 y 12, Santa María del Mar, T7-971494, www.islazul.cu. This has 62 apartments, 93 rooms, a restaurant, bar, tennis and pool. Also car hire, currency exchange and buró de turismo for excursions. The HabanaBusTour stops outside, making it convenient for getting into the city.

B Hotel Tropicoco, Av Sur y Las Terrazas, Santa María del Mar, T7-797 1371, recepcion@htropicoco.nor.tur.cu. The architecture here is ugly, with lots of concrete and small windows, the rooms are basic but adequate with sea view but no balconies. It has a pool, restaurant, and 3 bars and is an all-inclusive. It is conveniently placed opposite the beach where most tourists are deposited on day trips from Havana so if you need drinks or the toilet, best stop here.

D Miramar, Av 7B 47614, entre 476 y 478, Guanabo, T7-796 2507. A small, pleasant hotel where the 3rd-floor rooms are the best in terms of quality and the view; some rooms can be joined up for family reasons. All have TV, fridge, clock and safety box. The pool is clean. Restaurant daily 0730-2300, bar daily 1000-2200 and 24-hr reception.

Casas particulares

Prices here are high, starting at CUC$30 per night for a double room with many at a lot more than that if they are on the beach or very close to the water.

B-C Nancy Pujol Av 1 50019 entre 500 y 504, Guanabo, T7-796 3062. Right on the waterfront, this house has 2 bedrooms but is only rented to 1 couple or 2 couples travelling together as the bathroom is shared. You also get your own kitchen and living/dining room, but if you don't want to cook Nancy will provide meals at the usual rates. Lovely location only steps from the sand, pleasant garden at the edge of the sea.

C Iriana Suárez y Rosa Machado, Av 1 50017 entre 500 y 504, Guanabo, T7-796 3959. Next door to Nancy and also on the waterfront, with a lawn going down to the seawall, Iriana and Rosa rent a room upstairs with independent access, while they live downstairs. Floor-to-ceiling windows in the living area with kitchen/bar lead out onto balcony overlooking the garden and the sea with sun loungers. Minimum stay 7 days in Jan-Feb.

D Alberto y Neisa, 500 5 D 08 entre 5 y 7, www.geocities.com/paseovedado/guanabo.html. 2 rooms, 1 in the house with own entrance, the other in a cottage in the back yard, each with a/c, fridge. Short walk to beach.

Jibacoa *p134*
Hotels

B SuperClubs Breezes Jibacoa, Playa Arrojo Bermejo, Vía Blanca Km 60, T47-295122, www.superclubscuba.com. Price per person per night depending on season and view, all-inclusive, no children under 16, 250 rooms and suites in 2-storey buildings, attractive setting with hilly backdrop and curved, sandy bay, comfortable, good bathrooms, nice beds, buffet, Cuban or Italian restaurants, vegetarian options, tennis, basketball, bicycles, hiking, snorkelling, diving, catamaran, sunfish, kayaks, gym, windsurfing, no motorized watersports to protect reef, excursions available, indoor games room, pool, piano bar, nightclub, beach bar, wheelchair accessible, 2 rooms for disabled guests, evening entertainment disappointing, but around the headland is a Cuban camping resort where they know how to party during the summer holidays.

E Campismo El Abra, further along rough track, T47-295120. Essential to book through

Cubamar in Havana, people who arrive without a reservation are turned away. 87, 2- to 3-bed cabins with fan or a/c, small rooms, very basic, hot, small shower, organized activities including bicycles, small horses, badminton, *pelota*, bar, restaurant and cafeteria, post office and *cambio*, computer lab, public phones, enormous but murky pool, small, rocky beach, best to walk east or west, extensive grounds, lots of greenery and mosquitoes. This resort does accept foreigners, but about 70% of guests are Cuban. Parking and facilities for campervans.
E Campismo Los Cocos, T47-295231. About the best campismo in the country, cabins of good quality, facilities for the disabled, swimming pool, children's pool, public phones, computer suite, games room, TV room, lots of activities such as dancing, bikes, horses, bar, restaurant and cafeteria.

❶ Eating

Cojímar *p132*
¶¶¶ **La Terraza**, Real 161 esq Candelaria, T7-939486, terrazas@cbcan.cyt.cu. Daily 1200-2300. Overpriced seafood meals, terrible fish, paella is the house speciality. Photographs of Hemingway cover the walls. Tourist trap for tour parties.

Playas del Este *p133*
Many reasonably priced *paladares* in Guanabo and elsewhere. There are cafés, bakeries, restaurants and *heladerías* on Av 5 entre 478 y 480 in Guanabo, including, **La Hatuey**, a chilled, dark, wooden bar, and **La Cocinita**, which has a pool table, on Av 5 esq 480 and **El Piccolo**, quite a good Italian. There's also a great little bakery just past the *Cadeca*.
¶¶ **Maeda**, Quebec 115 entre 476 y 478, Guanabo, T7-962615. Daily 1200-2400. This is a *paladar* in a beautiful setting on hillside with outside seating under flower-filled terracing. There is also seating in an a/c room. International and Cuban food is served as well as a *parillada* along with wines and a selection of puddings. They also have a wood-fired oven

for baking. Run by the welcoming Miguel. Reservations advised for the evenings as it's a popular spot for visiting *Habaneros*.
¶ **Pizza Al Mare**, Av 5 y 482, Guanabo. A huge variety of pizzas ranging from CUC$1.50-4, sold by the slice.

❶ Bars

Playas del Este *p133*
There are a/c bars indoors and open air bars on the beach at all the hotels, offering the usual range of Cuban cocktails or a cold beer.

❸ Entertainment

Playas del Este *p133*
There are several cabarets and night clubs on Av 5 in Guanabo, also **Guanabo Club** 468 entre 13 y 15, and **El Tucán** at the Hotel Bacuranao.

▲ Activities and tours

Playas del Este *p133*
At Playas del Este, the hotels provide some non-motorized watersports.
Marina Tarará, run by Marinas Puertosol, Vía Blanca Km 19, Tarará, Playas del Este, T7-971462, F7-971313, VHF77. Moorings for 50 boats, VHF communications and provisioning, yacht charters, deep sea fishing (CUC$250-450 per day depending on type of boat) and scuba-diving, all of which can be arranged through the hotel tour desks. Diving is surprisingly good here, considering its proximity to the capital city. The seabed drops off in steps and there are wrecks to explore as well as coral gardens and reef fish.
Mi Cayito Recreation Centre, Av de las Terrazas, Laguna Itabo, Santa María, near Boca Ciega, T7-971339. Daily 1000-1800. Equipment for hire includes a pedal boat (CUC$1 per person per hr) with 4 seats, water skiing in the lake, CUC$10 for 15 mins and kayak hire. Showers and changing rooms

available. The **Restaurant El Pelícano** is on site but set back from the lake.

Recreación Náutica, beach at the end of Av 474, Playas del Este. Daily 1000-1800. Run by a bunch of friendly guys. Pedalos, CUC$7.50 per hr, catamaran CUC$15 per hr with sailor, 2½-hr trip with snorkelling, CUC$15 per person. Sun lounger CUC$2 per day, umbrella CUC$2 per day. Bar service and food served on the beach.

San Antonio de los Baños p131

At **Hotel Las Yagrumas**, see Sleeping above, you can get a day pass to use the facilities. Use of the pool for day visitors is CUC$3 Mon-Fri, or CUC$5 at weekends when it it very busy with Cuban families. 2 people can get a day pass for CUC$15 to use the facilities and have lunch of a half chicken, vegetables and 8 beers. The tennis courts at the hotel are reasonable; rackets and balls are supposed to be available but don't rely on it, there is a gym and massage is offered, although not really worth the charge.

O Shopping

Playas del Este p133

There is a **farmers' market** in Guanabo selling fresh fruit and vegetables 6 days a week and a supermarket for bread and tinned goods. The **Centro Comercial de Guanabo** shopping centre, behind Recreación Náutica has a supermarket.

Transport

Around Havana p131
Bus

For the **Playas del Este**, the 400 bus (40 centavos) from Egido near the Estación Central de Trenes can get you to **Bacuranao**, **Santa María** and **Guanabo**. The 405 and the 464 also leave from **Guanabacoa**. The easiest, most comfortable, safest and quickest way to get out to the beach is to take the HabanaBusTour T3, which leaves every 35 mins from Parque Central 0900-2100, CUC$5.

Cycling

Cycling is a good way to get to the **Playas del Este**. Use the *ciclobus* from Parque El Curita, Aguila y Dragones, Centro, via the tunnel under Havana Bay, or the 20-centavo ferry to **Regla** from near the Aduanas building, and cycle through Regla and **Guanabacoa**. Be careful of the very poor road surfaces and frequent roadworks.

Taxi

The standard taxi price from Havana to the **Playas del Este** is CUC$20-25 (fix the price before you set off or insist on the meter being used); opposite Hotel Miramar in Guanabo is a taxi service, 476 esq 7B, open 24 hrs, T7-796 6666, T7-796 3939.

O Directory

Around Havana p131
Banks

Banco Popular de Ahorro, Guanabo, Playas del Este, open Mon, Thu, Fri 0830-1530. Wed 0830-1900. Visa and MasterCard accepted. **Cadeca**, Av 5 entre 476 y 478, Guanabo, Playas del Este, daily 0800-1300, 1400-1800. Visa and MasterCard accepted.

Medical services

All hotels have a doctor on permanent duty, CUC$25 per consultation. **Clínica Internacional Santa María del Mar (Clínica del Sol)**, Av de las Terrazas 36, Santa María del Mar, T7-796 1819, ext 102, www.servimed cuba.com, open 24 hrs all year. Includes all types of medical service from consultation to ambulance service to dentistry. A consultation between 0800-1600 is CUC$25, between 1601 and 0759, CUC$30. It also sells nappies, sanitary towels and medicines.

Post

At Playas del Este, the post office is on Av Las Terrazas entre 10 y 11, Santa María del Mar, Playas del Este. Here you will also find a **Telecorreos** and **Transtur** car hire.

Contents

Footprint features

At a glance

◯ **Getting around** On foot, by
bicycle, hired car, taxi and Víazul
long-distance bus.

◯ **Time required** 2 days to
2 weeks.

Pinar del Río

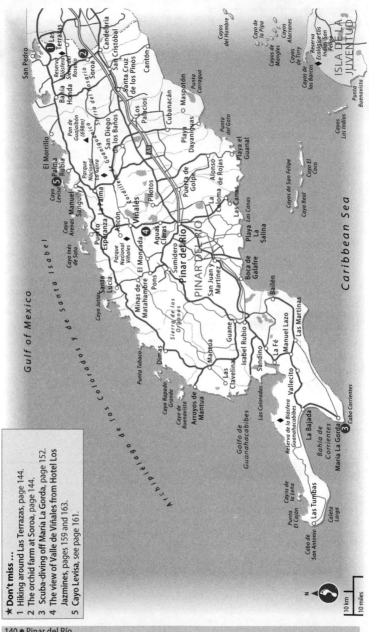

★ **Don't miss ...**
1 Hiking around Las Terrazas, page 144.
2 The orchid farm at Soroa, page 144.
3 Scuba-diving off María La Gorda, page 152.
4 The view of Valle de Viñales from Hotel Los Jazmines, pages 159 and 163.
5 Cayo Levisa, see page 161.

Gulf of Mexico

Caribbean Sea

ISLA DE LA JUVENTUD

The west of Cuba is blessed with an exotic landscape of limestone mogotes, caves and mountains, forested nature reserves and tobacco plantations. This is where you will find the world's best dark tobacco, which is hand-processed into the finest cigars. There is world-class scuba-diving, and there are good beaches and wetlands for migrant water fowl. The Sierra del Rosario contains the Biosphere Reserve at Las Terrazas, a must for anyone with an interest in ecology and tropical forests, as well as the orchidarium at Soroa.

The capital of the province and the major city west of Havana, Pinar del Río can be a good base for excursions as transport starts from here, while María La Gorda is a diver's dream, low key, laid back and friendly. The small town of Viñales attracts thousands of visitors, both independent and package tourists. Its position beside the mogotes provides spectacular views and good walking opportunities. Its beauty has been internationally recognized and the Viñales Valley has been declared a UNESCO World Cultural Landscape.

Ins and outs

Getting there

Pinar del Río is the main transport hub for the area. **Air** It has a domestic airport, the only one in the west, but flights are few and far between. **Rail** There is a railway line between Havana and Pinar del Río, with a slow and unreliable service. The line continues on to Guane for local services. **Road** There are daily **Víazul buses** to the city, continuing on to Viñales. Local services to smaller towns fan out from Pinar del Río. A dual-carriage highway has been completed almost as far as Pinar del Río. It takes two hours to get to Pinar del Río on the *autopista*, see Havana to Pinar del Río, below. Some slip roads are unsurfaced, just mud and stones. **Car hire** is available in Pinar del Río and Viñales for independent excursions. There are also plenty of tours to caves, cigar factories, tobacco farms and other local attractions.

Tourist information

Tour agencies such as **Cubatur**, **Cubanacán** and **Havanatur** operate as tourist information offices, although their main purpose is to sell tours. They can help with hotel reservations, tickets and transfers.

Best time to visit

The weather is wettest from September to November, but you can get rain in the hills at any time of year, usually in the afternoon. Pinar del Río holds its carnival in July and Viñales has one in March.

Land and environment

The western end of the island is dominated by one of the island's three main mountain ranges, the **Cordillera de Guaniguanico**, which is divided into the **Sierra del Rosario** in the east (rising to the **Pan de Guajaibón**, its highest point at 699 m) and the **Sierra de los Organos** in the west, which form a curious Chinese-looking landscape with steep-sided limestone hills and flat, fertile valleys. A fault line creates a sharp boundary between these mountains and a wide expanse of rolling farmland in the southern part of the province, centred on the pleasant but unspectacular provincial capital of Pinar del Río. The province contains three major nature reserves: a 260-sq-km biosphere reserve in the Sierra del Rosario, a 132-sq-km national monument in the Sierra de los Organos around Viñales, and a 1175-sq-km biosphere reserve in the Guanahacabibes peninsula at the western tip.

Pinar del Río grows about 70% of Cuba's tobacco crop and almost every agricultural area is dotted with *vegas*, curious tent-shaped windowless structures made of palm thatch, which are used for drying tobacco leaves, a process that takes at least 45 days (easy to enter and take photographs). The fields are ploughed, mostly with oxen, in September and October. The crop is transplanted into the fields in November, with the leaves picked over the following months. The cigar factory in Pinar del Río has regular tours and in the harvest season it is possible in most villages to visit an *escogida de tabaco*, where the best leaves are selected for further processing. The flat lands of San Juan y Martínez are where the very best tobacco is grown. See page 150.

Sierra del Rosario

→ *Colour map1, B4.*

Heading west from Havana the land is initially low-lying and unimpressive. Soon, however, green mountains come into view, stirring anticipation of exploration and discovery. The Sierra has a 260-sq-km biosphere reserve, giving recognition to its ecological diversity and richness. Birdwatching is rich and rewarding around Las Terrazas, the main centre for nature tourism. Lovers of flora will appreciate the orchidarium at Soroa and the many and varied plants to be found by anyone who has hiked up and down the hills. ►► *For listings, see pages 145-146.*

Ins and outs

Getting there The easiest way of getting to Soroa is to book yourself on an organized **tour** from Havana. A day trip (10 hours) to Las Terrazas, with walking, river bathing and a ghastly lunch is around CUC$50 at any tour agency. Other trips include overnight stays at the hotels and some take in Soroa as well. Alternatively, hire a **car** and take your time, but rooms at **Hotel Moka** need to be booked in advance. Public transport is negligible. Long-distance **buses** go along the *autopista* but not to Las Terrazas or other sites of interest. **Taxis** are expensive and can only be arranged in Havana, Pinar del Río or Viñales.

Best time to visit The driest time is from January to April, when it is easiest to hike in the mountains. The orchids at Soroa are good then too. The wet season begins around May, while storms can be expected between September and November.

Havana to Pinar del Río

The *autopista* journey from Havana to Pinar del Río is a rather surreal experience, with modern motorway junctions but virtually no traffic using them except horse-drawn buses running to nearby villages. Watch out for dogs sleeping peacefully in the fast lane or bicycles heading towards you in the wrong lane. Also take care when driving under bridges as people wait there for lifts and sometimes step out into the road to stop traffic, resulting in accidents. Vultures can be seen circling overhead. The *autopista* passes through flat or gently rolling countryside, with large stretches of sugar cane, tobacco fields and some rice fields, with scattered Royal palms and distant views of the Cordillera de Guaniguanico. There are also large uncultivated areas used as rough pasture, with hump-backed zebu and other cattle, as well as white cattle egrets which help rid them of parasites. You can see traditional houses built of palm planks, thatched with palm leaves, and plenty of *vegas*.

An alternative route is to leave the *autopista* at **Candelaria** or **Santa Cruz de los Pinos** for the Carretera Central, quite a good road, which adds only 20 minutes to the journey. It passes through more intensively farmed countryside, with citrus and other fruit trees. Villages straggle along the road, with colonnaded single-storey traditional houses and newer post-Revolution concrete block structures.

Las Terrazas

On the *autopista*, 51 km west of Havana, the Sierra del Rosario appears on the right and a roadside billboard announces the turning to Las Terrazas/Moka, 4 km north of the *autopista*. However, after that there is little signposting through a confusing series of side roads; you will have to ask the way. There is a barrier at the entrance to the **Biosphere Reserve** ① *admission CUC$7*, which covers 260 sq km of the eastern Sierra del Rosario. Admission to the reserve includes a horrible lunch, unless you have a reservation at the hotel. Las Terrazas was built in 1971 as a forestry and soil conservation station, with nearby slopes terraced to prevent erosion. It is a pleasant settlement of white-painted houses and a long apartment block overlooking the lake of San Juan, which now houses an ecological research centre. In Las Terrazas there is a *paladar*, as well as craft workshops, a gym, a cinema and a museum which sometimes holds *canturías* or folk music sessions. Nearby there are waterfalls where you can picnic.

Following the death in a car accident of the popular singer, Polo Montañez in 2002, his house was opened as a museum, run by his brother. In nearby San Cristóbal, a clay statue of the singer has been put on display. Once a woodcutter, he rose to fame as a singer/songwriter with many hits in the three years before his death, touring Latin America and Europe.

Hiking around Las Terrazas

The hills behind the hotel rise to the **Loma del Salón** (564 m). There are several easy hiking trails: to the partly restored 19th-century **Buenavista** coffee plantation (restaurant has *pollo brujo*, cheaper for hotel guests than for others); 3 km along the San Juan River to the old **La Victoria** coffee plantation and sulphur springs; 4 km along **La Serafina** path to the ruins of the 19th-century **Santa Serafina** coffee plantation, excellent for seeing birds like the Cuban trogon, the solitaire, woodpeckers and the Cuban tody; 8 km along the Cañada del Infierno valley to the **San Pedro** and **Santa Catalina** coffee plantations. There are also more demanding whole-day hikes: a day hiking with a professional ecologist as guide is CUC$33-41 for one person, falling to CUC$14-18 per person with six people. Other activities include riding, mountain bikes, rowing on the lake and fishing. There is also a zip line, **Canopy Las Terrazas**, which crosses the lake into the trees, CUC$25.

Soroa

If travelling by car, you can make a detour to Soroa, a spa and resort in the Sierra del Rosario, 81 km southwest of the capital, either by continuing 18 km west then southeast from Moka through the Sierra del Rosario, or directly from the *autopista*, driving northwest from Candelaria. As you drive into the area from the south, a sign on the right indicates the **Mirador de Venus** and **Baños Romanos**. Past the baths is the **Bar Edén** (open till 1800), where you can park before walking up to the **mirador** ① *25 mins, free on foot, CUC$3 on a horse*. From the top you get fine views of the southern plains, the forest-covered Sierra and Soroa itself. There are lots of birds, butterflies, dragonflies and lizards around the path; many flowers in season and birdwatching is very popular here.

Further north is a **Jardín Botánico Orchidarium** ① *T48-522558, guided tours daily 0830-1140, 1340-1555, CUC$3, birdwatching, hiking and riding CUC$3 per hr*, with over 700 species of which 250 are native to Cuba, as well as ferns and begonias (check if the orchids are in bloom before visiting). Alberto, at the desk, speaks good English and some French and there is also a restaurant, **Castillo de las Nubes** (1200-1900). There is an excursion to **El Brujito**, a village once owned by French landlords, where the third and fourth generations of slaves live. Across the road from the Orchidarium is a **waterfall** ① *250 m along a paved path, CUC$2*, worth a visit if you are in the area. You can do a day trip from Havana or stay overnight.

San Diego de los Baños

Nearer Pinar del Río, another detour north off the Carretera Central at Entronque de San Diego, also in fine scenery, is to the spa of San Diego de los Baños and the Parque Nacional La Güira. In the wet season a nearby irrigation lake, the **Embalse La Juventud**, often floods and then this diversion becomes compulsory. San Diego de los Baños is a pretty little village, with colonnaded houses and a tree-lined square, right on the southern edge of the Sierra del Rosario. Its mineral waters were discovered in the 17th century and public thermal baths were opened in 1951 but the buildings are closed and the place empty, although you can still get a massage. The area was badly hit by Hurricane Ike in 2008 and has not completely recovered yet.

Parque Nacional La Güira

A few kilometres west of San Diego, an impressive neo-Gothic gateway leads to the Parque Nacional La Güira. Inside, there are extensive neglected 19th-century gardens, pools and statues, with the ruins of a Gothic mansion. There is a small bar near the entrance. Behind, the road winds up through the hills to an army recreation centre; behind this there is an enormous, cheap and rather run-down restaurant. The **Cueva de las Portales** just north of here was Che Guevara's HQ during the Cuban missile crisis and there is a small exhibition of military and personal relics. The National Park covers an area of 22,000 ha and protects a number of endemic species.

Maspotón

To reach Maspotón, near **Alonso Rojas** in the mangrove wetlands close to the south coast, leave the *autopista* at Los Palacios and drive south for 25 km. This is an interesting wildlife area close to the bird migration route from North to South America, but is run as a 134-sq-km hunting resort, where migratory ducks, long-tail and white-wing doves, quail, guinea fowl and pheasant can all be shot, and there is also freshwater fishing.

◉ Sierra del Rosario listings

For Sleeping and Eating price codes and other relevant information, see Essentials pages 37-43.

● Sleeping

Las Terrazas *p143*
Hotels
A Hotel Moka, Km 51 Autopista a Pinar del Río, T/F48-578600, www.hotelmoka-lasterrazas.com. Run in cooperation with the Cuban Academy of Sciences as an ecotourism centre, breakfast and dinner packages available, transfers from Havana, a/c, satellite TV. Above the village is this 26-room hotel complex, beautifully designed and laid out in Spanish colonial style with tiled roofs. Staff are friendly and knowledgeable, gardens behind the hillside site have a tennis court and a pleasant pool where you can have food and drinks. Vegetarian restaurant just below the hotel. This is an unusual opportunity to stay in a nature reserve with tropical evergreen forests, 850 plant species, 82 bird species, an endemic water lizard, the world's 2nd smallest frog and world-class experts on tap. Even the hotel receptionist has an ecology PhD. For those wanting more adventure there is a zip line across the lake into the trees.

Casas particulares

D-E Villa Juanita, Las Pastora 601, Cayajabos, Artemisa, 3 km from las Terrazas. 2 rooms, small kitchenette, meals available, good food, very welcoming *casa particular*, no English, but expressive, slow Spanish spoken.

Soroa *p144*
Hotels

A-B Villa Soroa, T48-523534, 49 cabins and 10 self-catering houses, a/c, phone, radio, some have VCR and private pool, restaurant El Centro (quite good), disco, bar, Olympic-sized swimming pool, bike rental, riding nearby and handicrafts and dollar shop. A peaceful place. The hotel runs 1-day, 17-km, gently paced hikes around the main sights of the area with picnic.

Casas particulares

There are over 12 casas now in Soroa.
D Ana Lidia, on the road up to **Villa Soroa**, about 1 km from the autopista, T05-228 9372. Ana Lidia works at the orchid garden and her own garden is a mini botanical garden. She has 2 rooms each with double and single bed, rocking chairs on shady terrace, meals available, served by husband, Jorge Luis. A good casa, experienced hosts.
D Casa Azul, 300 m outside Soroa next to a primary school. 1 big room, balcony overlooking a huge garden, fruit trees, coffee bushes and mountains, free parking, meals available, daughter speaks some English.
D-E Hospedaje Estudio de Arte, Km 8.5, past **Villa Soroa**, next to **Casa Azul**, infosoroa@hvs.co.cu. Jesús is an artist and has a contract with UNEAC; the hotel organizes tours to his Estudio de Arte in the house, where he sells his paintings. His wife, Aliuska, runs the house, 1 room, large and decorated with Jesús' art, excellent *comida criolla*, food recommended by Cubans.

San Diego de los Baños *p145*
Hotels

C Hotel Mirador, on Calle 23 Final, T48-778338, carpeta@mirador.sandiego.co.cu. 3 star, run down, massage, pool, car rental, rooms have a/c, phone, satellite TV.

Casas particulares

D-E Carmen Suárez González, Calle 34 2310 entre 23 y 33. 1 room, 3 fans, no a/c, fridge, garage CUC$1, colonial architecture with tiled roof, huge garden, building a new room, meals available.
D-E Villa Julio y Cary (Caridad Gutiérrez y Julio Gil), Calle 29 4009 entre 40 y 42, opposite the *balneario*, T48-548037. 1 room, with private bathroom, a/c, fridge, meals and drinks available, garage CUC$1, porch overlooks garden, near river where locals swim, nice retired people.

⊘ Eating

Havana to Pinar del Río *p143*
There are *paladares* in some villages, including a rooftop one in Candelaria:
Fusilazo, 3 blocks south of the Carretera Central and 500 m east of the junction with the road for Soroa.

Soroa *p144*
Ranchón Criollo, a few hundred metres from the autopista on the left. Open 0900-2300. Food prices in pesos cubanos, drinks in CUC$. Better than the state restaurant right by the autopista for lunch or dinner.

San Diego de los Baños *p145*
Paladar Sorpresa opposite *Libertad*, the hotel for Cubans, west of the plaza.

Pinar del Río

→ *Colour map 1, B3.*

The capital of Pinar del Río province gives a good taste of provincial Cuba. It is a lively city and there is always something going on but it is not particularly attractive. The centre consists of single-storey neoclassical houses with columns, some with other interesting architectural detail. Under the porches, there is a thriving trade in one-person businesses, from selling snacks to repairing cigarette lighters. Horse-drawn vehicles vie for space alongside bicycles and battered old cars on the roads, while the pavements are full of people jostling and weaving in and out of the pillars and other obstacles.
▸▸ For listings, see pages 153-158.

Pinar del Río

Sleeping
José Antonio Mesa cp **5**
Pinar del Río **11**
Traveller's Rest cp **8**
Villa Lolo cp **10**
Vueltabajo **1**

Eating
Café Pinar **6**

Coppelia **1**
Doña Neli **3**
El Aguila de Oro **5**
El Marino **8**
El Mesón **9**
La Taberna **4**
Terrazina **7**

Entertainment
Bar La Esquinita **1**
Casa del Joven Creador **6**
Casa de la Cultura **2**
Casa de la Música **3**
Palacio de los
  Matrimonios **5**
Teatro José Jacinto
  Milanés **4**

Ins and outs

Getting there There is an **airstrip** but services are not well developed. There is a **train** from Havana, which is cheap but has the disadvantage of being very slow with lots of stops and is very dark, so there is a risk of theft. You have to hang on to your bags all the time and take particular care of your pockets in the tunnels. The **bus station** is reasonably central and all buses use the same terminal. **Víazul** air-conditioned buses come from Havana on a route that continues to Viñales. On arrival in Pinar del Río you must expect to be hassled by crowds at the bus or train stations, who are touting for your business (see Sleeping, page 153). Even if you come in by car they will be waiting for you at the road junctions. Young men on bicycles are a particular hazard and very persistent. Always say you have a reservation. ⮞ *See also Transport, page 157.*

Getting around The town is one of several that have changed street names but continue to use the old ones as well as the new official names. It can be confusing when names on the map conflict with what people really call the streets, for example 20 de Mayo is now Primero de Mayo, Vélez Caviedes is also Ormani Arenado, while Virtudes is also Ceferino Fernández. Pinar del Río is not large and it is easy to **walk** around the centre and to most of the places of interest, such as the rum and tobacco factories. For a short excursion out of the town, it is easy enough to get a **bus** to Viñales, but public transport is very limited to towns in other directions. **Car hire** is the most convenient way of getting about, or hire a taxi.

Best time to visit Carnival is in July but it is not on the scale of Santiago's or Havana's. At any time of year you can find something going on in and around the city. Expect storms between September and November, although heavy showers can happen at any time, usually in the afternoon. This area was badly hit by the hurricanes in 2008.

Sights

The main shopping street and centre of activities is José Martí, which runs west-east through the town. At the west end is the **Centro de Artes Visuales** ① *Martí, opposite Parque Independencia, T48-752758, Mon-Fri 1000-1700, Sat 0800-1200, CUC$1.* Walk along José Martí to the east to a renovated building opposite the Wedding Palace: the **Palacio de Computación** ① *Martí esq González Coro, Mon-Sat 0800-2100, theatre, cafeteria and classrooms for teaching computer skills,* which was inaugurated by Fidel Castro in January 2001. It is very photogenic if taken from Parque de la Independencia. The **Casa de la Cultura Tito Junco** ① *Martí esq Rafael Morales, Mon-Sat 0800-1800,* is in a huge colonial house and includes an art gallery, a hall for parties and seven classrooms for teaching dancing, painting, singing, etc. There are evening activities according to scheduled programmes. The old **Globo** hotel, right in the centre near the corner of José Martí and Isabel Rubio, is only for Cubans, but it has a beautiful tiled staircase worth a peep. The **Museo Provincial de Historia** ① *Martí 58 entre Isabel Rubio y Colón, T48-754300, Mon-Sat 0800-1700, CUC$1,* details the history of the town and displays objects from the wars of independence. On the same side of the street is the **Teatro José Jacinto Milanés** ① *Martí esq Colón.* Built in 1883, this is one of the most beautiful theatres in the country. Further along Martí is the **Museo de Ciencias Naturales Tranquilino Sandalio de Noda** ① *José Martí 202 esq Av Comandante Pinares, T48-753087, Mon-Sat 0800-1700, CUC$1,* with geological and natural history, not large, not much explanation, not much on typical Cuban animals. The great thing, however, is the eclectic building, formerly the Palacio Guasch, which is the most ornate in the region, with Gothic towers, spires and all sorts of twiddly bits.

There is a **cigar factory, Fábrica de Tabaco Francisco Donatién** ① *Maceo 157 y A Tarafa, T48-723424/773069, Mon-Sat 0800-1700, CUC$5 for a short visit, no photos or videos allowed*, one of the town's main tourist attractions. It reputedly makes the best cigars in Cuba and even when the factory is shut you can still buy the very finest cigars in the town. Avoid the youngsters selling cigars outside. Workers in the factory will also try and sell you cigars. Buy from the shop opposite, **Casa del Habano**, and you'll get the genuine article, even if it is pricey. Remember there is a limit on the number of cigars you can take out of the country without a receipt so any illegally bought cigars should be smoked in Cuba. Also worth a visit, if you're interested, is the **rum factory, Fábrica de Guayabita** ① *Isabel Rubio 189 entre Ceferino Fernández y Frank País, Mon-Sat 0800-1700, CUC$2, tour and stop at the tasting room*, which makes a special rum flavoured with miniature wild guavas, *Guayabita del Pinar*, which comes in either dry or sweet varieties. The bottles on sale are cheaper than those in the shops. Between the two is the pretty cream-coloured cathedral of **San Rosendo** ① *Maceo 2 Este esq Gerardo Medina*.

Around Pinar del Río

South to the coast

The nearest beach, 25 km to the south of Pinar del Río, is **Las Canas**, near **La Coloma**. From La Coloma you can take a boat trip to the **Cayos de San Felipe**. The Cays are unspoilt and fabulous. ➤ *See Activities and tours, page 156.*

The Carretera Central continues west from Pinar del Río through pleasant farming country with villages strung along the road, sugar and tobacco fields, citrus trees and pasture. There are distant views of the mountains to the north and clearly marked side roads lead south to the fishing town of **Boca de Galafre** and the beach for Cubans at **Bailén**, where there is a sprawling camping resort stretching 2 km along the sand, with small A-frame cabins on the beach and concrete houses with self-catering facilities behind, T48-496145. It is very popular with Cubans in the summer months. Cubans are allowed here April to September for a very basic beach holiday. The beach is spoilt by the run-off from the Río Cuyaguateje, which makes the water muddy and there is no reef to snorkel on. It is cleared at the beginning of April but then left to get dirty, muddy and smelly. Further east, away from the river, the beach is nicer, but it is all rather rundown.

There is a bus from Pinar del Río in the morning, returning in the afternoon, but it often fails to appear. Several kilometres down the road to Playa Bailén and 1 km before you get to the beach, there is a **crocodile farm** ① *daily 0900-1700, CUC$2, photographs CUC$3, video cameras CUC$5*, where they breed the American crocodile (*Crocodrylus acutus*). You can get uncomfortably close to the babies and can hold them. However, unless you are lucky, or come at feeding time, you are a 500 m telephoto lens away from the 4- to 5-m beasts. Note that small cars are likely to get bogged down in the sandy drive of the farm.

West to Península de Guanahacabibes

Back on the Carretera Central, **Isabel Rubio** has a gas station with a shop selling drinks, toiletries and canned foods. There is car rental in town and a place you can buy pizza at the junction of the road to Sandino. From Isabel Rubio, a very pretty way to return to Pinar del Río (about one hour) is through Guane, Los Portales and Sumidero. **Guane**, a large, attractive village with old houses and a little baroque church, is also the railway terminus.

Cuban cigars

During Columbus' second journey to the New World, he landed at Gibara in Cuba. Forays inland brought reports that the local inhabitants were smoking roughly rolled dried leaves for ceremonial or religious purposes, which they called *cohibas*. The Spaniards soon acquired the taste for tobacco and in the 17th century introduced it to the European market with great success. The first tobacco plantations in Cuba were established by the Río Almendares (Havana), in the centre of the island and around Bayamo. Tobacco planting spread in the 18th century, becoming particularly successful in the west and by the 19th century tobacco planters and merchants were extremely prosperous. By the time Cuba achieved its independence there were 120 cigar factories around the island.

Nowadays tobacco is cultivated in the west of Cuba in the province of Pinar del Río, in the centre in the provinces of Villa Clara and Sancti Spíritus and in the east in the provinces of Granma and Santiago de Cuba, although the tobacco regions are known as Vuelta Abajo, Semi Vuelta, Partidos, Remedios and Oriente. Only Partidos and Vuelta Abajo can grow tobacco of a high enough quality for the Grandes Marcas of cigars (*Habanos*), and only Vuelta Abajo produces all the leaves necessary for a cigar. Lower quality tobacco is made into cigarettes. Tobacco is extremely labour intensive and in Cuba it is grown, harvested and processed entirely by hand. Seedlings are transplanted from the nursery between October and December when they are 18-20 cm, taking great care not to damage the delicate roots. After a week they are weeded and after two weeks they are earthed up to maintain humidity and increase the plants' assimilation of nutrients. This is done with the help of oxen rather than a tractor, to avoid compacting the soil. When the plant reaches 1.4-1.6 m, side shoots are removed and the plant is encouraged to grow tall with only six to nine pairs of leaves. Harvesting takes place in January-March, during which time the leaves are collected by hand, two or three at a time, every five days, starting at the bottom. They are then taken to a huge, thatched barn, where they are sewn together in pairs and hung on a pole to dry. The leaves turn yellow, then reddish gold and are considered dry after about 50 days. They are then piled in bundles or stacks for about 30 days, during which time the first fermentation takes place at a temperature not exceeding 35°C, before being classified according to colour, size and quality for wrappers or fillers. At this stage the leaves are stripped off the main vein, dampened, flattened and packed in bigger stacks for up to 60 days of fermentation at a temperature not exceeding 42°C. Finally they are stored and aged for months, or maybe years, before being taken to be rolled by the expert hands of factory workers.

Five types of leaves are used in the manufacture of a cigar. In the middle (*tripa*) are a mixture of three types, *ligero*, *seco* and *volado*. These are wrapped in the *capote*, which is then enveloped in the *capa*, which is the part you see and determines the appearance of the cigar. There are two types of tobacco plant: the *corojo*, and the *criollo*. The former produces only the *capa*, but it comes in several colours. It is grown beneath vast cotton shrouds to protect it from the sun's radiation and keep it soft and silky. The latter provides the other four leaves needed to make up the cigar, which determine the flavour. It is grown in full sunlight to get intense flavours. Each of the five leaves is processed and aged differently before reaching the factory floor for mixing according to secret recipes and rolling.

Hundreds of workers sit at tables in the factory, equipped only with a special knife called a *chaveta*, a guillotine and a pot of gum. A skilled artisan (*torcedor*) makes an average of 120 cigars a day as he or she sits and listens to readings from the press or novels, a tradition which has carried on since 1865 and has never been replaced by the radio or taped music. Although many of the people rolling cigars are women, it is unfortunately a myth that Cuban cigars are rolled on the thighs of dusky maidens. The women sorting the leaves do, however, place them across their laps on each leg and this may have been where the erotic image originated.

Quality control is rigid. Any cigars which do not meet the standards of size, shape, thickness and appearance are rejected. Those which do make it are stored at a temperature of 16°-18°C at a humidity of 65-70% for several weeks until they lose the moisture acquired during rolling. A specialist then classifies them according to colour (of which there are 65 tones) and they are chosen for boxes, with the colours ranging from dark to light, left to right. They have to remain exactly as they are placed in the cedar wood box and the person who then labels each cigar has to keep them in the same order, even facing the same way.

Finally the boxes are stamped and sealed with the government's guarantee, which looks rather like a currency note and carries the words: 'Cuban Government's warranty for cigars exported from Havana' in English, French and German as well as Spanish.

Always buy your cigars from a state shop, not on the street, where they are bound to be fakes, no matter how good a deal they appear. Check the quality of each cigar. They should be tightly rolled, not soft; they should have no lumps or other protuberances; if you turn them upside down nothing should come out; the colour should be uniform and the aroma should be strong. The box should be sealed with the four-language warranty, which should not be a photocopy, and on the bottom you should find the stamp: Habanos s.a. HECHO EN CUBA *Totalmente a mano*. You may take only 23 cigars out of the country without a receipt, but if you buy them in a state shop and get a valid receipt you can buy cigars up to a value of CUC$2000 (unless you are returning to the USA, of course, where the embargo forbids you to import Cuban cigars of any worth).

Cigars are like fine wines or whiskies and there are many different types from which to choose. Castro used to smoke *Cohiba* cigars, which were created in 1966 exclusively for the diplomatic market. In 1982 the *Cohiba Lanceros*, *Coronas Especiales* and *Panatelas* were created for public sale, followed in 1989 by the *Espléndidos*, *Robustos* and *Exquisitos*, which together make up the Classic Line (*La Línea Clásica*). In 1992, to mark the 500th anniversary of the landing of Columbus, they brought out the 1492 Line (*La Línea 1492*), with its five centuries: *Siglo I, II, III, IV, V*. The *Espléndidos* now sell for up to CUC$385 a box.

As well as the *Cohiba* brand, there are *Montecristo, Romeo y Julieta, Bolívar, Punch, Hoyo de Monterrey, H Upmann, Partagás, Quintero, La Flor de Cano, El Rey del Mundo* and *Rafael González*, all of which have their company histories and logos, mostly dating from the 19th century.

The road runs through limestone hills, crossing the pretty **Río Cuyaguateje** several times and passing through the **Valle de San Carlos**, a spectacular narrow valley with cliffs and steep wooded hills rising on either side. Farmers grow fruit, vegetables and tobacco, with ox-drawn ploughs furrowing the bright red soil and tent-shaped tobacco drying sheds, *vegas*, everywhere.

After Isabel Rubio the countryside becomes completely flat. The villages are less lively and the agricultural landscapes less varied, with plantations of Caribbean pine in some stretches. On the north side of the road, 7 km west of Isabel Rubio, is the turning for **Laguna Grande**, a lake where you can fish or swim. A few miles further on at **Punta Colorada** is a small beach.

The main road continues through **Sandino**, where there are ten schools for Latin American students to study medicine, nursing and engineering, and **La Fé** to **Manuel Lazo**. After this village, potholes are more common. The last 15 km or so to the coast are through semi-deciduous dry coastal woodland. On reaching the coast at **La Bajada**, a very desolate little village, an immigration post will ask to see your documents.

The **Península de Guanahacabibes**, which forms the western tip of Cuba, is a Natural Biosphere Reserve. The reserve covers 1175 sq km but has not yet been developed for ecotourism. The peninsula is formed of very recent limestone, with an irregular rocky surface and patchy soil cover. There are interesting fossil coastlines, caves and blue holes; but with dense woodland on the south coast and mangrove on the north, the peninsula is uninviting for the casual hiker. However, for keen naturalists there are 12 amphibian species, 29 reptiles including iguana species, 10 mammals (including *jutía carabalí* and *jutía conga*) and 147 bird species, including nine of the 22 that are endemic to Cuba. There is a scientific station at La Bajada. Permits are required for entering the reserve. The Science Academy offers a Safari Tour with an English-speaking guide, Osmani Borrego, for CUC$25 per person. You can climb to the Radar for CUC$1 for a good view of the forest and the sea.

To the west of La Bajada, a good new road continues for 52 km to **Cabo de San Antonio**, where there is a new hotel, a few houses and a lighthouse built in 1849 and named after the then Spanish governor, Roncali. A marina opened in 2009, offering provisioning and refuelling for yachts, fishing and a dive shop. The coastline has several pretty white-sand beaches and clear waters with several suitable spots for snorkelling, but is otherwise lonely and desolate. There are some caves to explore, the main one being **Cueva La Sorda**, 1 km northwest of the lighthouse, where three different levels have collapsed into a central hole. There are many legends attached to the cave, where archaeological finds have been made. More recently an endemic frog was discovered after Hurricane Ivan: the 20-mm *Eleutherodactylus guanahacabibes*.

The main road continues 12 km south, hugging the coast, to **María La Gorda**, in the middle of nowhere, reputedly the best diving centre in Cuba and an idyllic spot for relaxing or doing nothing but **diving**. There are several wrecks off the western peninsula and freshwater cave diving in the blue holes is also possible, though not on offer as an organized activity. The dive boat tours usually go a short distance to dive sites, mostly reef or wall dives with caves, tunnels, drop-offs and even bits of old Spanish galleons, where there are lots of fish of all sizes, rays, moray eels, lobsters, grunts, groupers, turtles, barracuda and maybe whale sharks. The sea is very clear, very warm and calm, even when it is too rough to dive anywhere else in Cuba. There is good snorkelling with small coral heads close to the white sand beach, or you can go out on the dive boat, but from September to December there are sometimes jelly fish. They inflict only a mild sting, but they make swimming uncomfortable. ▸▸ *See Activities and tours, page 156.*

For Sleeping and Eating price codes and other relevant information, see Essentials pages 37-43.

◒ Sleeping

Pinar del Río *p147, map p147*
Hotels
B Pinar del Río, José Martí final, torwards the autopista but within walking distance of the city centre, T48-750707. Under renovation in 2009.

B Vueltabajo, Calle José Martí 103 y Rafael Morales, T48-759381, reserves@vueltapr.co.cu. Reopened in 2007 after total renovation, pleasant hotel, nice rooms but avoid those facing the noisy street, safety deposit box, satellite TV. Pricey meals of poor quality but fast service, restaurant open 0715-0930, 1200-1445, 1900-2145. Bar open 1700-2330, very crowded with locals, who offer cigars to foreigners (beware fakes), drink inside or outside, but the porch is close to the road. Car rental, excursions, tourism bureau, currency exchange.

Casas particulares
The number of *casas particulares* has declined following damage by the 2008 hurricanes and the subsequent shortage of food. There is a mafia of young men on bicycles who will meet you on arrival, whether by car, bus or train, and pester to take you to a *casa particular*, *paladar*, or whatever. Sometimes they say they are from **Formatur**, the tourism school. Sometimes they tell you there is a salsa festival in town to get you to stay here rather than go on to Viñales. They are after a commission, set by them at CUC$5 per person per night and have been known to be violent with Cuban landlords who refuse to pay. Avoid them if you can and make your own way using the map. If you accept any help with directions they will ask the Cuban family for money. Taxi drivers are in the same game; if your driver says he can't find the address, refuse to pay unless he goes to the

right house. He will try and take you somewhere else to get his commission.
D-E Casa Yusimi, Martí 154, T48-752818. Balcony overlooks street, good facilities with kitchenette and fridge.

D-E José Antonio Mesa, Gerardo Medina 67 entre Adela Azcuy y Isidro de Armas, T48-753173. Colonial building, spacious, breakfast available, nice family but involved in paying commissions so unpopular with other renters.

D-E Traveller's Rest, Isidro de Armas 70 entre Pedro Tellez y Primero de Mayo, sign outside, T48-777349 (call between 1000-1800), customerservice1@gmx.us (guide Juan Carlos Otaño, page 156). Colonial architecture, 2 rooms with 2 beds, fridge, a/c and fan, nice meals available, free welcome coffee, tea, *mojito* on arrival.

D-E Villa Lolo, Martí 57 entre Isabel Rubio y Colón. 1 room, private, a/c, fan, hot and cold shower, little English spoken, dog, watch out for hustlers seeking commission.

D-E Zunilda Rodríguez Hernández, Acueducto 16 entre Méndez Capote y Primera, Rpto Celso Maragota, T48-754639. 2 a/c rooms, private bath, hot water, breakfast and dinner, garage, her husband Julio fought with Che and Fidel.

West to Península de Guanahacabibes *p149*
Hotels
A Villa Cabo San Antonio, Playa Las Tumbas, T 48-757655, www.villacabosanantonio.com. Simple resort of 8 tasteful wooden lodges, 16 rooms with verandas, no disco or noise, just peace and quiet except for mosquitoes at sunset. On white-sand beach with crystal-clear water, marina 4 km from hotel with bar, scuba-diving, fishing. Car and bicycle hire, excursions, restaurant, shop, cooking facilities at the snack bar or the marina.

A-B María La Gorda, T/F48-771316, www.hotelmarialagorda-cuba.com. Jul-Aug are most expensive, Nov-Easter high season, buffet meals and diving can be included in packages. Lovely location, 55 rooms, some open onto the beach, hammocks between palm trees, nicely decorated, simple but comfortable, minibar, TV, while other *cabañas* are in the forest, but these attract mosquitoes. Service and cleanliness have been criticized as hit or miss. Eat in the restaurant (probably the best option) or at the expensive buffet, or have sandwiches in the bar. There are no places to eat outside the hotel. Not much entertainment, shop, *Telecorreos*.

Casas particulares
D-E Carmin, Calle de las Ambulancias 9, Sandino. No phone. Beside the road to María La Gorda, 1 room, a/c, garage, patio with fruit trees.
D-E Casa Alexis, Zona L 33, Sandino, T48-423282. 2 rooms with a/c, run by neighbour Carmen Cordero since Alexis went abroad. On the road to María La Gorda, the house has a sign.
D-E Tony, Zona M41, Sandino, T48-423843. 2 rooms with all the standard fittings, TV, patio, garage.

❷ Eating

Pinar del Río *p147, map p147*
Restaurants
❢❢❢ **Café Pinar**, Gerardo Medina e Isidro de Armas, opposite Coppelia, T48-778199. Open daily 1800-0200. Expensive restaurant, a show at 2130, Afro-Cuban show Tue. Full of *jineteros* and pickpockets. Beware of theft.
❢❢-❢ **El Aguila de Oro**, Rafael Morales esq Antonio Maceo. Open daily 1100-2300. Colonial architecture, looks like a hacienda, pleasant atmosphere, new bar and restaurant, prices in pesos cubanos, close to the cigar factory so watch out for *jineteros* hanging around.
❢ **Coppelia**, Gerardo Medina. Open daily 0800-2330. Ice cream can be bought in pesos, very cheap.
❢ **Doña Neli**, Gerardo Medina 24. Bakery. Open daily 0700-1900 for bread, 0830-2300 for pastries and cakes.

❢ **El Marino**, Isabel Rubio esq Martí, T48-750381. Daily 1200-2300. Nicely decorated with nautical theme, fast service, only Spanish spoken, charges in pesos cubanos but *jineteros* hang around to charge you in CUC$. *Enchilado de langosta* costs 45 pesos cubanos (CUC$2), *arroz con vegetales* 12 pesos, *filete de pescado* 35 pesos. Dress code, no shorts, no sandals, no smoking
❢ **FrutiCuba**, Isidro de Armas y Gerardo Medina, next to the ice cream parlour. Open daily 1000-2200. Fruits, milkshakes and fruit juices, pay in pesos cubanos.
❢ **La Taberna**, González Coro 103 opposite El Paquito amusement park for children, T48-750588. Open daily from 1800. Bar and restaurant with Spanish influences, house speciality *favada gallega y lacón*. Pesos only, very cheap, but they try and get you to pay for drinks in CUC$, which is not necessary. The one place in town where you can have a quiet meal free from *jineteros*, a/c, but very slow service, allow plenty of time for your meal, arrive early.
❢ **Mar Init**, José Martí, opposite Parque de la Independencia, T48-754952. Open Tue-Sun 1930-2130. Pay in pesos, fish is the speciality of the house.
❢ **Terrazina**, Antonio Rubio y Primero de Mayo, open 1130-1500 and 1800-2200. Pay in pesos. Pizza, spaghetti, beer, all-you-can-eat for less than CUC$1.

Paladar
❢ **El Mesón**, Martí, opposite the Museo de Ciencias Naturales, T48-752867, Mon-Sat 1100-2400. A *paladar* run by Rafael, a former teacher, nice place, the only place outside a *casa particular* where you can get a decent meal, lunch or dinner.

West to Península de Guanahacabibes *p149*
Paladar
❢ **La Magistral**, Zona M41, Sandino, T48-423843. Open daily. Price negotiable. Run by Tony, who also has a *casa particular*, see above.

⚙ Entertainment

Pinar del Río *p147, map p147*

Cinema

Cine Praga, Gerardo Medina 31, next to Coppelia, T48-753271. Mon-Sun 1400-2400. 2 pesos cubanos.
Cine Zayden, Martí 111. 1 peso.

Music

The town is very lively on Sat nights and, to a lesser extent, on Fri. There is live music everywhere, salsa, *son*, Mexican music, international stuff. During the day in Parque Roberto Amarán you can hear traditional music (mambo, rumba, cha-cha-cha, danzón) Sun 0900. Baseball fans gather here for heated discussions about sport. Late at night it is a gathering spot for the gay community.

Parque de la Independencia is quieter and a place to enjoy the breeze at night, a popular hangout for the young crowd.

Opposite the **Hotel Vueltabajo** is a bar where locals gather to drink draft beer made from grapefruit and perform *canturias*. Open daily but best on Fri evening.
Bar La Esquinita, on Isabel Rubio. Daily 2000-0200. Live music, usually guitar.
Callejón de Corina, Primero de Mayo. A *Proyecto Socio-Cultural*, held at weekends (Sat or Sun) 1500-1730, show of folkloric music (rumba, guaguancó) and children perform with dance and a fashion show.
Casa de la Cultura, Rafael Morales esq Martí. Band play every Sun evening with a dance contest for the elderly, fantastic, free, photos allowed.
Casa de la Música, on Gerardo Medina next to Coppelia. Live music daily except Mon.
Casa del Joven Creador, José Martí 113A, opposite the Chess Academy, T48-774672. Free entry, free tea. An organization for music and the arts where young musicians gather at night and arrange concerts. The popular (metal/Latin/thrash) band is **Tendencia**, www.tendencia.co.nr, led by singer and director Kiko, a high school teacher. They have travelled abroad a few times and have a national reputation.
Disco Pista Rita, on González Coro. An open-air venue popular with teenagers, where they play loud, US-style disco music and rock, entry 2 pesos, the only drink on sale is neat rum at 25 pesos a bottle. Pinar Rock, a national rock festival, is held here the 2nd weekend of Mar.
La Picuala, at the back of the Teatro Milanés, Wed 1630, Sat, Sun 2100 for the best bands and a fashion show.
Rumayor, 2 km on road to Viñales. Restaurant (1200-2200, closed Thu). A *Tropicana*-style show, Fri, Sat and Sun CUC$5, very good, lots of security. Starts 2300 (get there before 2200 to get a table) and lasts about 1½ hrs, followed by disco until 0300 or so. Held in small amphitheatre with proper sound and lighting system. No photography or videos allowed. The complex is in a pleasant garden with lots of trees. Don't bother with mid-week *Noche Cubana*, held on a different stage, the show is no good and the place is full of *jineteros*.

Nightclubs

Artex, Martí 36, opposite Photo service. Open daily 0900-0200.
Palacio de los Matrimonios (The Wedding Palace), Martí 125, T48-757653. Bar open Tue-Fri 0800-2400, Sat and Sun 1000-0200. Beer, rum, snacks, TV, a/c, a lovely place, CUC$1 entry.

Theatre

Teatro José Jacinto Milanés, Martí entre Isabel Rubio y Colón, T48-753871. There are 3 theatre groups, 1 for children and 2 for adults, which give occasional performances.

⚙ Festivals and events

Pinar del Río *p147, map p147*
1st week of Jul Carnival lasts for for 5 days, Wed-Sun.

O Shopping

Pinar del Río *p147, map p147*
Art gallery
Galería de Arte Yoruba, Rafael Ferro 119.
Open 0900-1900, CUC$1, coffee or tea
included. Local artists displaying and selling
Afro-Cuban cultural works. Run by Enrique
Machín, a Babalao, who is also a painter.
Many languages spoken here.

Bookshop
Vietnam, Martí 5, Mon-Fri 0800-1700,
Sat 0800-1200.

Cigars and rum
Casa del Habano, opposite the cigar factory,
for all brands of cigar from the Vueltabajo
region. Smart, upmarket, bar at the back,
open same hours as the factory.
Casa del Ron, Maceo esq Antonio Tarafa, 50 m
from cigar factory, for all your rum needs.

Handicrafts
There is a craft shop on Martí esq Gerardo
Medina. Daily 0800-1700.

Markets
There is a fruit market opposite the railway
station on Av Rafael Ferro, Mon-Sat 0800-1600,
Sun 0800-1300, pay in pesos. An even better
farmers' market is on Av Alameda, near
Parque Independencia, on the left before
the cemetery on the road to Luis Lazo,
open Tue-Sat 0800-1800, 0800-1200 Sun.
A new a/c market is opposite the Banco
Financiero Internacional, next to Coppelia
on the corner of Gerardo Medina and Isidro
de Armas, daily 0900-1700.

▲ Activities and tours

Pinar del Río *p147, map p147*
Boat trips
Ecotur, Km 2.5 Carretera Luis Lazo, T48-
753844, ecoturpr@enet.cu, contact Norges
Pérez Santos. From Coloma there are boat trips

to the Cayos de San Felipe. Prices range from
CUC$38, if there are 10 of you, to CUC$166 per
person if there are only 2, for a day trip that
includes a visit to a lobster ground, a coral reef
for snorkelling, Cayo Sijú, birdwatching, fishing,
lunch and a spell on the beach. In winter you
can watch turtles and at any time you can see
crocodiles and iguanas watching you while
you have lunch. The boat doesn't always run,
so make sure you confirm beforehand.

Diving
Dive shop at María La Gorda, T48-771306,
T/F84-78131, see page 152. Doctor
specializing in hyperbaric medicine. Good
boat with shade, pleasant Spanish-speaking
staff. The dive boat leaves 0930 and 1530 for
the offshore reef (CUC$40 per dive, plus
CUC$10 a day to rent equipment for those
not on a package).
 The new marina (opened 2009) at Cabo
de San Antonio has a dive centre with 27
dive sites to explore. They also offer fishing
at the marina and berths for yachts.

Guides
Juan Carlos Otaño, T48-777349 (**Traveller's
Rest** *casa particular*, call between 1000-1800),
customerservice1@gmx.us, also known as
'The Teacher', speaks French, English, Italian
and some German, very friendly and helpful.
Excursions and trips locally and around the
island. He works as a tour guide on a tobacco
plantation Nov-Apr and is a connoisseur of
Cuban cigars.

Sailing
For visitors arriving by yacht, María La Gorda is
a port of entry. There are 4 moorings, max draft
2 m, VHF channels 16, 19, 68 and 72. The new
Marina Gaviota Cabo de San Antonio has
refuelling and provisioning facilities for visiting
yachts, T48-750123, www.gaviota-grupo.com.

Tour operators
Cubanacán, Chucho Valdés y M Gómez,
T48-773015. Tours, reservations, tickets,
internet 0830-2100.

Cubatur, Martí 115, T48-778405, daily 0800-1700.
Ecotur, T48-753844, ecoturpr@enet.cu. Contact Norges Pérez Santos for full-day tours taking in birdwatching, hiking, trips to tobacco plantations, the crocodile farm, horse riding, fishing, jeep safaris, caving and hunting.
Havanatur, Martí, T48-778494.

⊖ Transport

Pinar del Río *p147, map p147*
Air
Alvaro Barba airport is on the road to La Coloma, 8 km from town, T48-755542/750106. Domestic flights only and not many of them.

Bus
The bus station is on Colón, north of José Martí, near Gómez. It has been recently renovated and is under constant police surveillance. Downstairs for tickets for provincial buses and trucks, upstairs for buses to **Havana**. A new boulevard has opened at the bus terminal, where you can get a quick meal, lunch for 30 pesos cubanos, just by where the buses from Havana come in. Also a 24-hr café opposite the bus station. **Víazul**, T48-752572/755255, runs a daily bus service from Havana to **Viñales**, see page 32. It stops on request at **Las Terrazas** and **San Diego de los Baños**. There are no buses to María La Gorda; you have to get an official transfer from Havana with a package tour or rent a car.

  If you get a local peso bus your name has to be on the list. To **La Palma**, 1730, 2 pesos, **Bahía Honda**, 1820, 4 pesos, **Puerto Esperanza**, 1930, 2.60 pesos, **Sandino**, 1800, 2 pesos, **Guane**, 2 pesos, **Mantua**, 3 pesos.

Car hire
Transtur, Martí 109 near Restaurant La Casona, T48-750104, commercial.pri@transtur.cu. Distances from Pinar del Río are 157 km to Havana, 159 km to María La Gorda, 103 km to Las Terrazas, 88 km to Soroa, 25 km to Viñales. From Havana to Pinar del Río takes

around 2 hrs 50 mins by the highway, 4 hrs 10 mins on the main road. **Servi Cupet** station on Calle Rafael Morales esq Frank País, on the road to San Juan y Martínez.

Taxi
Long-distance travel by taxi is possible but you will need very good Spanish to negotiate effectively. **Cubataxi** has an office in the bus station at Pinar del Río with an a/c waiting room and an officer who can show you a brochure of trips and fares (no English spoken), open 0700-1800 Mon-Sat 0700-1200 Sun. Taxi to Havana bus terminal CUC$100, to María la Gorda CUC$120 (4 passengers), to Viñales CUC$20 one way, CUC$60 round trip with waiting time.

Train
The railway station in Pinar del Río is on Av Comandante Pinares, T48-752106/752272. From **Havana** at 2140, arriving at 0310. Take a torch, hang on to your luggage, don't sleep, noisy, train stops about 29 times, very slow. The line continues to **Guane**, CUC$3, 1830. Trains to Havana leave at 0800 on alternate days, and cost CUC$7. There is also an overcrowded train to Bailén for the beach, departs 0720, returns 1630, 2 pesos cubanos.

ⓘ Directory

Pinar del Río *p147, map p147*
Banks Banco Financiero Internacional (BFI), Gerardo Medina, opposite Coppelia, T48-778183, open Mon-Fri 0800-1500. Cadeca, Gerardo Medina 43N, next to Coppelia, T48-778247, open 0830-1800. Also on Martí 46 next to Artex bar, T48-778357. Banco Popular de Ahorro, Martí 113, opposite the chess academy, Mon-Fri 0800-1700. **Chess academy** Martí 110, Mon-Sat 0800-2000. **Internet** Etecsa, on Av Alameda. CUC$6 for 1 hr with *tarjeta*. Cubanacán, Martí, internet access 0830-2100, 3 terminals, prepaid cards CUC$6 for 1 hr. **Language schools**

Andrés Bello, Maceo 20, Mon-Thu 1730-2030. French, German, English, Italian and Spanish classes. **Medical services** Policlínico Turcios Lima, opposite cathedral, Gerardo Medina 112, open Mon-Sat 0800-1700. **Dentist**, Martí 162, T48-773348, open 0800-1700. Pharmacies: Camacho, Martí 62, daily 0800-2300. Piloto, under El Globo Hotel, daily 0800-2400 with emergency service.

Post Martí esq Isabel Rubio, Mon-Sat 0800-1700. **Telephone/fax** Etecsa, Av Alameda IIA, Parque de la Independencia, T48-754585-7. A **Telepunto** 24-hr phone centre is at Gerardo Medina esq Juan Gualberto Gómez, T48-754051, domestic and calls abroad, phone cards for sale.

Viñales

→ Colour map 1, B3.
North of Pinar del Río, the road leads across pine-covered hills and valleys for 25 km to Viñales, a delightful, small town in a dramatic valley in the Sierra de los Organos. Viñales itself is a pleasant town, with single-storey houses with red-tiled roofs and wooden colonnades along the main street. The once-impressive avenue of pine trees along the main street was sadly destroyed by the hurricanes in 2008. Visitors come here to relax, hike in the hills and maybe visit a beach on the north coast. The valley has a distinctive landscape, with steep-sided limestone mogotes rising dramatically from fertile flat-floored valleys, where farmers cultivate the red soil for tobacco, fruits and vegetables. As in so much of rural Cuba, horses, pigs, oxen, zebu cattle and chickens are everywhere, including on the main road. ►► *For listings, see pages 162-165.*

Ins and outs
Getting there There is no **airport**, but the one at Pinar del Río is not far away. The nearest train station is at Pinar del Río. **Víazul** has a daily **bus** service from Havana via Pinar del Río and there are local buses between villages.

Getting around The town is little more than a village and it is easy to **walk** around. A tour bus goes round the hotels and town which you can hop on and off, 0830-1800, CUC$5 for a 40-minute round trip. Many visitors hire a **car** or **scooter** to get around the nearby attractions, although there are also **horses** for hire.

Best time to visit The mountains attract a fair amount of rain and you can expect wet afternoons, particularly from September to November. Carnival is in March.

Tourist information There is a visitor centre, **La Casa del Visitante**, on the main road heading out to Pinar del Río, near **Hotel Los Jazmines**, open daily 0730-1800.

Sights
The main street is Salvador Cisneros and a walk along it will reveal nearly all the attractions Viñales has to offer. Streets running parallel or across it are residential and contain many *casas particulares*. **Víazul** drops you off half way along the street, opposite the main square with a little-used church. There is also a little municipal museum on Salvador Cisneros and a **Casa de la Cultura** on the square with an art gallery. An informative curator here speaks English. There are several bars and restaurants along Salvador Cisneros, but hardly of the quality to warrant the thousands of visitors who come here every year.

On the edge of Viñales is **Caridad's Garden** ① *turn left at the gas station at the end of Salvador Cisneros on the road to Cueva del Indio, no entry fee, but a tip of CUC$1 is appreciated*. The garden contains a beautiful collection of flowers from Cuba and around the world and fruit trees. Chickens scratch about in the shady undergrowth with their chicks. The garden was first planted in the 1930s. A guide will show you around, pointing out all the different species and you will be invited to try all the different fruits. They are generous with their produce but appreciate contributions to the upkeep of the garden.

Around Viñales

Mural de la Prehistoria

Two kilometres west of Viñales is the Mural de la Prehistoria, painted by **Lovigildo González**, a disciple of the Mexican Diego Rivera, between 1959 and 1976, generally disliked as a monstrous piece of graffiti. If you are fit and active you can climb up the rocks to the top for a great view. No guide needed. One hundred metres before the

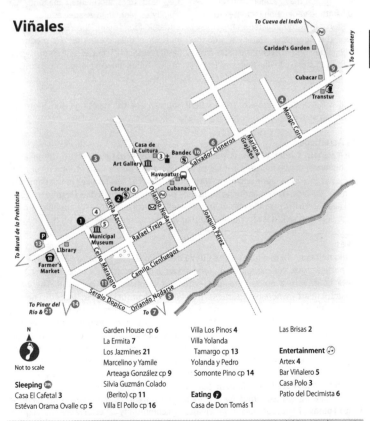

Viñales

N

Not to scale

Sleeping 🛌
Casa El Cafetal cp **3**
Estévan Orama Ovalle cp **5**

Garden House cp **6**
La Ermita **7**
Los Jazmines **21**
Marcelino y Yamile
  Arteaga González cp **9**
Silvia Guzmán Colado
  (Berito) cp **11**
Villa El Pollo cp **16**

Villa Los Pinos **4**
Villa Yolanda
  Tamargo cp **13**
Yolanda y Pedro
  Somonte Pino cp **14**

Eating 🍴
Casa de Don Tomás **1**

Las Brisas **2**

Entertainment 🎭
Artex **4**
Bar Viñalero **5**
Casa Polo **3**
Patio del Decimista **6**

Rocks, caves, valleys and mogotes

The rocks around Viñales are pure limestones formed in the Jurassic period around 160 million years ago. Unlike most other rocks, limestone can be dissolved by rainwater. Rivers and streams often flow underground through extensive cave systems; most of the 10,000 recorded caves in Cuba are in the western province and one cave system in the Valle Santo Tomás consists of a total of 25 km of underground passages. Where a valley is formed in tropical limestone, often by downwards faulting of the rock, it may be filled with fertile red soil. Rotting vegetation increases the acidity of the groundwater on the valley floor. This 'aggressive' water eats into the valley sides, undercutting the rocks and producing steep cliff-like features. The valley floor is broken by isolated steep-sided hills, known to both English- and Spanish-speaking geologists by their Cuban name: mogotes. Other valleys (narrow gorges) are produced when the roof of a large cave collapses. Similar tropical limestone landscapes can be seen in parts of Puerto Rico and Jamaica.

Rapid drainage of rainwater into the rock produces dry growing conditions for plants. The limestone hills have a distinctive vegetation type, with palms (including the curious cork palm), deciduous trees, succulents, lianas and epiphytes. More than 20 species are endemic, found only in the Viñales area. The isolation of the mogotes has also produced distinctive animal species, with some types of snail found only on a single mogote.

mural is **Restaurant Jurásico**, from where you can see the paintings and there is a swimming pool nearby.

Los Acuáticos

Four kilometres from Viñales is the community, **Los Acuáticos**, where the villagers worship water. It was founded in 1943 by Antoñica Izquierdo, a *santera*, who recognized the importance of hygiene and clean water for health. The few families in the hamlet on the mountainside are self-contained and they bathe three times a day. Despite excellent rural healthcare in Cuba, the community refuses medical assistance for anyone who has an accident or is sick. It is recommended that women do not come here on their own.

Caves

Six kilometres north of Viñales is the **Cueva del Indio** ① *CUC$5, avoid 1130-1430 when tour parties arrive, not enough boats, long delays*, a cave which you enter on foot, then take a boat, with a guide who gives you a description, very beautiful. There is a restaurant nearby where tour parties are given a lunch of suckling pig (*lechón*). The tour includes lunch but not the cave, and no drinks; even water is an 'extra'. Beyond the restaurant is a small farm, well kept, with little red pigs running around, oxen and horses. There are trips to a disco in the **Cueva de San Miguel**, west of Cueva del Indio (much better to go on your own and have the cave to yourself), short hiking trips to a *mogote*, visits to various caves and **El Palenque de los Cimarrones**, a restaurant and craft shop with a display of Cuban folklore. These are advertized as daily events, but don't rely on it. ▸▸ *See Entertainment, page 164.*

The **Valle de Santo Tomás** (with 25-km cave system) contains the **Gran Caverna Santo Tomás** 17 km southwest from Viñales in a community called El Moncada. A guide will show you the cave; prices depend on which walk you choose. Near El Moncada is the 3-km ecological path, **Maravillas de Viñales**.

North of Viñales to the coast

It is a lovely drive southwest through the valley and then north up to the coast through El Moncada, Pons and the former copper mining centre of **Minas de Matahambre** up to **Cayo Jutías** on the north coast near Santa Lucía, 50 km. The road is well signed on the way there, but not at all on the way back. The road east of Santa Lucía to San Cayetano is in very poor condition and travellers have to detour through Viñales to regain the coast. The coastal road around the western end of Cuba through **Mantua** to Guane is long and rather tedious, too far inland to see the sea. It is mostly good but you can't relax, it is full of potholes and other surprises.

Cayo Jutías
① *CUC$5.*
Cayo Jutías, a 6.7-km cay, is attached to Cuba by a long causeway through mangroves. There is a restaurant/bar on the beach (open daily 1300-1800, bar 1000-1800) and there are thatched shade umbrellas, a beach volleyball pitch and a toilet. The beach is a narrow strip of curving white sand with mangroves at either end. The far west end is the quieter with the better beach. The sea is calm, warm and multi-coloured but there is weed and not much snorkelling unless you can swim quite far out to the reef, which is marked by buoys. There is some good brain coral and anemones and, although there is a good variety, the fish are quite small. There is a lot of sand and sea grass on the way out to the reef, which can get stirred up with poor visibility, but this changes once you are over the reef, which is shallow with excellent visibility, especially when the sun is shining. A kiosk rents snorkelling equipment for CUC$2.50 per hour or CUC$5 per day (individual bits can be rented separately) on production of identity documents. Sunbeds cost CUC$1.50 per day. **Mégano**, an islet just offshore, is reached by boat, 12 minutes. An excursion there with lunch costs CUC$50 for the whole day.

Cayo Levisa
Puerto Esperanza, 24 km from Viñales, is a fishing town and not worth going to for beaches. There are *casas particulares* and plenty of food on offer, eg lobster and fish.

Further east is Cayo Levisa, part of the **Archipiélago de los Colorados**, with a long, sandy beach and reef running parallel to the shore, with good snorkelling and scuba diving (lots of fish). There are about 23 dive sites between 15m and 35 m deep and no more than 30 minutes away by boat. The underwater scenery is characterized by big sponges and enormous black coral trees. Angel fish are very numerous, as are barracuda and schools of jacks. The current is generally quite gentle so it is an ideal place for beginners and experts alike. There are several bits and pieces of old galleons, most of which have been covered by corals. Diving costs CUC$40, including a drink and a packed lunch, snorkelling trips are CUC$14, equipment included. In season you can windsurf or go on sailing and snorkelling trips to other cays and beaches, but from September when the sea gets rougher there is less available. Check beforehand: if you pay in advance for diving but the boat does not go out, it is time consuming to get a refund. The island is very quiet and peaceful with nothing much to do except dive or walk around the island, which takes about three hours. It is very relaxing and charming. To get to Cayo Levisa go to Palma Rubia, from where it is 15 minutes by boat to the island. There are two ferries, at 1000 and 1800, returning from Cayo Levisa at 0900 and 1700 (CUC$15 includes drink). The jetty is on the south side and you follow a boardwalk through the mangroves to get to the hotel on the north side. Take insect repellent. Hired cars can be left at the terminal building at Palma Rubia.

◉ Viñales listings

For Sleeping and Eating price codes and other relevant information, see Essentials pages 37-43.

● Sleeping

Viñales *p158, map p159*
Casas particulares
There are more than 280 registered *casas particulares* and people meet you off the buses. Most charge CUC$20-25 a night with breakfast at CUC$3-4 and dinner at CUC$7-10, depending on your menu choice. Many offer juice, coffee or *mojito* but do not say whether it is free or not. Best to ask to avoid nasty surprises on the final bill.
D-E Casa El Cafetal, Calle Adela Azcuy Norte Final s/n, T015 223 9175 (mob). Lovely rural and peaceful location, detached cottage in a lush garden which produces lots of fruit and coffee for the household. Marta and Amador Martínez run this casa with Edgar Rivery, an expert climber. 1 bedroom with 2 double beds and private bathroom.
D-E Estévan Orama Ovalle, Orlando Nodarse 13, T48-793305. Very knowledgeable and friendly hosts, big room, clean and safe, excellent breakfast and dinner, good *mojitos*.
D-E Garden House, Salvador Cisnero 44, T48-793297. 1 room, terrace overlooking big garden, garage CUC$1, meals available.
D-E Marcelino y Yamile Arteaga González, Salvador Cisneros 6, near the Cupet station, on the road to the cemetery, no phone. Welcoming and kind, great breakfast CUC$3 and tasty dinner CUC$6.
D-E Oscar y Leida, Adela Azcuy 43, T48-793381. Oscar Jaime Rodríguez and Leida Robaína Altega offer a friendly and welcoming home shared by 3 generations of family, including cousins, which is a mecca for climbers. Oscar was one of the first local

people to get involved in climbing the *mogotes* and is very experienced and knowledgeable about routes.
D-E Silvia Guzmán Collado (Berito), Camilo Cienfuegos 60A, T48-793245. 1 room, sleeps up to 6, fans, private, hot shower, garden, English spoken, meals available, try 'Berito's chicken', drinks (beer, *mojito*).
D-E Villa Azul, Km 25 Carretera Pinar del Río, T48-793288 (neighbour). Large room for up to 5 people, private bath, parking, fruit and coffee from own garden overlooked by terrace, caring couple offer security and comfort.
D-E Villa El Pollo, Salvador Cisneros, by Bandec. Run by nephew of Garden House owner and often used as overspill. Suite at back of house with independent entrance, very large room, dining room and bathroom. No hanging space for clothes but lots of room to spread out. A/c, no fan, rocking chairs outside front door, good food, fish excellent, chickens in back yard.
D-E Villa Ernesto/Traveller's Rest, Salvador Cisneros 20 Este, on the road to the cemetery (sign outside), T48-793261 (call for reservation 1500-1900), customerservice1@ gmx.us. 2 rooms with 2 beds, a/c and fan. Described as a 'generous, warm and obliging host', Don Ernesto makes the best *mojito* in Viñales, having worked for over 30 years as barman at Los Jazmines. Contact him direct or through his nephew, Juan Carlos, see Guides page 156.
D-E Villa Los Pinos, Cisneros 36, T48-796097. Sandra Fernández Mesa is a tour guide in the Viñales National Park and speaks English, while her husband, René, also speaks French. 1 bedroom with 2 double beds in colonial house dating from 1892, a/c, good bathroom, independent access or door from the house.
D-E Villa Milagro e Ivan, Salvador Cisneros, Edif Colonial Apto 7, T48-793222. Friendly

and pleasant family, extremely helpful, amazing views over the valley from their balcony, excellent cooking, delicious *mojitos* with honey, a/c, 24-hr hot water.

D-E Villa Mirtha, Rafael Trejo 129. Run by Martha Fernández Hernández, double room with 2 double beds, bathroom, hot water, good breakfast included, dinner CUC$6 for fish, beans, rice and salad, son David speaks French but no English.

D-E Villa Sol, Calle C Final 1, T48-695591, T015-2832018 (mob). Deborah Alfonso and Juan Carlos are friendly and both speak English. They offer 1 airy room with independent access, lovely view of the mogotes from the terrace at the back.

D-E Villa Tery, Calle 4/5 y 7 31, La Colchonería, T48-696662. Simple house but clean, with friendly, honest family. Guillermo, the father, will answer all your questions, Yolli, his daughter is an excellent cook, while her grandfather will show you how to make cigars. English spoken.

D-E Villa Yolanda Tamargo, Salvador Cisneros 186, T48-793208. 1 large room, hot and cold shower, fan, colonial architecture, parking CUC$1, terrace overlooking garden with fruits and orchids, nice place, meals.

D-E Yolanda y Pedro Somonte Pino, Interior 7A (behind the *Secundaria*), no phone. Nice family, quiet, relaxing, little garden, 1 room with 2 beds, fan, bathroom, hot water, simple but clean, good breakfast with lots of fruit from the garden, dinner available.

Around Viñales *p159*

B-C La Ermita, Carretera de la Ermita Km 2, 3 km from town with magnificent view of the valley and town, especially at sunset, T48-796100/796071, www.hotelescubanacan.com. 62 rooms, a/c, phone, radio, shop, tennis court, wheelchair access, pool (not always usable), food not recommended, walk into the village for evening meal, breakfast included, nicer public areas than at **Los Jazmines**.

B-C Los Jazmines, Carretera de Viñales Km 23.5, 3 km before the town, in a superb location with travel brochure view of the valley,

T48-796210/796205, www.hotelescubanacan. com. 62 nice rooms and 16 *cabañas*, nightclub, breakfast buffet CUC$5 if not already included, unexciting restaurant, bar with snacks available, shops, swimming pool (CUC$5 including towels for day-visitors and CUC$5 in vouchers for bar drinks), riding, easy transport.

B Rancho San Vicente, Valle de San Vicente, near Cueva del Indio, T48-796201, www.hotelescubanacan.com. 54 a/c rooms in *cabañas*, bar, restaurant, breakfast included, nightclub, shop, tourist information desk, nice pool, open to day-visitors, good for lunch after visit to caves, spa with warm sulphurous waters, mud baths with steroids, hormones, antibiotics and vitamins, other facilities on offer include physiotherapy, massage, acupuncture, digitopuncture, medical checkups, a full-body massage is CUC$25, with mud pack on the face CUC$5, mineral baths CUC$5 with use of pool. Usually closed in the low season.

North of Viñales to the coast *p161*

AL-B Cayo Levisa, T48-756501, www.hotel cayolevisa-cuba.com. Packages include transport from Havana, some or all meals and often watersports, book in Havana through any tour agency that deals with **Cubanacán**. 33 cabins on beach, thatched, with verandas, built in 2 rows but staggered so that each gets a sea view, a/c, TV, fridge, comfortable but not luxurious, spacious, also some new apartments which don't have the same charm, restaurant serves bland food, bar, live music.

🍴 Eating

Viñales *p158, map p159*

🍴 **Casa de Don Tomás**, Salvador Cisneros 140, T48-796300. The oldest house in Viñales (1879), totally renovated after the 2008 hurricanes. Food very average, eggs the only option for vegetarians, cocktails are good and it's pleasant to sit and listen to live music with a Ron Collins or Mary Pickford. Most cocktails are CUC$1.50, but the house special, *Trapiche*, is CUC$2 (rum, pineapple juice, honey, sugar cane syrup). A bottle of rum is not much more than in a shop and a shot of rum starts at CUC$0.20. Begging dogs can be a nuisance although they are regularly chased away by staff and security guard.

¶ **Las Brisas**, on the main street. Fully renovated after the hurricanes. Food charged in pesos cubanos, drinks in CUC$, not much on the menu, food poor, dogs begging at table, only Spanish spoken, a/c.

Around Viñales *p159*
¶ **Jurásico**, Mural de la Prehistoria, T48-796260. Bar open daily 0800-1630 for lunch CUC$7-8 and drinks.

North of Viñales to the coast *p161*
¶ **Paladar Jesús Carus Gallardo**, Frank País 87, Puerto Esperanza. Tasty food, inexpensive, help with accommodation if needed.

⊕ Entertainment

Viñales *p158, map p159*
Live music
Artex, Salvador Cisneros, bar, live music, shop 1000-2000.
Bar Viñalero, Salvador Cisneros, next to the museum. Under renovation in 2009 with only a kiosk on the porch serving drinks, but usually there is live music in evenings, inside and outside seating. Varied music, from traditional to rock.
Casa Polo, next to Casa de la Cultura on the plaza, CUC$2. Live music every night with different bands, followed by disco until 0200.
Patio del Decimista, Salvador Cisneros 112A, T48-796014, bar, live music, CUC$1.

Around Viñales *p159*
Los Jazmines, see Sleeping, above. Disco 2000-0300, CUC$5.
Palenque de los Cimarrones, 4 km north of Viñales at Km 32 Carretera a Puerto Esperanza. Fri-Sat there is a cabaret show and after midnight a disco, very popular. Take a sweater with you in case you stay until very late.

⊕ Festivals and events

Viñales *p158, map p159*
Mar Carnival is in the middle of the month lasting for 4 days, Thu-Sun.
Jul Parades including beauty pageant.

○ Shopping

Viñales *p158, map p159*
El Mogote, open daily 0900-1900. A *Caracol* shop on main street. There is also a **bakery** close to the farmers' market. The best bakery is on the road to the Mural de la Prehistoria at the outskirts of town, open Mon-Sat 0700-1700, Sun 0700-1300 for very fresh Cuban bread, 4 pesos cubanos a loaf.

▲ Activities and tours

Viñales *p158, map p159*
Climbing
The *mogotes* are a magnet for climbers. There is a local climbing group of men and women, very enthusiastic, who are equipped mostly with gear left behind by foreign climbers. One of the first and therefore most experienced is **Josué Millo Gómez**, Calle Rafael Trejo 108A. Other possible contacts include **Oscar Jaime Rodríguez**, Calle Adela Azcuy 43, T48-793381, who has a *casa particular* often used as a base camp by visiting climbers and knows all the best climbing (*escalando*) spots in Viñales and the rest of the country. Be wary of *jineteros* offering to take you to a man called Oscar but who take you somewhere completely different for a commission. Alternatively, Edgar Rivery at **El Cafetal**, see above, is very experienced. For more information on routes and hazards, see www.cubaclimbing.com.

Diving
Cayo Levisa Diving Centre,
www.cayolevisa.org. Dives at 0830, 1100 and 1430. 1 large boat for up to 20 divers and 1 smaller one for 10 go out to 23 dive sites:

coral, wall and wreck diving. SSI courses are available for Open Water and Advanced qualifications. The nearest hyperbaric chamber is at the Naval Hospital in Havana, 35 mins away by helicopter. Snorkelling equipment CUC$5 per day. Get to the dive shop early to make sure of a set.

Hiking

Hiking in the valleys is perfectly safe, however if venturing into the mountains themselves, it would be sensible (particularly for women) to take a local guide, but they don't all speak good English. You can find one at the Visitor's Centre for CUC$10-20, depending on the chosen trail, or at the museum opposite **Artex, or ask at your casa particular.** Martín Luis López is recommended; a former ecology and geography university lecturer, he speaks English, French and some German and knows Viñales like the back of his hand. You may find him at La Casa del Visitante.

Riding

Yosbel Reyes Crespo, Camilo Cienfuegos s/n. CUC$5 per hr. Yosbel does a 5-hr tour taking in the Cueva del Indio, which is probably more than enough on a horse. 3-hr tours also offered. Well worthwhile and a good way to see the countryside.

Tour operators

Cubanacán, on Salvador Cisneros 63C, next to the bus terminal, 0800-1700. Motocross rental, CUC$30 per day, phone cards, lodgings, car rental. Excursion to Cayo Jutías CUC$21 including lunch of main course and a drink. **Havanatur**, Salvador Cisneros 65, T48-796161. Tours, reservations and ticket sales. **Paradiso**, bureau on the porch of Casa de la Cultura, Cisneros 76, T48-796164. Wide variety of tours and excursions around town. The representative, Bravo, is a former English teacher and speaks good English.

⊖ Transport

Viñales *p158, map p159*
Bus
Bus terminal at Salvador Cisneros 63A. **Viazul**, T48-793195, daily from **Havana** via Pinar del Río, see page 32. Local buses from **Pinar del Río** to **Puerto Esperanza**, **La Palma** and **Bahía Honda** all pass through Viñales. Tour buses from Havana will drop you off if you want to stay more than a day and collect you about 1600 on the day you want to return.

Bicycle/scooter
On the plaza **Cubanacán**, daily 0900-1900. Rents bicycles and scooters by the hour, the day or longer. Alternatively rent a bike on the street for CUC$10 for the afternoon. It is illegal to rent bicycles from *casas particulares*, but it happens and is cheaper.

Car hire
Havanautos and Transtur at the end of Salvador Cisneros by the gas station, T48-796305/796330, Mon-Fri 0830-1800, cars and small jeeps. Cubacar, also by the gas station, T48-796060, Mon-Fri 0800-1700, Sat 0900-1300, not always open, but good rates.

Taxi
Cubataxi to **Cayo Jutías** is CUC$60-70, as they charge by distance and for waiting time, with a surcharge later in the afternoon. To **María la Gorda** costs CUC$75 (tour agencies charge CUC$90-100 with commission). Private taxis are now rare because of police surveillance.

⊙ Directory

Viñales *p158, map p159*
Banks
Banco Popular de Ahorro, Salvador Cisneros 54A, does not do credit cards, open Mon-Fri 0800-1200 and 1330-1630. Bandec, Salvador Cisneros 58, for credit card transactions. Cadeca, Salvador Cisneros 92, open Mon-Sat 0800-1800.

Contents

Footprint features

At a glance

◉ **Getting around** On foot, by bicycle, hired car, taxi, Matanzas BusTour and Víazul long-distance bus.

◉ **Time required** 2 days to a week.

Matanzas

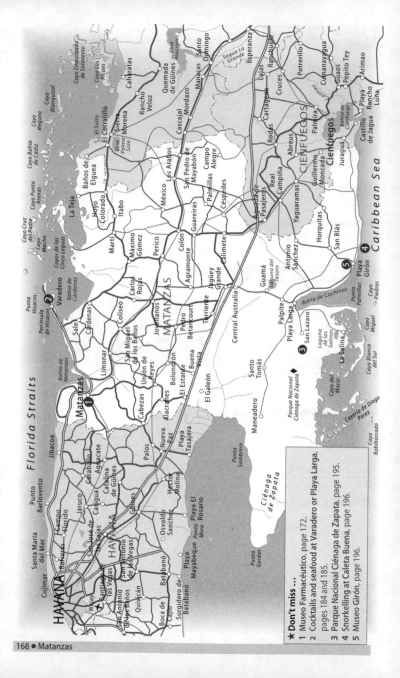

★ Don't miss ...
1 Museo Farmacéutico, page 172.
2 Cocktails and seafood at Varadero or Playa Larga,
   pages 184 and 185.
3 Parque Nacional Ciénaga de Zapata, page 195.
4 Snorkelling at Caleta Buena, page 196.
5 Museo Girón, page 196.

Matanzas province, to the east of Havana, is mainly associated with the mega-resort of Varadero beach. This tourist enclave incorporates some 17,000 hotel rooms squeezed onto a finger of land stretching out into the Caribbean. All budgets are catered for but you won't find a double room under CUC$50-60 in high season. The white sand, the handsome palm trees and the inviting sea, along with watersports, some good hotel food in a few places and some winning deals at all-inclusives make this a popular holiday spot. However, for all that it represents of Cuba it might as well be another country. Close to Varadero and in contrast to it are the low-key towns of Matanzas and Cárdenas where there is no engineered tourism. Both have had their heyday: Matanzas as the birthplace of rumba and danzón and Cárdenas as an industrial superstar. The outstanding Cuevas de Bellamar and the luscious Valle de Yumurí, studded with thousands of Royal palm trees, are also worth visiting.

The second largest province in the country also has a southern coast with one of Cuba's most notable geographic features, the Ciénaga de Zapata, a huge marsh covering the entire coast and the peninsula of the same name. It is a nature reserve, protecting many endemic species of flora and fauna, as well as numerous migrating birds. The diving in the deep-blue sea off Playa Girón and Playa Larga is exceptional. Also here, in the Bay of Pigs, the disastrous American-backed invasion is remembered in two museums.

Getting there

Air There is an international airport at Varadero, which receives scheduled and charter flights from Europe and Canada. **Rail** Connections by rail are reasonable with Matanzas on the main line between Havana and Santiago and on local lines to other towns, however service is poor. A feature of rail transport is the Hershey electric line between Havana and Matanzas, which used to service the Hershey chocolate factory before the Revolution, but it breaks down frequently and timings are very approximate. **Road** There is a good road out from Havana along the north coast to Matanzas and Varadero with an excellent bus service provided by **Víazul**. Local buses run to other towns such as Cárdenas but public transport is limited to the Zapata peninsula. **Viazul** stops at Entronque de Jagüey and Girón with non-state taxis as an option for onward transport. There are plenty of tour buses to take you there on an excursion, but car hire is recommended if you want flexibility. ▸▸ *See also Matanzas, below, Varadero, page 179, Cárdenas, page 189, and Zapata Peninsula and the Bay of Pigs, page 193.*

Tourist information

State tour agencies can be found in all the hotels in Varadero and the Bay of Pigs. They operate as tourist information offices although their main purpose is to sell tours. They can help with hotel reservations, tickets and transfers. **Infotur** can also be found in Varadero and at the airport.

Best time to visit

The winter season between December and April has the best weather but the highest prices. The wettest time of year is between September and November, but if there is a cold front off the eastern seaboard of the USA in the winter you can expect rough seas and a smaller expanse of sand as a result. The Bay of Pigs is more protected from the weather but has been hit in the past by hurricanes between September and November.

Matanzas

➜ *Colour map 2, A1. Population: 115,000.*

Matanzas is a sleepy city with old colonial buildings, a remarkable pharmacy museum and a legendary musical history. It sits on the Bahía de Matanzas and is freshened by the sea breeze. On the opposite side of the bay is the busy, ugly industrial zone (there are oil storage facilities, chemical and fertilizer plants, sugar, textile and paper mills and thermal power stations). Both the rivers Yumurí and San Juan flow through the city and you can walk along the riverside at dusk and watch the fishermen or take in the tranquillity and murmur of fellow observers.

Most of the old buildings are between the two rivers, with another colonial district, Versalles, to the north of the Río Yumurí. This area was colonized in the 19th century by French refugees from Haiti after the revolution there. The newer district, Pueblo Nuevo, also has many colonial houses. ▸▸ *For listings, see pages 176-178.*

Ins and outs

Getting there The town lies 104 km east of Havana along the Vía Blanca, which links the capital with Varadero beach, 34 km further east. If you are travelling by **car** the drive is

Music in Matanzas

Matanzas is a quiet town in all senses but one. If you listen carefully you can hear its unique heartbeat: one, two, one two three.

With its docks and warehouses, Matanzas provided the ideal birthplace for the rumba and it is still the world capital of this exhilarating music and dance form. Families here are virtually born into the rumba: the latest incarnation of the *Muñequitos de Matanzas* has a young boy keeping the beat on the bamboo *guagua*. The *Muñequitos* are the fathers and mothers of contemporary rumba, having set the standards for *rumberos* on their tours across the globe. Of course, the *rumba Matancera* bears not the slightest resemblance to its ballroom namesake.

The rumba at the *Casa de la Trova* was famous for its intricate drumming, vocal improvisations and dancing, which is by turns graceful, audacious, devotional and downright dirty. Rumba is a communal art form – the *Columbia* style was created by workers on the Columbia railway line; however, great names of the past are recalled in *Columbias* such as 'Malanga Murió'. On your way to a rumba, don't forget to stop at a bar and put a record by Matanzas' own Arsenio Rodríguez on the 1950s jukebox. Without Arsenio, there would have been no *conjunto son* and thus no Latin salsa. If you've got time, go and pay homage at the site of the dance hall where on a hot January night in 1879 Miguel Faílde created the *danzón cubano*, still the only authentic, unselfconscious marriage of orchestral sounds with African rhythms. It is now the (closed) *Sala de Conciertos José White de Matanzas*, Calle 79 entre 288 y 290. *Danzón* is currently enjoying a revival: across Cuba, music is being reissued and orchestras formed and there is a European *danzón* orchestra based in Holland. The world has much to thank Matanzas for.

unattractive along the coast and can be smelly because of the many small oil wells producing low-grade crude en route, but once you get into the hills there are good views of the countryside. There is a spectacular lookout with a view of the Yumurí valley, called the **Mirador de Bacunayagua**, overlooking a viaduct spanning a gorge, the highest bridge in Cuba. Most buses make this a rest stop. Long-distance **buses** between Havana and Varadero all pass through Matanzas and you can request a stop here. You can also get here by **train** en route from Havana to Santiago. However, the 2½ to four-hour journey via the Hershey Railway, the only electric train in Cuba, which runs from Havana to Matanzas, is memorable and scenic if you are not in a hurry. ▶▶ *See also Transport, page 178.*

Getting around Most of the places of interest are within walking distance, but if you get tired you can board a **horse-drawn coche**, hail a **bicitaxi** or you can hire a **local driver** to take you around for a day trip out of town. Some of the main sights can be reached using the hop-on hop-off MatanzasBusTour between Varadero and Matanzas which passes the city centre historic sights, the San Severino fort, Cuevas de Bellamar and Tropicana. ▶▶ *See Transport, page 178, for details.*

History

The town dates from 1693, when immigrants from the Canary Islands founded a settlement they called San Carlos y Severino de Matanzas, between the rivers San Juan and Yumurí. Before that, the area was known mainly for an attack on the Spanish fleet in

1628 in the Bahía de Matanzas, by the Dutch Admiral Piet Heyn. Spain and Holland were at war at the time and the fleet was considered war booty, with the four million ducats of gold and silver captured being used to finance further battles. The name Matanzas is thought to come from the mass slaughter of wild pigs to provision the fleets, but it could also refer to the killing of the Amerindians who lived here and called the bay Guanima. Around the time of the founding of the city, a fortress, the Castillo de San Severino, was built on the northern shore of the bay to keep out pirates and any other invaders.

The town became prosperous with the advent of sugar mills in the 1820s, followed by the railway in 1843. Most of the buildings date from this time and by the 1860s it was the second largest town in Cuba after Havana, with all the trappings of an important city, such as a theatre, newspaper and library. It even became known as the 'Athens of Cuba' because of all the musicians and writers living there. The **Sala de Conciertos José White de Matanzas**, on Contreras (79) on the plaza, was formerly the *Lyceum Club* and is famous for being the place where the *danzón* was danced for the first time in 1879 (there is a plaque outside but it is now closed), see page 171.

Sights

City centre

Parque de la Libertad is the main square, with a statue of José Martí in the middle and dominated by the former **Palacio del Gobierno** on its eastern side. The **Sala de Conciertos José White** (see above) is on the northern side and next to it is the abandoned **Hotel Velasco**. Just beside the hotel is the **Teatro Velasco**, now a cinema.

On the south side of the plaza is the beautifully preserved **Museo Farmacéutico** ① *Milanés 4951 entre Santa Teresa y Ayuntamiento, T45-223197, Mon-Fri 1000-1800, Sun 0800-1200, CUC$3, camera charge, CUC$1 per picture,* containing the original equipment, porcelain jars, recipes and furnishings of the Botica La Francesa, opened in 1882 by the Triolet and Figueroa family. Both men founded a pharmacy in Sagua la Grande before visiting Matanzas together and establishing the new pharmacy; Triolet later married into the Figueroa family. The pharmacy shelves are all made of cedarwood and divided by Corinthian columns – all made from one tree trunk. All the shelves are filled with 19th-century French porcelain jars, which are full of medicinal plants and imported European products and North American goods. The museum exhibits lists with all the formulas on it, displays pill makers, the original telephone, baby bottles, gynaecological equipment and scorpion oil. It was a working pharmacy until 1964, when it was nationalized and then converted into this fascinating museum, believed to be unique in Latin America. Curator Patria Dopico is very helpful.

East of the plaza is the former home of local poet, José Jacinto Milanés (1814-63), on the street that bears his name; it is now the **Archivo Histórico**. There is a statue of the poet outside the elegant **Catedral de San Carlos Borromeo**, further down on Milanés (83), first built in 1693, but rebuilt in 1878 after a fire in a neoclassical style with frescoed ceilings and walls. Now undergoing restoration, the frescoes will disappear.

Further east is the **Plaza de la Vigía**, dominated by the **Teatro Sauto** ① *daily 0830-1600, CUC$2.* There are 14 performances a month and ticket prices vary. A magnificent neoclassical building, built by Daniel Dallaglio, an Italian, who won the commission by competition; Dallaglio also built the church of San Pedro Apóstol, see page 175. The theatre dates from 1862-63 and seats 650 people in cream, wrought-iron seats in three-tiered balconies for performances that have included in the past Enrico

Matanzas

Valle de Yumurí

(Estero) 292

Río Yumurí

AREC HAVALETA

Mirador de Monserrate

la Ermita de Monserrate

BALCON DEL YUMURI

Carretera Yumurí 67

Humbolt Cespedes

(Cuarta)

(Tercera) 23

(Segundo) 27

(Primero) 37

(Arostegui) 41

(San Hipólito) 47

VERSALLES

(San Juan) 49

(Versalles) 51

(Santa Rita) 53

(San Alejandro) 55

San Pedro Apóstol

(Gómez) 59

(Isabel) 63

(Arostegui) 69

SIMPSON

57

(Reforma) 59

(Fortuna) 61

(Jesús María) 63

Seminario

Methodist

(Jáuregui) 65

Hershey Terminal

MATANZAS ESTE

(Salamanca) 71

(Daoíz) 75

(Maceo) 77

LOS MANGOS

Pentecostal

Contreras (Bonifacio Byrne)

Los Carmelitas

Presbiteriana

Parque Libertad

Catedral de San Carlos Borromeo

Bahía de Matanzas

Parque René Fraga

(Milanés) 83

MATANZAS OESTE

La Caridad

(Río San Severino) 93

(Cuba) 95

(Alvarez) 97

(Embarcadero Blanco) 99

(Zaragoza) 101

Río San Juan

(Recurso) 103

(Refugio) 105

101

A

(San Andrés) 119

(San Sebastián) 115

(San Juan Bautista) 117

(San Francisco) 119

(La Merced) 121

PUEBLO NUEVO

(San Juan de Dios) 123

(Santa Rita) 125

Estadio Victoria de Girón

Interprovincial

(San Rafael) 127

(Espíritu Santo) 131

Long Distance (Viazul)

ARMANDO MESTRE

(San Fernando) 135

(Buen Viaje) 139

(Tenaza) 145

Destino

Palmar del Junco

NARANJAL SUR

LA JAIBA

(Maurguil)

(Av 1) 175

(Av 3) 177

(Av 5) 179

(Av 7) 181

(Av 9) 183

CAMILO CIENFUEGOS

MIRET

Matanzas maps

1 Matanzas, page 173

2 Matanzas centre, page 174

N

500 metres

500 yards

Entertainment 😊

Cabaret Restaurante Monserrate 1

Caruso and Anna Pavlova, who toured Cuba in 1917. French actress Sarah Bernhardt, musician José White, singer Rita Montaner and Alicia Alonso, director of the Cuban National Ballet, have all appeared here. It was restored after the Revolution. In the entrance there are Carrara marble statues of Greek goddesses (and a painting of Piet Heyn, the Dutch admiral) and, in the hall, the muses are painted on the ceiling. Most unusually, the floor can be raised to convert the auditorium into a ballroom. Opposite the theatre is the restored, pale orange **Palacio de Justicia**, built in 1826 and rebuilt in 1911.

The **Museo Palacio de Junco** ① *Milanés entre Magdalena y Ayllón, T45-243464, Tue-Fri 1000-1800, Sat 1300-1900, Sun 0900-1200, CUC$2*, a royal blue building overlooking the theatre, houses the provincial museum, built by a wealthy plantation owner and dating from 1840. The historical exhibits include an archaeological display and the development of sugar and slavery in the province. It includes the remains of a slave who was thrown into a pit with his chains still attached and stocks to hold the feet of slaves. There are guns and pistols from the capture of silver boats of Dutchman Piet Heyn on 8 September 1628.

There are several bridges in the town, but the one you are most likely to notice is the steel **Puente Calixto García**, built in 1899 at the edge of Plaza de la Vigía and next to the neoclassical fire station, **Parque de los Bomberos**. Just below the bridge is a **mosaic memorial to Che Guevara**. Opposite the fire station is **Ediciones Vigía** ① *daily 0900-1600*, where you can see books being produced, ranging from fairy tales to those commemorating important events. These are all handmade and in first editions of only

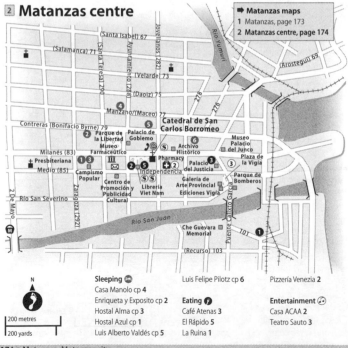

2 Matanzas centre

➡ **Matanzas maps**
1 Matanzas, page 173
2 Matanzas centre, page 174

Sleeping
Casa Manolo cp 4
Enriqueta y Exposito cp 2
Hostal Alma cp 3
Hostal Azul cp 1
Luis Alberto Valdés cp 5
Luis Felipe Pilotz cp 6

Eating
Café Atenas 3
El Rápido 5
La Ruina 1
Pizzería Venezia 2

Entertainment
Casa ACAA 2
Teatro Sauto 3

200 copies, so they are collectors' items, particularly if you get one signed. The **Galería de Arte Provincial** ① *also on the plaza, daily 0900-1700*, has rotating displays of contemporary Cuban art.

North of the city centre

North of the Río Yumurí in Reparto Versalles near the Hershey terminal is the **Iglesia de San Pedro Apóstol** ① *Calle 57 y 270, open Mon-Sat mornings and 1530-1930*. Cross the park in front of the terminal and walk up the street in the far corner. The church will soon be towering above you on the left. There is a rather lovely stained glass of Saint Peter. The interior is mustard yellow and there is an imposing altar piece with four Ionic columns.

Beyond Reparto Versalles, towards the northeast on Avenida del Muelle is **Castillo de San Severino** ① *Mon-Sat 0900-1700, Sun 0900-1300, CUC$2, CUC$1 for pictures, CUC$5 for a video camera*. This muscular, colonial castle was a solid lookout post on the Bay of Matanzas built to prevent pirate attack. The original coat of arms is still above the main entrance. Originally water lapped at the castle entrance but a road was built in front of it in 1910. The moat, however, was never filled with water. San Severino was also used as a prison until the 1980s. A man was incarcerated here for six years for being a Jehova's witness. It is said the prison was divided by a wall: on one side were political prisoners and on the other homosexuals. The castle was built in 1693 and, with UNESCO support, is being turned into a **museum of slavery**. This will include displays of ceramics and pipes and other materials found at the castle as well as exhibits on Afro-Cuban religion.

La Ermita de Montserrate, a good hike north up Domingo Mujica (306), northwest of the Parque de la Libertad, was built in 1872 in honour of the Virgin of Monserrat. The roof caved in after storm damage and it is now being rebuilt. From the hilltop it is perched on, you can see the city and the bay rolled out before you and on the other side the verdant **Valle de Yumurí** although the perfection of the view is slightly marred by the pylons marching towards the horizon. This is an excellent place to walk.

Around Matanzas

Castillo del Morrillo and Caves

The road out to Varadero goes past the university and the Escuela Militar. One kilometre past the university you come to the **Río Canímar**, which flows into the Bahía de Matanzas. Trips along the river can be arranged from Varadero. Just before the bridge over the river, take the road running alongside the river towards the bay to the **Castillo del Morrillo** ① *Tue-Sun 1000-1700, CUC$1 entrance, CUC$1 for guide*, built in 1720 to protect the area. The castle is now a museum in memory of Antonio Guiteras Holmes, who was shot with the Venezuelan revolutionary, Carlos Aponte Hernández, by Batista's troops near the bridge. Bronze busts of the two men can be seen underneath a mahogany tree. Guiteras Holmes was a student leader who started a revolutionary group called *Joven Cuba* (Young Cuba) in 1934. He served briefly in the government that replaced Machado, but fell foul of the rising Batista. It was when he and Aponte came to Matanzas in 1935 to try and find a boat to take them into exile in Mexico that they were caught and executed. The castle also has a *sala* of aboriginal archaeology and a large rowing boat.

Southeast of town at Finca La Alcancía are the **Cuevas de Bellamar** ① *T45-261683, Mon-Sat 0900-2030, Sun 0900-1700, tours daily at 0930, 1030, 1130, 1315, 1415, 1515, 1615, CUC$5, CUC$8 includes the extra 100-m stretch, parking CUC$1, CUC$5 for cameras with flash and video cameras. Take bus No 12, 1 peso cubano, from Parque Libertad to the caves,* *leaves every 2 hrs*. This cave system, discovered in 1862 by somebody working the land, stretches for 23 km, and is stuffed full of stalactites, stalagmites (one 12 m tall) and underground streams. Tour parties come from Varadero so you may get herded along with a bus load but, in any case, you are not allowed in unaccompanied along the 750-m trip through the caves; you can go a further 100 m with torches. There is a small museum with items found in the caves and explanations in English and Spanish. The complex has a restaurant, shop and children's playground.

There are also caves at **Las Cuevas de Santa Catalina**, near Carbonera, 20 km east of Matanzas, where there are believed to be 8 km of tunnels. Amerindian paintings have been found here, close to the entrance, and the caves were used as a burial site. Another cave, **Refugio de Saturno**, is a large cave often visited by scuba-divers, although anyone can enjoy a swim here. It is 1 km south of the Vía Blanca, 8 km east of the Río Canímar.

◉ Matanzas listings

For Sleeping and Eating price codes and other relevant information, see Essentials pages 37-43.

● Sleeping

Matanzas *p170, maps p173 and p174*
Casas particulares
All the casas listed here offer food and their rooms have a/c and fans, hot and cold water, but not all have private bathrooms. Those with shared bathrooms are cheaper, with rates starting at CUC$15, while those offering private bathrooms charge CUC$20-25.
D-E Enriqueta y Exposito, Contreras 29016 entre Sta Teresa (290) y Zaragoza (292), T/F45-245151. Enriqueta has 2 pleasant rooms although 1 is up a precarious staircase. Both rooms have use of a fridge. This place is often full and so it might be wise to ring in advance.
D-E Hostal Alma, Milanés (83) 29008 Altos entre Sta Teresa (290) y Zaragoza (292), T45-242449, hostalalma@gmail.com. Huge and grand 19th-century house with beautiful *vitrales*, terrace and fabulous roof view, with 2 rooms on the 2nd floor with private bathroom, fridge, minibar. 1 room can hold a couple and child. Dinner is also offered to non-guests, but ring beforehand to book. The friendly family and their attractive house make this a very popular option.
D-E Hostal Azul, Milanés (83) 29012 entre Santa Teresa (290) y Zaragoza (292), T45-242449, T5-273 7903 (mob), hostalazul.cu@

gmail.com. Well-preserved 1870s mansion with original tiles. Very spacious, 2 rooms with large private bathrooms. Run by husband and wife team Yoel Baez and Aylin Hernández, who are very helpful. Having worked 12 years in Sol Meliá hotels in Varadero, Yoel is experienced in hospitality and speaks English and Italian.
E Casa Manolo, Manzano (77), (also known as Maceo) 28805 entre Ayuntamiento (288) y Sta Teresa (290), T45-247893, 1 block from the centre. This is a basement house (enter a large entrance hall and then take the steps down to the right), with 1 clean room. The bathroom is shared with the owner who provides amusing company.
E Luis Alberto Valdés, Contreras (79) 28205 (2nd floor) entre Jovellanos y Ayuntamiento (288), T45-243397, anatapanes@gmail.com. Luis has 2 rooms, 1 able to house a couple and a child. Shared bathroom in clean, 1st-floor flat.
E Luis Felipe Pilotz, Cuba esq Manzanera. An 1882 house with beautiful taupe and blue tiles. The 2 rooms have use of a fridge, washing machine, and 2 shared bathrooms. Large patio. There is also use of a parking spot 30 m away. Welcoming family.

Around Matanzas *p175*
Hotels
C Canimao, Km 4.5 Carretera Matanzas a Varadero, T45-261014, www.islazul.cu.

A modern, but nice-looking hotel on the outskirts of Matanzas opposite the **Tropicana** cabaret. It has 120 rooms on a hill above the Río Canímar, with good restaurant, breakfast included, nightclub, pool, excursions offered on the river or to caves. Nearby is a natural canyon, the Cueva de Los Cristales, which had evidence of aboriginal infanticide.

Casas particulares

There are several rooms to rent along the coast road to Varadero, right on the sea front, in Reparto Playa, once you get past all the bridges. They are quite a long way from the town centre with a good view of the tankers.

Eating

Matanzas *p170, maps p173 and p174*
You are better off eating in your *casa particular* in Matanzas.

La Ruina, just past Puente Calixto García on Calle 101. Open 24 hrs. Very attractive restaurant converted from sugar warehouse, dinner, delicious pastries, great ice cream, pesos and CUC$ accepted, live music at weekends.

Café Atenas, Calle 83 y 272 (Plaza de la Vigía). Daily 1000-2200. A modern, highly a/c all-plastic café opposite Teatro Sauto, snack food, but also pizzas, spaghetti, grilled fish, chicken and ice cream.

El Rápido, behind the cathedral. Open 24 hrs. Serves up the usual pizza, snacks and cola combinations. Service is very quick.

Pizzería Venezia, Calle 85 entre 282 y 288, T45-242789. Pizza and pastas.

Entertainment

Matanzas *p170, maps p173 and p174*
The Centro de Promoción y Publicidad Cultural, Independencia (85) entre Ayuntamiento (288) y Sta Teresa (290) has a *cartelera* in the window displaying all entertainment fixtures.

Live music and dance

The Plaza de la Vigía is the place to go in the evenings; locals congregate here to chat, play dominoes or draughts, or make music. The **Teatro Sauto**, see Sights, page 172, usually has live performances at the weekends.

Casa ACAA (Asociación Cubana de los Artistas Artesanos), Calle 85 entre 282 y 280. Live music with trios and pianists. Also has a café.

Around Matanzas *p175*
Cabaret

Cabaret Las Palmas, Calle 254 esq 127, T45-253252. Wed, Thu, Fri 2030-2400, Sat 2030-0200. Live show Thu, Sat, comedy Fri, taped music Wed. Entry usually CUC$2, depending on the event.

Cabaret Restaurante Monserrate, Mujica (306) final, T 45-244222. Wed, Fri, Sat, Sun 2100-0200. CUC$1 or pesos cubanos. Bus No 12 takes you there.

Tropicana Matanzas, Autopista Varadero Km 4.5, T45-265380, reservas@tropimat.co.cu. Daily 2030-0230, show Wed-Sun 2200-2330, CUC$35 which includes a cocktail, ¼ bottle of rum and 1 soft drink. The Matanzas version of the famous cabaret in a spectacular outdoor setting opposite the Hotel Canimao.

Festivals and events

Matanzas *p170, maps p173 and p174*
20-26 Aug From the Tue-Sun is the Carnival de Matanzas.

Shopping

Matanzas *p170, maps p173 and p174*
Next door to the Galería de Arte Provincial, on Plaza de la Vigía, is a large building housing **Vigía Crafts**, Mon-Fri 0900-1800, for crafts, ceramics and clothing. **Librería Viet Nam** on Calle 85 y 288 for books, behind El Rápido. **Photo Service** on Ayuntamiento (288) esq Independencia (85). **Supermercado La República** Calle 85 (Independencia) esq 288.

Daily 0830-2030. A fairly well-stocked, but small, CUC$ supermarket.

⊖ Transport

Matanzas *p170, maps p173 and p174*
Bus
The bus station, T45-291473, open 24 hrs, is at Calle 131 y 272, Calzada Esteban esq Terry (Coppelia is opposite the terminal). There are taxis and *coches* at the bus station. However, if you arrive later in the day you might just be left with a *taxi particular*, in which case, if you have an address when you arrive at the house insist that you did so by your own means otherwise the taxi driver will get a CUC$5 commission for every day you stay in a casa.

Víazul, T45-916445, passes through on its **Havana–Varadero** route, 3 daily, see timetable, page 32. There's a hop-on hop-off MatanzasBusTour that leaves Matanzas' Parque Libertad at 1115, 1445, 1545, and 1715. It passes the city centre historic sights and goes on to the San Severino fort, Cuevas de Bellamar and Tropicana arriving at Varadero at 1245, 1415, 1715 and 1845. It returns from Varadero at 0930, 1100, 1400 and 1530. CUC$10. **Transtur** operates the service and has confirmed that passengers wishing to return from Varadero later can take any **Transtur** bus heading to the city.

Car hire
Servi Cupet, T45-253594.

Taxi
There are no official taxis in Matanzas; they have to come from Varadero and will charge extra. **Cubataxi**, T45-611616, charges CUC$25 Matanzas–Varadero.

Train
There are 2 stations: the Hershey terminal and main terminal. There are 5 trains daily on the electric Hershey Railway to and from Casablanca in **Havana**. It uses a station north of the Río Yumurí in Versalles at 282 y 67. There are no facilities here and the ticket office, T45-244805, has erratic opening hours. Trains from **Hershey** leave at 0433 (getting in to Casablanca at 0720), 0830 (1102), 1243 (1532), 1633 (1918), 2034 (2318), returning from Casablanca at 0606, 0947, 1411, 1805, 2204. Tickets CUC$2.80, children half price, but you may never get charged. If there is no electricity it doesn't run.

The newer, main station south of the town at Calle 181, Miret (open 24 hrs, T45-292409), receives trains from Havana en route to Santiago. Horse-drawn *coche* to market area, CUC$1.

⊕ Directory

Matanzas *p170, maps p173 and p174*
Banks Banco Nacional, at 83 (Milanés) y 282, diagonally opposite the cathedral. Bandec, esq 282 y 85, Mon-Fri 0800-1500. Visa and MasterCard. **Banco Popular,** Medio (Independencia) (85) opposite the church, Mon-Fri 0800-1530. **Medical services** Facilities for foreigners are available in Varadero, but there is a **pharmacy** here, open 24 hrs, at 85 y Matanzas (282). **Post** At 85 entre 290 y 288, daily, 24 hrs. **Telephone/internet** Etecsa, Milanés y 282, daily 0830-2130. Telephone service and internet, *tarjetas* available, CUC$6 per hr for internet.

Varadero

→ *Colour map 2, A1.*

Cuba's chief beach resort, Varadero, is built on the Península de Hicacos, a 23-km-long thin peninsula, along the length of which run two roads lined with dozens of large all-inclusive hotels, some smaller ones, and several chalets and villas, many of which date from before 1959. Sadly, some of the hotel architecture is hideous.

Varadero is still undergoing large-scale development and joint ventures with foreign investors are still being encouraged. The latest area for development is Laguna Mangon at the far end of the peninsula. Despite the building in progress it is not over-exploited and is a good place for a family beach holiday. The beaches are quite empty, if a bit exposed, and you can walk for miles along the sand, totally isolated from the rest of Cuba, if not other tourists. ▸▸ *For listings, see pages 182-189.*

Ins and outs

Getting there Varadero's international **airport** is 26 km from the beginning of the hotel strip. If you are booked into one of the new hotels at the end of the peninsula, you will have a journey of some 40 km. The **Víazul** bus pulls in here on its way to the central bus terminal. If you are travelling **by car** from Havana there is a good dual carriageway, the Vía Blanca, which runs to Varadero, 142 km from the capital. The toll at the entrance to the resort is CUC$2 for cars. The easiest way to get to and from Havana is on a **tour** or **transfer bus**, booked through a hotel tour desk, which will pick you up and drop you off at your hotel. There are daily **buses** from Havana, and also from Trinidad via Sancti Spíritus and Santa Clara with **Víazul** (see timetable, page 32). A taxi from Havana to Varadero airport costs CUC$80. ▸▸ *See also Transport, page 188.*

Getting around Distances are large. Avenida 1, which runs southwest–northeast the length of the peninsula, has a tourist **bus** service, see Transport, page 188. It takes about an hour to cover the length, taking into account dropping-off times. Calle numbers begin with lowest numbers at the southwest end and work upwards to the northeast. Car rental is available at the airport and at numerous hotel and office locations along the peninsula. Most hotels rent **bicycles**, or **mopeds**, which will allow you to get further, faster. **Taxis** wait outside hotels, or you can phone for one. There are also **horse-drawn carriages** for a leisurely tour and a handful of *cocotaxis*.

Tourist information Infotur has an office at Calle 13 esq Av 1, T45-662966, infovar@ enet.cu. There are also offices in the airport, at Calle 44 esq Av 1 and Calle 20 esq Av 1. Most are open daily 0800-1700. Your hotel tourist desk should also be able to answer all your questions. If not, all tour operators can help. Some places in Varadero accept euro.

History

Salt was the first economic catalyst in the area, followed by cattle, timber and sugar. A plan was drawn up in 1887 for the foundation of a city, but development of the peninsula did not really begin until 1923, when it was discovered as a potential holiday resort for the seriously rich. There are some old wooden houses left, with rocking chairs on the verandas and balconies, but the village area was not built until the 1950s. The Dupont family bought land in the 1920s, sold it for profit, then bought more, constructed roads and built a large house, now the **Mansión Xanadú**.

Sights

The relatively recent development of Varadero means there is little of historical or architectural interest; visitors spend their time on the beach, engaging in watersports or taking organized excursions. The southern end of the resort is more low key, with hustlers on the beaches by day and *jineteros* in the bars at night. The village area does feel like a real place, not just a hotel city, and, in contrast to some other tourist enclaves (such as the northern cays), Cubans do actually live here. The far northeastern end is where international hotels are; you can pay to use their facilities even if you are not staying there. Apart from their own hotel shops, they are very remote from the shopping area and independent restaurants. As a result, most of the hotels at the far end are all-inclusives.

The **Museo de Varadero** ① *C 57 y Av de la Playa, daily 1000-1900, CUC$1*, is worth a visit if you want something to do away from the beach. The house itself is interesting as an example of one of the first beach houses. Originally known as *Casa Villa Abreu*, it was built in 1921 by architect Leopoldo Abreu as a summer house in blue and white with a lovely timber veranda and wooden balconies all round, designed to catch the breeze. Restored in 1980-81 as a museum, it has the usual collection of unlabelled furniture and glass from the early 20th century, stuffed animals in a natural history room (a revolutionary guard dog, Ima, appears to be suffering from mange), and an Amerindian skeleton (male, aged 20-30, with signs of syphilis and anaemia). However, the most interesting exhibit is a two-headed baby shark washed up on these shores. There are several old photos of the first hotels in Varadero, including Dos Mares (1940), Internacional (1950) and Pullman (1950), as well as items of local sporting history, a shirt of Javier Sotomayor and a rowing boat from the Club Náutico de Varadero. The **Parque Josone**, Avenida 1 y 57, is a large park with pool and several restaurants.

At the far end of the peninsula the land has been designated the **Varadero Ecological Park** (Parque Ecológico Varahicacos) ① *Centro de Visitantes for the reserve is at the road entrance to Hotel Paradisus Varadero, 0900-1630, CUC$3*. The reserve includes 700 m of beach with different plant species including scrub and cactus, with a lagoon where salt was once made, several kilometres of sandy beach and two caves. The **Cueva de Ambrosio**, 30 mins walk from the main road, is where dozens of Amerindian drawings

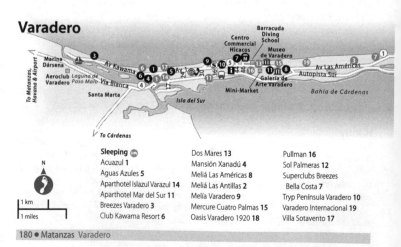

Varadero

Sleeping 🛏
Acuazul **1**
Aguas Azules **5**
Aparthotel Islazul Varazul **14**
Aparthotel Mar del Sur **11**
Breezes Varadero **3**
Club Kawama Resort **6**

Dos Mares **13**
Mansión Xanadú **4**
Meliá Las Américas **8**
Meliá Las Antillas **2**
Meliá Varadero **9**
Mercure Cuatro Palmas **15**
Oasis Varadero 1920 **18**

Pullman **16**
Sol Palmeras **12**
Superclubs Breezes
  Bella Costa **7**
Tryp Península Varadero **10**
Varadero Internacional **19**
Villa Sotavento **17**

were discovered in 1961. **Cueva de Musulmanes** contains aboriginal fossils. Nearly opposite Marina Chapelín is a Dolphinarium, see Activities and tours, page 187.

Beaches, watersports and the cays

Varadero's sandy beach stretches the length of the peninsula, broken only occasionally by rocky outcrops which can be traversed by walking through a hotel's grounds. Some parts are wider than others and as a general rule the older hotels have the best bits of beach. For instance, the **Internacional**, which was the **Hilton** before the Revolution, has a large swathe of curving beach, whereas the brand-new, upmarket **Meliá Las Américas** and its sister hotels, **Meliá Varadero** and **Sol Palmeras**, have a disappointingly shallow strip of sand and some rocks. However, the sand is all beautifully looked after and cleaned daily. The water is clean and nice for swimming but snorkelling is not worth the effort. For good **snorkelling**, take one of the many boat trips out to the cays. There are three **marinas**, all full service with **sailing tours**, restaurants, **deep-sea fishing** and **diving**. All services can be booked through the tour desks in hotels. You can indulge in almost any form of watersport, including **windsurfing and kitesurfing** and **non-motorized pedalos** but these are not practised in the open sea for environmental and safety reasons (you might get blown over to Miami). If you are not staying in any of the Varadero hotels you may organize activities yourselves, but it will be a bit more difficult.

There are many **sailing tours** to the offshore cays, which usually include lunch, an open bar and time for swimming and snorkelling.

Varadero is one of the most developed areas for diving. There are several sites around the offshore cays suitable for novice or advanced divers. Interesting sites include the wreck of the *Neptune*, a 60-m steel cargo ship thought to be German, lying in only 10 m. This is home to a number of fish including massive green moray eels and very large, friendly French angelfish. The wreck is very broken up, but the boilers are still intact and there are places where the superstructure (shaft and propeller) is in good condition and interesting to explore with good photo sites. Among the many reef dive sites in the area are Clara Boyas (Sun Roof), a massive 60-sq-m coral head in 20 m of water, with tunnels large enough for three to four divers to swim through. These connect with upward

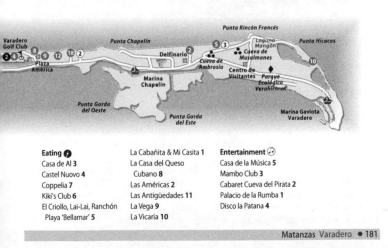

Eating 🍴
Casa de Al **3**
Castel Nuovo **4**
Coppelia **7**
Kiki's Club **6**
El Criollo, Lai-Lai, Ranchón
  Playa 'Bellamar' **5**

La Cabañita & Mi Casita **1**
La Casa del Queso
  Cubano **8**
Las Américas **2**
Las Antigüedades **11**
La Vega **9**
La Vicaria **10**

Entertainment 😊
Casa de la Música **5**
Mambo Club **3**
Cabaret Cueva del Pirata **2**
Palacio de la Rumba **1**
Disco la Patana **4**

passages where the sunlight can be seen streaming through. Another site, Las Brujas (the Witches), is only 6 m deep. Large coral heads protrude from the sandy bottom, with coral holes and crevices, adorned with sea fans, home for large schools of snappers. Playa Coral is a site on a 2-km barrier reef west of Varadero, beginning at Matanzas Bay, with a large variety of fish and coral. This is usually a shore dive, although if you go over the wall, where you can find black coral and gorgonians in deep water, it can be a boat dive. If you are based in Varadero on a dive package, you may be offered a trip to Playa Girón for good shore diving, and to the Saturno Caves for an inland cave dive, as part of your package.

The **cays around the Hicacos Peninsula** were once the haunt of French pirates and it is supposed that the name 'Varadero' comes from the fact that ships ran aground here, becoming *varados* (stranded). **Cayo Mono** lies five nautical miles north northeast of Punta de Morlas. During the nesting season in mid-year it becomes a seagull sanctuary for the 'Gaviota Negra' (*Anous stolidus*) and the 'Gaviota Monja' (*Sterna fuscata* and *Annaethetus*), during which time you can only pass by and watch them through binoculars. **Cayo Piedra del Norte** is two miles southeast of Cayo Mono. On the cay is a lighthouse. Other cays visited by tour boats include Cayo Blanco, Cayo Romero and Cayo Diana. ➤➤ See Activities and tours, page 187.

◉ Varadero listings

For Sleeping and Eating price codes and other relevant information, see Essentials pages 37-43.

● Sleeping

Varadero *p179, map p180*
Casas particulares are not legal in Varadero but they do exist. Between Cárdenas and Varadero there are oil wells. The air smells of sulphur, which drifts as far as Varadero if the wind is in the wrong direction when gas is released from the wells, often in the middle of the night. It is particularly obvious if you stay at the southwestern end of the peninsula.

The building of new hotels and renovation of older ones is continuing all along the Varadero peninsula, with some encroaching on the edge of the nature reserve. Overdevelopment is a real issue. Unless you want an all-inclusive beach holiday in an international hotel, it is best to stay in the mid-town area, where restaurants, bars and shops are within walking distance, hotels are smaller and more intimate and the beach is just as good. Someone booking from abroad as a package will get a better deal than those who try and book from Havana where you'll get a rack rate. Prices quoted here are rack

rates. There are weekend deals, mid-week deals, daily rates, etc.

LL-L Breezes Varadero, Carretera de las Americas Km 3, T45-667030, www.superclubscuba.com. 270 fully equipped rooms for singles and couples; no children under 16. Lots of activities and sports (all included), plenty of equipment, 5 bars, 3 restaurants, disco, themed parties, indoor games room, gym, sauna, jacuzzis, Olympic-size pool, tennis, diving and other watersports, such as sailing and waterskiing. Popular and crowded even in low season. Discount golf rates available.

LL-L Meliá Las Américas, Carretera de Las Morlas, T45-667600, www.solmeliacuba.com. One of the most expensive hotels on the strip, with 290 rooms, suites, but cleanliness and quality of the rooms has been criticized. Don't be afraid to ask to see another room. Comfortable, glitzy public areas, 5 restaurants, a recommended breakfast, nice pool. Golf, tennis, watersports, gym, and disco offered. The hotel is conveniently next to the **Plaza América** shopping centre and the Varadero golf course where a discount on the golf is available. Children under 18 are not permitted to stay here.

LL-L Meliá Varadero, Autopista del Sur Km 7, Carretera Las Morlas, T45-667013, www.solmeliacuba.com. Close to the strip's shopping complex, with 490 rooms, sits on a rocky promontory. Tennis, watersports, nightclub, spa offered. Prices reflect this hotel's lush splendour.

LL-L SuperClubs Breezes Bella Costa, Carretera Las Américas, Km 4.5, T45-667210. An attractive all-inclusive with 386 rooms at the end of one section of a sandy beach with rocky shore, landscaped gardens. Pool with swim-up bar, watersports and tennis. They have some lovely palapas on the beach. Formerly an Iberostar hotel, it is hoped that service will improve under SuperClubs' management.

LL-L Tryp Península Varadero, Autopista del Sur Km 17.5, Punta Hicacos, T45-668800, www.solmeliacuba.com. This is the most attractive all-inclusive hotel on the entire peninsula. It is built in wooden, Caribbean plantation-style villas painted in pastel and white shades. The lobby bar is attractive with wicker chairs. There are 591 rooms and 5 suites which are in bungalows, some with sea view. There are excellent facilities for children with a large pool area with children's play equipment and good à la carte restaurants.

LL-AL Mansión Xanadú, Carretera Las Americas, Km 8.5, T45-668482, www.varaderogolfclub.com. The beach house built for the Du Pont family in the 1920s is now the clubhouse for the golf course, offering the smartest, boutique-type accommodation in Varadero. The mansion sitting on a bluff overlooking the sea and backed by the golf course offers 5 doubles and 1 single room, each with balcony. Furnished with period pieces and very prettily decorated, golf is usually included in the package. Restaurant and bar. Away from the hustle and bustle of the beach resorts. Guests use all the facilities and the beach at the next door Meliá Las Américas.

LL-A Club Kawama Resort, Av 1 and Calle 1, Reparto Kawama, T45-614416, www.gran-caribe.com. A good mid-range all-inclusive hotel on the beach, 440 rooms with balcony or terrace. Buffet and à la carte restaurant, disco, entertainment, watersports included, kids' club, pool, tennis, gym, sauna, massage, hairdresser, medical services, PO, cambio, internet, moped and car rental, taxis, tourism bureau.

L-AL Varadero Internacional , Av Las Américas Km 1, T45-667038, www.gran-caribe.com. Formerly the Hilton, renovated in 1999-2000 when many of its period features were obliterated and instead of the garish pink it is now painted in tasteful but characterless shades of cream. It still has a bit of glamour though and its entrance is a wonderful 1950s grand style. There are 162 rooms. Watersports are not included if you take the all-inclusive option. There is a famous cabaret, Cuban art gallery, and it has one of the best stretches of sand on the whole peninsula. The Cabaret Continental stars Tue-Sat at 2200, CUC$25. On Sun there is a smaller one.

L-A Dos Mares, Calle 53 y Av 1, T45-612702, www.islazul.cu. One of the oldest hotels, dating from 1940 in Spanish style. It's small, friendly and full of character, across the road from the beach. Breakfast is included, rooms are adequate if a little dark and some come with good-sized bathrooms, others are small. No credit cards accepted.

L-A Mercure Cuatro Palmas, Av 1 entre 60 y 64, T45-667040, www.mercure.com. 282 rooms, some in bungalows and villas, hacienda style, on the beach, opposite Centro Comercial Caimán and good for shops and restaurants. Very pleasant hotel with a pool that has built-in sunbeds just under the water and an attractive hacienda-style sitting room and bar overlooking the pool area. Lots of services. This is definitely one of the more attractive places to stay.

AL Aguas Azules, Carretera Las Morlas, Km 14, Punta Francés, T45-668243, www.hotelesc.es. An expanded hotel with 411 rooms, 24-hr drinks and snacks, non-motorized watersports, day and night entertainment. A well-run, 4-star all-inclusive, formerly called Club Amigo Varadero.

AL-A Oasis Varadero 1920, Autopista Sur Km 11, T45-668288, www.oasishotels.com. 534 rooms and 30 suites, 5 restaurants and 3 bars, of which 1 is reserved for cigar smokers, lots of sports including catamarans, windsurfing, kayaks, aerobics, gymnasium, volleyball, basketball, 8 tennis courts, 4 pools including one for children, dancing lessons, pétanque and indoor games, other things can be arranged outside the *Club* such as horseriding, deep-sea fishing and scuba-diving and the usual excursions offered by all the hotel tour desks.

A Meliá Las Antillas, Carretera Las Morlas Km 14, T45-668470, www.solmeliacuba.com. All-inclusive nicely designed hotel with 350 rooms. Avoid the junior suite economy and opt for a more expensive, more attractively furnished room. There are 4 restaurants, 4 bars, banana boat, fitness centre, sauna, tennis, car rental, watersports (all included), lots of services and entertainment.

A-B Acuazul, Av 1 entre 13 y 14, T45-667132, www.hotelacuazul.com. 78 rooms in a blue and white concrete block, with pool. Older-style hotel, but quiet and one of the more reasonably priced all-inclusives (bed & breakfast also available). The kitsch aquaerobics entertainment is unmissable. **Villa Sotavento** and **Aparthotel Islazul Varazul** are part of the same group with interchangeable facilities.

A-B Pullman, Av 1 entre 49 y 50, T45-612702, www.islazul.cu. One of the oldest hotels in Varadero notable for its turret and style of a castle. It's small with only 16 rooms, low-key, limited facilities and not directly on the beach, so not great value. Breakfast is included and there's a small patio restaurant.

B-C Aparthotel Mar del Sur, Av 3 y Calle 30, T45-612246, www.islazul.cu. Friendly staff, 366 small, acceptable apartments and rooms available, mostly for package deals booked from abroad. It's a smartish and clean hotel 3 blocks from the beach, with pool, kids' pool, bar, buffet breakfast included but it's terrible as is all the food served. Convenient for the **Víazul** bus and the banks. It has its own

stretch of beach with free (limited range) alcoholic and non-alcoholic drinks at the rustic bar. One of the best value places in the lowest price range on the peninsula.

❼ Eating

Varadero *p179, map p180*
There are a handful of good restaurants outside the resorts and many mediocre ones. Note that à la carte restaurants in the all-inclusive hotels need to be reserved in advance. They are popular and you should reserve your tables soon after checking in to avoid disappointment.

Along Camino del Mar
♔ **Mi Casita**, Camino del Mar entre 11 y 12, T45-613787. Daily 1800-2300. Meat and seafood.
♔ **La Cabañita**, Camino del Mar esq 9, T45-616764. Daily 1900-0100. This is right on the beach under a thatched roof with a lovely bit of sand opposite.

East on Avenida Primera and Playa
♔♔♔ **Las Américas**, Mansión Xanadú, Av Las Américas, T45-667388, www.varadero golfclub.com. Daily 1200-1600, 1900-2230. International food that is acceptable but not outstanding. You come for the beautiful setting in the lovely old mansion (built between 1928 and 1930) and upstairs bar with wide-sweeping views.
♔♔♔ **Las Antigüedades**, Av 1 y C 59, T45-667329. A lovely restaurant stylishly decorated inside with plenty of figurines and statues to keep you interested. It serves good seafood and criollo cuisine.
♔♔♔-♔♔ **Casa de Al**, in among Villa Punta *Blanca*. A stone building with blue painted wooden attributes, which used to belong to Al Capone. It's a quiet spot for a sunset drink (with outdoor tables on the terrace) or a meal of Mafia Soup, Godfather Salad, Fillet Mignon 'Lucky Luciano' and cold blood ice cream. The service is a little on the slow side but not annoyingly so. Worth a visit.

Cuban cocktails

Most bars have their own specialities, but there is a range which is fairly common to all. However, even the standard cocktails will taste different when made by different barmen, so don't expect a *Mojito* in Havana to be the same as a *Mojito* in Varadero. Cocktails come in all colours and flavours, short or long, and some are even striped or multicoloured. All should be presented as a work of art by the barman, who has probably spent years at his training.

To make a **Mojito**, put half a tablespoon of sugar, the juice of half a lime and some lightly crushed mint leaves in a tall glass. Stir and mix well, then add some soda water, ice cubes, 1½ oz light dry rum and top up with soda water. Serve with a garnish of mint leaves and, of course, a straw.

A **Cubanito** is a Cuban version of a Bloody Mary, with ice, lime juice, salt, Worcester sauce, chilli sauce, light dry rum and tomato juice. Note that tomato juice is not always available everywhere.

An **Ernest Hemingway Special** is light dry rum, grapefruit juice, maraschino liqueur, lime and shaved ice, blended and served like a *Daiquirí*.

An **Havana Special** is pineapple juice, light dry rum, maraschino liqueur and ice, shaken and strained.

A **Mulata** is lime juice, extra aged rum, *crème de cacao* and shaved ice, blended together and served in a champagne glass.

The old favourite, **Piña Colada**, can be found anywhere: coconut liqueur, pineapple juice, light dry rum and shaved ice, all blended and served with a straw in a glass, a pineapple or a coconut, depending on which tropical paradise you are in.

Another old recipe best served in a coconut is a **Saoco**, which is just rum, coconut milk and ice.

One to finish the day off, and maybe even yourself, is a **Zombie**, a mixture of ice, lime juice, grenadine, pineapple juice, light dry rum, old gold rum and extra aged rum, garnished with fruit.

♙♙♙-♙♙ La Casa del Queso Cubano, Av 1 entee 62 y 64, T45-667747. Daily 1200-2300. A highly a/c restaurant with smart tables serving a variety of fondues including lobster and chocolate as well as breaded pork, chicken and grilled fish. Vegetables sometimes lacking although advertised on the menu.

♙♙♙-♙ El Criollo, esq 18 y Av 1, T45-614794, daily 1200-2400. A thatched-roof bar with ambient Cuban music and efficient service. Offerings include, *filete de res mechado con bacon*, *camarones* and roast pork.

♙♙ Castel Nuovo, Av 1 y 11, T45-667786. Daily 1200-2345. Italian restaurant with a smart-ish indoor dining area and a rundown, but pleasant, outdoor area. The pizzas are massive and the service is very efficient.

♙♙ Lai-Lai, Av 1 y 18, T45-667793. Daily 1200-2400. Bar/restaurant serving up spring rolls, Chinese soup and other oriental cuisine as well as the usual Cuban fare.

♙♙ La Vega, Av Playa entre 31 y 32, T45-611430. Daily 1200-2300. A charming, wooden restaurant with baskets hanging from the staircase and with outdoor seating on wooden decking. Serving a large range of *mariscos* including squid, paella and crêpes for pudding. Cheaper dishes are available. There is a gorgeous giant leaf sculpture outside.

♙♙ Ranchon Playa "Bellamar", Av 1 entre 16 y 17. Pleasant, thatched-roofed roadside restaurant delivering up large portions of food, including breaded fish fillet, pizza, red snapper and lobster. Don't eat anything for hours beforehand and bring earplugs if you can't bear blaring western 1970s hits.

♙ Kiki's Club, Av 1 y 8, T45-614115. Daily 1200-2345. Sports theme. Serves Italian food in a restaurant that's partially open air.

La Vicaria, Av 1 y Calle 37, next to Los Delfines hotel, T45-614721. A part-thatched covered restaurant, which, apart from doing a whole heap of chicken like everywhere else on the strip, actually serves salads, which are hard to come by.

Bars

Varadero p179, map p180

Every hotel has several bars to choose from and it can be fun to work your way through the barman's list of cocktails during your holiday. Even here, however, you may be told 'no hay', with tomato juice and other mixers often unavailable. Stick to the traditionally Cuban and you won't be disappointed. Outside the hotels, the **Bar Mirador Casa Blanca**, on the top floor of the **Mansión Xanadú** at the Golf Club is worth a visit for the view and relaxed atmosphere, if not the prices.

Entertainment

Varadero p179, map p180

Casa de la Música, Av Playa entre 42 y 43, T45-667568. Open Tue-Sun 2230-0300, CUC$10 entrance. Run by EGREM, the state music company. A cartelera in the window advertizes events.

A Buena Vista Social Club group performs live every 1st and 3rd Wed of the month at 2200 at Plaza América. Call Paradiso travel agency to reserve, T45-614759.

Nightclubs and cabaret

Cabaret Continental, at Hotel Varadero Internacional. See Sleeping, above.
Cabaret Cueva del Pirata, Autopista Sur Km 11, T45-667751, Tue-Sat 2230-0300. Show in a cave, CUC$15.
Mambo Club, Carretera Las Morlas Km 14, next to Aguas Azules Hoteles C (formerly Club Amigo Varadero), T45-668565. CUC$15.

Palacio de la Rumba, Av Las Américas, Km 4, T45-668210. Daily 2200-0300, CUC$15. Includes bar, live salsa bands at weekends. Popular with Cubans and foreigners.

Festivals and events

Varadero p179, map p180

Jan Carnival involves lots of tourist participation, encouraged by the hotel entertainment teams.
Nov Some years an arts festival is held in Varadero, lasting a week, which attracts some of the best artists in South America.

Shopping

Varadero p179, map p180

Arts and handicrafts

Handicraft markets offer all manner of souvenirs, from elaborately decorated wooden humedores to keep your cigars temperature-controlled, to T-shirts and keyrings, which are easier to pack. The main market area is in the Parque de las Mil Taquillas.
Artesanía, Av 1 entre 12 y 13, Av 1 entre 15 y 16, Av 1 esq 47 and Av 1 esq 51.
Galería de Arte y Taller de Cerámica Artística, Av 1 entre 59 y 60. Daily 0900-1900.

Cigars

Casa de Habanos, Av 1 esq 39. Also **Casa del Habano** next to La Casa del Queso Cubano, Av 1 esq Calle 64. Daily 0900-2300.

Shopping centres

Centro Comercial Caimán, Av 3 entre 61 y 63; **Plaza Caracol**, Av 1 esq 54; **Plaza América**, by the Sol Meliá hotels. The **Centro Comercial Hicacos**, Av 1 entre 44 y 46, originally the Parque 8000 Taquillas, has reopened with 6 modules that include a variety of shops, Etecsa office and an **Infotur** office.

▲ Activities and tours

Varadero p179, map p180

Diving

Centro Internacional de Buceo Barracuda, C 59 y 1 Av, T45-613481, www.nauticamarlin. com. Daily 0800-1900. There are some 30 dive sites off Varadero. Bay of Pigs excursion offered too as well as night diving, cave diving, wreck diving (including a 100-m-long Russian wreck) and lessons off Varadero. 1 dive CUC$50, 3 dives CUC$92, 10 dives CUC$258. ACUC Open Water Diver US$365, Dive Master US$800. English, Italian, French, German, Russian and Hungarian spoken. Most trips are 0830-1430 but a trip to Playa Girón lasts all day. All the marinas offer diving. Barracuda also offers kitesurfing, windsurfing, wakeboarding and catamaran use. Kitesurfing and windsurfing classes are CUC$150 for 6 hrs.

Dolphinarium

Delfinario, Autopista Sur Km 12, T45-668031, daily 0930-1700. Shows 1100, 1530. Show is CUC$15, swimming with the dolphins CUC$93, camera CUC$5.

Fishing

Offshore: *Peto* (wahoo) Oct-Feb, *Dorado* Apr-Sep; Sierra (sailfish) Apr-May; *Atún, bonito* Apr-Sep. **Reef:** Barracuda all year; *Aguají* (grouper) all year; *Pargo* (snapper) May-Jul best, Aug-Apr good. **Bay:** *sábalo* (tarpon); *jinawa* (yellow jack) Feb-Apr best, rest of year good. Contact the marinas for fishing, usually CUC$250-300, including open bar and equipment for half a day.

Golf

There is a Canadian-designed golf course on Av Las Américas Km 8.5, upgraded in 1996 to 18 holes, par 72. The original 9 holes were set out by the Du Ponts around their mansion, built in 1928-30, which is now the **Mansión Xanadú**, and the new ones extend along the **Sol Meliá** resorts.

Varadero Golf Club, T45-668482, www.varaderogolfclub.com. Daily 0700-1900. With 2 putting greens, a chipping green and a driving range and Pro-shop and equipment rental at Caddie House. Green fee 18 holes, CUC$70. Beginner's lessons available. Special offers are available at certain times of the year with shared powered golf carts (which are compulsory) thrown in. Reservations with 24 hrs notice are advised especially Sep-Dec.

Hotel sports facilities

The large hotels all offer **tennis** courts, some have **squash** courts and **volleyball** is played on the beach, usually organized by the hotel entertainment staff. **Table tennis**, **billiards** and other indoor games are available if the weather deteriorates or you have had enough sun.

Marinas

Marina Chapelín, Autopista del Sur, Km 12.5, T45-667550, www.nauticamarlin.com. VHF 16 and 72, daily 0800-1900. **Moorings** for 20 boats, maximum draft 30 m, boat rental and laundry. There's an on-site restaurant and staff are friendly. Ring at least 1 day beforehand to book your activity. This is by far the busiest marina. **Snorkelling** is offered at a coral beach and in Saturno Cave; a **seafari** to Cayo Blanco includes a dolphin show, transfer, equipment, open bar, lunch and an Afro-Cuban show, CUC$75 per person, for a full day's trip. **Boat Adventure**, is an Aqua-Rays adventure through the canals CUC$39 and **Discover Tour**, a jeep and boat safari which involves off-roading, swimming in a cave and speedboating along the river Canimar, CUC$73.

Marina Dársena Varadero, Carretera de Vía Blanca Km 31, T45-667550, www.nautica marlin.com. VHF 16. Moorings for 113 boats, maximum draft 4 m, boat rental, showers, laundry, internet, restaurants, bar, fishing, shops, day charters, diving, liveaboard for 20 people.

Marina Gaviota Varadero, Península de Hicacos Km 21, T45-667755, www.gaviota-grupo.com. VHF 16. Moorings for 35 boats with more coming soon, 3 m draft, showers, laundry, restaurant, bar. Sea safaris in catamarans with a visit to Cayo Cangrejo, yacht rental, fishing, swimming with dolphins and diving.

Sky diving and parachuting

Centro Internacional de Deportes Aéros, Km 1.5, Vía Blanca, opposite Marina Dársena Varadero, T45-667256. Courses or tandem jumps are on offer, see the price list on the wall at the airstrip. It is approximately CUC$150 for a jump/fall/fly.

Tour operators

Every hotel has a tour agency on site offering local and national excursions (to Havana, Cárdenas (see page 189), Valle de Yumurí, Pinar, Cayo Largo, Bay of Pigs, Guamá-Cienfuegos-Trinidad, Pinar by plane, Tropicana, Santa Clara), boat trips, multi-lingual guides, transfers, booking and confirmation of air tickets, air charters, car rentals, reception and representation service. Excursions can all be booked at all hotel tourism bureaux and through tour operators. Note that most agencies close for lunch. **Cubanacán**, C24 entre Av 1 y Av Playa, T45-667836, www.cubanacan.cu. **Gaviota**, Calle 56 y Av Playa, T45-611844, www.gaviota-grupo.com.

◉ Transport

Varadero *p179, map p180*
Air

The Juan Gualberto Gómez **airport** (VRA), T45-247015, receives international scheduled and charter flights.

Bus

The interprovincial bus station is at Autopista Sur y C 36.

Víazul, T45-614886, has daily buses **Havana–Varadero**, **Varadero–Trinidad** and **Varadero–Santiago de Cuba**, see timetable, page 32.

Tourist bus Varadero BeachTour, run by Transtur, T45-668212. There are dozens of bus stops along the peninsula (all clearly marked). The bus passes every hour (a red open-top double decker). CUC$5 for a day ticket where you can get on and off. The hop on hop-off MatanzasBusTour leaves Varadero at 0930, 1100, 1400 and 1530 arriving in Matanzas at 1100, 1230, 1530 and 1700. It returns to Varadero at 1115, 1245, 1545 and 1715. CUC$10 per day.

Car/moped hire

Hire a car rather than jeep to avoid having your spare wheel stolen, insurance covers 4 wheels, not the spare. Agencies have offices all over town and in nearly all the hotels. **Cubacar** at many of the hotels, main office: T45-667326. **Transtur**, T45-667715. **Vía Rent a Car**, T45-619001. **Havanautos**, T45-614409. **Petrol stations** Servi Cupet, 54 y Autopista, 17 y Autopista, Vía Blanca Km 31.

Moped/bicycle hire

Hiring a moped is a good way to see the peninsula but you will have no insurance and no helmet. Many of the hotels do moped rental and bicycle hire, CUCS$12-15 per hr, CUCS$24-30 per 24 hrs.

Taxi

Cubataxi, T45-614444. Most trips cost from CUC$5-15 depending on where you need to go along the peninsula. The best place to hail a taxi is at any hotel as they usually wait there for fares. Horse-drawn vehicles act as taxis, usually just for a tour around town, CUC$10.

◉ Directory

Varadero *p179, map p180*
Banks Banco Popular de Ahorro, esq Av 1 y 36, has an ATM, Mon-Fri 0830-1530. **Banco Financiero Internacional**, Av 1 y 32, Mon-Fri 0900-1500, last working day of month 0900-1200. Cash advance service with Visa and MasterCard available. **Bandec**, Av 1 y 36, has an ATM. **Immigration and police** 39 y Av 1, T45-613494. Immigration, Mon-Fri

0900-1200, 1350-1630 for visa extensions. Canadian consulate, 13 y Av 1, close to a mini grocery store. **Internet/telephone** DHL, next to Casa del Habano, Av 1 y 39, daily 0800-2000. Etecsa, Av 30 y 1, open daily 0830-1930 for internet and phone booths. **Medical services** Clínica Internacional Varadero, Av 1 y 61, T45- 667711/667226, www.servimedcuba.com. International clinic and pharmacy, doctor on duty 24 hrs, a medical consultation in your hotel is possible at a cost. **Post** Av 1 entre 36 y 37, open at 0800. Most hotels have post offices where you can buy stamps for use and for collectors. Internet, phone and fax services are usually available but rates vary.

Cárdenas

→ Colour map 2, A1. Population: 75,000.
Cárdenas is 18 km southeast of Varadero on the Bahía de Cárdenas. The town's architecture is attractive, in the traditional 19th-century Spanish colonial style of houses with tall windows, intricate lattices, high ceilings inside, ceramic tiled floors and interior gardens. However, its glory days are over and it's a good place to come to see a working Cuban town. It is trapped in a time warp, empty of tourists, friendly and a good place to meet Cubans. There is none of the aggressive hustling found in hotel districts or more tourist-oriented cities and no police harassment of Cubans associating with foreigners. However, the flip side of this relaxed attitude is that romantic liaisons, which once took place in Varadero, are being squeezed out to Cárdenas. ▸▸ *For listings, see pages 192-193.*

Ins and outs
Getting there Most long-distance transport is via Varadero where you will find the nearest **airport**. The **railway** is for local services only and there is not much in the way of long-distance **bus** transport, although there are **Astro** services from Havana, Matanzas and Varadero, and **Víazul** stops here on its way between Varadero and Trinidad.

Getting around Cárdenas is a slow city, with traffic moving at the pace of the horse. Transport is limited to **coches**, **bicycles** and pedestrians. The city is set out in very regular grid form, with Calles running parallel to the sea in consecutive numbers and Avenidas crossing them. The main street is Avenida Céspedes and Avenidas are numbered from here, with those running northwest starting from Avenida 1 oeste in odd numbers, and those running southeast starting from Avenida 2 este in even numbers. However, as in many places, people refer to old names rather than the numbers. Use the TV tower as a landmark. The tower is on Avenida Céspedes y Calle 11, called Coronel Verdugo. The three main museums are around Plaza Echeverría, just two blocks from Avenida Céspedes.

Best time to visit Like Varadero, hurricane season can be wet and stormy although there are plenty of fine, bright days. Between December and April is the driest time.

History
Cárdenas was founded in 1828. It was once one of the most important cities in Cuba with its wealth built on sugar. It had the first alcohol refinery, the first electricity plant and the first gynaecological hospital in Cuba; and its Plaza de Mercado is unique in Latin America. Its main claim to fame is that the Cuban flag was first raised here in 1850 by the revolutionary General Narciso López, a Venezuelan who tried unsuccessfully to invade

Cuban rum

Sugar was first introduced to Cuba by Christopher Columbus, who brought sugar cane roots from the Canary Islands on his second transatlantic voyage. The first rudimentary mills produced sugar cane juice, but as they became more sophisticated the juice was turned into alcohol. A clear wine was made, which, when distilled several times, became a basic rum. In the 19th century a new manufacturing process was developed, which considerably improved the quality of Cuban rum, and the industry rapidly expanded with the construction of hundreds of sugar mills all over the country. The cities of Havana, Santiago de Cuba, Cienfuegos and Cárdenas all produced rum of export quality under the labels of *Havana Club* (founded in 1878), *Bacardí, Campeón, Obispo, San Carlos, Jiquí, Matusalem, Bocoy* and *Albuerne*.

The family firm of *Bacardí* was the largest in Cuba for nearly 100 years, building substantial wealth on the back of rum. After the 1959 Revolution, when the sugar industry and the distilleries were taken over by the state, the family left the island and took the Bacardí name with them. The Bacardí rum, now found worldwide, is not distilled in Cuba. Many labels can be found in Cuba, including the venerable *Havana Club, Caribbean Club, Caney, Legendario, Matusalem, Varadero, Bucanero* and *Siboney*.

Rums of all different ages can be found. Generally, the younger, light rums are used in cocktails and aged, dark rums drunk on the rocks or treated as you might a single malt whisky. Light, dry rum in Cuba is aged (*ron añejo*) for three years, has little body and is between 40° and 60° proof. Old gold, dry rum is aged for five years, is amber in colour and can be drunk straight or added to cocktails for an extra kick. Extra aged rum is aged for seven years and is usually drunk neat in a brandy glass or on the rocks.

Cocktails first became popular after the development of ice making in the USA in 1870 and were introduced to Cuba soon afterwards. The first Cuban cocktails were the *Cuba Libre* and the *Daiquirí*, the former developed when US intervention forces brought in bottled cola drinks during the war of independence against Spain at the end of the 19th century, and the latter invented by an engineer in the *Daiquirí* mines in eastern Cuba.

Cocktails boomed in the 1920s with an influx of bartenders and global visitors, many of whom were escaping prohibition in the USA. Recipes were named after visiting film stars and other dignitaries and developed at *La Bodeguita del Medio* or *El Floridita*, bars still flourishing today. The *Hemingway Special* was created for the writer by the famous bartender, Constante, at *El Floridita*. Others include a Greta Garbo, Lilian Gish and a Mary Pickford.

Cuba by landing at Cárdenas with an army of 600 men (only six of whom were Cuban), who had sailed from New Orleans. Cárdenas was also thrust onto the world stage in 1999-2000 after the Miami boat boy Elián González was finally returned to his home town after a geopolitical wrangle involving the USA, Cuba, the families and the law. His story is commemorated in a new museum, see below.

Sights

Cárdenas is a city with a sense of humour: it commemorates the mundane with bizarre memorials. On Calle 13 there is a *coche* statue, equipped with a white, stone horse. Behind the **Fuerte Roja** (a bar in a tower) is a bicycle that stands high on a thin metal plinth as if it was balancing on the gymnastics beam. Outside the hospital a large, fibreglass nose provides a bus shelter: its giant nostrils the gaping way in to the waiting area. (Apparently, the *nariz* is in homage to the majority black population of Cárdenas); and at the entrance to the city (approaching from the Varadero end) a giant crab welcomes visitors. However, the sculptor's lack of marine knowledge has left a biological mutant on the roadside: the Cárdenas crustacean has a large right pincer (normal *cangrejos* sport the large claw on the left).

Where Avenida Céspedes ends at the sea, there is the **Monumento a la Bandera** with a huge flagpole commemorating the flag-raising event on 19 May. There is also a plaque at the **Hotel Dominica**, which Narciso López occupied with his men and is now a National Monument. Unfortunately, the General's attempts to free Cuba from colonial rule were unsuccessful, as he failed to get local support. One of the town's other claims to fame is that it contains the oldest **statue of Christopher Columbus** in the Western Hemisphere, now in front of the cathedral in Parque Colón on Avenida Céspedes, five blocks from the flagpole. It was the work of a Spanish sculptor, Piquier, in 1862. **Plaza Malacoff** is worth a visit to see the decaying, iron market building, put up in the 19th century on Avenida 3 oeste and Calle 12. It was built in the shape of a cross and the two-storey building is surmounted by a 15-m dome made in the USA. The market is a great public gathering place for gossip and beer-drinking. On Calle 2, overlooking the water, is the **Fábrica de Ron Arrechabala**, which makes both the *Varadero* and *Bucanero* label rums. The site has been a rum factory since 1878, when the *Havana Club* company was founded here.

One of Cárdenas' most celebrated residents is the boy, Elián González, who hit the headlines in 1999 (aged six) when he was shipwrecked off the Miami coast (see History, page 417). His father, who works locally in the tourism industry, was finally able to take him home from the US after seven months of legal wrangling, and Ellán resumed near-normal life in school. In July 2001, Fidel Castro opened the **Museo a la Batalla de Ideas** ① *C 12 y Plaza Echeverría, Tue-Sat 0900-1700, Sun 0900-1300, CUC$2, kids free, camera CUC$5, guide CUC$2, mirador CUC$1*. This small museum, housed in the 1873 fire station, is a veritable shrine to Elián. Everything Elián and his family said or did is featured here. The display includes the T-shirt worn by the fisherman, Sam Ciancio, who hauled Elián out of the sea. There are also letters from the likes of Guatemalan Nobel Prize-winning author Rigoberta Menchú and the Uruguayan exiled writer, the late Mario Benedetti saying that Elián must be reunited with his father. There is a *maqueta* (model) of the Tribuna Antiimperialista José Martí, a demonstration ground built in front of the US Interests section in Havana during the whole saga. The large bronze statue of José Martí in the museum foyer was the original statue on the parade ground during the demonstrations against his staying in Florida. The one in Havana is a replacement statue. There is also a large display about the Miami Five.

The **Museo Municipal Oscar María de Rojas** ① *Plaza Echeverría entre Av 4 y 6 este, Tue-Sat 0800-1600, Sun 0800-1200, CUC$2*, exhibits art, geology specimens and local and natural history. A local, 20th-century hero is remembered in his birthplace, now a museum. **Museo Casa Natal José Echeverría** ① *Av 4 este y Plaza Echeverría, Tue-Sat 0900-1700, Sun 0800-1200, CUC$1, guide CUC$2, CUC$1 per photo*, dates from 1703, but Echeverría was born here in 1932. He was a student leader killed by Batista's troops in 1957. Exhibits are scarce but those on show relate to 19th-century independence struggles downstairs and the 20th-century Revolution upstairs. Of note are a giant doll used to hide clandestine objects and a photo of the man himself, blood-drenched in the street after being mown down. The park outside is named after Echeverría and there is a monument to him in the park. The

Salón Massaguner art gallery ① *Av Céspedes 560, 1 block south of the TV tower*, has high-quality works from Matanzas province artists. There is the *art naif* of Olga Vallejo and political works of Francisco Rivero, among others, including sculptures.

Around Cárdenas

About 10 km from town is the museum sugar mill **Central Azucarero José Smith Comás**, where an 1888 steam engine is still used for tourist trips. Take the road to Santa Clara, turn right at the fork by an old paper mill. Some 24 km south of Cárdenas is **Jovellanos**, a large town with a pleasant colonial centre, Parque Central and church. It is a junction of the roads from Varadero to the Zapata peninsula and from Matanzas to Santa Clara. It is of no particular interest to travellers except that as a result of slavery and enforced migrations, the Arara people of Benin came here via Haiti and brought the sort of music with them that is normally only heard around Santiago de Cuba.

The main road from Matanzas runs east from here to **Colón**, on the main railway line from Havana. This is another 19th-century town with abundant neoclassical architecture and faded grandeur. For adventurous independent travellers exploring rural Matanzas, you will be well off the tourist trail; you can spend pesos cubanos in restaurants and on transport. Carnival is 15-17 October.

⊙ Cárdenas listings

For Sleeping and Eating price codes and other relevant information, see Essentials pages 37-43.

❷ Eating

Cárdenas *p189*

There are a couple of *cafeterías* where you can get a sandwich and a beer and peso snack stands along Av Céspedes, but otherwise Cárdenas is not a great culinary experience. The public market has seasonal fresh fruit and vegetables.

❡ **Café Spiriu**, Plaza Echeverría, 2 blocks east of Av Céspedes. Daily 0800-2200. Popular, attractive with lovely *vitrales* above its doors, *criollo* food, great ice cream, reasonable prices, best place in town.

❡ **El Rápido**, diagonally opposite the cathedral and another branch opposite Plaza Malacoff. Good for a quick fix.

❡ **Las Palmas**, Av Céspedes y 16. In large, walled, colonial building with imposing dining room, mostly a drinking place, sometimes drunken brawls late at night.

❶ Bars

Cárdenas *p189*

There's a beer bar opposite El Rápido, see above, which seems popular at weekends. **La Fuerte Roja**, a small turret, that's more of a dusty pink than red, is a popular and quirky spot for a beer with wooden, roadside tables standing firm in the middle of a small and quiet traffic island in front of the memorial to a bicycle.

❸ Transport

Cárdenas *p189*
Bicycles/coches

There is not much in the way of local transport; bicycles, or *coches*, are the only carriers. Cárdenas is an easy bike ride from **Varadero** and there are bike park areas where a guard will watch your bike for CUC$1.

Bus

The bus station is on Av Céspedes y 22, with services to **Matanzas, Colón, Jagüey**

Grande, **Havana** and **Santa Clara**. To get to **Varadero** catch a bus from the corner of Av 13 oeste y Calle 13, they should leave every hour, but as the principal demand is from hotel workers they are more likely to run according to shifts.

Víazul stops in Cárdenas on its **Trinidad–Varadero** route. Get there early, or buy a reserved ticket.

Taxi

Taxi from **Varadero** CUC$40 round trip with waiting time.

Zapata Peninsula and Bay of Pigs

This is one of the most famous places in the world: for every Cuban it signifies a great victory; for the Americans, a failure of monumental proportions. Historian of Cuba, Hugh Thomas, said the disaster of the CIA-backed invasion in April 1961 was so politically dismal for JFK that he went out and ordered the US space agency to land a man on the moon before the decade was out. In his history epic 'Cuba' he wrote, "perhaps a victory for the US in Cuba might have deprived mankind of that achievement in 1969". Unfortunately, there is little to see at the Bay of Pigs (Bahía de Cochinos) relating to the air and sea attack except monuments on the roadside marking the fallen and a museum about the invasion. However, this is extremely interesting and is full to overflowing with photos for those who don't read Spanish and there is a feeling of achievement and importance in making it to such an historical site that is a little off the beaten track.

Nowadays, there is more to the region than just its history. The whole of the south coast of the Matanzas province is taken up with the Zapata peninsula, an area of swamps, mangroves, beaches and much bird and animal life. Much of it is a national park – Parque Nacional Ciénaga de Zapata, the largest ecosystem on the Island containing the Laguna del Tesoro, a 9.1-sq-km lagoon over 10 m deep. It is an important winter home for flocks of migrating birds. There are 16 species of reptile, including crocodiles. Mammals include the jutía and the manatee, while there are more than 1000 species of invertebrate, of which more than 100 are spiders.

Near Playa Girón is a stunning natural pool area, Caleta Buena, brimming with sapphire-coloured water and teeming with tropical fish. Between Playa Larga and Playa Girón the sea is an exceptional colour, like lapis lazuli flecked with aquamarine. The diving in these beautifully coloured waters is highly rated and there are several marked spots where you can dive and snorkel.
▶▶ *For listings, see pages 196-198.*

Ins and outs

Getting there and around Entronque de Jagüey on the main highway marks the 'entrance' to the peninsula. There is also a road from Cienfuegos. Public transport is limited. **Viazul** runs a Havana-Entronque–Girón–Cienfuegos route. A few local **buses** run to Playa Girón and Playa Larga **Tour buses** and **taxis** are the usual method of transport but the most convenient way of getting around is to hire a **car** so that you can get to out-of-the-way places and stay as long as you like. **Hiking** is good in the National Park, but you will need to carry water as it is very hot in the swamps.

Tourist information The **Centro de Información La Finquita** is next to the **Cubanacán** Café at Entronque de Jagüey, on the national highway, T45-913224, daily 0800-2000, and provides local information and sells a map of the zone. It can arrange non-state taxis down to Playa Larga, CUC$20, and to Playa Girón, CUC$30. For national park information, see below. The dry season is from December to April. Winter is also the time when migratory birds visit the peninsula so birdwatching is especially rewarding.

South to the Bahía de Cochinos (Bay of Pigs)

Due south of Jovellanos you head towards the Zapata peninsula and the countryside becomes flat and uninteresting. This area was particularly badly hit by Hurricane Michelle in November 2001, with lots of houses damaged or destroyed. The storm ripped through the Zapata peninsula and its tourist attractions. **Jagüey Grande** is just north of the central highway from Havana to Santa Clara.

Finca Fiesta Campesina ① *just south of the Entronque de Jagüey, daily 0900-1800*, is a large country farm. The large, shady garden contains caged animals as well as a bar, shops and toilets. You can watch a man push sugar cane through a mangle so that you can try a glass of *guarapo* (sugar cane juice) mixed with lime (and rum if you want it). Animals include a snake called a *Majá de Santa María*, the *jutía*, a large-eared rat, and a prehistoric fish called a *manjuarí*, which has a long bill with lots of teeth and eyes set far back, making it look a bit like a platypus crossed with a crocodile. There is a *cabaña* complex in the grounds providing accommodation.

Central Australia, is a sugar mill that looks like an ailing dinosaur, built in 1872, and decommissioned in 2002. It had its moment of fame when Castro used the administration office (built 1915) as his centre of operations to repel the Bay of Pigs invasion (Operation Pluto). The office is now the **Museo Memorial Comandancia de las FAR** ① *T45-912504, Mon-Sat 0900-1700, Sun 0800-1200, CUC$1 plus CUC$1 with guide plus CUC$1 to take pictures.* It is a singularly unimpressive museum considering its historical importance. There are photos of destroyed planes and victory pictures and one showing the name of Fidel written on a wall in the blood of one of the Cuban victims. There are also some pictures of José Ramón Fernández, Director of Operations, who has been a Vice President of the Council of Ministers since 1978. The phone used by Fidel is still in situ and there is an anti-missile machine in the lobby. Outside the museum is the wreck of a plane shot down by Castro's troops. The guide will tell you that the dead American pilot was kept frozen in an institute in Havana as the US did not want to claim him and thereby admit responsibility for the invasion. The serviceman was not reclaimed until his daughter came to collect him in 1989.

Boca de Guamá

① *T45-913224, daily 0900-1800. Entrance to the crocodile farm CUC$5, CUC$3 for children, shows 0900-1630 including crocodile capture. The boat trip (8 people minimum, return after 1 hr) from Boca de Guamá to Villa Guamá is CUC$12, CUC$5 for children under 12. A speed boat runs at 0900, life jackets on board.*

At Boca de Guamá is a tourist centre of shops, a ceramic factory, a restaurant and a crocodile farm (*Criadero de Cocodrilos*) where they breed the native Rhombifer (*cocodrilo*; see also page 455) and which is also home to turtles (*jicotea*), *jutía* and what they call a living fossil, the *manjuarí* fish. From here it is possible to take a boat to **Villa Guamá**, a hotel (see Sleeping, page 196), and **Aldea Taína**, an Amerindian complex in the **Laguna del Tesoro**. On one of the islets a series of life-size statues of Amerindians going through their daily routines has been carved by the late Cuban sculptor Rita Longa, which you can see by following a boardwalk. In the middle is a replica of a *caney*, a large house belonging to the *cacique* (chief), where actors do a lot of wailing, blow a conch, daub your face black and expect you to give them a generous tip. This is not obligatory. Birdwatchers are advised to spend a few nights, or go on a tour one day and return with the next tour the following day. You will see most at dawn before the tour buses arrive.

Playa Larga → *Colour map 2, B1.*

The road south down the peninsula meets the coast at Playa Larga, at the head of the Bahía de Cochinos, commonly known as the **Bay of Pigs**. The US-backed invasion force landed here on 17 April 1961 but was successfully repelled. There is a small monument but most of the commemorative paraphernalia is at Playa Girón (see below). See History, page 410, for more information. The beach is open and better than that at Playa Girón. Some *casas particulares* have beach access.

Playa Larga is also a good place to come to explore the **Parque Nacional Ciénaga de Zapata**, also known as Parque Natural Montemar, a bird lover's paradise. There are 21 endemic species of birds inside the park. The smallest of these is the hummingbird. The best time to see flamingos and migratory birds is from December to March. Other sightings include magnificent frigates, sandhill crane, Cuban parakeet, nighthawks, owls and pied billed grebe. Sport fishing is also offered. The park Headquarters office, is just before you reach Playa Larga on the main road, indicated by a sign.

The **Laguna de las Salinas**, 25 km southwest, is the temporary home of huge numbers of migratory birds from December to April. The rest of the year it is empty. At the end of the road, at the forest technical station at La Salina, you can get a boat to one of the outlying islands, **Cayo Venado**, where there are iguanas and *jutías*. West of Playa Larga, a track leads to **Santo Tomás** where, in addition to waterfowl, you can see the Zapata wren, the Zapata rail and the Zapata sparrow.

East around the bay, **Cueva de los Peces** ① *daily 0900-1600, CUC$3 (but not always applied), restaurant and bar,* is a cenote that is full of fish and is good for diving (CUC$40) and snorkelling (CUC$5), particularly early in the day. A dive off the coast here in front of the Cueva is CUC$25. The snorkelling off the coast here is very good. Two kilometres southeast of Playa Larga is **Playa de la Máquina**, a sandy beach frequented by locals where you can see lots of old trucks, caravans and other 'machines'. Between Cueva de los Peces and Playa Girón is **Punta de Perdiz** ① *0900-1630*, where there is a restaurant, excellent snorkelling, a dive centre (CUC$25 per dive) and boat trips. See also Caleta Buena, below.

Playa Girón → *Colour map 2, B2.*

The resort at Playa Girón is isolated and small with little entertainment or nightlife. It is named after a 17th-century French pirate, Gilbert Girón, who frequented the area and presumably also appreciated its isolation. A stay of a few nights would be plenty to explore the area, visit the Bay of Pigs museum and take advantage of the scuba diving and snorkelling. The beach is walled in and therefore protected, but the sea is rocky. The **diving** and **snorkelling** is excellent and you can walk to the reef from the shore. Diving from Punta Perdíz (Bay of Pigs) is an easy beach entry if you are in the area, although the nearest dive shop is at Playa Girón. Nearby there is a 15- to 18-m-long Fisheries Division shipwreck, sitting in 20 m of water on a sand slope. The wreck was intentionally sunk by the government in 1995. The boat, known as a Cayo Largo boat, was built in the early 1980s from concrete and wire. Cuba is well known for building ships like this, which are expected to have a life of around 10 years and are then gutted, with everything of use being removed for a newer model. These 'throw away' boats used to be sunk in deep water, but as diving developed as a sport on the islands, the wrecks were placed in shallow waters to allow divers to explore them. The dive operation at the resort offers courses and packages of dives which can be tied in with accommodation, see Sleeping below. Further along the shore, however, there is another long sandy beach, and 8 km southeast is **Caleta Buena** ① *1000-1700, CUC$15 (CUC$7.50 children) for all drinks all day and lunch (1230-1500) also diving CUC$25 for 1 dive*, a pretty cove with lots of coral and fish. There is a small tourist centre, perched on some craggy rocks and the water is excellent for snorkelling. The pale blue, natural swimming pools are teeming with shoals of multi-coloured fish. There are also **caves** in the area for divers to explore. If you have your own transport, find a beach along the road between Playa Girón and Caleta Buena, there will be no people and good snorkelling 100 m offshore. ►► *For watersports, see also Hotels Playa Girón and Playa Larga, below and on page 197.*

At the site of national pilgrimage where, in 1961 at the **Bay of Pigs**, the disastrous US-backed invasion of Cuba was attempted (see History, page 410), is the **Museo Girón** ① *T45-984122, daily 0800-1700, CUC$2, plus CUC$I for Spanish-speaking guide, under 12s free, video show CUC$1, use of camera CUC$1, video camera CUC$5*. It shows how the invasion was repelled within 72 hours, with 200 CIA-trained Cuban exiles killed, 1197 captured and 11 planes shot down. Monuments to those who died are scattered along the coast. Outside the museum is a British Sea Fury fighter aircraft, used by Castro's air force against the invaders. The tank outside is a replica of the original in Havana that destroyed *USS Houston*. The remains of an American B-26 are also in the gardens. It came down on the *pista* on 17 April 1961. There are also tanks and boats belonging to the mercenaries (Brigade 2506).

◉ Zapata Peninsula and Bay of Pigs listings

For Sleeping and Eating price codes and other relevant information, see Essentials pages 37-43.

● Sleeping

South to the Bahía de Cochinos *p194*
Hotels
D-E Bohío de Don Pedro, T45-91-2825. Next to the Finca Fiesta Campesina is a complex of 12 very attractive fan-cooled *cabañas*. It's a lovely relaxed spot with a restaurant (0700-2130) and would be great for families with young children who need to run around.

Casas particulares
D-E Violeta Pita, Calle 58 1718 entre 17 y 19, Jagüey, T45-912690. 2 rooms, cooks wonderful fried bananas.

Boca de Guamá *p194*
Hotels
A-B Villa Guamá, Laguna del Tesoro, T45-915515, www.hotelescubanacan.com. 59 a/c rooms in thatched *cabañas* on stilts

on islands in the style of a Taíno village, with bath, phone, TV, restaurant, bar, cafeteria, shop, information desk, excursions, fishing in the lake. Take plenty of insect repellent.

Playa Larga *p195*
Hotels
A-B Hotel Playa Larga, at Playa Larga, T45-987294, www.hotelescubanacan.com. Sometimes fully booked with tour groups, 68 a/c spacious rooms in 1- or 2-bedroomed bungalows with bath, TV, restaurant, bar, shop, pool, tour desk, bicycle rental, birdwatching and watersports. undergoing a major but very slow revamp in 2009 and the finished rooms are quite attractive with sitting rooms, TV and desks. The beach in front of the hotel here is more pleasant than at Playa Girón where the view is broken by an enormous ugly breakwater.

Casas particulares
All the *casas particulares* are in Barrio Caletón which is just west of the public park

in Playa Larga. When you arrive in Playa Larga take an immediate right in front of the public park and swing round the edge until you arrive at the small residential area. Ask directions as you go. Nearly all casas are charging CUC$53 for a room for 2 including dinner (CUC$10 per person) and breakfast (CUC$4 each). Feel free to negotiate if you want smaller suppers or if you are staying for a while. Bear in mind there are no other eating options apart from at the hotel.

D Enrique Rivas Fente, Caletón, Playa Larga, T45-987178/0152 251117, yosvanyspcz@ yahoo.es. Enrique offers 2 rooms with TVs, storage area and shared bathroom. There's secure parking, rocking chairs and it's said the best food in town. They do indeed make an extra special effort when it comes to the food preparation and its serving.

D Ernesto Delgado Chirino, T45-987278, ernestodccz@gmail.com. Waterfront property, with waterside patio and great views of the boats. He has 1 generously sized, very nice self-contained apartment with a small kitchenette and a high standard of furnishings. Run by the cousin of Roberto Mesa Pujol, see below.

D Fidel Silvestre Fuentes, Barrio Caletón, T45-987359, fidelsfcaribe@yahoo.es Very friendly and welcoming family with 1 a/c room with hot and cold water in a shared bathroom and access right onto the beach from a pleasant patio. *Comida criolla* for supper.

D Roberto Mesa Pujol, Caletón, Playa Larga, T45-987307, casamesa@gmail.com. 2 rooms, a/c, private bathroom, hot water, secure parking. Marvellous location with garden opening onto white-sand beach, palm trees and volleyball net. Probably the best bit of beach fronting a house in the barrio. There's a billiards table indoors and a hammock in the garden.

Playa Girón *p195*
Hotels
A-B Hotel Playa Girón, T45-987206, www.hotel escubanacan.com. Just half the rooms in this

large resort are in use as the buildings undergo a much-needed renovation programme. All the rooms are in bungalows scattered around the grounds and look like a communist campsite. It's all-inclusive with buffet meals, bar, pool, diving, tour desk, shop and car rental. There's a disco opposite. Reception staff are very unhelpful. Caleta Buena is part of the hotel but the entrance is only free if you have booked your accommodation through certain tour operators.

Casas particulares
When you enter the village from the north, on your left are 2 apartment blocks. The 1st block is edificio 2, while the one behind, at an angle, is edificio 1. Opposite are a line of houses, some of which are *casas particulares*.

D-E Casa Luis, Carretera a Cienfuegos esq Carretera a Playa Larga, T45-984258. This is the best house in the Zapata area recognizable by its lion-topped columns on the gates. It is close to the hotel. Owned by Luis A García Padrón and his wife, they have 2 comfortable bedrooms. They also offer secure parking. It's a lovely, super-friendly and helpful household. The food is delicious too. Good English spoken.

D-E Miguel A Padrón y Odalys Figueredo, behind edificio 1, T45-984100 or T01-5227 9625 (mob). A modern house off the main road with 1 room; exceptionally clean, a/c and fan, helpful.

🍴 Eating

Boca de Guamá *p194*
The restaurant by the crocodile farm caters for tour parties and you get a bland and uninteresting set lunch with either fish, pork or chicken. However, if you ask, you can try a small portion of crocodile, CUC$5, which is chopped and fried. It tastes like fishy chicken with the texture of tough pork.

Playa Larga and Playa Giron *p195*
There are restaurants at Cueva de las Peces, Punta Perdíz and at Caleta Buena, see above.

O Shopping

South to the Bahía de Cochinos *p194*
Opposite the Museo Girón is a block of shops including **Tienda Playa Girón**, daily 0830-1630 (food, drinks and souvenirs).

▲ Activities and tours

Zapata Peninsula and Bay of Pigs *p193*
Diving
See **Hotel Playa Girón**, and **Hotel Playa Larga**, Sleeping above, for details. Diving is also possible at Cueva de las Peces, Punta Perdíz and Caleta Buena where there are state-run outfits. 1 dive costs CUC$25.

Birdwatching and wildlife watching
Parque Nacional Ciénaga de Zapata, Playa Larga, T45-987249, pnacionalcz@enet.cu, daily 0800-1630 Trips to the Río Hatiguanico, Las Salinas, Los Sábalos, Bermejas and Santo Tomás. Each trip costs CUC$10 per person. The guides are all bird specialists and some speak English. Visitors need their own transport and tips are not included. Call beforehand if you want a particular specialist. Sport fishing is also offered but you need to ring the office for information and prices. Minimum price is CUC$190.
Orestes Martínez Garcías (known as El Chino), T45-987373, T5253 9004 (mob), www.ourexplorer.com, chino.Zapata@gmail.com. Has been working in the Zapata peninsula for 35 years. He has expert bird knowledge.

Tour operators
Both hotels **Playa Girón** and **Playa Larga** have tour desks, see Sleeping above. See also **Cubanacán**, Tourist information, page 193.
Tourist centre, Caleta Buena, no phone, call Hotel Playa Girón (T45-984110), daily 1000-1700. Entrance to the cove CUC$15 adults, CUC$7.50 children, including lunch (1230-1500) and all drinks (1000-1700). There are sun loungers and *casitas*. Snorkelling

CUC$5 per day, diving CUC$25 per dive. There's also a volleyball net. Highly recommended day or half-day trip. You need your own car or a taxi to get here.

A 1-hr boat trip along the Río Hatiguanico can be organized at Cubanacán, CUC$19 per person and the launch point is at Km 102, some 38 km towards Havana from Jagüey Grande.

⊖ Transport

Zapata Peninsula and Bay of Pigs *p193*
Bus
Víazul runs a daily bus **Havana–Jagüey Grande–Guamá–Girón–Cienfuegos–Trinidad**, see timetable, page 32.

Car hire
Havanautos, opposite Hotel Playa Girón, daily 0800-1200 and 1300-2000. Between **Playa Girón** and **Playa Larga** in a car is 30 mins; from **Guamá** to **Playa Larga** is 10 mins; from **Entronque de Jagüey** to **Guamá** is 15 mins.
Petrol station Servi Cupet, opposite Museo Girón, open 24 hrs. There's also a Servi Cupet outside Boca de Guamá.

Taxi
For **Playa Larga**, organize a taxi with Cubanacán at Entronque de Jagüey. **Playa Girón** and the **Bay of Pigs** can also be reached by taxi from **Cienfuegos** (1½ hrs).

A private taxi will charge about CUC$70 to **Havana**. Better to get a lift with a tour bus returning to **Havana** or **Varadero**, CUC$30. The hotel also runs day trips to Havana, but ring to check days and times beforehand, a 1-way ride will cost about CUC$25.

⊕ Directory

Zapata Peninsula and Bay of Pigs *p193*
There is a **post office** near the Museo de Girón.

Contents

Footprint features

At a glance

◉ **Getting around** On foot, by
bicycle, hired car, taxi and Víazul
long-distance bus.

◉ **Time required** 1-2 weeks.

Centre West

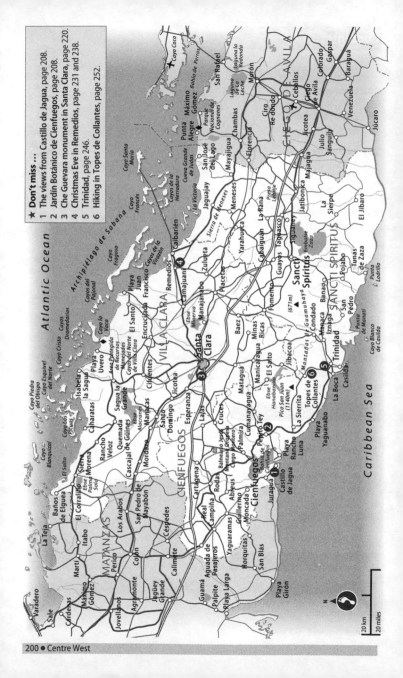

★ **Don't miss ...**
1 The views from Castillo de Jagua, page 208.
2 Jardín Botánico de Cienfuegos, page 208.
3 Che Guevara monument in Santa Clara, page 220.
4 Christmas Eve in Remedios, page 231 and 238.
5 Trinidad, page 246.
6 Hiking in Topes de Collantes, page 252.

From the early Spanish settlements and sugar plantations built on slavery to magnificent 19th-century merchants' mansions and opulent theatres, this region is generously endowed with architectural delights. The memories of heroes of the wars of independence and other struggles for liberation including the Revolution, are preserved in monuments and street names. The three provinces of Cienfuegos, Villa Clara and Sancti Spíritus in the centre west share the lush, forested Montañas de Guamuhaya, their boundaries meeting close to the highest point, Pico San Juan, in the legendary Sierra del Escambray. The mountains are a habitat for many birds, butterflies, frogs and other creatures of the forest and offer great hiking, river bathing and birdwatching.

The coastal city of Cienfuegos has some architectural highlights, particularly the theatre and the Palacio de Ferrer, both late-19th-century masterpieces. The diving is good, with some pleasant dive lodges. The 1958 battle for the city of Santa Clara was crucial to the outcome of the Revolution and this lively university city is now a shrine to the Argentine guerrillero and icon, Che Guevara.

The northern part of Villa Clara is mostly flat and the coastline is protected by an archipelago of cays with some spectacular white coral sandy beaches. Heading south, the provincial capital of Sancti Spíritus was one of the seven towns founded by Diego Velázquez in 1514, but the star attraction is the colonial town of Trinidad, awarded UNESCO World Heritage Site status to protect its cobbled streets, single storey, pastel-coloured houses with red tiled roofs, its churches and its planters' mansions. It also has the advantage of being close to a beach, with access to the mountains, and has some outstanding live music performances.

Ins and outs

Getting there

There is an international airport outside Santa Clara which receives mostly charter **flights** from Canada in season, otherwise you fly to Havana or Varadero and transfer from there overland. Santa Clara is on the main east-west highway from Havana to Santiago and communications by land are excellent, with frequent **buses** in both directions. Direct buses run daily to Cienfuegos from Havana, continuing to Trinidad, or you can get to Trinidad from Varadero via Santa Clara and Sancti Spíritus. There is also a daily service Trinidad–Santiago de Cuba, with several stops along the way. Santa Clara and Cienfuegos can be reached by **train** from Havana, but Trinidad is not on the main line and only a tourist service operates from here.
▸▸ *See also Getting there, below and pages 216, 231, 239 and 246.*

Tourist information

Tour agencies such as **Cubatur**, **Cubanacán** and **Havanatur** can be found in all the main towns and operate as tourist information offices although their main purpose is to sell tours. They can help with hotel reservations, tickets and transfers.

Best time to visit

If you enjoy watersports and festivals related to the sea, then March is a good time to go to Cienfuegos. May is busy in Santa Clara, where there are film, music and dance festivals, but the best time is around 28 December, when the populace celebrate the end of the Revolution and the Plaza de la Revolución is alive with revellers enjoying a concert. The week leading up to Chrismas Eve is the time to be in Remedios, when the *parrandas* are in full swing, and September is ceremonial in Trinidad, with followers of Catholicism and *Santería* joining parades through the streets in honour of the Virgen del Cobre, patron saint of Cuba, whose day is 8 September.

Cienfuegos

→ *Colour map 2, B3. Population: 386,100.*

Cienfuegos, on the south coast, is an attractive, breezy seaport, sometimes described as the pearl of the south, with a Caribbean feel to the place. Once known as Fernandina de Jagua, it has its fair share of legends about pirates and corsairs. A couple of dive lodges to the south, a marina and a naval museum add to its nautical emphasis, although the beaches in this area are pleasant but not worth going out of your way for. Most of the city's festivals are based on seafaring activities and there are many regattas and races for yachts, power boats, kayaks and rowing boats. French immigrants at the beginning of the 19th century influenced the development and architecture of the city, which is a fascinating blend of styles including a heavy presence of art deco buildings in its residential streets. Highlights are the Tomás Terry theatre and the Ferrer palace both remarkable buildings from the 1890s, the heyday of Cienfuegos' prosperity. The city was granted UNESCO World Heritage Site status in 2005. ▸▸ *For listings, see pages 209-215.*

Ins and outs

Getting there **Trains** run to and from Santa Clara, where you connect with trains to Havana or to the east. The railway station is on Calle 49 esquina Avenida 58, not far from the old centre. Cienfuegos is 80 km from Trinidad and 70 km from Santa Clara. There are regular **buses** from both these cities as well as from Havana, Varadero, Santiago de Cuba and Camagüey. The bus station is on Calle 49, esquina Avenida 56, close to the railway station. → See also Transport, page 214.

Getting around Much of the city can be seen **on foot**, or you can use a horse-drawn **coche** for longer distances. For excursions out of the city, **car hire** is the most convenient, or hire a **taxi** to take you around, or take a **tour**.

Tourist information Infotur has an information desk on the Parque Martí outside **Bar El Palatino** with a few leaflets. **Ministerio de Turismo** in Cienfuegos, T43-551631, www.cubatravel.cu. However, if you are staying in a *casa particular*, you will find your hosts very knowledgeable about what is going on in the area.

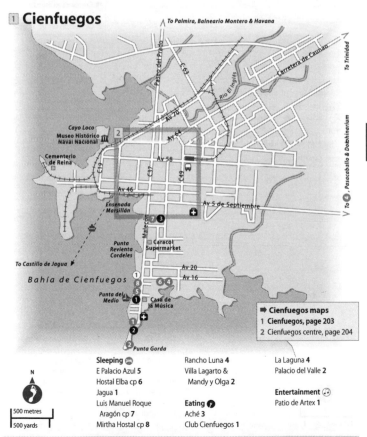

1 Cienfuegos

Sleeping
E Palacio Azul **5**
Hostal Elba cp **6**
Jagua **1**
Luis Manuel Roque
  Aragón cp **7**
Mirtha Hostal cp **8**

Rancho Luna **4**
Villa Lagarto &
  Mandy y Olga **2**

Eating
Aché **3**
Club Cienfuegos **1**

La Laguna **4**
Palacio del Valle **2**

Entertainment
Patio de Artex **1**

→ Cienfuegos maps
1 Cienfuegos, page 203
2 Cienfuegos centre, page 204

500 metres
500 yards

Sights

City centre

The city is designed on a grid system with even-numbered Avenidas running from west to east and odd-numbered Calles running south to north. Part of Avenida 54, from Calle 29 to Calle 37, is closed to traffic. Known as the Boulevard, it has small trees, cafés and restaurants as well as many shops, banks and other services and is the hub of city centre life. The main street is Calle 37, called the **Prado** with a central promenade down the middle of the road where people stroll or sit. It is called the **Malecón**, further south, between Avenida 40 and Avenida 22, where the Prado runs beside the water. The palm

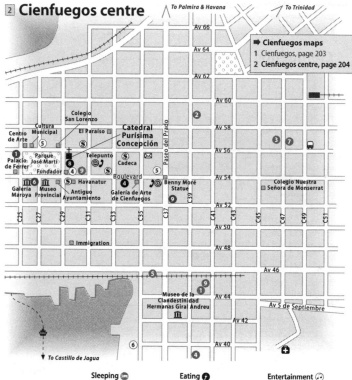

2 Cienfuegos centre

➡ Cienfuegos maps
1 Cienfuegos, page 203
2 Cienfuegos centre, page 204

200 metres
200 yards

Sleeping	Eating	Entertainment
Adelaida y Migue cp **1**	El Polinesio **8**	Café Cantante **5**
Amileidis y Waldo cp **2**	La Verja **4**	Centro Nocturno
Casa Las Golondrinas cp **3**		Costa Sur **6**
E La Unión **9**	**Bars**	Club El Benny **4**
Hostal Plus cp **4**	Bar Jardines de la UNEAC **1**	Teatro Tomás Terry **5**
Hostal Ramiro cp **5**	El Palatino **6**	
Iván y Lili cp **7**	La Fernandina **9**	
Milagros cp **9**		

trees and the view across the Bahía de Cienfuegos make this a lovely walk. The bay can be seen from quite a few places in the centre of the city, but there is no beach and the land by the water is usually dirty.

The central square is **Parque José Martí**, which is a pleasant plaza with benches, a rotunda bandstand and a statue of the ever-present José Martí. Formerly the Plaza de Armas, the first 25 blocks of the city were laid out from here and all the most important colonial buildings are around it. The arch on the west side of the square symbolizes the entrance to the city and is supposed to be similar to the Arc de Triomphe in Paris, having been built by the French founders of Cienfuegos. On the east side on Calle 29 is **La Catedral Purísima Concepción** ① *Mon-Fri 0700-1200, Mass daily at 0730, at 1400 on Sat and at 1000 on Sun* built in 1868, which has a somewhat neo-Gothic interior with silvered columns. On the north side, on Avenida 56, is the majestic building of the old **Colegio San Lorenzo**, now a secondary school, **5 de Septiembre**, not open to the public but a site of former resistance. A civilian and naval uprising in Cienfuegos was quashed by Batista on this day in 1957 and there are several memorials and references to the event across the city. If you do get permission to enter, there is a memorial to the martyrs who died and their pictures are in a glass cabinet.

Next door is Cienfuegos' *pièce de résistance*, the **Teatro Tomás Terry** ① *Av 56 2701 entre 27 y 29, T43-551772, www.teatroterry.azurina.cult.cu, daily 0900-1700, CUC$1 including a guided tour, CUC$2 photos/video, see also Entertainment, page 213,* built in 1889 after the death of the Venezuelan Tomás Terry, with the proceeds of a donation by his family. It was inaugurated in 1890 in front of an audience of 1200 with a performance of Aída. Great artists such as Enrico Caruso, Sarah Bernhardt and Ana Pavlova all performed here. The lobby has an Italian marble statue of Terry and is decorated with fine paintings and ornate gold work. The interior is largely original with wooden seats. Note the ceiling with exquisite paintings of muses and also two portraits of Cuban writers. Over the stage is a large grinning mask representing comedy. The two sets of theatre boxes nearest the stage were traditionally used by mourners who were not supposed to be at the theatre, but did not wish to miss the performance. They had a separate door so that they could enter and leave the theatre and watch the performance unseen by the rest of the audience.

The most notable building on the west side is the Palacio de Ferrer, now the **Casa de Cultura Benjamín Duarte** ① *T43-516584, closed for renovation in 2009.* It is a beautiful building dating from 1894, with a magnificent tower on the corner designed to keep an eye on the port and shipping (great views of the park and the sea if you climb the tower). The opera singer, Caruso, stayed at the Palacio de Ferrer when he came to Cienfuegos to sing at the theatre in 1920. It is worth seeing for the marble floor, staircases and walls, carved in Italy and assembled at the palace. Also note the Italian ceramic wall tiles in gold, white and blue, which change colour in the sunlight, and the plasterwork on the walls and ceiling.

The grand grey and white building on the south side of the square is the **Antiguo Ayuntamiento**, the former town hall where Fidel Castro spoke to the people on 6 January 1959. The **Museo Provincial** ① *Av 54 2702 entre 27 y 29, on the south side of Parque Martí, T43-519722, patrimonio@azurina.cult.cu, Tue-Sat 1000-1800, Sun 0900-1300, CUC$2, tour CUC$1, photos CUC$1,* was formerly the Casino Español, a cultural-political institution, built in 1894 for meetings and gatherings and now a Monumento Nacional. It has a grand staircase with lots of marble and its rooms contain furniture and art as well as archaeology and history of the region and city; exhibits include an aboriginal skeleton, a necklace made from vertebrae, small zoomorphic statues and stones, art nouveau doorways, a *maqueta* of the 5 September 1957 uprising and plenty of explanations about the event, but one of the most interesting things in the museum is a gigantic pair of red, fibreglass, high-heeled shoes – the vast heels hanging over the toilet walls.

At the junction of the Boulevard (Avenida 54) and Paseo del Prado (Calle 37) is a bronze lifesize statue of Benny Moré, who looks like he's strolling down the Prado. The musician was born in the province and Cienfuegos was his favourite city. Famous musicians from here include the Orquesta Aragón, which unleashed the Cha-Cha-Cha upon the world, while the oldest band in the country, Los Naranjos, founded in the 1930s, also hails from here.

Ten minutes' walk south along Prado is the **Museo de la Clandestinidad Hermanas Giral Andreu** ① *Av 42 entre 37 y 39, Tue-Fri 0900-1800, Sun 0900-1200, free*, which has a few exhibits about the Revolution, and some grainy black and white pictures of the 5 September 1957 uprising. Revolutionaries Lourdes and Cristina Giral were born here but later moved to the capital to earn a living, getting involved in raising funds and obtaining medicines for the Revolutionaries. The sisters were murdered in Havana in 1958 during the Batista regime. The museum preserves their bedroom, some photos and a few personal possessions.

Some ten minutes walk west along Avenida 62 is the **Museo Histórico Naval Nacional** (Naval Museum) ① *Cayo Loco, T43-516617, Tue-Sat 0900-1800, Sun 0900-1300, CUC$1 for foreigners, free for Cubans*, painted a dusky pink and white like a fairy tale castle. This is a much more interesting museum than it looks and is not entirely military, including many exhibits with more commercial links to the sea. Outside, there are old weapons in the garden. Inside, there are rooms dedicated to the 1957 uprising and then a number of interesting documents, such as Cuba's declaration of war against Germany, Tokyo and Rome; the *bandera* that was on the Maine and on the Granma; items and documents relating to the Granma and the Playa Girón invasion; archaeological items including pre-Columbian indigenous artefacts; models of boats, fishing memorabilia; items relating to the Wars of Independence; natural history, lighthouses and local artwork.

Paseo el Prado (Calle 37) runs straight from the town centre down the peninsula to **Punta Gorda**. In this area are hotels, restaurants, nightlife and some of the largest houses, built for the wealthy families in the first half of the 20th century. One of the most photographed buildings, **El Palacio del Valle** ① *T43-551226, daily 1000-2300, terrace bar 1100-0200, entry CUC$1 includes a drink on the terrace*, is right at the end of Calle 37 in a beautiful location with sea views all around. The building dates from 1894, with a mixture of architectural styles but with Arab influences predominating. It has incredibly ornate ceilings and other decorations. Designed by Italian architect Alfredo Collí Fanconetti, it was created with the help of Cuban, French and Arab artists. Materials were imported from Spain, Italy and the USA. The building was bought by Alejandro Suero Balbín and given to his daughter as a wedding present upon her marriage to Sr Valle. It is now used as a restaurant, but you can wander in during the day for a look around. Another eclectic building is the **Club Cienfuegos** ① *Calle 37 entre 10 y 12, T43-512891*. Inaugurated in 1920 as the Cienfuegos Yacht Club, it is painted a brilliant white and can be identified by the twin domes on the towers at the front, linked by a balcony and a grand staircase. It is still a centre for sailing, with also tennis courts, a playground, a *sala de fiestas* for public events, two restaurants, free parking and scooter rental.

There is an old cemetery, west of the centre of town in Reparto Reina, opened in 1839 as the municipal burial ground. The **Cementerio de Reina** ① *daily 0600-1800*, has some interesting 19th-century tombs with lots of marble and works by local sculptors. You can find here the tombs of the French founders of the city and Spanish soldiers who died in the wars of independence on the left of the entrance as well as relatives of the dictator

Batista. The largest statue is that of the Sleeping Beauty, for a woman who died in 1907 aged 24, who has some opium plants in one hand and a poisonous snake in the other. Although it was declared a Monumento Nacional in 1986, the cemetery is suffering from lack of maintenance and is in a poor state. About 3 km east of the centre is the newer **Cementerio Tomás Acea** ① *Av 5 de Septiembre entre Km 3 y 4, Mon-Sat 0700-1800, free or CUC$1 with guide*, built by one of the most powerful families in the city and noted for its grand replica of the Parthenon at the entrance. There is a striking monument to the fallen of 5 September 1957 inside and there are avenues of fruit trees and ornamental trees.

Around Cienfuegos

The bay of Cienfuegos, at 88 sq km, is the third largest in Cuba and has attracted industry and shipping, which you will see around the city. A large shrimp fleet sails from here, the port is a major exporter of sugar with 12 sugar cane refineries in the area as well as the largest cement plants and oil refineries in Cuba. A huge nuclear plant lies unfinished since the fall of the USSR.

Palmira

The Parque Central of **Palmira**, about 12 km north of Cienfuegos, is rather unusual. The church looks like it is decorated with *Terry's Chocolate Orange* segments and the southern side features an ornate Grand Masonic Lodge. The fascinating lodge interior features statues of Minerva, Venus and Hercules and the severed John the Baptist's head as well as unusual swords. There are human skulls on display, although questions about their origins are sidestepped. Ask at the lodge social club next door if you would like to be shown around. Palmira is famous for its *Santería* processions and the time to be in town is 3-4 December. On 3 December animal sacrifices are made; on the following day processions can be seen in the streets. At the **Museo Municipal de Palmira** ① *southeast corner of the park, T43-544533, Tue-Sat 1000-1800, Sun 0900-1300, CUC$1*, the very friendly staff will explain all the exhibits in the three sections dedicated to *Santería* especially the three principal sects in the area: Cristo (dating from 1913), San Roque (1915) and Santa Barbara (1917). The museum also arranges folkloric shows. Ring for information or ask at one of the tour operators in Cienfuegos.

Balneario Jesús Montane Oropesa Ciego Montero

① *North of Palmira, open all year except the last 2 weeks of Dec, T43-542236. There is a train from Cienfuegos (0700) on alternate days, 1 hr, to Baños station, which is a few mins' walk from the balneario, return train 1700, bus at 1420 from Cienfuegos, returning 0600, daily.*

These thermal baths are close to the famous water factory from where millions of bottles of mineral water are transported around the country. The sulphurous waters with temperatures of 37-38° are supposed to be good for rheumatism, arthritis, psoriasis and traumas. Treatments last from 10 days to six months and range from hydromassage, body massage (CUC$25), fangotherapy (CUC$10), immersion in thermal pools alone or in groups (CUC$4-6) to acupuncture. There are 28 rooms, CUC$27.50 per person per night, including all food. There are no facilities nearby except, bizarrely and incongruously, a small store selling alcohol (which is not permitted at the *balneario*) and fast food the other side of the railway track.

Playa Rancho Luna and Castillo de Jagua

ⓘ *Castillo open Mon-Sun 0900-1600, CUC$1, guides are available. There is a ferry from Cienfuegos to the castle from Av 46 entre 23 y 25, 0800, 1300, 1700, 45 mins, returning 0630, 1000, 1500, CUC$0.50. Regular crossings, 5 mins, CUC$0.50 from close to Hotel Pasacaballo to the village around the castle. There is also a guagua (bus) from Pasacaballo to Cienfuegos every 1½ hrs, 1 peso cubano.*

If you are in need of some sea and sand, the Playa Rancho Luna is about 16 km from Cienfuegos, on a road lined with mango trees, near the **Hotel Rancho Luna**, see Sleeping, page 211. The beach is quite nice but nothing special and there is a rundown restaurant with little to offer. However, the diving, organized at the hotel is very good. There are lots of reef sites and a variety of modern wrecks, including seven sunk as diving sites just outside the harbour. One of the best is *Camaronero II*, a shrimp boat only five minutes from the dive shop. Most of the wrecks have been stripped of everything, but the *Camaronero II* still has her propellers which makes an interesting photo. Built in 1974 from steel, she is 22 m long and was sunk deliberately between 1983 and 1984 in 18 m of water, totally intact. The wreck is adorned with small coral growth, small gorgonias and sponges, and seasonally large schools of red snapper, grouper, hog fish and jacks are found there. However, during the rainy season the visibility is not good because she lies near the mouth of the river. Other wrecks include: the *Camaronero I*, an 8-m wreck lying in shallow water close to shore but very broken up; the cargo ships, *Panta I* and *II*, sunk in 1988; the *Barco R Club*, a 20-m cement and steel passenger ship sunk in 1992 in 8 m; also the 20-m passenger boat *Barco Arimao* sunk in 1992 in 18 m, and the steel fishing boat *Itabo* sunk in 1994 in 12 m. The best reef sites include *El Bajo* in 4 m, *El Laberinto*, *La Guasa* and *Rancho Luna II* all in 12 m, and *La Corona* in 15 m (divers often see whale sharks here).

If you continue along the road for about 3 km past the beach you get to the **Hotel Pasacaballo**. There is a jetty here and another further along a rough track to the left, from where you can get a little ferry which plies across the mouth of the Bahía de Cienfuegos to the village on the western side, site of the **Castillo Nuestra Señora de los Angeles de Jagua**. The castle was built at the entrance to the bay in 1733-1745 by Joseph Tantete of France. There is only one entrance via a still-working drawbridge across a dry moat. There are views of the narrow entrance to the bay and the Escambray mountains beyond. The vista is impressive minus the eyesore of the **Hotel Pasacaballo** and the eerie structures and housing projects of Ciudad Nuclear, which were built for a nuclear power station whose construction was abandoned halfway through the project. The courtyard of the castle has a prison and a chapel. Inside the castle is the **Museo Nuestra Señora de los Angeles de Jagua** ⓘ *T43-965402*, with five exhibition rooms full of legends and historical explanations.

Close to the **Hotel Faro Luna** (closed 2009), is one of Cuba's controversial **Dolphinariums** ⓘ *Km 17 Cienfuegos-Pasacaballo, T43-548120, Fri-Wed 0930-1700 (subject to change), shows at 1000, 1400, CUC$10 adults, CUC$6 children*. The four dolphins are kept in seawater pens. You can swim with the dolphins for a few minutes – CUC$50, under 12s CUC$33 (including entrance and show). There is a bar, restaurant and showers on site. ▸▸ *See page 22 for further details about dolphinariums in Cuba.*

Jardín Botánico de Cienfuegos

ⓘ *Pepito Tey, T43-545115, daily 0800-1700, CUC$2.50, children CUC$1, bar for drinks. Look out for 2 rows of palm trees leading to the garden from the entrance at the road. Bus from Cienfuegos stops outside, 20 centavos, or take an organized tour.*

Some 23 km east of Cienfuegos, on the road to Trinidad between the villages of San Antón and Guaos, is the Cienfuegos botanical garden, a national monument founded in 1901 by Edwin F Atkins, the owner of a sugar plantation called Soledad, nowadays called Pepito Tey. Atkins turned over 4.5 ha of his sugar estates to study sugar cane, later introducing other trees and shrubs that could be used as raw materials for industry. In 1919 Harvard University became involved in the studies and the site became known as the Harvard Botanical Station for Tropical Research and Sugar Cane Investigation. After the Revolution, the State took charge of the gardens in 1961, renaming them and employing scientific personnel to preserve and develop the many tropical species now found there. Different sections of the gardens are devoted to areas such as medicinal plants, orchids, fruit trees, bamboos and one of the world's most complete collections of palm trees. It is a fine garden and a nice place to wander around. See if you can get a guide (Spanish speaking, tip welcomed) as it will be much more interesting.

Eastern Cienfuegos
In the east of the province at **Martín Infierno**, off the road between Cienfuegos and Trinidad there is a 67-m-high stalagmite, said to be the tallest in the Americas. You will need a 4WD vehicle for this trip and so it's recommended to take a tour. This could also include an excursion to **El Nicho**, a series of cascading waterfalls up to 35 m high surrounded by forest in the Escambray mountains (see also page 222). Situated on the western spur of the lake in Cienfuegos province, 46 km from Cienfuegos, there are pools, caves and paths and, of course, a lunch stop. A beautiful spot in the forested hills on the edge of the Parque Natural Topes de Collantes where coffee is grown. There is almost no public transport to the lake despite assurances of the occasional bus from Manicaragua, so car hire or private transport is essential.

◉ Cienfuegos listings

For Sleeping and Eating price codes and other relevant information, see Essentials pages 37-43.

◉ Sleeping

Cienfuegos *p202, maps p203 and p204*
Hotels
AL-A E La Unión, 31 entre 54 y 56, T43-551020, www.cubanacan.cu. Built in 1869 and recently restored, this very attractive hotel in colonial style is painted in duck-egg blue with white, wrought-iron balcony railings. 49 rooms and some suites are equipped with pleasant, dark-wood furniture and all mod cons. The hotel is decorated in pretty tiles and the swimming pool is beautifully sunken into the patio. There's also a sauna, jacuzzi, gym, laundry, pharmacy, internet centre, tourism bureau, car hire, shop, 3 bars and the 1869 restaurant,

see Eating, below. Non-guests can use the pool for CUC$10 including food and drinks (*consumo*) of up to CUC$7.
AL-A Jagua, 37 entre 0 y 2, Punta Gorda, T43-551003, www.gran-caribe.com. Modern block design but in great location at the tip of the peninsula. 147 a/c rooms (most with twin beds), 2 suites, with views over the bay. Restaurant Escambray and 24-hr café next to a very nice pool. Non-guests can use the pool for CUC$10, which includes food and drinks (*consumo*) to the value of CUC$9. The Palacio del Valle restaurant is also next door to the hotel. There is a shop, internet access and nightly cabaret (except Wed), 2200, CUC$5 includes one cocktail, which is extremely colourful, good and worth the entry fee.
B E Palacio Azul, Calle 37 1202 entre 12 y 14, Punta Gorda, T43-555828, www.cubanacan.cu. Designed by an Italian architect in 1920 as a

private home, this delightful little hotel is definitely the best in town. 7 rooms, all individually named after flowers, double, twin or triple beds, some with balconies, very comfortable, high standard of fixtures, fittings and furnishings, TV, safe, minibar, room service, parking, dining room for breakfast and snacks only, bar, roof terrace for sunbathing. Painted blue and white outside, the building is distinguished by a turret, from where you can get a fabulous view of the bay.

Casas particulares

All the casas listed offer a/c, fan, private bathroom, hot and cold water and fridge. They nearly all charge CUC$20-25, depending on the season, but lower rates can be negotiated for long stays.

D-E Adelaida y Migue, Av 44 3925 entre 39 y 41, T43-513595. Colonial-style house with high ceilings and tiled floors, 2 rooms off passage with no windows, 1 room larger than the other, double or twin beds, firm mattress. Tables and chairs on roof terrace, under cover or in full sun.

D-E Amileidis y Waldo, Calle 39 5818 esq 60, T43-518991, wrodriguezdelrey@yahoo.es. 1950s house designed by the Dean of the Faculty of Architecture in Havana and built by a former mayor for his niece as a wedding present, all furniture, lamps, etc date from then. 2 rooms, one of which has independent entrance, terrace with lovely garden and views of city and sea, garage, very good food, friendly and helpful family, English and Italian spoken, dogs kept in the family quarters, their son likes to chat and play games such as dominoes with visitors.

D-E Casa Las Golondrinas, Calle 47 5613 entre 56 y 58, T43-515788, drvictor61@ yahoo.es. 100 m from bus terminal and train station. Dr Víctor Sosa Rodríguez del Rey and his family offer 2 spacious rooms with large windows and private bathrooms in this 1910 house with terrace and sunbathing area. Good food, friendly and helpful family.

D-E Hostal Elba, Av 16 4315 entre 43 y 45, Punta Gorda, T43-516140. Tania and Manolo

Fernández have a beautiful and well-maintained house built by Manolo, an engineer. Great hospitality, 2 bedrooms, wonderful *criollo* food, excellent quality all round.

D-E Hostal Plus, Calle 39 3818 entre 38 y 40, T43-519037, www.cuba-rent.com. Friendly and welcoming Kuki and Lázaro offer 2 comfortable rooms tastefully decorated in white but unmistakably Cuban. 1 is very large with TV and small bathroom, the other is a good size with huge bathroom, good double beds with foam mattress topper, table and chair, safe deposit box, hanging rail. On the roof is a delightful covered terrace for dining or relaxing with extra bathroom, loads of plants, plenty of fresh and tasty food.

D-E Hostal Ramiro, Av 46 4410 entre 35 y 37, T43-513406, T01-5271 0598 (mob). Ramiro Suárez Pérez and his English-speaking doctor wife have 2 rooms, 1 bigger than the other, on the ground floor, not attached to the family rooms, independent. Large terrace for dining, off-street car parking. Often used by groups as there are lots of casas in this area.

D-E Iván y Lili, Calle 47 5604 entre 56 y 58, T43-527256. Completely independent upstairs suite, family lives downstairs, nice room, balcony, wardrobe, TV and video, CD player, kitchen/diner, terrace at the back with table and chairs on roof, meals available, Iván works for UNEAC and can tell you what events are planned in town.

D-E Milagros, Calle 41 4407 entre 44 y 46, T43-518590. A well-kept house with patio and pretty garden, eat inside or outdoors, car parking, double bed, good bathroom, lots of wardrobe space, rooms open onto corridor so no windows.

D-E Mirtha Hostal, Calle 37 1205 entre 12 y 14, Punta Gorda, T43-526286, T01-5292 9936 (mob), dailynh12@yahoo.es. Mirtha Bango Trujillo is a charming and efficient hostess at this spacious modern house next to Palacio Azul, set back off the road in its own garden with safe car parking. 1 room with double and single beds on ground floor, 2nd room upstairs with terrace and sea view. A balcony upstairs has chairs and is great for drinks, sunbathing, etc. Plenty of storage space, laundry service, lots of good food.

E Mandy y Olga, Calle 35 apto 4D entre Litoral y 0, Punta Gorda, T43-519966. Next to **Villa Lagarto** and part of the same family. There are 2 rooms with an adjoining shared bathroom. Each room has a fridge, closet, TV and a/c. There is an independent entrance but you only 1 to the 2 rooms and bathroom. Coffee and juice are free.

E María Elena Terre, Av 54 5504 entre 55 y 57, T43-517440. Nice house, bedroom very good and very clean, excellent cooking and huge breakfasts, more than enough food, served on a very pleasant terrace. Conveniently close to Víazul, with garage if you arrive by car.

E Villa Lagarto, Calle 35 apt 4B entre Av 0 y Litoral, Punta Gorda, T43-519966, villalagarto@yahoo.es. Tony and Maylin have 2 upstairs rooms with open balcony. 1 has 2 beds, fridge and a/c, the other has a double bed and fridge. There is a pretty patio with fabulous views over the water and towards the mountains. There is a small, salt-water swimming pool with a lizard sculpture that spouts water from its mouth. The pool is also home to 2 beautiful turtles. Welcome cocktail on arrival.

Around Cienfuegos *p207*
Hotels

AL-B Club Amigo Rancho Luna, Carretera a Rancho Luna Km 18, T43-548030, www.cubanacan.cu. 222 all-inclusive small rooms, 2 restaurants, massage, jacuzzi and gym facilities. The pool is very large but in an older style. Mini-golf, horseriding, car hire, watersports, internet and diving centre, see Diving, page 214. Entertainment organizers busy in the pool, on the beach and with night time shows. Popular with Canadians in winter.

B Villa Guajimico, Carretera a Trinidad Km 45, Cumanayagua, T43-450947, best to book through **Cubamar**, in Havana, www.cubamarviajes.cu. Overlooks mouth of Río La Jutía, great location, surrounded by cliffs, caves, coral reefs and small beaches accessible only by boat. 3 star, 51 cabins, of which 3

are triples, white with red tiled roofs, a/c, bathroom, pool, restaurant serving average food, bar, parking, hobicats, good for excursions, but more than anything it is a great dive resort, see Diving, p214.

🍴 Eating

Cienfuegos *p202, maps p203 and p204*
Restaurants

🍴🍴🍴 **Club Cienfuegos**, Calle 37 entre 8 y 12, Punta Gorda, T43-512891, contacto@club.cfg.cyt.cu. Daily 1000-0100. Beautiful white building formerly the Cienfuegos Yacht Club, opened in 1920. 2 restaurants, 1 is Italian and the other offers *comida criolla*.

🍴🍴🍴 **Palacio del Valle**, Calle 37 y Av 0, next to Hotel Jagua, T43-551226. Daily 1200-2200, terrace bar 1100-0200. The place to go for its style, if not for the food. Speciality seafood, including *paella Cienfuega* and lobster, with cheaper options such as fried shrimps and omelettes. There is a lovely view of the bay from the bar on the terrace. Live music at weekends and the pianist Carmencita plays in the restaurant.

🍴 **1869**, Hotel E La Unión, T43-551020. Daily 0700-2145. The service is good and the decor handsome but some of the food is 2nd rate. Oyster in creole sauce and squid in tomato sauce are better options than the chicken dishes.

🍴 **El Polinesio**, 29 5410 entre 54 y 56, T43-515723. Daily 1200-1500, 1800-2200. Serving international and Cuban food, the restaurant also has a shop on the corner, selling handicrafts, rum, cigars, music, etc. There are tables outside for a drink, pleasant for people watching during the day or evening.

🍴 **La Verja**, Boulevard (Av 54) entre 33 y 35, T43-516311. Daily 1100-1500 and 1800-2400. Offers fried fish, breaded shrimp, goulash and salads (a rarity) plus all the usual culprits in a lovely dining room with dark wood carved features in an old house, with scarlet tablecloths and curtains. There's a bar as well as patio dining. A bronze chandelier hangs from the ceiling and the floor is studded with blue, diamond-shaped tiles. Also does *bocaditos*. Good service.

†Î-Î Covadonga, opposite **Hotel Jagua**, T43-518611. Daily 1230-1500 and 1800-2130. Large restaurant in a pleasant seaside setting but very run down with poor service. Long established, founded by María Covadonga, of Asturias, Fidel came here in 1959 on his victory tour towards the capital.

†Î-Î El Cochinito, Calle 37 entre 4 y 6, Punta Gorda, T43-518611. Open 1200-1400, 1800-2100. All dishes based on pork.

†Î-Î El Pollito, Calle 37 (Prado) y 56 (San Carlos), T43-513523. Chicken in all its various forms. Closed for renovation 2009.

†Î-Î La Laguna, Av 10 y Calle 47, Laguna del Cura, T43-517452. Seafood on the waterfront. Specialities include *Filete Canciller* and *Arroz Laguna*.

†Î-Î Pizza Nova, Calle 31 5418 entre 54 y 56, T43-452020. Italian food.

Paladares

†Î Aché, Av 38 4106 entre 41 y 43, T43-526173. Mon-Fri 1200-2200. In operation since 1996, this is now the only legal *paladar* for foreigners. A professional establishment, very well appointed with matching tables and chairs, local artwork on the walls, rustic decor, comfortable, nice bar. Soups and salads for starters followed by main course of chicken, pork, fish cooked in a variety of ways. There is the usual 'flan' or ice cream for dessert, or try *cascas de huevo con queso*. Excellent cocktails, very generous with the rum and will add more to your daiquirí if you want it, Chilean or Spanish wine, Cuban wine is used in the sangría.

○ Bars

Cienfuegos *p202, maps p203 and p204*
Bar Jardines de la UNEAC, on the west side of Parque José Martí, Calle 25 5411 entre 54 y 56, T43-523272, www.uneac.co.cu. Daily 0900-2200 or later, depending on event.

Set in a tranquil garden/patio covered in bougainvillea, renovated 2009. A centre for cultural nightlife with live music (trova, Afro-Cuban, folk) Sat nights, film shows 3 nights a week, Sun *peña folklórico*, an art gallery for more experimental art. Always something going on, events are posted on the gates. No entry fee for the bar but they sometimes charge depending on the activity.

El Palatino, on the south side of Parque José Martí, Av 54 entre 25 y 27, T43-551244, www.palmarescuba.com. Bar open 1000-2300. Built in 1842 as a private residence, it has been used as a bar and restaurant since the beginning of the 20th century, recently renovated with an olde worlde atmosphere, decorated with the works of local caricaturists. Light meals and snacks available. Live traditional music and jazz.

La Fernandina, Prado y 52. A small, popular, but cosy bar.

Palacio de Valle, see Eating, above. On the roof is a bar, open daily 1000-1700. Good views and another restaurant in the garden, CUC$1 to enter *terraza* and get a cocktail.

● Entertainment

Cienfuegos *p202, maps p203 and p204*
Live music
Café Cantante, Calle 37 esq Av 54. Traditional Cuban music with cocktails, you may be charged in pesos cubanos.

Casa de la Música, Calle 37 entre 4 y 6. T43-552320. Entrance price varies according to band/show but is posted outside on the ticket booth. This is a large venue on the seafront with afternoon and evening entertainment posted outside the entrance. There is a rather lovely seafront stage with great views across to the Escambray mountains. Also a music shop with helpful staff, Mon-Sat 0830-1700, Sun 0830-1200.

Centro Cultural El Cubanísimo (Centro Nocturno Artex), Calle 35 entre 16 y 18, Punta Gorda, T43-551255. Daily 0930-0200, CUC$1. Also known as the **Patio de Artex**. The place for the most important musical events in Cienfuegos, including the **Festival Internacional Benny Moré de Música Popular** and **Cubadisco**.

Centro Nocturno Costa Sur, Av 40 entre 33 y 35. Restaurant open 1100-140, 1800-2100. Nightclub 2200-0100 weekdays and until 0200 at weekends. Cabaret CUC$2. Live music and disco.

Club El Benny, Av 54 2904 entre 29 y 31. Mon-Fri 2100-0100, Sat 2100-0200, CUC$3 per person, couples CUC$8, *consumo mínimo*. Nightclub with live entertainment. Nightly offerings of comedy, karaoke and *bolero*. Men must dress smartly, no T-shirts or sandals.

Cultural Municipal, Av 56 entre 25 y 27. Boleros, *peñas* and danzón.

Parque Villuenda, between 62 y 64. Live music by *Guajiros* in this park on Sun at 1000.

Theatre

Teatro Tomás Terry, 56 2701 entre 27 y 29, T43-551772. *Cartelera* is posted outside. Tickets usually cost CUC$5 for a *silla* and CUC$40 for a *palco*.

⊛ Festivals and events

Cienfuegos *p202, maps p203 and p204*
Mar Late in the month there is a national moto boat competition for the **Copa 26 de Julio**.
Apr International **rowing** competition. On 22 Apr there are celebrations for the **founding of the city** of Villa de Nuestra Señora de los Angeles de Jagua, or Cienfuegos.
End of May A **sailing** tournament.
Jul In the first week is the **Fiesta de los Amigos del Mar**, with sailing regattas and races as well as exhibitions of water sports including sailing, rowing, water skiing, motor boats, kayaks, swimming, as well as cycling, beach volleyball, karting, etc. The bay of Cienfuegos roars to the sound of speed boats mid-July when the **Grand Prix, Formula T-1**, is held, with competitors from the USA, Mexico, Venezuela, Costa Rica and Cuba, among others.

Jul/Aug Carnival with stalls and plenty of boozing along the partially shut off Malecón.
Sep Festival Internacional Benny Moré, every other year, celebrating Cuban music in honour of the great sonero, who was born in Santa Isabel de las Lajas in Cienfuegos province.
5 Sep Fiesta in Parque José Martí and a procession to the Tomás Acea cemetery to commemorate the fallen heroes of the failed insurrection of that day in 1957.
Dec Christmas is celebrated with a huge street party; rum is drunk from all manner of containers and there is dancing to a band on the **Hotel Jagua** promenade.

O Shopping

Cienfuegos *p202, maps p203 and p204*
Art and souvenirs
Artex, Av 54 entre 35 y 37. Daily 0800-1800. Music, clothing, drinks and souvenirs.
Casa del Fundador, Av 54 esq 29. Daily 0900-1900. Rum, music, handicrafts, cigars.
El Embajador, Av 54 esq 33. 0930-1900 daily. Cigars, rum and coffee.
Galería Maroya, Fondo Cubano de Bienes Culturales, Av 54 2502 entre 25 y 27, south side of park. Mon-Sat 0900-1830, Sun 0900-1300. Original art works, papier mâché goods, wooden items, jewellery, clothes, T-shirts, bags, baskets, leather, etc, antiques, showcase for local artists, courtyard at the back of large colonial house dating from the 1890s with art on the walls. The appropriate export documents for works of art are available. Maroya is the indigenous word for moon. The shop is a magnet for tour parties.

Bookshops
Librería Bohemia, Av 56 entre 33 y 35. Mon-Sat 0800-1630. Second-hand and antique books.
Librería Dioniso San Román, Av 54 esq 37. Mon-Sat 0900-1700, Sun 0900-1200. Reasonable selection of books in CUC$ and a section sold in pesos cubanos.

Food
Caracol, Prado. Daily 0900-1900.
A well-stocked supermarket.
El Paraíso supermarket, Av 58 esq 33.
Mon-Sat 0830-1730, Sun 0830-1200.

▲ Activities and tours

Cienfuegos *p202, maps p203 and p204*
Diving
There are 2 dive operations in the area: at **Club Aringo Rancho Luna** and **Villa Guajimico**.
Villa Guajimico, see page 211, www.cuba marviajes.cu. Offers various dive packages with accommodation.
Centro Internacional de Buceo Faro Luna at Hotel Rancho Luna, T43-548020. English, French, German and Italian spoken. Diving 0900-1130 daily, 1 dive CUC$30, 2 dives CUC$59, 3 dives CUC$87, equipment rental CUC$10 daily. Courses available. There are 40 sites including wall, caves, pillars (La Dama del Caribe) and 6 sunken ships.

Sailing
Club Cienfuegos, Calle 37 entre 10 y 12 Av, Punta Gorda, T43-512891, contacto@ club.cfg.cyt.cu. Sun-Fri 1000-0100, Sat 1000-0200. A pure white Parisian-style mansion built in 1920 is now this club/ marina where you can arrange excursions on a catamaran or yacht. There are 2 restaurants, tennis, a shop selling sporting and fishing equipment, car and moped hire, billiard table, bumper boats, go-karts and minigolf.
Marina Puertosol (also known as Marlin Cienfuegos), Calle 35 entre 6 y 8, T43-551699/ 551241, VHF 16, operativo@nautica.cfg.cyt.cu, mpsolcfg@ip.etecsa.cu. Full-service marina 1 km from town centre with 36 slips, maximum length 60 m, maximum draught 30 m, fuel, water, electricity, ships, chandler, car hire, taxis, restaurant, bathrooms, waste disposal. Cienfuegos is a port of entry so Customs are here too. You can rent catamarans for CUC$8 per hr, pedalos CUC$5

per hr and kayaks CUC$3 per hr. Sailing and diving excursions also available.

Tour operators
Excursions and tours usually depend on a minimum number of people. Prices for a tour of Cienfuegos CUC$10, Jardín Botánico CUC$10, Castillo de Jagua CUC$15 (with transport), cigar factory CUC$4, El Nicho, Hanabanilla or Topes de Collantes CUC$27 with lunch, Trinidad CUC$17, Varadero CUC$27, Havana CUC$33, Guamá CUC$27, Santa Clara CUC$17.
Cubanacán, Av 54 2903 entre 29 y 31, T43-551680, cuba.viajes@cfg.cyt.cu. Mon-Fri 0800-1700, Sat 0800-1200. Also at Calle 37 1208 entre 12 y 14, T43-551191. Reserve tours a day in advance. Can arrange taxis, diving and fishing.
Cubatur, Calle 37 5399 entre 54 y 56, T43-551242 and in Hotel Jagua, T43-551242.
Ecotur, T43-550575, yusy@jagua.cfg.sld.cu, contact Francisco Román.
Havanatur, Boulevard (Av 54) 2906 entre 29 y 31, T43-511393. Mon-Fri 0830-1200, 1330-1630, Sat 0830-1200. Also at Hotel Jagua. They also offer tours to Yaguanabo CUC$29, Hacienda La Vega CUC$17 and Finca La Isabela CUC$15.

⊖ Transport

Cienfuegos *p202, maps p203 and p204*
Bus
Terminal at Calle 49 esq Av 56, T43-515720/516050. **Víazul**, office inside the main bus station, T43-518114/515720, daily 0800-1700, passes through Cienfuegos on its **Havana–Trinidad** route.

Car/moped hire
Havanautos, Calle 37 entre 16 y 18, Punta Gorda, in front of Servi Cupet, and at the Hotel Jagua T43-551154, 551211. Daily 0800-1200, 1300-2000. As well as car hire, you can also hire mopeds at CUC$22 per day.

Petrol stations: Servi Cupet Cimex petrol station is at Calle 37 entre 16 y 18, and also on the way to Rancho Luna. The Bahía filling station, at Autoimport, is at Calle 37 esq Av 40.

Coches
Coches charge a couple of pesos.

Taxi
Cubataxi, T43-519145. To **Rancho Luna**, CUC$8, to **Pasacaballo** CUC$11. A private but illegal **taxi** for **Playa Girón** can be bargained down to CUC$25.

Train
Terminal at Calle 49 esq Av 58, T43-528328. All services generally slow, unreliable and uncomfortable. To **Havana**, via **Santa Clara**, to eastern destinations (**Santiago**, **Bayamo**, **Holguín**) change trains in Santa Clara.

❶ Directory

Cienfuegos *p202, maps p203 and p204*
Accident and emergency Ambulance: T104. Fire: T105. Police: T106. **Banks** Banco Financiero Internacional, Av 54 esq 29, Mon-Fri 0800-1500. Cash advances on credit cards. **Bandec**, Av 56 esq 31, Mon-Fri 0800-1500. Visa and MasterCard accepted. **Cadeca**, Av 56 entre 33 y 35, Mon-Sat 0800-1700, Sun 0800-1200. Quickest for changing currency. **Immigration** Av 48 entre 29 y 31. Open for visa extensions, Mon-Fri 0800-1200, 1300-1500.
Insurance Asistur, Av 54 y 31, T43-551624.
Internet Etecsa, see below, CUC$6 per hr, can be easier and quieter in hotels which offer internet access. **Medical services** Clínica Internacional, Calle 37 202 entre 2 y 4, opposite Hotel Jagua, T43-551622, www.servimedcuba.com. Offers 24-hr emergency care, consultations, laboratory services, X-rays, pharmacy and other services. There is usually someone who speaks a language other than Spanish. If the front door is shut, knock. Visa and MasterCard accepted. **Farmacia Principal Municipal**, Av 54 entre 35 y 37, pharmacy open 24 hrs. **Santa Elena**, 37 esq Av 60, also open 24 hrs. There is also a pharmacy at the Clínica Internacional. **Post** Av 56 esq 35, 0800-2000. Sells phone cards as well as postal services. **Telephone** Etecsa/Telepunto, Calle 31 entre 54 y 56. Phone, fax and internet, daily 0830-2200. Internet costs CUC$6 per hr, available until 1900.

Santa Clara

→ *Colour map 2, B4. Population. 238,000. Altitude: 112 m.*
Santa Clara is best known for being the site of the last and definitive battle of the Revolution, when Che Guevara and his men captured an armoured troop train and subsequently the city. Che's body is interred here and his mausoleum is a major visitor attraction. Long underestimated by tourists on their way to somewhere else, Santa Clara is a pleasant university city lying in the heart of Cuba, with a sense of urgency and purpose. It is a cultured city and, as well as the monumental mausoleum, there are several art galleries and museums to stroll around and parks to sit and take in the atmosphere. Santa Clara's nightlife is humming, with any number of clubs and music venues where you can take in traditional or more contemporary Cuban styles, or there is the beautiful old theatre where you can find dance or drama performances of an international standard. South of the city, the land rises gently to the Alturas de Santa Clara, a range of hills reaching 464 m at its highest point, and then the magnificent Sierra de Escambray. There are lakes and reservoirs in the hills, where you can hike, birdwatch or fish in a peaceful and picturesque landscape. ▸▸ *For listings, see pages 223-230.*

Ins and outs

Getting there There are no domestic **flights** to Santa Clara but international charters come from Canada and Italy. On the cays, an airstrip receives short-hop flights and air taxis (**Gaviota**). Santa Clara is on the main cross-island railway line. **Train** services join the city with Havana and Santiago de Cuba and with most of central Cuba's towns. The railway station is quite near the middle of the town. If you are travelling by **car**, the arterial *autopista* running from Havana to Santiago de Cuba links the city with these two major urban centres and other provincial capitals. Lesser roads go north to the cayos and south to Trinidad. Daily **bus** services make Santa Clara easy to get to on any route through the island. The long-distance bus station is about 2.5 km from the centre (a taxi to the centre is CUC$2-3). ▶▶ *See also Transport, page 229.*

Getting around It is easy enough to **walk** round the town centre but the main attraction, the Che Guevara mausoleum in Plaza de la Revolución, is some way out. Walking takes about 20 minutes. **Car hire** is available if you want to make excursions further afield, or there are guided tours for the cays from some of the travel agencies in town. If you are staying in a *casa particular* ask if anyone in the family offers their services as a driver and/or guide, which will be cheaper than an official taxi.

Tourist information There is no tourist office as such, but several state tour agencies in town can give you information on trips and excursions, as well as make hotel reservations and reconfirm flight tickets. If you are staying in a *casa particular* you will probably find your hosts to be a mine of information worth tapping into. They will usually make phone calls for you to arrange transfers or accommodation at your next destination. The hotels all have a *buró de turismo*, which sells organized tours and little else.

History

The village of Santa Clara was founded on 15 July 1689, when 17 families from San Juan de los Remedios migrated from the coast to the interior. Land was parcelled out and a powerful landholding oligarchy was formed. The settlement grew and the economy prospered on the fortunes of stockbreeding, tobacco, sugar, other crops and the exploitation of the Malezas copper mines, while taking advantage of the favourable location on the main trading route through the island. In 1827 when the island was divided into three departments, Santa Clara was one of the sections of the central department. In 1867 the town became a city and in 1873 the railroad arrived, linking it with Havana. In 1895 when the island was further divided, this time into six provinces, Santa Clara became the capital of Las Villas, which included within its boundaries what is now Villa Clara, Cienfuegos, Sancti Spíritus and the Península de Zapata. The 1975 administrative reorganization sharply reduced the provincial territory, renaming it as Villa Clara, with Santa Clara as its capital and dividing it into 13 municipalities. Aside from Santa Clara, where most of the heavy industry is concentrated, other important urban centres are Caibarién, Camajuaní and Remedios to the northeast, Placetas to the east and Sagua La Grande to the north.

Santa Clara was the site of the last battle of the Revolution in December 1958 before Castro entered Havana. Batista was on the point of sending an armoured train with military supplies, including guns, ammunition and soldiers, to Santiago de Cuba to counter-attack the revolutionaries. However, when the train arrived in Santa Clara on 24 December it could go no further because the rebels had destroyed several bridges. Che Guevara had his command post in the university and his troops were hiding in the outskirts of Santa Clara. The train was parked near the Loma El Capiro and soldiers on board climbed up the hill to see Che's troops advancing. They opened fire but were defeated and the rebels took the Loma. Che moved his command post to the building which is now the seat of the PCC Provincial and from there made plans to derail the train, which took place at dawn on 29 December. At around 1500 the same day, the train retreated but was ambushed by 23 men. Fighting for the train was over within an hour, but the battle for the city lasted until 1 January 1959 when news spread that Batista had fled the country. It is said that the capture of the train was the decisive factor in the triumph of the Revolution and it is now a major tourist attraction (see under Sights, below).

Sights

City centre

Parque Leoncio Vidal is the central plaza of the city, a pleasant park with trees, a central bandstand, and a bronze statue of **Marta Abreu de Estévez**, one of the benefactors of Santa Clara. It is busy day and night and local people love to listen to the band playing or just stroll around in the evening with their friends and families. The municipal band plays a variety of music for about an hour Thursdays and Sundays at 2000. There is also typical Cuban music played live outside the theatre, with traditional music played on Saturdays at 2200. There are plenty of benches where you can sit and take in the atmosphere but be prepared to be joined by interested Cubans. The roads around the edge are for pedestrians only and until 1894 there was racial segregation, with a fence dividing the inner and outer footpaths: white people walked in the centre of the park, while blacks were only allowed around the edge. In 1996 the plaza was declared part of the National Heritage. In one of the fountains on the north side of the Parque is a sculpture by José Delarra dating from 1989 (replacing a statue placed here in 1925 which was damaged in 1959), called **El Niño de la Bota Infortunada**. It is of a boy of about six or seven years old, representing those who, during the war of secession in the United States, used their boots to carry water to the sick and injured, much of it often spilt or lost through holes in the shoe. There are plans to renovate some of the buildings around the square and turn one or two into hotels and shops. Handicrafts and fresh flowers are sold around the Parque.

On the north side of the Parque, on the corner of Calle Máximo Gómez, is **Teatro La Caridad** ① *Parque Vidal, T42-208548, Tue-Sun 0900-1700, CUC$1, tickets for performances around CUC$4-10.* It was built in 1884-85 with money raised by Marta Abreu de Estévez containing frescoes by artist Camilo Salaya (Philippines). In its heyday it attracted artists such as Enrico Caruso, Libertad Lamarque, Lola Flores, Alicia Alonso, El Ballet Nacional de Cuba, Chucho Valdés, etc. It is a Monumento Nacional and has been restored several times, most recently in 2009, but contains more original features than any other theatre in Cuba, such as furniture, mirrors, paintings and busts in the lobby. You can also see the original stage machinery, with over 4.5 km of ropes, levers, pulleys and counterweights, possibly the only machinery of this period still in use anywhere in the world.

Round the corner from the theatre is the largest art gallery outside Havana, the **Galería Provincial de las Artes Plásticas** ① *Máximo Gómez 3 entre Marta Abreu y Barreros, T42-207715, Tue-Thu 0930-1800, Fri-Sat 1400-2200, Sun 1800-2200, free.* Originally built in the 19th century as a family house, it became the headquarters of the Colonia Española at the beginning of the 20th century. After the 1960s it was used for other purposes and has recently been rebuilt with all its former glory. There are three rooms for temporary exhibitions of paintings, drawings, crafts, sculpture and other works by national and international artists. There is sometimes live music in the form of *peñas culturales* at around 1500.

On the same side of the Parque as the theatre is the **Museo de Artes Decorativas**, ① *Parque entre Lorda y Luis Estévez, T42-205368, Mon, Wed-Thu 0900-1800, Fri-Sat 1300-2200, Sun 1800-2200, check times as they can vary, CUC$2*. The house was built at the end of the 18th century and belonged to a *criollo* family. Furniture, paintings, porcelain and glassware are exhibited in rooms around a central courtyard, each furnished in the style of the 18th, 19th or 20th centuries. The courtyard is also used for small concerts, fashion shows, etc. Half a block away, just off the Parque is the **Centro Provincial de Patrimonio** ① *Céspedes 10 y Plácido, T42-205051, Mon-Fri 0900-1630, free*. Dating from the beginning of the 19th century when it was a domestic building on two floors, the first floor is now an art and photographic gallery. There is evening entertainment the first Saturday of the month at 2100. A little further on and round the corner is the **Casa de la ACAA** (Asociación Cubana de Artesanos y Artistas) ① *Maceo 7 entre Bulevard y Céspedes, T42-223969. 0900-1600*. Here you can find locally made high-quality cultural handicrafts and works of art for exhibition and sale in a recently restored colonial house (1840). On Saturdays there is live entertainment: *peñas* by handicraft artists at 1930, while on the third Saturday of the month ceramicist musicians hold a *peña* at 2100. Two blocks from the Parque is the Catholic church, **Nuestra Señora del Buen Viaje** ① *Pedro Estévez (Unión) esq Buen Viaje, T42-206332, daily 0700-1130, Mass Tue-Fri 0800, Wed 1700, Sat 1630, Sun 0800, 2000*. Some of its architectural elements date from the 18th century, although the building was deeply modified later, especially during the 20th century and it is a mixture of styles. Next to the church, the former monastery built by the priests is now the Bishopric of Santa Clara. Another Roman Catholic church to the south of the Parque is **la Santísima Madre del Buen Pastor**, or 'La Divina Pastora', built in the 19th century and part of the Capuchin Order.

Also on the Parque is the **Biblioteca Provincial José Martí**, housed in the neoclassical **Palacio Provincial** ① *T42-206222, Mon-Fri 0800-1800, Sat 0800-1600*. It was the seat of provincial government (Las Villas) and one-time headquarters of Batista's police force. It was attacked by the Revolutionaries on 29 December 1958, surrendering the next day. It was also the place from where General Máximo Gómez addressed the people on 13 February 1899. A 72-hour wake for Che Guevara and his guerrilla comrades was held here in 1997. Its stock of books is limited but the architecture rewards a visit. There is a concert hall, usually used on Thursdays at 2100, but check the 'cartelera' on the door for other events. Temporary art exhibitions are also hosted here. On the west side of the Parque is the **Hotel Santa Clara Libre**, an ugly green tower block whose bullet-marked, art deco façade is a reminder of Che's battle for the city. Art exhibitions and cultural events are held during the day and evenings at the **Casa de la Cultura** ① *T42-217181, daily 0800-2300*. The building is architecturally interesting and worth a look. A variety of cultural events are held here. ▶▶ *See Entertainment, page 226*.

Just behind Teatro La Caridad runs Santa Clara's main commercial thoroughfare, best known as the Boulevard, which heads east as Calle Independencia to the Tren Blindado. If you walk two blocks away from the Parque along Marta Abreu and then turn right along Zayas, heading up to the Boulevard, you enter what has traditionally been the Chinese part of town. The architecture ranges from traditional colonial to art deco and you won't find Chinese temples here, but around 20% of the residents are of Chinese origin and until recently the Chinese Consulate was here (now a school, 13 de Marzo). The **Casa de la**

Ciudad Atípica ① *Boulevard esq Zayas, T42-205593, Mon 0800-1200, Tue-Fri 0800-1200, 1300-1700, 2000-2200, Sat 1400-2200, or later, Sun 1700-2100, CUC$1*, is mostly an art gallery showcasing local artists. Built in the 19th century, it has beautiful stained-glass windows and colonial architecture. It was initially a family house belonging to a man called Rivalta, from Barcelona; it became the Casa de la Ciudad in 1990. There are 12 exhibition rooms (permanent and temporary) containing art, furniture, photography

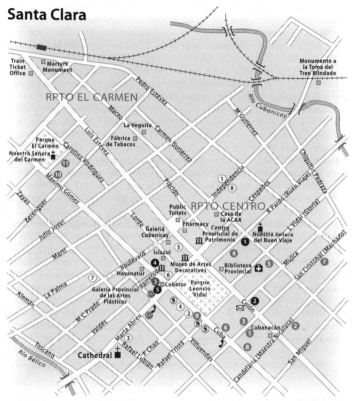

Santa Clara

500 metres (approx)
500 yards (approx)

Sleeping
Alba Hostal cp **3**
Casa Mercy cp **1**
Héctor Martínez cp **4**
Hostal El Patio cp **5**
Hostal Florida Center cp **2**
Hostal La Bugambilia cp **6**
Hostal María Isabel
　Obregón cp **7**
Hostal Rosita cp **8**
José Ramón de
　Zayas Lara cp **10**
Olga Rivera Gómez cp **11**
Santa Clara Libre **9**

Eating
1878 Colonial **4**
Coppelia **2**
El Alba **1**
Salón Juvenil **3**

Bars & clubs
Las Terrazas de la
　Marquesina **3**

Entertainment
Bar Club Boulevard **1**
Casa de la Ciudad **7**
Casa de la Cultura **4**
Cine Teatro Camilo
　Cienfuegos **2**
Club Mejunje **3**
Piano Bar **5**
Teatro 2 **8**
Teatro La Caridad **6**

(provincial social and political themes), local heraldry and local folkloric legends. Other artists of national and international stature are hung here, including several paintings by Ruperto Jay Matamoros (1912), Amelia Pelaez (1896-1968) and Wifredo Lam (1902-1982). Concerts and *peñas* are held in the central patio. ▸▸ *See Entertainment, page 226.*

Some 425 people, of which three quarters are women, work at the **Fábrica de Tabacos** ① *Maceo entre Julio Jover y Berenguer, T42-202211, visiting hours Mon-Fri 0900-1100, 1300-1500, workers go home at 1600, CUC$4, get a ticket in advance from a tour agency (eg Havanatur) or at the shop on the opposite corner and then wait your turn at reception for a guided tour,* the largest cigar factory outside Havana occupying most of one block. Tours are available during working hours. Note the cigar labels used as paper chain decorations.

The cathedral, **Iglesia Parroquial Mayor de las Santas Hermanas de Santa Clara de Asís** ① *Calle Marta Abreu, entre Alemán y Lubián, T42-202078, Mon-Fri 0900-1200, 1400-1700, Sat 1500-1700. Mass Tue 2015, Thu 1700, Sun 0800, 1000, 1700,* dates only from the 20th century. It was consecrated in 1953 after a decade of works, and has some interesting stained-glass windows donated in the memory of loved ones. It became the cathedral of the new Diocese of Santa Clara in 1995. The main attraction is the 3-m-high white marble statue of the Virgin Mary at the main door, officially known as La Inmaculada Concepción, but also called La Virgen de la Charca (Virgin of the pond). The statue was commissioned by a local association of Roman Catholic women and blessed on Mother's Day, 12 May 1957. It stood originally at the entrance to the city but in the 1960s it was discarded in a ditch. It remained there until 1986 when it was disturbed by road building machinery and attracted huge interest with hundreds of people helping to clean up the Virgin. However, it was not until 1995 that the rather damaged and soiled Virgin was put inside the cathedral.

There are other churches scattered around the city, such as **Nuestra Señora del Carmen** ① *Parque El Carmen, T42-205217, 0900-1200, 1500-1700, Mass Mon-Tue, Thu-Fri 1700, Wed 2030, Sat 1430, Sun 0730, 2100.* This small church with a beautiful altar was built in the 18th century on the same hill where the founders of Santa Clara celebrated the first Mass, in 1689. It was used as a prison for women in 1868-1878. Part of the Silesian Order, there are connections with Don Juan Bosco and Italian saints, whose portraits adorn the walls. Father José Vandor, a Silesian priest and deeply holy man, was a mediator in the historic Battle for Santa Clara in December 1958. He was much loved by his parishioners and the process for his canonization has recently been opened. In the pleasant square, Parque El Carmen, outside, there is a 1951 marble monument to the 12 families who founded the city. It is a semi-circular spiral construction supported by 12 pillars and in the middle is a tamarind tree. Also in the square is a monument to Roberto Rodríguez 'El Vaquerito', a troop commander who was killed here in one of the battles for Santa Clara in December 1958.

Plaza de la Revolución

A monument to Che has been built on one side of the **Plaza de la Revolución Ernesto Guevara**, about a 20-minute walk from the city centre, and this is the focal point of the national obsession with the Argentine *guerrillero*. A huge bronze statue of Che carrying a machine gun stands on top of a large concrete plinth, a bas-relief scene depicting Che in battle and an inscription of a letter from Che to Fidel when he left Cuba. It is on Prolongación Marta Abreu after the Carretera Central forks to the south; entrance on Calle Rafael Tristá, which runs parallel. Major speeches and commemorative events take place here, such as on May Day or 8 October, the day of Che's death. On 28 December there is an annual concert with Cuban and Latin American singers.

Ernesto 'Che' Guevara: rise and fall of the 'New Man'

Every visitor to Cuba learns to recognize the face of Che Guevara, the Cuban Revolution's unofficial emblem. Born in Rosario, Argentina, Ernesto Guevara was a medical student when he began travelling around Latin America by motorcycle, bus, truck and even as a stowaway on ships. In 1954, Guevara was in Guatemala when the CIA toppled that country's elected government. His hopes for peaceful change in the hemisphere were dashed and Guevara found his enemy: imperialism. Months later in Mexico he met his natural ally, the exiled Cuban lawyer, Fidel Castro. Guevara joined Castro's invasion force as a doctor, but once in Cuba quickly showed himself a brilliant field commander as well and rose during three years of warfare to lead the guerrilla army's second column.

Repeatedly wounded, Che led from the front lines and was lionized by his Cuban soldiers, many of whom would follow him for the rest of their lives. On 27 December 1958, Che's badly outnumbered guerrillas ambushed a troop train at Santa Clara, Cuba, the victory that sealed the fate of the Batista regime. It was the apogee of Guevara's career. Within days he had entered Havana and revolutionary politics, a field of battle far more dangerous than the mountains of the Sierra Maestra.

Following the triumph of the Revolution on 1 January 1959, Cubans rallied to Guevara. Nicknamed 'Che' after an Argentine figure of speech, Guevara routinely spoke at Castro's side and was seen as the Revolution's second leader. His position was won through public support; a charismatic orator, Guevara appealed to the idealism of the young, calling for the birth of a 'New Man', or a revolutionary society based on moral, rather than material incentives. His eloquence on behalf of the poor and dispossessed made him a global spokesman for the Third World.

Once in power, Guevara endorsed show trials and summary executions of opponents and later, as head of the Central Bank and the Ministry of Industry, his Socialist economic reforms produced chaos even by his own account. Frustrated by Fidel Castro's increasing reliance on the Soviet Union, Guevara quit Cuba in 1965, first to join a doomed rebellion in the Congo, then, in late 1966, to launch his own guerrilla column in Bolivia.

On 8 October 1967, in an operation coordinated by the CIA, Guevara was captured and executed by Bolivian troops. His remains were repatriated to Cuba 30 years later, to be interred in a bronze mausoleum at the site of his great victory in Santa Clara.

Guevara remains an enigmatic figure, seen as both an inspiring idealist and an inflexible ideologue. Despite his position as the Revolution's greatest hero, 'El Che' has also become a symbol of dissent for those Cubans who recall his energy and optimism at a time when the Cuban Revolution seems to lack both. See also page 426.

The monument complex, inaugurated on 28 December 1988, was designed by **José Delarra** (1938-2003), who went on to construct 14 further sculptures symbolizing the feats of the guerrilla and his invading forces in Villa Clara province. Under the monument is a **Mausoleum**. The remains of Che and his comrades who fell in Bolivia have been interred at this site, with architecture designed to be in keeping with the harsh surroundings in which they fought. Fourteen Royal palms to the left represent the date, 14 June, while the additional 14 Royal palms to the right, making a total of 28, represent the year of Che's birth: 1928. The mausoleum is open to the public, numbers limited to 20, and the chamber is a place of contemplation and calm. There are now 38 tombs but only 30 are occupied. Beside the mausoleum is the **Museo Histórico de la Revolución** ① *T42-205985, Tue-Sun 0900-1700, free, bags should be left at the entrance.* The museum has good displays in Spanish and sometimes a video about Che's life and role in the Revolution, with many photos, uniforms and personal effects, including his famous leather jacket, the clothes he wore when he was murdered in Bolivia, as well as displays of the battle in Santa Clara. Recommended. Behind the complex construction work is underway on a cemetery for all the guerrillas under Che's command during the Revolution. To get to the museum from the city centre, you can walk or take a *bicitaxi* (illegal), CUC$1 per person, but agree on a price in advance, as the drivers are notorious for moving the goalposts.

Monumento a la Toma del Tren Blindado
① *Independencia, heading east towards Camajuaní, between Río Cubanicay and the railway line, T42-202758, Mon-Sat 0800-1700, CUC$1, photos inside the wagons CUC$1.*
Three of the five carriages of Batista's troop train and a bulldozer used to derail the train are preserved here. Is Cuba the only place in the world where a bulldozer sits on a plinth? The train, carrying 408 heavily armed troops and weapons, was attacked and taken on 29 December 1958 by 23 guerrillas under the command of Che Guevara in a heroic battle lasting only one hour. The carriages are arranged in a small park among clusters of angular pillars and an inscription on an obelisk describes the event. There is a museum inside the wagons showing weapons and other things carried on the train as well as photos of the aftermath.

El Che de los Niños
On the outskirts of Santa Clara as you head towards the cays (opposite the PCC offices, which were Che's HQ in 1958), there is another statue of Che, a bronze cast by Casto Solano of Spain. It is known as El Che de los Niños and shows Che striding along holding a small child in one arm, a cigar in the other hand and lots of tiny details reflecting events in his life. On his shoulder is an Amerindian man on a goat, signifying him telling his story to the child. On one of his boots is the bike he travelled on through South America with his friend Alberto Granados. Don Quijote is on one of his pockets, while on his belt is his troop.

Around Santa Clara

Embalse Hanabanilla
The **Sierra del Escambray**, part of the Montañas de Guamuhaya, occupies most of the land between Santa Clara and Trinidad and can be visited from either city. Although not the highest mountain range in Cuba, it is one of the most beautiful, being coated in forest and home to a variety of plant and animal species. The peaks are intersected by streams, waterfalls and fertile valleys, where thatched *bohíos* are home to farming families eking out a living from growing bananas, coffee and livestock. There are several lakes and dams in the province of Villa Clara and the province boasts the largest river to drain into the Atlantic, Río Sagua la Grande, at 144 km long. Embalse Alacranes, 45 km north of Santa Clara, is the second largest reservoir in the country, while man-made Embalse Hanabanilla, the third largest, is very attractive and used for recreational purposes as well as water supply, with hunting and fishing both popular. Some 30 km south of Santa Clara, the road to Trinidad passes through **Manicaragua**, a large town of 80,000 inhabitants set in rolling hills covered

with tobacco fields, and then rises into the mountains. **Hanabanilla reservoir** has the largest hydroelectricity station in the country, but looks like a natural lake. It is in a very attractive landscape with lovely views. The lake is stocked with largemouth bass and other fish and there are plenty of wild duck, quail, pheasant and other game birds. You can take a boat trip on the lake to the **Restaurante Río Negro** (7 km from the **Hotel Hanabanilla** and accessible only by boat CUC$7.50 per person, Tuesday to Sunday), to the Trucha Falls (five-hour boat trip including Río Negro and the falls, CUC$60), to a farmer's house, or go hiking or horse riding in the mountains. There are several options and tours available. The resort area can get crowded with Cubans at the weekends, but you don't need to walk far to get peace and quiet. Embalse Hanabanilla can be visited as a day trip from Santa Clara, Cienfuegos, Trinidad or Sancti Spíritus, but an overnight stay would be more rewarding and it is a convenient place to stay between the towns.

⊙ Santa Clara listings

For Sleeping and Eating price codes and other relevant information, see Essentials pages 37-43.

● Sleeping

If you want to be in the city centre then you are recommended to stay in a *casa particular*, of which there are several excellent ones to choose from with knowledgeable and helpful host families. For a more rustic feel, there are state hotels on the outskirts of the city and in the hills, but these are usually booked for people on package tours.

Santa Clara centre *p217, map p219*
Hotels
D Santa Clara Libre, Parque Vidal 6, T42-207548, www.islazul.cu. Central, 1956 dilapidated metal-concrete building on Parque Vidal with bullet holes on the façade, preserved from the December 1958 battle when some of the police were using the building to defend the city from the revolutionaries. 145 spartan rooms, but comfortable, with a/c, phones, TV, water shortages, lifts also erratic and ancient, straight out of Batman's Gotham, noisy, car rental, observation deck with bar on top of the building from where you get a great view of the city, cinema.

Casas particulares
Casas charge CUC$20-25, although occasionally you can negotiate a lower rate, depending on the season and demand. All those listed offer meals, private bathrooms, hot water, a/c, fan, fridge. Beware of *jineteros* outside who may tell you the house is full and offer to take you somewhere else, or concoct some other story so they can get a CUC$5 commission. Ring the bell and get the facts from someone inside. If you come by bus with a prior reservation, the casa owner will meet you at the terminal with a taxi, CUC$3.
D-E Alba Hostal, San Cristóbal (E Machado) 7 entre Cuba y Colón, 142-294108. A beautiful old house, high ceilings, tiled floors, colonial style, lovingly renovated and run by Wilfredo Alba Contreras and his family. 2 rooms each with 2 antique beds (new mattresses) which open on to a small patio with tables and plants. Period furniture and light fittings complete the restoration.
D-E Casa Mercy, San Cristóbal (E Machado) 4 entre Cuba y Colón, T42-216941, T5283 6076 (mob), isel@uclv.edu.cu. Very central casa run by experienced hosts, Omelio (engineer) and Mercedes (social worker) Moreno and family, who speak several languages, are helpful, knowledgeable and friendly. 2 good rooms, upstairs overlooking the street, private and separate from the rest of the house, double bed, single available if needed, laundry, iron, good home cooking, vegetarians and children catered for, cocktail menu and rum tasting, roof terrace with view of the Che mausoleum in the distance. Parking, taxis and tours arranged.

D-E Héctor Martínez, Rolando Pardo (Buen Viaje) 8 entre Maceo y Parque, T42-217463. Room in house dating from 1902, original floor tiles, double and single beds, good fixtures and fittings, pleasant patio with tables, rocking chairs, plants.

D-E Hostal El Patio, Maceo 102 entre Gloria (Leoncio Vidal) y Mujica, T42-207054, pedroval@capiro.vcl.sld.cu. Lourdes and Pedro Valdés run this pleasant casa with high ceilings and a small, cosy interior patio with rocking chairs and shady plants. Room with twin beds which can be pushed together plus bed for child.

D-E Hostal Florida Center, Candelaria (Maestra Nicolasa) 56 entre Colón y Maceo, T42-208161. Delightful colonial house dating from 1876, which was the first ever private house to win the architectural conservation prize in 2008. 2 rooms with antique furniture open on to large, verdant patio garden where there are orchids, parrots, caged songbirds, a dog and cats. Hospitable host Angel Rodríguez Martínez is an excellent cook and speaks some English, French and a little Italian. Parking for CUC$2, car guarded all night and washed.

D-E Hostal La Bugambilia, Cuba 5 entre Tristá y San Cristóbal, T42-222945, 052898101 (mob), kkrodrigueszamora@yahoo.es. Enrique Rodríguez Zamora has 1 room with 2 double beds off a passage at the back of an old house, good facilities, music centre, elaborate bar in main part of house with dining area, or eat outside under the bougainvillea which gives the house its name.

D-E Hostal Las Jimaguas, Independencia 104 entre Sayas y Esquerra, T42-215471, lasjimagua104@yahoo.es. English-speaking Carlos and Belkis and their 2 daughters offer 2 rooms in a colonial house on the corner of the Boulevard and are kind, warm and generous. Garage available.

D-E Hostal María Isabel Obregón, San Cristóbal 118 entre Unión y Maceo, T42-206346, joanrd@uclv.edu.cu. Rooms are at the back of the house through the main patio where there are tables and chairs among the plants, with another patio beyond

that for the guest rooms, which have double and single beds, quiet and private. María Isabel is a vet and has a tiny dog, tropical fish, parrot and other birds.

D-E Hostal Rosita, Cuba 55 entre Candelaria y San Cristóbal, T42-294318. Rosa García Sánchez runs this *casa particular* in a colonial house with extraordinarily high ceilings and antique tiles. 1 room has a bathroom in the corner of the room behind a curtain, the other has a separate, bigger bathroom. Services include internet access, a microwave oven, washing machine or hand washing area, TV in lounge, 220v for recharging phones.

D-E José Ramón de Zayas Lara , Máximo Gómez 208 altos entre Yanes y Berenguer, T42-207239, T5281 4972 (mob), josedzayas@ yahoo.es. Short walk from Parque Vidal and train station. Private and independent suite upstairs with kitchen/diner, alcove with child's bed, fenced in and tiled terrace with good view. Ideal for long stays or people with small child who need to self-cater. Meals available. Family lives downstairs.

D-E Olga Rivera Gómez, Evangelista Yanes 20 entre Máximo Gómez y Callejón del Carmen, T42-214973. Lovely art deco house in front of Nuestra Señora del Carmen church. A lush green vineyard in the inner patio is home to a dozen parrots and canaries singing in their cages. 2 rooms, TV, parking, terrace, helpful owner.

Around Santa Clara *p222*
Hotels

A-B Los Caneyes, Av de los Eucaliptos y Circunvalación, T42-218140, www.cubanacan.cu. Thatched public areas with 96 rooms in cabins designed to look like Indian huts in a park-like setting, a/c, hot showers, TV, facilities for disabled people, pool, disco 2200-0200, enthusiastic evening entertainment by the pool, good buffet, breakfast included, excellent value, medical services, shop, popular hotel for tour parties and hunters. Day passes (1000-1700) are available whereby you can use the pool for CUC$5, including CUC$3 of food and drink, but note that although they are sold as

all-inclusive deals (CUC$10 Fri-Sun, CUC$5 Mon-Thu), they are in fact credit slips and anything you eat or drink over that amount will be charged at the end of your visit.
A-B Villa La Granjita, outside town at Km 2.5 on Maleza road, T42-218191, www.cubanacan.cu. 75 rooms in thatched *cabañas* among fruit and palm trees, emphasis on nature and tranquillity, TV, a/c, phone, internet access, bar, shop, buffet restaurant, breakfast included, horses, nighttime entertainment around the pool. Pool open to visitors for CUC$5, which includes food and drinks of CUC$3 (*consumo*) *Sala de fiestas*. 24-hr medical services, massage (45 mins CUC$10, 20 mins CUC$5).
D Hanabanilla, Salto de Hanabanilla, Manicaragua, on the northwest edge of the lake, T42-202399, www.islazul.cu. 125 rooms in Soviet-style block, a/c, phone, radio, pool, bar and cafeteria, restaurant with Cuban and international food, breakfast included.
Mirador Bar on the top floor, excellent view, tours offered with sailing trips on the lake to various sights including a farmer's house, waterfall and lunch at the Río Negro restaurant, fishing tackle available.

❶ Eating

Most *casas particulares* offer food, with breakfast at around CUC$3, dinner CUC$7-10, depending on what meat you choose, recommended, better than restaurants. In the city centre you can find snack bars such as **Rápido** and **Di-tú** serving sandwiches, biscuits, ice cream and little else. Begging can be persistent if you eat outside at a street café.

Santa Clara centre *p217, map p219*
Restaurants
⁕⁕⁕-⁕ 1878 Colonial, Máximo Gómez 8, near the Boulevard, T42-202428. Daily 0900-1100 for snacks, 1200-1445 lunch, 1900-2245 dinner. Offers a variety of *criollo* dishes, mainly pork in different styles, bar in the patio, long trousers required for men at night.

⁕⁕⁕-⁕ Dimar Sandino, San Miguel y Av 1, T42-201375. Daily 1000-2200. 10-min walk east of the centre, light meals, pastas, fish and seafood specialities, bar, charges in CUC$.
⁕⁕⁕-⁕ La Concha, Carretera Central esq Danielito, 1 km to the east of the centre, T42-218124. Daily 1100-2300. Good international and *criollo* cuisine, Italian speciality, extensive range of bar drinks, pleasant place. Parking.
⁕⁕-⁕ El Marino, Paseo de la Paz y Carretera Central, T42-205594. Daily, with lunch at 1200-1445, and dinner 1900-2245. Seafood, paella a speciality, snacks available outside formal meal times (1000-2200), CUC$ or pesos accepted.
⁕ Coppelia, Colón esq Mujica just off Parque Vidal, T42-206426. Tue-Sun 1000-2330, ice cream, seriously cheap, sweets and drinks.
⁕ Doña Neli, Maceo y San Miguel, T42-218189. Coffee shop serving fast-food meals. The bar/restaurant is open 0900-2100, the bakery 0700-1900. There is another outlet at Villuendas e Independencia, T42-203881, open 0900-1930.
⁕ Salón Juvenil (Palmares), Marta Abreu 10 entre Máximo Gómez y Villuendas, T42-200974. Mon-Fri 0900-2230 and Sat-Sun 0930-2230. Dinos Pizza, *cafetería*, drinks, cocktails, cybercafé (internet use CUC$0.10 per min).

Paladares
⁕ El Alba, Rolando Pardo (Buen Viaje) 26 entre Maceo y Parque. Daily 1200-1500 and 1800-2030. Standing counter only catering mainly for Cubans and charging in pesos, although CUC$ are accepted. Takeaway food also available. Meals are mostly pork dishes with *congrí* and green salad, cheap and practical.

❶ Bars

Santa Clara centre *p217, map p219*
Las Terrazas de la Marquesina, in the patio of Pizzería La Toscana, opposite the theatre, M Gómez y M Abreu, T42-224848. Mon-Fri

1000-0045, Sat-Sun 1000-0145. Snacks and drinks, avoid the spaghetti, tea and coffee charged in pesos cubanos, beer, rum and other drinks in CUC$, pleasant place for a drink, popular with young people at night, live traditional music 2100-2400.

🎭 Entertainment

Santa Clara centre *p217, map p219*
Cartelera is a pamphlet with what's on in Santa Clara, Remedios, Caibarién.

Cinema
Cine Teatro Camilo Cienfuegos, on the ground floor of the Hotel Santa Clara Libre on Parque Vidal, T42-203005. Check billboard outside for show times and what's on. This is Santa Clara's only cinema and entering is like stepping back in time. Seriously cheap, 2 pesos.

Live music
You don't have to go to a club or bar to hear live music in Santa Clara as there are regular performances in the parks. As well as the municipal band playing Thu and Sun evenings in the bandstand, on Sat at 2200 there is usually a band or *orquesta* playing outside the theatre at the edge of the park, while on Sat at 2100 in Parque Las Arcadas, Independencia y Luis Estevez, there is dancing to a good band playing Cuban music from the 1950s or thereabouts. Aimed mainly at senior citizens, it is wonderful to watch even if you don't join in.
Bar Club Boulevard (Carishow), Independencia 225 entre Maceo y Unión, T42-216236, Thu-Tue 2000-0230, Carishow CUC$5, includes drinks of CUC$2. Nightclub, very trendy, small, phenomenal dancing and lethal supplies of rum although drinks more expensive than other places, also used for social occasions, birthdays, etc, show with different acts, singers, comedians.
Casa de la Ciudad, Boulevard esq Zayas. Typical Cuban music in the inner courtyard of a lovely colonial house. Be sure to pin down

what's going on and when. Usually, *Trova* on Sun except the last in the month 1700-1900, *Música de Concierto* on 3rd and 4th Fri of the month at 2100, *Concierto entre Cuerdas* 1st Sat of the month at 2100, *Baile del Danzón* 2nd Fri of the month 1500-1700, *Concierto de Boleros* last Sun of the month 1800-1900, *Folklor Cubano con Tambores* 3rd Wed of month 1000. Seriously cheap, CUC$1.
Casa de la Cultura, Parque Vidal, T42-217181. A variety of cultural activities with local and provincial artists, including: *Danzón* 1st and 4th Thu in the month 2100, *Noche de Trova Tradicional* 3rd Wed 2100, *Café Cantante* Fri 2100, *Peña de la Música* 1st and 3rd Sat 1400, *Tarde de la Rumba* 3rd Sat 1600, every Sat at 2100 there are Boleros, Septets, choirs, etc, *Los Fakires* with dancing every Sun 1600, very popular, *Peña Campesina* 2nd Sun 1400 and 4th Sun at 2000, *Peña Artesenal* 3rd Sun 1000.
Club Mejunje (mishmash), 2½ blocks west from Parque Vidal, Marta Abréu 107 entre Alemán y Juan Bruno Zayas, T42-282572, bar open weekdays at variable hours, 2-5 pesos. The best place to go to sample what Santa Clara has to offer in the way of nightlife. Cultural centre in a backyard full of trees, ruins, artefacts and graffiti-covered walls. Composers, singers, musicians and friends sing, play and drink together, friendly, welcoming, enjoyable. Mon 2100 *Noches de Victrola*, music from the 50s and 60s; rock night Tue 2100 with live or taped music; 1st and 4th Wed of the month 2100 *Cuando Eramos Niños*, with music from the 90s to the present; 2nd Wed 2100 *Todo Mezclado* with alternative music; 3rd Wed 2100 theatre performance; Thu 2200 *Trovuntivitis* with very good *trovadores*, both young and traditional; Fri 2200 is *Viernes de la Buena Suerte*, traditional Cuban music and occasionally the internationally famous *Los Fakires* and *Son Aché*; 2nd Sat of the month at 1000 *Tambor*, live Afro Cuban folkloric music; every Sat 1800 *Tarde de los Feelinbusteros* for fans of 'Feeling', followed at 2100 by *Disco Mejunje*, this is the night for gays with a transvestite show, live

and taped music; and Sun there is dancing 1700 to live groups and orchestras. Larger events are staged in the courtyard, wide variety ranging from concerts to theatre, from shows for kids to transvestite shows for gays (popular at weekends).

El Bosque, Centro Cultural, Av El Sandino y Carretera Central, Vigía, 1 km from Parque Vidal, T42-204444. Tue-Sun 2100-0100, Mon 1800-2030 *Peña del Feeling*, Fri music of the decade. Tree-ringed, outdoor venue for live and taped music and nightlife, cabaret, fun shows, CUC$5, of which CUC$3 includes drinks. After midnight it eventually becomes a disco. Heady atmosphere and good dancing. 24-hr patio bar, à la carte menu available.

Piano Bar, Luis Estévez 13 entre Independencia y Parque, T42-215215. Restaurant daily 1045-2245, *comida criolla*, the piano bar opens 1000-1800 for drinks, cocktails and snacks and 2100-0100, live music Wed-Sun with the pianist Freyda Anido and band, invited singers, national and international music.

Theatre

Teatro 2, Independencia entre Maceo y P Estévez, T42-204038. Base for Teatro Estudio Teatral and Teatro 2, both from Santa Clara. Experimental or alternative theatre, occasionally visiting companies from abroad. 2 theatre halls seat 120 and 60 people, varied programme, see billboard at the theatre, 2 pesos.

Teatro Guiñol, Tristá entre Alemán y Carr Central, T42-207860. Children's theatre and entertainment, Sat 1700, Sun 1000 and 1700, children 1 peso, adults 2 pesos.

Teatro la Caridad, Calle Máximo Gómez, Parque Vidal, T42-208548. Under renovation 2009 but expected to open by year end. Look in *Cartelera* or the billboard outside for what's on, you might catch a performance by a top ballet company and the annual National Dance Festival is held here. Tickets CUC$4-10, performances at 2100.

❀ Festivals and events

Santa Clara centre *p217, map p219*
The dates of festivals vary from one year to the next and new festivals may be added.

There are 2 **film festivals**: in **Nov** and **May**, dates variable, with premières, critics and discussions.

Jan A *trova* festival is held, called the **Festival Longina Canta a Corona**, with subsidiary events in Caibarién.

Mar Santa Clara is the base for the **Festival 'A Tempo' con Caturla**, a young people's concert also held in Remedios.

Apr At the **Festival Nacional de la Danza** (National Dance Festival) there is traditional music and dancing in theatres and all around Parque Vidal, and every 4 years international groups participate.

May **Festival del Cine Profilm** is held every other year.

12 Aug There is a popular jazz festival called **La Verbena de la Calle Gloria**, celebrated since the beginning of the 20th century in honour of Santa Clara de Asís, patron saint of the city.

End of Oct-beginning of Nov The week-long **Festival de Rock Ciudad Metal** held on Calle Tristá and Carretera Central.

Nov **Festival de Cine Cubanacám.**

Dec Every 2 years the **Festival de Creación Musical 'Gustavo Rodríguez'** In Memoriam is held, in which composers and songwriters release their new works.

28 Dec Lots of commemorative activities in the Plaza de la Revolución and in the Parque Vidal, celebrating the last successful battle of the **Revolution** in 1958 with concerts and music festivals attracting Cuban and Latin American singers and musicians. From 28-30 Dec, early in the morning, hundreds of children dressed in rebels' uniform commemorate the battle, marching from the Monumento al Tren Blindado to different parts of the city, including Parque Vidal.

O Shopping

Santa Clara centre *p217, map p219*
The road behind the theatre, which runs between Maceo and Juan Bruno Zayas, is known locally as *Boulevard*. It is pedestrianized and locals shop here in CUC$ for clothes, electrical, domestic and household goods, some food and other items. Shops are open daily 0900-1700 unless otherwise stated.

Bookshops
Pepe Medina, Colón y Parque Vidal, T42-205965. 1 of the best in town.
Viet Nam Heróico, Independencia 106, T42-203233. Reasonable selection with **Artex** shop next door selling souvenirs and postcards.

Cigars
La Veguita (Cubanacán), Maceo 176 entre Berenguer y Martí, T42-208952, veguita@vcl.cyt.cu. Opposite the tobacco factory, sells cigars, rum and coffee, English spoken, very informative, large stock.

Markets
Agromercado Buen Viaje, Rolando Pardo (Buen Viaje) Final. Mon-Fri 0900-1800, Sat 0800-1700, Sun 0800-1200, and **Mercado 26 de Julio**, Calle San Miguel, Mon-Sat 0800-1800, both sell fruit, vegetables and pork, in pesos. Buen Viaje has the best variety.

Souvenirs
Next to the theatre on the corner of Parque Vidal and Lorda is a small shop selling T-shirts, books about Che, cassettes and CDs, nicknacks and maps.
Artex Ilusión, Colón 18 entre Machado y Parque, T42-214397, Mon-Sat 0900-1700, Sun 0900-1200. Sells artesanías, Che souvenirs, percussion (drums, bongos) instruments, cassettes, CDs, toiletries, drinks, T-shirts and nicknacks. There is another Artex, **El Bazar**, Carretera Central y Prolongación de Marta Abreu s/n, near the Plaza de la Revolución, T42-206505, also sells books, food, good choice.

Galería Cubanicay, Luis Estévez 9. Daily 0800-1830. Wide choice of handicrafts, art as well as furniture and shoes made locally.

▲ Activities and tours

Santa Clara centre *p217, map p219*
Baseball
Played from Nov until around Apr at the **Augusto César Sandino** stadium, Av Sandino y 6, T42-206461. Tickets 1-2 pesos. Take drink and snacks. The local team is Villa Clara. Nearby is the **Natilla Jiménez** mini-stadium built for children's baseball, great matches, unforgettable.

Fishing and shooting
Expeditions are organized to Embalse Alacranes and Embalse Hanabanilla, contact **Flora y Fauna/ Ecotur**, Carr Central Km 306, Banda Placetas, T42-206285, www.ecoturcuba.co.cu. Mon-Fri 0800-1630, equipment rental, guide. For sports fishing contact **Ecotur**, in Caibarién, T42-350570, ffaunavc@enet.cu.

Tour operators
Cubanacán, Colón 101 esq Maestra Nicolasa, T42-205189, Mon-Fri 0830-1730, Sat 0830-1230. Excursions, hotel reservations, transfers, car hire. Prices of tours at all the agencies depend on numbers in the party and any additional features added.
Cubatur, Marta Abreu 10 entre Máximo Gómez y Villuendas, T/F42-208980, cubatur@tur.cu. Mon-Fri 0900-1800, Sat 0800-1200. Also at Cayo Santa María. Excursions to every possible tourist site in west and central Cuba as well as **Víazul** tickets, flight confirmations, etc. Helpful and informative personnel.
Flora y Fauna/Ecotur, Carr Central Km 306, Banda Placetas, T42-206285, www.ecotur cuba.co.cu. Mon-Fri 0800-1630, contact Leonides Luis Fleites. Hiking, birdwatching, jeep tours, horseriding, lots of tours into the countryside as well as fishing and shooting.
Havanatur, Máximo Gómez, 13 entre Independencia y Barreras, T42-204001,

Mon-Fri 0830-1730, Sat 0830-1230. Air tickets, tours, etc. Excursions to Cayo las Brujas (transfer, lunch and beach time), Cienfuegos (city tour, lunch and beach), Trinidad (city tour, lunch and beach), to Hanabanilla on demand.

Islazul, Lorda 6 entre Parque Vidal y Boulevard, just off Parque Vidal by the theatre, T42-217338, Mon-Fri 0800-1130, 1300-1600. Dealing mainly with Cubans, hotel reservations.

⊖ Transport

Santa Clara centre p217, map p219
Air
Abel Santa María international airport is on Carretera de Malezas, Km 11, north of the city, T42-209138. Charter flights come in from Canada and Italy, at the moment there are no domestic flights.

Bus
Local There are some buses, 20 centavos. Horse-drawn *coches*, or taxi-buses, go all over town and down Marta Abreu to the bus stations, 1-2 pesos. They stream up and down the main streets, taking 8 passengers and there are always queues. Buses and coches are reserved for Cuban nationals. Tourists have to take taxis.

Long distance The provincial bus station for destinations within Villa Clara is on Carretera Central esq Pichardo, T42-222823/T203470, 1 km from centre, white building. The interprovincial bus station for long distances is on Carretera Central (Av Cincuentenario) 483 entre Independencia y Oquendo, Virginia, T42-222523 for reservations, 1 km further out, a/c, snack bar.

For Víazul services, see page 32, to **Havana**, **Santiago**, **Varadero**, **Camagüey**, **Trinidad**, and to most of the provincial capitals. Astro services are not available to tourists, except occasionally foreigners are permitted on buses to **Remedios** and **Caibarién**. Get a numbered ticket, stay near

departure gates until bus is ready and then join the scrum, avoiding pickpockets.

Car hire
Havanautos/Cubacar, Marta Abreu 130 entre JB Zayas y Alemán, T42-218177, daily 0800-1700; Tristá y Amparo, T42-202040, daily 0800-2000; Carretera Central (Banda Esperanza), T42-201377; Abel Santamaría airport, T42-209118, open when there are flights; Placetas, T42-884444; Remedios, T42-395555. Small cars CUC$75 per day for up to 6 days, less for each subsequent week, CUC$45 per day for over 30 days, including insurance and 20 litres of fuel.

Rex, Marta Abreu 130 entre JB Zayas y Alemán, daily 0830-1730, luxury cars, rates variable over 1-30 days, with or without driver.

Scooters from **Havanautos/Cubacar**, Marta Abreu 130 entre JB Zayas y Alemán, T42-208534, daily 0800-1700, CUC$12 for 2 hrs, CUC$15 for 3 hrs, CUC$24 for 24 hrs, CUC$17 1700-0900, CUC$22 per day for 2-4 days, cheaper for longer, weekend rate CUC$45 Fri 1700-Mon 0900.

Petrol stations Servicentro Oro Negro, Carretera Central y San Miguel, T42-218174, open 24 hrs daily, shop, fuel, repairs (0800-1700), payment in CUC$. Also **Servicentro El Capiro**, Av Liberación, Santa Catalina, T42-208224, and **Servicentro Las Villas**, Carretera Central y Maceo, T42-208879, offering the same services. 6km on the Autopista towards Havana is **Servicentro Km 259**, T42-208953, 24 hrs, self-service, shop, drinks. Further on, **Servicentro Km 270**, offers the same services.

Taxi
Cubataxi, T42-222555/T210363, good drivers, reasonable prices, the only legal form of local transport for foreigners, about CUC$70 for a whole day's tour to the cays and Remedios.

Bicitaxi costs CUC$1 to most places in town, fix a price beforehand or they will overcharge you. It is illegal for them to take foreigners, so you might like to take down his ID registration number (on the back) if there are any problems.

Train

The Martha Abreu railway station is north of Parque Vidal on Estévez at Parque Mártires, and is much more central than either of the bus stations. It is a very impressive station with a shady square outside, the usual bust of Martí and a monument to martyrs that looks like a stone totem pole which someone has taken a bite out of where it has eroded at the top. The ticket office (and a post office) is across the square. Information T42-202895-6. Reservations T42-200853, open Mon-Fri 0830-1800, Sat 0830-1200. There are trains to **Havana** (CUC$10) and to **Santiago** (CUC$20); also trains to **Bayamo** (CUC$17.50), **Camagüey** (CUC$9), **Sancti Spíritus, Holguín** and other towns, timetables are unreliable and the train may not even appear at any time, so call beforehand. In 2009 they were running every 2 days, to eastern towns at 0119 and 0418, and to the west at 2345, 1316 and 1528.

❶ Directory

Accident and emergency Ambulance: T104, for 24-hr emergencies. **Police:** the police station is on Colón entre Serafín García (Nazareno) y Morales (Síndico), near Parque Vidal, T116/106. **Banks** Banco Financiero Internacional, Cuba 6 entre Tristá y E Machado, just down from Parque Vidal, T42-207450, open Mon-Fri 0800-1500, but closes at 1200 on the last working day of the month, also Visa and MasterCard. **Bandec,** Vidal esq Cuba, Visa, MasterCard, Mon-Fri 0800-1500. The **Cadeca** office for changing currency and TCs is at Parque Vidal, Rafael Tristá esq Cuba, T42-205690, Mon-Sat 0830-1800, Sun 0800-1300; **Western Union** services carried out at 0830-1600 Mon-Sat, 0800-1200 Sun. **Western Union** branches also at La Riviera, opposite the bus station, Carretera Central, Bda Esperanza, T42-218166, and at Tienda Praga, Independencia

y Máximo Gómez, T42-209134, open Mon-Fri 1000-1200, 1300-1700, Sat 1000-1200. **Immigration** There is an immigration office for visa extensions on Sexta 9, entre Carretera Central y Av Sandino, T42-212523. English spoken, but patience required, Mon-Fri 0900-1630, Sat 0800-1200. **Internet** Salón Juvenil (Palmares), Marta Abreu 10 entre Máximo Gómez y Villuendas, T42- 200974, daily 0930-2100, CUC$0.10 per min, **Dinos Pizza,** cafeteria, drinks, cocktails. See also Etecsa, below, CUC$6 per hr. No printing service is offered anywhere. **Medical services** The best hospital for foreigners is the **Arnaldo Milián Castro Hospital,** referred to as Hospital Nuevo, at Circunvalación and Av 26 de Julio in the Reparto Escambray area to the southeast of the town, T42-272016, information T42-271234. Pharmacy: Farmacia Campa, Independencia y Luis Estévez, T42-206924, 24 hrs, 0800-2200 sales of medicine to the public, after 2200 only official prescriptions, charges in pesos. Farmacia Internacional, Colón 106 entre 9 de Abril y Maestra Nicolasa, T42-208069, Mon-Fri 0830-1630, Sat 0830-1230. Medicines, cosmetics and health products, charges in CUC$. **Post** Colón 10 entre Parque y E Machado, T42-203862, just off Parque Vidal, opposite Coppelia ice cream parlour, Mon-Sat 0800-2200. DHL and EMS, known as Cubapost, at Telecorreos, Cuba 7 entre Tristá y E Machado, T42-214069, for courier service, Mon-Fri 0800-1600, Sat 0800-1100. **Telephone** Etecsa, Marta Abreu esq Villuendas, T42-201010/T206000, daily 0830-1930, sale of phone cards in pesos cubanos and CUC$, telephones and accessories, domestic and international phone calls and fax service, internet access 0830-1930. Etecsa has a *cabina* on Cuba esq Machado (San Cristóbal), T/F42-217898, daily 1030-1800. For domestic, foreign calls, fax (42-204050). **Cubacel,** Callejón Barreros 4 entre M Gómez y Villuendas, T42-200000, Mon-Fri 0830-1600. Sells cell phones and services in CUC$.

Remedios and the north coast

The province of Villa Clara has plenty of lesser known attractions to offer including the delightful colonial town of Remedios, famous for its Christmas-time festival but a pleasant place to visit at any time of year. Off the main tourist drag, it is a fine example of an unspoilt provincial town, where foreigners are welcomed but not hassled. Its museums, churches and galleries are well cared for and worth visiting. Caibarién, an old fishing town on the coast, has fewer charms but work is being done to restore its old buildings to their former glory. The northern coast is low lying and there are mangroves and swamps, but it is fringed with coral cays with sandy beaches and crystal clear water in the Archipiélago de Sabana. Some of the cays are being developed as a major new beach resort, while the most northwesterly point of the province is an established health spa. ▶▶ *For listings, see pages 235-239.*

Ins and outs

Getting there There are domestic **flights** to the Abel Santamaría international airport north of Santa Clara from Havana and Varadero and international charters from Canada and Italy. It is 116 km from the airport to Cayo Santa María, the furthest resort. On the cays, an airstrip receives short-hop flights and air taxis. **Train** services are slow (two hours) and designed for local people to get to work in Santa Clara, rather than for tourist excursions. If you are travelling by **car**, a good road leads northeast from Santa Clara through Camajuaní to Remedios and Caibarién, from where a stone causeway has been built to link several cays. The causeway is a toll road. There are no **buses** to the cays.

Getting around Hiring a car or a taxi is the best way of touring the region as public transport is intermittent and unreliable. In any case, there is no other way of visiting the cays except on an organized tour.

Best time to visit The driest time of year is from December to April, generally considered high season with the best weather, but if a cold front comes down from the north the cays can get cool and windy. Later in the year the weather gets hotter but wetter. There are fascinating and enjoyable festivities in the week running up to Christmas Eve in both Remedios and Caibarién.

San Juan de Remedios → *Colour map 2, B4. Population 30,000.*

The colonial town of San Juan de Remedios is 43 km northeast of Santa Clara. Remedios was the eighth *villa* founded by the Spaniards, around 1513-1515, by Vasco Porcallo de Figueroa and for 160 years it was the main settlement in the area. It was never given the status of one of the original *villas* because Porcallo de Figueroa refused to allow the construction of a city hall. Its location was changed a couple of times, however, in 1544 and 1578, and when pirate attacks and other commercial incentives encouraged some of the inhabitants to move inland to Santa Clara, it began to decline. Not long after the founding of Santa Clara, a fire in 1692 hastened this trend. The present town was built following the fire and there are many beautiful colonial buildings, particularly around the pleasant Plaza Martí, which has some Royal palms and a gazebo in the centre. Traffic is very light and moves at the pace of the many *bicitaxis*, which can be found for hire around the Plaza.

Sights

This is the only town in Cuba where there are two churches on the plaza. **Iglesia Buen Viaje** is in a poor state and leaking, so it is unused and awaiting funds for renovation. The **Iglesia Parroquia Mayor San Juan Bautista de Remedios** ① *office open Mon-Fri 0900-1200, 1400-1700, when visitors are allowed entry, Mass Mon-Wed 0830, Thu-Sat 0800, Sun 1630, donations requested,* was built in 1692 on the remains of a 1570 church, making it one of the oldest churches in Cuba. It was renovated in 1944-1953 by an American millionaire who traced his family roots to Santa Clara. He discovered that one of his ancestors had been a founding member of the town and therefore must have come from Remedios, where he found birth records in the church. He spent US$1 million renovating the roof and walls and altar, taking off a false ceiling and whitewash on the beams to reveal gloriously painted and carved beams. The altar is cedar and was covered in gold leaf, but it shone so much you couldn't see the detail, so some of it is now painted over to give more definition and contrast. Buried in the church are Juan de Loyola (parish priest 1685-1775) and 17 of his relations.

Also on the square is the **Museo de Música Alejandro García Caturla** ① *Mon-Sat 0900-1200, 1300-1700, Sun 0900-1300, CUC$1.* García Caturla was born in 1906 and in the 1920s he studied both music and civil law at the university of Havana. He formed the jazz band *Caribe* with a group of students but he was strongly influenced by the Grupo Minorista which contributed to bringing the African influence into Cuban mainstream music. He met the writer Alejo Carpentier, and under his protection he went to Paris where he continued his cultural education by going to the *Ballet Russes* and the *Folies Bergères*. On his return to Cuba he created the *Orquesta de Conciertos de Caibarién*, which gave its first concert in 1932. His music then took a back seat and he concentrated on law, rising through the ranks of the local judiciary, but he was murdered in 1940, aged 34, shot by an unknown assassin allegedly for upsetting the local social order by working with the poor. The museum has copies of newspaper articles about his death, including one by Nicolás Guillén, the poet. There are also displays on other prominent local musicians and bands with lots of photo boards, and art exhibitions.

There is also an interesting **Museo de Arte Popular Las Parrandas** (festival museum) ① *walk past the Hotel Mascotte down Máximo Gómez away from the plaza, the museum is 1 block on the right, Tue-Sat 0900-1200 and 1300-1800, Sun 0900-1300, CUC$1, with guide CUC$2, photos CUC$1 each, special rates for media professionals,* which should not be missed. Two sections of the town compete against each other in games and festivities in the week leading up to 24 December, with the winning district being the one to make most noise, although no one really wins. The event originated with the local priest telling children to wake everyone in the town for midnight mass by making as much noise as possible and it soon became a tradition. The mayor complained to Spain about the 'music from hell' and asked for it to be banned, but the *parrandas* continued and developed into what they are today. The two districts, named Carmen and San Salvador, prepare long in advance, building towers in secret, which have a different theme each year and are transported and erected at the corners of the plaza. There is music, based on the *polka*, which varies slightly between Carmen and San Salvador, fireworks and floats. However, in contrast to carnival elsewhere, the people on the floats do not dance, in fact they do not even move, they are there simply as a tableau. An informative guide will explain all about the *parrandas* in English or Spanish, starting with a model and map of the city showing how the festival boundaries have changed over the years from eight groups to two, Carmen and San Salvador. There are replicas of several towers constructed during the 20th century, photos, costumes, musical instruments and mascots.

Museo de Agroindustria Azucarero Marcelo Salado (Museo del Vapor)
① *Reforma village, 400 m on the left of the road from Remedios to Caibarién, T42-363286, Mon-Fri and alternate Sats 0700-1600, CUC$3, CUC$9 with return steam train trip to Remedios (call early to find out what time the steam train leaves, its operation depends on numbers of visitors).*

Many redundant sugar mills in the country are now being converted into museums and this is one of them, in the old Central Marcelo Salado. This interesting museum is dedicated to the history of the sugar industry in Cuba with an exhibition area made up of all the different installations of a sugar mill, its tools, machinery and boiling rooms. There are several working steam engines, a video room and you can even clamber up on to some of the machinery. The train stops at the **Finca Curujey** restaurant, see below.

Caibarién and around → *Colour map 2, B5.*

The town's full name is Cayo Barién, but it is always referred to as Caibarién. It is a fishing town and the main port for the province. There is an unappealing beach on the edge of town; beach tourism for foreigners is now being directed offshore to the cays. Founded in 1832, Caibarién, a small town, with distinctive 19th-century architecture, has become rundown and scruffy in parts. Many buildings have fine wooden porches with a French influence, and some are quite grand, although there is an atmosphere of the Wild West, emphasized by the number of horses in town. The pavements, unusual in Cuba, are made of large stone slabs set in concrete. Caibarién has been bypassed by tourism and the visitor can wander around unmolested by hustlers. The Malecón is lined with numerous warehouses used for storing sugar cane in the 19th century, most of which are now in ruins. Recent investment in the seaside boulevard has led to the construction of a new Malecón to the fishing zone in the east with a new road, coconut palms and several bars and cafés where you can sit and admire the view. At the centre of the town there is a large square, with an 1850 church and the impressive neoclassical Lyceo (1926), where the **Museo Municipal de Caibarién María Escobar Laredo** ① *Av 9 entre 8 y 10, Parque Central, T42-352189, Tue-Sat 1000-1800, Sun 0900-1300, free,* is on the second floor. There are permanent and temporary exhibitions as well as the furniture belonging to María Escobar Laredo, who was one of the benefactors for the city. The gazebo in the centre of the plaza was built in 1915, the largest in Cuba and famous for its excellent acoustics. There are concerts by local bands on Thursday and Sunday nights. Also on the plaza is a store, which was, during the first decade of the 20th century, a bespoke tailor's called **London City**.

There is a legend that says recently transported slaves who escaped from their masters in Santa Clara fled northwards towards the coast, believing that they were still in Africa but had merely been shipped along the coast of their own continent. Upon reaching Caibarién, they despaired to find that they could not go any further, and reluctantly settled there. Much of the local culture is influenced by slavery and African traditions. Like Remedios, Caibarién also has its *parrandas*. Christmas Eve is a non-religious celebration, inaugurated in 1892 with the banging of a drum by a 110-year-old former slave called Juan de Jimagua. The public then followed him plus many other conga players around the town, a tradition still maintained today. The members of each *barrio* build an artistic creation on the plaza, based on local legends and folklore; they are ostensibly judged, but this is usually just a friendly, heated discussion of which is the best creation.

The cays

The nearest cay to Caibarién is **Cayo Conuco**, accessible by ordinary road (not the new causeway) just offshore. This is a biosphere reserve with lots of flora and fauna, and a campsite. Take insect repellent. There are the ruins of a former cholera hospital, built by the slaves in the 19th century to quarantine victims of the disease.

Extensive development is underway off the coast, with several new hotels being added to the existing small collection of all-inclusive resorts. Fidel Castro used to fish here when he was younger and for many years he kept the Villa Clara cays undeveloped. A 48-km stone causeway, from Caibarién to the three cays off the north coast, was completed in 1996 having taken seven years to build. If driving from Santa Clara, when you reach Caibarién turn right at the statue of a huge crab at the entrance to the town and then right at the next junction, avoiding the town centre. Carry on to a bridge, go under it and turn right in order to go over the bridge and effectively turn left. There are signs. There is a toll booth (*peaje*) at the start of the causeway, CUC$2 per vehicle, one way. Passports are checked. The road takes you through mangroves and open water and it is an impressive drive. If you want a few days of peace and quiet on unspoilt beaches then the cays are perfect, but they are remote and you need to be aware that there are no facilities outside the hotels, which sell day passes (Villa Las Brujas has the cheapest). You can still use the public beaches, La Salina, Punta Madrugilla and Perlas Blancas, but take your own food and drink.

At bridge 36 is the airport at **Cayo Las Brujas**, the first of the cays to be developed for tourism. There is a small hotel, **Villa Las Brujas**, on the cay, pleasant restaurant and bar, open to non-guests, and with a wooden observation deck up on the rocks overlooking the beach and the sea. You can buy a day pass and visit the hotel for the day, and have use of their facilities, including the hotel beach; this a recommended way to experience the cays. Watch out for biting insects at dawn and dusk. **Scuba-diving** trips can be arranged for around CUC$35 at the adjacent Marina Cayo Las Brujas, and there are other trips which leave from the jetty, eg to San Pascual, a moored American cargo ship built in 1920 has been here since 1933. It was once used as a molasses warehouse and there are still barrels of molasses (*miel*) in it, being used as ballast. There are murals by the famous Cuban artist Leopoldo Romañach. Both he and Ernest Hemingway stayed here. After bridge 42 you will see the vast Occidental Royal Hideaway Ensenachos, that has privatized the best beach on the cays, **Playa Ensenachos**, previously just several stretches of perfect soft sand between rocks, sea grapes and mangroves.

The last and largest cay, **Cayo Santa María**, is under major development, with a 9000-room hotel village opening in 2009 under the Barceló label, joining the three Sol Meliá all-inclusive resorts already there. The beach here is long, sandy, wild and unspoilt, but it does get rough at certain times of the year. The sea is calmest from June to August, it can be rough after then if there is a cold front off the eastern seaboard of the USA, and then in January and February the waves can be huge. Playa Ensenachos faces a different direction and is quieter.

Camajuaní

The road from Santa Clara to the cays and the coast leads first to Camajuaní, a typical 19th-century town stretching along the main street of Independencia. All the houses in Camajuaní have columns and verandas and an extremely grand railway station evokes a prosperous past, built on making shoes.

Baños de Elguea

ⓘ *Circuito Norte, Corralillo, Villa Clara, see also Sleeping, below.*

In the extreme west of the province, 136 km from Santa Clara, is Baños de Elguea. The Elguea *balneario* is a hotel and health resort with sulphur springs which are used to treat arthritis, rheumatism, skin diseases and tourists in need of pampering. The waters healing properties were discovered accidentally when a slave of the Elguea family was freed. He had a skin disorder and it was feared he might contaminate the rest of the slaves. He was later found to be cured after he had frequently bathed in the springs. A small hotel was then built to exploit the waters' beneficial properties, now replaced by the hotel and spa. Thermal waters are different temperatures (average 45°C) and there are medicinal muds for a variety of complaints including stress and obesity. The waters at the hotel's Thermal Centre are claimed to be hyper-mineralized, with chlorine, sodium, bromine, and a small amount of radon and sulphur. Qualified medical assistance is available, along with masseurs for general pampering. To say that the hotel is remote is understated and you will need your own transport to get there.

There are beaches at **El Salto** and **Ganuza**, nearby, where there are no hotels but you can find accommodation at local resorts and at local *campismo* resorts, if there is space for non-Cubans. Hiring a car in Santa Clara is a good idea and you will need a good road map.

⦿ Remedios and the north coast listings

For Sleeping and Eating price codes and other relevant information, see Essentials pages 37-43.

⦿ Sleeping

San Juan de Remedios *p231*
Hotels

B Hotel E Mascotte, Máximo Gómez 112, T42-395144, www.hotelescubanacan.com. Closed for renovation and expansion in 2009, lovely rooms in colonial mansion, those in front overlook the square, those at the back look over old tiled roofs, bar, restaurant, charming patio used for entertainment.

Casas particulares

There are over 30 *casas particulares* in Remedios and there is plenty of choice in the centre.

D-E Gladys Aponte Rojas, Brigadier González 32 altos entre Independencia y Pl Margall, T42-395398, apontegladys_44@yahoo.es. Central apartment on 1st floor up 2 flights of stairs, decorated with santería paraphernalia, close to main square. 1 huge room with good view, 2 double beds and a single bed, large bathroom, the 2nd room is smaller with 1 bed,

private bathroom, terraces on roof and on main floor of apartment, internet access.

D-E Hostal El Chalet, Brigadier González 29 entre Independencia y José A Peña, in front of the old post office, T42-396538, www.particuba.net. Jorge Rivero Méndez and his family run this casa in a smart house dating from 1950. The rooms are upstairs on the roof, with double and single beds, one is a suite with sitting room, all in very good condition, fabulous views over the town and the tiled roofs around, terraces up and downstairs, lots of space for sitting and relaxing, laundry service, parking for 2 cars with a guard at night, meals CUC$7-10, or CUC$5 for vegetarians.

D-E Hostal La Caridad, Brigadier González 3 entre Alejandro del Río y Margall, T42-396427/ 395030. An enormous and beautiful double/ triple room in a colonial home. Friendly and chatty host Jesús Crespo Camejo is very obliging and helpful in organizing excursions. Excellent cook, meals a treat.

D-E Hostal La Estancia, Camilo Cienfuegos 34, in the town centre beside Teatro Villena, T42-395582. Manuel Antonio (Noly) Garcías Rodríguez (artist and photographer) and his wife have lovingly restored this colonial house which was, in 1878, the house of the *Procurador* (Attorney) of the town. Large living room with grand piano, spacious dining room opens on to leafy patio with caged songbirds and a small swimming pool. 2 rooms, each with 2 double beds and modern bathrooms.

D-E Hostal Las Chinitas, Independencia 21 entre Brigadier González y Maceo, T42-395784/395316, perezandro@yahoo.ca. Greisy Fong Gómez offers 2 rooms in a colonial house, 1 with double and single bed, new bathroom and high ceilings, windows on to street, the other has 2 single beds, is smaller but quieter and opens on to the dining room and the patio. Next door, her parents Deisy Gómez Montenegro and Gregorio Fong Seuc have another room on the street with small but adequate bathroom in the corner. The family is friendly and keen to please.

D-E Hostal Octavo Villa, Av Heriberto Duquesne 9 entre Céspedes y Morales Lemus, T42-395102. At entrance to town, opposite the police station. Alberto Piloto and Mireya Fraginas run this well-thought-of *casa* in a quiet neighbourhood. 1 room with 2 beds, food served on patio or indoors, parking, plunge pool.

D-E Hostal Villa Colonial, Antonio Maceo entre Gen Carrillo y Fe de Valle, T42-396274. Frank and Arelys are very friendly hosts at this wonderful colonial home with a front room stuffed with antique furniture and beautiful tiles. 2 bedrooms, a small patio where *mojitos* are made for guests and a dining room where delicious dinners are served.

D-E La Casona Cueto, Alejandro del Río 72 entre Enrique Malaré y Máximo Gómez, T42-395350. Spectacular colonial house from the 18th century with its original façade, floors and roof, beautiful interior windows and wooden spiral staircase leading from the vast living room with piano and antiques to rooms upstairs, as well as medallions symbolizing the Soles y Rayos de Bolívar conspiracy. Jenny Cueto (Kaky) has 2 large rooms with 2 beds in each and modern bathrooms, interior patio with fountain as well as roof terrace, dogs, doves and turtles, safe car parking.

Caibarién *p233*
Hotels
Accommodation is hard to find when Cubans are on holiday in the summer.
D-E Brisas del Mar (Villa Blanca), Reparto Mar Azul, T42-351699, www.islazul.cu. On small beach away from centre but with lovely sea views although only 7 of the 17 rooms look over the sea, mostly Cuban guests (who pay in pesos), intermittent water, restaurant, bar, few facilities.

Casas particulares
There are many families offering rooms in their houses; touts will find you when you get off the bus or stop you as you drive into town.
D-E Casa Jorge, Av 7 1815 entre 18 y 20, T42-364277. A modern house run by Jorge F Amador, upstairs, 2 rooms with shared bathroom, hot water, a/c, fan, seafood and typical Cuban food.
D-E Casa Virginia, Ciudad Pesquera 73, T42-363303, virginiaspension@aol.com. Run by Osmany and Virginia, he is a former fisherman and can lend you snorkelling gear, she is very kind and chatty. Private downstairs area for guests, 2 rooms with private bathroom, hot water (solar panels), fridge, a/c, fan, TV, terrace with hammock and plants, independent entrance. Very good food, seafood a speciality. Osmany is helpful with excursions and transport.
D-E Casa Yayo, Av 35 10-16B entre 10 y 12, T42-364253. 50 m from the sea with sea view, terrace, 2 rooms with private bathroom, hot water, fridge, a/c, fan, parking, breakfast and dinner offered. Run by Eladio Herrara Bernabeu, the house is in an area where fishermen live.

The cays *p234*
Hotels
LL Barceló Cayo Santa María Beach Resort
T42-350400, www.barcelo.com. This new 5-star resort has 624 junior suites, 3 restaurants, 4 bars, 2 swimming pools, tennis courts, and day and night-time entertainment. Children are welcome. This is the 1st part to open of a

mega hotel city made up of 4 resorts; the 2nd will open end-2009.

LL Occidental Royal Hideaway Ensenachos, Cayo Ensenachos, T42-350300, www.occidental hoteles.com. Elegant and luxurious, this resort spans 2 of the best beaches in the area as a vast metropolis in 3 sections: the Royal Hideaway, Royal Spa, and Royal Suites. All the rooms are huge, with marble floors, balconies and every luxury. The spa facilities are superior. The beaches, Playa Ensenachos and Playa Mégano, are gorgeous stretches of soft fine white sand. Playa Ensenachos is reached by a long, attractive boardwalk. No children under 12. Food and service reported of intermittent quality, especially in low season.

LL-L Meliá Cayo Santa María, T42-350200, www.melia-cayosantamaria.com. All-inclusive, 5-star, 360 spacious and smart rooms for adults only (over 16). Rooms and bungalows (not many with ocean view) are in grounds of flourishing vegetation on a 400-m stretch of pristine beach. Loads of activities, gym, 3 swimming pools, watersports include catamarans, kayaks, paddle boats, snorkelling and windsurfing. Fishing and diving arranged.

LL-L Meliá Las Dunas, T42-350100, www.melia-lasdunas.com. 5-star all-inclusive mega-resort, 925 double rooms in 2-storey bungalows scattered around enormous grounds with exotic gardens; golf buggies are needed to get around. It's impersonal but those wanting anonymity may enjoy it. 7 restaurants, 5 bars, 3 pools and 2 tennis courts plus extensive watersports equipment.

LL-AL Sol Cayo Santa María, T42-351500, www.solmelia.com. Slightly smaller than the Meliá Cayo Santa María, rooms mostly in sets of 1- and 2-storey buildings scattered around the grounds with plenty of tropical vegetation. Beautiful beach but only about a 3rd of the rooms have sea view. There's also a private villa with pool, jacuzzi and butler service. Plenty of activities with 3 pools, a gym, sauna, tennis courts, kids' club, 4 restaurants and a watersports centre.

A Villa Las Brujas , Cayo Las Brujas, T42-350199, www.gaviota-grupo.com. One of the nicest small beach hotels in the country. A delightful complex of 24 good-quality red-roofed *cabañas* (19 have sea view) connected by a wooden boardwalk above rocks and between mature bushes. All have colour TV, a/c, balconies and verandas on stilts. Quiet and peaceful, with access to a good sweep of curving beach, soft, pale sand, a few umbrellas and hire of watersports. Restaurant with open air or a/c seating and view down to the beach. Car hire and tours arranged.

Baños de Elguea *p235*

B-C Hotel Islazul Elguea/Baños de Elguea, Circuito Norte, Corralillo, Villa Clara, T42-686298, www.islazul.cu. A remote hotel known for its 'healing' waters, with 99 rooms, gym, 3 pools, beauty salon and sauna as well as a Thermal Centre where a host of medical and therapeutic spa treatments are offered, see above.

🍴 Eating

San Juan de Remedios *p231*
Restaurants

There are several restaurants around the square and behind the church, charging CUC$ or pesos cubanos, but they are nothing special and it is better to eat in your casa, particular if staying overnight.

🍴🍴 Curujey, 1 km from the steam museum. Tour parties are taken here. Rural location, farm surroundings, large grove of trees, turkeys, chickens and you can watch them milking the cows.

🍴🍴 El Louvre, overlooking the square, T42-395639. Daily 0700-0200. Said to be the oldest restaurant in Cuba, colonial building with wooden bar and counter, tables inside and out, snacks and drinks, terrible coffee, nice place to stop for lunch and watch the school children on their break.

🍴 Di Tú , Máximo Gómez 098C. Mon-Fri 1000-2400, Sat and Sun 1000-0200. Light meals and drinks.

Caibarién *p233*

♥ **Pizzería al Mare**, Calle 8 entre 5 y 7. Daily 0900-1500, 1520-2120. Eat inside or out for people watching. The food is not good, but you can pay in pesos. Street food and drinks sold outside on the corner at lunchtime.

♥ **Saramar**, Calle 14 1502 entre 15 y 17. Open 1100-2300. Good prices and excellent cooking at this *paladar*, can be paid in pesos cubanos or CUC$, in which case prices start at CUC$5.

🎭 Entertainment

San Juan de Remedios *p231*
Live music

Centro Cultural Las Leyendas (Artex), on the square next to Louvre bar. Tables outside or inside, walk through the building to the stage at the back, live music at night, also recorded music, depending on the event.

🎉 Festivals and events

San Juan de Remedios *p231*
Dec Apart from its architecture, Remedios' other claim to fame is its **carnivals** (*parrandas*), held on 16-24 Dec; the best night being 24 Dec, when celebrations go on until dawn. This is a once-in-a-lifetime experience and well worth attending. Personal safety is not an issue (apart from the thousands of home-made fireworks), but do watch out for your personal belongings, particularly when fireworks are let off. The resulting crush and excitement is the perfect setting for wallets and cameras to go walkabout. Either make sure you hang on to your bags or get out of the crowd before the mayhem starts.

Caibarién *p233*
Last weekend in Aug Carnival.
Oct Caibarién has an annual fiesta, dating from 1999, celebrating the founding of the town on 26 Oct.
Dec Like Remedios, Caibarién also has *parrandas* at the same time.

🔺 Activities and tours

Remedios and the north coast *p231*
Marina

Marina Cayo Las Brujas, T42-350013, for scuba-diving, fishing and sailing excursions.

Tour operators
Havanatur, Av 9 entre 8 y 10, on plaza next to the Liceo, Caibarién, T42-351171, Mon-Fri 0830-1200 and 1330-1630, Sat 0830-1200.

🚌 Transport

Remedios and the north coast *p231*
Air
Cayo Las Brujas airport, T42-350009, receives Aerocaribbean charter flights. International flights use the airport north of Santa Clara.

Bus
The San Juan de Remedios bus station is at the entrance to the town on the right coming from Santa Clara, T42-395185. Taxis and *bicitaxis* wait outside. The Caibarién bus terminal, Calle 1 entre 6 y 8, has regular buses to **Remedios** and **Santa Clara**, if you can get on. *Carros particulares* (private cars) can be found for trips to other destinations. Fares are all in pesos, get a numbered ticket when you arrive at the terminal, seats are sold only when the bus arrives. If going to **Santa Clara**, many private cars will take you from outside the terminal for about CUC$2-3 per person. There is no public transport out to the cays, so you have to arrange car hire or pick up an official taxi.

Car hire
Transgaviota, Km 52 on the causeway at Villa Las Brujas, T42-350083/4.
Rent a Car Vía, at Hotel Ensenachos, T42-350384; Hotel Meliá Cayo Santa María. T42-350532; Hotel Sol Cayo Santa María, T42-350232.

Remedios and the north coast *p231*
Banks Cadeca, M Gómez 77, Remedios,
T42-397120. Banco Popular de Ahorro, at
Av 9 entre 6 y 8, Caibarién, T42-363256.
Bandec, Av 7 601, Caibarién, T42-363242, and
at Cienfuegos 2, Remedios, T42-395443.

Immigration Av 7 entre 6 y 8, Caibarién,
open 0800-1200, 1300-1500. **Post** Calle 10
entre 11 y 13, Caibarién, T42-363208, daily
0800-1200 and 1400-1800.
Telephone Etecsa, Av 11 y 10, Caibarién,
T42-353696, for all phone and internet
services. Card phones on the main plaza.

Sancti Spíritus

→ *Colour map 2, B4. Population: 133,000.*

Sancti Spíritus, the provincial capital, is one of Cuba's seven original Spanish towns and has a wealth of buildings from the colonial period, although many of them have been altered and there has been lots of new building. Tourism is now being developed around the town. Hotels have been renovated and remodelled and coach parties come for day trips. So far foreign tourists get little unwanted attention. The local people are friendly and helpful when approached, but are generally indifferent to foreigners. ▸▸ *For listings, see pages 243-245.*

Ins and outs

Getting there There are no scheduled **flights** to the airport north of town. Main line **trains** from Havana to Santiago stop at the train station 15 km away at Guayos, but you will be met by **taxis**, both state-owned and private. The former cost CUC$10 into town, the latter can be negotiated. About 70 km northeast of Trinidad and 80 km southeast of Santa Clara, the town can be reached by road from Cienfuegos, Santa Clara or Trinidad. Long-distance **buses** come to Sancti Spíritus from both ends of the island, but the bus station is 2 km from the centre, so if you are not up to walking with your luggage you will have to get a taxi. ▸▸ *See Transport, page 245.*

Getting around The old city can be toured **on foot** without much difficulty. For excursions by **car** ask at a *casa particular* for a private driver, or find one outside the bus station and negotiate a price. Trinidad can be visited as a day trip by bus or car, but it is better to stay in Trinidad and visit Sancti Spíritus as a day trip.

Tourist information There is no tourist office in Sancti Spíritus, but the office of **Havanatur** on the square can provide information.

History

The town was founded by Diego Velázquez in 1514. Originally situated on the Río Tuinicúe, it was moved to its present location on the Río Yayabo in 1522 and was sacked by pirates in 1665. The town grew as sugar and livestock became important and its geographical position made it an excellent agricultural market town. In the San Luis valley, or Valle de los Ingenios (Valley of the Sugar Mills), between Trinidad and Sancti Spíritus, are many ruined sugar mills, plantation houses and slave quarters, including Manaca Iznaga (see page 254). There are many sites commemorating those who fought in the 19th-century wars of independence, the local hero being Major General Serafín

Sánchez Valdivia. At the end of the Cuban Revolution in 1958, rebel forces were led into the city under the command of Armando Acosta Cordero and Sancti Spíritus was liberated on 23 December. Fidel Castro arrived on 6 January 1959 and spoke from the balcony of the library. With the administrative changes in 1976, Sancti Spíritus became the capital of the new province of Sancti Spíritus.

Sancti Spíritus

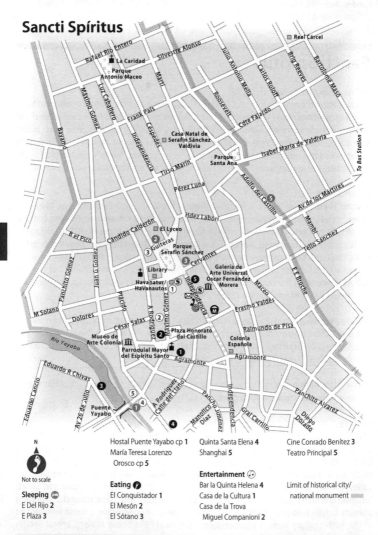

N

Not to scale

Sleeping 🛏
E Del Rijo **2**
E Plaza **3**

Eating 🍴
El Conquistador **1**
El Mesón **2**
El Sótano **3**

Hostal Puente Yayabo cp **1**
María Teresa Lorenzo
  Orosco cp **5**

Quinta Santa Elena **4**
Shanghai **5**

Entertainment 🎭
Bar la Quinta Helena **4**
Casa de la Cultura **1**
Casa de la Trova
  Miguel Companioni **2**

Cine Conrado Benítez **3**
Teatro Principal **5**

Limit of historical city/
  national monument ▬

Sights

Parque Serafín Sánchez is the centre of activity in the city where all major roads converge. Around the square are the cinema, library, banks, Havanatur/ Havanautos and the beautiful baby blue **Hostal del Rijo**, renovated to its colonial splendour. The **Museo Provincial de Sancti Spíritus** ① *Máximo Gómez 3, T41-327435, Mon-Thu 0900-1700, Sat-Sun 0800-1200, CUC$1* has the usual exhibits on local history and culture in a building that dates from 1740. There are collections of Amerindian artefacts, items from the colonization and African slavery, the wars of independence and the Revolution plus coins and decorative arts.

Just north of the square **El Lyceo/Sociedad Cultural de Negros**, Calle Luz Caballero, was the first school for blacks, opened in 1859. It is now a society for veterans of the Revolution.

The **Galería de Arte Universal Oscar Fernández Morera** is in the house of the local artist Oscar Fernández Morera on Céspedes 126 Sur, whose works are on permanent display. There are exhibits of originals as well as reproductions.

On Plaza Honorato, south of Parque Serafín Sánchez, the **Iglesia Parroquial Mayor del Espíritu Santo** ① *Jesús Menéndez 1 entre Honorato y Agramonte, Tue-Sat 0900-1100, 1400-1700*, dates from 1522 when it was a wooden construction. The present Romanesque and baroque building made of stone, replaced the earlier one, but it is acknowledged as the second oldest church in Cuba because it still stands on its original foundations. It was finished in 1680, having taken 60 years to build. The church has been declared a National Monument. Fray Bartolomé de las Casas gave a famous sermon here, marking the start of his campaign to help the indigenous people. He was a Dominican missionary and polemist, who devoted his life to the cause of Amerindian liberty. He spent many years on Hispaniola (now the Dominican Republic and Haiti), where he wrote the *Brief Relation of the Destruction of the Indies*, a horrifying catalogue of atrocities that took place at the time. He was appointed Protector of the Indians in 1516 and spent the next 10 years trying to prove that free Amerindians could be converted to Christianity without use of force or enslavement. However, the experiment came too late for the Amerindians of the Greater Antilles, as the Spanish could not do without slave labour and the Amerindians would not work without coercion.

The **Museo de Arte Colonial** ① *Calle Plácido 74 Sur entre Guairo y Pancho Jiménez, T41-325455, Tue-Sat 0900-1700, Sun 0800-1200, CUC$2, photos CUC$1*, is housed in the former palace of the Iznaga family, who made their fortune out of sugar and were hugely influential with links to the military and bureaucracy of the province. Built in 1744, the house has 100 doors. It contains collections of porcelain from France, England, Germany and Spain, oil paintings and decorative fans, and in the music room there is one of the oldest pianos in Cuba.

East of the church, a shopping mall has been established in the newly renovated 1926 building, **Colonia Española**, on Independencia Sur esquina Agramonte. It is a fine building in the eclectic style with neoclassical ceilings and CE on the windows, once a cultural centre for the high society.

The **Puente Yayabo** is considered a particular feature of Sancti Spíritus and is the only one of its type left on the island. The bridge was built in 1831 with five arches made of limestone, sand and bricks, which, according to legend was mixed with donkey milk. It is now also a National Monument. The river itself has given its name to the *guayaba*, or guava, which grows along its banks, and also to the *guayabera*, a loose man's shirt without a tail, worn outside the trousers and without a tie.

The former **Teatro Principal** next to the bridge was built in 1839 and was the scene of all the major cultural, social and political events of the city. **Calle Llano** is a twisty street, with cobblestones right to the edge of the Yayabo River.

Walk up Céspedes and you will pass the **Casa Natal de Serafín Sánchez Valdivia** ① *Céspedes 112 Norte, entre Sobral y San Cristóbal, T41-327791.* Sánchez Valdivia was born here on 2 July 1846, going on to fight in three wars in the 19th century. He collaborated with José Martí and reached the rank of Major General before being killed in battle in 1896. **Parque Antonio Maceo**, on which stands the **Iglesia de la Caridad**, was the place where the Communist Party of Sancti Spíritus was founded on 7 December 1930. If you head east along Frank País out of the historic centre, you will come to the old prison, **Real Cárcel** (Royal Prison) ① *Bartolomé Masó entre Anglona y Mirto.* The building has been preserved as a site of historical interest. It was built in the mid-19th century and used initially to incarcerate runaway slaves and then to imprison hundreds of Cubans who fought for independence.

Around Sancti Spíritus

Many of the excursions included in the Trinidad section, page 246, can also be done from here, particularly the Valley of the Sugar Mills, which lies between the two towns.
➤➤ *See Activities and tours, page 261, for excursions around Trinidad.*

The flatlands of the northern coast of the province rise to the Sierra de Meneses, and the flatlands of the southern coast rise in the west to the Montañas de Guamuhaya. Sugar is no longer grown in commercial quantities in the province and the sugar mills have closed, but there is some tobacco grown on the hills and rice in the low lying south, while cattle are also raised. A lot of the southeast of the province is flat, with mangroves and wetlands along the coast, and this area contains the largest man-made reservoir in the country, **Embalse Zaza**, through which flows the Río Zaza, 144.7 km long. Embalse Zaza is a popular excursion for hiking, birdwatching, shooting and fishing, or just to go to the hotel (see page 243) and laze around the pool. The hotel can get busy at weekends. In September there is an annual international fishing tournament here.

For those with their own transport (or hired private car), you can tour the north coast, where there is a beach at **La Victoria**, a spa at **San José del Lago** and a cave system at **Cueva Grande de Judas**. **Mayajigua** is the main town in this area, founded in 1820, and reasonable for a break in the driving.

The road to Playa Victoria is virtually the only road to the north coast where there are mangroves and caves of the **Parque Nacional Caguanes**, a UNESCO Biosphere Reserve. None of the park is over 25 m above sea level and it is notable for its caves, pictographs and underground treasures rather than its scenic beauty. **Lago Martí** in the park has fresh water sponges.

North of Mayajigua is **Punta de Judas** on a road which stops just short of the coast. Here there is the Cueva Grande de Judas, which is at the eastern side of the Parque Nacional Caguanes, where there are several caves: Cueva Grande, Cueva del Pirata, Cueva Humboldt and Cueva de los Chivos. There are archaeological sites in the caves and pictographs.

For Sleeping and Eating price codes and other relevant information, see Essentials pages 37-43.

⊜ Sleeping

Sancti Spíritus *p239, map p240*
Hotels
B E Del Rijo, Honorato del Castillo 12 esq Máximo Gómez, T41-328588, www.hotelescubanacan.com. Built in 1818-1827 the building has been converted from the ruins of the old family home of a doctor, Rudesindo García Rijo, facing onto the Parque. It is a typical example of colonial architecture with stained-glass windows, arches downstairs for shade and balconies with wrought iron fretwork upstairs, all painted in a variety of beautiful blues. An inner courtyard has a fountain, plants and dining tables outside, overlooked by the landing giving access to the 16 spacious (some bigger than others) and well-furnished rooms with wooden shutters at the windows, high ceilings, safety box, minibar, radio, room service, TV, facilities for wheelchairs, restaurant, *cafetería*, snack bar, currency exchange, post office, internet/fax, laundry.
B E Plaza, Independencia 1, Plaza Serafín Sánchez, T41-327102, www.hoteles cubanacan.com. 25 rooms, in an old colonial building, first built in 1854 but destroyed by fire in 1973 and subsequently restored and opened to the public in 1994. High-ceilinged rooms, refurbished in colonial style, some with balconies overlooking plaza, TV, bar, restaurant, car hire.

Casas particulares
C Hostal Las Américas, Carretera Central 157 Sur entre Cuba y Cuartel. T41-322984, hostallas americas@yahoo.es. Modern house with spacious rooms, TV, DVD, MP3, stocked minibar, safe box in wardrobe, hair dryer, national and international phone service, garage for 2 cars. Large, lush garden with fruit trees and ornamental plants and a swing where you can have a welcome drink, Las Américas *mojito*. Snacks, breakfast, lunch and dinner are available, any special requirements or tastes catered for, typical dishes of the region with lots of fruit and veg, house speciality *cordero espirituano*. English and Italian spoken.
D-E Hostal Puente Yayabo, Calle Jesús Menéndez 109 entre Padre Quintero y Río Yayabo, T0152408545, puente.yayabo@ yahoo.es. Totally renovated in 2008, this former ruin officially dates from 1840 but could be earlier. It is right beside the old bridge and the rooms have lovely views over the river. Elena and Víctor are most hospitable and offer unusual touches such as fishing rods, free tea, coffee, *mojito*, their son speaks English and French. Double and single beds, TV, roof terrace has tables and benches under cover, garage.
E María Teresa Lorenzo Orosco, Adolfo del Castillo 33 (Altos) entre Av de los Mártires e Isabel María de Valdivia, T41-324733. 2 rooms in upstairs apartment, double and/or single beds available, table and chairs also optional, wardrobe, TV, terrace with shaded dining area and rocking chairs in the sunshine overlooks neighbours' gardens. Experienced and knowledgeable hostess, in business since 1997, friendly family, English spoken.

Around Sancti Spíritus *p242*
A-C Rancho Hatuey, 4 km north of town, 2 km from the airport, just off Carretera Central at Km 383, T41-328315, www.islazul.cu. Modern hotel with 78 double and 3 triple rooms in main building or in modern *cabaña*, pool, various meal plans, restaurant, bar.
C Zaza, T41-328512, 10 km outside the town on the Zaza artificial lake, at Finca San José. 105 a/c (old and noisy) rather cramped rooms with balconies overlooking pool, phone, restaurant, bar, nightclub, games room, shop, car rental, medical services, tourism bureau, rather rundown but pleasant and good value, shooting and fishing can be arranged.

🍴 Eating

Sancti Spíritus *p239, map p240*
Restaurants
†††-† **El Conquistador**, Agramonte 52 Ote. Open until 2200, closed Mon. Delightful building, friendly staff, mainly Cuban dishes.
†††-† **El Mesón**, Máximo Gómez 34, on Plaza Honorato del Castillo, T41-328546. Daily 1000-2200 if there are customers. In a building that was the 1st post office, furnished with heavy wooden tables and chairs. *Criollo* food, probably the best restaurant in town, crowded at lunchtime, popular with tourists, live music. Good seafood, or try *garbanzo* soup or *ropa vieja*.
†††-† **Quinta Santa Elena**, Padre Quintero entre Llano y Manolico Díaz, T41-329167. Daily 0900-2400. Popular with tourists at lunchtime. Near the river and bridge in colonial house with patio garden, traditional Cuban food and music, show on Sat evening.
† **Saratoga**, on the plaza. Café serving drinks and snacks.
† **Shanghai**, Independencia, just off the plaza. 1200-1445, 1900-2245. On the Boulevard, Chinese, mostly Cuban clientele. You may be able to pay in pesos.

Paladares
There are several *paladares* just across Puente Yayabo, then turn left or right. Try:
† **El Sótano**, Eduardo R Chivas 18C entre 26 de Julio y Jesús Menéndez, T41-325654. Daily 1100-2400. Good peso *paladar*. One of the tables is on a balcony overlooking river (mosquitoes), ask in advance for vegetarian food, large portions, good food, nice family.

Street stalls also sell snacks including pizza, which are good value.

🎭 Entertainment

Sancti Spíritus *p239, map p240*
Cinemas
There are 3 cinemas on Parque Sánchez, 60 centavos for a film, 2 pesos cubanos for a video.

Live music
Most nightlife happens around the Parque.
Bar La Quinta Helena, on the left just before Puente Yayabo. Large, pleasant terrace, garden, patio, live music and concerts.
Casa de la Cultura. For all things cultural. Holds ad hoc art exhibitions, poetry readings and live music. There is usually rock music on Sat night and irregular performances of more traditional *boleros* on other nights.
Casa de la Música, Padre Quintero 32, T41-324963. Open-air seating and a stage, terrace overlooking Río Yayabo, CUC$1, shows Fri and Sat nights.
Casa de la Trova Miguel Companioni, Máximo Gómez Sur 26. Walk through a grand house past photos of all the local musicians, past and present, to the patio where there is a bar and stage and a mango tree in the centre. Live music. Artex shop.

🛍 Shopping

Sancti Spíritus *p239, map p240*
There are **CUC$ stores** on Independencia Sur and a peso **market** on Erasmo Valdés, good for meat, fruit and vegetables.
Fondo de Bienes Culturales, Independencia Sur 55. Art and handicrafts.
Librería Julio Antonio Mella, Independencia Sur 29. A reasonable bookshop; there is a second-hand bookshop nearby at Independencia Sur 25.

▲ Activities and tours

Sancti Spíritus *p239, map p240*
Sport

Sancti Spíritus has good sporting facilities, including the José Antonio Huelga baseball stadium, the Sala Polivalente Yayabo, which has a football pitch inside an athletics track, various soft ball stadia and rodeo. There is also a 6-lane bowling alley with a bar.

Tour operators

On the square, at Cervantes 1, are **Havanatur**, T41-328308, for flights and tours, **Havanautos**, T41-328403, for car hire, and **Islazul**, T41-326390, for hotels and tours. **Ecotur**, T41-357419, ffauna@yag.co.cu, contact Rodobaldo Hernández for countryside tours, birdwatching, hiking, horseriding, fishing or jeep safaris.

⊖ Transport

Sancti Spíritus *p239, map p240*
Bus

Local Horse-drawn buses for short journeys around town. **Long distance** The bus station is 2 km east of town on the Carretera Central. Walk out of town along Cervantes, follow signs to Ciego de Avila along Carretera Central, about 5 blocks past the zoo, the bus station is on your right. **Víazul** buses on the **Havana–Santiago** or **Trinidad–Santiago** routes daily, but you may not get a seat.

Taxi
Local *Bicitaxis* will get you around town if you don't want a taxi. **Long distance** A private taxi (*particular*) will take you to **Trinidad** for CUC$25 or less, and to **Santa Clara** for around CUC$30, depending on the quality of your Spanish. Find a driver outside the bus station.

Train

Station at Guayos, 15 km north. Taxi into town CUC$10. Touts offer transport and accommodation. Sancti Spíritus is on the main line service between **Havana** and **Santiago** and there are additional daily trains to **Camagüey**, 2-3 hrs, in theory.

⊙ Directory

Sancti Spíritus *p239, map p240*
Everything you need is on Independencia, a pedestrian street known as Boulevard. **Banks** Banco de Crédito, on the plaza, Mon-Fri 0800-1500. Cash advance on credit cards. **Cadeca**, Independencia 31, just off plaza, for TCs and currency exchange, Mon-Sat 0830-1800, Sun 0830-1230. **Pharmacy** Independencia Sur at the southwestern corner of Parque Maceo. **Post** Independencia Sur 8, south of Parque Serafín Sánchez. **Telephone/internet** Etecsa, Independencia, phone calls, phone cards, internet access.

Trinidad

→ *Colour map 2, B4. Population: 60,000.*

Trinidad, 133 km south of Santa Clara, is a perfect relic of the early days of the Spanish colony: beautifully preserved streets and buildings and hardly a trace of the 20th century anywhere. It was founded in 1514 by Diego Velázquez as a base for expeditions into the 'New World' and Hernan Cortés set out from here for Mexico in 1518. The five main squares and four churches date from the 18th and 19th centuries and the whole city, with its fine palaces, cobbled streets and tiled roofs, is a national monument. Architecturally, Trinidad is perhaps Cuba's most important town: its preserved and colourful colonial buildings are suspended in a time warp and since 1988 it has been a UNESCO World Heritage Site. Many of the families who live in the old houses rent out rooms and this is one of the best places to lodge privately. There is good hiking among picturesque waterfalls and abundant wildlife in the forests up in the mountains overlooking Trinidad. Playa Ancón, nearby, is a reasonable beach to relax on and a good base for boat trips and watersports. ▶▶ *For listings, see pages 255-262.*

Ins and outs

Getting there There is a small airport that only receives charter **flights**. Trinidad is not connected to the national **rail** network. The most convenient independent way of getting to Trinidad is by **Víazul bus** (see timetable, page 32), with services from Havana via Cienfuegos, or from Varadero via Santa Clara and Sancti Spíritus. Most visitors to Trinidad arrive on tour buses from Havana and Varadero and do a day trip, although it is possible to extend your stay and rejoin the bus a day or two later. The drive from Sancti Spíritus through the Valley of the Sugar Mills is very attractive. ▶▶ *See also Transport, page 261.*

Getting around The old city should be toured **on foot**. The cobbled streets make wheeled transport rather uncomfortable. All the main sites are within easy walking distance of each other. For local excursions many people hire a driver and **car**, although some prefer to **cycle** to the beach (fine on the way there, harder work on the way back), and organized tours are recommended for **hiking** in the mountains to avoid getting lost and to make sure you go to all the right places.

   Maps of Trinidad can be unbelievably difficult to follow because of the use of old and new street names. Locals of course switch from one to the other. The old ones have been painted over in white on the streets and are still legible. The new names are in black letters on white, often on the opposite side of the street.

Tourist information There is an **Infotur office** ① *Restaurante Santa Ana, Plaza Santa Ana, 0800-1800, T41-998257/8.* Information is also freely available from the state tour operators: **Cubatur** and others (see Tour operators, below). However, they are concerned to sell their own tours, so for impartial advice and for how to get off the beaten track it is worth asking your hosts, if you are staying in a *casa particular*. They will know of private, usually illegal, taxi drivers and guides who can show you something a bit different from the organized tours.

Best time to visit September is good for religious processions around the 8th of the month, Cuba's patron saint's day, but at any time of year you can find music, dance and other festivities. Semana Santa (Easter) is another good time for processions, with a huge event on Good Friday; Semana de la Cultura is the second week of January and Carnival is in June. Expect heavy rain between September and November, when the cobbled streets become awash with water, but in the mountains it can rain any day, turning paths into muddy slopes.

History
A thriving economy soon grew up around the settlement, originally based on livestock, exporting leather, meat and horses. This prize inevitably attracted the attention of adventurers and there was a particularly severe period of attacks between 1660 and 1688. Mansfield from Port Royal in Jamaica and Legrand from Tortuga, off Hispaniola, looted and set fire to the town, destroying the original archives of the church and the city hall. Unlike other populations who moved inland to escape pirate attacks, the inhabitants of Trinidad decided to stay and defend their wealth with their own fleet, inflicting several defeats on British and Dutch corsairs in the 17th and 18th centuries. After the British took Havana in 1797 they tried and failed to invade Trinidad and Sancti Spíritus, an event which is portrayed in the coats of arms of both cities.

After a time, sugar was introduced and by 1797 there were 56 sugar mills and 11,697 slaves imported to work in the sugar cane fields. Trade, the arts and sciences all expanded on the back of the sugar prosperity: Alexander von Humboldt visited and studied the fauna and flora around Trinidad; the first printing press was opened and the first newspaper began to circulate; schools of languages, music and dance were opened; a wide variety of artisans set up businesses, including gold and silversmithing; and in 1827 the Teatro Cándamo opened its doors. The well-off patricians built huge mansions for themselves (now museums) and sent their children to European universities. However, the Industrial Revolution and the increase in sugar beet grown in Europe sounded the death knell for an economy based on slave labour and in the second half of the 19th century Trinidad went into decline. Construction ceased and the city remained frozen in time with its cobbled streets and red-tiled roofs.

Sights

Plaza Mayor
The Plaza Mayor is the centre of the town, an elegantly adorned square with white wrought-iron railings and ornate lamp posts in the middle shaded by a few towering Royal palms. Some of the very few two-storey buildings can be found here, denoting the importance of the plaza and all are painted in pretty pastel colours with red-tiled roofs. On the east side of the plaza is the cathedral, **Iglesia Parroquial de la Santísima Trinidad** ① *Casa Parroquial at Fco J Zerquera 456, opposite the church, T41-993668, F41-996387, daily 1030-1300 for sightseeing and photos; Mass daily at 2000, Sun at 0900, during which no sightseeing is allowed*. The church was built between 1817 and 1892. The later altars are made of precious woods, such as cedar, acacia, mahogany and grenadine and were built in 1912-22 by a French priest, Amadeo Frieory, a Swiss Brother Lucas and two Cuban carpenters. On the left of the altar is a crucifix of the brown-skinned Christ of Veracruz, who is the patron of Trinidad. It is the largest church in Cuba and is renowned for its acoustics. The church choir, called Piedras Vivas, composes and sings religious music and hymns with a Cuban rhythm, wonderful to hear on Sundays and holidays. Visitors who can play an instrument or sing are welcome to participate in rehearsals and then performances. Travelling musicians have included members of the London Philharmonic Orchestra. If you want to make a charitable donation of any sort, the church is the place to do it.

Trinidad

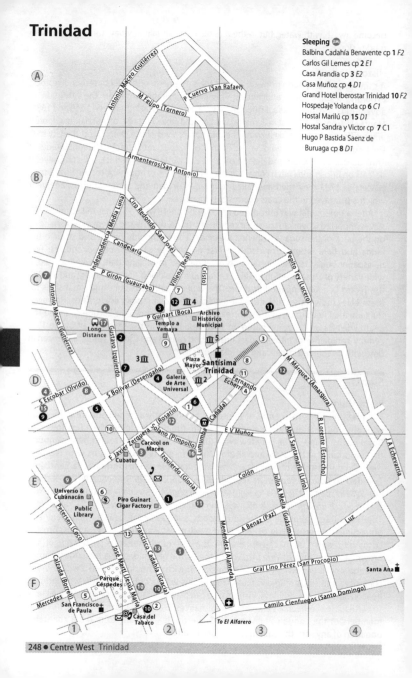

Sleeping 🛏
Balbina Cadahía Benavente cp **1** *F2*
Carlos Gil Lemes cp **2** *E1*
Casa Arandia cp **3** *E2*
Casa Muñoz cp **4** *D1*
Grand Hotel Iberostar Trinidad **10** *F2*
Hospedaje Yolanda cp **6** *C1*
Hostal Marilú cp **15** *D1*
Hostal Sandra y Victor cp **7** *C1*
Hugo P Bastida Saenz de
 Buruaga cp **8** *D1*

N

100 metres
100 yards

⑤

Next to the church is the **Museo Romántico** ⓘ *Hernández 52, T41-994363, Tue-Sun 0900-1700, CUC\$2, no cameras allowed*. The museum has an excellent collection of porcelain, glass, paintings and ornate furniture, which belonged to several families from the area. The ground floor was built in 1740 by Santiago de Silva and in 1808 the second floor was added by Don José Mariano Borrel y Padrón. The Conde de Brunet family lived there from 1830-1860, during what is known as the Romantic period. The Conde de Brunet, a local dignitary, whose full name was Nicolás de la Cruz Brunet Muñoz, made his fortune from sugar and cattle. At his death he owned 700 slaves and two sugar mills as well as lots of land and cattle. The exhibits are displayed in the colonial mansion, with beautiful views from the upper-floor balconies. Locals come here for their wedding photos.

Other museums worth visiting around Plaza Mayor include the **Museo de Arqueología Guamuhaya** ⓘ *Simón Bolívar 457, esq Villena, Plaza Mayor, T41-993420, Sat-Thu 0900-1700, CUC\$1*, which presents a general view of developments from pre-Columbian to post-conquest times. **Museo de Arquitectura Colonial** ⓘ *Desengaño (Ripalda) 83, T41-993208, Sat-Thu 0900-1700, CUC\$1*, exhibits specifically on the architecture of Trinidad, particularly aspects of the 18th and 19th centuries. It also offers tours of the city with a guide and video showings. The **Museo Nacional de Lucha Contra Bandidos** ⓘ *Hernández esq Piro Guinart, T41-994121, Tue-Sun 0900-1700, CUC\$1*, housed in the old San Francisco de Asís convent, features exhibits on the 1960s counter-revolutionary campaign in the Escambray mountains. There is a small shop selling T-shirts of Che, postcards, etc. **Museo Municipal de Historia** ⓘ *Calle Simón Bolívar 423, T41-994460, Sat-Thu 0900-1700, CUC\$2*, is an attractive building, but with rather dull displays, walk up the tower for a good view of Trinidad instead.

Also close to Plaza Mayor is the **Casa de la Cultura** ① *Francisco Javier Zerquera 406 entre Muñoz y Lumumba, T41-994308, daily 0700-2300*, which has an art gallery and a *sala* for teaching drama, painting, music and dance, open for special events. The **Casa de la Música** next to the church has two entrances. Its main entrance is at the top of the steps next to the church. Its other entrance, leading to a large 'greenhouse' venue is on JM Márquez. There is a music shop selling CDs, cassettes and also instruments, with a small display of the history of music in Trinidad. These two places join back to back. Located in an open-air shell of a house is the **Casa de la Trova** ① *entrance on Fernando Echerrí, Mon-Sat from 2200 until late for music performed by live bands, Sun from 1400 until late for singing groups, followed by* música mecánica. See also Entertainment, page 258, for live music venues. The **Galería** ① *Plaza Mayor, free,* exhibits local art. Upstairs, a shop sells paintings, clothes and handicrafts.

The **Templo a Yamaya** ① *Villena 59 entre P Guinart y S Bolívar*, is an Afro-Cuban shrine with dolls on the altars and Afro-Cuban symbols on the walls. It is open to the public and you can watch *Santería* celebrations take place. Initiations are held here for anyone who wants to become a *Santero*. In September 2003 the first procession was permitted through the streets of Trinidad, coinciding with the celebrations on 8 September for the Día de la Caridad de Cobre, patron saint of Cuba. After lighting candles in the temple, the Virgin was paraded around the block to the accompaniment of trumpet and drums, similar to many Catholic processions. However, it was followed by ceremonies back at the Templo involving *Santería* drumming when dancers became possessed by spirits.

Parque Céspedes

Parque Céspedes to the southwest of the centre has shaded archways of vines and trailing plants. To the west is the fine building of the local government, Poder Popular Municipal, and to the south is the **Iglesia de San Francisco de Paula**. There is also a cinema and telephone offices. The corner of the park at Calles Francisco J Zerquera y Martí is known as La Esquina Caliente (the hot corner) because it is where heated discussions are held between sports fans as they argue over baseball. The **Plaza Santa Ana** is at the extreme southeast of the colonial zone. On the north side is the ruined church, the **Ermita de Santa Ana**, and on the east, a yellow colonial building houses the **Restaurante Santa Ana**, see page 258.

You can also visit the **Piro Guinart Cigar Factory** ① *Maceo esq Colón, opposite Restaurante Colonial, Mon-Sat 0700-1200, 1300-1600*. It is not very big and the tour is free; note that only a few people work on Sat. Tips are gratefully received; it is acceptable to take photos. Note that the **Fábrica de Tabacos** makes tobacco for cigarettes while the **Casa de Tabaco** makes cigars.

South of Parque Céspedes is **El Alfarero** ① *Calle Andrés Berro, go east on Maceo until 1 block after the hospital you get to a blue house on a corner, turn left, El Alfarero is the low yellow building 2 blocks on the right, Mon-Sat 0730-1200 and 1300-1600*, which is a ceramics factory, making earthenware pots. There is no organized tour but it is open for you to wander around, watch the pots being thrown and glazed, and buy anything if you want. The factory used to belong to the Santander family, but was taken over by the government. The standard of pottery declined and only utilitarian pieces are now produced. The elderly Sr Santander still lives opposite the factory, but now devotes his time to breeding birds. He has 400 or so birds in his house and yard: finches, budgerigars, parakeets, etc, which are exported around the world by the government. The Santander family have now been allowed to set up their own factory again on the other side of the road and are successfully making pots and souvenirs at **La Casa del**

Alfarero (Casa Chichi) ① *Andrés Berro 51, T41-993146.* The house is very smart and prosperous with urns on the wall. Go down side entrance to the left of the house to the workshop at the back. Cuba is known for its old 1950s American cars, but this family owns a 1914 Ford model T car, which has been used in several movies.

Around Trinidad

South of Trinidad to Playa Ancón

About 8 km west of Trinidad is the small, pleasant fishing village of **La Boca**. The beach here is not cleaned daily as it is on Playa Ancón in front of the hotels, but Cubans come here on holiday and there is a cheerful if rough and ready atmosphere about the place. Many people prefer it to Playa Ancón as it is lively with the facilities of *casas particulares* and places to eat. There are some buses to La Boca or you can get a taxi, or rent a bicycle from local people for about CUC$3 a day. You can also hire a private car or taxi for about CUC$5 one way or a *cocotaxi* for CUC$2 to take you from Trinidad to La Boca. In summer there is a bus stop and taxi rank on Simón Bolívar by the railway line.

Casilda is a rather scruffy fishing village 5 km south of Trinidad across a tidal flat where there are lots of birds. It is a run-down port used mainly for exporting sugar. Its sights include the ruined Catholic church, **Ermita de Santa Elena**. There is private accommodation available, but it is still about 11 km to the beach. If you are cycling this route you may be pleased to know that there is a breezy bar at the point where the road La Boca–Ancón meets the road Casilda–Ancón, where you can get a coke for CUC$1.

The best beach resort near Trinidad is **Playa Ancón**, not a town as such, just three resort hotels of varying quality. The beach is white sand with clean turquoise water, but sandflies appear after 1600. Inland there are swamps and lakes, so be prepared for mosquitoes at certain times of the year. The best part of the beach is right in front of the **Hotel Ancón**, where there are straw sunshades, some seagrape trees and beach loungers (CUC$2). The rest of the beach has little shade. People are sometimes disappointed when they come here and expect something more spectacular, but it is very pleasant for a day trip out of Trinidad. There is a beach bar for drinks and snacks. There is a bus with a rather erratic schedule. Departures are supposed to be 0900, 1100, 1400, but don't rely on it. A taxi fare is CUC$8 one way, but you can share the car between four people. There are usually plenty of taxis and *cocotaxis* waiting in the public car park next to the hotel for the return journey. There is good **diving** less than 300 m offshore. The drop-off is at about 25 m and there is plenty to see.

Cayo Blanco de Casilda

Offshore and southeast of Playa Ancón is Cayo Blanco de Casilda, where there is a beautiful beach with lovely white sand, 1½ hours by boat. A small cay to the east, **Cayo Macho**, is excellent for watching seabirds and pelicans, while to the west of Cayo Blanco there is some lovely coral 18 to 40 m deep where you can find a wide variety of fish, turtles, lobster and crab. In places the coral has been damaged by storms but in other patches it is plentiful with brain coral, sea fans and lots of fish and starfish. A day trip on a catamaran with snorkelling is organized by hotels and tour companies for CUC$45 with lunch. Huge iguanas and hermit crabs clean up all the leftovers round the back of the kitchen. Sometimes the iguanas come round to the tables and effectively beg for fruit. You get a lovely view of the Sierra Escambray from the sea and it is a worthwhile excursion. ▸▸ *See Activities and tours, page 261.*

Parque Natural Topes de Collantes

Inland from Trinidad are the beautiful, wooded Escambray mountains, whose highest point is **Pico San Juan**, also known as La Cuca, at 1140 m. Rivers have cut deep valleys, some of which, such as the Caburní and the Guanayara, have attractive waterfalls and pools where you can swim. The **Parque Natural Topes de Collantes** ① *entrance to the National Park CUC$6.50,* is a 110-sq-km area of the mountains which contains many endemic species of fauna and flora. There are several paths in the area and walking is very rewarding with lovely views and lush forest. There is no public transport, but day trips are organized to Topes de Collantes by **Cubatur** or **Cubanacán** which are recommended.

A **Jeep Safari** for six hours costs CUC$55 per person, minimum two passengers, lunch included. There is a fair amount of hiking, which is hard work when the return journey is uphill. The trip includes a stop at a farm house for fruit, mashed plantain with garlic and lime, *guarapo* (sugar cane liquor) and coffee for an extra CUC$1. A **Truck Safari**, minimum eight passengers, including lunch, costs CUC$43. All take in swimming in a waterfall. You can see lots of wildlife, butterflies, hummingbirds and the *tocororo*, the national bird of Cuba. These are great days out in luscious surroundings. Recommended. Hiring a private car with driver to Topes de Collantes and the **Salto de Caburní** will cost you about CUC$25-35 with up to four people. Private tours do not go to the same places as jeep tours, whatever anybody tells you. Bargain hard for a good price but do not go if it has been raining recently, it gets very muddy and it is dangerous to walk in the hills. A walking stick is recommended, as is a guide. Make sure the driver takes you to the right place. The path which begins at the village of Topes is not the right place. The official start of the path to the waterfall is at the **Hotel Escambray**, but private cars cannot take you to it, so you have to walk from the village to the hotel and ask for directions there. Guides can be picked up in the village, or take an official tour at the hotel, which is much better value as you go to all the right places. You may find horses for hire half way up the hill if the climb is too much for you. ▸▸ *For further details, see Activities and tours, page 261.*

To get to the **Salto Vegas Grandes**, another waterfall, turn right immediately after the barrier when entering the village from Trinidad. You go into a cul-de-sac with several high-rise apartments. Continue along the track at the end of the last block for about 1.5 km. Eventually the track descends steeply along a narrow path (very tricky, good footwear required – do not attempt after rain). Another 2-km walk leads west from the hotels to **La Batata**, a cave with an underground river making pools in which you can swim. The temperature of the water never exceeds 20°C. Just northwest of here, but best reached on another path, is the restaurant at **Hacienda Codina**, T42-540117 (serving *comida criolla*) often combined with a trip to the Cueva del Altar, the orchid gardens and a mirador.

Some 12 km north of Topes near Guanayara, there is another waterfall, the **Salto El Rocío**, with swimming in the Poza del Venado by the Río Caballero. There is a restaurant nearby, the **Casa de la Gallega**, where you can have a chicken lunch Galician style.

Off the beaten track is the **Salto Javira**, reached on horseback across the Valle de los Ingenios from Trinidad, up into the Escambray mountains. A very pretty and pleasant trip through farmyards, bean fields and other crops. You can go by horseback up to the National Park entrance and from there you have to walk, 40 minutes. Start at the Restaurant El Cubano, where you buy your CUC$6.50 National Park entrance ticket. This is 5 km out of town down a track next to the Río Guaurabo. The attractive 40-minute walk is marked along a tributary of the river and you cross pretty streams in the forest until you climb a rocky path to get to the waterfall. At one point you pass a cliff face covered with hundreds of hanging wasps' nests. The river cascades down a smooth rock face into a

Horse riding around Trinidad

Horse riding is a popular excursion around Trinidad and a good way of covering long distances into the countryside, giving access to rivers, waterfalls, mountains, forests and other natural attractions. Within a relatively short time you can also get a feel for the way local farmers live and work and see what they produce. Many of the routes take in rivers and waterfalls where you can bathe, cool off and relieve any aches and pains from the exercise. The drawback is the quality of the horses, which would often be rescue cases in the countries from where we tourists come.

Unofficial, private guides are now illegal as the government has withdrawn their licences. This has not stopped the practice and there are often police crackdowns when they impound the horses and their saddles. Knowing that they are in danger of losing their property, guides offer their poorest animals and saddles to tourists which can be dangerous for both horse and rider. Prices range between CUC$10-20 depending on the guide and where you go. The official tours usually have horses and saddles in better condition. The animals are fitter and healthier and are less likely to have sores from ill-fitting tack. Prices start from CUC$15 at Rancho el Cubano or CUC$20 from Flora y Fauna.

Whether you opt for legal or illegal guides, the most important thing is not to accept horses or tack in poor condition, thereby encouraging the owners to look after their property

better. Think also of your own safety (and travel insurance). A thin, poor animal is more likely to fall. A horse with sores can often make a sudden movement when in pain and unseat its rider. An unofficial guide once offered me an ex-racehorse, which had previously won its owner sizeable amounts of money at *fiestas*, but now had one back leg twice the size it should be, with an untreated wound. All the horses in the group had sores from their rough saddles and bridles and festering wounds in other places. However, their feet were shod and in reasonable condition and I was told that they are treated once a year against parasites. As long as the horse can still stand up and do its job, many Cubans appear to care little for its wellbeing. This is partly through ignorance and lack of education about horse welfare and partly because of a lack of funds for veterinary medicine, including basic items such as wormers. Veterinary care has not kept pace with the standard of health care enjoyed by the Cuban people.

It is up to tourists to complain and campaign for better treatment of the horses. Changes have been made in other areas of tourism when foreigners have made their feelings known. There are some Cubans who appreciate the work which has to be done and are linking up with charities, trainers and vets overseas to get help. For further information in the Trinidad area and suggestions of how you could help, see www.diana.trinidadphoto.com.

deep green pool, surrounded by cliffs and caves inhabited by bats, which fly in and out of the darkness. It is great for a cool swim and very photogenic. If you don't want to go to the waterfall, you can carry on through the valley on horseback. There is a nice ride passing farmers' houses so you can see how they live and work, chat with them, maybe be offered a cup of coffee, and there are several rivers where you can bathe. This trip can also be done on foot.

Alberto Delgado monument

About 4 km from Trinidad, on the Cienfuegos road on the way to the turning for the Topes de Collantes National Park, there is a small monument to Alberto Delgado. Turn south on the road by the stone wall with his name on it and there is a small monument and cave by the Río Guaurabo. Alberto Delgado was a revolutionary who infiltrated the group of US-backed counter revolutionaries known as G2, working from the Escambray mountains. As a result of his activities, a group of 90 counter-revolutionaries was caught in the early 1960s. However, intelligence sources in Cuba and Miami identified him as a spy and a message to that effect was sent from *Radio Swan* (on Swan Island near Miami) to G2 in the mountains. Delgado was captured and executed by the counter-revolutionaries by being hung from a tree in the vicinity of the monument. On the other side of the river from the monument is the house of the Finca Maisinicú, where Alberto Delgado lived.

Torre de Manaca Iznaga and Valle de los Ingenios

① *15 km from Trinidad on road to Sancti Spíritus, daily 0900-1600 or 1700, CUC$2.*

The Torre de Manaca Iznaga in the village of the same name has now been given UNESCO World Heritage status alongside Trinidad city, because of its historical importance The legend goes that there were two rival brothers, one who wanted to build a tower and the other who wanted to dig a hole as deep as the tower was high. In fact there is only a tower, which was built between 1835 and 1845. It is 43.5 m high, has seven floors and 136 steps to the top. It was built as a lookout to watch the slaves working in the valley at the sugar mills. There were two bells in the tower, one was rung when it was time for the slaves to stop work and take a meal in a communal eating house, the other was rung if an escape was discovered, alerting the slave catchers, or *rancheros*. One of the bells, dating from 1846, can be seen on the path leading to the tower. There is a great view of the surrounding countryside, including the Valle de los Ingenios (Valley of the Sugar Mills) and the Escambray mountains as well as the rooftops of the village below. Look out for the large sugar cauldrons lying around the village. The **Manaca Iznaga** restaurant is in the old plantation house, a yellow colonial building (daily 0900-1700, meals CUC$6-15) and there is a small shop. Tour operators offer day trips, see page 261, or you can hire a private car to take you for about CUC$15-20. See Transport, page 262, for train details.

On the same road, 5 km from Trinidad, is a mirador, from where you get a fine view of the Valley of Sugar Mills and the Escambray mountains, with the sea on the opposite side. There is a nice bar at the mirador, and if a tour group turns up there is often a demonstration of a sugar press.

For Sleeping and Eating price codes and other relevant information, see Essentials pages 37-43.

● Sleeping

Trinidad *p246, map p248*
Hotels
L-AL Grand Hotel Iberostar Trinidad,
José Martí y Lino Pérez, T41-996070,
www.iberostar.com. 35 rooms and 4 suites
with view from balcony of plaza, no pool,
nowhere to sit outside, no children under
15, a/c, TV, minibar, room service, laundry,
safety box, internet, international phones,
24-hr cambio, gourmet restaurant with
international rums available, good buffet breakfast,
smokers' bar with cigars and rums available.
A Las Cuevas, Finca Santa Ana, T41-996133,
www.cubanacan.cu. On a hill 10 mins' walk
from town (good road), with caves in the
grounds and a caving museum, nice view of
the sea and lovely sunsets. 114 comfortable
rooms and mini-suites in chalets and
apartments with a/c, phone, radio, minibar,
TV, very clean, 2 swimming pools, bar with
excellent *daiquirís* and great view, show in
the hotel 2100, disco in cave below.
Reception 2230-0230, entrance CUC$3 (most
rooms are not disturbed by noise), tennis,
shop, post office, exchange facilities,
2 restaurants, à la carte or buffet meals,
breakfast included, evening meal CUC$12.
A Villa de Recreo Ma Dolores, Carretera
Circuito Sur, T41-996481, www.cubanacan.cu,
1.5 km from Trinidad on the road to
Cienfuegos. Garden setting near Río Guarabo,
19 brick *cabañas* and 26 bungalows with
kitchen, a/c, shower, clean, restaurant, shop,
pool bar, quiet spot but noisy in the evening
as it is an all-dancing, all-singing tour group
destination, horse riding, river excursions.

Casas particulares
There are hundreds of *casas particulares* in
Trinidad but even so, at peak times they can
all be full and you will need to book ahead.

They are generally more expensive than
in other towns, so expect to pay around
CUC$25 for a room. All those listed here
offer 'hot' water, a/c and fans with en suite
bathrooms unless otherwise stated.
C Casa Muñoz, José Martí 401 entre Fidel
Claro y Santiago Escobar, T/F41-993673,
www.casa. trinidadphoto.com. Very friendly,
English speaking, run by Julio César Muñoz
Cocina and Rosa Orbea Cerrillo with their
family, horse and splendid dogs. Julio has a
charity project for horse welfare. Great house,
one of the grandest in Trinidad, built in 1800
with lofty ceilings and cool, intricately tiled floors,
2 rooms with 2 double beds, new bathrooms,
minibar, roof terrace, patio, parking, very popular
so book in advance. Base for photographers
and film makers; Julio is a photographer and
can arrange workshops and study groups.
D Balbina Cadahía Benavente, Maceo
355 entre Lino Pérez y Colón, T41-992585.
Extremely pleasant family, old colonial house, 2
rooms, will arrange trips, friendly, good reports.
D Carlos Gil Lemes, José Martí 263 entre
Colón y Fco J Zerquera, T41-993142, carlosgl
3142@yahoo.es, next to library. Beautiful
late-19th-century house with sumptuous
tile decoration, English spoken, 2 rooms with
shared bath, garden courtyard, neighbour
has a garage for rent, CUC$1 per night.
D Doña Ramonita, Camilo Cienfuegos 68
entre Pedro Zerquera y Frank País, T41-
993637. Mother and son owners are friendly
and welcoming. Charming house with lovely
leafy inner patio.
D Gisela Borrell Bastida, Frank País (Carmen)
486 entre Fidel Claro y Santiago Escobar,
about 200 m from bus station, T41-994301.
2 rooms with double and single bed on
ground floor, use of own dining room, sitting
room, own entrance, lots of space.
D Hospedaje Yolanda, Piro Guinart 227
entre Izquierdo y Maceo, opposite the bus
station. Very nice rooms in enormous colonial
house including 1 with 2 double beds, terrace
and views of sea and mountains.

D Hostal La Candelaria, Antonio Guiteras (Mercedes) 129 entre P Zerquera y A Cárdenas, T41-994239. Run by Elvira and Eddy, both teachers but no English spoken, friendly and generous, humble accommodation, but spotlessly clean, 2 rooms, nice garden, great food.

D Hostal La Rioja, Frank País 389 entre Simón Bolívar y Fco J Zerquera, T41-994589, T53-5271 1776 (mob), tereleria@yahoo. com.mx. Run by friendly and helpful Teresa Leris Echerri, 2 rooms with double and single beds, the 1 upstairs has access to a small kitchen, bathrooms, patio garden at rear, table outside in the shade for meals, dachshund, garage, some French and English spoken.

D Hostal Marilú, Santiago Escobar 172 entre Frank País y José Martí, T41-992899, hostalmarilu@yahoo.es. Small room with firm double and single beds, bathroom has new fittings but no door yet. Nicer large room on roof with 2 double beds, eat outdoors upstairs on terrace with iguana and dog or indoors downstairs. Marilú, Carlos and family are very friendly and pleasant and serve good food.

D Hostal Roca Verde, Simón Bolívar 166 entre Pereira y Zerquera, T41-994807. 2 basic rooms with bathrooms, friendly and helpful owners, pleasant patio for meals, excellent food if a bit pricey at CUC$6 for breakfast and CUC$12 for dinner plus drinks.

D Hostal Sandra y Víctor, Maceo (Gutiérrez) 613 entre Piro Guinart (Boca) y Pablo Pichs (Guaurabo), T41-996444, hostalsandra@ yahoo.com. Family lives downstairs, 2 guest rooms upstairs, gives privacy and security, well-cared-for property, good bathrooms, fridge, balcony to the front off the dining room, spacious and comfortable with friendly hosts who provide delicious and hearty meals.

D Hugo P Bastida Saenz de Buruaga, Maceo 539 entre Santiago Escobar (Olvido) y Piro Guinart (Boca), name above the door, T41-993186. Typical dark colonial home with high ceilings run by elderly gentleman, 1 lovely room, very friendly dog, Sr Bastida speaks English and his wife is an excellent cook, good-value meals.

D José y Fátima, Francisco J Zerquera 159 (Rosario) entre Frank País y Francisco Petersen, T41-993898. Upstairs rooms, 1 with double bed, the other with double and single beds, nice new bathrooms, door and windows open onto balcony for lots of fresh air, table on the patio for meals (lots of dishes, whatever you want) and roof terrace with laundry facilities and washing machine and a great view over the rooftops.

D Lazara Borrell Farías, Colón 312 entre Maceo y Jesús Menéndez, T419-2454. 2 rooms each with bathroom, huge house in historic centre, friendly, good English.

D Mabel Ortíz Durán, Francisco J Zerquera 360 entre Ernesto V Muñoz y Gustavo Izquierdo, T419-2220. Own key to room and house, huge room with 2 double beds, huge portions of food with lots of fruit and vegetables, will cook whatever you want, beautiful colonial building 2 mins from main square, feels almost like a museum, generous and hospitable family.

D María Esther Pérez, Francisco Cadahía 224 (Gracia) entre Colón y Lino Pérez, T41-993528. Nice extension with 2 rooms attached to old colonial house, antique beds in both, fabulous fish meals, run by herbalist, using plants from her own garden, parking 5 doors away.

D Pedro Aliz Peña, Gustavo Izquierdo 127 (Gloria) entre Piro Guinart y Simón Bolívar, T5251 2096 (mob), just by bus station. Old house with high ceilings, patio, quiet, 2 spacious rooms, simple but clean, new bathrooms, Pedro and Teresa are sociable and helpful, only Spanish spoken.

D Teresa Cerrillo, Frank País 372 entre Mario Guerra y Francisco J Zerquera, T41-993673 (Casa Muñoz), teresacerrillo@yahoo.es. Pink house with patio at the rear full of plants and greenery, 2 double beds in large room, fridge.

South of Trinidad to Playa Ancón p251
Hotels

AL Brisas Trinidad del Mar, Playa Ancón, T41-996500-7, www.cubanacan.cu. 4-star all-inclusive hotel, 241 rooms and junior suites in 2/3-storey multicoloured blocks in a circle around free-form pool, 2 rooms for wheelchair users, a/c, TV, phone, radio, internet access, medical centre, massage, beauty parlour, shops, laundry, fax and email, car and bike rental, tourism desk, buffet and à la carte restaurants, jacuzzi, tennis, gym, sauna, games room, watersports, entertainment including, disco 2230-0200, on good beach, reef-protected sea, nice sand with sea grapes behind.

AL Club Amigo Ancón, Playa Ancón, T41-996120, www.cubanacan.cu. Concrete block of 279 rooms, showing its age, price room only, although they encourage you to go all-inclusive, including extras such as snorkels, internet access. The hotel has an hexagonal pool, disco and many facilities, including watersports, best beach here, lots of families stay, but lots of complaints. Offices of **Cubanacán** and **Transtur** for excursions.

B-C Club Amigo Costa Sur, Playa Ancón, T41-996174-8, www.cubanacan.cu. Standard (73) or superior rooms (39) in a block or chalets (20) in front of them, built above rocks with beach to north of hotel where there is a natural swimming pool and bar on the sand. Price room only, but all-inclusive if you stay more than 3 nights. Gym, nightclub show at 2145, pool, billiards, shop, internet access.

Casas particulares

D Elsa Hernández Monteagudo, Av del Mar, Casa 5, La Boca, T41-993236. 2 double rooms, 2 bathrooms (ants on floor, harmless), huge, tasty meals, bike rental, rocking chairs on terrace for sunset watching, great hospitality.

D Hostal Vista al Mar, Calle Real 47, La Boca, T41-993716. Owned by Manuel Menéndez, 2 rooms, parking, overlooking the sea.

D Rancho Florida, Calle Real 78, La Boca, T41-993535, hostalranchoflorida@yahoo.es. Run by Eloy Acosta and Sonia Pérez, Eloy speaks reasonable English and is friendly. Small room with good bathroom (watch out for tree frogs in toilet!) overlooking sea, good food, direct access from garden to sea, parking, hammocks and sun loungers under huge fig tree just metres from water's edge.

D Segundo Valledares, Calle D 1 entre Av del Sol y Av del Mar, La Boca, T41-996883, christhian_dares@yahoo.com. Excellent food, friendly, 1 room, sitting room, parking.

D Villa Dalia, Real 158 entre Iglesia y Perla, Casilda, T41-995382, juanmayor@yahoo.es. 2 rooms, minibar, patio, terrace, parking.

D Villa Sonia, Av del Mar 11 entre D y E, La Boca, T41-992923. 2 rooms, parking, overlooking the sea, porch with hammocks, meals.

Parque Natural Topes de Collantes *p252*
Hotels

A Kurhotel Escambray, Topes de Collantes, T42-540180, www.gaviota-grupo.com. A huge, multi-storey hospital/hotel in the mountains offering special therapeutic treatments for patients from all over the world, but with the usual hotel services, too. Lots of Cuban art from the 1980s displayed on the walls of public areas. Excursions, disco, pool, squash court.

B Los Helechos, T42-540330, www.gaviota-grupo.com, southwest of Topes de Collantes village. 48 a/c rooms, restaurant, bar, *cafetería*, thermal pool, gym, massage, sauna, steam baths, bowling alley, shop, tourism bureau, car hire.

B Villa Escambray, T42-540335. Villas for tourists behind the Dirección General by the path to Salto de Caburní.

❼ Eating

State-run restaurants are OK but nothing special. Family-run restaurants, *paladares*, are not as numerous as before because most people eat in *casas particulares* where the food is excellent and cooked to order. Breakfast is usually CUC$3-5 and dinner CUC$6-15.

Trinidad *p246, map p248*
Restaurants

▾▾▾-▾▾ Colonial, Maceo 402, esquina Colón. Daily 1200-2215. Nice place, popular. Fri at 2200 is Viernes Vino, when they offer wine and canapés with live music.

♥♥♥-♥♥ Don Antonio, Izquierdo 118 entre Piro Guinart y Simón Bolívar, T41-996548. Daily 1100-2300. A nice old colonial house with ornate columns and tiled floor.

♥♥♥-♥♥ Plaza Mayor, Villena 15, just off Plaza Mayor, T41-996470, plazamayor@enet.cu. Daily 1200-2130. Elegant setting with pink tablecloths, live music, lobster CUC$24, steak and seafood, buffet CUC$8, pleasant courtyard at the rear.

♥♥♥-♥ El Mesón del Regidor, Simón Bolívar 426 entre Ernesto V Muñoz y Villena, opposite Toro, T41-996572. Daily 0900-2200. Lovely patio. *Criollo* cuisine.

♥♥ El Jigüe, Real 69 esq Guinart, T41-996476. Daily 1200-2245. Live music, good food and atmosphere, most dishes CUC$7-8, chicken special CUC$8.

♥♥ Las Begonias, Maceo esq Simón Bolívar. Daily 0900-2200. The only café in town with the added attraction of 6 computer terminals for internet access. Also **Cubanacán** bureau. Fast-food dishes. Ice cream parlour opposite.

♥♥-♥ Ruinas de Leonci, Gustavo Izquierdo entre Simón Bolívar y Piro Guinart. Daily 1030-2300. Bar and restaurant with cosy small garden, pleasant wooden tables and chairs inside.

♥♥-♥ Santa Ana, Plaza Santa Ana. Daily 1200-2200. House special pork CUC$4.65, other dishes CUC$7-9. Live show at 2200. Scooter rental. **Infotur** office 0800-1800, T41-998257/8.

♥ El Rápido, Martí esq Lino Pérez. Fast food.

♥ Villa Real, Real 74, T41-997664. Italian and *criollo* food.

Paladares

♥♥♥-♥♥ Estela, Simón Bolívar 557, T41-994329. Open from 1900 Mon-Fri. Garden setting among trees and variegated shrubs, surrounded by very high walls at the back of a colonial house. Excellent and plentiful food, lots of variety with salads, rice, beans, vegetables, well-cooked meats, friendly hosts, get there early to avoid queues in high season, this is the best and most popular place to eat in town. Menu changes according to what's available and fresh.

♥♥♥-♥♥ Sol y Son, Simón Bolívar 283 entre Frank País y José Martí. Daily 1900-2300. Run by English-speaking ex-architect Lázaro in 19th-century house, nice decor, courtyard, popular, vegetarian special, excellent pork, tasty stuffed fish.

Peso restaurants

There is a sit-down pizza restaurant where tourists can pay in pesos cubanos on Martí at Parque Céspedes. Lots of pizza stalls on Lino Pérez entre Martí y Maceo, but the best are on Francisco Cadahía y Lino Pérez.

South of Trinidad to Playa Ancón *p251*
There are several bar/restaurants all along the beach in La Boca. In Playa Ancón there is very little choice apart from the hotels listed above.

♥♥♥-♥♥ Grill Caletas, Playa Ancón between Playa la Boca and Hotel Costa Sur. 0900-2100. Seafood specials, CUC3-12.

♥♥♥-♥ Grill del Caribe, Playa Ancón, along the beach northwest of the Hotel Ancón, T41-996241. Makes a change from hotel food but is poor value. There is a little beach behind it.

🍸 Bars

Trinidad *p246, map p248*
Bar Daiquirí, Lino Pérez entre Cadahía y José Martí. Daily 0900-2300. Beer CUC$1.15, *mojito* CUC$2, daiquirí CUC$4.

Bar Las Ruinas de Segarte, Alameda entre Márquez y Galdós. Open 1000-2400. Set in a ruined courtyard, also does snacks.

Círculo Social de Obreros, Martí. Serves rum in pesos cubanos, tourists welcome, an authentic drinking experience.

🎭 Entertainment

Trinidad *p246, map p248*
Cinema
Cine Romello Cornello, Parque Céspedes. Show at 2000, 40 centavos. For up-to-date times and programme see the billboards

just inside the doors. Some American action films are shown here.

Music and dance

Lots of people offer 'unofficial' salsa lessons for about CUC$4 an hr; Trinidad is a good place to learn and you'll soon be dancing with Cubans in local bars.

Casa de la Música, up the steps past the church in Plaza Mayor, T41-996622. Restaurant daily 1000-2200, show 2200-0200, piano bar 1800-0600. Full of tourists and Cubans, salsa, live performers, shop selling CDs, cassettes, music magazines.

Casa de la Trova, daily 0900-0100. Entry free during the day, CUC$1 at night. 1 block from the church is the excellent live Cuban traditional music and *trova* with a warm, vibrant atmosphere. There are mostly Cubans here, of all age groups, and it's a great place to watch, and join in with, the locals having a good time. Excellent fresh lemonade, local cocktails, refreshing pit stop after a stroll through the artesanía market. Live music day and night.

Centro Cultura Sandunga (formerly Artex), Lino Pérez 306 entre Cadahía y José Martí, T41-996486. Outdoor bar 0900-0100. In a nice old colonial house built in 1870, CUC$1 for show at 2200 with *parrillada*, dancing, live music and karaoke.

Coppelia, Martí, opposite the public library. Still open after everything else is closed, music, popular with Cubans, restaurant food 0900-2100, disco at 2200-0300, special show Fri-Sun at 2300, CUC$1 for show and disco.

La Bodeguita de Trinidad, Colón entre Martí y Maceo. Daily 0900-2400. Not as legendary as its Havana namesake, but a nice little music bar, open courtyard and with quaint sheltered booths for couples, *trova* group every night 2100-2400, entry free, beer CUC$1, food available.

La Canchánchara, Villena 78. Daily 1000-2245. Another venue for live music, fast food, serves a drink of the same name created out of rum, honey and lime in small earthenware pots. More touristy than **Casa de La Trova** (cigar and souvenir shop), but good traditional music with different groups playing.

La Escalinata, T41-996622, on the terrace leading up the steps next to the church, before you get to the Casa de la Música. Bar 0900-0200, cafeteria 1600-0400, show 2100, live bands 0900-2000, but not when it rains. Great place for a sunset cocktail.

La Parranda, Villena 59, in the patio of the Templo de Yemaya just off Plaza Mayor. Open 0900-2400. An outdoor bar/music venue, very ad hoc farmyard atmosphere, but excellent live music every night, good place to learn salsa, watched from semicircle of seats, cocktails CUC$2, dancing.

Las Cuevas (see Sleeping, p255). Good disco, dance merengue and salsa with Cubans between the stalactites in a cave below reception, from 2230, entrance CUC$3.

Las Ruinas de Brunet, Maceo entre Colón y Francisco Javier Zerquera. Daily 0900-2400. Nightly Afro-Cuban show at 2100 for tourists in ruined colonial courtyard, very tacky and unauthentic, also *trova* from 1600, percussion classes 0900-1100, dance classes 1300-1600. Bicycle and scooter rental.

Palenque de los Congos Reales, Fernando H Echerri entre La Escalinata y Casa de la Trova, T41-994512. Bar daily 1000-2400 (Sat until 0100). During the day there are sometimes groups playing and an Afro-Cuban show. Nice shady open air space for day time or evening drink.

⊛ Festivals and events

Trinidad *p246, map p248*
Jan Semana de la Cultura is in the second week of the month, with art exhibitions, live music in the streets and other cultural activities. Following Semana de la Cultura there are several Santería festivals, including **Mamalroko**, a rite where offerings are made to the Orisha Iroko living in the Ceiba tree to ask for health and peace, which often include street parades and the beating of Batá drums.

Mar/Apr Semana Santa (Easter) is celebrated with an enormous procession on Good Fri. Special attention is given to the statue of Cristo de la Veracruz, which is thought to work miracles, and the choir sings its heart out.

24 April Fiesta Cukalambiano is a folkloric festival with music, dancing and horse competitions.

Jun Carnival, with traditional festivities and contests, including one for the Carnival Queen.

18 Aug Santa Elena, the patron saint of Casilda, is celebrated with a mass in the ruins of the church, festivities, fairs and horse competitions.

8 Sep Día de la Caridad de Cobre, Cuba's patron saint's day. There are lots of religious processions around the town, accompanied by music and dance.

22 Nov Santa Cecilia, the patron saint of music, is a fiesta with music on the streets and a special mass in the church with the emphasis on music.

Dec Santa Bárbara (Chango), an important Santería festival, with a Velada on 3 Dec and procession and Bembé (drum beating for the saints) on 4 Dec. San Lázaro (Babalú Ayé) on 17 Dec, another of the principal Orishas, with procession and Bembé. The week before Christmas you will see **Posadas**, nativity processions when children dress up as Mary, Joseph and shepherds and sing carols on the streets with Mary on a donkey.

O Shopping

Trinidad *p246, map p248*
Art
Casa de los Conspiradores, Cristo 38, to the right of La Escalinata. Gallery-studio of the painter and sculptor, Yami Martínez. The name of the house comes from being the base, in 1848, of Cuban patriots fighting against the Spanish government in a conspiracy known as the Conspiración de la Mina de la Rosa Cubana.

Galería de Arte Universal, Villena 43, opposite the Plaza Mayor, T41-994432. Fri-Wed 0800-1700. Contemporary Cuban art for sale.
Tienda de Arte Amelia Pelaez, Simón Bolívar esq Valdés Muñoz, T41-993590.

Bookshop
Tienda de Libros, José Martí 273. Mon-Fri 0900-1700, new and second-hand books for sale.

Food
There is a store on Zerquera esq Izquierdo, daily 0930-2130, which sells some food and drink with a good selection, and another on Maceo esq Lino Pérez which sells food, clothes and toiletries. Fruit and vegetables are bought from vendors in the street or at doorways. Look out for what is on offer or in season and pay in pesos cubanos.

Handicrafts
All along S Lumumba and EV Muñoz are handicraft stalls, especially crochet and needlework, with jewellery, beads, carvings, hats, baskets and boxes. It is called Candonga, or Mercado Popular de Artesanía. The standard of handicrafts has improved and they are cheaper than in Havana, but avoid coral, shell or any other items taken from the sea.

Souvenirs
Bazar Trinidad, Maceo 451, esq Zerquera, on the opposite corner from Caracol. Postcards, curios, pictures, T-shirts, typical Cuban handicrafts.
Caracol, on Maceo esq Zerquera. Souvenirs, T-shirts, postcards, etc.
Tienda La Cochera, on Simón Bolívar, round the corner from the Museo Romántico. A small selection of souvenirs, drinks, postcards, toiletries, T-shirts.
Tienda Panamericana, Lino Pérez entre Cadahía y José Martí. Food, clothes and toiletries, sold in CUC$.
Universo, Martí entre Rosario y Colón. Sells shoes, clothes, department store, also Cubanacán tour company on site.

▲ Activities and tours

Trinidad *p246, map p248*
Marina and watersports
Marina Marlin Trinidad, Península Ancón, opposite Hotel Ancon, T41-996205, marinastdad@enet.cu, VHF 16, 19, 68, 72. Six moorings, 1.8-m draft, showers, laundry, rental. All boat excursions and water activities are based here and you can buy direct from the marina or through any tour operator. A seafari to Cayo Blanco on a catamaran costs CUC$45, 5 hrs with lunch, open bar and snorkelling, to Cayo Macho on a catamaran is CUC$40, 5 hrs with lunch, open bar and snorkelling. **Diving** costs CUC$35 for 1 dive, CUC$64 for 2, night diving CUC$45 for qualified divers. All types of **fishing** available including deep-sea fishing, CUC$280 for 6 hrs for 6 people.

Tour operators
There are 4 tour operators and all offer the same tours at the same prices. There is a wide variety of tours as Trinidad has access to the sea, mountains, valleys, rivers, waterfalls, etc, so just head for the nearest agency and see what takes your fancy. Prices vary according to what options you choose, such as lunch and transport. Opening hours vary according to the season, but they are usually 0830-1700. Excursions to the most popular places, for example: to the Valley of the Sugar Mills on the steam train, 5 hrs, CUC$10; 5-hr horseback ride in the Valley CUC$23; truck Safari to the Parque el Cubano, 6 hrs, CUC$35; jeep Safari to Guanayara (Topes de Collantes), 6 hrs, CUC$35; truck Safari to Topes de Collantes, CUC$43; Jeep Safari Trinitopes to Salto del Caburní, CUC$29; Salto de Javira, 6 hrs, CUC$16. Excursions further afield include Guamá and Playa Larga, 12 hrs, CUC$69; Santa Clara, 8 hrs, CUC$45; Sancti Spíritus, 8 hrs, CUC$39; nature tour including the Valle de los Ingenios, Parque Natural Jarisco in Banao, CUC$55; Cienfuegos, 8 hrs, CUC$43. **Cubanacán**, Colón esq Frank País, T41-996320/996590, with bureaux in the Universo store on Martí entre Colón y Francisco J Zerquera, T41-996142; at Cubacar, Lino Pérez 366 entre Maceo y Cadahía, T41-994753; and at Begonias, Simón Bolívar esq Maceo, T41-996736.
Cubatur, Maceo esq Zerquera, T/F41-996314, with a bureau at Simón Bolívar 430 esq Maceo, T41-996368, and in all the beach hotels.
Infotur, Restaurante Santa Ana, Plaza Santa Ana, T41-998257-8. Open 0800-1800.
Paradiso, Lino Pérez 306 entre Cadahía y José Martí in the Centro Cultural Sandunga (formerly Artex), T41-996345, paradiso@artextdad.co.cu.

⊖ Transport

Trinidad *p246, map p248*
Air
No regular flights, only charters.

Bicycle/scooter hire
Cycling on cobbled streets is difficult to say the least. Scooters and bicycles can be hired from **Las Ruinas de Brunet**, see Entertainment, page 259. Bicycles can also be hired through tour companies or *casas particulares*. Trinidad is on a hill, so cycling to the beach is easy, coming back is hard work. Make sure your bike is in good condition.

Bus
Long distance Terminal entrance on Gustavo Izquierdo, near the corner with Piro Guinart, office daily 0600-1700, T41-994448, T44-996676 (after 2000), T53-5251 2165 (mob, for international calls and text messages), economica@trin.palmares.cu. Transport (other than with **Víazul**) to the east of Cuba is difficult from Trinidad as it is not on the Carretera Central. Best to go to Sancti Spíritus through beautiful hilly scenery (see below) and take the bus or train from there. For Víazul timetable and prices, see page 32. In addition, Víazul runs an irregular transfer service to **Havana airport**, to **Varadero** and to **Viñales**, using minibuses. Go to the Víazul office a couple of days in advance to organize it.

Transtur also runs a bus service from Parque Céspedes. You can make reservations at any tour agency or go straight to Parque Céspedes if you want to travel the same day. To **Havana**, 0715, CUC$25, stopping in **Cienfuegos**, CUC$6; to **Viñales**, 0700, CUC$35.

Car hire
Cubacar, at Servi Cupet on the way out of Trinidad towards Casilda, T/F41-996301; at the Cubatur office, Maceo esq Zerquera, T41-996110; at Lino Pérez 366 entre Maceo y Cadahía, T41-996633; at Simón Bolívar 430 esq Maceo, T41-996257. **Rent a Car Vía** (Gaviota), at the airport, T41-996388. **Rex**, at any Cubanacán agency.

Petrol stations Servi Cupet on the way out of Trinidad towards Casilda.

Taxi
Cubataxi, Camilo Cienfuegos on the way out to Casilda, T41-998080, or T41-992214, at the bus station. Also *cocotaxis* and taxis parked on Maceo entre Simón Bolívar y Colón.

Train
The station is south of the town, walk south straight down Lino Pérez until you get to the railway line, then turn right, T41-993348. Tourists can take a trip on a 1907 steam train to **Manaca Iznaga** daily in high season at 0900, CUC$10. Call beforehand to see if it is running as it does sometimes break down.

❶ Directory

Trinidad *p246, map p248*
Accident and emergency Police: the main police station is 1 km from the centre of town on Calle 1 in Reparto Armando Mestre. There is a sub-station at the corner of Colón and José Martí. For any problem ring T41-996900 or 106. Fire: T105. **Banks** Bandec, José Martí 264 entre Zerquera y Colón, T41-992405, Mon-Fri 0800-1500, Sat 0800-1100. Changes TCs for dollars and cash advances on credit cards. **Cadeca**, Martí 164, T41-996262, half a block from Parque Céspedes, open Mon-Sat 0830-1800, Sun 0830-1200. There are *cambios* in Hotel Las Cuevas, Hotel Ancón and Hotel Costa Sur, where you can change TCs. **Immigration** T41-996950. **Internet** Las Begonias, Maceo entre FJ Zerquera y Simón Bolívar, 6 terminals, CUC$6 per hr, Mon-Fri 0900-2100. **Etecsa**, on Parque Céspedes. Email facilities, plenty of terminals but can get busy, early morning best, CUC$6 per hr, fax, phones and cards. **Medical services** The Clínica Internacional is on Lino Pérez 103 esq Anastasio Cárdenas, T41-996492, www.servimedcuba.com. Modern, with out-patient consultations, laboratory tests, X-rays, pharmacy, dentistry, massage and 24-hr emergency care. It is better to go there rather than to the general hospital as they have more medical supplies. They will contact your travel insurance company and arrange ambulance transfers. A consultation fee is CUC$25, a call-out fee CUC$50. **Post** Antonio Maceo 418 entre Zerquera y Colón, Mon-Sat 0800-1700, Sun 0900-1700. Another small post office on Gral Lino Pérez, Parque Céspedes, beside Iglesia San Francisco, daily 0800-1700. **Telephone** Etecsa office on Parque Céspedes for telephones, mobiles, fax and internet service.

Contents

Footprint features

At a glance

◉ **Getting around** On foot, by bicycle, hired car, taxi and Víazul long-distance bus.

◉ **Time required** 1-2 weeks.

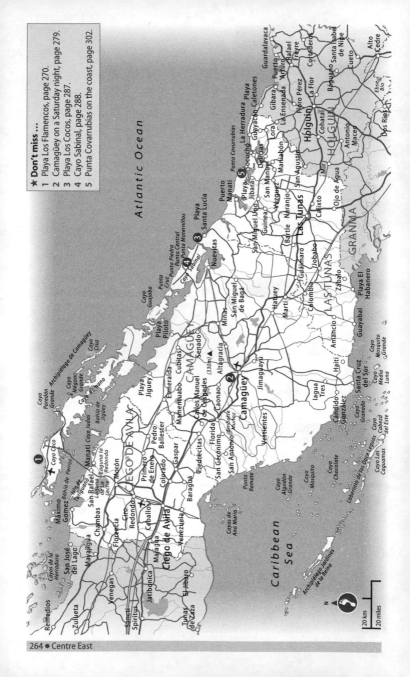

★ **Don't miss ...**
1 Playa Los Flamencos, page 270.
2 Camagüey on a Saturday night, page 279.
3 Playa Los Cocos, page 287.
4 Cayo Sabinal, page 288.
5 Punta Covarrubias on the coast, page 302.

Atlantic Ocean

Caribbean Sea

N

20 km
20 miles

The three provinces of Ciego de Avila, Camagüey and Las Tunas make up a large area of mostly flat, agricultural land with few natural features of outstanding beauty, although the landscape is pleasing with livestock grazing in the meadows. The city of Ciego de Avila, also known as the pineapple town, is not a tourist attraction, but the centre is being improved with many changes for the better. North of the city, however, is one of the island's main beach resorts: the cays of Jardines del Rey, principally Cayo Coco and its neighbour, Cayo Guillermo. Extensive beaches of pale sand are now a magnet for the all-inclusive tourist market. Other cays in the Jardines del Rey archipelago are also lined up for development.

The only city of note in the region is Camagüey, a UNESCO World Heritage Site since 2008, which is an ideal place to stay a few days if travelling from one end of the island to the other. The old colonial heart of the city with its labyrinthine streets has been restored to its former splendour while the shopping area is full of magnificent 19th-century buildings which have stood the test of time better than in seaside cities such as Havana or Santiago. North of the city is the long-established beach resort of Playa Santa Lucía, with hotels now starting to show their age. However, this beach and the nearby cays are irresistible for lovers of sun, sea and sand, while the diving is superb, especially if you like sharks. Las Tunas is another city which people mostly just pass through, preferring instead to visit the north-coast beaches, which are so far relatively undeveloped with few facilities.

Ins and outs

Getting there
Air There are international airports north of Ciego de Avila, on Cayo Coco (Jardines del Rey), Las Tunas and Camagüey, and a domestic airport near Playa Santa Lucía. Charter flights from Canada, Argentina and the UK bring visitors to the cays. **Rail** The three provincial capitals are linked by rail and road, being on the main routes from Havana to Santiago de Cuba. Trains are unreliable and some services are not available to foreigners. **Road** Víazul has a good daily bus service either from Havana, Varadero or Trinidad to Holguín or Santiago, stopping at all major towns along the way. ▸▸ *See also Ins and outs for Ciego de Avila page 267, Camagüey page 279 and Las Tunas page 300.*

Tourist information
State tour agencies can be found in all the main towns and at hotels in the beach resorts and these operate as tourist information offices although their main purpose is to sell tours. They can help with hotel reservations, tickets and transfers.

Best time to visit
You will find plenty of wet weather if you come here between June and November, with most of the rain falling in the three months at the end of that period when there is also a significant hurricane risk. The area was badly hit in 2008 by hurricanes which impacted seriously on farming and food supplies. Snow birds come in the winter months to the north-coast beaches but there can be rough seas bringing weed and debris from November to February if there is a cold front further north. Generally the driest time of year is between December and April. There are several cultural events in Ciego de Avila worth a look if you are in the area at the right time, including the International Book Fair in February/March, the Piña Colada Music Festival in April, the Carnival of Flowers in the second half of May and the market for Arte Popular in the second half of November.

Ciego de Avila

➜ *Colour map 2, B6. Population: 130,000.*

Ciego de Avila was founded in 1840 on the site of an hacienda granted to Alonso de Avila, one of Velázquez' commanders, and consequently is short of fine historical architecture and monuments although there are plenty of columns, portals and tiles to decorate the 19th-century buildings. It is an agricultural market town with a large thermal electricity plant. The main road from Havana to Camagüey and Santiago passes straight through the middle of town; most people just keep going. The Province of Ciego de Avila is most often visited for the beach resorts off its northern coast. The islands of Cayo Coco and Cayo Guillermo, which make up part of a 400-km coral reef, have excellent deep sea fishing, diving and snorkelling. Many new luxury hotels have opened for package tourism but they are very remote and isolated from the rest of Cuba. Scuba-divers also rate highly the cays off the south coast that make up the western half of the Jardines de la Reina archipelago. Dive packages must be organized in advance but the unspoilt underwater environment makes the effort well worthwhile. Elsewhere in the province, birdwatching in the countryside is good, with 234 species, of which 18 are endemic, game shooting is organized and there is some freshwater fishing. ▸▸ *For listings, see pages 271-278.*

Ins and outs

Getting there The airport 24 km north of Ciego de Avila was closed in 2009. The international airport on Cayo Coco is convenient if that is your destination, saving a long bus ride out to the cays. So far it is receiving scheduled international flights from Argentina, the UK and Canada, as well as domestic flights from Havana, and charter flights according to season and demand. The railway station is central and **trains** on the Havana to Santiago route stop here, but are unreliable and foreigners are often not allowed on. **Víazul buses** are more convenient, running from Havana to Santiago, Havana to Holguín, Varadero to Santiago and Trinidad to Santiago, several daily. However, if you break your journey here, make sure you have a reservation well in advance for the onward bus, as the long-distance buses are usually full when they go through town.

Getting around Much of the city can be seen **on foot**, or you can use a **bicitaxi** or **coche** for longer distances. For excursions out of the city, **car hire** is the most convenient, or you can hire a state or private **taxi** to take you around, or take a tour.

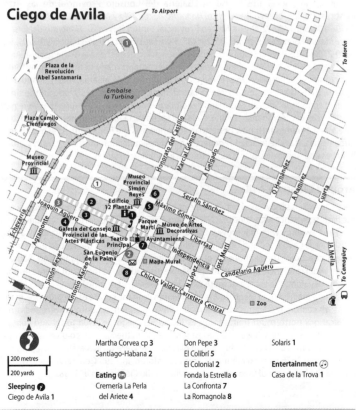

Ciego de Avila

200 metres

200 yards

Sleeping 🛏️
Ciego de Avila 1

Martha Corvea cp 3
Santiago-Habana 2

Eating 🍽️
Cremería La Perla
del Ariete 4

Don Pepe 3
El Colibrí 5
El Colonial 2
Fonda la Estrella 6
La Confronta 7
La Romagnola 8

Solaris 1

Entertainment 🎭
Casa de la Trova 1

Tourist information The hotels have *burós de turismo* which can give information, although their main purpose is to sell tours. These can be convenient if you do not have a car. **Infotur** has an office in the international airport in Cayo Coco and another in Ciego de Avila beneath the Edificio de 12 plantas, Honorato del Castillo esq Libertad, T33-309109, www.infotur.cu. Maps and phone cards are for sale while information and leaflets are free.

Sights

The main square is the **Parque Martí**, with a statue of José Martí dating from 1925 in the centre. On the south side are the church, **Iglesia de San Eugenio de la Palma**, patron saint of the city, and the former town hall, **Ayuntamiento**, built in 1911, and now the municipal government headquarters. The **Teatro Principal** ① *Joaquín Agüero y Honorato del Castillo, T33-222086*, built in 1927, is considered one of the best in the island for its acoustics and is an interesting eclectic style. Also on Parque Martí is the **Museo de Artes Decorativas** ① *T33-201661, Sun-Tue 0800-1600, Wed-Sat 0800-2100, CUC$1.* Dating from 1930, when it was opened as the Liceo society, it now showcases Cuban and foreign furniture, china, porcelain, silver, marble and ivory from the 19th and 20th centuries. For an insight into local artists, visit the **Galería del Consejo Provincial de las Artes Plásticas** ① *Calle Independencia entre Honorato del Castillo y Maceo, T33-223900, Sun-Fri 0830-2100, Sat 1400-2200.* The **Museo Provincial Simón Reyes** ① *Honorato del Castillo entre Máximo Gómez y Libertad, T33-204488, Mon-Tue 0900-1700, Wed-Sat 0830-2200, Sun 0830-2100, CUC$1,* is in a restored building that was formerly the seat of the Spanish Army Command during the War of Independence and contains many items of local historical significance. At the place where the city was founded, Marcial Gómez y Joaquín de Agüero, there is a 19th century **Mapa Mural**, depicting the first 25 blocks of the rising town. It shows the Spanish command headquarters and some of the forts that were part of the Júcaro to Morón military line. Calle Independencia, from Honorato del Castillo to José María Agramonte, is now pedestrian and known as the Boulevard. As in many other Cuban cities, it is the focus of regeneration and beautification in the city, with statues, benches and decorative plants along the busy commercial street.

Around Ciego de Avila

Ciego de Avila is sandwiched between the provinces of Sancti Spíritus and Camagüey. It is the flattest province with none of its land rising above 50 m. The northern coastline is low lying and swampy with mangroves. Offshore, but connected to the mainland by a long causeway, is Cayo Coco and other cays where tourism has been developed and several large hotels built. The central part of the province is used for cattle ranching. Sugar is grown widely and there are citrus and pineapple plantations. To the south, there are more mangroves along the coast and more cays with a wealth of marine life.

The two main cities of Ciego de Avila and Morón lie in the centre of the province. In the late 19th century the Spanish built a road, railway line, fence, sentry towers and other fortifications north-south from Morón to Júcaro via Ciego de Avila to try and contain independence fighters. It was the largest fortification in the Spanish colonies in the 19th century and the ruins can still be seen in places. They were unsuccessful in keeping out the rebels: in 1876 General Manuel Suárez took Morón, in 1895 General Antonio Maceo crossed the line north of Ciego de Avila, as did Camilo Cienfuegos in 1958.

Morón → *Colour map 2, B6. Population: 60,000.*

Morón was founded in 1750 and is about 36 km northeast of Ciego de Avila. The nearest urban centre to the Jardines del Rey, some people stay here as a less expensive alternative to the mega hotels on the cays. It is promoted as the Ciudad del Gallo (Cockerel City) with a monument to the bird by sculptor Rita Longa which is a replica of the rooster at Morón de la Frontera in Spain. There is a **Museo de Arqueología e Historia** ① *Calle Martí 374, T33-504501, Mon-Tue 0800-1600, Wed-Sat 0800-2100, CUC$1,* showcasing Indo Cuban and Meso-American archaeology as well as the archaeology and history of the city, with a good panoramic view. The railway station is also considered architecturally important. Built in 1923 in an eclectic style with a neo-classical influence, resembling many buildings of the first years of the Republic.

Apart from visitors passing through here on their way to Cayo Coco, the main visitors to this area are here for the **shooting** for game birds and waterfowl and **fishing**.

About 3 km north of Morón to the west of the road is the **Laguna de la Leche** (Milk Lake), Cuba's largest natural lake at 68.2 sq km and part of a system of lakes, marshes and low-lying wetlands. It is so called because of its cloudy white appearance, caused by lime deposits under the water. Its salinity makes it very popular with several thousand flamingos. It is the location for the **Aquatic Carnival** of Morón held in August or September.

About 11 km from Morón, beside the road and before the Isla de Turiguanó, is **Laguna La Redonda**. It covers an area of 26 sq km, with four main canals and a channel network, with an average depth of 1 m. Red mangroves grow in abundance and you may see the *tocororo*, the national bird. The northern wetlands which include Laguna de la Leche and Laguna La Redonda are the ideal habitat for a number of endemic and migratory birds and birdwatching is excellent for the range and quantity of species. At the lake you can arrange fishing trips and hire rods, boats and guides (T33-302489, guided 45-minute motorboat tour to see the fauna and flora, CUC$4 per person, minimum four passengers). Fishing (principally for catfish) is available all year, there is no closed season. There is a restaurant/bar where you can sit and watch the water if you don't want to fish. At the **Isla de Turiguanó** you can visit the International Centre for Quarter Horses, often included on tours of the area, contact **Gaviota Tours**, T33-302260, or **Ecotur**, T33-308163. Horse riding is possible.

About 40 km west of Morón, where the land becomes more hilly and picturesque, is **Florencia**. This is a place where organized excursion parties come from the cays to sample Cuban country life. Horse riding is available in the hills, you can swim in the mineral waters of a river pool, have a lunch of suckling pig on the banks of the river and watch a rodeo. Independent travellers may not get the rodeo, but if a visit is timed not to coincide with a tour party, they could benefit from all the other activities in peaceful surroundings.

Cayo Coco → *Colour map 2, B6.*

Cayo Coco is the largest cay in the Jardines del Rey archipelago which was named by Diego de Velázquez in honour of the king of Spain. The cays were isolated and visited only by fishermen until the white sand beaches and turquoise water attracted the attention of the tourist industry and a causeway was built in 1988 allowing access by land. Since then, Cayo Coco has become a focal point in the government's 'ecotourism' interests, although the hotels are large, luxury resorts built and operated with foreign investment. It is very remote and nearly all foreigners are here on a package of a week or so. Cayo Coco is 374 sq km, of mostly mangrove and bush, which shelter many migratory birds as well as permanent residents. There are some 150 species of bird, of which some are considered endemic. Cayo Coco gets its name from a bird, the Coco Blanco, or white ibis, standing less than 50 cm tall, which lives in remote areas of Cayo Coco and Cayo Romano.

The first hotels on Cayo Coco are 62 km from Morón. The island is connected to the mainland just north of Morón by a 27 km causeway cross the Bahía de Perros, which continues to connect Cayo Guillermo and Cayo Paredón Grande. Drivers must stop at the checkpoint, show passports and pay a CUC$2 one-way toll. At the rotonda on Cayo Coco there is a gas station, shop and fast food bar. Contact tour operators, see Activities and tours, page 275, to arrange excursions.

The Atlantic side of the island has 22 km of excellent beaches, particularly **Playa Los Flamencos** (15 minutes' drive from hotels), with some 5 km of white sand and shallow, crystalline water. Year round it is possible to see Roseate flamingos (Phoenicopterus ruber ruber), after whom the beach is named. Flamingos nearly died out here in the 1970s but, with some encouragement, have increased to some 30,000 birds in the cays. There's a beach bar and grill. This lovely spot won't remain quiet for long: Gaviota are to build three hotels here. The beaches are quite difficult to get to and some of the hotels restrict access to guests only.

Anyone looking for solitude can explore **Playa Prohibida**, appropriately named as the government has banned construction here in the interests of ecology. A nature trail starts from near here leading into the centre of Cayo Coco, ending at the dune, Loma del Puerto, the highest point in the area. **El Bagá nature park** ① *T33-301062 ext 103, baga_director@ fica.inf.cu*, is a recently protected 70-ha area designed to preserve the wildlife as well as make it accessible to visitors. It is named after a local tree, the roots of which are used for floats in fishing nets. You can take a guided tour through the forest along trails or a boat trip through the mangroves and canals, good for birdwatching. **Sitio La Güira** ① *performing animal show at 1000 and 1500 Mon-Sat, children's circus show 0900-1300 Thu, horse riding, campesino fiestas*, is an attractive purpose-built ranch in the middle of the cay where there used to be a charcoal maker at the beginning of the 20th century. Güira is the local name for calabash, and there are many calabash trees growing here, the fruit of which are used to make maracas. There are cabins, *bohíos*, where you can stay. **El Parador de la Silla**, near the entrance by road to Cayo Coco, is a rustic mirador from where you can see water birds, flamingos and the local topography.

Cayo Guillermo

Cayo Guillermo, a 13-sq-km cay with 5 km of beach, is connected to Cayo Coco by a causeway. Cayo Guillermo is protected by a long coral reef which is good for diving with plentiful fish and crustaceans, while on land there are lots of birds. Sand dunes, covered in palms and other vegetation, are believed to be among the highest in the Caribbean. **Playa Pilar** at the far western tip is spectacular and one of the best beaches in Cuba. Resorts on Cayo Coco arrange day trips for CUC$5. The environment is protected by the **Santa María National Park**. Ernest Hemingway came here to fish, which is why there are frequent references to him. Fishing is still superb around here and if you tire of deep sea fishing you can make an excursion to one of the freshwater lakes mentioned above. Across a narrow channel to the north of Cayo Guillermo is **Cayo Media Luna**, a small islet with excellent snorkelling on the reef offshore, where you can see a wide variety of fish and coral as well as a few wrecks. The dictator Fulgencio Batista had his holiday home here.

Jardines de la Reina

The Jardines de la Reina is an archipelago of 3000 sq km of cays and mangroves, running along the south coasts of the provinces of Ciego de Avila, Camagüey and Las Tunas. Unapproachable for years as they were Fidel Castro's favourite fishing spot, these islands have now been declared a natural park. There are birds, iguanas, turtles and loads of fish (and mosquitoes, bring insect repellent). The archipelago is uninhabited and generally visited only by liveaboard dive boats and fly fishermen. There are about 40 dive sites along the southwest side of the archipelago. The reef runs parallel to the shore and usually drops down in three 'steps': the first at 10-15 m, very exposed to the surf; a second at 20 m on a sandy bottom, and a third that starts at 40-45 m and drops downward. You will find all the reef fishes here including tarpons. The sea is often rough. Access is usually from **Júcaro** on the coast. Dive boats leave from here and Marlin has the largest fly-fishing fleet in the country here. Fishing and diving is promoted among these virgin cays with empty beaches by **Avalon**, which also runs a floating hotel. **Cayo Caguama** is just off the south coast of the province of Camagüey. There is a beach where turtles nest and iguanas run around under the trees but tours are no longer offered.

◉ Ciego de Avila listings

For Sleeping and Eating price codes and other relevant information, see Essentials pages 37-43.

◉ Sleeping

Ciego de Avila p266, map p267
Hotels

C Ciego de Avila , Carretera de Ceballos, about 2 km outside Ciego de Avila, T33-228013, www.islazul.cu. 143 standard, functional rooms in a modern, 5-storey block, large pool, taxis, car hire, good food, shooting arranged with guide and dog.

C-D Santiago-Habana, Honorato del Castillo entre Joaquín Agüero y Chicho Valdés, T33-225703. www.islazul.cu. 76 rooms on the main road through town, under renovation in 2009 but still open, convenient, car hire.

Casas particulares

D-E Dr A de Armas, Independencia 317 entre 1 y 2, Reparto Vista Alegre, T33-228451. A superb 1950s house with lovely period accents owned by a doctor. Modern room at the back of the house of a big patio.

D-E Iris Marrero Cano, Cuba 265 entre 5 y Soto, T33-225571, bellkiss265@yahoo.es. A 1966 yellow and chocolate brown home with a spacious double room and plenty of facilities. Guests have use of a kitchen. Parking.

D-E Martha Corvea, José M Agramonte 19 entre Joaquín Agüero e Independencia, T33-201327, T015-294 6041 (mob). Martha is friendly and has a lovely house close to the town centre with a rooftop terrace and 2 comfortable en suite rooms.

D-E Omar Valdés, Soto 212 entre Cuba y Ciego de Avila, Reparto Díaz Pardo, T33- 225417. This casa with a small fully equipped room with a dining room and kitchenette attached has a small swimming pool too.

Morón p269
Hotels

Many people stay in Morón because it is a cheaper option than staying on the cays at the big hotels.

C Morón, off Av de Tarafa, T33-502230, www.islazul.cu. 3-star, concrete block type of hotel, 144 rooms and suites with balcony but only 1 block in operation in 2009, restaurant, coffee shop, bars, disco, large pool, games room, good a/c and food, tourism bureau, medical service, car hire, shop, shooting arranged with guide and dog.

D La Casona de Morón, Cristóbal Colón 41, T33-502236. A very attractive, yellow colonial building in the town centre, remodelled in 2009 as a boutique hotel, restaurant and bar stayed open throughout building works, operated by Palmares.

Casas particulares

There are currently about 70 *casas particulares* in Morón for you to choose from. Breakfast usually costs CUC$3-5 and evening meal CUC$6-10.

D-E Alcides Pérez Torres, Calle 11 edif 9 Apto 23, entre 10 y 4 (micro sur), T33-504552. Tiny apartment (hard to find) with comfortable room and bathroom opposite. Separate room for study/eating with pull-down table. Miniscule terrace (with a parrot) overlooks the street. English, Italian, Portuguese and German understood.

D-E Casa Xiomara, Calle 8 2C, entre Sordo y C, T33-504236, ysary@moron.cav.sld.cu. This super-friendly and kind family offer 1 room in an independent *casita* with small kitchen and bathroom in the back patio surrounded by gigantic hibiscus flowers. Food is served on the back terrace. A lovely place to stay. Nothing is too much trouble. Xiomara Machado Moreno's daughter, Lisbeth, speaks English and can offer a lot of advice.

D-E Hostal Lalita, Av Tarafa 174, esq 7, T33-503523. A lovely casa right on the main road run by a friendly family. The ample bedroom is upstairs with large terrace overlooking the street, large bathroom, huge sitting room, kitchen and dining area. There's also a sun terrace surrounded by bougainvillea.

D-E Juan Clemente Pérez, Castillo 189 entre Serafín Sánchez y San José, T33503823. Nice family, helpful and friendly, 2 rooms, a/c, private bathroom, simple but clean, hot water available, Spanish only.

D-E Maite Valor Morales, Luz Caballero 40B entre Libertad y Agramonte, T33-504181, maite69@enet.cu. Large house with a rooftop terrace, 1 large apartment with 2 beds, and a small kitchenette; the other bedroom is smaller and the bathroom is next door. Large dining room in the converted garage. Parking for 4 cars, garage CUC$2. Maite and her partner offer superb and abundant food and often cater for tour parties. English and Italian are spoken. Very professional business.

D-E Onaida Ruiz Fumero, Calle 5 46 entre 6 y 8, T33-503409. Not far from city centre with own private parking. Attractive, small yellow bungalow framed by huge frangipani. 2 rooms, 1 next to terrace.

Cayo Coco p269

All the hotels on Cayo Coco and Cayo Guillermo are all-inclusive. Some of them are huge. At the end of 2008 there were 4247 hotel rooms available. All offer several restaurants, entertainment and watersports. The rate will vary depending on how long you are staying and the time of year. Although most people who stay here are booked on packages from abroad, independent travellers can book their own stays at short notice once they are in the country. In high season there is limited availability for rooms of less than a week's rental, but out of season rooms are filled on a daily basis. There are lots of 2- to 3-day packages or weekend breaks offered from Havana. A day pass is available from all the hotels, allowing you use of all the facilities, meals and drinks, usually around CUC$40, depending on the hotel and how late you are allowed to stay.

Hotels

LL-L Hotel Meliá Cayo Coco, Playa Las Coloradas, T33-301180, www.solmelia cuba.com. Attractive resort on lovely beach with wonderful tropical setting and beautiful rooms. Many in bungalows around a natural lagoon. Huge swimming pool with hydromassage, great restaurant. Guests can use the dance club and other facilities at the Sol Meliá hotel next door.

L-AL NH Krystal Laguna Villas & Resort, T33-301470, www.nh-hotels.com. This vast resort complex is a metropolis, with 3 amphitheatres, landscaped grounds and a variety of restaurants and bars. Most rooms in unattractive blocks but there are more exclusive rooms in wooden villas built over the lagoon. The complex is a 5-min walk from the sands. Shame about the 6 captive flamingos in reception.

L Sol Cayo Coco, T33-301280, www.solmelia cuba.com. The only hotel in the area with access to 2 beaches: Playa Las Coloradas and Playa Larga; a rocky outcrop divides the two. Good for familes with a great kids' programme, club, minigolf, soccer field, a kids' corner restaurant and 2 pools with children's sections. Plenty of family entertainment, alongside sailing, canoeing, water bikes, windsurfing, snorkeling and water polo.

AL BlueBay Cayo Coco, T33-302350, www.bluebayresorts.com. New at end-2008, so vegetation is still growing. Stunning beach (Playa La Jaula) with wooden beach bar and *palapas*. 328 rooms and studios in dull, square buildings dominated by an uninviting boxy mirador. Only 60 rooms have a beach view, the rest face the gardens, pool or laguna. Some rooms have outdoor showers. It has several restaurants and a swim-up pool bar. Fenced-off baby pool and play room for children.

C Villa Jardín Los Cocos, Ensenada Bautista, T33-308121/31, www.islazul.cu. This small resort is in a strange place beyond the line-up of hotels and surrounded by the workers' village. You'll need your own transport. There are 21 rooms (only 5 with a/c) in bungalows around the grounds. Rooms are spacious but spartan and dated; they come with TV, fridge and large old-fashioned bathrooms.

C-D Villazul, T33-301278/9, www.islazul.cu. Just 10 rooms in the cream, green and brown blocks of this hotel are available to foreigners. There's a restaurant and café on site. Staff are lifeless and the whole place feels abandoned. It's set in vegetation way back from the beaches so you'll need your own transport.

D-E Sitio La Güira, T33-301208. 4 *cabañas* and 2 rooms sit in this delightful, peaceful rustic setting worlds apart from the resorts. The *cabañas* are newly refurbished and come with a small private bathroom and a/c. The 2 cheaper rooms in a classic bohío are more rustic with fans and share a bathroom and a central dining area. Restaurant on site (open 0800-2300). Best to reserve in advance. You'll need your own transport to get to the beach.

Cayo Guillermo *p270*
LL-L Iberostar Daiquirí, T33-301650, www.iberostar.com. A handsome, large resort set amid palms and very attractively landscaped grounds. Rooms are in standard blocks around a large pool with a more intimate feel than the next door Meliá Cayo Guillermo. Great for families with a children's programme.

LL-L Meliá Cayo Guillermo, T33-301680, www.solmeliacuba.com. A large and fairly luxurious complex with a beach lined with palms and a picturesque wooden pier that stretches out into the sea. (This was damaged by the 2008 hurricanes and in mid 2009 had yet to be fully restored.) There are extensive facilities and most people's interests are catered for. Rooms are spacious and decorated in a nautical theme.

LL-AL Sol Cayo Guillermo T33-301760, www.solmeliacuba.com. A more laid-back low-key resort with rooms in bungalows or blocks. Most accommodation is decorated in sea blue; the best rooms are in the individual bungalows set near the beach. There is a whole range of activities and a children's pool, popular with families.

AL-A Villa Cojímar, T33-301712, www.gran-caribe.com. Multi-coloured bungalows with standard rooms are set in a quiet beachfront location at the eastern end of Cayo Guillermo. It's low key and a reasonable budget option. Restaurants, bars and watersports are offered but it does not compare with the larger, better-equipped resorts on Cayo Guillermo.

🍴 Eating

Ciego de Avila *p266, map p267*
🍴 **Cremería La Perla del Ariete**, Joaquín de Agüero y Simón Reyes. Open daily 1200-2400. 8 flavours of ice cream, also pastries and sodas, electronic games.

🍴 **Don Pepe**, Independencia 103 entre Simón Reyes y Maceo, T33-223713. Cuban food, pesos cubanos, open for lunch and dinner until there are no customers.

El Colibrí, Honorato del Castillo y Máximo Gómez, T33-266219. Daily 1100-2100. Recorded music and videos to accompany your meal costing about CUC$2.50-3.80. Starters of fruit juice, ham and cheese, main courses of *comida criolla* such as fried chicken, pork steak, beef, shrimp, spaghetti, served with rice, salad and chips. Also live music venue, see below.

El Colonial, Independencia 110, entre Simón Reyes y Maceo, T33-233595. Open for lunch and dinner. Nice courtyard but Spanish food nothing to write home about, pesos cubanos.

Fonda la Estrella, Máximo Gómez esq Honorato Castillo, T33-266186. Open daily 1200-2400. Wooden chairs and tables afford street views at this small restaurant in a colonial building. Bargain *menú del día* or the house dish of *ropa vieja*. Prices from CUC$1.50.

La Confronta, Marcial Gómez entre Independencia y Joaquín de Agüero, T33-200931. Open for lunch and dinner. Cuban food, pork served in a variety of ways with all the traditional trimmings. A 2-course meal can cost up to 40 pesos cubanos.

La Romagnola, Carretera Central entre M Gómez y Honorato del Castillo, T33-225989. Lunch and dinner, Italian, pesos cubanos.

Solaris, Honorato del Castillo entre Independencia y Libertad on the west side of Parque Martí, top floor of 12-storey building, T33-222156. Tue-Sun 1200-1500 for lunch, 1800-2200 for dinner. Bar serving drinks, cocktails and Cuban food charged in pesos cubanos. Live piano music and an excellent view of the city.

Morón *p269*

La Atarraya, outside town in the middle of Laguna de la Leche, T33-505351. Dishes are based on seafood and fish, the restaurant operates in pesos cubanos, but some items can only be paid for in CUC$.

La Fuente, Martí 169 entre Libertad y Agramonte, T33-5505758, 1000-2400. Cuban food. 2-course meals with fried chicken or pork, with rice, chips, dessert and coffee for around CUC$2, but you can

order more expensive dishes such as fish for CUC$10 or mixed seafood, which will include lobster and shrimp, for CUC$13.

Parrillada La Cueva, Laguna de la Leche, T33-502239. Tue-Sun 1000-1745. Prices vary from CUC$2 for fried chicken to CUC$7 for seafood and fish, all accompanied by rice, salad and fried vegetables. Light meals and other typically Cuban dishes available.

Rancho Palma, Carretera a Bolivia, 3 km north of Morón. Rural setting surrounded by vegetation, house speciality is a whole roast pig (hog roast), although there are cheaper options for around CUC$5, such as pork casserole with rice, chips and salad.

Cafetería El Jardín de Apolo, Martí entre Sergio Antuña y Enrique José Varona, open 24 hrs. Light food and drinks.

Paraíso Palmeras, Martí 382, T33-502030, 1200-1400, 1900-2100. A la carte restaurant serving international food, house speciality paella Valenciana for CUC$3.60. Other paellas and rice dishes are cheaper and there are also meat dishes on the menu.

Cayo Coco *p269*

Ranchón Las Dunas, Playa Academia, just north of the rotunda. Open1100-2300. Run by Islazul Motel Jardín Los Cocos. Seafood served under a thatched roof.

Ranchón Playa Flamenco, Playa Los Flamencos. Open 0900-1600, food served 1200-1500. Attractive beach bar and grill run by friendly staff in lovely isolated spot, for the time being. A full lobster meal will cost you around CUC$15. There are other, similar, Ranchón offering the same sort of things.

Cayo Guillermo *p270*

Ranchón Cuba Libre, between Iberostar Daiquirí and Meliá Cayo Guillermo hotels, T33-301522. Open 0830-1830. Restaurant and bar with international food and drinks.

Ranchón Media Luna on a little cay off Playa Pilar, reached by boat. Bar and grill, seafood, drinks and natural juices.

Ranchón Playa Pilar, Playa Pilar. Thatched beach hut overlooking idyllic sands.

🎵 Bars

Ciego de Avila *p266, map p267*
El Patio del Mulato Acelerao,
Independencia entre Simón Reyes y José M
Agramonte, T33-227786. Open weekdays
0900-2000 and weekends until 2400. Bar
with recorded music, drinks, sodas, sweets.

🎭 Entertainment

Ciego de Avila *p266, map p267*
Music and dance
Batanga, Hotel Ciego de Avila, T33-228013.
Hotel disco, open Wed-Mon 2200-0200, Sun
1600-2100. Admission CUC$5 per couple
including drinks of CUC$3, or CUC$3.50 per
person including drinks of CUC$2.50.
Casa de la Trova, Libertad 130 y Simón
Reyes, T33-222107. Fri-Sun open until 2100.
Traditional and folklore live music.
El Colibrí, Honorato del Castillo y Máximo
Gómez, T33-266219. 2200-0200. Cuba
Ritmos show, dancers, singers, comedy and
cabaret. Admission per couple Mon-Thu
CUC$3 including drinks of CUC$2, Fri,
Sat CUC$5 (consumo CUC$4), Sun CUC$7
(consumo CUC$5).
El Patio de Artex, Libertad entre Honorato
del Castillo y Maceo, T33-266680. Open daily
1000-0200. Shows, boleros, singing, comedy,
circus, dancing, a wide range of artistic and
cultural events, lively, entertaining, attractive
and very Cuban atmosphere. Admission
varies according to the event. Cafetería serves
light food, snacks, fries and drinks.
La Cima, Hotel Santiago-Habana,
T33-225703. Open daily except Tue.

Morón *p269*
Casa de la Trova (El Patio del Gallo), Calle
Libertad entre Martí y Narciso López, T33-
504602. Open Mon-Sat 2200-2400, Sun 1800-
0100. Traditional music with local trova singers.
Admission varies according to the event. Also
other singers, comedians, bands and shows.

Disco en La Casona, Hotel La Casona.
Outdoors, shows, dancing, salsa under the
stars, lots of people, popular. Renovated 2009.
Discoteca, Hotel Morón, T33-503901. Open
daily 2200-0200. Nightclub with Cuban and
Latin music. Admission per couple CUC$5
(consumo CUC$3), or per person CUC$3.50
(consumo CUC$2.50). Sat *Noche Moronera*
with music and *parrillada* 2100, advance
reservations required.
El Patio de Artex, Libertad esq Narciso
López. Open-air entertainment, boleros,
comedians, dancing, national and local artists.

Cayo Coco *p269*
All the hotels offer nighttime activities, night
clubs, discos, piano bars, etc.
Cueva Jabalí, 6 km from Tryp Cayo Coco
hotel, T33-301206. Daily 2300-0200. A cave
with several interconnecting rooms where
shows and discos are held. Usually CUC$15
admission with open bar.

🎉 Festivals and events

Morón *p269*
Mar Feria Internacional del Libro, with book
sales, lectures and seminars.
Jun There is a Festival Internacional del
Bolero in the 1st 2 weeks of the month, usually
dedicated to a single singer and his works.
Sep Carnaval is an aquatic festival held on
the Laguna de la Leche, where some 14 floats
from all over the country compete.

🏔 Activities and tours

Ciego de Avila *p266, map p267*
Diving
Diving is rewarding in the Jardines del Rey,
with 32 km of coral reef made up of pillars,
walls and sandy channels, including 28 dive
sites of between 4-30 m where you can see
coral gardens, invertebrates, lots of fish,
turtles, dolphins, sharks and other large
pelagics. The 3 dive centres on Cayo Coco

and Cayo Guillermo are run by Marlin Náutica y Marinas, www.nauticamarlin.com. 1 dive costs CUC$40, dive packages available which are cheaper per dive, CUC$450 for 20 dives. An Open Water course costs CUC$310 and a Resort course CUC$70.

Avalón off the south coast at Júcaro, Jardines de la Reina, www.divingincuba.com, www.avalonfishingcenter.com. Liveaboard boats, complete packages for several days of dedicated diving or fishing. This is the only operation in the area, where there is also a small floating hotel, **Hotel Tortuga**, for divers and fishermen.

Blue Diving, Hotel Meliá Cayo Coco, T33-308179, bluediving@marlin.cco.tur.cu.

Coco Diving, Tryp Cayo Coco, T33-301020, cocodiving@marlin.cco.tur.cu. Equipment rental for diving and snorkelling. Resort courses and open water certification with CMAS, ACUC, SSI. Capacity for 32 divers a day on the boats.

Green Moray, at Meliá Cayo Guillermo, T33-301627, greenmoray@marlin.cco.tur.cu.

Fishing and shooting

Hotels can organize fresh-water fishing trips to Laguna La Redonda, Morón, where you can hire rods, boats and guides. Non-fishing visitors can hire *lanchas*. Fishing is available all year, there is no closed season. Fresh-water fishing is not as good as it used to be, due to the disappearance of the trout and their replacement by catfish. Deep-sea fishing offshore can be arranged at the marinas on Cayo Coco and Cayo Guillermo (see below) and costs around CUC$290 per boat (up to 4 people) for a half day (4 hrs) or CUC$450 for a full day (7 hrs) including lunch and open bar. Inshore fishing for fish such as mackerel and snapper to the east of Cayo Paredón Grande costs CUC$129 per boat for 2 passengers for 4 hrs and CUC$179 for 7 hrs. The shooting season for pigeon is 15 Jul-1 Sep; for duck 15 Oct-31 Mar.

Ecotur, Cayo Coco, T33-308163, www.ecoturcuba.co.cu, organizes fresh water fishing and shooting for game birds and waterfowl at Presa de Chambas and other lakes close by, as well as sea fishing.

Pagurex, ugartesc@yahoo.es, offers shooting packages including accommodation in Morón and Ciego de Avila, shooting permits and transfers. Rifle hire is CUC$15 per day, ammunition is CUC$15 for a box of 25 imported cartridges or CUC$10 for Cuban cartridges. You can bring your own equipment with prior permission.

Marinas

Marina Aguas Tranquilas, Cayo Coco, www.nauticamarlin.com, VHF 16 and 72, commissary, minor repairs, fuel, water, boat rental, fishing, dive centre.

Marina Internacional Cayo Guillermo, Faro Paredón Grande, Cayo Guillermo, T33-301411, www.nauticamarlin.com, VHF 16, 19. 6 berths, 30 m draft, fuel, water, electricity, commissary, restaurant, bar, boat rental, fishing, diving, snorkelling, excursions.

Sailing

Catamaran tours to Playa Pilar, the coral reef with snorkelling, lobster lunch and open bar cost CUC$75 for adults and CUC$38 for children under 12 for a full day or CUC$43 and CUC$22 for a half day; a 4-hr sail to Cayo Baliza on the route followed by Hemingway which he described in *Islands in the Stream*, costs CUC$29 for adults and CUC$14.50 for children with lunch, open bar and snorkelling. Private charters for up to 6 people with crew, fishing tackle, snorkelling equipment, open bar and lunch cost CUC$290 for a half day and CUC$480 for a full day (7 hrs). A trip to Cayo Paredón Grande with a visit to the Diego Velásquez lighthouse, Playa Los Pinos and a beach bar, followed by a boat trip around the cay is CUC$25pp, children half price. You can also go by boat on a 3-hr birdwatching trip to see the flamingos, CUC$29 adults, CUC$22 children. There are several other options, including sunset cocktail trips with live music.

Spa

Centro Spa-Talaso Acuavida, Av de los Hoteles, T33-302157, www.servimed cuba.com. At the eastern end of the hotel strip on Cayo Coco, this new spa offers mud therapy, massages and hydro treatments.

Tour operators

Excursions (including lunch at a hotel) from Ciego de Avila or Morón to the cays are available from state tour operators for foreigners and Cubans but do not include transport. You can hire a state or private taxi to take you there. It will cost you CUC$45-60 from Morón and CUC$60-75 from Ciego de Avila which, if hiring a private taxi, will in effect cover the driver's lunch package. Cubans can only visit the resorts if they pre-book a tourist lunch voucher with a tour operator.

Cubanacán, T33-301215/6 in Ciego de Avila; T33-504720 in Hotel Morón; Hotel Tryp Cayo Coco, T33-301215, combinado@viajes.cav.cyt.cu.

Cubatur, T33-301436/301029 in Ciego de Avila with a bureau in Kikere ice cream parlour on Parque Martí in Morón, T33-505519; Cayo Coco. T33-301436, cleon@cubatur.cu.

Ecotur, Parque El Baga Cayo Coco, T33-301062/308163, www.ecoturcuba.co.cu. They organize jeep or scooter tours of Cayo Coco and Cayo Paredón, visiting the lighthouse, Playa Prohibida, the sand dunes, Parque El Bagá, crocodiles, iguanas, turtles and horseriding, CUC$39 adults, CUC$20 children by jeep, CUC$29 adults, CUC$15 children by scooter, minimum 2 people with guide.

Gaviota Tours, Hotel Playa Coco, T33-302259, gaviotatourscc@playacoco.co.cu.

Havanatur, T33-308235/301371 in Ciego de Avila; Hotel Sol Cayo Coco, T33-266342, vgomez@cimex.com.cu.

Ciego de Avila *p266, map p267*
Air

The Jardines del Rey international airport is on **Cayo Coco**, T33-309161-5. Cayo Coco airport receives **AeroCaribbean** flights from **Havana** as well as international flights from Canada, the UK and Argentina. In 2009 the international airlines landing here were **Cubana, Sunwing, Thomas Cook, Airtransat, Canjet** and **Air Canada**. The terminal has banking services, tourist information and shops selling handicrafts, cigars and rum.

Airlines Cubana, Carretera Central 83 entre Maceo y Honorato Castillo, Ciego de Avila, T33-201117. AeroCaribbean at Cayo Coco airport, T33-309106, cocodr@enet.cu. Aero Club Palmares offers microlight flights from Cayo Coco hotels, CUC$30, 10 mins. Tandem parachute jumps taking off from the airport and landing on the beach are available for CUC$120 per person. Tandem paragliding from a boat and landing on the beach is CUC$40.

Bus

The Ciego de Avila bus station is on the Carretera Central just east of the zoo. Víazul, T33-225109, stops here on its **Havana–Santiago** route. Víazul, to **Havana, Trinidad, Varadero, Holguín and Santiago**. For timetable and prices see page 32. Only tour buses go to **Cayo Coco**, there are no public buses.

Morón bus terminal is at Martí entre Poi y Céspedes, but Víazul does not come here.

Car hire

Cubacar, in Ciego de Avila: Hotel Ciego de Avila, T33-200102; Hotel Santiago Habana, T33-266169; Libertad s/n entre Honorato del Castillo y Maceo, T33-212570; Candelario Agüero entre Arnaldo Ramírez y Onelio Hernández, T33-207133; Terminal de Omnibus, Carretera Central Este, T33-225105. In Morón: Hotel Morón, T33-502028; Cristóbal Colón 32, T33-502020; Parque Echeverría, Serfio Antuña s/n, T33-502152. On the cays in most of the hotels. Rent a Car Vía, T33-222050. Rex, at Hotel Sol Cayo Coco, T33-302244; Hotel Ciego de Avila, T33-228013, specializing in the luxury end of the market. Mopeds can be hired on the cayos at most of the hotels for CUC$15 per hr or CUC$40 for 24 hrs.

Petrol stations At Carretera de Morón, Circunvalación Km 2.5, Ciego de Avila; at Carretera Central e Independencia Km 444, Ciego de Avila; Crucero Campo Hatuey, Majagua (Carretera Central); at Carretera de Bolivia, Vía Cayo Coco, Morón; and at the roundabout at Cayo Coco.

Taxi
Cubataxi, Reparto Ortiz, Ciego de Avila, T33-266666, central office on Cayo Coco, T33-308202, reservations T33-302222; Av Tarafa, Morón, T33-503290. A taxi from the airport on Cayo Coco to Cayo Coco hotels is CUC$10-15; from the airport to Cayo Guillermo, CUC$15-25. *Bicitaxis* in Ciego de Avila charge in pesos cubanos, making them a very cheap form of local transport for foreigners. A taxi from Ciego de Avila to Morón is CUC$10.

Train
Daily train to **Ciego de Avila** to and from **Havana** and **Santiago**. In theory it arrives from Havana at 1230 and from Santiago at 0440 but is technically reserved for Cubans. **Morón** is on the **Santa Clara–Nuevitas** railway line; the train runs one day to Santa Clara and the next day to Nuevitas, uncomfortable but if you can get on you pay in pesos cubanos. You can also get to **Camagüey** by train daily from Morón, paying in pesos cubanos.

❶ Directory

Ciego de Avila *p266, map p267*
Banks Banco Financiero Internacional, Honorato del Castillo, Ciego de Avila, T33-225274, Hotel Sol Cayo Coco, T33-301252 and Hotel Iberostar Daiquirí, Cayo Guillermo, T33-301607. **Cadeca**, Independencia 118, Ciego de Avila, T33-266009, 0900-1730; Honorato del Castillo e Independencia, Ciego de Avila, T33-266418; Calle Martí, Morón, T33-502246, as well as in the airport and in hotels on the cays. **Customs** Aduana at Cayo Coco, T33-309107. **Immigration** Independencia esq La Cruz Verde (store), Ciego de Avila, T33-223665, phones manned 24 hrs, tourist card extensions CUC$25. **Medical services** Clínica Internacional de Cayo Coco, next to Hotel Playa Coco, open 24 hrs, T33-302158, www.servimedcuba.com. Facilities for tourists also at the provincial hospitals in Ciego de Avila and in Morón, where there are rooms reserved for foreigners. **Post** At the corner of Chicho Valdés y Marcial Gómez. DHL and Cubapost, Carretera Central y Marcial Gómez, Ciego de Avila, T33-222096, for documents and packets, Mon-Fri 0800-1700, Sat 0800-1200, and at Calle 5 entre Carretera de Morón e Isabel, T33-223126, 0800-1800. In Morón, Calle Martí esq Serafín Sánchez. **Telephone** Etecsa, on Parque Martí, Ciego de Avila, in the 12-storey building, providing phone, fax and internet service. Telepunto, Joaquín de Agüero entre Honorato del Castillo y Maceo, Ciego de Avila, T33-207201, on Parque Martí, Morón and the cays also sells prepaid cards for internet access, CUC$6 per hr, and cards for national and international phone calls, open 0830-1930 daily.

Camagüey

Camagüey is the largest of Cuba's 14 provinces and is an excellent place to break your journey if you are crossing the island from one end to the other. The attractive countryside is flat and fertile, with cattle roaming the grasslands which are dotted with Royal palms. The colonial capital city of Camagüey is recommended for a stay of a few days, as there is much of historical importance and lots of sites of revolutionary interest from the 19th and 20th centuries. Significant restoration works are taking place in the old city, a UNESCO World Heritage Site, on churches, plazas and mansions. Culturally, Camagüey has lots to offer, with an excellent ballet company and lots of music and art. Camagüey has been politically and historically important since the beginning of the 16th century. Many generations of revolutionaries have been associated with Camagüey and several key figures are commemorated, the most notable being Ignacio Agramonte, who was killed in action in 1873. However, most tourists head instead for the north coast to Santa Lucía beach resort for sun, sea and sand. This is another of Cuba's remote hotel developments and it can be difficult to organize worthwhile excursions unless you have a car. ▶▶ *For listings, see pages 289-299.*

Ins and outs

Getting there All major routes pass through Camagüey province and as the city is squarely in the middle, it is well located as far as communications are concerned. The international **airport** is 9 km north of the city and you may be lucky enough to find a bus that will bring you into Parque Finlay, otherwise you will have to catch a taxi, state or private, CUC$5. Most tourists arriving at the airport are taken by bus straight to their resorts on the north coast, not into Camagüey. There are **flights** from Havana and international scheduled and charter flights, although these vary with the season. The **railway** station is just north of the centre, within walking distance of several hotels and *casas particulares*, and on the main line from Havana to Santiago. The **bus** station is further out, the other side of the river from the centre, with several daily buses from Havana and Santiago, as well as good connections with neighbouring towns. Taxi from here to the town centre, approximately CUC$5. ▶▶ *See also Transport, page 297.*

Getting around The active will be able to **walk** to most sites of interest in the city, otherwise you can pick up a **bicitaxi**. Note that many streets have two names, one an old colonial religious name and the other a replacement from the early 20th century. People use both (see map, page 280). Many provincial towns and Playa Santa Lucía can be reached by **bus**, but check your return journey before setting off. **Car hire** is available, or you can arrange for a Cuban to drive you in his car.

Tourist information All the main hotels have tourist agencies who can provide information, although their main aim is to sell tours. *Casas particulares* are usually better informed than agencies in Camagüey and often more helpful.

History

The capital of the province was originally called Puerto Príncipe, until 9 June 1903. The village of Santa María de Puerto del Príncipe was first founded in 1515 at Punta del Guincho in the Bahía de Nuevitas, but the site was unsatisfactory for development because of a lack of water and poor soil fertility. In 1516 the first settlers moved to Caonao (an Amerindian word for gold or place where gold can be found), an aborigine chiefdom

Camagüey

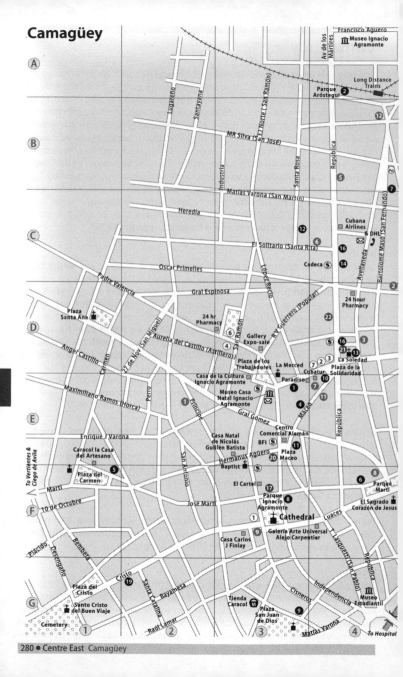

Francisco Aguero

Museo Ignacio Agramonte

Av de los Mártires

Long Distance Trains

Parque Aróstegui

MR Silva (San José)

Lugareño
Santayana
El Norte (San Ramón)
Industria
Heredia
Santa Rosa
República

Matías Varona (San Martín)

Cubana Airlines & DHL

El Solitario (Santa Rita)

Oscar Primelles

Cadeca

Padre Valencia

Gral Espinosa

Plaza Santa Ana

24 hr Pharmacy

24 hour Pharmacy

Aurelia del Castillo (Astilleros)

Gallery Expo-sale

Angel Castillo

Carmen

27 de Nov (San Miguel)

San Ramón

López Recio

RV Guerrero (Popular)

Bartolomé Masó (San Fernando)

Avellaneda

La Soledad

Plaza de los Trabajadores

La Merced

Paradiso

Cubatur

Plaza de la Solidaridad

Casa de la Cultura Ignacio Agramonte

Museo Casa Natal Ignacio Agramonte

Gral Gómez

Perro

Príncipe

Maximiliano Ramos (Horca)

Enrique J Varona

Centro Comercial Alemán

Maceo

Casa Natal de Nicolás Guillén Batista

BFI

Plaza Maceo

Caracol la Casa del Artesano

San Antonio

Hermanos Aguero

Baptist

República

To Vertientes & Ciego de Ávila

Plaza del Carmen

Martí

El Cartel

Parque Ignacio Agramonte

Parque Martí

El Sagrado Corazón de Jesus

10 de Octubre

José Martí

Cathedral

Luaces

Lasqueti (San Pablo)

Plácido
Bembeta
Tesangano
Cristo
Santa Lofalma
Bayamesa
Raúl Lámar

Plaza del Cristo

Santo Cristo del Buen Viaje

Cemetery

Tienda Caracol

Plaza San Juan de Dios

Casa Carlos J Finlay

Galería Arte Universal Alejo Carpentier

Cisneros

Independencia

Museo Estudiantil

República

Matías Varona

To Hospital

Short Distance Trains

Parque Finlay

Francisquito Quiñones

MR Silva (San José)

Palma

Fidel Céspedes (San Rafael)

Padre Olalio (Pobres)

Pablo Lombido

Loret de Mola

Oscar Primelles (San Esteban)

Cnel Labrada

Jaime

Ignacio Agramonte

Felix Caballero

Angel Cirio Betancourt

Vate Morales

Plaza de la Revolución

Baseball Stadium

Olympic Stadium

To Sports Centre

Plaza Casino Campestre

To Bus Station

Sleeping

Casa Caridad **2** D4
Casa Láncara cp **3** D4
Colón **5** B4
Deysi Leyva cp **6** C4
Gran **7** E4
Eduardo y Geraldine cp **1** E2
Estela Mugarra Carmona cp **9** F3
Hospedaje Colonial Los Vitrales cp **8** F4
Juan E Crespo Mulén cp **11** E4
Plaza **12** B4

Eating

Cafetería Ditú **2** A4
Club Ecos **13** D4
Coppelia **4** E3
El Ovejito **5** F1
Impacto **14** C4
La Bigornia **16** C4 & D4
La Isabela **1** F3
La Mandarina Roja **7** B4
La Volanta **8** F3
La Tinajita **19** G2
Papito Rizo (La Terraza) **12** C3
Parador de los Tres Reyes **9** G3
Pizzería la Piazza **10** E4
Rancho Chico **6** F4
Rancho Luna **11** E3

Bars

Bar el Cambio **17** F3
Bar Las Ruinas **20** E3
Bodegón San Calletano & Callejón de la Soledad **21** D4
Club Oxio **22** D4

Entertainment

Casa de la Trova Patricio Ballagas **1** F3
Cine Encanto **2** D4
Cine Casablanca **7** D4
Galería Colonial **3** D4
La Casona **4** D3
Teatro Principal **6** D3

N

Not to scale

near the Río Caonao. However, in 1527 enslaved Amerindians rose up against the Spanish colonizers and burned down the town. The settlers then moved again, further inland, between the Río Tínima and the Río Hatibonico, where the village was finally established.

Moving inland was no protection against pirate attacks. During the 17th century, as the settlement became prosperous on the back of raising livestock, and later sugar, it was the target of the Welshman Henry Morgan in 1668 and of French pirates led by François Granmont in 1679. However, despite the looting, the town continued to grow throughout the 18th century, although its architects took the precaution of designing the layout to foil pirate attacks. No two streets run parallel, and this creates a maze effect, which is most unlike other colonial towns built on the grid system. On 12 November 1817, Fernando VII, the king of Spain, declared Puerto Príncipe a city with a coat of arms.

Several revolutionary events of the 19th century are remembered in Camagüey. In 1812 eight black slaves fighting for independence under the command of José Antonio Aponte, were executed. In 1826, revolutionary Agüero Velazco was hanged in what is now Parque Agramonte. Joaquín de Agüero y Agüero and his followers took arms against the colonial power in 1851, but their movement failed and they were executed by firing squad. In 1868, when Carlos Manuel de Céspedes initiated the struggle for independence, many Camagueyans supported him, including Ignacio Agramonte, Salvador Cisneros Betancourt, Maximiliano Ramos, Javier de la Vega and others who are remembered in street names, monuments and museums.

Land and environment

Camagüey is the largest province in the country covering more than 14,000 sq km. It is mostly low lying. Its highest point, at 330 m, is in the Sierra de Cubitas to the north of Camagüey city. The Atlantic north coast is broken by a series of large coral cays, which make up the Archipiélago de Camagüey. There are long sandy beaches, crystal-clear water and fantastic diving on the reef, but so far there has been little development except at Playa Santa Lucía in the east. Behind the protective cays, the land is marshy, until it rises gently to the Sierra de Cubitas where there are caves and rocky spurs. Nuevitas is the main port on the north coast and there is considerable heavy industry in the area. The southern, Caribbean coast of the province is mostly swampy. There is a fishing port at Santa Cruz del Sur, but otherwise little habitation in the wetlands. Offshore, the sea is dotted with tiny uninhabited cays. Previously one of Fidel Castro's favourite fishing spots, the cays are now visited mostly by scuba-divers on liveaboard boats.

Beef and dairy farming occupies much of the land and many of the province's traditions revolve around cowboys and their activities, such as rodeos. There are also many poultry farms in the central part around Camagüey and Minas. Sugar cane is grown in the north and south of the province, with sugar mills near Florida, Carlos Manuel de Céspedes, Brasil, Vertientes, Batalla de las Guásimas and Cándido González. Several other mills have been demolished as the economy moves away from the monoculture of sugar. There are also rice fields in the west around El Trece and El Alazán. Some citrus is grown and processed in the north near Sola.

Sights

City centre

Colonial buildings of the 17th to 19th centuries are interspersed with more modern constructions of the 20th century and walking around the city will reveal many architectural

Tinajón – vessel of love and bondage

The logo of Camagüey is the *tinajón* and the city is known as the city of the *tinajones*. This story goes back to the time when the first settlers had serious problems with their water supply. However, it rained a lot in the region and the Spanish potters found a solution by storing water in pots similar to those brought from Spain containing wine and oil. From that time on the *tinajón* became a feature of every Camagüeyan house or patio. Legend has it that if a girl offers a visitor water from a *tinajón* he should not refuse it but, before accepting, he should know that if he drinks he will fall in love with the girl and never leave the city.

gems being used for everyday purposes. There are plazas, museums and churches being restored to attract tourism, but this is not a tourist city. Declared a World Heritage Site in 2008, UNESCO reported that 'the town developed on the basis of an irregular urban pattern that contains a system of large and minor squares, serpentine streets, alleys and irregular urban blocks, highly exceptional for Latin American colonial towns located in plain territories. The 54-ha Historic Centre of Camagüey constitutes an exceptional example of a traditional urban settlement relatively isolated from main trade routes. The Spanish colonizers followed medieval European influences in terms of urban layout and traditional construction techniques brought to the Americas by their masons and construction masters. The property reflects the influence of numerous styles through the ages: neoclassical, eclectic, art deco, neo-colonial as well as some art nouveau and rationalism.'

Santa Iglesia Catedral is on the south side of Parque Ignacio Agramonte. Construction was started after the town fire of 1616 with the intention that it should be the largest parish church in Puerto Príncipe, with two chapels and a cemetery. In the 19th century the chapels were demolished and a different shape was given to the building in 1875. In 1937 the sculptor Juan Albaijez carved a statue of Christ, which was placed inside the church. After being closed for some time for renovations it reopened in 2001 with a newly painted exterior and very smart interior. The Parque has also had a facelift, with lots of marble and a cleaned up statue of Ignacio Agramonte on horseback. The Casa de la Trova is on the west side of the square, together with the library. One block away is the **Casa Natal de Nicolás Guillén Batista** ① *Agüeros 58 esq Cisneros, T32-293706*. The building may have been the poet's birthplace, but he only lived here until he was two. The building is now used as an art and cultural studies school although staff are very happy to show you round and there are a few pictures and some of his poems on the walls. See also page 428. Another famous son of Camagüey is remembered at the **Casa Carlos J Finlay** ① *Cristo 5 entre Lugareño y Callejón del Templador, T32-296745*. Born in 1833 in the city of Puerto Príncipe, as it then was, Finlay was of French and Scottish descent and studied in Philadelphia, Havana and Paris. As a result of his scientific research in the 1870s, in 1881 he was the first to come up with the theory that a mosquito of the genus Aedes was the vector for yellow fever and that the mosquito population should be controlled. From 1902 to 1909 Finlay was the chief health officer of Cuba and his findings were used to control the spread of both malaria and yellow fever during the construction of the Panama Canal at the beginning of the 20th century. He died in Havana in 1915.

A couple of blocks south of the Parque is **San Juan de Dios**, another national monument, built in 1728 as a church with a hospital attached, the first hospital in the village for men. It also contained a home for the aged. Apparently this is the only church in

Latin America that has the Holy Trinity as its central image. The **Plaza San Juan de Dios** was created at the beginning of the 19th century when two houses were bought to make the plaza. At around this time the San Juan de Dios church tower was moved to the front. On 12 May 1873 the body of Ignacio Agramonte was deposited in the hospital for identification before being taken to the cemetery. In 1902 the hospital was closed and later converted to a military infirmary. It was used to house the homeless after the hurricane in 1932 and was inaugurated as a modern hospital in 1952. Cobblestones were laid in the plaza in 1956. The hospital building changed hands several times before the **Centro Provincial de Patrimonio Cultural** occupied it. The plaza is closed to traffic. There is a small handicraft market, **Tienda Caracol**, and a couple of restaurants.

Casa Jesús Suárez Gayol, now the **Museo Estudiantil Camagüeyano** ① *República 69, T32-297744, closed lunchtime*, was the home of one of the Cuban guerrillas who lost his life in Bolivia alongside Che Guevara. The museum has exhibits about Camagüeyans, particularly students, who were active revolutionaries in the struggle for independence.

East of the cathedral along Luaces is the **Parque Martí**, also known as the **Plaza de la Juventud**. The **Sagrado Corazón de Jesús**, on Luaces, overlooking the Parque Martí, is a beautiful neo-Gothic church built in 1920. It used to have wonderful stained-glass windows depicting scenes from the gospel, but most were destroyed by stone throwing after the Revolution. Restoration work started here in January 2001, with a new roof among other works. Good progress is being made on the church and a building on the west side of the square is also shored up with timber supports prior to its renovation.

North of Parque Ignacio Agramonte, if you walk up Independencia, you come to Plaza Maceo, a busy junction of several roads with shops, banks and places to eat. One block north of here is the **Plaza de los Trabajadores**. **Nuestra Señora de la Merced**, a National Monument on Avenida Agramonte on the eastern edge of the Plaza de los Trabajadores, was built in 1747 as a church and convent at what was then the edge of town but is now in the centre. Over the years it has been transformed into a baroque church and a diocesan house. In the courtyard there are abandoned cannon used by the Spanish military in the 19th century. In 1906 a fire burned the altar, which was reconstructed in Spain in a neo-Gothic style. As the city expanded, the cemetery had to be closed, but the catacombs can still be seen. The entrance is either side of the altar; you will be followed by a warden down the steps into the mini-museum. The original wooden cross on the bell tower was moved into the catacombs in 1999. You can also see bones, skulls and several 18th-century artefacts from the church. The ceiling of the church shows early 20th-century paintings in a swirling pre-Raphaelite style, although it badly needs to be restored. On the walls are four 17th-century and eight 18th-century paintings, but the most important treasure in the church is the Santo Sepulcro, a silver coffin, constructed in 1762 with the donation of 23,000 silver coins. Before the Revolution, it was carried in procession along the streets of Camagüey; now it is kept inside the church. The church has been under restoration for many years and is still not completed. It has an external clock, which was the first public clock in Camagüey, and a library. There is always someone around to show visitors the church and provide information.

Also on the square is the **Museo Casa Natal Ignacio Agramonte** ① *Av Ignacio Agramonte 459, opposite the church on Plaza de los Trabajadores, T32-297116, Tue-Sat 0900-1900, Sun 0830-1130, CUC$2, musical activities Sat 0800-1500*. The museum is for students of revolutionary history. Ignacio Agramonte y Loynaz, one of the national heroes of the struggle against the Spanish, was born here on 23 December 1841. Agramonte, a lawyer and cattle rancher, led the rebellion in this area and in July 1869 forces under his

Brother Olallo

José Olallo Valdés (1820-1889) was abandoned as a tiny baby in an orphanage in Havana but at a very young age joined the Order of St John of God and spent the rest of his life helping the sick and wounded. At the age of 15 he was moved to Camagüey to tend to those suffering from the cholera epidemic of 1835 and continued to work in the San Juan de Dios hospital, later taking care of the wounded from both sides of the war. It is believed that he attended the body of Ignacio Agramonte in 1873. Religious orders suffered persecution under Spanish law but because of his popularity at the hospital the civil authorities allowed him to remain, thus becoming the only remaining Brother of St John of God in Cuba. He was beatified in the Plaza de la Caridad on 29 November 2008 in the first such ceremony ever to take place on Cuban soil.

command bombarded Camagüey. However, he died on 11 May 1873 after being wounded in action. When he took up arms against the colonial power in 1868 shortly after finishing his studies at university in Spain and Havana all his goods were confiscated by the state. The ground floor and courtyard of this lovely house were turned into a market while the second storey was occupied by the Spanish council. Later the ground floor became a bar and a post office. In the second half of the 20th century the house was restored and now the top floor is a museum exhibiting objects relating to the life of this revolutionary, while other rooms are used for lectures, art exhibitions and offices.

East along Ignacio Agramonte is the tiny Plaza de la Solidaridad, formerly Plaza del Gallo, little more than a junction of five roads. **Nuestra Señora de la Soledad** is on República esquina Ignacio Agramonte on the edge of the Plaza. It is the oldest church in town. In 1697 the Presbyterian Velasco started the construction of a hermitage which was concluded in 1701 and transformed into a parish by the bishop Diego Evelino de Compostela. In 1733 the current church was started, although construction was not finished until 1776. The outside is of brick, while inside there are attractive painted friezes on the arches, a carved wooden roof and a painted cupola (which needs renovation).

Quinta Amalia Simoni ① *Gen Gómez 608 entre Simoni y Plaza de la Habana, T32-292469, Tue-Sat 0930-1500, CUC$1,* was the family residence of the woman who became the wife of Ignacio Agramonte. The Spanish set fire to the house during the Ten Years' War, damaging most of its opulent furnishings such as the Carrara marble, and it never fully recovered its former glory. After the war, the Simoni family had their property restored to them, but Agramonte's widow and two children lived there only intermittently, spending much of their time in the USA. The house with its six neo-classical arches has been recently restored and in 2005 was opened as a museum. It is considered the symbolic home of the Camagüeyan family and activities take place for local women and children.

West of the centre

Iglesia Nuestra Señora de Santa Ana, along General Gómez, was started in 1697 with a single nave. Over the years it was gradually enlarged with a tower added in the middle of the 19th century.

Nuestra Señora del Carmen, on the west side of Plaza del Carmen, was started in 1732 by Eusebia de Varona y de la Torre, who wanted to build a three-nave temple for the Jesuits. However, they did not like its location, which at that time was on the outskirts of the town, so they demolished it. One hundred years later, her heirs with the help of Padre Valencia, built the women's hospital of Nuestra Señora del Carmen, which was finished in 1825. A church was built alongside the hospital, originally with only one tower, but a second was added in 1846, making it the only two-towered church in Camagüey. Part of the church collapsed in 1966 but restoration started in January 2001. The façade has been replastered and work continues inside. The hospital alongside is now the **Sede del Historiador de la Ciudad**. The whole of the **Plaza del Carmen** has been renovated, a task which included housing as well as smart new restaurants and tourist shops. An amusing feature are the clay statues of very lifelike people going about their ordinary tasks: women gossiping over coffee, a man pushing a cart, another man reading a newspaper and a couple with their arms around each other. It's pleasant to sit on a bench with them and watch the world go by.

At the west end of Calle Cristo is **Santo Cristo del Buen Viaje**, built as a small hermitage in 1794 by Emeterio de Arrieta with one nave. In the 19th-century two naves and a tower were constructed. It is rather dilapidated, but the large cemetery behind it is kept very smart with grand tombs. The square in front of the church, **Plaza del Cristo** or **Parque Gonfaus**, is not as interesting as some of the older squares in town as it has no buildings of architectural interest and even the benches are broken.

North of the centre

Museo Provincial Ignacio Agramonte ① *Av de los Mártires 2 esq Ignacio Sánchez, T32-282425, Tue, Wed, Thu and Sat 1000-1800, Fri 1200-2000, Sun 1000-1400, CUC$2*, first built as a cavalry barracks in 1848, was converted into the **Hotel Camagüey** from 1905-1943, but there are still cannon, water troughs and *tinajones* in the garden. After considerable restoration the museum was inaugurated on 23 December 1955 (the anniversary of Agramonte's birth). There are exhibitions of archaeology, with copies of drawings and artifacts found in the caves of the Sierra de Cubitas (see below), natural history (lots of dusty stuffed animals and birds), paintings and furniture of the 19th and 20th centuries, but nothing special.

At the far end of Av de los Mártires is Plaza Joaquín de Agüero (Plaza de Méndez), the second largest square in the city. Joaquín de Agüero and his followers were shot by a firing squad here on 12 August 1851. In 1913 a monument was erected to honour the heroes.

East of the centre

The **Parque Casino Campestre**, on the eastern side of the Río Hatibonico, was the first place in Cuba to hold cattle shows. In the 19th century it was used for fairs, dances and other social activities but in the 20th century its purpose and structure was changed. Trees have been planted and there are monuments to independence fighter Salvador Cisneros Betancourt, to the Unknown Soldier, and to teachers. Next to the park there is a monument erected in 1941 to Barberán and Collar, the first pilots to cross the Atlantic at its widest point, in a flight from Seville. It took them 39 hours and 55 minutes.

Around Camagüey

Without your own transport, it may be easier to take an excursion, for further details see Activities and tours, page 296. There is a **Crocodile farm** ① *9 km from Senado, just north west of Minas, Mon, Wed, Sat, 0900-1700, CUC$1, other days with prior reservation through Ecotur, or through Cubanacán, CUC$14*, where endangered species are preserved. On the farm there is also an Amerindian village and you can visit a cave which is a burial site. You can take a boat trip on the Río Máximo and watch a santería ritual being performed. The farm has a restaurant for lunch, offering traditional Cuban dishes for CUC$6-8.

There are walking tours of the **Sierra de Cubitas**, a protected area 35 km north of Camagüey, where you can visit caves with Amerindian drawings and see much endemic wildlife and lots of birds. The tour lasts all day and is hot and tiring, minimum eight people, two expert guides, take a hat, good walking boots and lots of water.

A road heads northeast out of Camagüey past the airport through pastures and chicken farms to the coast. The first town of any size is **Minas**, with a population of about 20,000. There is no reason to stop here except to see the **Fábrica de Instrumentos Musicales** ① *Calle Camilo Cienfuegos, Minas, T32-696232*, where they make and sell violins, guitars and percussion instruments. **King Ranch**, 80 km from Camagüey on the way to Santa Lucía, offers rodeo, horse riding and cheap accommodation.

Some 54 km southeast of the city is **Najasa** and **Hacienda La Belén** ① *T32-274995, www.ecoturcuba.co.cu, head east on the Carretera Central, at Jimbambay turn south to Najasa, the Hacienda is 5 km from town, entrance CUC$5, horse riding CUC$6, lunch CUC$8, see Sleeping, page 290, for accommodation*, covering an area of 4500 ha in the Sierra de Najasa. This is a protected area of geological and biological diversity, including caves and the second finest forest reserve in the country. The Hacienda is a stud farm and offers horse riding through the reserve and the forest. Birdwatching is good on the trails where you can see the tocororo, the national bird, as well as other protected endemic species. Tours of the area include a visit to a typical farmer's house, and the Gaspar-Najasa caves.

Playa Santa Lucía → *Colour map 3, B3.*

Santa Lucía is a beach resort 112 km northeast, or two hours by road, from Camagüey, where the sand stretches some 20 km along the northern coast near the **Bahía de Nuevitas**. This is a beautiful beach, protected by an offshore reef that contains over 50 species of coral and is much sought after by divers. The water is clear and warm, with an average temperature of 24°C. You can sometimes see dolphins near the shore and there are flamingos in the *saliñas* (salt flats) inshore. The province is the second largest salt producer in the country (after Guantánamo) and the area is principally scrub, swamp and salt flats. It is a lovely place to come and relax but be aware that it is remote, there is no real town as such, although plenty of people live here, and excursions inland can therefore be time-consuming and expensive. Most people who stay here are on all-inclusive package tours for a week or so and see little of Cuba. However, hotel tour desks can offer you day trips or longer excursions by land, sea or air to anywhere in Cuba.

Eight kilometres from Santa Lucía there is **Playa Los Cocos**, which is even better than Santa Lucía. There is a broad sweep of beach with a fishing village, La Boca, at one end and beach bars at the other end by the channel which leads to Nuevitas. Shark feeding takes place near wrecks in the channel, see Activities and tours, page 296. There are lots of coconut palms after which the beach gets its name. The sand here is very white and the water crystal clear. There are a few rocky bits at the edge of the water but it is mostly sandy, gently sloping and safe for children. The bars and seafood restaurants (fresh lobster for less than CUC$11) will rent you sunbeds, CUC$1. Use insect repellent against the small, black, biting insect known as a *jején*; the bites hurt at the time you are bitten but they only start to itch like mad the next day.

Across the channel, west of Playa Los Cocos, is **Cayo Sabinal**, reached by road from Nuevitas. Boat trips will be organized by hotel tour desks in Santa Lucía. Hemingway was inspired to write that it was a marvellous place where the wind from the east blows night and day, and the territory as virgin as when Columbus arrived on these shores. Things haven't changed much since then. There are beautiful beaches of white sand which are practically deserted and the cay is a wildlife reserve housing the largest colony of pink flamingos in the Caribbean, plus many other birds that are rare or endangered elsewhere. There is pleasant accommodation available in cabins, but lots of mosquitoes. There are seafood restaurants along the beaches of Playa Brava (the better beach) and Playa Los Pinos.

Florida → *Colour map 3, B1.*

Some 46 km northwest of Camagüey on the road and railway to Ciego de Avila, is Florida, a town of some 40,000 inhabitants, with hospitals and clinics, a museum, art gallery, *Casa de Cultura*, cinema, hotel and restaurants. There are a couple of sugar mills, some factories making construction materials and textiles and a brewery. Tour buses pass through here, but few foreigners stop long. However, there are a number of lagoons in the area and Florida is used as a base for shooting and fishing expeditions. The **reservoirs Porvenir** and **Muñoz** nearby and **Mañana de Santa Ana**, southeast of Camagüey, are used for organized six-hour trout fishing sessions. The area is also popular for shooting duck, quail, doves and guinea fowl, among other game birds, so if you stay at the local hotel, **La Casona de Florida**, you may find your fellow guests are hunters. The other hotel, **Hotel Florida**, is used by **Víazul** as a pit stop for lunch on the way from Trinidad to Santiago, but the guests are all Cubans on a family holiday.

Guáimaro → *Colour map 3, B3.*

Heading southeast by road towards Las Tunas, you can stop in Guáimaro, just before the provincial border. It is a small town about 80 km from Camagüey, with a population of about 20,000 and a lively agricultural fair, *Feria Agropecuaria*, every early October, when stalls are set up in the park and rows of people sell roast pork at the side of the street. However, it is notable for its historical connections: Carlos Manuel de Céspedes was elected first president of the Republic here by the constituent assembly of 1869. The assembly's other task was to draw up the first Cuban constitution. Seventy years later the town got round to commemorating the event with a monument in Parque Constitución dedicated to the men who fought for Cuban independence including Céspedes and José Martí.

For Sleeping and Eating price codes and other relevant information, see Essentials pages 37-43.

● Sleeping

Camagüey centre *p282, map p280*
Hotels

B Gran Hotel, Maceo 67, entre Ignacio Agramonte y General Gómez, T32-292093-4, www.islazul.cu. Colonial style, built 1939, when it was the most luxurious hotel in the country, perhaps even in Latin America, renovated 1997, very smart now, central, breakfast included, a/c, fan, cable TV, fridge, good bathroom, best rooms with balcony overlooking Maceo, security box rental, car hire, small swimming pool with children's area, restaurant on top floor, good view, also piano bar, 24-hr café.

C Colón, República 472 entre San José y San Martín, T32-283346/241727, www.islazul.cu. Old style built in 1920s, beautifully painted in blue and white, marble staircase, long thin hotel on 2 floors around central well, rocking chairs overlook patio bar and restaurant, breakfast included, rooms with 1 or 2 beds, a/c, TV, phone, good bathroom, lobby bar, friendly staff.

C Plaza, Van Horne 1, entre República y Avellaneda, T32-282413/282435, www.islazul.cu. 67 rooms with TV, fridge, colonial building right by railway station, grim exterior, brown and cream, not all rooms have a/c, more expensive rooms face the front, with balcony, but rooms at the back are away from traffic noise, mediocre restaurant, breakfast included, bar

Casas particulares

Rooms cost CUC\$20-25, negotiable, depending on the time of year and length of stay, although some go as low as CUC\$15, with breakfast at CUC\$3-5 and evening meal CUC\$6-10, depending on what you eat. All the casas listed here offer a/c, fan, private bathroom with hot and cold water and usually a fridge. Those in Rpto La Vigía, north of the centre, are some distance from the centre, but being in a residential neighbourhood they are quieter.

D-E Casa Caridad, Oscar Primelles 310 A entre Bartolomé Masó y Padre Olallo (Pobres), T32-291554, abreucmg@enet.cu. Caridad García Valera runs this colonial house with 2 rooms, 1 with double and single bed, the other with 2 double beds. Very clean, regularly fumigated. Delightful garden at the back with climbing and trailing plants not affected by the hurricane because of high walls, eat indoors or outside, more than enough food, garage, safe parking. If she is full, Caridad's son and daughter-in-law **Eduardo y Geraldine** also rent a room, **E**, on Gollo Benítez (Príncipe) 61 entre Gen Gómez y San Ramón, T32-296759, with 2 beds, TV, garage, patio.

D-E Casa Láncara, Avellaneda 160 entre Ignacio Agramonte y Jaime, T32-283187, T528 10375 (mob), casalancara@yahoo.es. Built 1910 in colonial style with high ceilings and wonderful blue and yellow tiles on walls. 1 room with small bathroom, off passage and patio with trailing plants and rocking chairs. Half-board packages available. Friendly family with children and small dog.

D-E Deysi Leyva, Santa Rita (Solitaro)16A (Altos), entre República y Santa Rosa, T32-293348. Tiny, friendly Deysi offers 1 room, new double and single bed, large bathroom, not modernized yet, closet, bedside light, room opens out onto passage to back of apartment, dining room alongside, laundry service, meals available.

D-E Estela Mugarra Carmona, Cisneros 161 Apto 2 entre Cristo y San Isidro, T32-295053. 2 rooms in 1st-floor apartment built in 1958 with all original fixtures and fittings, a period piece with solid wood wardrobes and folding doors, all in excellent condition. 1 room larger than the other but both can fit 2 beds, TV, no view from bedrooms but small balcony overlooks busy street for people watching, food available and complimentary juice, tea and coffee. Very central, 20 m from Parque.

D-E Hospedaje Colonial Los Vitrales, Avellaneda 3 entre Gen Gómez y Martí, T32-295866, requejobarreto@gmail.com. Run by Rafael Requejo, and his family. Rafael speaks English and is full of stories about the architectural history of the house, which has a courtyard and colonial kitchen off it as well as a modern kitchen alongside. Good traditional meals are served, with beans and rice cooked the way they have been for centuries. 2 very high ceilinged rooms which open onto patio where lush plants are recovering from hurricane damage, new bathrooms, new beds, hanging space for laundry, do it yourself or they will do it for you, own water tank giving good pressure, garage. In case of overspill, Rafael's sister has a legal room for rent upstairs through the garage. Serious trouble with *jineteros*, take care not to be taken to other house by tricksters, they even copy the house name and number to fool you into thinking that you are at Los Vitrales.

D-E Juan E Crespo Mulén, Maceo 68 (Altos) entre República y Gen Gómez, T32-298049, jcrespo@finlay.cmw.sld.cu. Very central, apartment above shops, 1 very blue room overlooking busy street, run by architect with great style. Fabulous iron bed head, foldaway bed for child against wall, disguised to look like artwork, light and bright bathroom, 1950s tiles, TV outside room in sitting area with balcony.

West of the centre p285
Casas particulares

D Mayra y Gaspar, Gen Gómez 546 entre Damas y Plaza Habana, T32-296725. Family lives in colonial house at the front, 2 rental rooms built in garden at back of house with kitchen for guests' use or ring bell for service. Lovely big rooms, double and single bed, wardrobe, bedside lights, TV on request. Both rooms open on to huge garden with mature trees and palms, swings for children, very private and comfortable.

D-E Reyes y Carolina, Damas (Sabino Monte) 221 entre Horca y Medio,

T32-298907. Amazing decor with ornaments, plastic flowers and soft toys everywhere. 2 rooms, 1 in house with double bed, TV, brown bathroom, good quality fittings, the other upstairs at the back of the house, more independent and private with white bathroom, off terrace with view over tiled roofs, lots of plants. Carolina, a former history teacher, serves very good food and specializes in cocktails, particularly Canchanchara.

North of the centre p286
Casas particulares

D-E Casa Miriam, Joaquín de Agüero 525 entre 25 de Julio y Perucho Figueredo, Rpto La Vigía, T32-282120, T0527 03252 (mob), miriamhouse29@yahoo.com. Modern house, excellent accommodation. Miriam Guerra de la Cruz lives upstairs with guests while her extended family lives downstairs. Well-maintained house, 2 light and airy rooms each with private bathroom (1 has bathtub), large wardrobes, TV/DVD, internet. Large terrace on roof with lots of plants, dogs and cats, great views of city. Miriam is a knowledgeable and efficient English-speaking hostess, she will collect you from the bus terminal, arrange excursions and transport and serves good, hearty 3-course meals with lots of fruit and fresh veg.

E Raúl Pérez Bahamonde, Alfredo Adán 355 entre Joaquín Agüero y Capdevila, Rpto La Vigía, T05-2302 916 (mob), rimbasuarez23@yahoo.es. Independent studio apartment with separate staircase up from family sitting room, bedroom, living room, bathroom and kitchenette, TV, fridge, rocking chairs, garage. Food available if you don't want to cook on limited facilities.

Around Camagüey p286

B Hacienda La Belén, 5 km from Najasa, 54 km southeast of Camagüey, T32-864349/274995. Small hotel operated by Ecotur, www.ecoturcuba.co.cu. 10 double rooms for nature lovers, a/c, private bathrooms, breakfast included, meals available, pool, lovely rural location, horseriding, hiking, birdwatching.

C Hotel Camagüey, Carretera Central
Este Km 4.5, T32-287267/8, www.islazul.cu.
Good condition, modern, Soviet-influenced
architecture, pool, disco show, bar in the
lobby and on 2nd floor, cafeteria, buffet
restaurant, car hire.

Playa Santa Lucía p287

The Santa Lucía resort is part of the Cubanacán
group (www.cubanacan.cu), including
joint-venture hotels, restaurants, shopping
centre, watersports, discos and other
amenities. All the hotels are all-inclusive and
prices are per person sharing a double room.
Standards vary, but they all offer a/c, TV,
entertainment, sports and tours. It is possible
to stay in *casas particulares* at Playa Santa Lucía
and Playa Los Cocos, but they are illegal.
AL-A Gran Club Santa Lucía, T32-365145,
aloja@club.stl.cyt.cu. Newish, low buildings
and cabins, 3 star, considered one of the best
with 108 rooms and suites on the beach,
144 garden rooms and suites, buffet and à la
carte restaurant, snack bar, disco, pool with
children's area and swim-up bar, games
room, bicycle and scooter hire, lots of
activities and trying to cater for all ages.
A Brisas Santa Lucía, T32-336140, aloja@
brisas.stl.cyt.cu. 400 rooms of which 4 are
wheelchair accessible, 8 suites. All the usual
facilities you'd expect of a 4-star hotel and
among the best here. Good bit of beach, friendly
staff, lots of entertainment and nightlife, buffet
OK, 3 à la carte restaurants to choose from.
C Escuela Santa Lucía, T32-336310/336410,
ariel@eht.stl.cyt.cu. The furthest hotel north
and also a staff training centre. 2-star, 1 of
the cheapest (CUC$ room without breakfast),
very basic, 30 rooms, rather tatty but
redeemed by personal touches, TV,
restaurant, bar. Helpful staff, but services
rather erratic. Decent budget option.
C-F Casas Islazul Santa Lucía, for
reservations contact Alejandro at the Islazul
office at ECOS café beside Iglesia Soledad in
Camagüey, T32-292550/295817, bturcmg@
enet.cu. Houses for rent on Playa Residencial,
1-4 rooms, good for groups.

D Club Sabinal Los Pinos, Playa Los Pinos,
Cayo Sabinal, T32-287047. Price (per person)
includes 2 meals, 2-star cabins, bathroom,
radio, bar, restaurant, horse rental, taxis,
credit cards accepted.
D Costa Blanca, Playa Residencial, T32-336373.
A comfortable, very cheap little Islazul hotel.

Nuevitas

C-D Caonaba, Calle Albaisa esq Martí,
Nuevitas, T32-414803, recepcion@
caonaba.co.cu. 38 rooms, on high ground
overlooking the bay, breakfast included.

🍴 Eating

Restaurants have a reputation for reheating
leftovers, *paladares* can be expensive, *casas
particulares* are best for fresh, wholesome
cooking. In the city centre renovation of
colonial buildings has led to a proliferation
of smart, state-run restaurants with fairly
mediocre food but in very attractive locations.
Some restaurants allow tourists to pay in
pesos cubanos and a plate of food there will
cost around 30-60 pesos (CUC$2-3), with
mojitos at some 2-5 pesos, making them
extremely cheap, but quality is variable and
fresh ingredients are not always available.
There are several shops where you can buy
food, but to find out how the locals cope, go
to the *Agromercado* near the river. As well as
fruit and vegetables there is a small place
where you can order cooked food and lots
of people will try to sell you snacks.

Camagüey centre p282, map p280
Restaurants

🍴 **Don Ronquillo**, in covered area at the back
of Galería Colonial, Ignacio Agramonte 406
entre República y López Recio, T32-285239.
Daily 1200-2200. Used by tour parties with set
lunch and live music for CUC$10, reasonably
priced, most dishes CUC$5-10, national beer
CUC$1.20, *mojito* CUC$2.
🍴 **La Isabela**, Ignacio Agramonte near Plaza
de los Trabajadores and Casa Natal Ignacio

Agramonte, T32-221540. 1100-1600, 1830-2200. Italian food, founded in honour of an actress from Camagüey, each chair bears the name of a Cuban film-maker.

Parador de los Tres Reyes, T32-286812, and **Campana de Toledo**, T32-286812. 2 small colonial-style restaurants on Plaza San Juan de Dios serving Spanish food, pleasant, live music. The latter has tables overlooking the square or in the courtyard, chicken/fish CUC$5-7, *moros y cristianos* CUC$1.50. The former is cheaper but has smaller portions. Open for lunch and dinner, but tour parties mean they are busy at lunchtime.

Bucanero, República 420, T32-253413, open 24 hrs. Decorated like a tavern with buccaneer theme, restaurant, bar and private room for parties, lots of different dishes charged in either CUC$ or pesos cubanos, drinks in CUC$.

El Rincón, López Recio esq Callejón Sin Salida, T32-292903. Mon-Fri 1530-2400, Sat-Sun 1200-2400. Restaurant, bar and a private room for parties by reservation, specialize in chicken, many other dishes too, pesos cubanos.

La Volanta, Parque Agramonte, Independencia 160, T32-291974. Daily 1200-2300. Basic Cuban food, traditional menu, no frills, pay in CUC$ or pesos cubanos, but tell the waitress first which currency you want to pay in. Restaurant bar and patio used as a sort of cabaret.

Pizzería La Piazza, Agramonte on the corner with Maceo. Daily 1200-2100. Italian food. Restaurant upstairs, reservations required, pizza downstairs. You can pay in pesos but there may be a queue at lunchtime.

Rancho Chico, Martí 54 esq República, T32-292253. Daily 1200-2200. Charges in pesos cubanos and specializes in beef dishes.

Rancho Luna, on the east side of Plaza Maceo, T32-294361. Daily 1400-2230. Serves basic Cuban food specializing in pork dishes, pay in pesos cubanos.

Paladares

El Cardenal, Martí 309 entre Hospital y San Antonio, 1100-2300. The most expensive *paladar* in the city, but not necessarily the best, Cuban dishes.

El Califa, San Clemente 46A esq Cisneros. 1200-2300. Cuban food, charges in pesos cubanos.

La Mandarina Roja, San Fernando 382 entre San Martín y San José, T32-292067. Fri-Sun 1200-2200. Chinese food.

Papito Rizo (La Terraza), Santa Rosa 8 entre Santa Rita y San Martín, 1 block from República, T32-298705. Open 1100-2300 or later. Several different sections for waiting, drinking or dining, sit upstairs to eat in the fresh air, under roof, pleasant, popular, considered by locals to be the best *paladar* in town, fast service, young and friendly staff speak English and Italian, Cuban dishes priced in pesos cubanos but you can also pay in CUC$.

Cafés and snack bars

Cafetería Ditú, on República by Parque Aróstegui overlooking the railway line, T32-282880, 24 hrs. Convenient if waiting for a train, music. Alternatively you can sit on one of the shady benches in the Parque and train spot. Other branches 1 block from the bus station and on Av Finlay on the way to Playa Santa Lucía.

Club Ecos, Agramonte beside Iglesia La Soledad, T32-298947. Open 1000-0200.

Coppelia, Independencia opp Casa Natal Ignacio Agramonte, T32-294851. Ice cream and other snacks in pesos cubanos.

Impacto, República, opposite Cadeca, T32-286339. Ice cream and snacks.

La Bigornia, República y Callejón de Correa, T32-284784. Sun-Thu 1000-2200, Fri, Sat 1000-2400. Live traditional music Fri and jazz Sat from 2100, bar, café and complex of shops.

Las Arecas, Gran Hotel, Maceo. A good 24-hr snack bar on the ground floor, entrance on Maceo.

West of the centre p285
Restaurants
♜♜♜ **El Ovejito**, at the entrance to Plaza del Carmen, T32-242498. 1200-2145. Quite elegant and lovely situation, CUC$10-30, *moros y cristianos* CUC$4, *mojito* an extortionate CUC$5.50.
♜ **La Tinajita**, Cristo 177 entre Bembeta y Santa Catalina, near cemetery, T32-296323. Daily 1000-2200. Bar and restaurant with colonial decor, speciality *Tasajo* Cuban dishes, pay in pesos cubanos.

Paladares
♜ **Rancho Casas**, Carretera Central oeste 786 entre 2 y 3, Rpto Iman, T32-295679. Open 1100-2300. Rustic style in natural environment, take care on rocky path up to the house, windy. Good food, local dishes.

North of the centre p286
Restaurants
♜ **Corderito**, Julio Sanguily esq 1 paralela, Rpto La Vigía, T32-283383. Daily 1200-2200. Restaurant, bar and cafeteria, Cuban food, lamb a speciality, pesos cubanos.
♜ **Vicaria El Pollito**, Av Finlay Km 5.5 on the way to Playa Santa Lucía, T32-261384. Open 1000-2200. Restaurant, grill and bar.

Paladares
There are several offering reasonable Cuban food ♜, including **Doble Vía**, Bella Vista 54 entre Andrés Sánchez y Av Finlay, Rpto La Vigía, daily except Wed, **La Sirena**, Call 2 13A entre A y B, Rpto La Guernica, T32-251989, 1200-2300, and **Luly Lunch**, Calle B 1 entre Av Finlay y Calle 2, Rpto La Guernica, 1200-2300 daily.

East of the centre p286
Restaurants
♜♜♜ **Di Mar**, Carretera Central este entre Puente de la Caridad y Puente Caballero Rojo, on the edge of Río Hatibonico, T32-256674. 24 hrs daily. Specializes in fish and seafood, serves wine and beer, charges in CUC$ so comparatively expensive.

♜♜-♜ **Dinos Pizzas Casino**, Humboldt 3 entre Av de la Libertad y San Joaquín, T32-298790. Open 24 hrs. Italian food, wine available, charges in CUC$
♜♜-♜ **La Paella**, Av de la Libertad 214 entre Domingo Puentes y C Montejo, T32-293152. Daily 1200-2400. Lovely colonial decor, tables upstairs, also garden and ground floor, pesos cubanos, fish, seafood and of course, paella.
♜ **Complejo Parrillada Taberna**, Carretera Central y Calle 4, Rpto Garrido, opposite Copacabana Disco, T32-295719. Daily 1200-2400. Rustic architecture, 3 rooms for dining, roast and grilled meats cooked on charcoal fires, buy meat by weight, pork 2.50 pesos cubanos per ounce, chicken 1.67 pesos. If you have a group of friends you can arrange with the staff to roast your own pig, or whatever you want, and pay them for the service.
♜ **Hatibonico**, Carretera Central, next to Di Mar, T32-294953. Daily 1200-2400. Reservations essential. Italian food charged in pesos cubanos, the most expensive dish is the shrimp pizza, which costs about 20 pesos. There can be a queue for pizza at any time.
♜ **Jayama**, Edificio 12 Plantas 1, Rpto Julio Antonio Mella, T32-271917. On top floor of 12-storey building, good view of city, particularly at night, modern decor, Cuban food, best to go early as after 1900 most dishes have gone and you have to eat whatever is left, pay in Cuban pesos.
♜ **Ming King**, Carretera Central 102 opp Parque Casino Campestre, T32-291785. Daily 1200-2100. Mainly Chinese food but plenty of other dishes available, 2 dining rooms, bar, garden with tables and bar and a private dining room, charges in pesos cubanos.

Playa Santa Lucía p287
There are good café grills at Playa los Cocos, serving good fish and seafood at reasonable prices. As well as the state-run restaurants and cafés, there are also *paladares*, ask *coche* drivers for recommendations, which are better value, although beware that not all of them are legal.

Ħ Las Brisas, near the junction in the residential area, T32-336349. Creole.
Ħ Luna Mar at the Centro Comercial, T32-336284. Passable pizzas, but avoid the fish.
Ħ Vía Appia, Residencial Santa Lucía, T32-336101. Italian, open lunch and dinner.
Ħ Alondra, T32-336146. Ice cream on the beach.

🍸 Bars

Camagüey centre *p282, map p280*
Bar El Cambio, on the northeast corner of Parque Ignacio Agramonte. This one-time gambling den now has lottery artwork on the walls, designed and decorated by artist Oscar Lasseria, see the toilet and bathroom ceramics, *mojito* CUC$2, you can expect to be approached here with offers of 'private' restaurants. A good view of the cathedral.
Bar-café Las Ruinas, on west side of Plaza Maceo. Set in ruins and shady trees.
Bodegón San Calletano and **Callejón de la Soledad**, República y Callejón de la Soledad, T32-291961, both at same location, the former open 1230-2300, the latter 1030-2300. Musicians will play at night if asked, but they will wait for a tip.
Club Oxio, República 277 entre San Esteban y Finlay, T32-287384. A complex with bar, grill, dancing, small pool, **Piscina BBQ**, 1000-1800, CUC$10 includes drinks and food up to CUC$8 (children 5-12 half price, under 5 free), games room, bowling CUC$1 per hr, photo studio, electronic games for children and adults. **Rincón del Bolero** every Sat, Sun 2100-2400, free. **Spot Café** 1000-2200 Mon-Fri, 1000-2400 Sat, Sun.
Gran Hotel (see Sleeping) has several bars with entertainment: **Piano Bar Marquesina**, CUC$5 for 2 people Mon-Fri, CUC$10 per couple on Sat and Sun, includes 2 meals and beer or rum; **Bar Piscina 1920**, CUC$3 per person (CUC$1 entrance, CUC$2 drinks), or CUC$10 Sat and Sun per couple including meal, beer/rum, with ballet acuático at 2130; **Bar El Mirador**, CUC$1 per person.

🎭 Entertainment

Camagüey centre *p282, map p280*
To see what is on, check www.pprincipe.cult.cu/actividades.

Cabaret
Galería Colonial, Ignacio Agramonte 406 entre República y López Recio. Cabaret show daily 2200-0200, live music sometimes, CUC$5 for the show but after it is over at about 2400 the charge drops to CUC$1. Can be rented for private functions.

Cinema
3 cinemas, none of which has a/c and they can be very hot, entrance 60 centavos-1 peso cubano: **Casablanca**, T32-292244 and **Encanto**, T32-295511, next door on Ignacio Agramonte, and **Guerrero**, T32-292874.

Live music and disco
Casa de la Trova Patricio Ballagas, on the west side of Parque Agramonte between Martí and Cristo. Mon-Thu 1200-1800, 2100-2400, Fri-Sun 2100-0200. Folk and traditional music. Courtyard and bar, while at the entrance is a souvenir shop where you can buy music.
La Casona, Padre Valencia 65 opposite Teatro Principal, proejo@pprincipe.cult.cu. Fri-Sun 2030-0100, 20 pesos cubanos per couple. Colonial house in which you can hear different types of music, traditional, folk music and others, temporary art exhibitions, snacks and drinks also available.

Theatre
Compañía de Magia, Gen Gómez 364, Plaza de Santa Ana, T32-293105/295544.
La Edad de Oro, Cisneros 259, T32-296420. Performances for children and teenagers.
Teatro El Viento, Plaza Joaquín de Agüero (Plaza de Méndez), beside Casa de la Cultura, T32-291701. Often has plays for children, youth theatre, Sat and Sun 1.20 pesos cubanos.
Teatro Guiñol, Lugareño esq San Clemente, T32-286438.

Teatro José Luis Tasende, Popular entre Padre Valencia y Lopez Recio, T32-292164. The Camagüey Dramatic Company performs here. **Teatro Principal**, on Padre Valencia 64, T32-293048. The Ballet de Camagüey, ranked 2nd in the country after Havana's ballet company, often performs here.

East of the centre *p286*
Cabaret
Cabaret Caribe, near Parque Casino Campestre. Daily show 2100-0200, CUC$5 (includes drinks of CUC$3) but this can change depending on the season. Very popular. Men should wear long trousers and shirts with collars or pullovers, women should not wear shorts. On Sun 0900-1200 there is kids' entertainment with clowns, magicians and games.

Live music and disco
On Sun morning there are activities in Parque Casino Campestre, including live music. **Copacabana**, Carretera Central este, near bus station and ballet school, T32-253858. Tue-Sat 2130-0200, background music and disco, Sun 1500-2000 for kids. Entrance CUC$3 includes drink of CUC$1.

Playa Santa Lucía *p287*
Live music and disco
Hotels lay on lots of daytime and evening entertainment and organized activities. **Disco La Jungla**, Centro Comercial, by Hotel Club Santa Lucía, T32-365145. **Disco La Corona**, near Hotel Las Brisas.

⊛ Festivals and events

Camagüey centre *p282, map p280*
Feb The 1st week celebrates the foundation of the village with lots of street parties.
24-29 June Carnival.

O Shopping

Camagüey centre *p282, map p280*
Artex and other CUC$ shops are on Maceo, Agramonte, República and on Cisneros, just north of Parque Agramonte. Maceo is a particularly busy street, with the **Centro Comercial Alemán** on Plaza Maceo, selling clothes, furniture and electro-domestic goods and other stores, **Coppelia** ice cream, fast food outlets and the **Gran Hotel** running up to Plaza de la Solidaridad. **Galería Colonial**, Ignacio Agramonte esq República is located in a restored colonial mansion. Shops and services include **Casa del Tabaco**, restaurant **Don Ronquillo**, café **Mamá Inés**, snack bar **Las Arcadas**, nightclub **Patio Colonial**, tourist bureau, toilets. It is used by tour parties but is a pleasant place to pause around town.

Art
El Cartel, Cisneros entre Hermanos Agüero y Martí. Marvellous collection of original screen prints from the 1960s and 1970s, many featuring Che and Fidel, as well as countless movie posters in the distinctive Cuban style. Some of the original prints are for sale, kept in a dusty cupboard and in poor condition. The owner will show you around the workshop if you ask.
Estudio Nazario Salazar Martínez, Padre Valencia 74 entre Tatán Méndez y Lugareño, T32-297682, nsm@anec.cmw.inf.cu. A noted artist with over 40 years of experience in drawing, painting, pottery and graphic design, his works are collected worldwide. He is known principally for his ceramics.
Galería Taller Larios, Independencia 301 esq Gen Gómez, T32-291575, larios@pprincipe.cult.cu. Gallery and workshop where you can see artists working on paintings, ceramics, ironwork, etc, under the direction of local artist, Orestes Larios Zaak, who specializes in drawing and painting and has been exhibited in Europe and the USA. Free entry, works for sale.
Galería Taller Lorenzo Linares Duque, Pintor 56. Internationally exhibited painter

since the 1970s, known for his landscapes and paintings of cockerels.

Galería Taller Martha Jiménez Pérez, Gen Gómez 274B entre Masvidal y Lugareño, T32-291696, Martha@pprincipe.cult.cu. A painter and sculptor, Martha's sculptures can be seen in Plaza del Carmen, models of real people who can be seen around the square. Some of them actually sit beside their representation, seeking tips from tourists.

Jardín del Edén, Bellavista 420 entre Alfredo Adám y 25 de Julio, Rpto La Vigía, T32-286909. Workshop and gallery of Oscar Lasseria, a painter, sculptor and ceramicist. If he is there he will show you around and you can buy anything he has for sale. Lasseria's works can be found decorating places such as Bar El Cambio, Cafetería La Bigornia, Ovejito restaurant on Plaza del Carmen and several ceramic murals around the city.

Handicrafts
Gallery Expo-sale on the side of the Plaza de los Trabajadores.

West of the centre p285
Caracol La Casa del Artesano, on Plaza del Carmen. Mon-Sat 0930-1720. Handicrafts.
Casa Taller de Cerámica Yasmín, Calle Primera 33 entre 1 y 2 transversales, Rpto San Miguelito, on the road out to Vertientes, T32-273254. Ceramics workshop where you can see how the *tinajón* is made as well as other domestic pottery.

Playa Santa Lucía p287
Centro Comercial, T32-365291. The usual tourist shops selling clothes, rum, cigars, souvenirs, etc, with ice cream, bar and snack bar to help pass the time.

▲ Activities and tours

Camagüey centre p282, map p280
Diving
At Playa Santa Lucía there are 37 dive sites at depths of 5-40 m in the area including a

shark feeding site in the channel between Playa Los Cocos and Cayo Sabinal about 20 m offshore. There is a concrete area by the *guardia* station and steps down into the water. Up to 20 bull sharks congregate at a depth of some 26-30 m by the wreck of a Spanish merchant ship at 35 m (the 66-m *Mortera* sank in 1905 on a slope of 7-27 m and is home to a host of marine life); some of them swim in between the divers. They have been hand fed by the dive masters from Shark's Friends Dive Shop since the early 1980s (very exciting to watch, no body armour worn). However, you have to wait for the current, when the tide is on the turn and there is only a 45-min window of opportunity. Other dive sites include caves, tunnels and a very picturesque and healthy coral reef. Other wrecks include the *Sanbinal* in 17 m and the British steel ship, *Nuestra Señora de Alta Gracia*, sunk around 1973 and completely intact, allowing divers to penetrate the entire ship, entering the engine room where all the machinery is still in place. An exciting historical site is Las Anforas, under an old fort dating from 1456. The fort was attacked several times by pirates, and artefacts from Spanish ships are scattered across the sea bed. (4 anchors were seen on 1 dive, with the largest being at least 2 m).

Shark's Friends, Playa Santa Lucía, T32-365182. Instructors hand-feed bull sharks Aug-Feb, depending on weather conditions. The sharks migrate elsewhere for the rest of the year. Dives cost CUC$30 for a single dive, cheaper for more, CUC$140 for 5 dives, CUC$255 for 10 dives. ACUC and SNSI courses are offered with 5 instructors: Open Water CUC$299, Advanced CUC$250. They use a 41-ft yacht and 2 13-ft motor launches, tanks and weight belts included, other equipment available.

Snorkelling
Catamarans leave twice daily at 1000 and 1400, weather permitting, from the pier just north of Escuela Santa Lucía, for the reef. CUC$25 including all gear and soft drinks on board and transfers from your hotel, about

3 hrs from collection to drop-off.
Recommended for a great snorkelling trip.

Tour operators

Cubanacán, tourism bureau in Hotel Plaza, contact Mairelis, T32-297374. Same tours and prices as Havanatur. Also in Playa Santa Lucía, Av Residencial, T32-336406/336449, each hotel has a bureau.

Cubatur, office on Ignacio Agramonte, opposite Cine Casablanca, T32-254785, cubatur@cmg.co.cu. Daily 0900-1200 and 1300-1700 and at Playa Santa Lucía T32-336291/335333 at entrance to Club Santa Lucía. Tours for individuals start from Playa Santa Lucía, nothing available from Camagüey except for groups. Many tours, including to Cayo Sabinal and Santa Lucía advertised, but unhelpful staff make it almost impossible to book anything.

Havanatur, Monteagudo entre Carretera Central y Cuba, Alt Casino, Camagüey, T32-281564/283606 and at Playa Santa Lucía, T32-365332. Also a desk in the **Ecos Café**, next to Iglesia Soledad, contact Jorge Omar Miranda Sánchez, T32-203664. He is very knowledgeable but out on tours most of the time. He should be at the desk, daily 0730-0930 and 1630-2000. They offer trips to Belén, Playa Santa Lucía for groups of 6+ people, hotel reservations all over the country and flight tickets.

Paradiso, Ignacio Agramonte, opp Cine Encanto, beside Cubatur. Guided city tours, also music and dance courses.

Watersports

Most watersports are available at the hotels but **Marlin** has boat rental and other watersports, T32-336404.

◎ Transport

Camagüey centre *p282, map p280*
Air
Any bus/truck going to Nuevitas, Minas or Playa Santa Lucía from Parque Finlay by the railway station will pass the Ignacio Agramonte International Airport (CMW). The airport is 9 km from the centre on the road to Nuevitas, T32-261000. There are 2 terminals, for domestic flights, T32-267202, and for international flights, T32-267150. **Cubana** flies daily from Havana, and once a week from **Montréal**. There are also charter flights from **Toronto**, Venezuela, Miami and **Europe** depending on the season. There is a small airstrip at Playa Santa Lucía, Joaquín de Agüero. There are car rental agencies at the airport.

Airlines Cubana, República 400 esq Correa, T32-292156/291338, Mon, Wed, Fri 0815-1600, Tue, Thu 0815-1830, Sat 0830-1130. Also at Playa Santa Lucía, in Club **Mayanabo**, T32-365352.

Bus
The Interprovincial bus station is southwest of the centre along the Carretera Central Oeste, esq Perú. **Víazul**, T32-270396 (24-hr service for reservations at the terminal or go to Cubatur), stops here on its **Havana–Santiago, Havana–Holguín, Varadero–Santiago** and **Trinidad–Santiago** routes. Buses and trucks to Playa Santa Lucía and other municipalities leave from opp Parque Finlay. Bus to Playa Santa Lucía 0500 and 1400, 3.25 pesos cubanos.

Car hire
Havanautos is at Céspedes y Carretera Central opp Hotel Camagüey, T32-272239, at Plaza Joaquín de Agüero (Plaza de Méndez), T32-257537, and at the airport T32-261010/287068. **Cubacar**, manager's office at Av Jayama y Carretera Central este, opp fuel station near Hotel Camagüey, with branches at Hotel Plaza, T32-282413, at Parque Casino Campestre beside Restaurante DiMar on the edge of the Río Hatibonico, T32-297472, at Plaza de los Trabajadores, Ignacio Agramonte 448, T32-285327, at Martí y Carretera Central oeste T32-257538, and at the airport, T32-287067. **Rex** at the airport, T32-262444, the best for luxury cars such as Audi, with

prices from CUC$70-160 a day, although other makes are available for less. **Vía Gaviota**, at the airport, T32-241806, probably the cheapest in the city, with good deals on weekly rentals. At Playa Santa Lucía, there are rental desks at the hotels or just outside them. **Havanautos**, T32-26188, commercial office at Av Residencial, T32-336368. **Cubacar**, T32-336109, commercial office, T32-365216. Also offices at Martí y Medrano, Nuevitas, T32-416486; Carretera Central, Florida, T32-516260; Martí 89 entre Victoria y Olimpo, Guaimaro, T32-813290.

Petrol stations: There are **Servi Cupet** 24-hr gas stations: Libertad, by the river on Carretera Central with Av de la Libertad; Vía Blanca, a couple of blocks further south on the other side of the Carretera Central; at Carretera Central este, beside Hotel Camagüey; at Av Saratoga, 300 m from Av Finlay; at Carretera Central oeste y Gen Gómez by the hospital; at Carretera Central este by the provincial bus station, and several others around the city; at the junction as you arrive at Playa Santa Lucía; Carretera Central y Francisco V Aguilera, Florida; Carretera Central y Martí, Guáimaro; Agramonte entre Albisa y Medrano, Nuevitas; Carretera de Santa Cruz del Sur 304 and Carretera Central y Vía Blanca, Camagüey.

Taxi
Cubataxi, Av de los Mártires in the same block as Hotel Puerto Príncipe, T32-281247/298721 in Camagüey. Av Principal La Concha, T32-336196 in Playa Santa Lucía. An official taxi will cost CUC$60 (CUC$0.50 per km) from **Camagüey–Playa Santa Lucía**, 1 way. You can probably negotiate a round trip with waiting time for CUC$70, depending on your bargaining skills, as the driver can earn extra money while you are at the beach. A private car will cost about the same as it is illegal and if caught by the police the driver will have to pay a fine or a bribe. You may have to call a **Cubataxi** for the rest of your journey. Ask at your *casa particular*. From **Playa Santa Lucía** to **Playa los Cocos**, expect to pay CUC$5-6.

Bicitaxis in the city charge CUC$0.40 per block, double that at night (plus surcharge after midnight), see list on back of bike. However, it is illegal for tourists to travel in private bicitaxis. There is an official, state-run agency: **Andariegos**, which tourists can use. Contact the manager, Alcides, at Calle Cristo, beside Restaurante Tinajita, T32-295484/295598. If you are in a group he can arrange for a fleet of bicitaxis to take you around town in a caravan.

Horse-drawn carriages are used in Camagüey and at Playa Santa Lucía for local taxi journeys; around town on official routes the price is 1-2 pesos cubanos, fix price in advance, **Playa Santa Lucía** to **Playa los Cocos**, CUC$20 return; a 2-hr tour is also CUC$20.

Train
Schedules and fares must be confirmed, trains cannot be relied on. Railway station, T32-292633/281525. Train ticket agency, T32-283214. Foreigners pay in CUC$ at **Ladis** office upstairs above the main ticket office opposite Hotel Plaza. The station is divided into long distance, south of the railway by Hotel Plaza, and short distances within the province, north of the railway between Joaquín de Agüero and Manuel Benavides. Camagüey is on the routes **Havana–Santiago**, **Havana–Bayamo** and **Havana–Guantánamo**.

❶ Directory

Camagüey centre *p282, map p280*
Banks Most banks are open Mon-Fri 0800-1500, Sat 0800-1100, except Banco Popular de Ahorro on Av Mártires, T32-283268, which is open Mon-Sat 0800-1900, with ATM. Other branches of BPA at República 294 entre San Estéban y Callejón de Magdalena, T32-297687, ATM; Cisneros 224 entre Hermanos Agüero y Martí, T32-296777, ATM; Av Libertad 33, T32-292632, ATM. **Banco Financiero**

Internacional is on Plaza Maceo, T32-294846. For all financial and exchange services including cash advances on credit cards. Efficient, cool, Mon-Fri 0800-1500 except last working day of the month 0800-1200. There is a **Cadeca** for currency exchange and TCs on República 353 entre Primelles y Santa Rita, T32-295220, Mon-Sat 0800-1800, Sun 0800-1300, also at Av de la Libertad inside the grocery, T32-286840, same hours, at the airport, in Hotel Camagüey and in hotels at Playa Santa Lucía. Charges are higher at the Cadecas in hotels and at the airport than in town. The **Banco de la República** is on República opposite Iglesia La Soledad. **Bandec** is on Plaza de los Trabajadores, T32-291875, ATM, Cisneros esq Plaza de los Trabajadores, T32-293932, Joaquín de Agüero 2, T32-288537, and Residencial, Playa Santa Lucía, T32-336383. **Immigration** T32-336225. **Internet** Etecsa, Avellaneda 271, daily 0830-1630 and **Telepunto**, República entre San Martín y San José, near Hotel Colón, T32-251559, daily 0830-1930, both offer internet access at CUC$6 per hr. The hotels have internet service for guests. **Medical services** The Policlínico Finlay is on Av Carlos J Finlay heading towards the airport. **Policlínica Pirra** is squeezed between the railway station and the Agramonte museum. The **Provincial Hospital** is west of the centre, T32-291902 /282012. **Amalia Simoni Clinic** is out on the road to Nuevitas, just past the junction with Circunvalación, T32-261051/261041. **Surgery,** Ignacio Agramonte 449, beside Isabela restaurant,

T32-251952, Mon-Fri 0900-1700, Sat 0900-1300, consulting room and pharmacy, pay in CUC$, Dr Víctor Sousa (T32-287476 home phone) and dentist Dr Yadira Ulloa (T01-5233 4087 mob) are in charge of medical services for tourists in Camagüey. At Playa Santa Lucía there is an **International Clinic**, Residencial 14, T32-336203, www.servimedcuba.com. **Pharmacy,** Maceo 8, 15 m from Plaza Maceo, 0900-1700 Mon-Fri, 0900-1500 Sat, CUC$. There are lots of pharmacies where Cubans pay in pesos cubanos, but it is illegal to sell medicines to tourists, who have to pay in CUC$ at the places listed. **Post** The central post office is just on the corner of the Plaza de los Trabajadores on Cisneros, next to Casa Natal Ignacio Agramonte, T32-293277. There are others on Los Mártires entre Julio Sanguily y Tomás Betancourt, T32-282309, on the corner of Plaza Joaquín de Agüero opp the children's theatre and on Carretera Central opp Hospital Provincial. At Playa Santa Lucía there is a post office by Servi Cupet at the main junction, the main post office is in Residencial and all hotels have an office. **Telephone** Etecsa Is on Avellaneda 271 and 308, T32-281709, daily 0830-1630, phones, accessories, pre-paid cards, internet and fax. Telepunto, República entre San Martín y San José, near Hotel Colón, T32-251559, daily 0830-1930, phone cards, accessories, international calls, fax, internet access, CUC$6 per hr. At Playa Santa Lucía **Etecsa** is by Servi Cupet at the main junction. Email is available.

Las Tunas

→ *Colour map 3, B4. Population: 120,000.*

Victoria de las Tunas, also known as Las Tunas, or even just Tuna, was founded in the 1750s, but was never more than a market town until Las Tunas became a province in its own right in 1975 and needed a provincial capital. Travellers could be forgiven for not noticing this small, agricultural province on their way from Camagüey to Holguín or Bayamo, as only about 65 km of the road actually passes through it. On the other hand, the provincial capital would make a convenient break in the journey, or you could get well off the beaten track by visiting the beaches of the irregular northern coast, indented by three large bays. Las Tunas boasts 35 virgin beaches, of which the main one, Playa Covarrubias, has fine, white sand and is protected by a 3-km coral reef. Hotel construction is making it easier to stay in this area, which so far does not have the enclave atmosphere of many of Cuba's beach resorts. ►► *For listings, see pages 302-304.*

Ins and outs

Getting there The Carretera Central linking Havana with the east of the country runs through the middle of town, although there is now a Circunvalación running round the south so that you can avoid the centre all together if you want to. There is a domestic airport outside **Las Tunas**, but no international flights land here. Las Tunas is on the long-distance **bus** and **train** routes from Havana to Santiago de Cuba. It is easy enough to get there but more difficult to get out, as most of the buses are full when they pass through. The long-distance bus terminal is 1 km from the town centre and closer than the railway station, 2.5 km away, but both are within walking distance if you haven't got much luggage. **Bicitaxis** and **coches** are available. ►► *See also Transport, page 303.*

Getting around The town of Las Tunas is small and you can **walk** around it in a day at a leisurely pace. Motorized or horse-drawn **taxis** are available if you are based further out at **Hotel Las Tunas**, where there is also **car hire**. The provincial bus station for bus services to local towns and villages is beside the railway station. Taxis will take you on excursions.

Tourist information The large hotels have information bureaux but there is not much on offer here.

Sights

City centre

The town centre is effectively the junction of three roads, the tree-lined Vicente García (the Carretera Central), Angel Guardia and Francisco Varona, at the Parque Vicente García, where there is a small church. There is a memorial to General Vicente García just off the Parque and his name crops up frequently in the town, because he led the struggle for independence in the area in 1868 and captured the town in 1876. The old centre of Las Tunas, the *casco histórico*, has received a certain amount of investment recently and the town has been beautified considerably, largely with the introduction of some 70 sculptures permanently exhibited around town. One, by Rita Longa, is of a naked woman lying in the shape of the island of Cuba, called 'Venus Stretching Out'. Las Tunas is known as the Cuban capital of sculpture and every two years has a major sculpture festival. Buildings, such as the 1945 Hotel Cadillac, have been completely renovated and an attractive pedestrian boulevard created, linking Plaza José Martí with the theatre, the provincial museum and the Memorial Mayor General Vicente García González (see below).

In 1976 a **Cubana** plane en route from Caracas to Havana was blown up just after take-off from a stop in Barbados by a bomber who left a device under his seat when he disembarked in Barbados. Seventy-three people, including the Cuban fencing team, were killed. To this day no one has been charged in connection with the incident. The **Memorial a los Mártires de Barbados** ① *Calle Lucas Ortiz 344 entre Teniente Peiso y Mártires de Barbados, T31-347213. CUC$1*, located in a museum in the park along Vicente García by the river, contains photos of all the victims around the walls. Three members of the fencing team came from Las Tunas and the museum is in the house of one of them. The 25th anniversary of the bombing, in 2001, coincided with the terrorist attack on the World Trade Center in New York, providing Cuba with extra publicity in its campaign for justice.

Opposite the Parque, the **Museo Provincial General Vicente García** ① *Calle Francisco Varona entre Angel Guerra y Lucas Ortiz, T31-348201*, displays local history. Built in 1921, it was originally the Town Hall, before becoming the municipal public library in 1951, a high school after the Revolution in 1959 and a museum in 1984 after extensive remodelling. The **Memorial Mayor General Vicente García González** ① *Calle Vicente García 5 entre Francisco Vega y Julián Santana, T31-345164*, is the birthplace of the general. The present house dates from 1919, as the General's house was burned down in 1876 when he ordered the burning of the city before turning it over to the Spanish. It is used for local ceremonies and houses various historical exhibits, old weapons, documents and art.

The birthplace of a local 19th-century poet has been made into a museum, the **Casa Natal Juan Cristóbal Nápoles y Fajardo**, on Lucas Ortíz. He was one of the greatest creators of the Cuban *cucalambé* style, which started in the 19th century but continues today as a niche cultural genre based on improvization. Nápoles wrote *décimas*, songs of ten sentences long. He vanished in 1862 and no one knows what happened to him. Every year a music festival is held in Las Tunas, *La Jornada Cucalambeana*, with singers of country music, improvization and other artists honouring this and other writers of *cucalambé* (see Festivals and events, page 303). There is also plenty of salsa and dancing, local food stalls and lots of beer and rum.

Around Las Tunas

The province is only 6589 sq km of mostly low-lying farming land, although the central part of the province around the city is part of the Holguín ridge and more hilly. There are three large bays on the northern coast: **Bahía de Manatí**, **Bahía de Malagueta** and **Bahía de Puerto Padre de Chapata**, which offer safe harbour and fishing ports. You can see flamingos and other water birds in the Bahía de Malagueta, which is one of the largest protected areas in the country, at 23,262 ha, of which 9210 are underwater. It includes the Cerro de Caisimú and Yariguá hunting reserve (Coto de Caza), where shooting and fishing are permitted in season. To get there, drive yourself, hire a driver for the day or see if there is an organized tour from one of the hotels.

The southern coast opens onto the **Golfo de Guacanayabo** and is marshy with mangroves. Beef cattle and sugar cane are among the main agricultural activities, while the UN Development Programme (UNDP) is helping to develop milk production. Close to Las Tunas you can get out to the **Motel El Cornito**, see Sleeping, where you can relax, walk or fish in the river and reservoir.

The main town on the north coast, 56 km from Las Tunas, is **Puerto Padre**, tucked in at the end of the bay of the same name. Unusually there are fresh water springs here, right next to the sea shore. Cooking salt for industrial purposes is extracted here. Severely damaged by Hurricane Ike in 2008, production was eventually resumed in June 2009. Overlooking the water is the **Fuerte de la Loma**, a stone fortress built in 1869 with four circular towers, a moat and a drawbridge. It saw active service during the Wars of Independence and during the Revolution, when it was used by Batista's troops until it was taken on 25 December 1958. Some colonial buildings dating from the 1860s remain in the town, which has a wide boulevard leading down to the Malecón where there is a restaurant. If you ask around there will no doubt be a *casa particular* where you can stay if you have to. There are two daily buses from Las Tunas from the provincial bus station next to the railway station, but it is easier to hire a driver for a day trip and take in a beach as well.

Further afield, you can drive to the north coast to the beaches on **Punta Covarrubias**, **Playa Las Bocas** or **Playa La Herradura**. There are no buses and little tourist development along this stretch of coast and you are likely to have the place to yourself. On **Playa Covarrubias**, 26 km west of Puerto Padre, there is an all-inclusive hotel, **Brisas Covarrubias**. So far this is the only hotel. The beach is white sand and protected by a reef which has created sand banks and shallow water, beautifully clear and safe. The Laguna Real, at the end of the resort, has pink water, coloured by the micro-organisms which live in it, attracting flamingos among other water birds. **Playa Las Bocas** is at the eastern bank of the mouth of the Bahía de Puerto Padre on a small bay with golden sand and a few palm trees. Crowds are almost non-existent although at weekends you will find Cubans who have their own transport enjoying themselves here. A basic beach bar sells pizza and soft drinks for pesos, but don't rely on it, take some supplies of your own. **Playa La Herradura** is east of here and is another unspoilt sandy beach with few facilities. There is no public transport to any of these beaches and it is best to hire a car or taxi.

◉ Las Tunas listings

For Sleeping and Eating price codes and other relevant information, see Essentials pages 37-43.

● Sleeping

Las Tunas city centre *p300*
Hotels
B Hotel Cadillac, Colón esq Francisco Vega, T31-372791, www.islazul.cu. 3-star hotel, totally renovated and reopened 2008. Built 1945 in the shape of ship which looks like it is anchored to the boulevard. 8 standard rooms, 2 junior suites, bar, Balcony Restaurant, roof terrace, nightclub planned in the basement.
D Las Tunas, Av 2 de Diciembre y Carlos J Finlay, T31-345014, www.islazul.cu, on a hill on the road out to the hospital, southeast of the town. 142 basic rooms in modern

4-storey block, restaurant, cafeteria, large pool (not always filled), car rental.

Casas particulares
D-E Villa Rosalba, Av 2 de Diciembre 3 entre Frank País y J Agüero, 31-349042. 1 room with bathroom, central location not far from bus station, Rosalba Guerra Cruz is very kind and hospitable as well as a good cook.
E Alejandro Cordero Pupo, Calle 50 entre Francisco Varona y Francisco Vega, La Loma, T31-348198. Alejandro is a civil engineer and his wife Maylyn live in a house which they designed and built a few years ago. 2 rooms to rent with ensuite bathrooms, a/c, 2 mins' walk from bus station, only Spanish spoken, helpful, kind.
E Elizabeth Rivero Mancebo, Lico Cruz 87 entre Villalón y Gómez, T31-347952

(neighbour). Upstairs apartment overlooking quiet street on airport side of town, 1 room, clean and newly decorated, new bathroom, good food, packed lunches available.
E Marianela Santiago, Lucas Ortiz 101 Altos, T31-343259. Central, 1 room, a/c, TV, radio, large terrace on roof, parking, friendly.
E Rodrigo y Yosi, Coronel Reyes 41 esq Gonzalo de Quesada, T31-348760. 1 room, clean and comfortable, good food. Rodrigo has a car and can drive you around town.

Around Las Tunas *p301*
Hotels
AL-B Brisas Covarrubias, Playa Covarrubias, west of Puerto Padre, T31-515530, www.cubanacan.cu. All-inclusive hotel, 180 rooms in *cabañas* on the beach with lots of sporting facilities available on land and in the water, massages and mud therapy, and a nightclub. Remote, so excursions can be time-consuming. Under renovation in 2009, due to reopen end-year.

⦿ Eating

Las Tunas city centre *p300*
Casas particulares are a better bet than the state restaurants.
♯ **1876**, Vicente García, near the park by the river, T31-344736. Daily 1200-2300. Restaurant and bar, specializes in pork.
♯ **Rey Mar**, Francisco Varona entre Colón y Carretera Central, T31-344923. Fish and seafood, open for lunch and dinner.

Around Las Tunas *p301*
♯ **Sierra Cristal**, on the Malecón, Puerto Padre. Daily 1130-0100. Seafood restaurant.

⦿ Entertainment

Las Tunas city centre *p300*
Casa de la Cultura, Vicente García 8 entre Francisco Vega y Francisco Varona.

Around Las Tunas *p301*
Anacaona, Puerto Padre. A nightclub on the Malecón esq Paco Cabrera, which accepts credit cards.

⦿ Festivals and events

Las Tunas city centre *p300*
Jun/Jul There is a Fiesta Cucalambé at the Motel El Cornito, 7 km west of town off the Carretera Central, for folk music, see page 301.
Dec Agricultural fair in La Tunas.

⦿ Transport

Las Tunas city centre *p300*
Air
There is an airport, Aeropuerto Hermanos Ameijeiras (VTU), T31-342484, 11 km from Las Tunas, which receives Cubana flights twice a week from **Havana**.
    Airlines Cubana, Lucas Ortiz esq 24 de Febrero, T31-346873.

Bus
The bus station is just south of the main Parque on Francisco Varona, T31-342444. Long-distance buses are already full when they pass through Las Tunas and you just have to hope that someone is getting off here. Local buses use the terminal near the railway station.

Car hire
There is a Havanautos desk in the Hotel Las Tunas, T31-349328.
    Petrol stations Servi Cupet fuel stations at Carretera Central Oeste Km 2, Las Tunas, and at Av Libertad 156, Puerto Padre. Oro Negro service station at Francisco Varona entre Lora y Menocal, Las Tunas.

Taxi and local transport
Most local transport is by horse and cart or other non-motorized transport such as *bicitaxis*.

Train

The railway station is northeast of the centre, with trains to **Holguín, Santiago** and **Havana**. Unreliable.

❸ Directory

Las Tunas city centre *p300*
Banks Banco Financiero Internacional on Vicente García y 24 de Febrero on your left as you head out towards Camagüey in a modern concrete and dark glass building, Mon-Fri 0800-1500. **Cadeca** Colón 141, Mon-Sat 0830-1800, Sun 0830-1300. **Post** Vicente García 6. **Telephone** Etecsa on Angel Guardia, just east of the Parque.

Contents

Footprint features

At a glance

◉ **Getting around** On foot, by bicycle, hired car, taxi and Víazul long-distance bus.

◉ **Time required** 1-2 weeks.

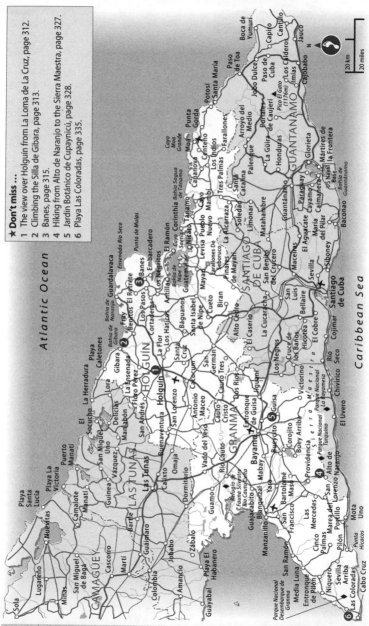

★ Don't miss...
1 The view over Holguín from La Loma de La Cruz, page 312.
2 Climbing the Silla de Gibara, page 313.
3 Banes, page 315.
4 Hiking from Alto de Naranjo to the Sierra Maestra, page 327.
5 Jardín Botánico de Cupaynicú, page 328.
6 Playa Las Coloradas, page 335.

Atlantic Ocean

Caribbean Sea

20 km
20 miles

N

The countryside of Holguín is attractive, hilly and covered with luxuriant vegetation. There are picture-book views of hillsides dotted with Royal palms, towering over thatched cottages, called *bohíos*, while the flatter land is green with swathes of sugar cane. The city of Holguín is unassuming and pleasant, with a huge central square. The local people take pride in the tourist developments of Guardalavaca; but unlike Varadero, there is no wall-to-wall hotel strip. The north coast is indented with pretty horseshoe-shaped bays and sandy beaches, protected by a coral reef.

Columbus is believed to have landed at the Bahía de Bariay on 28 October 1492, which he claimed was the most beautiful country he had ever seen. The indigenous people probably thought so too, since archaeological explorations have shown that there were primitive cultures here some 6000 years ago. Seboruco man is thought to have been the first inhabitant of what is now the province of Holguín.

The province of Granma occupies the western end of the Sierra Maestra and the flatlands and swamps to the north of the mountains. It was named after the boat that brought Castro and his comrades to Cuba to launch the Revolution. The area is studded with memories of the guerrilla struggle and the hills are full of evocative plaques commemorating the events immediately after their landing in 1956, but it has been largely neglected as far as tourism is concerned. This is one province where you will need to buy a few pesos cubanos and where hassling of tourists is rare. The capital of the province is Bayamo, which has good transport links and from where hiking into the mountains is organized, while Manzanillo is its main port.

Getting there

Air Holguín has an international airport accessible for either the north-coast hotels or Bayamo. It is a useful airport for a circuit of the eastern end of the island, taking in Holguín, Bayamo, Manzanillo, Santiago, Guantánamo and Baracoa. Manzanillo has an airport which receives charter flights from Canada and Venezuela and scheduled flights only once a week from Havana. **Rail and road** Rail connections to Holguín have been replaced by more efficient bus services. The railway line is 19 km from Holguín at the village of Cacocum; the service Holguín–Santiago and Holguín–Guantánamo have been suspended indefinitely because of repairs to the line. Both Holguín and Bayamo are on the main bus routes from Havana to Santiago de Cuba on the Carretera Central and transport links are good with Viazul buses for foreigners and Astro for Cubans. Manzanillo is less accessible, as you have to change bus or train in Bayamo. ▸▸ *See also page 325 and page 334.*

Tourist information

All the hotels around Guardalavaca have tourist desks which can provide information as well as tours. There are tour operators in Holguín and Bayamo (see Activities and tours, page 322), but you will get better advice from your *casa particular* if that is where you are staying.

Best time to visit

The driest season is from December to April. Hurricane season technically starts in June, but most storms arrive between September and November. Rain can fall at any time of year, usually in the afternoons. Holguín is developing a reputation as a good venue for festivals, with a local cultural event in January, the Romerías de May in the first week of May and an Ibero-American festival in October.

Holguín

→ *Colour map 3, B5. Population: 300,000.*
Holguín was founded in 1545 as Hato San Isidro de Holguín, but most of the architecture in the centre dates from the 19th and 20th centuries. There are many statues and monuments to national heroes, several of which are around Plaza de la Revolución, on the edge of the city, the location of the modern City Hall and the Provincial Communist Party building. The town was named after García Holguín, a captain in the Spanish colonization force. It officially received the title of Ciudad de San Isidro de Holguín on 18 January 1752, when the population numbered 1426. The city has two universities, two big hospitals, a paediatric hospital, brewery and baseball stadium and is busy, although all traffic moves at the pace of the thousands of bicycles that throng the streets. There are several attractive excursions to be made from the city, with easy access to some of the best beaches in the country. ▸▸ *For listings, see pages 317-324.*

Ins and outs

Getting there Holguín has the Frank País García international airport 12 km from town, a taxi ride into the centre. Most foreigners are on their way to the Guardalavaca beach resort and are transported by tour bus to their hotels. There are **flights** from Amsterdam, Dusseldorf, Frankfurt, Helsinki, London, Miami, Milan, Montréal, Toronto, Havana (CUC$101-105). The city is 19 km from the main Havana–Santiago **railway** line with daily train services in each direction. It is better served by long-distance buses. **Víazul** stops here on its Havana–Santiago and Trinidad–Santiago routes and runs **buses** to Guardalavaca in July and August for a day on the beach. ›› See Transport, page 323.

Getting around It is easiest to **walk** around the centre as traffic is very slow, but for going further afield you can hop on a horse-drawn **coche**, or hire a **bicitaxi**. Tour agencies offer organized excursions but if you want to go on your own, **car hire** is available.

Sights

City centre

Holguín is known as the 'city of the parks', five of which, **Parque Infantil** (also known as Ruben Bravo), **Parque Carlos Manuel de Céspedes** (also known as Parque San José), the **Plaza Central** (Plaza Gen Calixto García), **Parque Gen Julio Grave de Peralta** (Parque de las Flores) and **Parque José Martí**, lie between the two main streets: Antonio Maceo and Libertad (Manduley). There is a statue of **Carlos Manuel de Céspedes** in the park named after him: he is remembered for having freed his slaves on 10 October 1868 and starting the war of independence. The 1820 church, **Iglesia de San José**, is in **Parque Carlos Manuel de Céspedes** where there is a monument to the former president.

The Plaza Central is named after **General Calixto García Iñiguez** (statue in the centre), who was born in Holguín in 1839 and took part in both wars of independence. He captured the town from the Spanish in 1872 and again occupied it in 1898 after helping the US forces defeat the colonial power in Santiago de Cuba. His statue is in the centre and his birthplace, one block from the plaza, is now a museum, **Casa Natal de Calixto García** ① Calle Miró 147, T24-425610, Tue-Sat 0900-1630, Sun 1000-1800, CUC$1. The building is a National Monument, but the museum has a collection of dusty, faded exhibits and newer models of battles for lovers of army games. The inner courtyard is used for cultural activities after 2000.

Around the plaza are the **Commander Eddy Suñol Theatre** (he fought against Batista) and the **library** ① Mon-Fri 0800-2100, Sat 0800-1800, Sun 0800-1300, a modern building with a spiral staircase, which hosts special events on Sundays. Also on the plaza is **Galería Bayado** where you can buy ceramics, carvings and furniture. To the rear of the Galería, there is a courtyard where you can enjoy music and singing in the evening. At the **Casa de Cultura Dositeo Aguilera** ① T24-422084, there are handicrafts for sale, and dancing (danzón). On the north side of the square is the **Museo Provincial de Historia** ① Mon-Fri 0900-1700, Sat 0900-1300, CUC$1, CUC$3 with camera, known as La Periquera (parrot cage) because of the brightly coloured soldiers known as periquitos (parakeets) who used to stand guard outside when the building was used as an army barracks in the 19th century. It was built between 1860 and 1868 and is now a National Monument. On 30 October 1868, 500 armed independistas attacked the building shouting ¡Viva Cuba! but failed to take it because of its strategic defences. The most important item on display here is the Hacha de Holguín, a pre-Columbian axe head carved with the head of a man, measuring 350 mm in length and 76 mm at its widest point. It was found in 1860 on a hill around the city and is believed to be about 500 years old. It has become the symbol of Holguín. A replica is given to visiting dignitaries as the highest honour bestowed by the province.

The plaza is most active at night when families, friends and lovers enjoy the cooler air, sitting on the hundreds of benches or strolling around. Children leap all over the place and it is great for rollerskates, while music from the Casa de la Trova El Guayabero, named in honour of the local trovador, competes with a heavy-duty sound system on another

Holguín

Sleeping 🛏
Don Santiago cp **1** *F6*
Germán González
  Rojas cp **4** *F3*
Isabela Sera Galves cp **7** *C5*
Luis Turbay y Marya
  Ferrás cp **5** *B6*

Pernik **2** *B6*
Villa El Bosque **3** *B6*
Villa Liba cp **14** *A3*

Eating 🍴
1720 **1** *C4*
Casa del Cheff **13** *E4*

Coppelia **6** *D5*
El Piropo **8** *D4*
El Tocororo **9** *D5*
Jelly Boom **4** *E3*
La Begonia **5** *D4*
La Crema **10** *C4*
La Gran Vía **15** *E5*

N
🧭
Not to scale

corner. Calle Manduley, which runs along the eastern side of the square, has been converted to a pedestrian boulevard between Luz Caballero and Martí, and between Frexes and Arias. All along here are banks, cultural venues, restaurants and cafés; most charge in pesos cubanos.

Off the square, the **Museo de Ciencias Naturales** ⓘ *Maceo 129, Sun-Thu 0900-1700, Sat 1300-1700, CUC$1*, is full of stuffed animals, including a manatee, snakes, giant turtle, nearly all the indigenous birds of Cuba and a huge shell collection. Rather macabre, with human and horse foetuses in jars, but popular. The building is almost more interesting than the exhibits, with neoclassical pillars, pretty turquoise tiles on the outside, sitting lions and two 'moorish' turrets, all newly painted greeny turquoise and white.

Parque Peralta is another square between Maceo and Manduley, named after Julio Grave de Peralta, who led the Holguín independence struggle against Spain in 1868, although it is usually called the Parque de las Flores. Flowers are sold here; it is close to the cemetery and the cathedral. The **Cathedral** is on this square, built in 1720 but frequently altered or improved. It has recently been renovated and a statue of Pope John Paul II, who visited in 1998, has been erected in his memory. On 8 September there is a procession celebrating the day the Virgen de la Caridad appeared in the Bahía de Nipe, before she was taken to the Sanctuario del Cobre outside Santiago. The oldest house in Holguín (the first government house where the Governor lived), is now the **Museo de Arquitectura** ⓘ *Morales Lemus entre Arecochea y Cables*.

Major renovation work has been undertaken in the city centre, mostly between Calles Arias and Aricochea. Known as the Plan Imagen, it is still ongoing, and includes the restoration of historic hotels, such as the Majestic (for Cubans only), where Fidel Castro stayed in room 13 and the actor

Jorge Negrete also stayed. The **Plaza de la Maqueta** southwest of Plaza Central between Mártires and Máximo Gómez has become a major tourist attraction. The old market has been reconstructed in the centre to become a theatre, the Lírico de Holguín, and shops, art galleries and a hotel are in progress around the outside. It has been designed with artists in mind and round the square are humorous touches: telegraph poles are carved like totem poles; another statue depicts a woman with a shopping basket and on a balcony is a man looking over the railing. On the south side is the **Instituto Cubano del Libro** ① *Mon-Sat 0800-2000, Sun 0900-1200*, a printing house and an art shop stocking oils, acrylics and other art materials, as well as the Tienda Mona Lisa (Artex) for music, books and souvenirs. On the east side work is in progress on a new hotel, **Don José**, with an *artesanía* downstairs. On the north side, **EGREM** has a music shop, **La Flor de Holguín**, selling CDs and musical instruments, while next door is Caracol's **La Cohoba**, for cigars, rum and coffee, very smart, credit cards accepted.

North of the centre

Above the city is **La Loma de la Cruz**, a strategic hill and emblem of the city, which used to have a cross on top until Hurricane Georges blew it down in 1998. On 3 May 1790, a Franciscan priest, Antonio de Alegría, came with a group of religious people and put up the cross, 275 m above sea level, 127 m above the town. All the streets of the town were laid out from that strategic point, which has a lookout tower, built by the Spanish during the 10 Years' War. In 1929, stone steps were begun up the hill, not finished until 3 May 1950. Every 3 May locals celebrate the *Romerías de la Cruz de Mayo*. There is a road round the side of the hill, but if you wish to walk up straight up the 458 steps, there are lots of benches for resting on. There are also a couple of restaurants about 150 m up, one charging in CUC$ and the other in Cuban pesos. The way is lit up at night with street lights. Candles are lit and offerings of coins are made, but you are more likely to meet gangs of boys waiting for tourists than religious devotees. A policeman is usually on patrol in the morning. Women should not walk up alone in the evenings or at night.

An interesting local industry you can visit is the doll factory, **Fábrica de Muñecas Cubanas** ① *Av Cajigal entre Narciso López y Cervantes, Mon-Fri 0900-1600*. Further along the same road, Av Cajigal, about 2 km from the Parque Infantil on the road to Gibara, is an organ factory, **Fábrica de Organos**, the only one in the country, which you can also visit during working hours to see how they make the instruments.

Around Holguín

Holguín lies in the east of the country, stretching along the north coast and indented by many bays. The capital, Holguín, lies in a range of hills that stretch from Las Tunas to the coast at Punta de Mulas, while the eastern part of the province takes in the foothills of the Sierra del Cristal and the Montañas de Nipe-Sagua-Baracoa. The highest point in the province of Holguín is Pico Cristal, at 1813 m, found in the Sierra Cristal to the northeast of Mayarí and on the border with the province of Santiago de Cuba. Further to the east of the province is the hugely important nickel and cobalt plant with shipping facilities at Moa, which is receiving large amounts of foreign investment, particularly from Canada.

Mirador de Mayabe

The Mirador de Mayabe is a popular excursion. A restaurant and hotel have been built on a hillside a few kilometres out of town with a splendid view over the valley and the whole city. Water towers stand out like mushrooms in the distance. The restaurant has good Cuban food, open air but under cover and the usual strolling musicians. There is a swimming pool perched on the edge of the hill and beside it a bar, where Pancho, the beer-drinking donkey entertains guests. He is confined in a very small pen beside the bar and it is unlikely that the quantity of beer does him any good, but apart from an air of boredom he seems quite healthy and happy. This is actually Pancho II, as the first Pancho was killed in a car accident and a younger model had to be found and trained to drink beer. **La Finca Mayabe** has a second restaurant, normally open only for tour parties, with a *bohío*, and a collection of chickens, turkeys, ducks, etc, which you might find around a typical farmer's house.

Gibara → *Population: 30,000.*

About 32 km north of Holguín on the coast is the pretty little town of Gibara, still recovering from the damage wrought by Hurricane Ike on 7 September 2008. It is believed that Columbus first landed near here at Cayo Bariay on 28 October 1492, where a monument was erected to mark the 500th anniversary (see below). The hill nearby, the **Silla de Gibara**, he referred to as shaped like a saddle and it became a landmark and navigation reference point. Hike up to **El Cuartelón** (El Mirador) from where you get an excellent view of the Bahía de Gibara, the Fernando VII battery and the Colonial battery, the town with its higgledy piggledy deep red-tiled roofs punctuated by palm trees and the beach to one side. The town was not founded until 1817, but it became an important port for the area and there is still a thriving fishing industry, specializing in lobsters. It is also known for its links with cinema, hosting the annual Festival Internacional del Cine Pobre (low-budget movie festival) in April, a project of the late Humberto Solás, who died in 2008. The main square has a fine row of big African oak trees around it and in front of the pretty yellow church with two red domes there is a Carrara marble replica of the Statue of Liberty. In the town there are many large and pleasant old houses with open porches and stained-glass windows dating from the 19th century and there is a sweeping Malecón. On Independencia there are two museums, the **Museo Municipal** ① *CUC$1*, and the **Museo de Historia Natural** ① *CUC$2*, which have exhibitions about the area. One of the foremost artists in Cuba, Cosme Proenza Almaguer, comes from Gibara. He is a post-modernist painter, taking his inspiration from legends and fantasies and depicting phantasmagorical creatures, gnomes, medieval lakes and caravels. His gallery at Independencia 32 was closed after Hurricane Ike in 2008, but it is worth checking if it has reopened, T24-423934.

The area is noted for its extensive network of caves, tunnels and pools. If you walk up the hill from Independencia and ask for directions you will come to the Cavernas de Panaderos, consisting of 19 galleries and an underground trail of about 11 km. About 18 km northwest of Gibara along the coast, you come to **Playa Caletones**, a reasonable beach where natural rock pools have formed to make swimming pools.

Cayo Bariay

Cayo Bariay is not an island, but a round peninsula hanging onto the main island by a spit of land. At the tip is the **Monumento Encuentro entre Dos Culturas**, a monument erected in 1992 to Columbus' landing and the meeting of two cultures in 1492. There is a beach, Playa Cayo Bariay, and a restaurant, **El Mirador** with a good panoramic view of the coast. The area is popular with Cubans on holiday. Across the water is Playa Blanca and the **Hotel Don Lino** (Islazul) on Playa Don Lino.

Guardalavaca and around → *Colour map 3, B6.*

Guardalavaca has been developed as a tourist resort along a beautiful stretch of coastline, indented with horseshoe bays and sandy beaches. Numbers of visitors have risen fast as new hotels have been built. In the winter season, some 10,000 tourists arrive on 45 to 50 flights a week. The name of Guardalavaca encompasses the resorts on Playa Guardalavaca as well as nearby Playa Esmeralda, Playa Yuraguanal and Playa Pesquero Playa Guardalavaca is the oldest part with apartments for workers, a few shops, small craft market, a disco (La Roca), photo service, restaurants, fast-food place (El Rápido) and bus stop. On the beach you can hire surfboards and sailboats and there are beach bars. This is where you come for a day trip from Holguín. The other beaches are very isolated and there is nothing to do outside the hotels. Nevertheless, Playa Esmeralda is a very pretty horseshoe shape with a river coming down to the sea in the middle and rocks at either end providing good snorkelling opportunities. There is a reef offshore for diving, which is very unspoilt and has a lot to offer. The hills surrounding the beach are green and wooded, helping to make the hotels here unobtrusive.

On the eastern shore of Bahía de Naranjo there is a nature trail, **Sendero Ecológico Las Guanas**, which has a cave and a mirador, with lots of information in English and Spanish on the vegetation, fauna and Amerindians, CUC$6. Just before the entrance there is a path down to your left, about 10 m to **Playa El Tiburonario**, a nice beach and despite its name there are no sharks.

Bahía de Naranjo

The lagoon in the Bahía de Naranjo has been developed as a small marina. Near the mouth of the lagoon is an **aquarium** ① *T24-430132, 0900-1200 daily dolphin and sea lion show, CUC$42 adults, CUC$21 children, CUC$99 to swim with the dolphins; Tue, Thu, Fri*

Guardalavaca

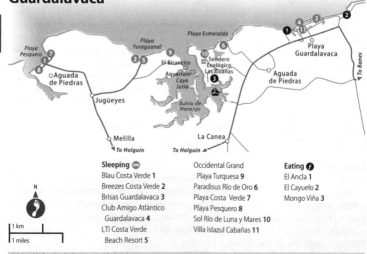

Sleeping 🛏
Blau Costa Verde **1**
Breezes Costa Verde **2**
Brisas Guardalavaca **3**
Club Amigo Atlántico
  Guardalavaca **4**
LTI Costa Verde
  Beach Resort **5**

Occidental Grand
  Playa Turquesa **9**
Paradisus Río de Oro **6**
Playa Costa Verde **7**
Playa Pesquero **8**
Sol Río de Luna y Mares **10**
Villa Islazul Cabañas **11**

Eating 🍴
El Ancla **1**
El Cayuelo **2**
Mongo Viña **3**

afternoon they put on a lobster party, CUC$116, including the show, meal, Afro-Cuban show and open bar until 1930-2000, depending on demand. It's 10 minutes by boat from the dock, with dolphins and a sea lion, and a **restaurant**. A visit here is often included in tours of the area with a show. At the mouth of the bay on the west side, is **El Birancito**, a replica *finca* of where Fidel Castro was born.

Chorro de Maita

A few kilometres from Guardalavaca on a hill with a wonderful view, is the **Museo Aborigen Chorro de Maita** ① *T24-430201, Tue-Sun 0900-1700, Mon 0900-1300, CUC$2 entrance,* a well-presented museum displaying a collection of 56 skeletons dating from 1490-1540, exactly as they were found. One is of a young Spaniard with his arms crossed for a Christian burial, but the rest are Amerindians, buried in the Central American style, lying flat with their arms folded across their stomachs. Excavations took place in 1986 and a total of 108 skeletons were found. The aborigines had malformed skulls from birth, which can be seen clearly. The tallest was 1 m 75 cm, although the average was 1 m 56 cm.

Almost opposite the museum is a replica of a **Taíno village** ① *T24-430422, open daily 0900-1700, CUC$3, children CUC$1.50, photos CUC$1, video CUC$5,* criollo *food available,* with statues of Amerindians going about their daily activities. If you are on an organized tour you may be taken to see the little village primary school just down the hill and you will pass the rural clinic where the doctor lives and works, looking after his allotted 120 families.

Banes

It is a pleasant drive about 30 km from Guardalavaca to Banes over the hills through rolling fields of sugar interspersed with Royal palms. This town is not usually on the itineraries of tour parties even though its church, **Iglesia de Nuestra Señora de la Caridad** was the site of the marriage of Fidel Castro to Mirta Díaz Balart on 12 October 1948. Banes was also the birthplace of the dictator Fulgencio Batista, giving it a second claim to fame with Cuba's leaders. When the Spanish gave way to the Americans in 1898, Banes became a dependency of the United Fruit Company and was owned by them until the Revolution. Having visited the Museo Aborigen Chorro de Maita (above), you may be interested to see the **Museo Indocubano Bani** ① *Gen Marrero 305 y Av José Martí, T24-802487, Tue-Sat 0900-1700, Sun 0800-1200, CUC$1,* which has a good collection of pre-Columbian artifacts, probably the best in Cuba, and a sizable collection of malachite. Explanations can be given by the curator, Luis Quiñones, who speaks English and French. The town of Banes was originally the site of the Bani chieftancy and the museum contains treasures discovered by the many archaeological digs in the area. Banes is considered the archaeological capital of the country.

Mayarí and around → *Colour map 3, B5/6. Population: 23,000.*

On the road from Holguín to Baracoa is the small town of Mayarí founded in 1814 on the river of the same name. It is the sort of place people pass through on their way round the coast to Moa or inland and up into the mountains to Santiago de Cuba, but hardly anyone bothers to stop. The setting is very pretty, with the Sierra del Cristal as a backdrop. Six kilometres from Mayarí is a large cave, **Farallones de Seboruco**, where, in 1945, an archaeological exploration revealed evidence that it had been used by people living there 5000 years ago. Inland and up in the hills the soil turns to a deep red; known as *mocarrero*; it is 85% iron. Visit the scientific station at the **Jardín de Pinare National**

Park. There are trails in the park through 12 different ecosystems. The **Salto de Guayabo** is 85 m high, one of the highest waterfalls in Cuba, and there is a tremendous view across the fall, down the valley to the Bahía de Nipe. Seek local information on where to walk. This whole area with the meseta of the Pinares de Mayarí, Cayo Saetía, the panoramic view from Alto del Carbón and Dos Bahías, Corintia beach and the Cabonico river contain a wealth of fauna and flora.

Finca Birán

① *T24-286102, to speak to Sulmai Vargas, in charge of visits (Florencio Martí is the director). Open Tue-Sat 0900-1600, Sun 0900-1200. Entrance CUC$10 adults, CUC$5 children, CUC$10 cameras, CUC$20 video cameras. You need your own car to get here as it is well off the beaten track and there is no food available, so take your own refreshments.*

In the foothills of the Sierra del Nipe, southwest of Mayarí, is the birthplace of Fidel Castro: Finca Birán. If coming from Holguín or Santiago de Cuba, take the turning east to Birán at Marcané Uno (just south of Loyaz Hechevarría) along a road with pot holes like caverns. If you can take your eyes off the road, the sierra provides a fantastic backdrop. On arrival in the village take the first left and drive for 1.5 km until on your left on the corner you come to a little white house with brown shutters and cactus in the fence. Turn left and drive to the end, where you arrive at the gateway of the Finca Birán (formerly Las Manacas) where Fidel grew up. Although he has written of happy childhood memories, Castro has shown little attachment to the place. It was the first farm to be expropriated after the Revolution, Castro had signed plans to flood the buildings under a reservoir in the 1960s before Celia Sánchez intervened to save it, and it was only in November 2002 that it was quietly opened to the public officially, in recognition of demand. In deference to his distaste for the cult of personality, it is called the **Birán Historic Site**, but was declared a National Monument in 2009. The houses are on stilts. The house where he was born and lived until he was 14 is straight ahead. It is a reconstruction as the original was destroyed by fire, but the walls are lined with family photos of Fidel as a boy. In the grounds are the former little school house, the teacher's house, bakery, cinema, and huts for the Haitian cane cutters. The tombs of Castro's parents are adorned by marble angels and can be clearly seen at the entrance to the buildings. The centenary of the birth of Castro's mother, Lina, was marked in 2003 by the presentation to the President at Finca Birán, of a book about the birth of the estate and its development by his father, Angel Castro: *Todo el Tiempo de los Cedros*, by journalist Katiuska Blanco. The presentation was attended by Fidel, his elder brother Ramón, and his sisters Angela and Agustina Castro Ruz.

Moa → *Population: 30,000.*

The coastal road continues east to Moa, where there is a huge nickel plant and it is very industrialized. Cuba has more than a third of the world's known reserves of nickel. The Pedro Soto Alba mine was built in 1944 by the Americans and the Moa Bay nickel plant was opened in 1959, but it was nationalized in 1960. **Cubaniquel** now produces an intermediate product in Cuba: nickel and cobalt contained in sulphide, which is then shipped to Canada and ends up as part of Canadian refined output.

The journey from Moa to Baracoa is 74 km and takes about two hours as the road is not in good order. There is no public transport for foreigners so you have to get a taxi or hire a car from Holguín to Baracoa via Moa. It is a spectacular ride along the coast with the mountains of the **Cuchillas de Moa** and the **Cuchillas de Toa** coming down to the sea, indented by many rivers and bays. The highest peak in the Cuchillas de Moa is the **Pico del**

Toldo, at 1175 m. From the Bahía de Taco to Baracoa the drive is beautiful, with luscious coconut palms, mountains, thatched houses and little coves with thin patches of white sand lapped by the aquamarine sea. It takes about one hour 25 minutes from Moa to Maguana, see page 379 for Playa Maguana.

⊕ Holguín listings

For Sleeping and Eating price codes and other relevant information, see Essentials pages 37-43.

● Sleeping

Holguín centre *p309, map p310*
Hotels
Praga, **Majestic Turquino** and **Santiago** hotels are reserved for national tourism and do not take foreigners.
C Pernik, Jorge Dimitrov y Plaza de la Revolución, T24-481011, www.islazul.cu. 202 rooms, mostly overnighters passing through, shops, bar, restaurant (food not recommended), swimming pool, TV, a/c, nice view from top-floor rooms, small bathrooms, adequate.
C Villa El Bosque, just off Av Jorge Dimitrov, Plaza de la Revolución, T24-481012, www.islazul.cu. 69 rooms in spread out villas, patio garden, fridge, basic shower room, TV, a/c, also 2 suites, good security, car rental, large pool, **El Pétalo** disco.

Casas particulares
D-E Arnold Alabart Freyre, Cables 18 entre Fomento y Peralta, Reparto Peralta, T24-424408. Spacious house built 1962 in large garden with lots of fruit and veg being grown. Set back from main road, garage and parking available. 2 good-sized rooms with huge wardrobes, solid wooden furniture, wonderful old exercise machines behind house, antique outdoor gym. Elderly Arnold has lots of family to help him, very hospitable, including dog.
D-E Don Santiago, Narciso López 258 Apto 3, p2, entre Coliseo y Segunda, T24-426146, visionatres@yahoo.es. Santiago Andraca Roblejo (formerly a civil engineer in the nuclear power industry) and his wife Consuelo (architect), offer 1 unexpectedly good room in an unprepossessing apartment block in walking distance of town centre. Double bed, reading lights, everything works, very homely. Excellent food, genial hosts, well-travelled in former Soviet block, very friendly and helpful, extremely knowledgeable about local tourism, can find alternative accommodation if they are full.
D-E Germán González Rojas, Angel Guerra 178 entre Camilo Cienfuegos y Carretera Central, T24-424075. Choice of room downstairs where Germán and his wife live, or upstairs in independent 2-bedroom apartment with separate entrance, terrace, kitchen and sitting room. Eclectic decor, Germán collects bottles of alcohol on display in kitchen. Good for long-term rental, room for bike storage, extra single bed for children, laundry facilities, TV.
D-E Isabel Sera Galves, Narciso López 142 entre Aguilera y Frexes, T24-422529. Large colonial house in town centre with wonderful old tiled floors, 2 rooms with high ceilings, 1 has 2 beds, shared large bathroom across passage, bedside lights, friendly dog, patio and lovely big garden at the back of the house with fruit trees, flowering plants, cats and chairs. Elegant Isabel is charming and serves great food.
D-E Luis Turbay y Marya Ferrás, Agramonte 68 entre Progreso y Río Marañón, T24-461000. The whole of the 1st floor is for guests, 1 bedroom, huge kitchen, a/c, TV, VCR, very good but often occupied by long-stay visitors. Friendly owners, very welcoming, good breakfast, laundry service.
D-E Miriam Grave de Peralta Bermúdez, Av de los Libertadores 22, esq Roosevelt, Reparto Peralta, T24-427425, miriamgdep@yahoo.es. Large modern house on a corner of busy road with a garden in front. 1 big room with double and single beds, large

bathroom, TV, all very spacious and popular with long-stay visitors.

D-E Villa Adelaida, Rastro 30 Altos entre Arias y Agramonte, T24-461708. 1 large room in modern apartment on 1st floor overlooking street, light and bright, lots of windows, TV. Adelaida Arias Ramírez is friendly and helpful with lots of contacts.

D-E Villa Liba, Maceo 46 esq 18, T24-423823. Modern house in quiet residential area within walking distance of the centre. Jorge Mezerene offers 2 rooms with double and single bed, a/c, fan, bedside lights, good wardrobe, phone interconnects with kitchen for room service, TV and video if you want it, patio with tables and rocking chairs under mariposa flowers and grapevines. Huge tank for constant water. Excellent food, good for vegetarians.

Around Holguín *p312*
Hotels
B El Mirador de Mayabe, T24-422160, www.islazul.cu, several kilometres outside the town. Has 24 rooms in cabins under the trees, tiled floors, a/c, TV, wooden furniture, fridge, hot water, adequate bathroom, quiet, fantastic view.

C Villa Don Lino, Playa Blanca, 8.5 km north of Rafael Freyre, T24-430259, www.islazul. cu. Good for the price (all-inclusive), quite clean, good beach, reasonable food, price includes breakfast. Cubans come here on holiday and there are 36 *cabañas* for rent. Car, motorbike and bicycle rental, excursions, sports and entertainment.

Casas particulares
D-E Hostal Las Brisas, J Peralta (Malecón) 61 entre Juan Mora y Mariano Grajales, Gibara, T24-845134. Great location on seafront with seaview from bedroom and roof terrace, comfortable house, newly painted and renovated after the hurricane, friendly hosts, 2 a/c bedrooms with bathrooms. Arnel Silvas Dominguez and Yvan Tamayo Aguilera have lived in France, speak good French, some English and cook good food.

D-E Hostal Vitral, Independencia 36 entre García y Peralta, Gibara, T24-844469. Right in the centre of town and close to the Malecón, this is a beautiful colonial house dating from 1876, with lovely stained glass (*vitrales*), tiled floors, massively high ceilings, arched hallway, antique furniture, flower-filled patios and roof terrace with hammocks and loungers. Nancy Pérez Pozo and her daughter, Rosi, are excellent hosts and are full of information on the area. 2 a/c bedrooms open on to patio. Garage.

Guardalavaca and around *p314, map p314*
Hotels
LL Paradisus Río de Oro Resort & Spa, Playa Esmeralda, T24-430090, www.solmelia cuba.com. A 5-star resort and one of the most luxurious and attractive beach resorts in Cuba. The food is a step up in quality and variety than at any other Sol Meliá property, with very good restaurants especially the Japanese restaurant where you can watch the food being cooked in front of you. Room blocks are set amid lush tropical gardens with quite a walk to the pool and down to the beach. The spa is very inviting.

LL-A Blau Costa Verde Beach Resort, T24-433510, www.blau-hotels.com. Unattractive hotel with room blocks around a large pool but the nautically themed poolside bar is nice. The beach is a walk away but is a lovely curve of white sand with thatched umbrellas and a small rocky section for kids to explore. Helpful staff.

LL-A Brisas Guardalavaca, T24-430218, www.hotelescubanacan.com. All-inclusive, good-sized sea view or inland rooms, attractive red-roofed villas, 4 restaurants (good buffet), 5 bars. The hotel is on a nice stretch of white sand but also has 2 lovely main pools for adults and 2 for children, organized entertainment, sports and kids' programmes, pleasant ambience, good facilities.

L-AL Playa Costa Verde, T24-433520, www.gaviota-grupo.com. Large but quite attractive with spacious rooms in 2-storey blocks scattered around the grounds. Excellent facilities for children with a pool, playhouse and a miniclub room, which is one of the nicest in Cuba. There is an attractive lobby bar with piano music in the evenings and a cigar lounge. Staff are very friendly here.

L-A Occidental Grand Playa Turquesa, Playa Yuraguanal, T24-430540, www.occidental-hoteles.com. Set apart from the other resorts and a fair walk away from the 700-m stretch of beach, but very smart with plenty of entertainment and sports and helpful, friendly staff. Rooms are in green and lemon blocks. The centrepiece is a series of stepped pools with some small waterfalls. The beach is pretty and there are a couple of massage huts but no shade.

L-A Playa Pesquero (Gaviota), T24-433530, www.gaviota-grupo.com. 1 of the largest all-inclusives in Cuba with almost 1000 rooms, all room blocks around a huge pool area. The hotel is packed to the hilt with entertainment, restaurants, bars and organized activities for children. Not the place to come for intimacy or charm and staff are the least friendly of the hotels in this area. The hammocks hitched to palm trees in the grounds are a nice touch, though.

L-A Sol Río de Luna y Mares Resort, Playa Esmeralda, T24-430060, www.somelia cuba.com. The former **Sol Río de Luna** and **Sol Río de Mares** are now run as 1 resort and guests are free to use the facilities at both resorts, which are adjacent to each other. The former is older and more attractive with more friendly and helpful staff. Lots of activities and facilities on offer. The water here is a stunning colour, best viewed from the hotel's terraces.

A-C Club Amigo Atlántico-Guardalavaca, T24-430180, www.hotelescubanacan.com. Amalgamation of 2 hotels, architecturally unappealing, low-rise 3 star. The older, 1970s complex is set back from the beach around a large oblong pool, although there are some comfortable rooms in the main hotel/reception block that are convenient for the beach, restaurants and social action. Newer, 2-storey villas with more updated furnishings are more attractive but a walk to the beach. The main complex of pools fronts the main hotel block. Plenty of facilities. Shop around for good deals, which can be a bargain.

Banes *p315*
Casas particulares
D-E Cary Hernández y Jorge Mulet, Augusto Blanca 1107 esq Bruno Meriño, T24-803718. Modernized colonial house, 2 bedrooms, independent and comfortable, terrace with pergola and sunbeds, car parking, good food, nice people.

D-E Dra Lisandra Naranjo García, Polo 28 entre Los Angeles y Ocuje, T24-802905. 1 comfortable bedroom and bathroom, good food and service, garage, patio and sea view, Lisandra is a surgeon with a very friendly manner.

D-E Gilma Quiñones Hernández, Calle H 1526 F entre Carretera de Veguitas y Francisco Franco, T24-802204. Colonial building dating from 1920 and in the same family ever since, 1 independent bedroom at the back of the house, with kitchen, parking, terrace, good facilities, charming hosts.

D-E Sonia Díaz Abaleen, Céspedes 119 entre Flor Crombet y Augusto Blanca, T24-802358. One large bedroom and bathroom, patio with ornamental plants, garage, centrally located, friendly and helpful hosts offering good food and service.

Mayarí *p315*
Hotels
B Villa Cayo Saetía (Gaviota), T24-516900, www.gaviota-grupo.com. On the island in the Bahía de Nipe, 12 spacious rooms in rustic bungalows. There are some lovely beaches here and it is popular with day-trippers from Guardalavaca hotels who come by noisy Russian helicopter. There are facilities for visiting yachts at the Base Náutica, VHF 16, and boat rental. It is also promoted as a place to shoot wild fowl and hunt introduced animals such as zebra and antelope. The restaurant specializes in exotic meat as well as creole food.

B-C Villa Pinares de Mayarí, La Mensura
National Park, T24-503308, www.gaviota-
grupo.com. Mountain lodge style, rustic
timber and stone, 2-star rooms and cabins for
couples and families, isolated, pool, tennis,
volleyball, gym, massage, bike rental, nature
trails, pine trees, lake, restaurant, bar, billiards,
horseriding, mostly used by eco-tour groups,
check before arriving that they are open as
they sometimes close if no party is expected.

Moa *p316*
Hotels
E Miraflores, Av Amistad, west of the town on
a hill, T24-606103, www.islazul.cu. Comfortable
hotel, a modern block of 148 rooms close to
the smelter workers' apartment buildings,
under renovation in 2009 and closed.

Casas particulares
There are no legal *casas particulares* and if
you arrive in a rental car you won't be able
to stay in an illegal one either as the car will
be a dead giveaway.

❶ Eating

Holguín centre *p309*, map *p310*
Restaurants
¶¶¶-¶¶ 1720, Frexes esq Miró. Restaurant,
bar, shows, information, souvenirs, in nicely
restored blue and white building. The
restaurant, on the right as you go in, is called
Les Parques and is gloriously elegant with
tablecloths, white china and roses on the
table, but you don't need to dress up.
The food is average but the service OK.
The menu ranges from chicken, pork and
lamb at CUC$5-6 to beef at CUC$8 and
lobster at CUC$22. Plenty of wine on display.
The bar is on the other side of the courtyard.
¶ Casa del Cheff, Luz Caballero entre Máximo
Gómez y Mártires, close to Plaza de la
Maqueta. Daily 1230 until everyone stops
eating. Good, simple seafood restaurant
with a good reputation.

¶ Coppelia, on Parque Peralta. Very popular.
Open 1000-2200, closes 1700 Thu.
¶ El Piropo, Maceo, on the park beside Luz de
Yara store. Good ice cream, well regarded.
¶ El Tocororo, on Parque Central, T24-468588.
Open 24 hrs. Cheap toasted sandwiches,
wooden sculpture above door.
¶ La Begonia, on Plaza Centralis. Outdoor
cafeteria under a flowering creeper, very
pretty, good for a Mayabe beer, meeting
place for *jineteras*.
¶ La Crema, on Libertad just north of Plaza
Central. A bakery and sweet shop.
¶ Pico Cristal, corner of plaza with Libertad,
T24-425855. Daily 1200-1500 and 1830-2245.
On 3 floors, cafetería on ground floor, open
24 hrs, usual range of fastish food, disco
Diskaraoke on 1st floor 2100-0100, restaurant
on top floor, international and Cuban food,
lots of chicken, some fish.

Paladares
¶ Jelly Boom, Martí 180, near the cemetery,
T24-424096. Daily 1200-2300, lunch only on
request so phone in advance. Supposed to be
one of the best in town, the usual *criollo* food,
ask around for others.
¶ La Gran Vía, Cables y Morales Lemus.
Reasonable food, open for lunch and dinner
until the last customer goes.
¶ La Pampa, Unión entre Cuba y Garayalde,
T24-422938. Daily 1200-2100. Run by Paco,
good *criollo* cooking.
¶ La Ternura, José A Cardet 293 Altos entre
Angel Guerra y Cables, T24-421223. Open
from 1800. Run by the charismatic and
professional Mirna Ruiz Nieves, *criollo* food,
mostly pork, chicken and eggs, served with
congrís and *mariquitas*. Prices in pesos
cubanos although she will accept CUC$ if
that is what you have; a beer or Cuba libre
is only 30 pesos. The heart-stopping house
speciality is the Uruguayo, a pork steak
stuffed with ham and cheese.
¶ Taberna Pancho, close to Plaza de la
Revolución on Av Jorge Dimitrov, round the
corner from the Hotel Pernik, T24-481868,
see Sleeping above. Daily 1215-1600 and

1815-2200. Serves beer and a reasonable burger, rustic style, heavy wooden furniture and lots of barrels, traditional music.

Around Holguín p312
Restaurants
Mirador de Mayabe, Villa Mirador de Mayabe, T24-422160. Open for lunch and dinner. Popular with tour parties for lunch.

Guardalavaca p314, map p314
There are restaurants in the *Centro Comercial* but no *paladares* in the area. Alternatively there are lots of beach bars on Playa Guardalavaca. Most restaurants in the hotels offer buffet meals. All have à la carte options but you have to reserve in advance.

El Ancla, at the western end of Playa Guardalavaca on a rocky outcrop, T24-430381. Daily 0900-2230. Nice location, dining overlooking the sea, speciality seafood.

El Cayuelo, short walk along coast from Las Brisas, T24-30422. Daily 0900-2300. Good for lobster.

Mongo Viña, on the road to Playa Pesquero, signposted beyond the mini zoo on the same road. Daily 0700-1700. There's a view of Bahía de Naranjo. Chef's choice includes fried chicken, *congrís* and salad.

⊕ Entertainment

Holguín centre p309, map p310
Music
Cabaret Nocturno, on road to Las Tunas, Km 2.5, T24-425185. Wed-Mon 2100-0200. Show with different Latin American music followed by salsa and dance music disco.
Casa de la Música, Frexes esq Libertad. Lots of different options. The **Salón Santa Palabra**, entrance CUC$3, 1500-1900, 2200-0400, live or taped music with food available; **Terraza Bucanero**, entrance CUC$3, 1900-0200, serving food with Bucanero and imported beers; **Video Piano Bar Las Musas**, entrance CUC$3, 1600-0400; **El Boulevar EGREM**, open 24 hrs outside, free entry. Buy entrance tickets

in the EGREM shop on Maceo esq Martí 1400-0200.
Casa de la Trova, on Plaza Calixto García between Casa de la Cultura and La Begonia, T24-453104. Daily 1100-0200, CUC$1. Good music and dance, notice board outside announcing what's on that night, small stage, bar, salón.
UNEAC, Libertad entre Martí y Luz Caballero, open until late, depending on the event. A magnificent restored colonial building with tables and chairs in central courtyard and now the major cultural venue in town. Art exhibitions, video shows daily except Mon, cultural and artistic events.

Theatre
Teatro Comandante Eddy Suñol, on Parque Calixto García. Due to reopen in 2009 following reconstruction.
Teatro Guiñol, Martí entre Maceo y Libertad, next to Telepunto, T24-427490.
Teatro Ismaelillo Maceo esq Coliseo opposite Parque Martí, T24-422695. Children's shows, films, concerts and drama.
A new concert hall is being built in Plaza La Maqueta.

⊛ Festivals and events

Holguín p308, map p310
Jan Semana de la Cultura Holguinera is a week of cultural activities with artists invited from other provinces. Prizes are given in poetry, art, video, theatre, etc.
Feb/Mar The Feria del Libro, a book fair.
Apr The Festival de Cine Pobre de Gibara, a cinema festival.
3 May Romerías de la Cruz de Mayo, see Sights, North of the centre, page 312.
Oct In the last week of Oct the Fiesta de la Cultura Iberoamericana is held, which each year is dedicated to one Latin American country and one province in Spain. There is a parade through the city and cultural events, organized by the *Casa Iberoamericana*, Arias entre Libertad y Maceo, Parque Céspedes.

O Shopping

Holguín centre *p309, map p310*
Centro de Artes, Martí 180 entre Maceo y
Mártires, T24-422392. Art gallery and main
location for the annual book fair.
Fondo de Bienes Culturales, Frexes, on
Parque Central next to museum. Arts and
crafts, prints and original art work, high
quality. In renovated mansion with patio
at rear where there is a café.
Galería Holguín, on Parque Céspedes,
under the chess academy, hosts art
exhibitions and sales.

Guardalavaca *p314, map p314*
Handicraft stalls are set up daily outside the
Club Amigo Hotel. Lots of wooden carvings
and crochet work. There are 2 Centro Comercial
shopping arcades, one next to the Club
Amigo, the other closer to Hotel Las Brisas.

▲▲ Activities and tours

Holguín centre *p309, map p310*
Caving and climbing
Get in touch with a local group of
espeleologists to explore the underground
rivers and pools found in caves about 10
and 18 km from Gibara by asking at the
Oficina del Historiador at the Fortaleza in
Gibara. An adventure park covering 36 sq km
has been built by **Gaviota**, which includes a
rocódromo, for vertical climbs, cave
exploration, potholing and cave diving
although there are other activities for the
less able too. A network of cable cars will
allow those who prefer not to climb to get
up the Silla de Gibara for a good view.

Diving
Mostly boat dives on the reef and wall
just offshore. There is lots of life here
underwater, you can see lobsters, moray
eels, huge crabs and angelfish, as well as
a variety of small, colourful, tropical fish,
grouper, snapper, triggerfish, eagle rays,

tarpon and sometimes sharks. This area is
not recommended during the wet season as
the sea is rough, visibility deteriorates, and
entry and exit is tricky with high waves.
Marlín, T24-430491, organizes scuba-diving
and prices are all much the same, depending
on the package you choose. A Resort Course
is CUC$70 (introductory pool dive), while an
Open Water course is CUC$370. There are
dive shops on the beaches. Most of the big
resort hotels offer diving as a package or on
an individual basis. On the western end of the
beach at Playa Guardalavaca is **Eagle Ray**,
T24-430316, marling.hlg@tur.cu, with a
capacity for 11 divers and visiting 32 named
sites between 5 and 40 m deep, CUC$35 for
1 dive. The **Sea Lovers Diving Centre** is at
Playa Esmeralda, T24-430060, several good
dive sites on the reef offshore, can be rough
at times. Good, well-maintained equipment
and safety record, CUC$30 for 1 dive.

Horse riding
Horse riding, T24-430117. Horses can be
found in the field behind the Brisas hotel.
From CUC$8 for 1 hr. Book through your
hotel as it could be easier.

Indoor games
Bolera, Calle Habana, Parque Infantil,
Holguín. Bowling, and other indoor games,
1000-0200, snacks and drinks in CUC$.

Marina
Marina Gaviota Oriente, Bahía de Vita,
Carretera a Guardalavaca Km 38, T24-430445/
430475, www.gaviota-grupo.com, VHF 16, has
38 slips, fuel and water, 220 and 110V power
supply, small repair shop and Customs office.
Deep-sea fishing trips leave from here, 0730
and 1300, boat rental CUC$270 plus CUC$20
per passenger, all equipment and lunch
provided. The lagoon in the Bahía de Naranjo
has been developed as a small marina with 9
moorings, fuel, water, electricity (VHF16),
where sailing trips and fishing expeditions can
be arranged. You can stay here, there are 2
rooms in **Bungalow Birancito** on Cayo

Naranjo (Gaviota), T24-430132,
www.villacayonaranjo.com.

Tour operators
The tour desks in the hotels have lots of
excursions on offer along the coast or inland,
even to Santiago de Cuba. Alternatively you
can hire a car, scooter or bike, or contract a
local private driver to take you wherever you
want. Private operators cannot pick you up
from a hotel in Guardalavaca, so meet in the
Centro Comercial or on the main road.
Cubanacán, behind the Club Amigo,
Guardalavaca, T24-430226, comercial@
viajes.gvc.cyt.cu.
Cubatur, behind Centro Comercial Los
Flayambones, Guardalavaca, T24-430171,
comercial@hog.cubatur.tur.cu. Tours and
excursions for hotel guests and other tourists.
Ecotur, Centro Comercial Guardalavaca,
T24-430155, www.ecoturcuba.co.cu.
Ecoturism, hiking, shooting and fishing.
Paradiso, Maceo y Martí, Holguín, T24-453104.

Watersports
Watersports are offered at Guardalavaca but
safety is not good with life-jackets not always
offered or worn. Hobie cats, windsurfers,
kayaks, pedalo bikes available. Catamaran trips
from Playa Guardalavaca CUC$42 with lobster
lunch. A sunset catamaran tour with seafood
and lobster dinner and 10 mins swim with
dolphins is CUC$100 adults, CUC$60 children.
For details of diving, fishing and boat
excursions, contact **Marlin Náutica**, Playa
Guardalavaca, T24-430491, marling.hlg@tur.cu.

⊖ Transport

Holguín centre *p309, map p310*
Air
The Frank País International Airport (HOG),
T24-425271 (international flight information
T24-474630, national flight information
T24- 474629), receives scheduled and
chartered flights from abroad and from
Havana to take visitors out to the beach at

Guardalavaca. Cubana has a weekly flight
from London and another from Toronto,
but is only 1 of 14 airlines flying here with 22
flights a week from Canada, the UK, Germany,
Italy and the Netherlands. There is also the
Orestes Acosta Airport (MOA), 3 km from
Moa, T24-607012, which has 1 scheduled
Cubana service a week from Havana.
    Airlines: Aerocaribbean, Libertad esq
Martí, Edif Pico Cristal, Holguín, T24- 468556,
aerocaribbeanhog@enet.cu. Cubana is
also in Edif Pico de Cristal, Libertad esq
Martí, Policentro, T24-468148, and at the
airport, T24-468114.

Bus
The interurban bus terminal, notable for
the number of horses, rather than vehicles,
is on Av de los Libertadores opposite the
turning to Estadio Calixto García. Buses or
shared taxis to **Gibara** leave from here at
0650 and 1750. The interprovincial bus
terminal is west of the centre on the Carretera
Central. You can walk along Frexes from the
centre, but it is a hot walk with luggage. A
bicitaxi costs CUC$2. Víazul and Astro buses
stop here. **Víazul**, T24-422994, runs buses to
Guardalavaca beach from this terminal daily
at 0830, 1 hr, CUC$6, returns 1900, be there
30 mins before departure and check in
advance that it is running.

Car hire
Available at the large beach hotels with
Transgaviota, which also rents scooters
(motos) for CUC$24 for 24 hrs. Cubacar, at
Guardalavaca, T24-430389, open 24 hrs, at
the airport, T24-468414, in Holguín, T24-
468217, ext 116. Havanautos, at the airport,
T24-468412 and in the Pico Cristal building,
T24-468559. Rex is at the airport, T24-464644.
    The road from Holguín past Rafael Freyre
to Guardalavaca is broad with a good
surface, lined with trees and empty of traffic.
The *Azules* are at every junction, organizing
lifts on trucks; other people improvise with
bikes or motorbikes.

Taxi

Cubataxi, Av Libertadores 74, Rpto San Field, T24-423290. Irregular service, check fares. At Playa Guardalavaca, T24-430139, CUC$35 1 way from Holguín to Guardalavaca, CUC$5 from Guardalavaca to Playa Esmeralda, CUC$12 to Playa Pesquero, CUC$7-10 to Chorro de Maita. There are a handful of horse and carts for local journeys around Guardalavaca: to Playa Pesquero CUC$30, Playa Esmeralda, CUC$15, Acuario, CUC$15.

Bicitaxi The family vehicle is a bicycle with side car – dad does all the work, mum sits alongside with the baby while seats on the cross bar and behind are for older children. There is very little motorized public transport. The city is choked with bicitaxis, horse-drawn buses and taxis, charging 50-80 centavos.

⊙ Directory

Holguín centre p309, map p310
Banks Bandec, Arias 159, T24-422512, Mon-Fri 0800-1500. **Cadeca**, just south of Cristal building on Boulevard, Libertad y Martí, T24-468503, Visa, MasterCard. **Banco Financiero Internacional**, Libertad 65 just north of the Plaza Central, T24-468034, Mon-Fri 0800-1500, last working day of the month 0800-1200, MasterCard, Visa.
Internet Telepunto, Martí esq Maceo, Holguín, 0800- 1930, CUC$6 per hr, as well as printing, fax service, prepaid phone cards and mobile phone services. Guardalavaca hotels have access for guests CUC$6 per hr. **Medical services** There are several hospitals in Holguín for different specialities: **Clínico Quirúrgico Lucía Iñíguez Landín**, Av Internacionalistas, T24-481013; **General Docente V I Lenin**, Av Lenin, T24-462011; **Pediátrico Octavio de la Concepción**, Av Libertadores 91, T24-462012. In Guardalavaca there is the **Clínica Internacional**, T24-430312, www.servimedcuba.com, open 24 hrs, with a pharmacy, T24-430291. There are also medical services at the resort hotels around Guardalavaca. **Post** Maceo 114 entre Arias y Agramonte, on west side of Parque Céspedes. There is a small post office with telephones and DHL office on Libertad, Plaza Central, Mon-Fri 1000-1200 and 1300-1600, alternate Sat 0800-1500.

Bayamo

→ *Colour map 3, C4. Population: approximately 150,000.*

Bayamo is a low-key, unexciting sort of place, where tourism is of little importance. For that reason it is worth stopping here to get a feel for local Cuban life. The city is clean, organized, friendly, cheap and undergoing renovation and beautification. It is the capital of the province of Granma, named after the boat that brought Castro and his comrades to Cuba to launch the Revolution. Visitors come here on their way to somewhere else, either to the Sierra Maestra for some hiking, or to the port city of Manzanillo and the Granma landing site on the coast. The history of the guerrilla struggle is palpable throughout the area with constant reminders of the landing in 1953. The province occupies the western end of the Sierra Maestra and the flatlands and swamps to the north of the mountains. Many of the country's major rivers drain into the Golfo de Guacanayabo, the longest being the Río Cauto. The southern coast has the best beaches and several resort hotels are clustered around Marea del Portillo at the foot of the mountains, where there are watersports, sailing and diving, but otherwise the area has been largely neglected as far as tourism is concerned.

Bayamo was the second town founded by Diego Velázquez in November 1513 and has been declared a Ciudad Monumento Nacional. However, it was burnt to the ground by its own population in 1869 as an act of rebellion against the colonial Spanish; consequently the town has little to offer in the way of very old colonial architecture, with many uninteresting low, box-like buildings reminiscent of provincial suburbs in Spain. Nevertheless, it is a cheerful town and there is often something going on, with makeshift stages put up for concerts or other festivities. Every Saturday there is a *Fiesta de la Cubanía*, when the whole of General García fills with stalls, ad hoc bars, pigs on spits, and the restaurants all put tables on the boulevard. ▸▸ *For listings, see pages 329-333.*

Ins and outs

Getting there There is a small airport, Carlos Manuel de Céspedes (BYM), 16 km from the centre, but it only receives **flights** from Havana, twice a week. International air passengers fly to Holguín and get the bus from there. Bayamo is on the main road between Havana and Santiago so there are regular **buses** from both ends of the island. Holguín is only 70 km away and there is frequent traffic between the two cities. There is also an irregular **train** service, which should not be relied on. ▸▸ *See Transport, page 333.*

Getting around Traffic is slow and moves at the speed of horses, as **coches** are a common and cheap form of transport. You will be able to **walk** around the centre, which is quite small, but a **coche** or **bicitaxi** is useful to get out to the **Hotel Sierra Maestra**, see page 330. A bicitaxi from the bus station to the centre is CUC$1-2. **Car hire** is available for excursions or there are organized tours.

Tourist information The tourist bureau at the **Hotel Sierra Maestra**, see page 330, is very helpful with information on all tours in this area. The **Hotel Telégrafo** also has a buró de turismo and occasionally maps. **Islazul** has an office on General García 207, daily 0830-1700.

Alternatively, if you are staying in a *casa particular*, your host family will probably know everything you want to find out.

Sights

City centre

The National Anthem of Cuba (*Himno Nacional*) was written by a poet from Bayamo and one of the city's squares is named the Plaza del Himno Nacional. On 20 October 1868, Bayamo was declared capital of the Republic in Arms and the National Anthem was sung. However, on 12 January 1869, the patriotic inhabitants set fire to the town rather than let it fall into the hands of the Spanish colonial rulers. This patriotism has led Bayamo to be called the 'birthplace of the Cuban nation' and it has been declared a National Monument. Background to this can be seen at the **Casa de la Nacionalidad Cubana** ① *Plaza del Himno 36 entre Antonio Maceo y Padre Batista, T23-424833.* The **Iglesia de Santísimo Salvador** in the Plaza del Himno Nacional is a 16th-century church which was badly damaged by the 1869 fire, but has been restored. It is a nice, cool, quiet place for a sit down. Beautifully painted, it is light and airy with a marble altar and a heroic and patriotic scene painted on the arch over it.

The main street is General García, now converted into a pedestrian boulevard known as Boulevard or Paseo Bayamez, a showcase for local artwork with intriguing and amusing street lights and benches. The Boulevard is lined with banks, museums, restaurants and cafés, the majority of which charge for their services in pesos cubanos. Among the new sites of interest along the Paseo are **La Galería de Cera** (waxworks) ① *Tue-Fri 1000-1800, Sat 1000-1500, 1900-2200, Sun 1000-1500, 1900-2130),* a small

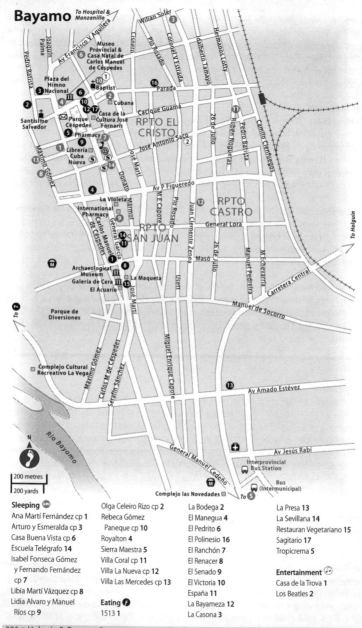

Bayamo

To Hospital &
Manzanillo

To Hospital &
Manzanillo

Museo Provincial & Casa Natal de Carlos Manuel de Céspedes

Plaza del Himno Nacional

Baptist

Cubana

Parque Céspedes

Casa de la Cultura José Fornaris

Pharmacy

Pharmacy

Librería Cuba Nueva

Parada

Cacique Guamá

RPTO EL CRISTO

Santísimo Salvador

José Antonio Saco

Av P Figueredo

La Violeta

International Pharmacy

RPTO CASTRO

General Lora

RPTO SAN JUAN

Masó

Archaeological Museum

Galería de Cera

El Acuario

La Maqueta

Carretera Central

Manuel de Socorro

Parque de Diversiones

Complejo Cultural Recreativo La Vega

Av Amado Estévez

Río Bayamo

General Manuel Cedeño

Av Jesús Rabí

Interprovincial Bus Station

Bus (Intermunicipal)

Complejo las Novedades

To Holguín

To 7

To 5

N

200 metres
200 yards

Sleeping
Ana Martí Fernández cp **1**
Arturo y Esmeralda cp **3**
Casa Buena Vista cp **6**
Escuela Telégrafo **14**
Isabel Fonseca Gómez y Fernando Fernández cp **7**
Libia Martí Vázquez cp **8**
Lidia Alvaro y Manuel Ríos cp **9**

Olga Celeiro Rizo cp **2**
Rebeca Gómez Paneque cp **10**
Royalton **4**
Sierra Maestra **5**
Villa Coral cp **11**
Villa La Nueva cp **12**
Villa Las Mercedes cp **13**

Eating
1513 **1**
La Bodega **2**
El Manegua **4**
El Pedrito **6**
El Polinesio **16**
El Ranchón **7**
El Renacer **8**
El Senado **9**
El Victoria **10**
España **11**
La Bayameza **12**
La Casona **3**

La Presa **13**
La Sevillana **14**
Restauran Vegetariano **15**
Sagitario **17**
Tropicrema **5**

Entertainment
Casa de la Trova **1**
Los Beatles **2**

aquarium, an **archaeological museum** ⓘ *Gómez 252 esq Masó, CUC$1)* and a Maqueta (scale model) of the city. You can enjoy a drink at a bar overlooking the plaza at one end of the Boulevard unmolested by *jineteros*, but here your *mojito* or *cuba libre* will cost you 5 pesos cubanos, not pesos convertibles.

The local museum is the **Museo Provincial** ⓘ *Maceo 55, T23-424125, Tue-Sat 0800-1400, Sun 0900-1300*, which has one room on natural history, an exhibition of architectural history, and a room on the war of independence. Next door is the **Casa Natal de Carlos Manuel de Céspedes** ⓘ *Maceo 57 entre Donato Mármol y José Joaquín Palma, T23-423864, Tue-Sat 0900-1700, Sun 0900-1200, CUC$1*, a museum dedicated to the life of the main campaigner of the 1868 independence movement. The 'Father of the Homeland' was born here on 18 April 1819. It is the only two-storey house to survive the fire of 12 January 1869. There are exhibits on the history of the founding of Bayamo up to the death of Céspedes in combat. Parque Céspedes is named in his honour.

On the corner of Amado Estévez and José Martí is the site of the first cemetery established in Cuba on 5 January 1798. Also here is the ruin of San Juan Evangelista, founded at the same time as the city, but destroyed by the 1869 fire. Only the tower survived. In the park is a monument to Francisco Vicente Aguilera, 1821-1877, one of the rebels in the 1868 war, and a *'retablo'* to *'los héroes'*. The first Baptist church in Cuba, founded 17 May 1705, is on the corner of Maceo and Marmol.

Bayamo is built above a very attractive river and it is a pleasant stroll down through a well-tended park. This large, open green space with plenty of trees also houses a market, and kiosks which sell fruit, vegetables, meat and snacks. Open-air events are often held here and there is a good swimming area in the river. It is very popular with Cubans, particularly at weekends.

Around Bayamo

Parque Nacional Sierra Maestra

From Bayamo the quickest way of getting into the mountains is to hire a driver, best with a group of you to share costs. Alternatively, if you want to cut costs, you need to get a *guagua* (if they will let you on, two a day) to Bartolomé Masó and hitch a lift from there (not much traffic) 20 km up into the hills to Santo Domingo. This is time consuming and hard work. If you are cycling it is strenuous and you will need a good level of fitness and cycling experience. The road is mountainous and there are several demanding hill climbs and steep descents. Take care to control your speed. You will pass **Camping La Sierrita** on the left after 4.5 km, then cross Río Providencia at 11 km. (You can stay at La Sierrita, but you will have to book at the **Campismo** office in Bayamo first, see below. It is not always open though.) In Providencia village, turn left at the T-junction and begin a steep 4.5-km climb. There are excellent views at the top and time to get your breath back before the very steep descent, with a left hand bend at the bottom crossing the bridge over the Río Yara, leading to **Villa Santo Domingo**. It is easier to hire a private driver, which will cost about CUC$40 to and from Bayamo, but he will take you direct to the National Parks office (just uphill from **Villa Santo Domingo**), which is some way from the village, in time to get a guide for the day.

All tours start at 0900, so you need to get there before then to arrange things. Prices have gone up steeply. To the Comandancia de la Plata costs CUC$20 per person (including guide), while to Pico Turquino it is CUC$33 extra for a two-day hike. You have to take a taxi, CUC$5, or join a tour party's truck (CUC$5 to the driver on the return) for the 5-km drive up the steepest road in Cuba to the car park at **Alto de Naranjo**, at 950 m.

Alternatively you can walk it. If you are all fit and fast walkers going by truck you can be back at the Parks office by 1400, but more likely it will take longer than that. From Alto de Naranjo, there is a path to the left to Pico Turquino and a path to the right for the 3-km walk to the **Comandancia de la Plata**, Castro's mountain base during the Revolution. Just 3 km does not sound like a lot, but this hike is not for the unfit. Parts are steep and can be either bone dry or very muddy. You need to be prepared to wash everything you stand up in afterwards, including your shoes. Take lots of water and snacks, there is no lunch.

Halfway along the path you come to the **Casa Medina**, where you rest for a bit in the shed where they dry coffee beans. The Medina family was the first to help the guerrillas during the Revolution and the Osvaldo Medina Quintet, which entertained the troops, still continues to perform. It is alleged that even now, Castro drinks coffee from this region to the exclusion of all others. Once you get to the command station you are shown a small museum and other wooden buildings in the camp. Castro's bedroom, campbed and kitchen are here. Some guides try to get home early by not showing you all the site, so ask to see the hospital and the Radio Rebelde installations, which are a further 15-minute walk to the top of the hill. It is all very evocative and atmospheric, helped by beautiful surroundings up in the mountains, where you can see the Cuban trogon and other birds in the forest. This trip is a highlight of any tour of Cuba and not to be missed. Photography was previously not allowed at the camp, ostensibly because Castro wanted people to come and see for themselves what it was like to hide out in the mountains during the Revolution, but now they charge CUC$5 for photos.

Pico Turquino (see page 356) can also be visited from Alto de Naranjo. This is a usually a two- or three-day hike, with one day to get up to the peak and the second day to come back the same way or carry on over the mountains to the coast west of Santiago, although it can be done in one day, even from Santiago. Camping Joaquín is the overnight stop. With some persuasion, is it also possible to do Pico Turquino one day and the Comandancia de la Plata the next, camping overnight rather than coming down to Santo Domingo. All trips have to be fully guided in the National Park, so if you want to do a two-day hike it is essential to arrange it in advance, often up to two weeks beforehand as only a limited number of people are allowed on the mountain overnight and it is often fully booked. There are other walks available on demand, depending on your abilities and what you are interested in. The guides are all knowledgeable but don't expect them to speak any languages other than Spanish.

Jardín Botánico de Cupaynicú

ⓘ *12 km from Bayamo on the outskirts of the town of Guisa. Look for signpost to Guisa on the right just after the electricity sub-station on the road to Santiago. Car or bicycle hire or private driver required to get here. CUC$2, Spanish-speaking guide, 2-hr tour, tip appreciated.*

The Jardín Botánico de Cupaynicú is just outside the village of Guisa. It is in a very mountainous region and difficult to get to but worth the effort for the beautiful setting and fascinating tour. There are 13 botanical gardens in Cuba, of which the most important is in Havana, followed by the gardens outside Cienfuegos and then these. It was started in 1981, but is the most natural, containing trees of over 300 years old and is good for birdwatching. Of the total 104 ha, 54.5 ha is a protected reserve, while the rest is divided into different specialities. The garden has a lot of ornamental plants but also a collection of edible and medicinal plants and 72 palms of all shapes and sizes, of which 16 are native Cuban. There is a large area of native forest and scientists are studying the flora to see what benefit they can be to man.

Guisa itself is also worth a visit. It is a pretty little town in the foothills of the Sierra Maestra, bedecked with colourful plants and gardens. It is known as a battle site of 1897 and also during the Revolution. The **Mirador de Guisa** is on top of the hill where Calixto García took up his position on 28-29 November 1897 in the War of Independence. The restaurant complex now on the hill affords lovely views of the mountains and a dam in the far distance which provides water and energy to the town and to Bayamo. The indoor restaurant and outdoor bars charge in CUC$ or pesos cubanos, a useful pit stop in a day trip out from Bayamo, but very busy at weekends.

Other excursions in the area include a morning's visit to the national monument where José Martí was killed on 19 May 1895 at **Dos Ríos** ① *Carretera Jiguaní–San Germán Km 21, to the northeast of Bayamo, reached by bus to Jiguaní at 0710, 80 centavos, 50 mins, then bus from Jiguaní to Dos Ríos at 0900, 1 peso; it arrives at 0950 and returns at 1015, but this gives you enough time to see the memorial.* The memorial path is lined with *lluvia de fuego* flowers and lots of yellow mariposas, the national flower. Note that the bus does not depart from where you got off, but from further up the road. You will probably see people waiting at the departure point along the former runway, now the road, created for Fidel's centenary memorial visit in 1995.

◉ Bayamo listings

For Sleeping and Eating price codes and other relevant information, see Essentials pages 37-43.

● Sleeping

Bayamo *p324, map p326*
Hotels
C-D Royalton, Maceo 53 y Joaquín Palma, very central location, T23-422246. The building dates from the 1940s but was closed in 2009 for remodelling prior to opening as a boutique hotel in the Cubanacán chain of hotels called Encanto, or Hoteles E.
D-E Hotel Escuela Telégrafo, Saco 108 entre Donato Mármol y Gen García, T23-427374. This is a small hotel school and if there are no classes they close the hotel, so reserve in advance. Suites and rooms, good restaurant. Buró de turismo.

Casas particulares
There are 40 registered casas in Bayamo, most of which are in the town centre. They nearly all charge CUC$15-20 per room in low season and CUC$20-25 in high season, occasionally CUC$30 with commission. The best rates can be found if you go direct to the casa and avoid commissions charged by

fixers. Breakfast is usually CUC$3-4, dinner between CUC$6-10, depending on what you choose to eat. Casa owners complain of *jineteros* who steal their guests before they arrive at the house, taking them somewhere else so they can charge commission, even if they have made reservations, so check the address and make sure you ring the bell at your chosen casa. You may be told that they have stopped renting or some other story to take you elsewhere. All those listed offer a/c, fan, private bathrooms and hot water.
D-E Ana Martí Fernández, Céspedes 4 entre Maceo y Canducha, Plaza del Himno, T23-425323, marti@enet.cu. Very quiet house and area, no traffic but cars can be parked safely outside. Colonial house with higgedly piggedly adaptations, 1 very blue room up metal ladder at front of house on mezzanine floor with low ceiling, 2nd room at the back up easier staircase, larger with bigger bathroom, window and balcony overlooking interior of house, TV, double and single beds. Ana and her husband live surrounded by antiques, old glass and china.
D-E Arturo y Esmeralda, Zenea 56 entre Wiliam Soler y Capote, T23-424051, www.casa-bayamo.com. Double or twin beds,

rooms newly equipped, nicely decorated and comfortable, TV, roof terrace, laundry service, one of the best casas in town. Friendly family, Arturo is very helpful and knowledgeable about tourism in the area and can arrange tours and transport. Good food and lots of it.

D-E Casa Buena Vista, Av Francisco Vicente Aguilera 106 entre Martí y M Corona, T23-423659, valiavista2002@yahoo.es. Valia López Sánchez has 2 rooms, 1 with double bed, the other with twin beds, garage and parking for car or bicycles, bike hire, dance classes.

D-E Isabel Fonseca Gómez y Fernando Fernández, Donato Mármol 158A entre Canducha Figueredo y Maceo, T23-429865. Upstairs apartment with terrace overlooking Baptist church and plaza, 1 nice room, comfortable, friendly and helpful couple.

D-E Libia Martí Vázquez, Máximo Gómez 56 Int entre Saco y León, T23-425671, lmartivazque@yahoo.es. 1 good-sized room upstairs at the back of the house with door to balcony and lovely view of a mature tree, gardens and the river. Bathroom in corner of room, walls do not reach to ceiling, double bed. Libia's family also rent in Santiago.

D-E Lidia Alvaro and Manuel Ríos, Donato Mármol 323 entre Figueredo y Lora, T23-423175, http://lydia.freeservers.com, nene19432001@yahoo.es. 2 old colonial houses in 1, family lives in 1 half, the other is rented to visitors, 1 room with double bed, sitting room with door to street, patio with flowers and caged birds, dachshund, use of kitchen, very private but family is there if you need them, charming elderly couple and their son.

D-E Olga Celeiro Rizo, Parada 16 (altos) entre Martí y Mármol, above Cubana office, T23-423859. Olga and her husband José Alberto are most hospitable and helpful in arranging excursions. 2 bedrooms with private bathrooms, 1 with 2 beds, comfortable, balcony off sitting room for watching the world go by in the plaza below. Good food, excellent sweet potato chips, substantial breakfast. Friendly dog.

D-E Rebeca Gómez Paneque, Maceo 105 entre Martí y Mármol, T23-422327, T01-5275 6803 (mob). Massive colonial house with high ceilings and huge rooms, large rented room up back stairs, very private, 2 beds, patios and terrace, quiet and central, TV in dining room.

D-E Villa Coral, Ruban Noguera 22 entre José A Saco y Cacique, T23-423165. Juana Varona Infante rents 1 room upstairs with dining room while she and her husband live downstairs. Independent access, very private, good accommodation, patio at back, balcony to front, lots of space, son lives in USA but occasionally uses 2nd room upstairs.

D-E Villa La Nueva, Zenea 330 entre Lora y Figueredo, T23-424395. Norma Ginarte Miranda and family live downstairs, while upstairs they have built 2 rooms with bathrooms, kitchenette, dining room and terrace, private, comfortable, good for family or groups.

D-E Villa Las Mercedes, Máximo Gómez 24 entre Maceo y Figueredo, T23-423959, mbaez@grannet.grm.sld.cu. Milagro de la M Martínez Medina and her young family and parrot offer 1 room with small bathroom, TV. The best thing about this house is the terrace on the roof with a magnificent view over the river.

Around Bayamo *p327*

C Sierra Maestra, Carretera Central Km 1.5 via Santiago de Cuba, 2 km from city centre, T23-427973, www.islazul.cu. Delightful post-Revolution 1960s building, kitsch interior, avoid rooms overlooking noisy pool, 3 bars, disco, mostly Cubans, helpful staff, car hire, credit cards accepted. Buffet restaurant open 0730-2230 for breakfast, CUC$4, lunch and dinner, about CUC$8.

C Villa Bayamo, Carretera a Manzanillo Km 5.5, T23-423102/423124, www.islazul.cu. 34 rooms and 10 cabins, 2 star, 2 km from the town centre, swimming pool.

C Villa Santo Domingo, Santo Domingo, Bartolomé Masó, www.islazul.cu. 20 rooms in cabins, some of which are damp, 1 star, a/c, TV, bar, restaurant, barbecue, games room, parking, credit cards accepted. There is good walking in the area along paths and trails and it is a great place to get close to nature with lovely views up in the mountains.

E Mirador de Guisa, Guisa, T23-391627. In the grounds beside the restaurant complex there are *cabañas* in pleasant gardens under the trees. Busy at weekends, but peaceful particularly during the week, these are usually let to Cubans and you may be able to pay in pesos cubanos, making them very cheap.

Camping

The Reservations offices for **Campismo Popular** are at Gen García 112, Bayamo, T23-424200; Villuendas 102, Manzanillo, T23-573662; Av Masó, Bartolomé Masó, T23-565679.

E La Sierrita, Carretera Santo Domingo Km 8, Bartolomé Masó, T23-565584, reservations at Campismo Popular in Bayamo, T23-424200. Technically for Cubans only, but foreigners are usually allowed if there is room and it is the base camp for hiking up Pico Turquino. You get a basic cabin with bathroom. Rural, beside the river, but Cubans on holiday can be noisy. This river is prone to flash flooding during rainstorms.

E Los Cantiles, Minas de Harlem, Jiguaní, T23-424862. Cabins by the Río Cautillo natural pools for river bathing.

⊘ Eating

Bayamo *p324, map p326*
Restaurants

There are a large number of restaurants along Gen García offering Cuban or international food, charged in pesos cubanos. State restaurants are cheaper than *paladares* because of the currency difference. Dress smartly, no shorts or sandals at night, men should wear long-sleeved shirts.

♔-♔ La Bodega, Plaza del Himno Nacional, by the church, close to Parque Céspedes. Daily 1100-0200. Colonial atmosphere, snacks and light meals, lunches, dinner, good food, CUC$.

♔ 1513, Gen García esq Masó, T23-425921. Daily 1200-2330. Small but recommended by Bayameses. Cuban and international cuisine, wide choice of dishes, good music.

♔ El Manegua, Figueredo entre Céspedes y Gen García. Daily 1200-2400. Wide choice of good-quality dishes in pesos cubanos.

♔ El Pedrito, Maceo entre Gen García y Donato Mármol, open 24 hrs. Pizzas and international food, bar, pesos cubanos accepted.

♔ El Ranchón, on the banks of the Río Bayamo at Balneario La Vega. Daily 1200-2100. Specializes in *comida criolla* and is a great place to try Cuban roast pork, country style. Food priced in pesos cubanos, drinks in either currency.

♔ El Renacer, Gen García, entre Lora y Masó. Daily 1800-2400. Wide choice of good-quality Cuban food, meat or fish, pleasant, pesos cubanos accepted.

♔ El Senado, Canducha Figueredo entre Gen García y Céspedes. Open 1200-0600. Renovated 2008, offers *comida criolla* using meats such as goat, lamb and rabbit, good quality, high-class atmosphere.

♔ El Victoria, Gen García esq Maceo at the start of Blvd Bayamez opposite Parque Céspedes. Reopened Jan 2009 after renovation offering tasty *criollo* food in a very Cuban atmosphere. Live traditional music at times.

♔ España, on Paseo Bayamez in the middle of Gen García. Daily 1200-2300. Very small and friendly, specializes in fish, look out for fish in *salsa perro*, a sauce made with fish stock, potatoes and chillies, typical of the Caibarién region in Villa Clara and apparently favoured by Fidel Castro. House or international wine. Charges in pesos cubanos.

♔ La Bayameza, Gen García entre Maceo y Canducha Figueredo, opposite Parque Céspedes. Daily 1200-2300. Pleasant and agreeable, local and international food at reasonable prices, live music occasionally.

♔ La Casona, Plaza del Himno Nacional, behind the church in a corner. Daily 1200-0100. Nice wooden bar, pasta, pizzas or meat dishes, very cheap, courtyard at the back covered with flowering vine, lots of green lizards, delightful.

¶ **La Presa**, Amado Estévez y Carretera Central. Daily 1200-2400. Specializes in seafood and fish dishes, even lobster and shrimp can be found here for 18-20 pesos cubanos – less than a dollar!

¶ **La Sevillana**, on Paseo Bayamez in the middle of Gen García. Daily 1200-2230. Pleasant atmosphere, good-quality food, plenty of choice although Spanish food is the house speciality.

¶ **Restauran Vegetariano**, Gen García esq Masó. Open 1200-2400. Very cheap vegetarian food, good selection of dishes.

¶ **Tropicrema**, Parque Céspedes. Daily 0900-2200. Cake and 2 scoops of ice cream, 1.80 pesos cubanos, very good and popular.

¶ **Yo Te Invito**, Rpto Jesús Menéndez, near Cabaret Bayamo. Daily 1200-2300. Good lunch and dinner service, pesos cubanos accepted.

Paladares

There are 2 *paladares*, both near Parque Céspedes. They have to charge in CUC$, making them more expensive, but the quality of cooking is better.

¶¶ **El Polinesio**, Parada entre Pío Rosado y Cisneros, T23-423860. Manolín runs this *paladar* on the upper floor of his house, serving Cuban and international dishes. At night a small group plays live traditional Cuban music on the terrace outdoors.

¶¶ **Sagitario**, Mármol entre Av Francisco Vicente Aguilera y Maceo. Tables in the patio of an old house, charming location, friendly owners serve traditional Cuban dishes.

☻ Entertainment

Bayamo *p324, map p326*
Cultural centres
Casa de la Cultura José Fornaris, Gen García 15, T23-422209.
Galería Provincial, Gen García 174 esq Luz Vázquez, T23-423109.

Live music and dancing

Sat nights all year round are given over to the Fiesta de la Cubanía, when Gen García becomes

an open-air bar and eating place with dozens of stalls setting out tables in the street and selling food and drinks in pesos, accompanied by traditional and modern music.

Amor Bayamés, Hotel Royalton, T23-422290. Night club, 2100-0100.

Cabaret Bayamo opposite Hotel Sierra Maestra, on Carretera Central, T23-421698. Daily 2100-0200. There is a restaurant at the entrance for a meal before the show, offering Cuban and international food in pesos cubanos, drinks in either currency.

Casa de la Trova, on the corner of Maspote and José Martí. Outdoor patio covered with creeping vine or a/c at the back. Shows during the afternoon and every night, quite touristy in high season. You can watch local groups such as Chacho y Sus Muchachos, who also tour abroad.

Complejo Cultural Recreativo Bayam, Carretera Central on the way out to Santiago. Live music, dancing, comedy, food. Also activities for children Sat and Sun mornings, ice cream parlour Tue-Thu during the day, becomes a restaurant at night.

Los Beatles, Juan Clemente Zenea esq Saco. Lifesize statues of the fab four standing outside the door waiting to go in. Live music and the cheapest mojito in Cuba at only 5 pesos cubanos. Mostly golden oldies played here, popular with the young and old.

Salón de Baile a Bayamo en Coche, Hotel Sierra Maestra, T23-482230. Disco, daily 2100-0200. Dancing, popular with young Bayameses, dancing, recorded Cuban and international music.

☻ Festivals and events

Bayamo *p324, map p326*
17-20 Oct La Fiesta de la Cubanía culminates in the Día de la Cultura Nacional on 20 Oct, celebrating the events of 10-20 Oct 1968 with the Grito de la Demajagua and the Himno Nacional. A host of cultural events are laid on, including theatre, ballet, concerts, art exhibitions, handicraft sales and book sales.

O Shopping

Bayamo *p324, map p326*
Markets
Complejo Cultural Recreativo La Vega,
on the banks of Río Bayamo, a large open
recreation area with swimming in the river,
fishing, restaurant, cafeterias, snack bars,
toilets, children's play area and market stalls
at El Chapuzón for food, selling whatever is
in season. On Sat, Sun they hold a *feria
agropecuario*, or farmers' market, which is
hugely popular. People come from far and
wide, even Santiago, to buy meat, fish, fruit
and veg, returning with their vehicles bulging.
Complejo las Novedades, just south
of bus station. Lots of kiosks, selling food
and refreshments.

O Transport

Bayamo *p324, map p326*
Air
Carlos Manuel de Céspedes domestic airport is
4 km out of town, T23-423695; 2 flights to
Havana a week, CUC$103.
   Airlines Cubana at José Martí 58 entre
Parada y Rojas, T23-423916.

Bus
The terminal is on the corner of Carretera
Central and Jesús Rabí, T23-424036. **Víazul**
(T23-427283) passes through Bayamo on its
Havana, **Trinidad** and **Varadero** to **Santiago**
routes, see page 32 for timetable and prices.

Car hire
Transtur offices outside Hotel Sierra Maestra.
   Petrol stations: El Especial, Carretera
Central y 2, T23-427331.

Horse and cart
CUC$1 to Hotel Sierra Maestra.

Train
Station is at Saco y Línea. Daily trains, in theory, to
Santiago, **Havana**, **Camagüey** and **Manzanillo**.

O Directory

Bayamo *p324, map p326*
Banks Banco Popular de Ahorro, Saco y Gen
García, Mon-Fri 0800-1700, Sat until 2000.
Bandec, Gen García 101, T23-426340. Visa and
MasterCard, Mon-Fri 0800-1500. **Cadeca**, Saco
101 y Gen García, T23-427220, Mon-Sat
0800-1700, Sun 0800-1200. **Pharmacy** There
are 3 pharmacies on Gen García, 1 is for
Cubans, charging in Cuban pesos, 1 sells
natural remedies (medicina verde) and the
3rd is international, charging in CUC$. **Post**
Parque Céspedes, with DHL. **Telephone**
Telepunto, Gen García 109, T23-428353,
0800-2100, for all phone and internet services.

Manzanillo

→ *Colour map 3, C3. Population: 100,000.*
*Manzanillo is a small seaside town and principal port of Granma province with not much to offer to
the foreign tourist. Its one advantage is that due to lack of tourism, visitors will not be subject to the
constant attention and hassle common in tourist destinations; the people of Manzanillo seem
completely uninterested in the activities of foreigners in their midst and you can stroll about the
town at your leisure virtually ignored. Another advantage of the absence of tourism is that you can
pay for nearly everything in pesos cubanos, so for the budget traveller who wants to hang onto
CUC$ for later, Manzanillo is a good stop-off point. During the Special Period the port was closed,
imports ceased and 3000 men were made redundant. Things have recently picked up a bit with
renewed imports of rice, building materials and fertilizers, but the harbour has silted up and big*

cargo ships can no longer come in, leaving it as principally a fishing town. Further proof of renewed interest in the town came with the reopening of the theatre after being closed for 30 years, together with the small Hotel Venus opposite for visiting stage artists. The universities are thriving and attracting foreign students. ▸▸ *For listings, see pages 336-338.*

Ins and outs

Getting there All long-distance transport is via Bayamo, unless you want to try for the once a week **flight** to and from Havana. At Bayamo you connect with **buses** and **trains** running from east to west along the island.

Getting around The town is not very big so you can walk around it or take a **bicitaxi** or **coche** for longer distances. Some streets are actually steps and therefore pedestrian. **Car hire** is available for excursions to the Granma landing site and other local attractions.

Tourist information The hotel is your best bet for information, or talk to local people. Tourism is not promoted in Manzanillo.

City centre

The centre of town is the **Parque Céspedes**. Here is the **glorieta** (gazebo), maintained in pristine condition and considered a symbol of the city, where concerts are held on Sunday afternoons. The square is surrounded by restaurants and snack bars, all of which charge in pesos cubanos. On José Martí there are cheap stalls selling essential commodities for Cubans, also the usual mini-*paladares*. The **Casa de la Trova** is the centre of nightlife on Saturdays, and you can mingle with Cubans in a natural environment, without feeling segregated in a tourist-only exclusion zone, as in the big cities. A small, colonial church, the **Iglesia de la Purísima Concepción**, is on Maceo, overlooking Parque Céspedes. The **Museo Histórico Municipal** is on José Martí 226, with artefacts of the *conquistadores* in one section and relics of the clandestine struggle in the other. The **Malecón** stretches

Manzanillo centre

Golfo de Guacanayabo

Sleeping 🛏	Eating 🍴	Entertainment 😊
Adrián y Tonia cp 1	El Golfo 1	Casa de la Trova 1
La Casa de Yordi cp 2	La Américas 2	Costa Azul 2

Not to scale

along the seafront from the town centre out to the Proyecto Recreativo, where there are night clubs, cabaret and lots of open air night life. Along the seafront you will find **El Ranchón** restaurant, fish restaurants and kiosks selling *minuto pescado*, small fillets of fried fish, while offshore little fishing boats bob about on the water.

Southwest Granma to Cabo Cruz → *Colour map 3, C3.*

From Manzanillo a road follows the coast along the Golfo de Guacanayabo to the tip of the peninsula at Cabo Cruz and the Parque Nacional Desembarco del Granma. There are several police checks along the way and if you are in a car driven by a Cuban he is likely to face a fine for carrying foreigners. He will pay it and carry on. Illegal taxi drivers usually factor this in to their price. About 10 km south of Manzanillo is the **Parque Nacional de Demajagua** ① *Mon-Sat 0800-1700, Sun 0800-1300, CUC$1, CUC$2 with guide.* The ruins of the **Demajagua sugar mill** are preserved in a park with neat lawns, palm trees and a visitor centre at the entrance. This is the place where, in 1868, Carlos Manuel de Céspedes cast the first stone in the First War of Independence by liberating his slaves and shouting "¡Viva Cuba Libre!". The mill was named after the bell used to call the slaves to work, which then became the symbol of the Revolution when Céspedes set off to rebel against Spanish rule. There is not a lot to see nowadays and a tree is growing up through the old machinery, but it is a pleasant stop on the hill with a view down to the sea and the cays offshore. The small one in the distance is Cayo Perla. Built in 1840, the mill was improved after 1868, but it didn't produce sugar, only molasses (*miel*).

After 50 km driving through sugar cane lands you come to the small town of **Media Luna**, home to the **Museo Celia Sánchez** ① *Tue-Sun 0900-1700*, in a green and white traditional wooden house on the main road out of town, a small but worthy testament to this influential player in the Revolution. Celia Sánchez was a key figure at the beginning of the Revolution and it was partly because of her support that the *Granma* landing was not a complete disaster. Contrary to expectations, Batista's troops were waiting for the yacht and the revolutionaries had to scatter into the hills. Despite being in great danger, Sánchez, who lived locally, managed to get messages to the different groups and they were able to reunite. The town is neat with hedges of hibiscus, bougainvillea and other flowering plants. The sugar mill still operates here.

Another 23 km brings you to **Niquero** where there is accommodation in a nice hotel with great views of the sea in one direction and a sugar mill in the other from its rooftop bar. Niquero bus station is full of horses and carts and *bicitaxis*; there are very few private cars in town. From Niquero a dirt road leads to the spot where Castro's 82 revolutionaries disembarked from the yacht *Granma*, on 2 December 1956 in a mangrove swamp just southwest of **Playa Las Coloradas**, a reasonable beach with a Campismo resort of cabins and entertainment for Cuban holidaymakers. By the dirt road is a small park where a replica of *Granma* can be seen and the house of Angel Pérez Rosabal, the first person to help Castro when he landed on 2 December 1956. A guide is obligatory. A 2-km concrete path through the swamp takes you to a rather ugly concrete jetty and a plaque marking the occasion of the landing (The real *Granma* is in Havana). It is a hot desolate walk there and back, but hugely atmospheric when you imagine the men wearing heavy fatigues and carrying enormous packs with guns and ammunition struggling through the mud, mosquitoes, mangroves and razor grass. Every year on 2 December, hundreds of youths re-enact the whole journey from Mexico, disembarking here and heading off into the Sierra Maestra, worth visiting at that time.

A few kilometres further on, just before you reach Cabo Cruz, is **El Guafe** ① *CUC$5 including guide*, where there is a 2-km, two-hour circular path, Sendero Ecológico, through the dry tropical forest. Along the path you can see evidence of Amerindian habitation, caves, burial sites and their ceremonial areas. Wildlife is also abundant, with butterflies along the path, birds in the forest and a wide variety of plants, including the tallest cactus in the country, called 'el Viejo Testigo', which was damaged by the 2008 hurricanes, but still lives to tell the tale. The dirt road ends at **Cabo Cruz** at the tip of the peninsula. There is a beach here, a mixture of stones and sand, with thatched parasols for shade, but it is not ideal for swimming because of the coral terraces just underwater. It is nice for a paddle after a hot walk at El Guafe, though. A ramshackle fishing fleet is parked under the eye of the 1871 lighthouse and there are a couple of kiosks selling fried fish if the restaurant is not open. A delicious fillet of freshly fried, piping-hot *minuto* in a bread roll will cost you about three pesos cubanos. Eat it sitting on the sea wall, then go back for another. The **Parque Nacional Desembarco de Granma**, which extends from the southwestern coast of the eastern region to the Sierra Maestra has been declared a UNESCO World Heritage Site, largely because of the Cabo Cruz marine terraces.

Between Niquero and Media Luna there is a turning southeast across the peninsula, following the Río Sevilla for much of the way, to **Pilón** (population 12,000), a small town with a harbour on the south coast. Just before **Ojo de Agua**, there are three separate signs and plaques marking the spots where three groups of men who disembarked from *Granma* crossed the road in underground water conduits, before heading into the Sierra Maestra. The signs have the emblems of five palms in a heart, because the men arranged to reassemble at a place called **Cinco Palmas**. The spot near Ojo de Agua has the actual conduit through which Fidel and his group went, sitting at the side of the road. At Pilón the road joins up with the coast road from Santiago de Cuba. The best beaches in this area are on the south coast around **Marea del Portillo** where there are a few hotels offering diving and other watersports. The sand is grey because of its volcanic origins and gets hot at midday, but the scenery is spectacular with palm-fringed bays at the foot of the mountains of the Sierra Maestra and the deep blue of the Caribbean Sea.

◉ Manzanillo listings

For Sleeping and Eating price codes and other relevant information, see Essentials pages 37-43.

● Sleeping

Manzanillo *p333, map p334*
Hotels
D-E Guacanayabo, Av Camilo Cienfuegos, T23-574012, www.islazul.cu. A multicoloured block hotel with 112 basic a/c rooms with private bathroom although only about 70 are in use, Visa/MasterCard, car hire, post office, 24-hr doctor, very helpful, changes TCs, views of pool from most rooms, full of noisy children during holidays, very loud disco music all day and evening, staff not used to

foreign tourists. To get to town centre, walk down steps to the right of the entrance, down the street to seafront and catch a horse and cart. The tourist bureau in the hotel has some day trips but out of Cuban holiday season they probably won't be running.

Casas particulares
Casas particulares can easily be arranged in the town centre, just hang around Parque Céspedes until you are approached. There were 5 legal casas in 2009.
D-E Adrián y Tonia, Mártires de Vietnam 49 esq Caridad, T23-573028. 1 room with small but good bathroom, pleasant roof terrace with shady vines from where you get a good

view down to the town and the bay. Quiet street, Caridad is a pedestrian street of steps. Charming hosts.

D-E La Casa de Yordi, Pedro Figueredo 121 entre Luz Luz Caballero y Mártires de Vietnam, T23-572127. A well-kept house with 2 rooms, run by helpful Caridad Romero Arias and her son Abelardo.

Southwest Granma p335

At Marea del Portillo 15 km east of Pilón, popular with Canadian package tours. Food and entertainment vary according to the season and numbers of guests, but bring items like syrup for your morning pancakes or ketchup for your hot dog if that is important to you as they often run out. There are few dining options outside the hotels and the buffet food is bland and boring. Tours of the local area are good, particularly to Cayo Blanco, when you get a decent lunch.

B-C Club Amigo Marea del Portillo, Carretera Granma Km 12.5, T23-597103, www.hotelescubanacan.com. All-inclusive, 3 star, 130 rooms, hot water, phone, tennis, beach volleyball, watersports, car rental, shop. This is the best of the 3 hotels in the group and if you opt for VIP you get the best rooms and some tours thrown in.

B-C Farallón del Caribe, Km 14, T23-597081, www.cubanacan.cu. All-inclusive, 3 star, 140 rooms, a/c, TV, hot water, phone for international calls, diving, watersports, tennis, car and bicycle rental, nice position.

B-C Villa Punta Piedra, Carretera Pilón, 8 km east of Pilón, T23-597009, www.cubanacan.cu. 2 star, part of the Marea del Portillo complex with shuttle buses 5 km to the other hotels and beach. Buffet restaurant, bars and pool, but all-inclusive means you can use the facilities of the sister hotels.

C-D Niquero, Martí 100 esq Céspedes, Niquero, T23-592368, www.islazul.cu. 2 star, 26 rooms, a/c, restaurant, bar, parking.

Camping

E Las Coloradas, Playa Las Coloradas, Carretera de Niquero Km 17, T23-578256, www.cubamarviajes.cu. Reservations at Campismo Popular in Bayamo or through Cubamar in Havana. International tourism is welcome here in the 28 1-star cabins that sleep 4-6. On the beach, very convenient for all the sights, with music, entertainment, bikes and horseriding. Spaces for camper vans.

Eating

Manzanillo *p333, map p334*
All the restaurants charge in pesos cubanos; most of them are in and around Parque Céspedes, but avoid the cheaper establishments with just a concrete bar and plastic plates as you run the risk of a stomach infection. Other restaurants have very basic menus of 2 or 3 dishes. There is a nice coffee bar on the corner of Maceo and Merchan and a snack bar with large terrace opposite. There are mini-*paladares* all along José Martí, selection not good, but ice creams (1 peso) are pleasant. There are also a couple of illegal *paladares*.

† **El Golfo**, Av 1 de Mayo y Aguilera, T23-575117. Open for lunch and dinner. Seafood a speciality.

† **Las Américas**, Maceo 83, T23-573043. Daily 1200-1500 and 1800-2100. *Criollo* menu.

Entertainment

Manzanillo *p333, map p334*
The **Casa de la Trova** is on the corner of Masó y Merchan. **Costa Azul** on Av 1 de Mayo y Narciso López, T23-573158, has a cabaret show 2100-0100. There is also a folklore music show at the art gallery building on the south corner of Parque Céspedes on Thu at 2030. The Danzón orchestra, La Original de Manzanillo and singer Cándido Fabré come from Manzanillo.

O Shopping

Manzanillo *p333, map p334*
2 souvenir shops on Parque Céspedes, 1 of them has Che Guevara T-shirts for CUC$4, compared with CUC$15 in the hotel, also a small but interesting selection of books, mostly on revolutionary history.

▲ Activities and tours

Manzanillo *p333, map p334*
Watersports
Watersports, scuba-diving, snorkelling and sailing can be arranged at the **Marea del Portillo** resorts. Scuba-diving is with **Centro de Buceo Albacora**, T23-597139, who take up to 8 divers to 17 sites at depths of 5-40 m.

⊖ Transport

Manzanillo *p333, map p334*
Air
The Sierra Maestra (MZO) airport is 12 km from the city, Carretera Jibacoa, T23-577520. It has international status and receives charter flights from Canada and from Caracas. It receives 1 scheduled **Cubana** flight a week from **Havana**, CUC$103.

Bus
The bus station is at Km 2 on the Bayamo road. To **Bayamo** at 0600, 1500, CUC$2.50; also daily buses to **Havana** and **Santiago de Cuba**. No **Viazul** services here.

Car hire
Transtur, Hotel Guayacanabo.
Petrol stations: La Bujía fuel station, Carretera Central y Circunvalación, Manzanillo, T23-577202.

Taxi and horse and cart
Plenty of 1950s American cars at the bus station, operate as local taxis. Horses and carts from the hotel to the centre, 1 peso.

Train
Station is 10 blocks east of Parque Céspedes on José Martí. It is at least 2 hrs to **Bayamo** where the train links up with the **Havana–Santiago** line and all stations in between. The train to **Santiago** is 2nd class, so services limited, no snacks available, take everything you need for a long journey. Departs 0625, should be daily but technical problems mean it is usually every other day, 8 hrs, CUC$5.75 (sometimes you can pay in pesos). If you have a bicycle go the day before to buy ticket, CUC$7.95, at the **Comercial de UB Expreso** office next to the train station, Mon-Fri 0800-1130, 1330-1700, Sat 0800-1130.

⊙ Directory

Manzanillo *p333, map p334*
Medical services Hospital Celia Sánchez Manduley, Av Camilo Cienfuegos, 10 mins' walk from Hotel Guacanayabo, T23-574011. Medical services for foreigners but take an interpreter if you don't have good Spanish. Doctor on call 24 hrs at **Hotel Guacanayabo**, can treat minor ailments. Prescriptions can be taken to the pharmacy in the hospital.

Contents

Footprint features

At a glance

⊜ **Getting around** On foot, by bicycle, hired car, taxi and Víazul long-distance bus.

◉ **Time required** 1-2 weeks.

Santiago & Guantánamo

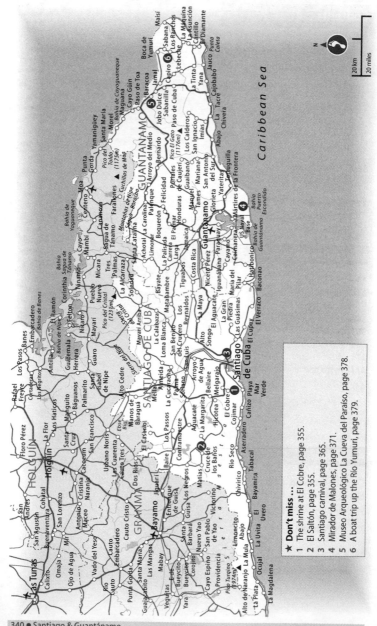

★ Don't miss...

1 The shrine at El Cobre, page 355.
2 El Saltón, page 355.
3 Santiago carnival, page 365.
4 Mirador de Malones, page 371.
5 Museo Arqueológico La Cueva del Paraíso, page 378.
6 A boat trip up the Río Yumurí, page 379.

N

20 km
20 miles

Caribbean Sea

This is the most mountainous part of the country, dominated by the Sierra Maestra, which runs along the foot of the island with several protected areas and National Parks, providing a habitat for many rare creatures. The highest point is Pico Turquino, 1974 m. The Sierra Maestra also provided shelter for Castro and his band of guerrillas during the Revolution and his command post can still be visited if you have enough puff and strength of leg. This part of the island is hot in more ways than one – there is no shortage of steamy nightlife. There is a very Caribbean feel to life here, partly because of the influx of migrants from other islands over the centuries, who brought their music and other cultural influences.

Santiago de Cuba, the second most important city in the country, is one of the oldest towns on the island, nestling in an attractive bay surrounded by mountains. It is a vibrant, cultured city with plenty of music. It is the place to come for carnival in July, a raw, ebullient celebration. Sleepy Guantánamo came to the world's attention in 2002 when the US naval base on the coast nearby was chosen to incarcerate prisoners from the conflict in Afghanistan. The crowd-puller in this most easterly province, however, is Baracoa, a laid-back, friendly place, hemmed in by pine-clad mountains. It's one of the best places to come for beaches, rivers, hiking, coconuts, chocolate and seafood, topped off by an active nightlife scene with lots of traditional and contemporary music.

Ins and outs

Getting there
Santiago is the end of the line for the main road and rail links from Havana and has domestic and international air services. There are several daily buses, trains and flights from the west end of the island and good connections if you want to fan out to Guantánamo, Baracoa and other towns in the region. ▶▶ *See also Getting there, Santiago below, Guantánamo page 369 and Baracoa page 375.*

Tourist information
Tour agencies such as **Cubatur** can give information on how to get to where you want to go and offer organized tours as well as make reservations for transport and lodging. *Casas particulares* are a good source of information on cultural and entertainment matters and often offer unofficial transport and recommend places to stay in other towns.

Best time to visit
Without doubt, July is the most exciting time of year to visit Santiago, for its carnival and anniversary celebrations for the attack on the Moncada Garrison in 1956. However, this is also the hottest time of year in an already hot city. The foundation of Baracoa is celebrated in mid-August and there is plenty going on. Although hurricane season officially starts in June, you are most likely to get storms from September to November, when you should be prepared for all your travel plans to be disrupted. The coolest time is from December to February, although if a cold front comes down from the eastern seaboard of the USA, anywhere on Cuba's north coast, such as Baracoa, can expect high seas and some rain.

Santiago de Cuba

→ *Colour map 3, C6.*
Santiago de Cuba, near the east end of the island, 970 km from Havana, is Cuba's second city, with its own identity and charm. Its culture is different from Havana's, with more emphasis on its Afro-Caribbean roots and Santería plays a large part in people's lives. There are regional differences in the music, partly because of past immigrants from the former French colony of Saint-Domingue, now Haiti. Carnival is an experience worth going out of your way for, with energetic dancing, parades, music and increasingly sophisticated costumes as the economy improves.

The city centre is cluttered, with the feel of an overgrown country village, featuring many beautiful pastel-coloured buildings in much better condition than many of those in the capital. It is not a colonial gem along the lines of Havana or Trinidad and there is heavy industry around its edge but it does have an eclectic range of architectural styles from colonial to art deco. The Vista Alegre barrio is an outstanding example of a leafy Cuban suburb, with grand art nouveau buildings, an early 20th-century contrast to the Mudejar style of the city centre. Visit the Maqueta de la Ciudad, a scale model of the city by the Casa de Velázquez, for an overview of the city's development. ▶▶ *For listings, see pages 356-369.*

Ins and outs
Getting there International and domestic **Cubana** and **AeroCaribbean flights** arrive at the Antonio Maceo airport, 8 km south of the city on the coast. On arrival you are greeted by several taxi drivers, some of whom even manage to get right into the arrivals building;

these are unofficial taxis but reasonably priced and safe. Official and unofficial taxis shuttle passengers into town for around CUC$5-8, depending on the company and the distance. Daily **rail** services to and from Havana link Santiago with all the major towns lying along the main rail route through the country. The railway station is central, opposite the rum factory on Avenida Jesús Menéndez, and within walking distance of many *casas particulares* and some hotels in the centre. There are several daily **Víazul buses** from Havana, with morning and afternoon departures, and one from Trinidad, via many places of interest worth stopping off along the way. The long-distance bus terminal is to the north of the city, by the Plaza de la Revolución, some 30 minutes' walk to Parque Céspedes. Outside you will find **taxis** to take you to your destination. Arriving at night is not a problem as there are always taxis waiting for business. ▸▸ *See Transport, page 367.*

Getting around Urban **buses** cost 20 centavos. There are also horse-drawn **coches**, 1 peso and **bicitaxis**, CUC$1, for short journeys around town, although tourists are supposed to take taxis. Plaza Marte is a central hub for lots of local transport. For excursions there are buses on some routes out of town but it is easier to negotiate a day trip with a driver who can take you to your destination. Make sure everything is agreed and clear before you set off, as drivers have a reputation for moving the goalposts when you're a long way from base. **Car hire** is available if you want to drive yourself. The city is easy to **walk** around with many of the sights congregated around the centre. It takes about 20-30 minutes to walk from Parque Céspedes to the Hotel Santiago and 30 minutes from the parque to the bus station.

Best time to visit Santiago's position at the foot of the mountains means that it is more protected from breezes than places along the north coast and is consequently several degrees hotter than Havana. This is not a problem in winter, but in the summer months of July and August it can be stifling. The song *Calor en Santiago* by Conjunto Rumba Habana sums it up perfectly: *"¡Candela, fuego, me quemo, el calor me está derritiendo!"* – "Candle, fire, I'm burning, the heat is melting me!" Unfortunately, this coincides with carnival in July, which just has to be the best time to visit Santiago. Nearly the whole month is taken up with festivities, starting with the Festival del Caribe, which runs into carnival in the third week with Santiago's patron saint's day on 25 July. Everything stops on 26 July, National Rebel Day and the anniversary of the attack on the Moncada barracks, then continues the next day.

History

Santiago de Cuba was one of the seven towns (*villas*) founded by Diego Velázquez. It was first built in 1515 on the mouth of the Río Paradas but moved in 1516 to its present location in a horseshoe valley surrounded by mountains. It was Cuba's capital city until replaced by Havana in 1553 and capital of Oriente province until 1976. During the 17th-century Santiago was besieged by pirates from France and England, leading to the construction of the Castillo del Morro, still intact and now housing the piracy museum, just south of the city. Because of its location, Santiago has been the scene of many migratory exchanges with other countries; it was the first city in Cuba to receive African slaves, many French fled here from the slaves' insurrection in Haiti in the 18th century and Jamaicans have also migrated here from the neighbouring island. Santiago is more of a truly ethnic blend than many other towns in Cuba.

It is known as the 'heroic city' (*Ciudad Héroe*), the cradle of the Cuban Revolution, the Rebel City, or '*capital moral de la Revolución Cubana*'. Many of Cuba's heroes in both the 19th

The Padre Pico steps in Santiago

The revolution in Haiti at the end of the 18th century brought a large influx of French immigrants to Cuba, many of whom settled in the south west of Santiago de Cuba in an area known as Loma Hueca. They built a theatre there called El Tivoli, the name by which the neighbourhood came to be identified. The hill leading up to the Tivoli area was so steep that it had to be paved in staggered form, and these steps were named Loma de Corbacho, after the grocery store on one of the corners.

Decades later, in the Republic's first year, Emilio Bacardí, in his function as mayor, had the steps renovated. Locals wanted them to be named in his honour, but he proposed the name 'Padre Pico', in memory of Bernardo del Pico, a priest who had helped the poor in Santiago.

The Padre Pico steps gained further historical status when Castro chose their strategic location to fire the opening shots in his first offensive against Batista in 1956. As well as all that history, the steps give commanding views of the bay and mountains around Santiago, and now form an essential part of any walking tour of the city.

and 20th centuries were born here and started insurrections in the city and the surrounding mountains. The national hero, José Martí, is buried in Santa Ifigenia cemetery, just west of the city. The city played a major role in the early days of the Revolution in the 1950s and boasts two major landmarks of the clandestine struggle: the Moncada Garrison, now a school and museum, scene of Fidel Castro's first attack on the Batista regime in 1953, and **La Granjita Siboney**, the farmhouse where 129 revolutionaries gathered the night before the attack on the Garrison, which is also now a museum.

Sights

City centre

The small **Parque Céspedes** is at the centre of the town and everything revolves around it. Most of the main museums are within easy walking distance. The **Hotel Casa Granda** flanks the east side while on the south side is the Cathedral, the white **Santa Iglesia Basílica Metropolitana** ① *Heredia entre Félix Pena y Gen Lacret (entrance on Félix Pena), daily 0800-1200, services: Mon, Wed 1830, Sat 1700, Sun 0900, 1830*. The first building on the site was completed in 1524 but four subsequent disasters, including earthquakes and pirate attacks, meant that the cathedral was rebuilt four times. The building now standing was restored in 1818, with more new decoration added in the early 20th century.

The west side of the park is occupied by a rather ugly bank, next to the beautiful 16th-century **Casa de Diego Velázquez**. The house where Diego Velázquez lived is now one of the best museums in Santiago, the **Museo de Ambiente Histórico Cubano** ① *Félix Pena 612, at the northwest corner of Parque Céspedes, T22-652652, Sat-Thu 0900-1700, Fri 1400-1700, CUC$1, with guided tour in English, French, German or Russian, camera fee CUC$1 per photo*. It is the oldest house in Cuba, started in 1516, completed 1530. Velázquez, Cuba's conqueror, lived on the top floor, while the ground floor was used as a contracting house and a smelter for gold. It has been restored after its use as offices following the 1959 Revolution and is in two parts, one from the 16th century, and one from the 18th century. Each room shows a particular period, demonstrating the development of Cuban material culture, featuring furniture, china, porcelain and crystal; there is also a 19th-century extension.

On the north side the **Casa del Gobierno** features a strong Moorish influence, particularly in the patio. This building is not open to the public, but is used for government functions.

The **Museo Provincial Emilio Bacardí** ① *entrance on Pío Rosado esq Aguilera, 2 blocks east of the Parque, opposite the Palacio Provincial, T22-628402, Tue-Sat 1000-2000, Sun 1000-1800, Mon 1200-2000, guided tour in English, CUC$1*, was named after industrialist Emilio Bacardí Moreau, its main benefactor and collector of much of the museum's contents. This was the second museum founded in Cuba and has exhibits from prehistory to the Revolution downstairs, one of the most important collections of Cuban colonial paintings upstairs, while outside on one side there is a reconstruction of a typical colonial street front and a nice courtyard. The archaeology hall has mummies from Egypt and South America, including a Peruvian specimen over 1000 years old. The Egyptian mummy dates back to the 18th dynasty, 2000 years ago, and was personally acquired by Emilio Bacardí and brought back to Cuba. There are also exhibits of ancient art, ethnology, documents of the history of Santiago and a hand-made torpedo used by the rebels during the first war of independence in the 19th century.

On Heredia near the Casa de la Trova is the **Casa Natal de José María Heredia**, the birthplace of Santiago's most famous poet (see box, page 348). It is now a cultural centre and there is a poetry workshop here on Fridays from 1700. The **Museo de Música** is above the Casa de la Trova (see Entertainment).

If you are not going to be in town in July, you can get a flavour of the carnival by visiting the **Museo del Carnaval** ① *Calle Heredia esq a Carnicería, T22-626955, Tue-Sat 0900-1800, Sun 0900-1200, CUC$1*. The museum exhibits a dusty collection of instruments, drums and costumes from Santiago's famous July carnival. There are also lots of photos and newspaper cuttings but with no explanation of their significance. Every afternoon except Saturday you can feel the beat of the *bata* drums when the folklore group, *19 de Diciembre*, perform in the courtyard, CUC$1.

Plaza Dolores is worth noting as a point of reference if walking east from Parque Céspedes. It is known as 'Bulevar', although it is really just a widening of Aguilera. It's the most popular of the plazas for an evening's gossip and where you're most likely to be approached by Cubans. It's also popular with musicians.

The **Museo de la Lucha Clandestina** ① *at the top of Padre Pico steps, Calle Gen Rabí 1 entre Santa Rita y San Carlos, T22-624689, Tue-Sun 0900-1700, free*, was founded to mark the 20th anniversary of the armed uprising in Santiago, Central Ermita and other parts of Oriente on 30 November 1956. The museum highlights the support given by the local urban population during the battle in the Sierra Maestra and has an exhibition of the citizens' underground struggle against the dictatorship. Housed on two floors, exhibits revolve around Frank País, from his early moves to foment a revolutionary consciousness to his integration into the Movimiento 26 de Julio under Fidel Castro. A guide speaking 'Spanglish' will take you round if you can't read Spanish. The building was originally the residence of the Intendente, then was a police HQ, a key target of the 26 July revolutionary movement. It is now completely restored after having been stormed and gutted during the Revolution. It is a beautiful yellow building with a marvellous courtyard and affords good views of the city. On Saturday afternoon the courtyard is the venue for conferences, performances and other cultural activities relating to the city's French roots. Many of the French staff of the Alliance Française attend.

① Santiago de Cuba

Museo de Holografía
& Monumento Gen
Antonie Maceo

Long Distance
Bus Terminal

Av Los Pinos

Av Mariana Grajales

SAN PEDRITO

LOS OLMOS

SAGARRA

SORRIBES

Paseo de Martí

Museo
Histórico
26 de Julio

Parque Abel
Santamaría

Museo Abel
Santamaría

Museo Casa
Natal de
Frank País

La Tumba
Francesa

Casa Natal de
Antonio Maceo

Santo Tomás

New Station

La Barrita
Rum Factory

Old Station

Bahía de
Santiago
de Cuba

San Francisco

Carmen

Plaza Dolores

Plaza
Marte

Parque
Céspedes

Aguilera

Cathedral

Centro Cultural
Francisco Prats

Bartolomé Masó

Maqueta de
la Ciudad

Castillo Duany

Santa
Lucía

Eduardo Yero (Rey Pelayo)

Museo de la
Lucha Clandestina

Padre Pico
Steps

Diego Palacios (Santa Rita)

Rafael P Salcedo (San Carlos)

Parque
Alameda

Desiderio Mesnier (Santa Rosa)

José de Diego (Princesa)

C García (San Fernando)

VILLALÓN

PALAU A (Ambrosio Grillo)

Gral Lahera

De los
Desamparados

Av 24 Febrero (Trocha)

➡ **Santiago de Cuba maps**
1 **Santiago de Cuba, page 346**
2 Ferreiro, page 350
3 Around Santiago de Cuba, page 352

N

200 metres
200 yards

Sleeping
Amparo Hernández
  Liranza cp **15** *F2*
Antonio Alonso
  Baldoneda cp **1** *D2*
Casa Colonial Maruchi cp **22** *D2*
Casa Colonial Tania cp **3** *F2*
Casa Dulce cp **6** *E3*
Casa Granda **17** *detail*
Dinorah Rodríguez Bueno
  & William Pérez cp **2** *E3*
E San Basilio **19** *detail*
Flor María González cp **20** *B6*
Garden House cp **4** *D2*
Gran Hotel **18** *detail*
Irma Jordana Valls cp **5** *E3*
Mario Nistal Bello cp **9** *F3*
Migdalia Gámez Rodríguez cp &
  André y Ramona cp **14** *D2*
Rita Guerra Bertolez y Renaldo
  Gascon Mirabent cp **23** *E4*

Eating
Café Ajedrez **2** *E2*
Café Catedral **11** *detail*
Complejo Don Antonio **3** *detail*
Coppelia **1** *D4*
El Baturro **10** *detail*
Garzón y K **13** *D5*
Isabelica **4** *detail*
Las Enramadas **6** *detail*
Las Gallegas **9** *detail*

La Taberna de Dolores **5** *detail*
Santiago 1900 **7** *detail*
Subway Aguilera **14** *E3*

Bars & clubs
Kontiki **12** *detail*
Las Columnitas **8** *detail*

Entertainment
Casa de la Música **1** *E2*
Casa de las Tradiciones **2** *F2*
Casa de la Trova (Museo
  de Música) **5** *detail*
Casa del Son **3** *E4*
Cine Cuba **11** *detail*
Cine Rialto **13** *E2*
Disco Bar/Club 300 **6** *detail*
El Patio de Artex **9** *detail*
El Patio de los dos Abuelos **12** *E4*
Sala de Conciertos
  Dolores **7** *detail*
Teatro Heredia **4** *A5*

Santiago de Cuba centre

José María Heredia

José Martí said of Heredia: "The first poet in America is Heredia. Only he has captured in his poetry the sublimity, fire and ostentation of its nature. He is as volcanic as its entrails and as calm as its mountain peaks." In his short but eventful life Heredia created a poetic canon that transformed the form and content of Latin American poetry.

José María de Heredia y Campuzano was born on 31 December 1803 in Santiago de Cuba, the city his parents had fled to from Santo Domingo in 1801 from the invading Haitian troops. He had an itinerant childhood, the family being constantly uprooted by his father's work; they left their first house in Santiago de Cuba when Heredia was only three years old. He then spent time in the USA and Santo Domingo, as well as Havana and Matanzas. At the age of 20 he was exiled to the USA for his involvement in an independence conspiracy. There he wrote his ode 'Niagara', establishing him as a world-class poet. His death in Mexico aged 36 cut short a tragic life in exile for a man devoted to his country.

The house where Heredia was born still stands, at Heredia y San Félix, in spite of efforts by the colonial rulers of the 19th century to have it demolished. An association made up of influential people like Emilio Bacardí succeeded in buying the house, agreeing to hand over its restoration to the municipal government in 1902. Today, it has regained its original prestige as a national monument and is the most important of the numerous other cultural sites on Calle Heredia, the street formerly called Calle Catedral. The house is a now museum dedicated to the poet's life, as well as a cultural centre and meeting point for contemporary local poets.

To get a good idea of the layout of the city, visit the **Maqueta de la Ciudad** ① *Corona entre San Basilio y Santa Lucía, Tue-Sun 0900-2100, CUC$1, drink included, small bar*. This is a scale model similar to the one in Havana. Nearby is the **Centro Cultural Francisco Prats** ① *Corona entre Heredia y San Basilio, guided tour*. This is a remodelled colonial house exhibiting personal belongings of the brilliant investigator.

There are several interesting churches in the centre: **Iglesia de la Santísima Trinidad (Carmen)**, on Félix Pena y San Jerónimo, built in the late 18th century with some neoclassical features; two blocks west is **Iglesia San Francisco**, on Calle San Francisco, also 18th century; **Iglesia de Santa Lucía**, Santa Lucía esquina Pío Rosado, a small church worth visiting in order to see the architecture in the surrounding streets; three blocks south of the Museo de la Lucha Clandestina is **Iglesia de los Desamparados**, on General T Prado; **Iglesia Santo Tomás** is an 18th-century church on Habana y Félix Pena.

North of the city centre

Ten minutes' walk north from the centre of Santiago is the **Bacardí rum factory**, or La Barrita, but you can only go in the shop and bar, the factory is closed to visitors since tourists 'stole' the technology by taking too many photos. Ron Caney is made here. There is also a small **Museo del Ron** ① *San Basilio 358 esq Carnicería, near Parque Céspedes, T22-623737, Mon-Fri 0900-1700, CUC$1 including 2 cl of rum*.

Also near the factory is the **Museo Casa Natal de Frank País** ① *General Banderas 226 y Los Maceos, T22-652710*. This museum is in the birthplace of the leader of the 26 July movement and of the armed uprising in Santiago on 30 November 1956, who was shot on 30 July 1957. He is considered a great hero of the Revolution and his face is often seen on posters and hoardings alongside that of Che, Fidel and other leaders. His tomb is in Santa Ifigenia cemetery.

Another revolutionary hero, but this time from the 19th century, is celebrated at the **Casa Natal de Antonio Maceo** ① *Los Maceo 207 entre Corona y Rastro, T22-623750, Mon-Sat 0900-1700, free.* The house was built between 1800 and 1830, and was the birthplace, on 14 June 1845, of Antonio Maceo y Grajales, one of the greatest military commanders of the 1868 and 1895 wars of independence. The museum houses his biography and details his 32 years' devotion to the struggle for independence.

Plaza Marte

Plaza Marte, a short walk up Aguilera from Parque Céspedes, is a pick-up and drop-off point for most urban transport. Go there if you want to get a taxi late at night. The bus stop for other *repartos*, including Vista Alegre, is on the corner of Aguilera and Plaza Marte. Plaza Marte is a quieter spot to sit than Parque Céspedes; sometimes musicians play and there's an ice cream stand. Baseball fans come here to dissect the latest matches and loudly proclaim their points of view. Children under 10 will enjoy the plaza at weekends in the late afternoon when there are rides around the square on kids' bikes or in little goat carts, as well as other entertainment paid for in pesos.

North of Plaza Marte, **Parque Abel Santamaría** is a small square commemorating one of Fidel's comrades who was captured by Batista's troops and had his eyes gouged out. Cuba's eye hospitals are now named after him. The park is on the site of the hospital he was occupying at the time of his capture. The remains of the hospital have been made into the **Museo Abel Santamaría** ① *Gen Portuondo (Trinidad) esq Av de los Libertadores, T22-624119, Mon-Sat 0900-1700, CUC$1.* It was inaugurated on the symbolic date of 26 July 1973 on the 20th anniversary of the attempted overthrow of the Batista regime and has seven rooms exhibiting furniture from the old hospital, clothing and personal possessions of the revolutionaries and other things linked with the history of the place. Two blocks east, the former Moncada Garrison is now the **Museo Histórico 26 de Julio** ① *Av Moncada esq Gen Portuondo, T22-620157, Tue-Sat 0900-2000, Sun 0900-1300, CUC$2, guided tour in English, French, Italian, camera fee CUC$1, video camera fee CUC$5.* The Garrison was attacked (unsuccessfully) by Castro and his revolutionaries on 26 July 1953. Most of the men were captured, tortured and murdered. Fidel was caught later and imprisoned before being exiled. When the Revolution triumphed in 1959, the building was turned into a school. To mark the 14th anniversary of the attack, in 1967 one of the buildings was converted to a museum, featuring photos, plans and drawings of the battle. Exhibits include personal items of the Revolutionaries, weapons used in the attack on the Moncada Garrison and during the battles in the Sierra Maestra. There is a homemade gun built by Che Guevara and a waistcoat that belonged to José Martí, an earlier hero. Bullet holes, filled in by Batista, have been reconstructed on the outer walls. A guided visit is highly recommended to help you understand the brutality and carnage of the Batista regime.

Plaza de la Revolución

One of Cuba's foremost revolutionaries of the 19th century, General Antonio Maceo, is honoured in the **Plaza de la Revolución Mayor General Antonio Maceo**. The plaza, to the northeast of the centre, has a dramatic monument to the Revolution made of galvanized steel in searing, solid Soviet style, and a gargantuan bronze statue of the general on horseback surrounded by huge iron machetes rising from the ground at different angles. Fidel has made many stirring speeches from the platform and you can picture the plaza filled to capacity to hear him. It was also where the Pope said Mass in his 1998 visit, where rallies were held demanding the repatriation of the Cuban boat boy Elián González in 2000, and the five Cuban heroes imprisoned in the USA in 2002-03, and where parades are held every 1 May on international Labour Day. The long-distance bus terminal is opposite the plaza and you can't miss the monument when departing by bus.

The **Museo de Holografía** ① *T22-643768, Mon-Sat, 0900-1700, Sun 0900-1300, CUC$1*, is housed below the monument in the Plaza de la Revolución. It features holograms, mostly of things associated with the Revolution and with General Maceo. A guided tour (in Spanish) shows you where the Pope rested after his speech in the plaza.

Ferreiro

The junction of Victoriano Garzón and Avenida Las Américas, where the hotels **Santiago** and **Las Américas** are situated, is known locally as Ferreiro, after the family that owned a large part of the surrounding area and emigrated to the USA after the

2 Ferreiro

➡ Santiago de Cuba maps
1 Santiago de Cuba orientation, page 346
2 Ferreiro, page 350
3 Around Santiago de Cuba, page 352

N

200 metres
200 yards

Sleeping 🛏
Jorge Juan Manchón Cusine cp **1**
José Luis Manzano cp **3**
Las Américas **2**
Meliá Santiago de Cuba **4**
Odalys Turro Tejeda cp **10**

Los Cactus cp **6**
San Juan **7**

Eating 🍴
El Mirador **5**
El Zunzun **1**
Helado Alondra **2**

Pizza Nova **3**
Tropical **4**

Entertainment 🎭
Casa del Caribe **1**

Revolution. From here, you can catch a bus to any part of town and get a taxi, official or otherwise. Take care at night, as the three small squares at this junction are not lit. North of here along Avenida de las Américas is the **Bosque de los Héroes** ① *Av de las Américas entre M y L, Ampliación de Terrazas, Mon-Sat 0900-1700*. In this park, a block from **Hotel Las Américas**, is the first monument in Latin America devoted to the memory of Che Guevara and his Cuban comrades who died in Bolivia. The architectural sculpture leaves shadows as the sun's rays change during the day, giving different images of the heroes. At night it is strikingly illuminated.

To the east of Ferreiro off Avenida Manduley, in Reparto Vista Alegre, are several interesting museums. The **Centro Cultural Africano Fernando Ortíz** ① *Av Manduley 106, 0900-1700,* displays items of African culture. The **Casa del Caribe** ① *Calle 13 esq Calle 8, T22-642285,* is a world-renowned cultural centre. If you are interested in *Santería*, there is a musical and religious ceremony at 0930 on Wednesdays.

The **Museo de la Religión** ① *Calle 13 206, esq Calle 10, 1 block from Casa del Caribe, Mon-Sat 0830-1700, free, knowledgeable English-speaking guide, CUC$2,* displays religious items particularly concerning *Santería*. There are no written explanations of the exhibits, not even in Spanish, so it is best to ask for a guide. The **Museo de la Imagen** ① *Calle 8 106, esq 5, T22-642234, Mon-Sat 0900-1700, CUC$1,* displays cameras, photographs, film and television.

Cementerio Santa Ifigenia

① *Av Crombet, Reparto Juan G Gómez, T22-632723, daily 0800-1730, CUC$1, CUC$1 for cameras, price includes guided tour in Spanish and English.*

This grand and well-kept cemetery northwest of the city features José Martí's mausoleum, a huge structure with a statue of Martí inside, designed to receive a shaft of sunlight all morning. Martí is surrounded by six statues of women, representing the six Cuban provinces of the 19th century. Along the path leading up to the mausoleum are signposts commemorating successful independence battles, each decorated with a quote by Martí. There is an elegant changing of the guard ceremony every 30 minutes, free. Also in the cemetery is the grave of Frank País, a prime mover in the revolutionary struggle, and other notable figures, such as Céspedes, the Bacardí family and the mother and widow of Maceo. There is a monument to the Moncada fallen and the tomb of Cuba's first president, Tomás Estrada Palma. More recently, it is the burial place of the famous musician, Compay Segundo, one of the stars of the *Buena Vista Social Club*, who was born in Santiago and died in Havana in 2003. It is said by some that Fidel Castro could be laid to rest here. Well worth a visit.

South of Santiago

The Ruta Turística runs along the shore of the Bahía de Santiago to the **Castillo del Morro**, a clifftop fort and World Heritage Site since 1997 with the **Museo de la Piratería** ① *T22-691569, CUC$4, CUC$1 for cameras, taxi to El Morro, CUC$25 round trip with wait, bus 212 from Plaza Marte or opposite the cinema Rialto, Parque Céspedes, stops in front of embarkation point for Cayo Granma,* a museum of the sea, piracy and local history, charting the pirate attacks made on Santiago during the 16th century. Pirates included the Frenchman Jacques de Sores and the Welshman Sir Henry Morgan and you can see many of the weapons used in both attack and defence of the city. The fort has many levels and fascinating rooms whose purpose can be guessed easily, such as the prison cells, the chapel and the cannon-loading bay. From the roof you can admire the thrilling views over the Bay of Santiago and Cayo Granma and you can follow some 16th-century steps almost down to the waterline. There is a narrow, grass-covered passage that eventually leads down to a small beach, which you can also get to by road. There is a good restaurant on a terrace with a great view, main dish CUC$6, and a cannon fire at sunset every evening.

Transport along the road passes the ferry at Ciudadmar to the resorts of **Cayo Granma** and **La Socapa** in the estuary (hourly, CUC$2 per person, 10 minutes). Cayo Granma was originally Cayo Smith, named after its wealthy owner; it became a resort for the rich. Now most of its 600 inhabitants travel to Santiago to work. There are no vehicles; there are a couple of *paladares* serving seafood in an idyllic setting looking across the bay towards Santiago, ask around, CUC$6 for a fish meal and a beer.

East of Santiago

La Gran Piedra and around
Excellent excursions can be made 26 km east to **La Gran Piedra** ① *CUC$1 to climb*. Unfortunately the road was closed in 2009, having been destroyed by the hurricanes of 2008 and everything cut off, so check before setting out whether it is open. From this viewpoint it

3 Around Santiago de Cuba

Sleeping	Club Amigo Carisol	El Saltón 4
Balcón del Caribe 1	Los Corales 6	Gran Piedra 5
Brisas Sierra Mar-	Club Bucanero 2	Versalles 8
Los Galeones 7	Costa Morena 3	

is said you can see Haiti and Jamaica on a clear day, more likely their lights on a clear night. It is a giant rock weighing 75,000 tonnes, the third largest solid rock in the world (according to the Guinness Book of Records), 1234 m high, and reached by climbing 454 steps from the road (only for the fit). The view is tremendous and buzzards circle around you. Hand-carved wooden curios are sold by artisans on the steps. There are no buses and official tours were suspended after the hurricanes. Two kilometres before La Gran Piedra are the **Jardines de la Siberia**, on the site of a former coffee plantation, an extensive botanical garden; turn right and follow the track for about 1 km to reach the gardens.

The **Museo La Isabelica** ① *Carretera de la Gran Piedra Km 14, closed 2009*, is a ruined coffee plantation once owned by French emigrés from Haiti, the buildings of which are now turned into a museum. It was named a World Heritage Site in 2000. It houses the former kitchen and other facilities on the ground floor with farming tools and archaeological finds. Upstairs is the owners' house in authentic 19th-century style. On view on the ground floor are instruments of slave torture. After the slave revolt in Haiti, large numbers of former slave owners were encouraged to settle in the Sierra de la Gran Piedra. This influx led to the impact of Haitian/French culture on Santiago, especially in music. Here they built 51 *cafetales*, using slave labour. During the Ten Years' War (1868-78) the revolutionaries called for the destruction of all the *cafetales*. The owner, Victor Constantin Cuzeau, named the

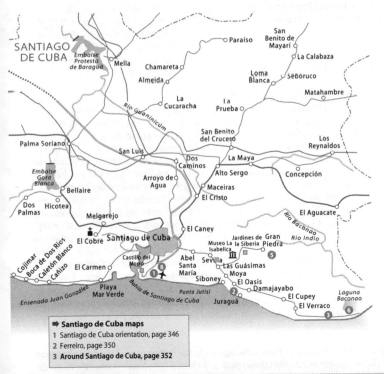

⇒ **Santiago de Cuba maps**
1 Santiago de Cuba orientation, page 346
2 Ferreiro, page 350
3 **Around Santiago de Cuba, page 352**

plantation after his lover and house slave, but when Céspedes freed the slaves he fled and Isabelica was thrown by the former slaves into a burning oven.

Siboney to Juraguá

On the Carretera Siboney at Km 13.5 is **La Granjita Siboney** ① *T22-639168, Tue-Sun 0900-1700, CUC$1,* the farmhouse used as the headquarters for the revolutionaries' attack on the Moncada barracks on 26 July 1953. It now has a museum of uniforms, weapons and artefacts used by the 129 men who gathered here the night before, as well as extensive newspaper accounts of the attack. The road is lined with stone tributes commemorating the spots where revolutionaries were killed.

Siboney ① *Cubans take bus 214 from near bus terminal, foreigners are expected to take a taxi or hire car,* 16 km east of Santiago, is the nearest beach to the city with a reef just offshore which is great for snorkelling, although the beach itself is stony and not particularly good. It gets very crowded at weekends when trucks disgorge passengers every 45 minutes. There is a certain amount of hassling on the beach. The accommodation office is at the entrance to the village. You will be approached with offers of private rooms to rent and there are numerous street food stalls and *paladares*, mostly frequented by Cubans, although you will be charged in CUC$.

About 20 km from Santiago, or half way between Siboney and Juraguá, look for a sign on the left to **Finca El Porvenir** ① *Carretera de Baconao Km 18, CUC$2 includes a drink,* a nice freshwater swimming pool with a bar and restaurant serving *comida criolla* from 1000-1800. The pool looks a bit green at first, but is actually clean and a wonderful place to stop off and cool down after sweating along the dusty highway. You can also go horse riding here.

Juraguá is a nicer beach than Siboney but it is a bit rundown and not really geared towards tourism although further development is projected in this area.

Valle de la Prehistoria and around

At Km 6.5 on the Carretera Baconao is the **Valle de la Prehistoria** ① *T22-639239, CUC$1, extra CUC$1 to take photos,* a huge park filled with life-size carved stone dinosaurs and stone-age men. Great for the kids but due to the total absence of shade it is like walking around a desert. Take huge supplies of water and try to go early or late. You can get quite a good view of the monsters from the main road as you pass by. Nearby is **Mundo de Fantasía**, a small amusement park also good for kids. Admission appears to be free, ask the stone clown at the entrance! Also in the area is the recommended old car and trailer museum, **Museo de Transporte Terrestre** ① *Carretera Baconao Km 8.5, Daiquirí, turn left at the junction for Playa Daiquirí, T22-639197, CUC$1 entrance plus CUC$1 for a camera and CUC$3 for video.* The old classic American cars are not particularly well kept, although some of the best of them are now being brought out to be used as taxis in Santiago to entertain the tourists. Others, however, are in serious need of proper restoration. **Daiquirí** beach is reserved for the military. The next beach, 1 km after Daiquirí, is **Colibrí**, featuring a seawater swimming pool and a pebble beach. However, this has now been developed as a treatment and rehabilitation centre for drug addicts and foreign tourists are no longer allowed entry. Continuing east at Km 35 is **Comunidad Artística Verraco**, a small artists' community, where you can buy original pieces of artwork, prices negotiable.

Baconao

On this stretch of the coast, there is the aquarium and dolphinarium **Acuario de Baconao** ① *CUC$7, sea-lion and dolphin shows daily, at 1030 and 1440, however small the audience,*

10-min swim with the dolphins CUC$39 extra . The show is of a high standard, although controversial as Cuba captures wild dolphins for its shows and for export. The aquarium has many species of fish as well as turtle and sharks (feeding time is spectacular). There is a basic refreshment bar where you can get a sandwich, and a beach, with trees for shade but no facilities. See also page 22 for further information about dolphinariums in Cuba. **Playa Cazonal** is a very high quality beach for this area, next to Hotel Corales. Wear something on your feet when swimming and avoid standing on the coral reef. **Laguna Baconao** ① *CUC$1 to enter the Laguna Baconao area,* is a large murky lake (5 km round) in a beautiful setting, used for dolphin breeding. Flanking the lake is a crocodile sanctuary, but they are kept in small enclosures with barely enough water to drink. Admission includes a boat ride to a floating bar in the middle of the lake.

West of Santiago

El Sanctuario de Nuestra Señora de la Caridad del Cobre
① *There is no bus, so either hire a private taxi, about CUC$20-25, or a Transtur taxi for CUC$30. You can also cycle. At Melgarejo turn left just after the petrol station, then in the village turn right at the crossroads; follow this road round to the right at the fork, leading to the church.*

Twenty-nine kilometres west of Santiago is El Sanctuario de Nuestra Señora de la Caridad del Cobre ('El Cobre'), where the shrine of Cuba's patron saint, the Virgen de la Caridad del Cobre, is built over a working copper mine. The story goes that in the 17th century, three fishermen were about to capsize in Nipe Bay, when they found a wooden statue of the Virgin Mary floating in the sea. Their lives were saved and they brought the statue to its current resting place above the altar. Downstairs there are many tokens of gratitude left by Cubans who have been helped by the Virgin in some way, for example, for their son to escape to Miami on a raft, in some medical problem or in some sporting event. It is quite common to see nuns dragging the infirm from a minivan into the church. There is a pilgrimage here on 7 September, the eve of the patron saint's day. Women with exposed shoulders are not admitted, so don't wear skimpy tops here, although they do hire rather attractive coveralls if you forget. Watch out for the touts swarming around you when you get out of the car; they will try to sell you souvenirs and pieces of copper. It is probably best to take a bit of copper and offer some pesos cubanos, otherwise they will be waiting for you when you leave the church. Fortunately they are not allowed inside.

Mar Verde to El Francés
There is a small, busy beach about 10 km west of Santiago called **Mar Verde**; then **Bueycabón**, which is nothing special, and then **Caletón Blanco** (30 km west of Santiago), which is a nice beach, mostly frequented by Cubans. Like all the beaches in this area, it is quite narrow, with beige sand. A seawater swimming pool next to the sea has the remains of a diving board. Hold your breath as youths throw themselves 2 m or so into the air above the pool, getting the distance they need over the water to avoid being smashed on the pool's edge. When they are not doing that, the pool is a pleasant place to take a dip if you want the Caribbean without the waves. There is a café and restaurant and Campismo for Cubans. Further along is **El Francés**, said to be the best beach in the west but reserved for the military.

El Saltón
About 35 km inland from El Francés, near **Cruce de los Baños**, you will find El Saltón (see Sleeping, below), a mini-resort advertized as 'stress relief', where there is a waterfall and

several natural pools to bathe in. Originally designed as a health spa, you don't have to be ill to stay there now. It is in a fantastic location in the Sierra Maestra and set into the side of a mountain some way down a track with a picturesque waterfall and nothing else around it. A great place for a massage in a very relaxing environment. Day trips are organized to include a swim, lunch, hiking with a guide and horse riding, contact Sol y Son, CUC$59 per person for a group of five, 0700-1700.

El Uvero and around

Further west from Santiago the wonderful coastal road runs along the base of the Sierra Maestra with beautiful bays and completely deserted beaches, some with black sand. It is only possible to visit by car and a sturdy one is recommended as parts of the road are gravel and unsealed. Many of the villages have connections with historical revolutionary events. **El Uvero**, about 60 km from Santiago, Carretera Granma, has a monument marking the attack by Castro and his men on the Batista troop HQ on 28 May 1957. The building that was attacked is now a small **museum** ① *s/n entre Escuela Simbólica y Campo Deportivo*.

It is 20 km from El Uvero to Ocujal and about 7 km from there to Las Cuevas (before La Plata), from where you can climb up to **Pico Turquino** (1974 m). This is the highest peak in the Sierra Maestra. There are only two legally established and maintained accesses to the mountain, from Las Cuevas and from Alto de Naranjo, see page 328. A guide is mandatory and costs CUC$15. You set out at 0630 and, depending on your level of fitness and speed, come down at 1730, just before dusk. It can often be difficult to get a guide without advanced booking and it is quicker and easier to go on a tour. Sol y Son, see page 366, offer a day trip for CUC$90 per person starting with jeep pick up at 0500, two hours to Las Cuevas then walk to Alto de Naranjo, four hours up, four hours down the other side, lunch on Pico Cuba, getting back to the jeep at 1700 and returning to Santiago at 1900. If you need accommodation in the area, you can ask around in Ocujal and Las Cuevas, or there is a campsite at La Mula, east of Ocujal.

◉ Santiago de Cuba listings

For Sleeping and Eating price codes and other relevant information, see Essentials pages 37-43.

◉ Sleeping

Santiago de Cuba centre *p344, map p346*
Hotels
L-B Casa Granda, Heredia 201 entre San Pedro y San Félix, on Parque Céspedes, T22-686600, www.gran-caribe.com. Elegant building opened in 1914 and patronized by many famous movie stars and singers, as well as sports champions Joe Louis the boxer and Babe Ruth the baseball player. Faded grandeur, many rooms in need of renovation and can be noisy at night with competing music. Laundry, car hire, satellite TV, pool, post office, business centre, 1 room for

disabled people, **Havanatur** and **Asistur** offices. Excellent central location with terrace bar and café, overlooking park, 5th-floor bar with even better views over city (CUC$2 to go up 2000-0100 if you are not staying at the hotel, but that buys your 1st cocktail), restaurant and café, open 0800-2400, good. Disco (karaoke) at the side of the hotel, CUC$1.
A-B Hotel E San Basilio, San Basilio 403 entre Calvario y Carnicería, T22-651702, www.cubanacan.cu. A 2003 hotel in baby blue, close to the historical centre, nice decor with lots of plants and stylish pieces of furniture. 8 large and very comfortable rooms, satellite TV, security box, minibar, 24-hr restaurant serving *criollo* and international food.

C Gran Hotel, Enramada 312 entre San Félix y San Pedro, T22-653020, www.granhotelstgo.cu. Training school for tourism workers (Formatur), 2 star, very central and newly rebuilt on a shopping street. 27 rooms, a/c, TV, hot water, mini bar, restaurant and cafeteria.

Casas particulares

Prices vary according to the season and whether commission is paid. In low season, or for long stays, you can pay as little as CUC$15, but this rises to CUC$20-25 in high season or with commission. Touts around Parque Céspedes, the bus station and at the railway terminal exit. Avoid casas on Corona, which is noisy with buses and other traffic. There are lots of casas on Enramada (Saco), the main shopping street and closed to traffic 0900-2100, if you care to browse. All casas listed here offer private bathrooms, hot and cold water, a/c, fan, fridge and meals are available.

D Casa Colonial Maruchi, San Félix 357 entre San Germán y Trinidad, T22-620767, maruchib @yahoo.es. Good location close to the centre, fabulous, well-preserved colonial house with large courtyard and beautiful vegetation. 2 large, quiet rooms, brick and plaster walls, exposed timbers, high ceilings, tiled floors. Maruchi is a researcher at Casa del Caribe with a wide knowledge of Afrocuban religions and Cuban culture. Speaks fluent English.

D-E Amparo Hernández Liranza, Santa Rita 161 entre Corona y Padre Pico, T22-656351, amparohl@yahoo.es. Extremely pleasant place and one of the best casas in terms of comfort and space. 2 rooms, very private and independent, double or twin beds, large and spacious, good bathrooms, lots of windows and fresh air. Each room has own patio/terrace on separate floors, great view of cathedral, city and bay, plants, table and chairs, deckchairs, rain and sun cover or sunbathing. Good food, plenty of fruit and veg. English and French spoken.

D-E Antonia Alonso Baldonedo, Morua Delgado (Rastro) 360 Bajos entre Gen Portuondo (Trinidad) y Lauro Fuentes, T22-622221. Smart, green and white, very spacious house built 1949 with all period features preserved. Double or twin beds, bathroom dated but good and clean, laundry service, good food, vegetarians catered for, English spoken, very friendly and helpful.

D-E Casa Colonial Tania, Castillo Duany (Santa Rita) 101 entre Callejón Santiago y Teniente Rey, T22-624490, aquiles@cultstgo. cult.cu. Tania García Terreno and family live in this huge old house, English, French and Italian spoken, 2 rooms, with windows, bedside lamps, desk, good bathrooms and furniture. Stairs up to roof terrace for sunbathing or great sunset watching with views over the bay and up to the cathedral.

D-E Casa Dulce, Bartolomé Masó (San Basilio) 552 Altos esq Clarín, T22-625479, gdcastillo20@yahoo.es. Delightful apartment, living room on corner has huge windows open to the breeze, 1 large bedroom with great view, one of the best casas, run by Gladys Domenech Castillo, who is helpful, friendly, speaks English and offers really good food and internet access. The roof terrace has a table for meals, sunbed, amazing views of the city and harbour.

D-E Dinorah Rodríguez Bueno and William Pérez, Diego Palacios (Santa Rita) 504 entre Reloj y Clarín, T22-625834. English and French spoken, William is a historian and full of knowledge on cultural matters, both of them are excellent sources of information and very helpful, 10-min walk from Parque Céspedes up steps on hillside, 2 independent rooms to one side of the house with ensuite bathrooms, rather small and dark, can connect for groups, laundry facilities, good food, patio with mature trees and seating.

D-E Garden House, Máximo Gómez (San Germán) 165 entre Rastro y Gallo, T22-653720. Run by María Abono Segura and Félix Correoso Castillo, a retired couple and their friendly Spaniel, who speak some English and Russian and can help with tours or travel problems. 2 rooms at the front of the house off the living room, TV, phone, comfortable, double and sofabeds. The garden at the back is really special, covered in trailing flowering plants, pots everywhere, bananas, while up on the roof is a terrace with more pretty garden and vines, swings for children, tables, benches, hammock.

D-E Irma Jordana Valls, Santa Lucía (Castillo Duany) 303 entre San Pedro y San Félix, T22-622391, close to Parque Céspedes. Huge colonial house, 1 room with double and single bed, access door to tiny patio, large bathroom with bathtub and bidet. 2nd L-shaped room with 2 double beds, smaller bathroom, high ceilings. Interior patio has flowering plants, the front room is cluttered with ornaments, dining room with TV opens onto patio. Meals and laundry service offered, only Spanish spoken.

D-E Mario Nistal Bello, Princesa (J de Diego) 565 entre Carnicería (Pio Rosado) y Calvario (Porfirio Valiente), T22-651909. 2 small rooms upstairs, double and twin beds, simple but clean and good. Dining area outside rooms with fridge and all crockery so you can prepare your own cold meals, good food offered, laundry service, doctor daughter speaks English and some Italian. Small patio with view of cathedral and larger terrace upstairs for sunbathing and great view all around. Secure parking opposite for small fee.

D-E Rita Guerra Bertolez and Reynaldo Gascón Mirabent, Padre Quiroga (Clarin) 157 A entre Rey Pelayo y Sta Lucía, T22-624859, ritag.guerra@yahoo.es. Up narrow staircase, 1 simple room with view of harbour, double bed and child's bed, windows on 2 sides for fresh air, small bathroom, 2 bedside lights, basic English and French, very friendly and helpful, Rita is a doctor.

E André y Ramona, T22-654349, offering a basic self-contained suite with bedroom, kitchenette, dining room, TV, roof terrace with amazing view of city and bay, covered table and chairs or sunny area. André has a 1949 car and offers tours or taxi service, English spoken.

E Migdalia Gámez Rodríguez, Corona 371 Altos entre San Germán y Trinidad, T22-654569. 2 rooms, both with 2 beds, one larger than the other with larger bathroom too, TV,

fan, daughter speaks English, quiet, friendly, good food. On the next floor, same family, live.

Ferreiro *p350, map p350*
Hotels

AL-A Meliá Santiago de Cuba, Av Las Américas entre 4 y M, Reparto Sueño, T22-687070, www.solmelia.com. Built in 1991, the 15-floor hotel's modern design stands out like a beacon and is quite a landmark with its red, white and blue colour scheme. 5 star, 302 rooms and suites, some for non-smokers and the disabled, 24-hr room service, excellent breakfast buffet CUC$9, lots of bars and restaurants, good view of city from roof top bar, swimming pools open to day visitors for CUC$10, tennis, sauna, car hire, business centre with internet access, post office and will change most any currencies into dollars, staff helpful and friendly.

B-C Las Américas, Av de las Américas esq Gen Cebreco, T22-642011, www.islazul.cu. 70 rooms, lively, high-quality restaurant, variety of dishes, non-residents may use pool where they have cultural shows every night, nice reception staff, safety deposit, car hire, **Cadeca**, shop, bicycle hire. Easy access to city centre, bus stop opposite hotel, taxis wait by bus stop.

B-C San Juan, Km 4.5 Carretera a Siboney, T22-687156, hotel@sanjuan.scu. cyt.cu. On edge of town, taxi to the centre CUC$3-4, but nice location, the former *Leningrado* is right beside the site of one of the last battles of the 1898 War of Independence. The remains of a huge ceiba tree are in the grounds, beneath which Spain and the USA signed the surrender of Santiago on 16 July 1898. 107 nice rooms, some triples, large, clean, smart and newly painted, large pool, bar, restaurants, good breakfast, high quality by Cuban standards, queues at weekends and during festivals, car hire, **Cadeca**.

Casas particulares

This area is more suburban, with wider streets, detached houses with gardens and lots of shady trees. It is quieter at night. Road signs are non-existent.

D-E Flor María González, J 314 entre Av Las Américas y 6, Reparto Sueño, upper floor, T22-645568, flor@ceefe.uo.edu.cu. 1 large room with 2 beds, TV, desk, fridge. Not a fancy house, but homely. Flor María is a professor at the Oriente University and her husband speaks English and Russian. They offer visiting students a half-board package for CUC$25pp, or you can pay-as-you-go for meals.

D-E Jorge Juan Manchón Cusine, 6 204 entre 7 y 9, Vista Alegre, T22-674827. House built 1933, colonial style with all original tiles and fittings, high ceilings, spacious and airy. 2 rooms, beds can be changed to suit, double, twin or child's bed. Front bedroom on corner has false ceiling but windows on 2 walls for breeze, new bathroom in corner of room, 2nd room has high ceiling, 1 window and huge bathroom, both with wardrobe. Large dining room can cater for groups, barbecue outside can roast whole pig, patio covered with vines, shady table and chairs. French spoken, a bit of English and lots of sign language.

D-E José Luis Manzano, 6 202 esq 7, Vista Alegre, T22-644272, josemanzano_22@ yahoo.com. Huge 1925 house with rocking chairs on front porch, next door to Jorge Juan Manchón on street corner shaded by trees, secure parking, son speaks English. 2 rooms with high ceilings and bathroom built into corner of rooms, tiled floors.

D-E Los Cactus, 10 410 entre 15 y 17, Reparto Vista Alegre, T22-642611. Run by Rubén Rodes Estrada, wooden house painted yellow and white, giant cactus outside. Independent room outside house in converted garage with roof terrace, all new fittings, TV, black bathroom, secure parking, good food, pleasant and quiet location.

D-E Odalys Turro Tejeda, 6 401 entre 15 y 17, Reparto Vista Alegre, T22-642911, odalis.xp@bpcaribe.ciges.inf.cu. Large, well-cared for house. 1 room on ground floor at front with windows on 2 sides, TV, massive bathroom, 2nd room upstairs at back with smaller bathroom. Eat in large kitchen or outside, terrace, guard dogs, parrot, fruit trees in front garden.

South of Santiago *p351, map p352*
Hotels
B-C Balcón del Caribe, Carretera del Morro Km 7.5, next to Castillo del Morro, T22-691011, www.islazul.cu. 94 rooms, of which 23 are in bungalows, on a cliff overlooking the sea, quiet, pool, simple Cuban food, cold water in bungalows, Cadeca, pleasant but inconvenient for the town.

B-C Versalles, Carretera del Morro Km 1, near airport, T22-691016, www.cubanacan.cu. 3-star, in residential area with views to mountains in the distance, 61 large and clean rooms, singles, doubles, triples and suites, minibar on request, staff can be unhelpful, CUC$1 for visitors to use pool, pool-side snack bar. Best if you have rental car, CUC$2 taxi from centre, difficult to get taxi into town.

East of Santiago *p352, map p352*
Hotels
AL-A Club Amigo Carisol Los Corales, T22-356113-5, www.cubanacan.cu. 3 star, 2 hotels now run as one, 310 rooms, a/c, minibar, TV, all-inclusive, 2 buffet and 2 à la carte restaurants, pool, lots of activities and watersports included but diving costs extra, animals on beach can be messy, wear water shoes to protect feet from rocks, tennis, disco and other night time entertainment, car and bicycle hire, childcare, near Playa Cazonal. Tours include trips to Santiago or horse riding to a waterfall.

B Club Bucanero, Carretera Baconao Km 4, Arroyo La Costa, 15 miles from the airport, T22-686363-4, www.gran-caribe.com. 3-star, 200 all-inclusive rooms (price code per person) with some triples set in pleasant gardens with pool over looking the sea. Food is reasonable but take your own tea bags or olive oil if it is important to you. Good dive centre here with dynamic instructors, beautiful dive sites and good visibility, also great snorkelling. CUC$5 for non-guests to enter the hotel including 2 drinks, CUC$25 each dive or less for more dives, nice little beach with canyon behind. Service criticized as over-friendly and prostitution is rife.

C Costa Morena, Carretera Baconao, Km 38.5, Sigua, T22-356126, www.islazul.cu. 2.5-star resort with 115 simple, functional rooms all ocean front. The beach is poor but there is a nice natural pool, good snorkelling and rock pools to explore. Short walk to Cactus Garden. Food monotonous, disco and entertainment.

C-D Gran Piedra, Carretera de la Gran Piedra Km 14, T22-686147, www.islazul.cu. Near the Gran Piedra, up in the hills, lovely setting, great views. 2 star, 22 simple rooms in stone bungalows with a bedroom, kitchen, sitting room, bathroom and balcony. You don't have to cook for yourself, though, as the restaurant and bar serve the usual Cuban fare. Check it is open as the road to Gran Piedra was closed in 2009 because of hurricane damage in 2008.

forests, with waterfall and natural pools in the hotel grounds. Sit and relax under the waterfall or go hiking, horseriding or birdwatching. Originally designed as a health spa, and still great for a massage, in a fantastic location in the Sierra Maestra and set into the side of a mountain some way down a track. The 24-room hotel is clean and nice with good service and an open air rustic restaurant, but the highlight is its picturesque waterfall, beside which you can have barbecues. If you are coming from Cruce de los Baños, there is a sign at the main junction to 'El Saltón y Filé', it is 3 km to Filé, cross the bridge in the village, at the crossroads turn left and it is a further 3 km to the hotel.

West of Santiago *p355, map p352*
Hotels
AL-A Brisas Sierra Mar-Los Galeones, on Playa Sevilla, Carretera de Chivirico Km 60, T22-29110, www.cubanacan.cu. All-inclusive rooms in 2 locations: **Sierra Mar** is on the beach, while **Los Galeones** is up on the hillside. **Sierra Mar** is a modern 200-room resort in terraced style, a/c, satellite TV, small beach, watersports, freeform pool on terrace with bar and good sea view, 2 restaurants, 3 bars, shop, rental bikes, many activities such as horse rental, helicopter ride into the mountains, sports, gym, kids' club, tours and car hire.
Los Galeones is for singles and couples over 16 only, marketed to honeymooners and considered by some to be the best of the coastal resorts in this area. 34 rooms including 1 suite on a cliff overlooking the Caribbean, lovely location, a/c and fan, satellite TV, 300 winding steps lead down to the sea, restaurant serves good food, bar, sauna, massage, gym, special scuba training pool, bowling, volleyball, car and bike rental, courtesy bus to **Sierra Mar**, a taxi from the airport costs about CUC$50. Snorkelling is good in this area.
C-D El Saltón, Carretera a Filé, Puerto Rico, Tercer Frente, near Cruce de los Baños, about 35 km inland, T22-566495, www.cubanacan.cu. In a beautiful valley surrounded by lush

Eating

Santiago de Cuba centre *p344, map p346*
Restaurants
All the hotels have restaurants, some of which are very good, such as in the **Meliá Santiago de Cuba**. In local restaurants the main dish is chicken, usually fried but sometimes with a garlic and onion sauce. A half chicken with fried green plantain (*tostones*), sweet potatoes (*boniato*) or chips costs 25 pesos, rice and beans (*congrí*) 2 pesos, salad 3 pesos, beer 10 pesos. You can find this sort of meal at the **Doña Yuya** chain, where they also serve things like smoked pork chops (*chuletas de cerdo ahumado*), veal (*ternera*) or thin steak (*bistec de palomilla*), costing around 25 pesos.
Complejo Don Antonio, Aguilera entre Calvario y Reloj, Plaza Dolores, T22-652205. Daily 1200-2300. A complex of restaurants, Chinese, Cuban, Italian, international. Nice decor, bar inside serving all kinds of Cuban cocktails, tasty *criollo* food, reasonable prices with dishes from CUC$3 for starters to CUC$28.
El Baturro, Aguilera esq San Félix, just off Parque Céspedes. Open 1200-2300. Cuban food, cheap, popular with foreigners.
Garzón y K, Av Garzón y K. Typical Cuban meals of meat, rice, beans and salad.

♥ **Las Enramadas**, Búlevar (Plaza Dolores), T22-652205. Good atmosphere, cheap, basic food, nice setting, open 24 hrs.

♥ **La Taberna de Dolores**, Aguilera esq Reloj, T22-623913. Spanish food. Open 1900-2400, reasonable at around CUC$5 for main course.

♥ **Santiago 1900**, San Basilio entre San Félix y Carnicería. Basic but excellent meals at bargain price of around CUC$4 including drinks, pesos and dollar equivalent acceptable.

♥ **Subway Aguilera**, Aguilera entre Reloj y San Agustín near Plaza Dolores. Open 0900-1700, 2000-0200. Charges in pesos cubanos, very cheap, snacks and cocktails.

Paladares

Most of the official *paladares* have closed because of taxes and regulations. However, you may get approached in the street by touts offering unofficial/illegal places to eat.

Street stalls

Street stalls sell snacks in pesos, usually only open until early evening, some only at lunchtime. Most things cost 1 peso. Avoid *fritos*, they are just fried lumps of dough; most reliable thing is cheese, pork or egg sandwich; pizza is usually a dry bit of dough with a few gratings of cheese. Lots of stalls along 'Ferreiro' or Av Victoriano Garzón, these are open later than others, especially up near **Hotel Las Américas**. Also lots around bus station on Libertadores and a few along the bottom part of Aguilera, between Parque Céspedes and Plaza Dolores. If you are in any doubt about the strength of your digestive system, avoid street stalls. The safest places to eat are *casas particulares*, where food is prepared fresh each day. It may cost you a bit more but it may save you a hospital bill.

Cafés and ice cream parlours

Café Ajedrez, Enramada y Santo Tomás. Open-air café in cool architectural structure designed by Cuban architect, Walter A Betancourt Fernández. Coffee only.

Café Catedral, underneath the Cathedral. Great coffee, tea, sandwiches, cheap.

Coppelia, Av de los Libertadores y Victoriano Garzón. Mon-Fri 1000-2100, Sat and Sun 1100-2200. No queuing if you have dollars.

Isabelica, Aguilera esq Plaza Dolores. Open 24 hrs. Serves only coffee, CUC$0.85, cigars rolled, bohemian hang-out, watch out for hustlers, serious hassling by *jineteros/as*. The local speciality *Rocío del Gallo* is coffee and rum – ask for it here.

Terrace Coffee Bar, Hotel Casa Granda. Open 24 hrs. A pleasant place for a drink. The **Roof Garden**, at the top of the same hotel, open 2000-0300, has *mojitos* CUC$1.

Ferreiro *p350, map p350*
Restaurants

♥♥♥ **El Zunzun**, Av Manduley, T22-641528. Open 0900-0200. International food, thought by some to be the best in town, but mixed reports on both food and service.

♥♥♥-♥♥ **Pizza Nova**, Hotel Meliá Santiago, T22-687070, outside by the shops. Open 1100-2400. Open air but under cover, serving surprisingly good pizzas and nothing like you get on the streets. Large variety of sizes and toppings from a small cheese and tomato pizza to a large one with lobster, also pastas chicken, meat or fish dishes if you are not seeking a pizza fix.

♥♥ **Tropical**, Fernández Marcane entre 10 y 9, upper floor. Open Tue-Sun 1800-2400. Open air, well decorated, excellent food, international style.

♥♥-♥ **El Mirador**, Calle 10 y Bravo Correoso, Sta Bárbara. Open 1200-0300, closed Wed. Open air café/ restaurant, state-run but charging in pesos cubanos as well as CUC$. Good food and popular, serving the usual chicken, pork and fish.

Paladares

Helado Alondra, Garzón y 6, T22-687078, near junction with Hotel Santiago. Great ice creams and milk shakes, 0900-2200.

East of Santiago *p352, map p352*
Restaurants

♥♥ **Jaiba Azul**, Carretera de Baconao, near Playa Cazonal. Tue-Sun 0900-1800.

Specializing in fish, lobster and other seafood, charges in pesos cubanos, very good value.

Sito de Compay Segundo, Calle Montenegro s/n, Siboney, T22-39325. Daily 1200-2100. The house where the musician, Compay Segundo, was born is now a restaurant serving international and *criollo* food, with dishes from CUC$1.50 to CUC$28.

Bars

Santiago de Cuba centre *p344, map p346*

El Baturro, Aguilera esq San Félix. Snacks, bar, nice atmosphere and reliable prices.

Kontiki, Enramada esq San Pedro. A dark bar popular with Cubans and visitors.

Las Columnitas, 1 block from Enramada, San Félix y Callejón del Carmen. Outdoor dollar bar and café. Beware of double measures.

Entertainment

Santiago de Cuba *p344, maps p346, p350 and p352*

Cabaret

Cabaret San Pedro del Mar, Carretera del Morro Km 7.5, T22-691287, CUC$20 taxi there and back. CUC$5 entrance, reasonable food.

Club Tropicana Santiago, Autopista Nacional Km 1.5, T22-642579 (restaurant 1200-2200), taxi, CUC$10. Local show with emphasis on the Caribbean and Santiaguerans, different from Havana's version and considered one of the best shows in Cuba, disco after the show, open 2000-0300, closed Mon, CUC$30, although you can get it for CUC$28 with Sol y Son, see page 366, or a package including transport and drink for CUC$44 per person for a group of 2-5 people. There is a restaurant with a limited menu and drinks aren't cheap.

Cinema and theatre

Cine Cuba, Gral Lacret entre Aguilera y Enramada.

Cine Rialto, Santo Tomás entre San Basilio y Heredia.

Teatro Heredia, Av de los Desfiles on the other side of Av de las Américas from the Plaza de la Revolución. You can hear live boleros and other traditional music in Café Cantante, in the theatre, Fri-Sun 2100, CUC$5.

Clubs and music venues

Buró de Información Cultural, also known as **El Patio de los dos Abuelos**, Pérez Carbo 5 frente a Plaza de Marte, T22-623302. EGREM agency, poetry, dance, live music in its patio bar. Rocks with live traditional son and boleros from 2130 until dawn and encourages visitors to join in. Also snack bar with tasty small meals, the *daiquirís* are a winner.

Casa de la Música, Corona 564 entre Aguilera y Enramada, T22-652227. Recorded music during the day 1000-1900. Live Cuban music every night 2200-0230 and Sat-Sun 1500-1900, a/c, CUC$5 entrance, sale of CDs and tapes, worth trying. Food available, reasonably priced.

Casa de las Tradiciones, Rabí entre José de Diego (Princesa) y García (San Fernando). Open 2030-0100, closed Mon, CUC$2. Also known as **La Casona**. Large colonial house with central patio, like going dancing in someone's living room, very cosy and local, rocking chairs and wooden stools around small tables made of barrels, music for listening and dancing to, 1500-2330 (good if you don't want a really late night), live *son, trova, boleros*, usually from 2000, small bar, CUC$2 entry.

Casa de la Trova, Heredia 208, around the corner from Casa Granda, T22-623943. Traditional Santiagueran *trova, son* and *boleros*. Most of the big names in Santiago music play here at night, all live, CUC$3-5. Great upstairs dance floor and seating area known as Salón de los Grandes Personas, with tables and chairs on the wooden balcony running the length of the room and overlooking the street below. Downstairs is also used, mainly for daytime concerts in the late morning and mid-afternoon, the room is open to the street and entry is only CUC$1. Tour operators offer night time packages

Daiquirí

The recipe for the Daiquirí cocktail was first created by an engineer in the Daiquirí mines near Santiago de Cuba. Known as a Daiquirí Natural (1898), it includes the juice of half a lime, half a tablespoon of sugar, 1½ oz light dry rum and some pieces of ice, which you put in a shaker, shake and serve strained in a cocktail glass, with more ice if you want.

The idea of using shaved ice came later, added by Constante, the bartender at the Floridita in the 1920s. It was a favourite of Ernest Hemingway; he described it in his book, *Islands in the Stream*, and drank it in the company of Jean-Paul Sartre, Gary Cooper, Ava Gardner, Marlene Dietrich, and Tennessee Williams among others.

The recipe for this Daiquirí includes 1½ tablespoons of sugar, the juice of half a lime, some drops of maraschino liqueur, 1½ oz light dry rum and a lot of shaved ice. Put it all in a blender and serve in a champagne glass.

Other refinements are the strawberry Daiquirí, the banana, peach or pineapple Daiquirí or even the orange Daiquirí, made with the addition of fruit or fruit liqueur. The resulting mound of flavoured, alcoholic, crushed ice should be piled high in a wide, chilled champagne glass and served with a straw – aaah!

---

including transport, drinks and a CD, Sol y Son is the cheapest at CUC$15 pp.

Casa del Caribe (see Cultural centres, below) on 13 154 esq 8, T22-642285. Live Afro-Cuban music and dance at weekends.

Casa del Son, Enramada, just off Plaza de Marte. Very popular, a/c, live bands and decent entry prices, CUC$2 for tourists, Cubans pay in pesos cubanos, drinks also reasonably priced. Live music on every night at time of writing.

Disco Bar/Club 300, Aguilera entre San Félix y San Pedro, behind Casa Granda hotel, T22-653532. Daily 1900-0300. Live and recorded music, snack bar.

El Patio de Artex, Heredia 304 entre Carnicería y Calvario, T22-654814. Former home of painters, Félix and José Joaquín Tejada Revilla, often live music with fantastic local bands, lots of dancing, friendly, 2200-0200. Free live son band at 1600 every day and live local bands at 2100, CUC$2.50. Meals available, lunch and dinner time.

Rincón de Santiago and **Café Cantante** in the Hotel Santiago. Daily 2000-0200, CUC$5 per couple including 1 drink each or CUC$6 including drinks if you book through Sol y Son.

Sala de Conciertos Dolores, Plaza Dolores. Classical and choral concerts.

Cultural centres

Casa de Africa, Av Manduley. Includes craftwork shop and has Afro-Cuban music in the evenings.

Casa del Caribe, 13 154 esq 8, Vista Alegre, T22-642285, www.casadelcaribe.cult.cu. Extensive library of Caribbean subjects, publishes magazine called *Caribe*, Afro-Cuban music and dance Sat nights, great authentic *folklórico*.

Centro de Estudios Africanos Fernando Ortiz, Av Manduley y 5, Vista Alegre. CUC$1 entrance, artefacts and research centre.

El Tívoli, Santa Rosa y Jesús Rabí. Promotes influence of French culture, named after neighbourhood where French settled in 18th century, fleeing from slave uprising in Haiti.

Hermanos Saiz, Heredia, cultural centre that promotes poetry.

La Conga de los Hoyo, Moncada y Av José Martí. Specializes in conga music, promotes the festival of 24 Jun with conga drummers in the streets.

La Tumba Francesa, Los Maceo 501 esq Gen Banderas, Mon-Sat 0800-1600, with dance displays Tue, and Thu 2030, CUC$2. Like its counterpart in Guantánamo, celebrates Haitian influence on Cuban

Music in Santiago de Cuba

Santiago is overflowing with musical talent. Even the cockerels crow in time to the *son*. Santiago is *son*'s spiritual home. At the **Casa de la Trova** on Calle Heredia images of old *soneros* look down on the musicians, as elegant Santiaguerans lose themselves in the dance and the rum flows freely. Although Cuba's most famous groups rarely venture out to Santiago (the impressive Heredia theatre has a reputation for turning on the sound halfway through the night), the city has enough supreme musicians of its own. The ancient and ironically named *Estudiantina Invasora*, the young *Grupo Turquino* and the multi-talented *Sonora La Calle* are all worth catching.

Rumba in Santiago has its place in the carnival parade. While the band takes a rest, the *Columbia Santiaguera* strikes up for the dancers. There is also *rumba* at the **Museo del Carnaval** on Heredia (almost opposite the *Trova*).

For a calmer session you can enjoy choral, orchestral and chamber music at the **Sala Dolores** (on Plaza Dolores). There is an annual *Festival Internacional del Coro* in December.

You can experience Santiago's African roots at the occasionally wonderful *peñas* at the **Casa del Caribe** on Calle B or the **Casa de Africa** on the evocatively named Avenida Manduley, both in Vista Alegre. Stunning shows by Orishas, Cocoyé and Guillermón Moncada celebrate all of Oriente's music and dance traditions. Other groups, such as the Cabildo Isuama and the Tumba Francesa, keep alive the memories of Africa.

July in Santiago is super hot, and so is the music. In early July, the Festival del Caribe brings groups from all over the Caribbean for street shows, theatre events and a big parade. Carnival follows almost immediately, when the *comparsas* and *paseos* parade their congas around the streets in spectacular style, past stages set up for live bands and kiosks selling beer and *frituras*. See Festivals and events, below.

To conga properly you'll need your wooden sandals (*chancletas*), curlers, shorts and a boob tube (*bajo y chupa*, literally 'down and suck'). To join the musicians you need the brake drum off a 1953 Chevy. Maybe it's better simply to *arrollar y gozar*.

culture, with traditional costumes, music, dancing and handicrafts.
UNEAC, Bartolomé Masó y Pío Rosado. National art and literature centre.

Dance performances
Cutumba, Trocha esq Santa Ursula. AfroCuban dance 0900-1300, free. Dance classes of all types by prior arrangement with an agency such as Càlédöñià, www.caledonialanguages.com, see page 369, and they have to be declared to the local arts council, but try contacting Odalis Calzadilla T0152267469 (mob). Private lessons can sometimes be arranged in the afternoon, CUC$10 per hr.

Orishas, at Museo del Carnaval, 2 blocks west of Parque Céspedes. There is a superb AfroCuban show Tue-Sun 1600, CUC$1 – unmissable.

⊛ Festivals and events

Santiago de Cuba *p344, maps p346, p350 and p352*
15-19 May Festival de Baile is a vibrant street festival.
Mid-May Festival de la Canción Francesa is a contest in which students of the Alliance Française sing in French. The 1st 3 places go to the national contest in Havana and the prize is a month's trip to France, all expenses paid.

1st week in Jul Festival del Caribe begins with theatre, dancing and conferences and continues later in Jul to coincide with the Moncada celebrations on 26 Jul.

18-27 of Jul Carnival is already in full swing by the Moncada celebrations on 26 Jul (as it was in 1953, the date carefully chosen to catch Batista's militia drunk and off-guard and use the noise of the carnival to drown the sound of gunfire). Carnival lasts 1 week between the 18 and 27 Jul, taking in Santiago's patron saint's day, 25 Jul and stopping for the rather more serious Moncada celebrations on 26 Jul, continuing on 27 Jul. This carnival is regaining its former glory and is well worth seeing. Wear no jewellery, leave all valuables behind. The other provinces are represented, installing an area in Reparto Sueño where they sell food and drink typical of each province. There are competitions and parades, with rivalry between the *comparsas* (congas) and *paseos* (*grupos de baile*). The whole city is covered in lights and all the doors are decorated. The parades and floats are judged from 2100 and pass down Garzón where there are seats for viewing. To get a seat go to the temporary Izlazul office behind the seating area on the south side of the road between 1800 and 2000. It starts at 2100, CUC$2 for a tourist seat. Good views possible if you queue early.

Sep Festival del Pregón is also known as *Frutas del Caney*, a festival of song when people dress up in traditional costumes and sell fruit in the street while singing.

Sep/Oct Festival de la Trova is a festival of folk music, the exact date each year depends on funding.

New Year's Eve *Son* bands play in Plaza Marte and surrounding streets. Just before midnight everyone moves toward Parque Céspedes and sings the National Anthem. On the stroke of midnight the Cuban flag is raised on the Casa de Gobierno, commemorating the anniversary of the first time it was flown in 1902 when the Republic of Cuba was proclaimed. Afterwards, there's all-night drinking and dancing on the streets and in local bars.

O Shopping

Santiago de Cuba centre *p344, map p346*
Art galleries and artesanía
Handicrafts and books are sold on the street on Heredia entre Hartmann y Pío Rosado.
Casa de la Artesanía, under cathedral in Parque Céspedes, T22-623924. Daily 0800-1730, also on Lacret 724 entre San Basilio y Heredia.
Fondo Cubano de Bienes Culturales, Lacret 704 esq Heredia, T22-652358, fbcstgo@cult. stgo.cu. Paintings, antiques and art works.
Galería 1927, Ateneo Cultural, Santo Tomás 755 entre Santa Rita y Santa Lucía, T22-651969. Daily 0900-2000.
Galería de Arte Universal, C entre M y Terrazas, Vista Alegre. Open Tue-Sun 0900-1700. Exhibition and sale of art work.
Galería la Confronta, Heredia entre Carnicería y San Félix. Contemporary art.
Galería Oriente, San Pedro (Lacret) 653 entre Heredia y Aguilera, underneath the Hotel Casa Granda on Parque Céspedes, contemporary art. Open Tue-Sun 0900-1700. Exhibition and sale of contemporary art.

Bookshops
Ho Chi Minh at the top of Enramada. Peso bookshop.
Librería Amado Ramos Sánchez, Enramadas y San Félix. Mon-Sat 0900-1800. Contemporary Cuban literature of all types, pay in pesos.
Librería Internacional, on Heredia under the cathedral. Open 0800-2000. A selection of paperbacks in English and postcards.

Food
Several stores can be found in the Parque Céspedes area, ask for 'shopping', especially on Saco. There are shops on Plaza del Marte and on Garzón near **Helado Alondra**. There is a food market on Ferreiro opposite **Hotel Las Américas**. Herbs, spices and *Santería* items can be bought on Mon and Thu at Gen Lacret y Gómez.
Casa de Miel, Gen Lacret. Sells honey.

Music
Artex, Heredia 304. Music and videos as well as postcards and cultural items for dollars.
Casa de la Música, Corona entre Enramada y Aguilera.
Casa de la Trova, Heredia y San Félix (see Clubs and music venues, page 362).
Enramadas and **Siglo XX**, Enramada. Records, books, clothes, jewellery, ornaments, etc in pesos.

▲ Activities and tours

Santiago de Cuba centre *p344, maps p346, p350 and p352*
Baseball
Played Nov-Apr at the Estadio Guillermo Moncada on Av Las Américas, T22-641090/641078.

Diving, fishing and waterports
The Sierra Maestra mountains all along this south-facing Caribbean coast offer a foretaste of what is to be found underwater, where the island platform gently shelves to a depth of 35 m and then the ocean wall drops straight down to a depth of over 1000 m in the channel between Cuba and Haiti. Popular wreck sites off Playa Sigua include the 30-m passenger ship, *Guarico*, lying in 15 m. She lies on her port side with the mast covered in soft sponges. A ferry/tug wreck lies upside down in 35 m of water and the 2 vessels together span around 150 m. The metal structure is covered with large yellow and purple tube sponges. The 35-m *Spring Coral* lies in 24 m. Most of the structure is still intact with a great deal of marine growth offering many photo opportunities. An unusual site is the *Bridge*. In 1895 a large bridge broke and fell into the sea in 12 m, along with a train. Later a ship sank and was blown into the bridge underwater, adding to the mass of structures. The **Sierra Mar Dive Shop** offers a special wreck dive on the *Cristóbal Colón*, a Spanish ship lying on a slope in 9-27 m. She was badly damaged by gunfire in 1898

by the US Navy during the Battle of Santiago in the Spanish American War after a long chase. Although initially beached, attempts to refloat her were abandoned. This is an excellent shore dive with hardly any current, although in the wet season visibility is affected by run-off from the Sierra Maestra. There are 4 other wrecks in shallow water and they are ideal for a snorkel.
Marlin Marina Punta Gorda, Calle 1 A 4, Punta Gorda, T22-691446, admin@marlin. seu.tur.cu, VHF 16 and 72. 30 moorings, boat repairs, commissary, fuel, water, showers, restaurant, boat rental, fishing (CUC$150 for 3 hrs, CUC$250 for 4 hrs, CUC$350 for 6 hrs), dive centre, windsurfing, catamarans, banana boat, waterbicycles. Also diving at the **Bucanero Hotel**, Juraguá and the **Sierra Mar Hotel**. All dive centres charge CUC$30 for 1 dive, CUC$59 for 2 dives, dive packages available, also resort course CUC$49, CMAS Open Water certification CUC$310, Advanced certification CUC$239, Rescue CUC$199.

Tour operators
Cubanacán, offices in the hotels **Meliá Santiago de Cuba**, **Versalles**, **Los Corales**, **Sierra Mar-Los Galeones** and at the airport. Head office T22-643445, F22-687209.
Cubatur, Victoriano Garzón entre 3 y 4, T22-652560, santiago@cubatur.cu. Daily 0800-1200, 1300-2000, is helpful with knowledgeable guides and excellent value. Also offices in **Hotel Meliá Santiago de Cuba** and at the airport. Easy to book Víazul tickets, air tickets as well as tours, car hire, tourist cards and hotel reservations.
Havanatur main office is on Av Raúl Pujol, T22-643603, with other offices at the airport, in the hotels **Meliá Santiago de Cuba**, **Casa Granda**, **Bucanero**. They have very good guides who are fluent in most European languages.
Sol y Son, Lacret 701 esq Heredia opposite Casa Granda, T22-687096, adelasolyson@ enet.cu. Open 0800-1700. Adela Acosta Vaillant is multilingual, efficient, helpful and knowledgeable. Lots of tours offered, cheaper than other agencies, domestic and

international air tickets, hotel bookings below rack rates.

✈ Transport

Santiago de Cuba *p344, maps p346, p350 and p352*
Air
Airport Antonio Maceo (SCU), is 8 km from town, T22-691014/691830, F22-86184. Flights most days to/from **Havana** with Cubana, CUC$108 and **Aerocaribbean**, CUC$115, 1 hr 45 mins, 2-hr check-in, also **Baracoa** (Sun), **Holguín** (Sat, Sun), **Trinidad** (Tue) and **Varadero** (Mon). Cubana also has international flights to **Santiago** from **Madrid**, **Paris**, **Canada**, **Rome** and **Milan**, and Aerocaribbean has flights from **Montego Bay**, **Jamaica**, **Port-au-Prince**, **Haiti** and **Santo Domingo**, **Dominican Republic**.

Airlines Aerocaribbean San Pedro entre San Basilio y Heredia. Cubana, Enramada esq Lacret, Mon-Fri 0900-1700, Sat 0900-1400, T22-651577/9. Local and inter-Caribbean flights (some destinations) can also be booked at tour operators while Cubanacán Express, Calle 6 entre L y M, Reparto Sueño, T/F22-687221, express@stgocub.scu.cyt.cu. Sells tickets for Aerocaribbean, Air France, Air Jamaica Express, Air Europa, Cayman Airways, Cubana, and Iberia.

Bus
Local There is a regular bus service between Plaza Ferreiro (top of Av Victoriano Garzón) and Plaza Marte/Parque Céspedes. Buses, 20 centavos. Horse-drawn *coches* are 1 peso. Bus No 214 goes to **Playa Siboney**; 207 to **Juraguá**; no bus at present to Parque Baconao or to El Cobre.

Long distance Terminal near Plaza de la Revolución at the top of Av de los Libertadores/Carretera Central. Víazul, T22-628484, is in an office to the left of the bus departure area, with a blue door, open 0700-2100, closed Sun afternoon, but if you turn up 30 mins before departure you can buy your ticket. Note that for buses to Baracoa demand can be great in high season. Get your ticket the day before (or Sat for a Mon journey). Once a busload of tickets has been sold no more will be sold that day but if you turn up at 0500 the next morning they usually put on more buses depending on demand. On your return you can only buy tickets on the day of travel because the number of seats depends on how many buses have come from Santiago, but queue early. See page 32 for timetable. For an overnight journey wear trousers and a fleece if you have one, as the a/c is very cold and even Víazul is not comfortable at night. Astro has more local services, but is reserved for Cubans and no longer available for foreigners.

Car hire
Cubacar and Vía Rent-a-Car at the airport and in the main hotels. Vía Rent a Car office opposite Casa Granda, T22-624646, also at Carretera del Caney y Calle 15, Reparto Vista Alegre, T22-641465. CUC$192 for 4 days plus CUC$40 for insurance. On return beware of CUC$10 charge for dirty exterior, CUC$20 for dirty interior and CUC$16 for scratches on the paint work caused by flying stones.

Taxi
Local Cubataxi, T22-651038/9, airport to town CUC$5, from the bus station to Plaza Marte is CUC$1, to Parque Céspedes CUC$2, from the centre out to Santa Bárbara CUC$3. You can also get a private taxi, lots hang around Parque Céspedes and Plaza Marte, but they will charge about the same as a Cubataxi. You will be continually offered private taxis every time you go out, particularly near any of the hotels or plazas.

Long distance Taxis can be a convenient way of covering long distances if there is a group of you to share costs, but for individuals is it worth investigating official transfers to places off Víazul's routes, eg Sol y Son can arrange door-to-door transfers direct to Holguín airport for the Fri, Sun flights, US$25 per person.

Bicitaxi Transport can be arranged at Plaza Marte for about CUC$1.

Train

The station is opposite the rum factory on Av Jesús Menéndez. Book tickets in advance from basement office in new terminal. Relatively easy and quick, unlike the journey itself when delays of 16 hrs or more are frequent. Do not enter the waiting room area but walk in from the left and there is a guard on the door. If there is a queue for tickets he will make you wait outside. Train travel is not as reliable or comfortable as bus travel and agencies have stopped selling tickets as a result of the irregular service. Take sweater for Havana journey, freezing a/c. Every other day to **Havana** in theory, 2000, 20 hrs, see also under Train, Havana, for fares and services.

● Directory

Santiago de Cuba *p344, maps p346, p350 and p352*

Accident and emergency

Fire Martí 517, T105. **Police** T106. Central police station is Unidad 2, Corona y San Gerónimo. Near to the hotels Santiago and Las Américas is **Unidad 4**, on Aguilera near the hospital and the market.

Banks

It is possible to get CUC$ cash advance on credit cards (non-US) at **Banco Financiero Internacional**, Av Las Américas entre I y J, Reparto Sueño, T22-686252, Mon-Fri 0800-1600, they also change foreign currency and TCs. **Banco de Crédito y Comercio**, Parque Céspedes, Santo Tomás entre Aguilera y Heredia and Lacret esq Aguilera, efficient service for credit card advances and changing TCs in European currencies. **BICSA**, Enramada opposite Plaza Dolores, for changing foreign currency and TCs. **Banco Popular de Ahorro**, Plaza Dolores, 0800-1500, Visa and MasterCard, ATM, prompt service, also a branch on Victoriano Garzón esq 3. TCs can

be changed in any hotel except those in the Islazul chain. **Meliá Santiago de Cuba** has a *Cadeca* in its shopping precinct (also post office, pharmacy, tour operators, gift shops) daily 0900-2000, will change virtually any cash currency into CUC$. TCs can be changed in the **Havanatur** office in Casa Granda. **Hotel Las Américas** has a *Cadeca* in the lobby open daily 0800-1800 (although there is often no one there at lunchtime), for currency exchange, TCs, Visa, MasterCard advances. In the **Asistur** office under Casa Granda you can get cash advance on all major credit cards including American Express and Diners Club; they will also change American Express TCs, the only place that will do so in all Cuba. Do not change currency on the street. There is a *Cadeca* on Aguilera close to Plaza Dolores. If you want to buy *pesos cubanos,* change no more than CUC$5-10 for a 2- to 3-week stay.

Immigration

Asistur, Hotel Casa Granda, Heredia esq San Pedro, T22-686600. For all health, financial, legal and insurance problems for foreign tourists. **Inmigración y Extranjería**, Calle 13 6 frente al despacho eléctrico, T22-641983, Mon and Fri 0900-1200, 1330-1630, Tue, Wed and Thu 0900-1200, in summer holiday mornings only. Go to **Bandec** on Parque Céspedes y Aguilera and buy special stamp (*sello*) for CUC$25, then return to Immigration for paper work (15 mins).

Internet

Etecsa has an office under the cathedral on the corner of Parque Céspedes, Félix Pena y Heredia, open 0700-2300 daily. Computers for internet access and phone booths for international and domestic calls. **Hotel Las Américas**, 2 terminals in the hotel lobby, CUC$3 per 30 mins. Bar alongside if you have to wait your turn. **Meliá Santiago de Cuba**, business centre off the entrance. The best place in terms of quality and quantity of machines where there are 6 computers, CUC$6 per hr, and connection is usually good. **Hotel Casa Granda** also has computers for internet access.

Language schools

The Universidad de Oriente, on the outskirts of town. Spanish language classes together with Cuban dance and percussion are offered by Càlédöñiâ Languages, The Clockhouse, 72 Newhaven Rd, Edinburgh EH6 5QG, T44-(0)131-6217721, www.caledonia languages.com. They also offer accommodation in *casas particulares*, hiking and tours in the Sierra Maestra.

Medical services

Clínica Internacional, Av Raúl Pujol esq 10, T22-642589. Outpatient appointments, laboratory, dentist, 24-hr emergencies, international pharmacy, especially for tourists, everything payable in CUC$, CUC$25 per consultation, the best clinic to visit to be sure of immediate treatment. There is a **pharmacy** next door to the Casa de la Trova on Heredia. The Hotel Meliá Santiago de Cuba has a well-stocked pharmacy but it is expensive.

Post

The main post office is on Aguilera y Clarín, daily 0700-2000, where you can make phone calls within Cuba and buy international phone cards. There is email service but no internet access. The Casa Granda has its own post office, as does Hotel Sol Meliá Santiago. For a courier service, Cubanacán Express, Calle 6 entre L y M, Reparto Sueño, T22-687221, express@stgocub.scu.cyt.cu. Offers good service at reasonable prices. There is also DHL, opposite the bar, El Baturro, near Plaza Céspedes, which also has email facilities.

Telephone

You cannot make collect calls from hotels, only from private houses. Etecsa is on Aguilera, just before Plaza Dolores, open 24 hrs. For calls outside Santiago, Centro de Comunicaciones Nacional e Internacional, Heredia y Félix Pena, by the cathedral.

Guantánamo

→ *Colour map 4, C1.*

Guantánamo, the capital of the most easterly and most mountainous province of the same name, has one major difference from other Cuban colonial towns. The large influx of Haitian, French and Jamaican immigrants in the 19th century means that the architecture has much less of a Spanish colonial feel; the narrow, brightly coloured buildings with thin wooden balconies and wrought ironwork are more reminiscent of New Orleans than Madrid. This is also reflected in the local musical rhythms, notably the Tumba Francesa, a colourful folk dance tradition originating in Haiti, based in the centre of the town. The city is close to the US naval base of Guantánamo (which cannot be easily visited from Cuba). It is so little a part of the town that you will not, except in conversation, come across it unless you make a specific trip to Mirador de Malones to view it through binoculars. The range of the Montañas de Nipe-Sagua-Baracoa runs through the province, ending at the Atlantic Ocean on the northern coast and the Caribbean Sea to the south. The area is notable for its many endemic species of fauna and flora and it is one of the most beautiful parts of the island. **⏵⏵** *For listings, see pages 372-374.*

Ins and outs

Getting there   There are **flights** from Havana six days a week, which then turn around and head straight back again. Guantánamo is some 80 km from Santiago on the Baracoa road. Víazul have **buses** from Santiago to Baracoa via Guantánamo. The Víazul bus is usually full at weekends and it can be difficult to get on another bus if you want to break your journey in Guantánamo, so seat reservation in advance is essential. **Train** services should be daily to and from Santiago, but you can't rely on them. **⏵⏵** *See Transport, page 374.*

Getting around The town is small enough to walk around but there are horse-drawn *coches* for longer distances. A taxi or organized excursion is required if you want to go to one of the look-outs to see the American base. A number of streets have had their names changed, but locals often do not even know the official title. Avenida de los Estudiantes is known as Paseo, while Bartolomé Masó is known as Carretera.

Best time to visit It is hot any time of the year, but humidity increases in the summer months and the risk of storms is higher from September to November.

History

The town of Guantánamo was founded in 1819 and was called Santa Catalina del Saltadero del Guaso until 1843. It lies north of the Bahía de Guantánamo, between the Jaibo, Bano and Guaso rivers which flow into the bay. Guantánamo is a pleasant, fairly well-restored colonial town.

The US naval base was established at the beginning of the 20th century, when Cuba was a protectorate of the USA following independence from Spain, in the area known as Caimanera at the mouth of the bay. Although the USA relinquished its right to intervene in Cuban affairs in 1934, it retained its naval base on a lease which expires in 2033. Cuba

Guantánamo

Sleeping
Lisette Foster Lara cp **1**
Elsye Castillo Osoria
   cp **2**
Guantánamo **4**

Osmaida Blanco
Castillo cp **3**

Eating
Oro Azul **1**

Taberna Las Ruinas **2**
La Bodeguita de Paseo **3**
Vegetariano **4**

100 metres
100 yards

considers the occupation illegal but has taken no action to eject the American forces. In early 2002, the US base came to the world's attention when al-Qaida and Taliban prisoners were transferred there from Afghanistan under heavy guard to await military trial following the war against the Taliban. Huge metal cages were built to incarcerate the prisoners and security at the base was tighter than ever. There was international condemnation of the treatment of the prisoners, who were not awarded the status of prisoners of war and while being held outside US territory were therefore outside the rule of law. In 2009 the new US President Barack Obama promised to close Camp Delta, where the prisoners were held, bringing to trial or repatriating the remaining prisoners. There was no mention of relinquishing the base to Cuba.

Sights

The central square is the **Plaza Martí**, shaded by laburnum trees, with a church, the Parroquial Santa Catalina de Ricci, in the centre. The two roads running north–south either side of the plaza, General Pérez and Calixto García, contain some of the most attractive colonial houses. The post office and the **Casa de la Cultura** are on the west side and the **Tumba Francesa** on the east. Two kilometres north, the **Plaza de la Revolución** has a modernist carved stone monument to the heroes of all the wars of independence. The **Museo Provincial** ① *José Martí 802 entre Francisco Aguilera y Prudencio del Prado, T21-325872, Mon 1430-1800, Tue-Sat 0830-1200, 1430-1800*, housing artefacts from the history of Guantánamo, is in a former colonial prison built in 1861-62. There is also a small museum near the Plaza de la Revolución which contains the space capsule in which the first Cuban went into space. South of the centre is the **Casa Natal Regino Boti** ① *Bernabé Varona 405, entre José Martí y Pedro Agustín Pérez*. Boti was a notable poet, essayist, historian and artist. He was born here on 18 February 1878 and lived and worked all his life in the same house.

Around Guantánamo

The **Zoológico de Piedra** ① *Carretera a Yateras Km 18, T21-865143. Mon-Sat 0900-1800, entrance CUC$1, with camera CUC$3, with video CUC$5*, is an outdoor museum of carved stone animals, set in a beautiful hillside location with tropical vegetation. Many are bizarre, from tiny stone lizards to huge bison. All are carved directly from the rocks in their natural setting and you can buy miniature replicas from the sculptor, Angel Iñigo Blanco, on the way out. There is a day tour taking in Guantánamo city, **La Tumba Francesa**, Zoológico de Piedra and Changüí (a traditional form of music played on a farm a short distance from the city while visitors have a good lunch, join in the dance and meet the musicians). The tour is organized by **Havanatur**, with an excellent guide in an air-conditioned minibus, daily during high season, Tuesday and Saturday in low season, 0900 outside **Hotel Guantánamo**, approximately CUC$30. There is also a trip, with the same sights, going on to Baracoa on the same day.

A trip to the **Mirador de Malones** to view the Guantánamo Naval Base can only be done as part of an organized excursion, as the area is controlled by Gaviota. The Cuban military has a command centre here and you will be shown round 'Castro's bunker'. Day trips from Santiago cost about CUC$15, depending on the size of the group. You can see the extent of the base through a US telescope and admire how the other half lives, with its golf course, cinema, McDonalds and other luxuries. There is a restaurant at the Mirador serving Cuban food.

For Sleeping and Eating price codes and other relevant information, see Essentials pages 37-43.

Sleeping

Guantánamo *p369, map p370*
Hotels
C-D Guantánamo, Calle 13 esq Ahogados, Plaza Mariana Grajales, Reparto Caribe, T21-381015, hotelgtmo@islazul.co.cu. 15 mins' walk from the centre. Plaza Mariana Grajales, created in 1985, is an important post-Revolutionary square, a complex of artistic and architectural monuments. 127 rooms, 8 suites, 12 cabañas, Soviet-style architecture, pool, clean, a/c, 2 bars and busy restaurant, food average, nightclub, disco, mostly Cuban clientele, staff pleasant and helpful, tours arranged to see the naval base.

Casas particulares
D-E Lisette Foster Lara, Gen Pedro A Pérez 661 entre Jesús del Sol y Prado, T21-325970. Central, close to plaza, blue façade, spacious with comfortable furnishings, a/c, balcony, roof terrace where you can have your meals or eat indoors, secure.
E Elsye Castillo Osoria, Calixto García 766 entre Prado y Jesús del Sol. Rooms with a/c, TV, fridge, sitting room, private and secure in central location.
E Osmaida Blanco Castillo, Gen Pedro A Perez 664 entre Paseo y Narciso Lopez, T21-325193. Bedrooms with a/c and private bathroom but one has no windows, the other is nicer. Outside seating.

Around Guantánamo *p371*
Hotels
A-D Caimanera, Loma del Norte, Caimanera, T21-499414, caimanera@enet.cu. On a slight rise overlooking the bay and the sea, single, double and triple rooms, suites and cabins but pleasant location, a/c, TV, bar, restaurant, pool. The closest you'll get to the US base.

D Villa La Lupe, Carretera El Salvador Km 3.5, T21-382612, recepcion@lupegtm.co.cu. 2-star, just outside Guantánamo on the Río Bano in a pleasant countryside location with lots of trees, 50 functional rooms in reasonably attractive modern blocks called cabins, reached by concrete staircases, a/c, TV, few luxuries but there is a decent pool and a squash court, peaceful atmosphere, bar, restaurant.

Eating

Guantánamo *p369, map p370*
Paladares on Av de los Estudiantes (Paseo) and a number of street stalls selling pork sandwiches for 5 pesos cubanos, some are there every day, all of them at weekends. Other *paladares* off Plaza Martí in the centre.

Restaurants
Oro Azul, Aguilera entre Los Maceo y Calixto García, T21-323853/328351. Open daily 1000-0300. Light meals and snacks, cafeteria with nightclub in El Patio, live music, small groups, CUC$2 Mon-Fri, CUC$4 Sat-Sun.
Taberna Las Ruinas, Calixto García esq Emilio Giro. Open daily 1000-0100. Bar and restaurant in a shell of a building, with wide ranging menu for lunch and dinner, live music at night with bands playing.
La Avellaneda, Bernabé Varona esq Calixto García, T21-324644. Open Wed-Mon (closed Tue) for breakfast 0700-0900, lunch 1200-1500 and dinner 1800-2300. Pork and chicken dishes.
La Bodeguita de Paseo, Paseo entre Beneficencia y Carlos Manuel, T21-323560. Open Tue-Sun for breakfast 0700-0900, lunch 1200-1500 and dinner 1800-2300, Sat and Sun open until 0045. Typical Cuban dishes such as *Ropa Vieja*.
Los Ensueños, Ahogados esq 16 Norte, T21-381601. Mon 1900-2200, Tue-Sun 1130-2330. A la carte menu, international and Cuban with the inevitable pork and chicken, house special is the chicken 'Gordon Blue'.

Music in Guantánamo

The name of Guantánamo is known the world over, thanks to the song 'Guajira Guantanamera' which is the climax of the show for all but the most principled groups. (The way to look cool and Cuban is to cry "AE SALA", after the first 'Guantanamera' and "SONGOLOQUESONGO" after the second). The words to the verses are noble and mournful, based as they are on the poetry of José Martí. 'Guajira' is a rural style of *son* and is similar to the simple, improvizing 'Nengón', which developed in the mountains surrounding Guantánamo. The Valera Miranda family, still living in the hills, have kept this style alive. In Guantánamo itself, *Nengón* became the 'Son Changüí' which, with its African thumb bass (*Marimbula*) and old style bongos, has stayed true to the roots of the original *son*. *Changüí* is tremendously complex, with backbeats, cross rhythms and constant bongo improvization but for many it is the most beautiful form of *son*. Catch it at the *Casa de la Trova*. Local grandad made good Elio Revé Matos (1930-1997), created a new *changüí* which brought him national fame (and a contract with Peter Gabriel) during the 1970s and 1980s. His background, like many Guantanamerans, is in the coffee plantations established in the sierra by French landowners following the Haitian Revolution in 1791. The *Tumba Francesa de Santa Catalina* was created during the 1890s by newly freed blacks in order to preserve the rich cultural heritage that had been developed on the plantations. One of only three such organizations still surviving (the other two being in Santiago and Sagua de Tánamo), the Tumba Francesa in Guantánamo still fulfils its original purpose. To the urgent rhythms of the Premier drums and the wooden percussion instrument the *Catá* (both of which originated in the Dahomeyan region of Africa), the elderly patrons recreate the dances of their great-great-grandparents. The singer (*Composé*) organizes the dance, calling the musicians to order and setting in train the ancient movements of the *Mason*, *Yuba* or *Frente*. Queen of *Composé* was Consuelo (Tecla) Benet Danger, the daughter of French-Haitian immigrant slaves and the only woman *Catá* player in Cuba, who sang and played until the age of 91.

🍴 **Vegetariano**, Pedro A Pérez esq Flor Crombet. Open daily for lunch 1200-1430 and dinner 1700-2300. A rare vegetarian restaurant.

⊙ Entertainment

Guantánamo p369, map p370
The is a **cinema** on Av de los Estudiantes, on the corner of the road to *Hotel Guantánamo* and a theatre, **Teatro Guaso** on Paseo esq Ahogados, T21-327240. Open Tue-Sun with performances at 1700 and 2030, also at 1000 on Sat-Sun. Local and national dance and drama companies perform here.

Live music and dancing
The Casa de la Cultura, Gen Pérez, southwest corner of Plaza Martí, has a varied programme of music and also holds exhibitions of photography and painting, usually run by UNEAC, José Martí near Plaza Martí.
Casa de la Trova Benito Odio, Pedro Agustín Pérez esq Crombet. Open Tue-Sun 0900-1200, 1400-1800, 1900-2400. Traditional music, guitar workshop.
Casa del Changüí Chito Latamble, Serafín Sánchez 710 entre Jesús del Sol y Narciso López, T21-324178. Tue-Fri 0700-2300, Sat-Sun 1000-0200. This is the place to hear Changüí bands playing. There are also other activities including children's entertainment.

Casa del Joven Creador, Calixto García entre Prado y Aguilera, T21-327695. Open 0800-1800, plus 1900-2400 when there are performances. The Compañía Danza Fragmentada performs here as well as other regional companies. Weekly performance Thu 2030.

Casa de Promociones Musicales Guantanamera (Casa de la Música), Calixto García 904 entre Crombet y Emilio Giro, T21-327266. Tue 1400-2400, Sat 1000-1200, 1400-0200, Sun 1000-1200, 1400-2400. Various cultural activities day and night including children's entertainment, comedians, traditional music and dancing.

Tumba Francesa, Serafín Sánchez 715 entre Jesús del Sol y Narciso López. Tue 0930-1300, Thu 0930-1200, Sat 0930-1400. Traditional folkloric music and dance. Shop sells good-quality Haitian-style handicrafts and souvenirs.

▲ Activities and tours

Guantánamo *p369, map p370*
Cycling
Contact **Josué Gaínza Matos**, Calle B 233 entre 7 y 8, Imías, Guantánamo, president of the local club, **Club de Cicloturismo La Farola**. He can also help with accommodation.

Tour operators
There are *burós de turismo* in the hotels in Guantánamo that can arrange tours to Mt Malones, where you can view the US base through Soviet binoculars. Islazul commercial office is on Aguilera entre Calixto García y Los Maceo, T21-327197, open Mon-Fri 0800-1200, 1400-1600.

⊖ Transport

Guantánamo *p369, map p370*
Air
Aeropuerto Mariana Grajales (GAO) is 16 km from Guantánamo, off the Baracoa road. Scheduled flight daily except Thu at 0800 from **Havana**, returning 1145 (1030 on Wed), CUC$118 one way. **Cubana** is at Calixto García 517 entre Prado y Aguilera, T21-355912.

Bus
The bus terminal, T21-326016, is 5 km southwest of the centre. Private cars and taxis run from the train and bus station to Hotel Guantánamo/town centre, CUC$1. Víazul stops here on its Santiago–Baracoa route, see page 32.

Car hire
Transtur is in the Hotel Guantánamo. Servi Cupet gas station at Prado esq 6 Este, the beginning of the Baracoa road. Oro Negro at Los Maceo y Jesús del Sol.

Train
The station is in the centre on Calixto García. Trains to **Santiago** and **Caimanera**, but you will have to check whether they are running.

⊕ Directory

Guantánamo *p369, map p370*
Banks Banco de Crédito at Calixto García esq Carretera, Mon-Fri 0800-1500. *Cadeca*, Calixto García 881 esq Prado, Mon-Sat 0830-1800, Sun 0800-1300. **Post** On the west side of Plaza Martí. DHL is in the post office.

Baracoa

→ *Colour map 4, B2. Urban population 41,200, rural population 40,500.*
Baracoa is the tourist hot spot of the east – small, low-key and attractive, surrounded by rich, tropical forests. It is the perfect place to come and spend a few relaxing days on the beach. Alternatively you can be more energetic and go hiking in the mountains or explore the many rivers that wind their way through canyons to the sea. It is well worth the trip from Santiago (five hours' drive) for the scenery of the 48-km section of road known as 'La Farola', a viaduct that winds through lush, bright green pine forests in the mountains and then descends steeply to the coast. If you are in an open truck it feels like a roller coaster as it bends and swoops at speed down the mountains. Look out for people selling cucurucho, *a delicious mixture of coconut, fruit and sugar served in a cone of palm leaves.* ▸▸ *For listings, see pages 380-384.*

Ins and outs

Getting there There is an airport with **Cubana flights** twice a week. In high season they can be notoriously difficult to book, even in Havana. It is usually easier to book a tour with an agency as they have greater access to seats, or you could fly to Moa, north of Baracoa, and hire a car to drive from there. There is no **railway**. It is best to travel by **road** from Santiago, with buses from there via Guantánamo. **Víazul** runs a daily bus service from Santiago. The bus station is within walking distance of the town centre. There is a road from Holguín round the coast through Moa, which is interesting if you are driving yourself and you can do a circular route via Guantánamo and Santiago back to Holguín, or vice versa. ▸▸ *See also Transport, page 383.*

Getting around The best way to get around Baracoa is on foot or by *bicitaxi*. Most of them wait around the Parque Central close to the Cathedral, outside the Manuel Fuentes Borges tobacco factory and outside the Banco de Crédito y Comercio, with fares depending on how far you want to go. Getting from the Hotel Porto Santo to town is difficult as there are no *bicitaxis* or taxis outside the hotel. Unless you get reception to call you a cab, walk down to the *barrio* at the bottom of the hill and wait around on the bridge for a *bicitaxi*.

History

Christopher Columbus arrived in Baracoa on 27 November 1492. He planted a cross, now housed in the church, and described a mountain in the shape of an anvil (*yunque*), which was thereafter used as a point of reference for sailors. The first maps of Cuba drawn by an Englishman showed the **Yunque de Baracoa** mountain, copies of which can be seen in the museum. Baracoa was the first town founded by Diego Velázquez. On 15 August 1511, he bestowed the settlement with the name Nuestra Señora de la Asunción de Baracoa and, for four years, it was the capital of Cuba. Between 1739 and 1742, Baracoa's three forts were built. The oldest, **El Castillo**, also known as Seboruco, or Sanguily, is now the **Hotel Castillo**. The others were **Fuerte de la Punta**, now restaurant **La Punta**, and **Fuerte Matachín**, now the municipal museum. Baracoa became a refuge for French exiles after the revolution in Haiti and they brought with them coffee and cacao farming techniques, as well as their own style of architecture, which contributed greatly to the buildings we can see now; as in Guantánamo, they have much less of a Spanish colonial style than in other towns in Cuba. The French also created the first drinking-water plant. In 1852, Carlos Manuel de Céspedes spent five months in isolation in Baracoa as a punishment. The war of independence of 1895 saw many revolutionaries disembarking at Baracoa. Up until the 1960s, it was really only accessible by sea until the viaduct, **La Farola**, was built. This is one of the most spectacular roads in Cuba, 30 km long, joined to the mountain on one side and supported by columns on the other.

Land and environment

The name Baracoa is an Amerindian word meaning 'existence of the sea', also known as 'land of water' – it is the wettest region in Cuba with annual rainfall of 2 m in the coastal zone to 3.6 m in the middle and upper Toa Valley. The Toa area is a UNESCO Biosphere Reserve, encompassing the Parque Nacional Alexander Von Humboldt. Baracoa has 29 rivers, including the **Río Toa**, 120 km long and the widest river in Cuba, see page 379. Another river, the **Río de Miel**, carries the legend that if you swim in it you will come back to Baracoa one day or stay here. There are many beautiful waterfalls, 120 different types of

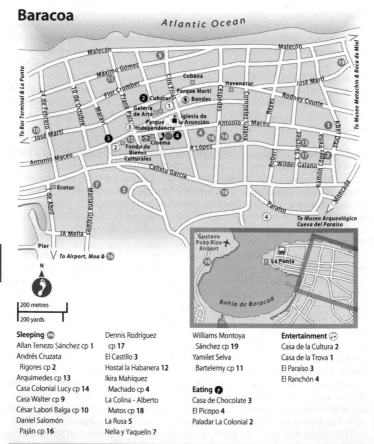

Baracoa

Atlantic Ocean

To Bus Terminal & La Punta

To Museo Matachin & Boca de Miel

Malecón
Malecón
Máximo Gómez
Cubana
José Martí
Flor Crombet
Parque Martí
Rodney Coutin
Cubatur
Havanatur
Galería de Arte
Bandec
Coroneles Galana
Parque Independencia
Iglesia de la Asunción
Antonio Maceo
Abel Díaz
Fondo de Bienes Culturales
Cinema
R López
José Martí
Antonio Maceo
Calixto García
Robert Wilder Galano
Ramón López Peña
Ecotur
Paraíso
Mariana Grajales
To Museo Arqueológico Cueva del Paraíso
JA Mella
Pier
To Airport, Moa &

N

200 metres
200 yards

Gustavo Pozo Rizo Airport
La Punta
Bahía de Baracoa

Sleeping
Allan Tenezo Sánchez cp **1**
Andrés Cruzata Rigores cp **2**
Arquimedes cp **13**
Casa Colonial Lucy cp **14**
Casa Walter cp **9**
César Labori Balga cp **10**
Daniel Salomón Paján cp **16**
Dennis Rodríguez cp **17**
El Castillo **3**
Hostal la Habanera **12**
Ikira Mahíquez Machado cp **4**
La Colina - Alberto Matos cp **18**
La Rusa **5**
Nelia y Yaquelín **7**
Williams Montoya Sánchez cp **19**
Yamilet Selva Bartelemy cp **11**

Eating
Casa de Chocolate **3**
El Picopo **4**
Paladar La Colonial **2**

Entertainment
Casa de la Cultura **2**
Casa de la Trova **1**
El Paraíso **3**
El Ranchón **4**

Myths and legends of Baracoa

Economic growth picked up in Baracoa at the beginning of the 20th century with bananas. A railway was built to transport them and trade in bananas was established with the USA. However, two diseases endemic to bananas wiped out the industry in 1945. Superstitious blame was placed on a mysterious man called 'El Pelú', who had arrived in Baracoa in 1897. Children had laughed at his strange appearance and people threw stones and, offended, he had placed a curse on the village. No one took any notice of it until the banana crisis of 1945. Even today, people still refer to the 'curse of El Pelú' and in Baracoa El Pelú is generally held to bring bad luck.

In the 1930s, 'La Rusa' arrived in Baracoa. Magdalena Rovieskuya was the daughter of a general in the Russian aristocracy, who had left Russia in 1917 to travel the world. She came to Baracoa, built a hotel (still called *La Rusa*) on the Malecón and became very popular with the local people, who affectionately called her 'Mimá'. In the 1950s she was on the point of leaving but

decided to stay and give her full support to the Revolution. She helped the Red Cross and supplied funds for the rebels to buy arms. Fidel and Che stayed in her hotel during the clandestine struggle. She died in 1978, on her deathbed donating a diamond bracelet to the *Festival Mundial de Los Estudiantes*.

There are many species of flora and fauna endemic to the Baracoa area and it is famous for its multicoloured snails, called *polimitas*. Legend has it that they came to Baracoa to find peace and took their bright colours from the sun, earth, sea and sky. They are sometimes sold around Boca de Yumurí, but they are now rather rare and you should not assist their demise by buying them.

A local story explains the origin and size of the Río Toa, the widest river in Cuba. It is believed there was an Indian tradition to banish naughty children to the mountains to learn good behaviour. Once there, the grief-stricken children cried so much that their torrent of tears formed a river.

tree and lots of coconuts. Some 80% of Cuba's coconut production comes from here. Rafting is possible down the Río Toa, with different levels of difficulty. Baracoa has 56 archaeological sites, with traces of the three Amerindian groups who lived there: the Siboney, the Taíno and the Guanahatabey (see page 402). **Caridad de los Indios** is the one surviving community of 300 Amerindians, called **Yateras** (now the Manuel Tames municipality), dating back to the Spaniards' arrival. Previous generations only married among themselves, but now they are integrated with the rest of society. They maintain many of their traditions and live in an isolated region with difficult access along the shores of the Río Toa.

Sights

The **Parque Central**, or **Parque Independencia**, is halfway down Antonio Maceo, one of the main streets in town. It has peso stalls selling good snacks and sandwiches at lunchtime and in the evening there is also a **Gaviota** café, **El Piropo**. There are other eating options on the Boulevard, as well as the karaoke bar, **El Paraíso**, the **Casa de la Trova** and the pizzeria, **La Baracoesa**, as well as other snack stalls. The **Iglesia de la Asunción** ① *Tue-Sat 0800-1200, 1400-1600, Sat 1900-2100, Sun 0800-1200*, on the Parque was built in 1511, burned down by the French in 1652, and rebuilt in 1807. The church contains the cross, known as the **Cruz de la Parra**, said to have been planted there by Columbus. Catholics and restorers have carved off slices over the years, with the result that the cross has diminished to almost half its former size. Belgian historians confirmed in 1989 that the cross did indeed date from Columbus' time and was made from the native seagrape tree (*cocoloba diversifolia*).

The **Museo Municipal** ① *Fuerte Matachín, Av Martí, T21-642122, daily 0800-1200, 1400-1800, CUC$1*, is in the Matachín fort at the end of the Malecón to the east of the town (turn right as you come in from La Farola). It is a small museum with interesting but rather antiquated displays on the history of the town from prehistoric times to memorabilia of La Rusa (see box, page 377) who died in 1978. There is a large cauldron for making sugar and the only armaments magazine of its type in Cuba dating from 1739. In 1838, the Queen of Spain presented Baracoa with its own coat of arms, now on display in the museum. The English-speaking conservation officer, Daniel Salomón Paján, is happy to give further information on local history and legends.

Above the town is the **Museo Arqueológico La Cueva del Paraíso** ① *Calle Moncada al final, 300 m uphill from the Hotel Castillo, Mon-Fri 0800-1700, Sat 0800-1200; CUC$3*. Located in a large and beautiful cave, which is part of the Majayara terrace system, its attractions include stalactites and stalagmites as well as petroglyphs and display cases containing archaeological finds from the area. The mirador at the museum offers stunning views of the town and the bay. In the second chamber there are graves of Taínos lying in the traditional foetal position, with their funereal offerings still in situ. One skeleton, which is currently undergoing testing, could be that of the cacique, Guamá, a rebel leader at the time of the Spanish invasion and the first known Cuban guerrilla, who fought against the Spanish for ten years. The dead man was clearly a dignitary, from the type of burial, and died from a fractured skull. It is believed that Guamá suffered a blow to the head, possibly by his brother after a dispute. The Yara-Majayara geological area is made up of three terraces, Yara, Majana and Majayara, in between which are many caves, used by generations of Amerindians before and after the arrival of Columbus and now becoming tourist attractions. More than 500 petroglyphs have been found, along with evidence of irrigation canals and tools. Archaeological tours of the area are available from the museum CUC$5-12. They include a visit to the Cueva Perla de Agua, east of Baracoa, containing rock drawings, which has been made into the first Parque Arqueológico Turístico de Cuba, and to the petroglyphs and other caves.

Around Baracoa

Boca de Miel and around
The delightful tropical village of Boca de Miel is within walking distance of Baracoa. Head east past the stadium, along the beach, and then turn north and cross a large bridge. You can buy fruit and watch the men fish. Around the bay is Playa Blanca, which is a bit rocky.

Playa Duaba
Playa Duaba is a point 6 km from Baracoa where the river meets the sea; you can swim in both and eat at **Finca Duaba**, where the food is good but the service not fantastic. Historically, Duaba is notable for being the place where General Antonio Maceo landed on 1 April 1895 to start the second War of Independence. There are waterfalls on the Río Duaba, reached by driving along a rocky road from Baracoa to the entrance by a campsite (**El Yunque**, Santa Rosa de Duaba 456), where you will be met by people wanting to guide you. A guide is needed for the 45-minute walk (take water) as you need to cross the river

at a certain point and scramble up rocks. Depending on your haggling skills you will have to pay CUC$5-8. Excellent excursion, unspoilt and no other tourists.

Playa Maguana

Playa Maguana, is a beautiful white-sand curving beach 22 km northwest from Baracoa, CUC$5 by bus. The trees come right down to the sand, so there is shade under them or among the sea grapes growing further along the beach. The sand shelves quite steeply into the sea, which can be rough at certain times of the year, particularly if there is a storm or a cold front coming down from the USA. This is the Atlantic, not the Caribbean, but the water is warm and inviting and, once you're in, there is a tremendous view looking inland to the mountains. Be very careful never to leave your things unattended and do not take valuables such as passports and tickets to the beach. There are many families living near the beach who will cook lunch for you and a *paladar* serving seafood. Hygiene is not a top priority. You can hire beach chairs, CUC$0.50 per hour or CUC$2 for the day, pedalos and snorkelling equipment from the beach bar and restaurant. There is a 16-room hotel, **Villa Maguana**, a short walk away; the only place where you can stay on the beach.

Río Yumurí

The Río Yumurí is 30 km east of Baracoa. This is the most spectacular of Baracoa's rivers, running through a deep canyon. There is an organized trip which includes a visit to a farm where they cultivate cacao, but even private drivers will do these sort of things too. If you don't want to take a tour, rent a private car (CUC$25-30) to the Río Yumurí where the road ends. A canoe will ferry you across or you can hire one to take you upriver for CUC$2 per person. There are always guides on hand. You can continue walking upriver and swim, very quiet and peaceful.

El Yunque

You can hire a guide to take you to the top of El Yunque, 575 m above sea level, to view the breathtaking scenery and panorama of banana and coconut palms. There are lots of birds, butterflies and other wildlife and a glorious view over the mountains, rivers and the bay of Porto Santo. Do not attempt it if you are not fit, it is a long, hard slog in tremendous heat and you will need plenty of water and good boots. Tours start from El Yunque Campismo, see above, CUC$13 with an official agency, and can include lunch or a snack and a bathe in the Río Duaba, CUC$16 with transport to the Campismo, minimum eight people. Easier is the long walk up the **Río Toa** through the UNESCO biosphere forest, followed by a 45-minute return boat journey along Cuba's widest river. Boat trips on the Río Toa cost CUC$5 per person, or CUC$18 with transport.

The most eastern point of Cuba, **Punta de Maisí**, is only 80 km from Haiti across the Windward Passage, and on a clear night it's possible to see the lights of the neighbouring island from the lighthouse here. However, the road is blocked and foreigners are not allowed access to this region. There are caves on the point: La Patana, Los Bichos and Jaguey, which the Taínos used for ceremonial purposes and have left drawings on the walls. They were first explored in 1945 by Dr Antonio Núñez Jiménez, who discovered that the temperature inside is very high.

For Sleeping and Eating price codes and other relevant information, see Essentials pages 37-43.

◉ Sleeping

Baracoa *p375, map p376*
Hotels
A-B Porto Santo, Carretera del Aeropuerto, T21-645106, www.grupo-gaviota.com. 80 rooms, 3 suites, a/c, TV, restaurant, bar, shop, beautiful swimming pool, car hire, next to airport, beach, peaceful atmosphere, friendly, night time entertainment with show.
B El Castillo, Calixto García, Loma del Paraíso, T21-645165, www.grupo-gaviota.com. 34 a/c rooms with bath, phone, TV in lobby lounge, pool (CUC$10 for use by non-residents, of which CUC$8 is for food) with great views, parking, friendly staff, food OK, excellent views, feeling of grandeur, very good breakfast included, decent restaurant.
B-C Hostal La Habanera, Maceo esq Frank País, T21-645273, www.grupo-gaviota.com. Glorious pink colonial building converted to a hotel in 2003. If you want a central hotel with style this is the place. Friendly staff, excellent service. 10 rooms, a/c, cable TV, room service, snack bar.
C-D La Rusa, a bright yellow building on the Malecón, Máximo Gómez 13, T21-643011, www.grupo-gaviota.com. Named after the Russian, Magdalena Menasse (see box, page 377), who used to run the hotel and whose photos adorn the walls; famous guests have included Fidel Castro, simple but updated rooms, average food, nice location.

Casas particulares
There are over 200 legal *casas particulares* in Baracoa now. Most charge CUC$15 in low season and CUC$20 in high season per room, before any commissions, but the better casas charge up to CUC$25. All those listed here offer hot and cold water in private bathrooms.
D-E Allan Tenezo Sánchez, Maceo 235 Alto entre Abel Díaz y Limbano Sánchez, T21-

643857. Pleasant house, 1 independent a/c room, fridge, blue and white terrace, lovely view, secure.
D-E Andrés Cruzata Rigores, Wilder Galano Reyes 23 Alto entre Abel Díaz Delgado y Ramón López Peña, T21-642697, T015-246 5755 (mob), cacaolog@enet.cu. Apartment upstairs, 1 comfortable a/c bedroom, own entrance, TV, modern bathroom, terrace with view over the town to the sea and awning for shade, nice place to sit and enjoy a *mojito* or *piña colada*, charming and helpful family offer lots of services such as laundry, good food, their son speaks English and Italian.
D-E Andrés Terrero Martínez , Martí 367, T21-642694. One room with independent access, terrace, a/c, private, friendly family, good food, secure car parking.
D-E Casa Colonial Lucy, Céspedes 29 entre Rubert López y Maceo, T21-643548. One of the nicest places to stay, Lucy has a delightful colonial house with lovely views over the town and the sea from the roof terrace. 2 rooms with high ceilings, fridge, a/c, great food, organizes trips.
D-E Casa Walter, Rubert López 47 entre Céspedes y Coroneles Galana, T21-642346, maribara@enet.cu. 2 a/c rooms with independent access, garden, terrace, good food.
D-E Daniel Salomón Paján , Céspedes 28 entre Maceo y Rubert López, T21-641443, 0152917403 (mob), fifi@toa.gtm.sld.cu. In town centre, 1 comfortable, quiet, a/c room with large bathroom, private, patio garden, friendly, knowledgeable and charming family where nothing is too much trouble, some English spoken. Daniel works at the town museum.
D-E Dennis Rodríguez, Rubert López 86 entre Ramón l ópez y Limbano Sánchez, T21-641373, dennys@toa.gtm.sld.cu. 2 a/c rooms, terrace with pleasant view and thatched roof umbrella for shade, TV, fridge, friendly family, good food.
D-E La Colina – Alberto Matos, Calixto García 158 Altos, T5-290-3651 (mob), yolandamll@ toa.gtm.sld.cu. Elegant house 2 mins from the

centre, terrace with view over the town and the sea, 2 a/c rooms with up to date fittings.
D-E Williams Montoya Sánchez, Martí 287, T21-642798. Very hospitable, colonial house, 2 rooms, good food, a/c, car parking, CUC$2, car cleaning CUC$2, also for non-guests.
D-E Yamilet Selva Bartelemy, Frank País 6 entre Máximo Gómez y Flor Crombet, T21-645357, yamile@film.cineclubes.com. Despite being a seaside town, this is one of the few houses to have a sea view from 2 light and bright rooms. The smaller room has the bigger bathroom, 2 beds, hot shower, sea breezes, a/c, fan, in hospitable household with charming couple, secure, comfortable, dinner CUC$6-8, breakfast CUC$2-3, excellent.
E Arquimedes, Rubert López 87 entre Limbano Sánchez y Ramón López, T21-643291. Run by Arquimedes and Bárbara, a/c, hot and cold water, great food with lots of fish in coconut and other local dishes, room has own entrance off the street or you can come in through the house.
E César Labori Balga, Martí 81 entre 24 de Febrero y Coliseo, T21-642507, T5-291 1314 (mob). A very welcoming and delightful family with a separate apartment with its own off-street entrance. 2 double bedrooms, a/c, small porch overlooking lush courtyard garden with chatty parrot. Eldest son, César, runs this casa and mother Concepción cooks lovely local dishes; fresh fish in coconut milk, lamb and excellent coffee from her father's farm.
E Ikira Mahíquez Machado, Maceo 168-A entre Céspedes y Ciro Frías, T21-643881. 1 room in separate part of the house with kitchen and garage, friendly family, terrace has sea view.
E Nelia y Yaquelín, Mariana Grajales 11 entre Julio A Mella y Calixto García, T21-642412. 3 generations of a delightful family offer a simple but comfortable place to stay, sea views, 2 small rooms, breakfast CUC$3, dinner CUC$7, both delicious and more than you can eat.

Around Baracoa *p378*
A Villa Maguana, Carretera a Moa Km 22.5, T21-641204, www.grupo-gaviota.com.

The only place to stay on the beach, Playa Maguana. Recently improved and expanded to 16 3-star rooms in 4 2-storey blocks, but still quiet, charming and simple. Restaurant for breakfast, lunch and dinner, and beach bar/*parrillada* with snacks and drinks 0700-2145. Snorkelling gear available.

🍴 Eating

Baracoa *p375, map p376*
The isolation of Baracoa has led to an individual local cuisine, mostly featuring coconut milk and fish. The best food can be had in *casas particulares*, which is where most people eat. Don't miss the *cucurucho*, also known as *dulce de coco* or *coco con chocolate*. These are wrapped in dried palm leaves in a clever cone shape with a carrying handle and are sold at the roadside up in the hills on La Farola. You can get 2 for CUC$1. They also sell cocoa balls the size of a tennis ball, 3 for CUC$1, which are delicious for making hot chocolate or using in cakes.

Restaurants
🍴-🍴 Fuerte La Punta. The fort at La Punta, which juts out into the bay west of the town, has been converted to a pleasant, breezy, open-air restaurant, with rustic tables and chairs inside the fort looking out through the cannon holes to the sea. Nice setting, reasonably priced food, fish in coconut milk CUC$6, *pollo frito* CUC$2.50, sandwiches CUC$2, spaghetti CUC$2.20.
🍴-🍴 La Colonial, José Martí 123, T21-645391. Excellent candlelit *paladar*, subdued atmosphere, extensive menu includes fish in coconut (*Pescado a la Santa Bárbara*).

Snack bars and cafés
Casa de Chocolate, Maceo esq Maraví. Serves a local version of hot chocolate with water, sugar and salt. Not to everyone's taste but worth trying just in case. Only 30 centavos a cup. Ice cream 1.60 pesos cubanos a scoop. Cuban pesos essential. Snacks, cakes and

sweets available. You can buy chocolate in town made by the Baracoa chocolate factory – a bit dry and gritty but with good flavour. The factory was opened by Che in 1963 on the Moa road out of town.

Costa Norte, 3 outlets on the Malecón: Costa Norte No 1 and Costa Norte Las Ruinas, are both cafeterias, set up to enliven the seafront area after it sustained serious damage in the 2008 hurricanes; Costa Norte No 2 offers restaurant service. All charge for drinks in CUC$ and for food in pesos cubanos.

El Picopo, Parque Independencia, T21-641665. 24-hr bar with outside seating. Fast food with occasional slow service, spaghetti, pizza, sandwiches, chicken. Also sells books, music, handicrafts, post cards and other miscellaneous items.

Pizzería La Baracoesa, Ciro Frías 155, T21-641010. Pizzas charged in pesos cubanos, so very cheap way of filling up. They run out of ingredients early, so don't rely on a late-night takeaway.

● Entertainment

Baracoa p375, map p376

Live music and dancing

Casa de la Cultura, Maceo 124, T21-642364. Open 2000-2300, free. Live music on its patio. Programme varies from day to day, with young local talent given the chance to shine. Nightly show of Afro-Cuban music by Bararrumba, which is highly recommended, very interesting to see all the costumes and instruments.

Casa de la Trova, Maceo 149B esq Ciro Frías. Traditional music, Tue-Sun from 2100, CUC$1 entry, CUC$2 for a *mojito* or *Cuba libre*, good *son* and friendly atmosphere. Seats around the edge but many people stand on the street and look through the windows (until it rains). Dancing in the centre. The local girls won't dance, so foreign women are approached to partner the men. Dancers always in demand.

El Paraíso, Maceo 141 esq Frank País, T21-643446. Karaoke and drinks bar, modern, entrance 20 pesos cubanos per couple.

El Patio de Artex, in the Fondo de Bienes Culturales (see Cultural centres), Maceo 120, opposite the Casa de Chocolate. Bar with live traditional music and other cultural activities, outdoor seating. Open 1000-2400, entry free.

El Ranchón, up the hill above Calixto García on Loma Paraíso, T21-643268. All the young people move up here after the Casa de la Trova and other places close. Open-air disco with live and recorded music, 2100-0130, although it doesn't really get going until after 2400. Great view over Baracoa and out to sea. Watch out for all the steps if you've been hitting the rum. Entrance CUC$1.

La Terraza de Cultura, at Casa de la Cultura, Martí 124, opposite Casa del Chocolate, T21-645197. Night club. Show starts at 2330, disco afterwards, CUC$1. Occasional comedy nights, good if your Spanish is up to it. A very popular venue.

Porto Santo and **El Castillo**. Nightly dancing and live music at these 2 hotels, the former is livelier, see Sleeping, above.

Cinema and events

Cineteatro El Encanto, Maceo, next to Parque Central. Shows movies and hosts cultural events.

● Festivals and events

Baracoa p375, map p376

Last week in Mar Semana de la Cultura promotes the cultural traditions of the area with lots of music and dancing going back to the roots of Cuban *son*. Fiesta del Kiribá is a farmers' fiesta, particularly coffee farmers.

Beginning of Apr Carnival.

12-15 Aug Fiesta de las Aguas celebrates the foundation of Baracoa on 15 Aug 1511. There are conferences and courses about history and tradition, architecture, archaeology, traditional dancing, environmental events related to the Humboldt National Park, *Cayambada* (legend of the Rio de Miel), demonstrations by *Treseros* (guitarists) and the Feria de Arte Popular.

O Shopping

Baracoa *p375, map p376*
There is a **bookshop** on José Martí 195. Most of the shops selling goods in CUC$ are on Martí. **Fondo de Bienes Culturales**, Maceo 120, T21-643627. Mon-Fri 0830-1700, Sat, Sun 0830-1200. Cultural centre promoting and selling art and handicrafts. As well as a tasteful souvenir shop full of local artists' work, wooden carvings, paintings, etc, there is information about local artists; Baracoa has its own school of *artesanía*, where artists train in traditional methods using wood and coconut shell, producing the work on sale in the shop. The very friendly and helpful English-speaking Alberto Matos Llime is worth talking to if you have any questions about local history and culture.
Galería de Arte Eliseo Osorio, Maceo 145, T21-641011. Mon-Thu 0900-2100, Fri 0900-2200, Sat 1600-2200. Art for sale, art exhibitions and special events, such as the Concurso Guayacán, wood carving demonstrations and exhibitions 6-8 Nov.

▲ Activities and tours

Baracoa *p375, map p376*
There are lots of guided tours on offer, taking you out into the countryside, up the mountains, into caves and archaeological sites, bathing in rivers, waterfalls and the sea, with or without transport, food and other extras. Most official tours, however, depend on a minimum number of people. Note that any tours taking you into the Humboldt National Park incur an entry fee of CUC$10. Baracoa city tour CUC$4, El Yunque CUC$13, Playa Maguana CUC$5, Rancho Toa CUC$5, Finca Duaba CUC$3 (Toa and Duaba, peasant farms and boat trips), Yumurí CUC$4 for guide, CUC$2 for boat trip (fishing village, cocoa plantation and boat trip). **Cubatur**, Maceo 149 esq Pelaya, T21-645306, cubaturbaracoa@enet.cu. Mon-Sat 0800-1200, 1400-1700, Sun 0830-1200. Tickets and reservations, transfers and tours.

Ecotur, Coronel Cardoza 24 entre Mariana Grajales y 1 de Abril, T21-643665, ecoturbc@enet.cu. Mon-Sat 0800-1200, 1400-1700, Sun 0830-1200. Contact Alexander Domínguez Abat for tours such as hiking and bird-watching, jeep excursions and other activities; extremely helpful.
Havanatur, Martí 202 entre Céspedes y Coronel Galano, T21-645358, laffita@cimex.com.cu. Mon-Sat 0800-1200, 1400-1700, Sun 0800-1200. The usual range of services, tickets and tours.

⊖ Transport

Baracoa *p375, map p376*
Air
Airport 100 m from **Hotel Porto Santo**. There are 2 scheduled **Cubana** flights a week from **Havana**, on Thu and Sun, at 1100, 2 hrs, arrives 1300, departs again 1400 back to Havana, CUC$135. In high season there is also a Gaviota flight on Fri from Havana with a stop in Holguín, arriving in Baracoa at 1300. Cubana, José Martí 181, T21-645374, open for ticket sales Mon-Wed, Fri 0800-1200, 1400-1700.

Bus
Main bus terminal at the end of Martí near Av de los Mártires, T21-643880/641550, for buses to **Havana, Santiago, Camagüey, Guantánamo**. Make sure you reserve in advance at busy times and that your name is down on the list, *plano*, otherwise your reservation will not be valid. It has been known for travellers to get stranded in Baracoa due to high ticket demand. Víazul has a service to **Santiago** at 1415, arriving 1900, CUC$15, departing Santiago 0700, arriving Baracoa 1230, via Guantánamo, see page 367 for details of tickets.

Car hire
Vía Car is the only car rental office in town, at Hotel Porto Santo, T21-641665, so if you are planning to end your self-drive journey here and fly back to Havana, make sure you

hire a car with this company (Gaviota). **Scooters** (Motos) can be hired at El Piropo on the Parque Independencia, T21-641671, 0800-1200, 1400-1700, CUC$24 for 24 hrs. There is a **Servi Cupet** station near the museum on Martí, closed Sun.

Playa Maguana *p379*
A battered Víazul **minibus** leaves Parque Independencia daily at 1000, returning 1700, CUC$2 1-way. A normal taxi charges CUC$17-20. Alternatively, hire a private car for about CUC$12-13, 1 hr on a terrible, unpaved road.

❶ Directory

Baracoa *p375, map p376*
Banks For currency exchange and credit card advances: **Banco de Crédito y Comercio**, Maceo 99 entre 10 de Octubre y 24 de Febrero, T21-642218, Mon, Tue, Thu, Fri 0800-1500, Wed 0800-1800, Sat 0800-1100; **Banco** Popular de Ahorro, Martí 166 entre Ciro Frías y Céspedes, T21-642286, Mon, Wed-Fri 0800-1500, Tue 1200-1900, Sat 0800-1100; **Cadeca**, Martí 241 entre Reyes y L Sánchez, T21-645345. **Internet** Etecsa, Maceo, opposite Parque Independencia, T21-643182, 0900-1900. Internet service with terminals using prepaid cards, CUC$6 per hour, valid only in Baracoa. **Medical services** Hospital Octavio de la Concepción y de la Pedraja, on Carretera Guantánamo at the entrance to the town. Clínica Internacional Baracoa, Martí 237 esq Roberto Reyes, T21-641038, open 24 hrs, medical services, laboratory and clinic. Policlínica, in the small *barrio* next to Hotel Porto Santo, there is also a dentist here. Clínica Estomatológica, Maceo, in Barrio de la Punta, near the fort. There is a 24-hr **pharmacy** on Maceo 132, T21-642271. **Post** Maceo 136, T21-642415, open 0800-2100. **Telephone** Etecsa Centro de Llamadas, Maceo, opposite Parque Independencia. Phone boxes for domestic and international calls using prepaid phone cards.

Contents

Footprint features

At a glance

◉ **Getting around** On foot, by bicycle, hired car and taxi.

◉ **Time required** 2 days to a week.

The islands

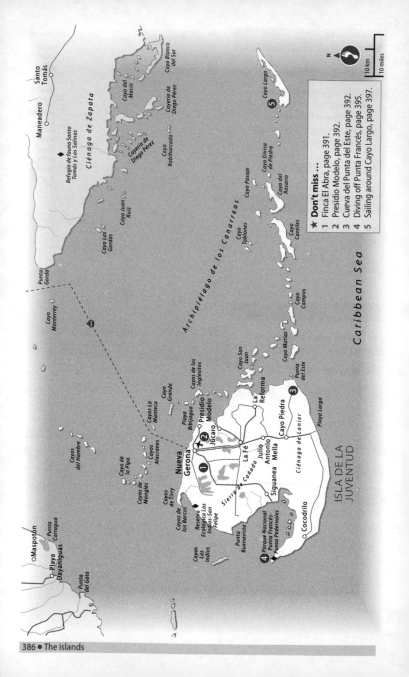

Santo Tomás

Maneadero

Ciénaga de Zapata

Cayo del Mico

Cayo Blanco del Sur

Cayería de Diego Pérez

Refugio de Fauna Santo Tomás y Las Salinas

Cayería de Diego Pérez

Cayo Rabihorcado

Cayo Largo

5

Cayo Divisa de Piedra

Cayo del Rosario

Archipiélago de los Canarreos

Cayo Juan Ruiz

Cayo Las Gordas

Punta Gorda

Cayo Pasaje

Cayo Tablones

Cayo Cantiles

Cayo Monterrey

Caribbean Sea

Cayos del Hombre

Cayo de la Pipa

Cayos de Mangles

Cayos La Manteca

Cayo Grande

Cayos de los Inglesitos

Playa Bibijagua

Presidio Modelo

Cayo San Juan

Cayo Campos

Cayo Matías

Punta del Este

Cayos de Tirry

Cayos Alacranes

Júcaro

Nueva Gerona

Cayos de los Barcos

Reserva Ecológica Los Indios–San Felipe

La Fé

La Reforma

Cayo Piedra

Playa Larga

2

1

3

Julio Antonio Mella

Siguanea

Ciénaga de Lanier

ISLA DE LA JUVENTUD

Cocodrilo

Parque Nacional Punta Francés–Punta Pedernales

4

Punta Buenavista

Sierra de Cañada

Cayos Los Indios

Maspotón

Playa Dayaniguas

Punta Caragua

Punta del Gato

N

10 km
10 miles

The Isla de la Juventud, or Isla, as it is known, looks as though it belongs on a scorched-edged pirates' map of old parchment bearing a single cross indicating buried gold. Apparently such tales of treasures still abound as it was once a lair for British and French *corsarios*. Its history as a temporary home for Castro (in prison), for Martí (in exile), for the US Navy (another naval base) and for residents from other communist countries (as students) makes the island a curious destination for the traveller keen to get off the beaten track. Its modern-day appeal lies in the exceptional diving off the west coast, the ancient caves and its natural setting.

As a one-time prison island, there has been very little development, and what there is has been concentrated around Nueva Gerona, its main town, and the port area. The island was badly affected by the hurricanes of 2008 and was low on the priority list for rebuilding. There are few reasons to stay here if you are not interested in diving, as the swimming is poor compared with other Cuban beaches. The island is a good place to go for a weekend out of Havana, although if you plan to see the whole island you will need more than one weekend.

Cayo Largo, on the other hand, is a sun, sea and sand destination, where all-inclusive is the order of the day and you are totally isolated from the rest of Cuba. It is so little a part of Cuba that Cuban pesos are invisible. Everyone comes here on a package deal, for one day, two days or a week, for no other reason than to enjoy the idyllic beaches with pale golden sand and perfect conditions for swimming, sailing and other watersports.

Ins and outs

Getting there
Air There are daily flights from Havana which connect with international flights, notably from 15 Mexican cities. Cayo Largo del Sur can be reached by air from other resort areas such as Varadero and there are charter flights from European and Canadian cities. **Sea** You can also get to Isla de la Juventud by sea, by ferry from Batabanó, but Cayo Largo del Sur can only be reached by sea if you have your own boat. ▸▸ *For further details, see Isla de la Juventud, below, and Cayo Largo, page 397.*

Getting around
Road Hired car or taxi is the usual method of transport, unless you book a tour through an agency. There are several public buses on Isla de la Juventud. If you are not in a hurry you can pick up a horse-drawn *coche*, or go by bicycle. The south of Isla de la Juventud is an exclusion zone and you need a permit to enter. **Sea** There is no inter-island transport and to get from the Isla to Cayo Largo you need a private yacht.

Tourist information
Ecotur agency on Isla de la Juventud is good for information and tours. The hotels on Cayo Largo have *burós de turismo* and **Cubanacán**, **Cubatur** and **Havanatur** are all represented. The website www.cayolargodelsur.cu is worth investigating and has a section on the Isla, although most of it is on Cayo Largo.

Best time to visit
The driest time of year is between December and April. From June you can expect increased humidity and rain, with the risk of tropical storms or hurricanes from September until November. There is usually a sea breeze at any time of year to cool things down and the islands are not as hot as the mother island of Cuba. Isla de la Juventud and Cayo Largo have both been hard hit by hurricanes, most recently by Gustav in 2008. The damage on La Isla was, according to Fidel Castro, worse than a nuclear explosion. On Cayo Largo the beaches have changed considerably in recent years as a result of storm action, but in mid-2009 all were reported in good shape.

Isla de la Juventud

The Isla de la Juventud (Isle of Youth) is in the Gulf of Batabanó, 97 km from the main island. Much of the island is flat, with a large area taken up with swamp in the Ciénaga de Lanier in the southern half of the island. The northern half is more hospitable and here there are marble hills near the capital, Nueva Gerona, and the slate hills of Sierra del Cañada in the west. The area around the Presidio (Model Prison) is particularly beautiful, with its low green hills and citrus plantations. Mangroves line much of the coast, a haven for wildlife and migrating birds. Some of the south coast's white-sand beaches are inaccessible because of a military zone, but others may be reached with appropriate permits. There is, so far, no infrastructure in the area and roads are virtually non-existent. The beaches on the west coast have black sand. ▸▸ For listings, see pages 393-396.

Ins and outs

Getting there The Rafael Cabrera Mustelier airport (GER) is nearly 5 km from town and there are three scheduled 40-minute **flights** a day from Havana. A testing way of getting to the island is by the passenger **ferry** from Surgidero de Batabanó on the mainland south coast. There are crossings at 1000 and 1500, but services and vessels are subject to change. It takes one to three hours depending on which boat is in use and costs CUC$50. It is usually crowded and the a/c is very cold. Do not even think about visiting the Isla without booking your transport off the island again. The plane and ferry are oversubscribed. ▶ *See also Transport, page 395.*

Getting around Travel to anywhere on the island can be difficult although nearly every car will turn into a **taxi** on request. Fares within Nueva Gerona and to main hotels and airport are about CUC$2-7. The best way to see the island is to hire a **private car** with a driver/guide, which costs about CUC$35-60 a day. It is worthwhile renting a car and driver/guide simply for the drive as there are some particularly beautiful areas with green rolling hills and citrus plantations. A good day's sightseeing will take in the Model Prison, the crocodile farm and the **Hotel El Colony**, where you can hire a kayak for an hour. If you hope to see the whole island, plan to spend more than a weekend, particularly if you want to see all the caves. Roads are generally in good condition. **Motorbike hire** from the hotels is CUC$20-30 a day (**Transtur**, T46-326666). Local transport is often by **horse and cart** (recommended for short distances), the drivers are willing to show you the sights and give you an impromptu history

Isla de la Juventud

Cayo de la Pipa
Cayos de Mangles
Cayos Alacranes
Cayo La Manteca
Cayo Grande
Punta de Tirry
Playa Paraíso
Cayos de los Inglesitos
Punta de los Barcos
Nueva Gerona
Playa Bibijagua
El Abra
Presidio Modelo
Cayos Los Indios
La Demajagua
Balneario Santa Rita
La Fé
Cayo San Juan
Sierra de Cañada
Punta Buenavista
Mina de Oro
La Jungla de Jones
La Reforma
Julio Antonio Mella
La Victoria
Argelia Libre
Punta Francés
Siguanea
Military Barrier
Cayo Matías
Cayo Piedra
Cueva del Punta del Este
Cayo Campos
Ciénaga de Lanier
Punta del Este
Cocodrilo
Playa Larga
N

| 10 km | **Sleeping** | Rancho el Tesoro **2** |
| 10 miles | El Colony **1** | Villa Isla **3** |

lesson. You cannot drive south of Cayo Piedra into the military exclusion zone without a permit, which can be obtained from **Ecotur** and other locations including the Buró de Turismo at Hotel Villa Isla, at car hire offices and at the Ministry of the Interior, Calle 16 at the harbour, see below. **Ecotur**, is recommended as a means of getting around the island, with trips to the south and chances of spotting a wild orchid that smells like chocolate.

History

The Isla was always an enclave, whether populated by pirates post-Columbus, or by US businessmen and communities of Japanese farmers in the first quarter of the 20th century. In recent decades, its population has been swelled by tens of thousands of Cuban and Third World students, giving rise to the modern name of **Isle of Youth**. Early aboriginal inhabitants called it Camaraco, Ahao or Siguanea. The abundant pine and later casuarina (Australian pine) trees gave rise it the name Isla de Pinos (Isle of Pines), by which it was known officially before the revolutionary authorities renamed it, and local inhabitants (and their baseball team) are still called *pineros* by other Cubans. It earned its place in world literature as the supposed model for Robert Louis Stevenson's *Treasure Island*. Yet another, unofficial, name, La Isla de las Cotorras (Island of the Parrots) is a reminder of just one of the feathered species that inhabit the island's pinewoods, though the Ciénaga de Lanier marshland extending east–west across the island is the chief magnet for ornithologists. Columbus named the island San Juan Evangelista (St John the Evangelist) when he arrived in June 1494. In the 16th and 17th centuries its use as a base by French and British pirates (including Welshman Henry Morgan who later gained respectability as governor of Jamaica) earned it another name, the Isla de Piratas (Isle of Pirates).

Place names like Estero de los Corsarios date from that era, as does Punta Francés, the lair of the French pirate Leclerc. Francis Drake also fought the Spaniards in the surrounding seas, and wrecked galleons from this era add interest to modern-day diving. The biggest draw, however, is the superb coral reef, acclaimed by Jacques Cousteau and others. Spain colonized the island in the 19th century, naming it Colonia Reina Amalia, but from the 19th century until the Revolution its main function was as a prison and both José Martí and Fidel Castro served time there.

After the Revolution, youth brigades were mobilized to plant citrus. Schools for international students, mostly from Africa (Mozambique, Angola, South Africa, Ethiopia) and Vietnam were built along the highway. Students started their studies at secondary level and returned to their countries at technical or postgraduate level. Their education was free. Students were taught on the basis of work and study and contributed to citrus cultivation. All the schools are now closed. Now the major economic activities are citrus cultivation and processing (in conjunction with Chilean capital), marble quarrying (mainly for tourism and export), fishing and tourism. The Delita mine has estimated deposits of 1,750,000 oz of gold and close to 14,000,000 oz of silver. The Isla is the centre of administration for the 2398-sq-km 'Special Municipality', which includes Cayo Largo and the Archipiélago de los Canarreos.

Nueva Gerona → *Colour map 1, C5.*

The capital, Nueva Gerona, dates from the 19th century and remains the only substantial settlement. Surrounded by small rounded hills, it is a pleasant, laid-back country town with a slow pace. The recent proliferation of private tourist-related businesses means that it is not as isolated as it used to be. Most development has taken place post-1959 (the island's entire population was just 10,000 in 1959), so there are few historically interesting buildings. The town centre is set out on the grid system where each block is about 100 m, with even-numbered streets running east–west and odd numbered ones north–south. The **Río Las Casas** runs through the town heading northwards out to sea; this has traditionally been the main route to the Cuban mainland. The boat that served as a ferry from the 1920s until 1974, *El Pinero*, has been preserved by the river at the end of Calle 28. It ferried Castro off the island when Batista's amnesty secured his release.

Sights

The **Parque Central** is two blocks west of the river, between Calles 28 and 30, and 37 and 39. The Parque attracts 'retired' men during the day and comes alive at night; it is also a good place to enquire about cars and guides. Ask anyone, as everyone has a contact. The church of **Nuestra Señora de los Dolores** is on the north side of the square. A church was first built on this site in 1853 but was blown away by a hurricane in 1926. The present one, in colonial style, was built in 1929. Padre Guillermo Sardiñas, parish priest here in the 1950s, was the only priest to join Fidel Castro on his revolutionary campaign in the Sierra Maestra, leaving the Isla in 1957 to take up arms. The **Museo Municipal** ① *Calle 30 entre 37 y Martí (39), T46-323791,* on the south side of the Parque Central, T46-323791, Mon-Fri 0900-2200, Sun 0900-1300, CUC$1, is housed in the former Casa de Gobierno, built in 1853, one of the oldest buildings on the island. It has a small historical collection of items of local interest.

To make the most of a day in town, you could ask the local ICAP (Cuban Institute for Friendship with the Peoples) office to arrange visits to places of social interest, where the rarity of visitors ensures a genuine welcome.

The **Museo de la Lucha Clandestina** ① *Calle 24 entre 43 y 45, T46-324582, Tue-Sat 0900-1700, Sun 0800-1200,* has a collection of photos and other material relating to the Revolution and the uprising against the dictator, Batista. The **Planetario y Museo de Ciencias Naturales** ① *Calle 41 4625 y 46, T46-323143, Tue-Thu 0800-1900, Fri 1400-2200, Sat 1300-1700, Sun 0900-1300, CUC$2,* has exhibits relating to the natural history, geology and archaeology of the island, with a replica of the Punta del Este cave painting.

Around Nueva Gerona

Outside the town, 3 km west just off the road to La Demajagua, is **Casa Museo Finca El Abra** ① *T46-396206, Tue-Sat 0900-1630, Sun 0900-1300, CUC$2, CUC$1 camera.* Excellent guide, only Spanish spoken. There are two white posts at the entrance otherwise it is not signed. It is a pleasant walk from town or take a horse-drawn *coche*. This is where José Martí came on 13 October 1870, after serving one year of a six-year sentence in prison in Havana. His father knew the *finca* owner, José María Sardá and his wife Trinidad Valdés Amador de Sardá and Sardá knew people in government. Martí's transfer to the *finca* was arranged on condition he did not leave it. He returned to Havana on 18 December 1870. In 1926 a hurricane destroyed the *finca*, which is in a lovely setting with a backdrop of hills, approached along an avenue of oak trees, and so most of it is not original. However, the floor of Martí's bedroom is original. You can see the contents of the house and kitchen and some of Martí's belongings. The 96 descendants of the Catalan military man-turned-*finca* owner still live in the area, some of them actually living at the *finca*. There are plenty of exhibits relating to the *finca* and the life of Martí but it's much more interesting if you speak Spanish as the guide can bring the exhibits to life, especially the stories about the love triangle that Martí found himself in between his wife-to-be and a Guatemalan lady.

About 4 km east of Nueva Gerona is the **Presidio Modelo** (Model Prison) ① *Reparto Chacón, T46-325112, Tue-Sat 0900-1630, Sun 0900-1300, CUC$2, CUC$1 camera,* built 1925-1932 by the dictator Gerardo Machado to a high-security 'panopticon' design first developed by Jeremy Bentham in 1791 to give total surveillance and control of the inmates. It is a sinister and impressive sight of huge circular buildings, very atmospheric, especially towards dusk and, although the building is now decaying, you can still imagine the horrors of incarceration here. You can wander around the guard towers and circular cell blocks and see the numbered, tiered cells. The four circulars had 465 cells with two men to a cell. On the sixth floor of each circular were 15 punishment cells. Men would be placed naked in the cell for nine days without bread or water and then sent to work outside. The circular in the centre was the dining room. All the wooden tables have been removed, but the metal supports remain. They randomly creak and moan, which is horribly eerie.

Pictures, beds and belongings have been carefully preserved. Inmates have included many fighters in the independence struggle, 350 Japanese Cuban internees in the Second World War, and Fidel Castro and fellow Moncada rebels imprisoned 1953-1955. Fidel and the other Moncada prisoners were held for 19 months in the medical wing, which is now the museum. Replacement beds have been installed and each bed is accompanied by a photograph and a potted history of all the Moncadistas including details of whether they are still alive. Fidel was removed from this wing to a separate room after singing to Batista through a window on one of his visits. Fidel's bed is not the original, but the bathroom with the chink of light with which Fidel read and wrote are authentic. Castro returned in 1959 to propose the development projects which were to transform it into the Isle of Youth. He closed the prison in 1967 and it became a school for a while before being turned into a museum.

The **Aguas Medicinales La Cotorra (Balneario Santa Rita)** ① *Centro de Rehabilitación y Aguas Termales, Calle 11, entre 16 y 18, near Santa Fé, T46-397961,* has three thermal pools with, it is claimed, highly restorative qualities. Massage, acupuncture and other therapies are offered. Close to Santa Fé is **La Jungla de Jones** ① *Tue-Sun 0900-1700, CUC$2.* North Americans Harry and Helen Jones came to the island in 1902 to set up a botanical garden with a wide range of trees from around the world. One of the most beautiful areas is a natural, bamboo cathedral. Mr Jones died in 1938 in an accident and Mrs Jones was murdered in 1960 by escapees from the Presidio Modelo. It is now in need of restoration.

Playa Paraíso is a white-sand beach in the north of the island with a restaurant, which is a little nicer, but not much, than **Playa Bibijagua**, which has black sand. You will be hassled on the beach here. The only hotel there is now a shell but there is a small café in the grounds, otherwise there are no facilities.

The **Cueva del Punta del Este** ① *59 km southeast of Nueva Gerona, transport by rental car or by an organized excursion,* contains paintings attributed to the original Siboney inhabitants. They were discovered in 1910 by a shipwrecked French sailor and contain 235 pictures on the walls and ceilings, painted long before the arrival of the Spanish. They are considered the most important pictographs in the Caribbean and have been declared a National Monument. It is believed that they might represent a solar calendar. There are seven caves in total.

Well worth a visit is the **Cocodrilo** (crocodile farm) ① *CUC$3,* a one-hour drive (any car) south and west from Nueva Gerona, including several kilometres of dirt road. You have a guided tour by the knowledgeable caretakers (in Spanish) of the hatchery and the breeding pens where the crocodiles stay for four to five years until they are released.

For Sleeping and Eating price codes and other relevant information, see Essentials pages 37-43.

◉ Sleeping

Nueva Gerona *p390, map p389*
The best option price-wise is to stay in *casas particulares*. People will approach you at the ferry dock, or at the bus terminal in Havana (they will get a commission), so don't fret if you haven't reserved.

Hotels
A Rancho el Tesoro, Carretera a La Fé Km 4, south of Nueva Gerona, in woods close to the Río Las Casas, T46-323035. 60 rooms in blocks. Unappealing. No pool but you can use the one at Villa Isla.
A Villa Isla, Carretera a La Fé Km 2.5, on the outskirts of Nueva Gerona beside the river, T46-323290. The foyer wins the ugliest and strangest foyer in Cuba award but the pool is great. 20 rooms, single and triple available, extra cots for children, a/c, fridge, TV, phone, pool where national swimming team trains, poolside bar, restaurants, squash court and gymnasium, disco Thu-Sun 2130-0400, young crowd, dance and aerobics classes advertized, the nicest hotel if you are not diving or on a package, Havanautos for car and motorcycle rental.

Casas particulares
E Bárbara García García, Calle 45 3606 entre 36 y 38, T46-324903. 2 a/c bedrooms with bath, home-cooked meals with Cuban dishes a speciality.
E Elda Cepero Herrera, Calle 43 2004 entre 20 y 22, T46-322774. Self-contained apartment behind Sra Elda's house, with a/c bedroom and bathroom, kitchen, living room and terrace.
E Villa Chave, Calle 45 3406 entre 34 y 36, T46-324292. Run by the kind family of Isabel y Onil. Good breakfasts and enormous suppers. Bathroom is shared between the 2 rented rooms.

E Villa Mas, Calle 41 4108 entre 8 y 10, T46-323544. 2 bedrooms, 1 with its own entrance and bathroom, the other in owners' house (Jorge Luis and Rey Mas), a/c, fridge, good meals, rooftop terrace. Another member of the family rents 2 bedrooms with shared bath, **Don Kike**, Calle 34 entre 43 y 45, near Parque Central, T46-321166.
E Villa Peña, Calle 10 3710 entre 37 y 39, T46-322345. 2 ground-floor rooms in Sra Odalis Peña Fernández' house, with private bath, a/c, breakfast and dinner available.
E Villa Viviana, Calle 32 4110 entre 41 y 43, T46-321255, zerep@web.correosdecuba.cu. Run by the friendly Viviana y Alina Pérez Castanedo. Occasionally their father Gilberto, a charming and interesting man, is there. Excellent self-contained apartment with 2 bedrooms above family home with separate entrance and kitchen and terrace with great views.

Around Nueva Gerona *p391, map p389*
B El Colony, T46-398282, www.hotelel colony.com (unofficial website). 40 mins by road from Nueva Gerona's small airport, very isolated, once part of the Hilton chain, established as a diving hotel before Cuba reappeared on the world tourist map, diving centre with access to 56 buoyed diving locations. Swimming and snorkelling not great because of shallow water and sea urchins, you have to wade a long way before it is deep enough to swim, but beach is white sand. 77 a/c rooms in main block and refurbished *cabañas*, single and triple available, discounts for stays of over a week, TV. Lovely setting, pool, basket ball, volleyball, tennis and squash courts, horseriding, car rental, excursions, busy with package tourists. In 2009 food was in short supply and very limited after the hurricane damage of 2008, so take snacks with you. Also take loads of insect repellent against sand flies and mosquitoes which make life most uncomfortable during the day and evening.

Ⓔ Eating

Nueva Gerona *p390, map p389*
Restaurants
There are very few *paladares*. The best bet is
to eat in your *casa particular*, where you can
get an excellent meal for CUC$6-8. At the
Mercado Agropecuario at Calles 24 y 35,
you can get fresh fruit and vegetables and
there are a few basic places to eat in this
area where you can pay in pesos.
♥♥-♥ Cabaret El Dragón, Calles 39 y 26,
T46-324479. Mon-Thu 1600-2200, Fri-Sun
1600-0030. Chinese and Cuban food, bar,
cabaret at weekends, deluxe atmosphere,
upscale crowd.
♥♥-♥ El Cochinito, Calles 39 y 24, T46-322809.
State run. Daily 1400-2200, specializes in pork
with dishes ranging from CU$1-9. There's an
airy dining room but food displayed in a cabinet
at the entrance looks really unappetizing. You
can sit on real cowskin chairs though.
♥♥-♥ La Insula, Calles 22 y 39, T46-321825.
Sun-Fri 1530-2230, Sat 1530-2100, café open
Sun-Fri 1200-0130, Sat 1200-2100. Probably
the most upmarket place in town and popular
with travellers. The food is of a high standard
and the staff are friendly. You might want to
avoid the karaoke nights as the staff will try
and get you to join in!
♥ Coppelia, Calles 37 y 32. Ice cream.

Ⓑ Bars

Nueva Gerona *p390, map p389*
Casa de los Vinos, Calles 20 y 41. Mon-Wed
1400-2200, Fri-Sun 1400-2400. Popular peso
drinking spot with grapefruit, melon, tomato
and grape wines, last orders 2300, so order
early, wine served in earthenware jugs,
advisable to take glasses, avoid the snacks.
Taberna Gerona, Calles 39 y 22. Daily
1100-2100. Cuban food and pub atmosphere,
very friendly, strictly pesos cubanos.

Ⓔ Entertainment

Nueva Gerona *p390, map p389*
Cabaret El Patio, Calle 24 entre 37 y 39. Daily
2100-0200, cabaret, 2 shows nightly at
weekends, at 2200 and 0100, entry CUC$3,
CUC$10, Fri, Sat, Sun, lots of Cubans, popular.
Casa de la Cultura, Calles 37 y 24. Check the
schedule posted outside for dance events.
La Movida, Calle 34 entre 18 y 20. Outdoor
disco, CUC$3, Cubans pay in pesos, young
student crowd, starts at 2200.
Villa Gaviota, Thu-Sun 2130-0400, entry
CUC$1. Disco next to the hotel, cave-like
atmosphere, picks up after midnight,
young crowd, techno music.

Ⓕ Festivals and events

Nueva Gerona *p390, map p389*
Mar Nueva Gerona has a grapefruit festival
and week-long fiesta around 13 Mar which
marks the end of the US hold on the island
(13 Mar 1926).

Ⓢ Shopping

Nueva Gerona *p390, map p389*
Art For local artwork there is the Centro de
Desarrollo de las Artes Visuales, Calles 39
y 26. **Bookshops** Librería Frank País, Calles
22 y 39. Mostly Spanish books.
Handicrafts Mercado Artesanal at Calles
24 y 35. **Photography** Photoservice Calle
39 entre 30 y 32, T46-324640.

⛰ Activities and tours

Isla de la Juventud *p390, map p389*
Birdwatching
There are many endemic birds on the Isla de
la Juventud and also many migrating water
fowl, particularly in the Ciénaga de Lanier,
the second largest swamp in the Cuban
archipelago, where you can also find

crocodiles. There are few facilities for birdwatchers and roads are very poor in the south, but on the other hand keen twitchers and birds find it remarkably unspoilt.

Diving

For diving information contact the Hotel El Colony, see above. The Centro Internacional de Buceo El Colony, T46-398181, has excellent facilities including underwater photography, and there is a recompression chamber. All dives (CUC$50-70) are boat dives. The area around **Punta Francés** in the west, about an hour from the marina, is probably the best, with caves, tunnels, deep canals and valleys and all manner of sea creatures including turtles and manatee, which are protected. There are over 40 different corals and innumerable fish. The west side of the island is protected from the prevailing winds so that the water is normally calm with temperatures ranging from 24°C in winter to 28°C in summer. The area is a marine reserve; you may only dive with an official operator. **Ecotur**, see below, offers cheap accommodation and diving deals. There are many exciting dive sites stretching east of the Isla de la Juventud towards Cayo Largo along the Archipiélago de los Canarreos, but these are really only possible on a liveaboard (some of which come from the Cayman Islands). The string of low-lying cays, with sandy beaches, mangroves, clear water and colourful reefs, has trapped many ships in the past. Divers have found the remains of over 70 ships and there is an area near Cayo Avalos, called Bajo de Zambo, that is full of them. Several would have been looking for turtle meat and today you can still find Green, Hawksbill and Ridley turtles, which are now protected in Cuba.

Fishing

Fishing is not allowed in the marine reserve, but the **Marina El Colony**, below, can arrange for a fishing trip to the south of the island.

Marina

Marina El Colony has mooring for 15 boats, maximum draft 2.5m, VHF channels 16, 19, 68 and 72, a liveaboard, *Spondylus*, with a capacity for 10 divers and other facilities. Watersports are available, such as catamarans, CUC$10 per hr, a 2-person kayak, CUC$6 per hr and a single kayak, CUC$4 per hr. Boat from marina to Centro Internacional de Buceo El Colony, CUC$8.

Tour operators

Ecotur, Calle Martí entre 24 y 26, T46-327101, ecoturpineroij@yahoo.es. Mon-Sat 0800-1700, contact the very helpful Pavel Martínez. Trips to the south of the island include La Cañada, Los Indios, El Cocodrilo, Punta del Este, Rincón del Guanal, Jacksonville, with chances to see chocolate-scented wild orchids and the tocororo bird plus deer. Prices are CUC$12.50-15 per person if you have a car or they can hire you a car for CUC$90 per day. If more than 4 people a minibus needs to be hired. All trips must be booked at least 1 day in advance because permits must be secured for visits to the southern part of the island. Also sells tours for Hotel Colony at cheaper prices: seafari, snorkelling, diving and you can take advantage of the hotel's transport service, CUC$3. Internet CUC$5 per hr, flights arranged. Guides speak English, Italian, French and German and are all naturalists.

⊖ Transport

Isla de la Juventud *p390, map p389*
Air

Rafael Cabrera Mustelier airport (GER), T46-322690. There are 3 scheduled 40-min flights a day from **Havana**, 0600, 1450 and 1715. They return at 0710, 1600 and 1825, so you could do a day trip if you wanted. Fare CUC$32 one way (but varies with season), book in advance.

Airlines Cubana at Calle 39 1415 entre 16 y 18, Nueva Gerona, T46-324259/322531, Mon-Fri 0800-1600, closed 1300-1400.

Bus

Buses run to **La Fé**, the **Hotel Colony**, **Playa Bibijagua**, and there is a bus marked 'Servicio Aéreo', which runs between the **airport** and the cinema in Nueva Gerona, but don't rely on any of these to run on a regular basis.

Car hire

Havanautos has an office in Nueva Gerona at Calles 32 y 39, T46-324432, but the hotels also have car hire desks, daily 0700-1900. About CUC$90 a day with insurance.
Petrol stations Cupet-Cimex fuel station is at Calles 39 y 30.

Ferry

Tickets for the bus and ferry to Nueva Gerona via Batabanó are sold from the **Naviera Cubana Caribeña (NCC)** kiosk at the Astro bus terminal near Plaza de la Revolución, Havana, T7-878 1841 or T7-860 0330, nccij@transnet.cu, to check times and to find out whether you need to go on the day of departure or several days beforehand because of availability problems. You must have your passport to travel. The bus fare from Havana to Surgidero de Batabanó is CUC$4. At the port, there are some small buildings to the right of the waiting room area where you need to go to buy your passage, CUC$50, 1 way. From there you and everyone else will be checked, rechecked, checked and checked again. There is a 20-kg weight limit and they are fairly strict about it. You will also have to pass your stuff through an X-ray machine. Bring all food and drink as the Cuban cafeteria will not sustain you (unless you imagine cigarettes will) should there be delays because of mechanical problems on the boat. If you have not organized your return trip, which is highly inadvisable, you need to go to the ferry port on Martí, Nueva Gerona, T46-324436, or **Agencia Sta María**, Oficina de Correo, Calle 53 entre 39 a y 8, Mercado de Abel, in Nueva Gerona, T46-322270, after 1400.

Taxi

Turistaxi, at Hotel El Colony, T46-398282.

❶ Directory

Nueva Gerona *p390, map p389*
Banks Banco de Crédito y Comercio, Calles 39 y 18, Mon-Fri 0800-1500. **Cadeca**, Calles 20 y 39, Mon-Sat 0830-1800, Sun 0830-1300.
Pharmacy Calles 39 y 24, Mon-Fri 0800-2200, Sat 0800-1600. Take plenty of insect repellent, particularly if you are heading for the Ciénaga or out to the Hotel Colony.

Cayo Largo

→ *Colour map 2, B1.*

Cayo Largo is at the eastern end of the Archipiélago de los Canarreos, 114 km east of Isla de la Juventud and 80 km south of the Península de Zapata. It is a long, thin, coral island, 26 km long and no more than 2 km wide. There are beautiful white sandy beaches protected by a reef, all along the southern coast which, together with the crystal clear, warm waters of the Caribbean, make it ideal for tourism. A string of hotels lines the southern tip of the island and these are practically the only employers on the island. The economy depends entirely on tourism. The northern coast is mostly mangrove and swamp, housing hungry mosquitoes as well as numerous birds (pelicans being the most visible) and iguanas. There are few Cubans on the island and the westernized, 'all-inclusive' nature of the place doesn't really recommend it to anyone wanting to see Cuba. On the other hand, if you want a few days on the beach with nothing but watersports to entertain you, then you should enjoy the resort. If you prefer your beach holiday with literally nothing, nudism is tolerated in certain spots. ►► *For listings, see pages 398-400.*

Ins and outs

Getting there and around **Flights** come in from Milan, Frankfurt, Toronto and Montréal and there are daily flights to and from Havana with weekly **excursions** from other tourist centres, such as Varadero, Cienfuegos, Pinar del Río, Trinidad and Santiago de Cuba. Day trips from Havana include transfers and lunch but you have to pay extra for watersports and boat trips; two-day, one-night packages with meals, drinks, transfers and a half-day snorkelling excursion are also available. You can hire a **car**, **scooter** or **bicycle** from your hotel to explore Cayo Largo, or book a place on an organized **tour** to see the island and some of the smaller cays. ►► *See Transport page 400.*

Tourist information There are tourist information bureaux in the hotels which will sell you excursions and tell you whatever you need to know. For online information, www.cayolargodelsur.cu; www.cayolargo.net, with information and a travellers' forum; www.cayolargodelsur.org.

Around the island

The best beach on the island is **Playa Sirena**, which faces west and is spared any wind or currents, which sometimes affect the southern beaches. It is also spared any hotels along its 2 km of white sand and so everyone comes on a day trip (a shuttle bus runs from the hotels). It has a restaurant, bar, shops and watersports. South of Playa Sirena are Playa Paraíso, which has a bar and *palapas*, also on the shuttle route, and Punta Mal Tiempo. The beach on which all the hotels are situated is Playa Lindamar. If there is a problem with the weather and the currents become dangerous, red flags will be flown to forbid swimming. Further east are the deserted beaches of **Playa Blanca**, **Playa Los Cocos**, and, in the northeast, **Playa Tortuga**, the main beaches where turtles lay their eggs. There is a turtle farm, **Criadero de Tortugas Granja de los Quelonios** ① *El Pueblo Turístico (El Pueblito) northwest of the airstrip, open 0900-1800, CUC$1, payable at the Marina – ask here about helping with releasing baby turtles back into the wild*. Tame iguanas can be spotted at the nearby **Cayo Rico** (day trips available from Cayo Largo) and also on the appropriately named **Cayo Iguana**. **Cayos Rosario** and **Avalos**, between Juventud and Largo, have not yet been developed. Catamarans make daily cruises to the neighbouring cays, CUC$75-80.

☉ Cayo Largo listings

For Sleeping and Eating price codes and other relevant information, see Essentials pages 37-43.

☉ Sleeping

All the hotels are all-inclusive and good-value package deals can be arranged from abroad as well as from Havana. Prices are only a guide. Packages can be as low as CUC$400 per person for 4 nights, including air and ground transport from Havana. You may have to wear a coloured plastic bracelet to indicate which package you are on. Prices include 3 meals and free use of all water sports and other activities such as tennis, horseriding and volleyball. Always check what is included in your package. Medical facilities, laundry, post office and fax services are all available. For more information, www.gran-caribe.cu, www.solmeliacuba.com. There is no private accommodation on the island and you will not need any pesos.

L Sol Cayo Largo, T45-248260, www.sol meliacuba.com. 296 cool blue, huge rooms with balconies and all the facilities for an active a beach holiday as you could imagine: diving, snorkelling, swimming pools for adults or children, tennis, volleyball, football, archery, bowls, boules, indoor games, gymnasium; and things to pamper yourself: jacuzzi, turkish bath, massage, beauty parlour. Rooms without ocean view are cheaper. Also several restaurants and bars, currency exchange, tour desk and taxis.

L-AL Eden Village Cayo Largo, T45-48111, www.edenviaggi.it. 112 rooms, package tours include 2 nights in Havana. Large rooms with balconies and 2 double beds. Lots of sports and entertainment and the usual facilities including tennis. Italian enclave, Italian and Cuban staff, Italian restaurant, Italian guests.

L-A Playa Blanca, www.gran-caribe.com. Formerly the Barceló Cayo Largo, was due to reopen under its new name in Nov 2009 with every facility and 306 rooms.

AL Club Cayo Largo, T45-248111, www.gran-caribe.com. Made up of 3 hotels, Villa Soledad, Villa Coral and Isla del Sur (reserved exclusively by an Italian tour operator), with 103 a/c rooms in total, 3 star, only a buffet restaurant here, watersports, taxi service.

AL Sol Pelícano, T45-248333, www.solmelia cuba.com. 307 colourful rooms, bright and cheerful with a huge pool and all the same facilities as the sister hotel. Good for families and scuba divers.

Cayo Largo

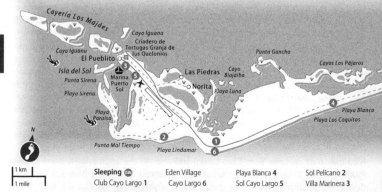

| Sleeping ☉ | Eden Village | Playa Blanca **4** | Sol Pelícano **2** |
| Club Cayo Largo **1** | Cayo Largo **6** | Sol Cayo Largo **5** | Villa Marinera **3** |

AL-A Villa Marinera, T45-248214, www.gran-caribe.com. 13 rooms in log cabins with veranda, 3-star, restaurant, pool, good sunset watching with view over sea. Diving packages are available here as the cabins are by the Marina and Diving Center.

🍴 Eating

There are several buffet restaurants and thatched snack bars (*ranchones*) attached to the hotels. The food is quite good and plentiful. A la carte restaurants have to be booked. You will not find any *paladares* here but there is lots of lobster. Alcoholic drinks are included in the all-inclusive package. Most of the cocktails are rum-based and sweet. Frequently essential ingredients are not available. Beer is often the best bet.

🎭 Entertainment

There is usually evening entertainment in the hotels. In El Pueblo Turístico **El Boulevar** is the main entertainment strip, with a couple of places to eat and drink, a **Plaza de la Artesanía** and a **Casa del Habano** (cigars hop); there are street parties at night.

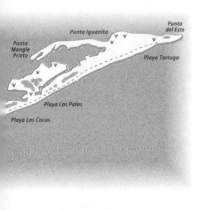

La Movida, Boulevar de Cayo Largo, by the Marina, T45-248305. Open 2000-0200, bar, disco and Centro Recreativo, recorded and traditional music, good meeting place. **Taberna El Pirata**, T45-248213. Bar open 24 hrs, recorded and traditional music.

🏃 Activities and tours

Diving

Good but perhaps not as spectacular as in some other areas of Cuba. There are 2 main diving areas: south of the island, along the reefs Los Ballenatos and on the nearby Cayo Rosario, there are some pretty coral patches rising from a sandy bottom in shallow water, rich in fish, gorgonians and sponges with easy diving, ideal for novice divers; north of the island, in the Golfo de Cazones, there is a deep drop-off with steep walls, ridges and caves where you can find large pelagics and black coral, but there is often a strong current so this is only really suitable for expert divers. Diving, snorkelling and glass bottom boats are all available. Hotels will arrange diving through **International Scuba Diving Center** at the Marina. See www.divingincayolargo.com. See also under **Villa Marinera**, in Sleeping, above.

Fishing

There is deep-sea fishing for marlin and other big fish, with international fishing tournaments held here. Contact **Casa Batida**, in the Marina, see below.

Marina

The **Marina Puerto Sol Cayo Largo del Sur** at El Pueblo Turístico has 50 moorings for visiting yachts, who don't have to buy a tourist card to come here if they are not going on to any-where else in Cuba, because the island is a free port. To clear customs, call the marina on VHF 6, or maritime security (*seguridad marítima*) on VHF 16. T45-248214, commercial.marina@ repgc.cls.tur.cu. There are showers, laundry service, restaurant and bar for yachties.

Sailing

Sailing is popular and there is a bareboat yacht charter fleet, available by the day for longer rental. Other watersports include windsurfing, kayaking, jet skis, catamarans, and banana rides at Playa Sirena.

Tour operators

Cubanacán, Hotel Sol Pelícano, T45-248302, roger@cayolargo.cyt.cu.
Cubatur, Hotel Sol Pelícano, T45-248258.
Havanatur, Hotel Sol Pelícano, T45-248215, freddy@cayolargo.cyt.cu.

⊖ Transport

Air

There are several charters and scheduled international flights to Vilo Acuña International airport (CYO). **Aerogaviota**, T45-248364, flies from Aeropuerto Playa Baracoa, **Havana**, a former military air base. There are also charter flights from **Varadero**.

 Airlines: AeroCaribbean at the airport, T45- 248364. **Cubana**, at the airport, T45-248141.

Car hire

Havanautos and **Transautos** at the Hotel Pelícano. Motorcycles, bicycles, and jeeps are also available. **Transtur**, T45-248245, direccion @transtur.cls.tur.cu. Scooters for hire at CUC$5 for 1 hr or CUC$3-4 per hr if hiring for more than 3 hrs, CUC$20 per day. Weekly rates available. Jeeps for CUC$11 for 1 hr or about CUC$50 for a day. Weekly rates available, including fuel and insurance. If hiring a vehicle or scooter, note that, other than the main road, trails are soft sand and that you can only go so far to the east before you have to walk. Taxi service at CUC$1, plus CUC$1 per km.

❶ Directory

Banks Bandec in the Pueblo Turístico, T45-248255, open 0800-1700. The hotels have currency exchange desks if you need them. Euros are accepted everywhere. You will not need Cuban pesos. **Medical services** Clínica Servisalud, Pueblo Turístico, T45-248238, clinica@cayolargo.cls. tur.cu. 24-hr emergency service, X-rays, pharmacy, home visits, massages.

Contents

Footprint features

Background

History

Pre-Columbian society in Cuba

The recorded history of the Caribbean islands begins with the arrival of Christopher Columbus' fleet in 1492. Knowledge of the native peoples who inhabited Cuba before and at the time of his arrival is largely derived from the accounts of contemporary Spanish writers and from archaeological examinations as there is no evidence of indigenous written records.

The Amerindians encountered by Columbus in Cuba and the other Greater Antilles had no overall tribal name but organized themselves in a series of villages or local chiefdoms, each of which had its own tribal name. The name now used, 'Arawak', was not in use then. The term was used by the Amerindians of the Guianas, a group who had spread into Trinidad, but their territory was not explored until nearly another century later. The use of the generic term 'Arawak' to describe the Amerindians Columbus encountered arose because of linguistic similarities with the Arawaks of the mainland. It is therefore surmised that migration took place many centuries before Columbus' arrival, but that the two groups were not in contact at that time. The time of the latest migration from the mainland, and consequently, the existence of the island Arawaks, is in dispute, with some academics tracing it to about the time of Christ (the arrival of the Saladoids) and others to AD 1000 (the Ostionoids).

The inhabitants of Cuba and the other Greater Antilles were generally referred to as Taínos, but there were many sub-groupings. The earliest known inhabitants of the region, the Siboneys, migrated from Florida (some say Mexico) and spread throughout the Bahamas and the major islands. Most archaeological evidence of their settlements has been found near the shore, along bays or streams, where they lived in small groups. The largest discovered settlement has been one of 100 inhabitants in Cuba. They were hunters and gatherers, living on fish and other seafood, small rodents, iguanas, snakes and birds. They gathered roots and wild fruits, such as guava, guanabana and mamey, but did not cultivate plants. They worked with primitive tools made out of stone, shell, bone or wood, for hammering, chipping or scraping, but had no knowledge of pottery. The Siboneys were eventually absorbed by the advance of the Arawaks migrating from the south, who had made more technological advances in agriculture, arts and crafts.

The people now known as Arawaks migrated from the Guianas to Trinidad and on through the island arc to Cuba. Their population expanded because of the natural fertility of the islands and the abundance of fruit and seafood, helped by their agricultural skills in cultivating and improving wild plants and their excellent boat-building and fishing techniques. They were healthy, tall, good looking and lived to a ripe old age. It is estimated that up to eight million may have lived on the island of Hispaniola alone, but there was always plenty of food for all.

Their society was essentially communal and organized around families. The smaller islands were particularly egalitarian, but in the larger ones, where village communities of extended families numbered up to 500 people, there was an incipient class structure. Typically, each village had a headman, called a *cacique*, whose duty it was to represent the village when dealing with other tribes, to settle family disputes and organize defence. However, he had no powers of coercion and was often little more than a nominal head. The position was largely hereditary, with the eldest son of the eldest sister having rights

Cuba fact file

Population 11,236,099 (2008).
Density 102.3 per sq km (2008).
Birth rate Per 1000 population 11.1 (2008). Urban 75.3% (2008). Male 50.1% (2008).
Ethnic composition White 65%, mixed 24%, black 10%, other 1% (2002).
Health Infant mortality 4.7 per 1000 live births (2008). 74,552 doctors,
1 per 151 inhabitants. 4.7 hospital beds per 1000 inhabitants (2008).
Life expectancy Male 76 years, female 80 years (2007).
Language Spanish.
Literacy 99.8% (2002).
National flower Mariposa, butterfly flower, a jasmine, symbol of purity and
rebellion in the Wars of Independence.
National bird Tocororo, Cuban trogon, with the red, white and blue colours
of the Cuban flag.
National tree Palma real, Royal palm, typical of the Cuban landscape.
Economy Gross domestic product (current prices) US$52.9 bn (2007, UN),
per capita US$4641 (2007, UN). Unemployment rate 1.6% (2008).
Average monthly salary 415 pesos cubanos (2008).
Tourism 2,348,000 visitors (2008). Tourism receipts CUC$2359 mn (2008).
Sources: ONE, Cuba; United Nations.

of succession, but women could and did become *caciques*. In the larger communities, there was some delegation of responsibility to the senior men, but economic activities were usually organized along family lines, and their power was limited.

The division of labour was usually based on age and sex. The men would clear and prepare the land for agriculture and be responsible for defence of the village, while women cultivated the crops and were the major food producers, also making items such as mats, baskets, bowls and fishing nets. Women were in charge of raising the children, especially the girls, while the men taught the boys traditional customs, skills and rites.

The Taínos hunted for some of their food, but fishing was more important and most of their settlements were close to the sea. Fish and shellfish were their main sources of protein and they had many different ways of catching them – from hands, baskets or nets to poisoning, shooting or line fishing. Cassava was a staple food, which they had successfully learned to leach of its poisonous juice. They also grew yams, maize, cotton, arrowroot, peanuts, beans, cacao and spices, rotating their crops to prevent soil erosion.

Cotton was used to make clothing and hammocks (never before seen by Europeans), while the calabash tree was used to make ropes and cords, baskets and roofing. Plants were used for medicinal and spiritual purposes, and cosmetics such as face and body paint. Also important, both to the Arawaks and later to the Europeans, was the cultivation of tobacco, as a drug and as a means of exchange. It is still of major economic importance in Cuba today.

They had no writing, no beasts of burden, no wheeled vehicles and no hard metals, although they did have some alluvial gold for personal ornament. The abundance of food allowed them time to develop their arts and crafts and they were skilled in woodwork and pottery. They had polished stone tools, but also carved shell implements for manioc preparation or as fish hooks. Coral manioc graters have also been found. Their boatbuilding techniques were noted by Columbus, who marvelled at their canoes of up to 75 ft in length, carrying up to 50 people, made of a single tree trunk in one piece. It took two months to fell a tree by gradually burning and chipping it down, and many more to make the canoe.

The Arawaks had three main deities, evidence of which have been found in stone and conch carvings in many of the Lesser Antilles as well as the well-populated Greater Antilles, although their relative importance varied according to the island. The principal male god was Yocahú, *yoca* being the word for cassava and *hú* meaning 'giver of'. It is believed that the Amerindians associated this deity's power to provide cassava with the mystery of the volcanoes, for all the carvings – the earliest out of shells and the later ones of stone – are conical. The Yocahú cult was wiped out by the Spaniards, but it is thought to have existed from about AD 200.

The main female deity was a fertility goddess, often referred to as Atabeyra, but she is thought to have had several names relating to her other roles as goddess of the moon, mother of the sea, the tides and the springs, and the goddess of childbirth. In carvings she is usually depicted as a squatting figure with her hands up to her chin, sometimes in the act of giving birth.

A third deity is a dog god, named Opiyel-Guaobiran, meaning 'the dog deity who takes care of the souls of the immediately deceased and is the son of the spirit of darkness'. Again, carvings of a dog's head or whole body have been found of shell or stone, which were often used to induce narcotic trances. Many of the carvings have holes and Y-shaped passages which would have been put to the nose to snuff narcotics and induce a religious trance in the shaman or priest, who could then ascertain the status of a departed soul for a recently bereaved relative.

One custom which aroused interest in the Spaniards was the ball game, not only for the sport and its ceremonial features, but because the ball was made of rubber and bounced, a phenomenon that had not previously been seen in Europe. Roman Catholicism soon eradicated the game, but archaeological remains have been found in several islands, notably in Puerto Rico, but also in Hispaniola. Excavations in the Greater Antilles have revealed earth embankments and rows of elongated upright stones surrounding plazas or courts, pavements and stone balls. These are called *bateyes, juegos de indios, juegos de bola, cercados* or *corrales de indios*. Batey was the aboriginal name for the ball game, the rubber ball itself and also the court where it was played. The word is still used to designate the cleared area in front of houses in the country.

The ball game had religious and ceremonial significance but it was a sport and bets and wagers were important. It was played by two teams of up to 20 or 30 players, who had to keep the ball in the air by means of their hips, shoulders, heads, elbows and other parts of their body, but never with their hands. The aim was to bounce the ball in this manner to the opposing team until it hit the ground. Men and women played, but not usually in mixed sex games. Great athleticism was required and it is clear that the players practised hard to perfect their skill, several, smaller practice courts having been built in larger settlements. The game was sometimes played before the village made an important decision, and the prize could be a sacrificial victim, usually a prisoner, granted to the victor.

The Amerindians in Cuba were unable to resist the Spanish invasion and were soon wiped out by disease, cruelty and murder, with only a few communities surviving in remote areas such as in the mountains behind Baracoa. The Spanish exacted tribute and forced labour while allowing their herds of cattle and pigs to destroy the Amerindians' unfenced fields and clearings. Transportation to the mines resulted in shifts in the native population which could not be fed from the surrounding areas and starvation became common. The

500 years since Columbus' arrival have served to obliterate practically all the evidence of the indigenous civilization in Cuba. Nevertheless, the legacy of the Taínos remains in names of places (Havana, Baracoa, Bayamo, Camagüey), rivers (Toa, Duaba, Yumurí, Caonao), domestic artefacts (*bohío* – farmer's cottage, *hamaca* – hammock, *cohiba* – tobacco) and in some areas farmers still use the same tools and plant the same crops (beans, yucca, maize) according to the four lunar phases as their forefathers did. Archaeologists and anthropologists have made significant discoveries around the country, but particularly around Baracoa, where a Taíno museum has recently been opened in a cave.

Spanish conquest

Cuba was visited by Cristóbal Colón (Christopher Columbus) during his first voyage to find a westerly route to the Orient on 27 October 1492, and he made another brief stop two years later on his way from Hispaniola to Jamaica. Columbus did not realize it was an island when he landed; he had heard from the inhabitants of the Bahamas, where he first made landfall, that there were larger islands to the south where there was gold, which he hoped was Japan. He arrived on the north coast of 'Colba', but found little gold. He did, however, note the Amerindians' practice of puffing at a large, burning roll of leaves, which they called *tobacos* or *cohiba*.

The Arawaks told Columbus of the more aggressive Carib tribe and he headed off towards the eastern islands to find them, discovering *La Isla Española*, or Hispaniola, which occupied the Spanish for the next few years with attempted settlements, feuds, rebellions and other troubles. On future expeditions, more settlers were brought from Spain to Hispaniola; adventurers who wanted to get rich quick and return to Spain. Although most died of tropical diseases, enough survived to impart their own European viruses on the Amerindians, decimating the local population. The Spaniards also demanded a constant supply of Amerindian labour which they were ill equipped to provide, having previously lived in a subsistence barter economy with no experience of regular work. The Spaniards' cruel treatment of the native inhabitants led to many of them losing the will to live. On the other hand, the need for a steady supply of labour pushed the Spanish into further exploration of the Indies. Slavers went from one island to another in search of manpower. Puerto Rico was conquered in 1508, Jamaica in 1509 and Cuba in 1511. From there they moved on to the mainland to trade in slaves, gold and other commodities.

Cuba was first circumnavigated by Sebastián de Ocampo in 1508, but it was **Diego Velázquez** who conquered it in 1511 and founded several towns, called *villas*, including Havana. From Cuba, Velázquez sent out two expeditions in 1517-1518 to investigate the Yucatán and the Gulf of Mexico. On the basis of their information he petitioned the Spanish Crown for permission to set up a base there prior to conquest and settlement. However, before the authorization came through from Spain, his commander, Hernán Cortés, set off without permission with 600 men, 16 horses, 14 cannon and 13 muskets to conquer Mexico, leaving Velázquez in the lurch.

The first African slaves were imported to Cuba in 1526. Sugar was introduced soon after but was not important until the last decade of the 16th century. When the British took Jamaica in 1655 a number of Spanish settlers fled to Cuba, already famous for its cigars. Tobacco was then made a strict monopoly of Spain in 1717 and a coffee plant was introduced in 1748. The British, under Lord Albemarle and Admiral Pocock, captured Havana and held the island from 1762-1763, but it was returned to Spain in exchange for Florida. Up until this point, the colony had been important largely as a refuelling depot for

Spanish ships crossing the Atlantic, but the British occupation and the temporary lifting of Spanish restrictions showed the local landowning class the economic potential of trading their commodities with England and North America.

Independence movement

Towards the end of the 18th century, Cuba began its transformation into a slave plantation society. After the French Revolution, there were slave revolts in the French colony of Haiti, which became the first independent black republic. French sugar planters fled what had been the most profitable colony in the Caribbean and settled across the water in Cuba, bringing their expertise with them. Cuba soon became a major sugar exporter and, after 1793, slaves were imported in huge numbers to work the plantations. The island was under absolute military control with a colonial elite that made its money principally from sugar. The tobacco monopoly was abolished in 1816 and Cuba was given the right to trade with the world in 1818. Independence elsewhere in the Spanish Empire bred ambitions, however, and a strong movement for independence was quelled by Spain in 1823. By this time the blacks outnumbered the whites in the island; there were several slave rebellions and little by little the Creoles (or Spaniards born in Cuba) made common cause with them. On the other hand, there was also a movement for annexation by the USA, Cuba's major trading partner, supported by many slave owners who had a common interest with the southern states in the American Civil War. The defeat of the South and the abolition of slavery in the USA ended support for annexation.

By the 1860s Cuba was producing about a third of the world's sugar and was heavily dependent on African slaves to do so, supplemented by indentured Chinese labourers in the 1850s and 1860s. Although Spain signed treaties under British pressure to outlaw the Atlantic slave trade in 1817 and 1835, they were completely ignored by the colony and an estimated 600,000 African slaves were imported by 1867. Independence from Spain became a burning issue in Cuba as Spain remained intransigent and refused to consider political reforms which would give the colony more autonomy within the empire.

On 10 October 1868, a Creole landowner, **Carlos Manuel de Céspedes**, issued the *Grito de Yara*, a proclamation of independence and a call to arms, while simultaneously freeing his slaves. The first war of independence was a 10-year rebellion against Spain in the eastern part of the island between 1868 and 1878, but it gained little save a modest move towards the abolition of slavery. In 1870, the **Moret Law** freed all children of slaves born after 1868 and any slave over 60, but complete abolition was not achieved until 1886. In 1878, the **Convention of Zanjón** brought the civil war to an end. This enabled Cubans to elect representatives to the Spanish *cortes* (parliament) in 1879, but did not suppress the desire for independence. Many national heroes were created during this period who have become revolutionary icons in the struggle against domination by a foreign power. Men such as de Céspedes, Máximo Gómez and the mulatto General Antonio Maceo have inspired generations of Cuban patriots and are still revered with statues and street names in nearly every town and city on the island. One consequence of the war was the destruction of much agricultural land and the ruin of many sugar planters. US interests began to take over the sugar plantations and the sugar mills and, as sugar beet became more important in Europe, so Cuba became more dependent on the market for its main crop in the USA.

From 1895 to 1898, rebellion flared up again in the second war of independence under the young poet and revolutionary, **José Martí**, who had organized the movement from exile in the USA, together with the old guard of Antonio Maceo and

Our Man in Havana

Graham Greene's first visit to Cuba was in 1957 to research his book *Our Man in Havana*. He was originally going to set it in Lisbon, but decided on a more exotic location; he planned to sell the film rights to the novel before it was even written. He immediately took a liking to the unlimited decadence Havana had to offer, and spent much of his time at the Shanghai Theatre, a club which featured live sex shows. Greene's former connections with the British SIS (Secret Intelligence Service) gave him access to political society. He based some of the characters in 'Our Man' on Batista's soldiers: Captain Segura, with his cigarette case made of human skin, was based on the real-life Capitán Ventura. The plot of the novel involves a vacuum cleaner salesman being mistaken for a secret agent, who for fear of being discovered as a fraud, tries to carry out the orders given to him by providing diagrams of vacuum cleaner parts, pretending they are in fact the plans for an arsenal of nuclear weapons.

Greene's training as a secret agent allowed him to infiltrate all levels of political life: he made contact with Castro's rebel forces in the Sierra, offering them any help they needed. He was asked to smuggle a suitcase of warm clothes, to help them survive the freezing night-time temperatures of the Sierra Maestra, through customs on a Havana–Santiago flight.

In 1959, when Greene arrived for the second time in Havana to assist director Carol Reed in the filming of his novel, the Revolution had already triumphed. Greene's small act of support in 1957 had not been forgotten, and Castro gave his personal seal of approval to the film, although he felt it didn't capture the full extent of Batista's evil.

Máximo Gómez. José Martí led the invasion but was killed in an ambush in May 1895 when the war had barely begun, and Maceo was killed in 1896. Despite fierce fighting throughout the island, neither the Nationalists nor the Spanish could gain the upper hand. However, the USA was now concerned for its investments in Cuba and was considering its strategic interests within the region. When the US battleship *Maine* exploded in Havana harbour on 15 February 1898, killing 260 crew, this was made a pretext for declaring war on Spain. Spain offered the independence fighters a truce but they chose instead to help the USA to defeat the colonial power. American forces (which included Colonel Theodore Roosevelt) were landed, a squadron blockaded Havana and defeated the Spanish fleet at Santiago de Cuba. In December 1898 peace was signed and US forces occupied the island. The Nationalists had gained independence from Spain but found themselves under **US military occupation** for four years and then with only limited independence granted to them by the USA.

During the occupation, the USA put the Cuban administration and economy back to rights. It eliminated a famine, introduced improved sanitation and helped to eradicate yellow fever with the scientific discoveries of a Cuban doctor, Carlos J Finlay. State education was introduced, the judiciary was reformed and an electoral system for local and national government was introduced. In 1901, an elected assembly approved a liberal constitution which separated Church and state and guaranteed universal adult male suffrage.

The **Republic of Cuba** was proclaimed in 1902 and the Government was handed over to its first president, **Tomás Estrada Palma**, the elected candidate of José Martí's Cuban

Revolutionary Party, on 20 May. However, the new Republic was constrained by the **Platt Amendment** to the constitution, passed by the US Congress, which clearly made it a protectorate of the USA. The USA retained naval bases at Río Hondo and Guantánamo Bay and reserved the right of intervention in Cuban domestic affairs, but granted the island a handsome import preference for its sugar. The USA intervened several times to settle quarrels by rival political factions but, to quell growing unrest and a reassertion of pro-independence and revolutionary forces, repealed the Platt Amendment in 1934. The USA formally relinquished the right to intervene but retained its naval base at Guantánamo. (The lease on Guantánamo Bay expires in 2033.) Resentment against the USA for its political and economic dominance of the island lingered and was a powerful stimulus for the Nationalist Revolution of the 1950s.

Dictatorship

Even after the repeal of the Platt Amendment, the USA dominated the Cuban economy. Around two thirds of sugar exports went to the USA under a quota system at prices set by Washington; two thirds of Cuba's imports came from the USA; foreign capital investment was largely from the USA and Cuba was effectively a client state. Yet, despite the money being made out of Cuba, its people suffered from grinding rural poverty, high unemployment, illiteracy and inadequate healthcare. The good life, as enjoyed by the socialites in the casinos and bars of Havana, highlighted the social inequalities in the country and politics was a mixture of authoritarian rule and corrupt democracy.

From 1924 to 1933 the 'strong man' **Gerardo Machado** ruled Cuba. He was elected in 1924 on a wave of popularity and set about diversifying the economy and investing in public works projects. However, a drastic fall in sugar prices in the late 1920s led to strikes and protests which he forcefully repressed. In 1928 he 'persuaded' Congress to grant him a second term of office, which was greeted with protests and violence from students, the middle classes and labour unions. Widespread Nationalist popular rebellion throughout Machado's dictatorship was harshly repressed by the police force. The USA was reluctant to intervene again, but tried to negotiate a deal with its ambassador. The Nationalists called a general strike in protest at US interference and Machado finally went into exile. The violence did not abate, however, and there were more strikes, mob attacks and occupations of factories, which the new government was unable to quell. In September 1933, a revolt of non-commissioned officers including **Fulgencio Batista**, then a sergeant, deposed the government and installed a five-member committee chosen by the student movement, the *Directorio Estudiantil*. They chose as president a professor, **Dr Ramón Grau San Martín**, but he only lasted four months before Batista staged a coup. Batista then held power through presidential puppets until he was elected president himself in 1940.

Batista's first period in power, 1933-1944, was characterized by Nationalist and populist policies, set against corruption and political violence. Batista himself was a mulatto from a poor background who had pulled himself up through the ranks of the military and retained the support of the armed forces. He was also supported by US and Cuban business interests while gaining control of the trade unions by passing social welfare legislation, building low cost housing and creating jobs with public works projects. The students and radical Nationalists remained opposed to him, however, and terrorism continued. In 1940, a new Constitution was passed by a constituent assembly dominated by Batista, which included universal suffrage and benefits for workers such as a minimum wage, pensions, social insurance and an eight-hour day.

Fidel Castro Ruz

Fidel Castro spent more than half his life as president, *jefe* (chief) and supreme *comandante* of Cuba. He passed from being the world's youngest ruler in 1959 to the longest serving head of state. He outstayed eight US presidents and survived hundreds of assassination attempts before handing power to his brother Raúl in 2006 at the age of 80. That year he had to undergo major abdominal surgery, the nature of which was kept a secret. The handover of power was originally temporary, but it became official and permanent in 2008. Although he no longer appears in public, he is actively involved in political life in Cuba, writing opinion pieces on world affairs for the *Granma* newspaper and meeting visiting dignitaries. His longest speech went on for seven hours, but Cubans were regularly called upon to listen to his rhetoric for four or five hours. Dramatic pauses gradually replaced the fire and arm waving of his youth and in many ways he mellowed with maturity. In 1996 he was received by the Pope in an historic photo opportunity which made him look almost sprightly in comparison with his host. He has always been instantly recognizable for his beard, now straggly and grey, and his military fatigues, although these were later occasionally replaced when abroad by a sober suit and, after his surgery, by a tracksuit.

In 1944, Batista lost the elections to the candidate of the radical Nationalists: Dr Ramón Grau San Martín, of the Partido Revolucionario Cubana-Auténtico, who held office from 1944-1948. His presidential term benefited from high sugar prices following the Second World War, which allowed corruption and political violence to continue unabated. Grau was followed into the presidency by his protégé, **Carlos Prío Socarrás**, 1948-1952, a term which was even more corrupt and depraved, until Batista, by then a self-promoted general, staged a military coup in 1952. Constitutional and democratic government was at an end. His harshly repressive dictatorship was brought to a close by **Fidel Castro** in January 1959, after an extraordinary and heroic three-year campaign, mostly in the Sierra Maestra, with a guerrilla force reduced at one point to 12 men.

Revolution

The dictator, Batista, was opposed by many, but none more effective than the young lawyer, Fidel Castro, the son of immigrants from Galicia and born in Cuba in 1926. He saw José Martí as his role model and aimed to continue the Revolution Martí had started in 1895, following his ideals. In 1953, the 100th anniversary of José Martí's birth, Castro and a committed band of about 160 revolutionaries attacked the Moncada barracks in Santiago de Cuba on 26 July. The attack failed and although Castro and his brother Raúl escaped, they were later captured and put on trial. Fidel used the occasion to make an impassioned speech, denouncing corruption in the ruling class and the need for political freedom and economic independence. The speech has gone down in history for its final phrase, "History will absolve me", and a revised version, smuggled out of prison on the Isle of Pines, became the basis of a reform programme. In 1955, the Castros were given an amnesty and went to Mexico. There Fidel continued to work on his essentially Nationalist revolutionary programme, called the **26 July Movement**, which called for radical social and economic reforms and a return to the democracy of Cuba's 1940 constitution. He met another man of ideas, an Argentine doctor called Ernesto Guevara (see box, page 221), who sailed with him and his brother Raúl and a band of 82 like-minded revolutionaries, back to Cuba on 2 December 1956. Their campaign began in the Sierra Maestra in the east of Cuba and after years of fierce fighting Batista fled to the Dominican Republic on 1 January 1959. Fidel Castro, to universal popular acclaim, entered Havana and assumed control of the island.

Communism and the 1960s

From 1960 onwards, in the face of increasing hostility from the USA, Castro led Cuba into socialism and then Communism. Officials of the Batista regime were put on trial in 'people's courts' and executed. The promised new elections were not held. The judiciary lost its independence when Castro assumed the right to appoint judges. The free press was closed or taken over. Trade unions lost their independence and became part of government. The University of Havana, a former focus of dissent, and professional associations, all lost their autonomy. The democratic constitution of 1940 was never reinstated. In 1960, the sugar centrales, the oil refineries and the foreign banks were nationalized, all US property was expropriated and the Central Planning Board (*Juceplan*) was established. The professional and property-owning middle classes began a steady exodus which drained the country of much of its skilled workers.

CIA-backed mercenaries and Cuban émigrés kept up a relentless barrage of attacks, but failed to achieve their objective. In March a French ship carrying arms to Cuba was sabotaged. At the burial of the victims, Castro first used the slogan, 'Patria o Muerte'. Diplomatic relations were re-established with the USSR, North Korea and Vietnam, while China and Cuba signed mutual benefit treaties. Meanwhile, the USA cancelled Cuba's sugar quota and put an embargo on all imports to Cuba.

At the beginning of 1961, the USA severed diplomatic relations with Cuba and encouraged Latin American countries to do likewise. This was the year of the **Bay of Pigs** invasion, a fiasco which was to harden Castro's political persuasion. On 14 April 1961, some 1400 Cuban émigrés, trained by the CIA in Miami and Guatemala, set off from Nicaragua to invade Cuba with the US Navy as escort. On 15 April, planes from Nicaragua bombed several Cuban airfields in an attempt to wipe out the air force. Seven Cuban airmen were killed in the raid, and at their funeral the next day, Fidel Castro addressed a mass rally in Havana and declared Cuba to be socialist. On 17 April the invasion flotilla landed at Playa Girón and Playa Larga in the Bahía de Cochinos (Bay of Pigs), but the men were stranded on the beaches when the Cuban air force attacked their supply ships. Two hundred were killed and the rest surrendered within three days. The invaders' aircraft also took a beating when 11 were shot down, including all the B-26 bombers flown from Nicaragua. A total of 1197 men were captured and eventually returned to the USA in exchange for US$53 million in food and medicine. In his May Day speech, Fidel Castro, who had personally taken control of the defence of Cuba, confirmed that the Cuban Revolution was socialist.

The US reaction was to isolate Cuba, with a full trade embargo and heavy pressure on other American countries to sever diplomatic relations. Cuba was expelled from the Organization of American States (OAS) and the OAS imposed economic sanctions. Crucially, however, across the border in both Canada and Mexico, governments refused to toe the line and maintained relations (a policy which has now borne fruit for many Canadian and Mexican companies at the expense of US businesses). Nevertheless, in 1961-1962, the trade embargo hit hard, shortages soon appeared and by March 1962 rationing had to be imposed.

An exploding cigar and other plots

The number of CIA-backed attempts on Castro's life is legendary, the most extraordinary stories so far published being about trying to kill him with an exploding cigar, or putting a special powder in his shoes to make his beard fall out. But, failing to assassinate or maim him, the US administration in the 1960s put an extraordinary amount of effort into trying to discredit him. Many covert plans were put forward to Operation Mongoose, an anti-Castro destabilization project at the Pentagon. One plan, codenamed Operation Dirty Trick, was to blame Castro if anything went wrong with US space flights, specifically John Glenn's flight into orbit in 1962. The Pentagon was to provide 'irrevocable proof' that if anything happened it was the fault of Cuban Communists and their electronic interference. Another idea was to sabotage a US plane and claim that a Cuban aircraft had shot down a civilian airliner. Yet another was to sink a US warship and blame that on Castro.

None of these came to anything, but sabotage did take place. Cuban émigré groups received help from a special CIA budget to destroy Castro's Cuba. In 1960, a French ship carrying a cargo of armaments from Belgium was blown up in Havana harbour, killing 81 people and wounding hundreds of others. Pressure was put on British companies by the USA to stop them trading with Cuba. Having 'discouraged' British ships from transporting a cargo of British Leyland buses and spare parts, but having failed to get the deal cancelled, it was therefore more than coincidental that an East German ship carrying the equipment was rammed in the Thames. Cuba has claimed other sabotage, such as supplying asymmetrical ball bearings to damage machinery, and chemical additives in lubricants for engines to make them wear out quickly. As classified documents of the Kennedy administration are released, more and more bugs keep crawling out of the woodwork.

At this stage, Cuba became entangled in the rivalry between the two superpowers: the USA and the USSR. In April 1962, Russian President **Kruschev** decided to send medium-range missiles to Cuba, which would be capable of striking anywhere in the USA, even though all Castro wanted were short-range missiles he could point at Miami to deter invasion. In October, President JF Kennedy ordered Soviet ships heading for Cuba to be stopped and searched for missiles in international waters. This episode, which became known as the **Cuban Missile Crisis**, brought the world to the brink of nuclear war, defused only by secret negotiations between JFK and Kruschev. Kennedy demanded the withdrawal of Soviet troops and arms from Cuba and imposed a naval blockade. Without consulting Castro and without his knowledge, Kruschev eventually agreed to have the missiles dismantled and withdrawn on condition that the West would guarantee a policy of non-aggression towards Cuba. In November, Kennedy suspended the naval blockade but reiterated US support for political and economic aggression towards Cuba. In the following year he made a speech in Costa Rica, in which he stated, "We will build a wall around Cuba", and Central American countries agreed to isolate the island.

Castro's decision to adopt Marxism-Leninism as the official ideology of the Revolution was followed by the fusion of the 26 July Movement with the Communist Party, at that time known as the Popular Socialist Party (PSP). The PSP had opposed the Revolution until the final stages of the overthrow of the Batista dictatorship and it took several years and two purges before the 'old' Communists were expunged and the new Communist Party was united behind the new official ideology. In October 1965, a restructured **Cuban Communist Party** (PCC) was founded and Cuba has been Communist ever since.

Economic policy during the 1960s was largely unsuccessful in achieving its aims. After a spell as head of the Central Bank, Che Guevara was appointed Minister of Industry, a key position given that the government wanted to industrialize rapidly to reduce dependence on sugar. However, the crash programme, with help from the USSR, was a failure and had to be abandoned. Sugar was king again but productivity plummeted and there were poor harvests in 1963-1964. The whole nation was called upon to achieve a target of 10 million tonnes of sugar by 1970 and everyone spent time in the fields helping towards this goal. It was never reached and never has been, but the effort revealed distortions in the Cuban economy which in effect increased the island's dependence on the Soviet Union. Castro jumped out of the frying pan into the fire: he escaped domination by the USA only to replace it with another superpower.

Social policy

Rationing is still in place and there are still shortages of consumer goods. However, the Revolution's social policies have largely been successful and it is principally these achievements that have ensured the people's support of Castro and kept him and/or his brother Raúl in power. Education, housing and health services have been greatly improved and the social inequalities of the 1940s and 1950s have been wiped out. Equality of the sexes and races has also been promoted, a major change in what was a *machista*, racially prejudiced society. Infant mortality is now on a par with many industrialized countries. In 1961 300,000 Cubans volunteered to go out into the countryside, as part of a literacy campaign, to teach their comrades how to read and write. On 22 December of the same year, Cuba was declared free of illiteracy. Considerable emphasis is now placed on combining productive agricultural work with study: there are over 400 schools and colleges in rural areas where the students divide their time between the fields and the classroom. Education is compulsory up to the age of 17, and free, while access to higher education has been granted to all.

1970s Soviet domination

During the second decade of the Revolution, Cuba became firmly entrenched as a member of the Soviet bloc, joining COMECON in 1972. Technicians came from Eastern Europe and Cubans were trained in the USSR. The Communist Party grew in strength and size and permeated all walks of life, influencing every aspect of Cubans' day to day living, while putting more central controls on education and culture. The Revolution was institutionalized along Soviet lines and the Party gained control of the bureaucracy, the judiciary and the local and national assemblies. Communist planners controlled the economy and workers were organized into government-controlled trade unions. A new socialist constitution was adopted in 1976. In 1971-1975 the economy grew by about 16% a year, but fell back after then and never recovered such spectacular growth rates again.

Cuba's foreign policy during this period changed from actively fomenting socialist revolutions abroad (such as Guevara's forays into the Congo and Bolivia in the 1960s) to supporting other left wing or third world countries with combat troops and technical advisers. Some 20,000 Cubans helped the Angolan Marxist government to defeat a South African backed guerrilla insurgency and 15,000 went to Ethiopia in the war against

Somalia and then the separatist rebellion in Eritrea. Cuban advisers and medical workers went to Nicaragua after the Sandinista overthrow of the Somoza dictatorship in 1979; advisers and workers went to help the left wing Manley government in Jamaica and to the Marxist government in Grenada (until expelled by the US Marines in 1983). In September 1979, Castro hosted a summit conference of the non-aligned nations in Havana, a high point in his foreign policy initiatives.

The decade also marked a period of intellectual debate at home and abroad about the path the Revolution was taking. In 1971, the poet **Herberto Padilla** was arrested for cultural deviation and forced to confess his crimes against the Revolution. His treatment and cultural censorship brought accusations of Stalinization of cultural life. The Padilla affair split the Hispanic intellectual world, with writers such as Octavio Paz and Carlos Fuentes of Mexico, Mario Vargas Llosa of Peru and Juan Goytisolo of Spain renouncing their support for the Revolution, while Gabriel García Márquez of Colombia and Julio Cortázar of Argentina reaffirmed their support. Free expression was stifled and during this time the best Cuban art and literature was produced by émigrés. The debate widened to include civil liberties and political rights, and official secrecy made it difficult to gauge accurately the persecution of political prisoners, religious believers, intellectual opponents and homosexuals.

1980s dissatisfaction and flight

By the 1980s, the heavy dependence on sugar and the USSR, coupled with the trade embargo, meant that the expected improvements in living standards, 20 years after the Revolution, were not being delivered as fast as hoped and the people were tiring of being asked for ever more sacrifices for the good of the nation. In 1980, the compound of the Peruvian embassy was overrun by 11,000 people seeking political asylum. Castro's answer to the dissidents was to let them go and he opened the port of **Mariel** for a mass departure by sea. He also opened the prisons to allow prisoners, both political and criminal, to head for the USA in anything they could find that would float. It was estimated that some 125,000 embarked for Miami, amid publicity that it was the criminals, delinquents, homosexuals and mental patients who were fleeing Cuba. At the same time huge demonstrations were organized in Havana in support of the Revolution. Some relaxation in controls was allowed, however, with 'free markets' opening alongside the official ration system.

This was the decade of the Latin American debt crisis and Cuba was unable to escape the pressures brought to bear on its neighbours. Development projects in the 1970s had been financed with loans from western banks, in addition to the aid it was already receiving from the USSR. When interest rates went up in 1982, Cuba was forced to renegotiate its US$3.5 billion debt to commercial banks and, in 1986, its debt to the USSR. The need to restrain budget spending and keep a tight control over public finances brought more austerity. The private markets were stopped in 1986 and the people were once more asked for voluntary labour to raise productivity and achieve economic growth. Excess manpower, or unemployment, was eased by sending thousands of Cubans abroad as internationalists to help other developing countries, whether as combat troops or technicians.

The **collapse of the Communist system** in the Eastern European countries in the late 1980s, followed by the demise of the USSR, very nearly brought the end of Castro's Cuba as well. Emigrés in Miami started counting the days until they would re-enter the homeland and Castro's position looked extremely precarious. There were signs that a power struggle was taking place at the top of the Communist Party. In 1989, General Arnaldo Ochoa, a hero of the Angolan campaign, was charged with drug trafficking and corruption. He was publicly tried and executed along with several other military officers allegedly involved. Castro took the opportunity to pledge to fight against corruption and privilege and deepen the process of rectification begun in 1986.

The Soviet connection

Before the collapse of the Soviet system, aid to Cuba from the USSR was traditionally estimated at about 25% of GNP. Cuba's debt with the USSR was a secret: estimates ranged from US$8.5 billion to US$34 billion. Apart from military aid, economic assistance took two forms: balance of payments support (about 85%), under which sugar and nickel exports were priced in excess of world levels and oil imports were indexed against world prices for the previous five years, and assistance for development projects. About 13 million tonnes of oil were supplied a year by the USSR, allowing three million to be re-exported, providing a valuable source of foreign earnings. By the late 1980s up to 90% of Cuba's foreign trade was with centrally planned economies.

US relations

Before the Revolution of 1959, the USA had investments in Cuba worth about US$1 billion, covering nearly every activity from agriculture and mining to oil installations. Today all American businesses in Cuba, including banks, have been nationalized; the USA has cut off all imports from Cuba, placed an embargo on exports to Cuba, and broken off diplomatic relations. Promising moves to improve relations with the USA were given impetus in 1988 by the termination of Cuban military activities in Angola under agreement with the USA and South Africa. However, developments in Eastern Europe and the former USSR in 1989-1990 revealed the vulnerability of the economy (see Economy, page 419) and provoked Castro to defend the Cuban system of government; the lack of political change delayed any further rapprochement with the USA. Prior to the 1992 US presidential elections, President Bush approved the Cuban Democracy Act (Torricelli Bill), which strengthened the trade embargo by forbidding US subsidiaries from trading with Cuba. Many countries, including EC members and Canada, said they would not allow the US bill to affect their trade with Cuba and the UN General Assembly voted in November in favour of a resolution calling for an end to the embargo. The defeat of George Bush by Bill Clinton did not, however, signal a change in US attitudes, in large part because of the support given to the Democrat's campaign by Cuban émigrés in Miami.

1990s crisis and change

In an effort to broaden the people's power system of government introduced in 1976, the central committee of the Cuban Communist Party adopted resolutions in 1990 designed to strengthen the municipal and provincial assemblies and transform the National Assembly into a genuine parliament. In February 1993, the first direct, secret elections for the National Assembly and for provincial assemblies were held. Despite calls from opponents abroad for voters to register a protest by spoiling their ballot or not voting, the official results showed that 99.6% of the electorate voted, with 92.6% of votes cast valid. All 589 official candidates were elected. Delegates to the municipal assemblies of people's power serve a two-year term. Delegates are directly nominated in neighbourhood meetings (the PCC does not put forward candidates), and ballot boxes are guarded by primary school children. Provincial delegates and national deputies are elected for a five-year term. The slate consists of up to 50% of the municipal delegates and the remainder selected by a national commission on

Castro and the UN

In 1960, Fidel Castro visited the UN for the first time since becoming leader of Cuba. Relations with the USA were becoming sour and the hotels in New York were wary of giving lodging to the new government in case of reprisals from Cuban exiles and other potential violence. Hotels refused to accept his booking without a large deposit, which he refused to pay. Undeterred, Castro led his party to buy tents and headed for Central Park, where he intended to pitch camp, declaring he was still a *guerrilla* comandante. They never got there, however, for a young black leader called Malcolm X persuaded them to come with him to Harlem, where he found them rooms in the rundown Hotel Theresa in the heart of the black district. In addition he promised them security and protection from the émigrés provided by his black Muslims. It was a great occasion and Castro held court at the hotel, receiving eminent visitors such as Nehru and his daughter Indira Gandhi, Nasser, Kruschev and others, while also mingling with the public. His performance at the General Assembly was memorable: the audience was forced to listen to a speech lasting 4½ hours.

Thirty-five years later, he made another visit to the UN and went back to Harlem, although he lodged at the Cuban UN mission. Discarding the sober suit he wore to the UN General Assembly (where this time he was limited to a five-minute address but received a longer ovation than President Clinton for a speech which expressed the broad resentments of the Third World), he donned his military fatigues and cap and went to talk to an all-ticket audience at the Abyssinian Baptist Church about Cuba's educational and health achievements. Although he was again excluded by polite society (he was not invited to President Clinton's reception for 149 heads of state and left off the guest list for Mayor Giuliani's dinner party) he was courted by no less than 230 US business people and invited to lunch by the Rockefeller family.

the basis of proposals from the mass organizations. In the October 1997 elections, 97.6% of the electorate voted and 92.8% of the votes were valid (7.2% blank or spoiled).

Economic difficulties in the 1990s brought on by the loss of markets in the former USSR and Eastern Europe, together with higher oil prices because of the Gulf crisis, forced the government to impose emergency measures and declare a special period in peace time (1990-1994). Rationing was increased, petrol became scarce, the bureaucracy was slashed and several hundred arrests were made in a drive against corruption. In 1993, Cuba was hit on 13 March by a winter storm which caused an estimated US$1 bn in damage. Agricultural production, for both export and domestic consumption, was severely affected. In mid-1994, economic frustration and discontent boiled up and Cubans began to flee their country. Thousands left for Florida in a mass exodus similar to that of Mariel in 1980 on any craft they could invent. It was estimated that between mid-August and mid-September 30,000 Cubans had left the country, compared with 3656 in the whole of 1993. In contrast, the number of US visas issued from January to August was 2059 out of an agreed maximum annual quota of 20,000. Eventually the crisis forced President Clinton into an agreement whereby the USA was committed to accepting at least 20,000 Cubans a year, plus the next of kin of US citizens, while Cuba agreed to prevent further departures.

As the economic crisis persisted, the government adopted measures (some of which are outlined below) which opened up many sectors to private enterprise and recognized the dependence of much of the economy on dollars. The partial reforms did not eradicate the imbalances between the peso and the dollar economies, and shortages remained for those without access to hard currency.

Cuba then intensified its economic liberalization programme, speeding up the opening of farmers' markets throughout the country and allowing farmers to sell at uncontrolled prices once their commitments to the state procurement system were fulfilled. Importantly, the reforms also allowed middlemen to operate. It had been the emergence of this profitable occupation which had provoked the government to close down the previous farmers' market system in 1986. Markets in manufactured goods and handicrafts also opened and efforts were made to increase the number of self-employed.

US pressure in the 1990s

In 1996, a US election year, Cuba faced another crackdown by the US administration. In February, Cuba shot down two light aircraft piloted by Miami émigrés, allegedly over Cuban air space and implicitly confirmed by the findings of the International Civil Aviation Organization (ICAO) report in June. The attack provoked President Clinton into reversing his previous opposition to key elements of the Helms-Burton bill to tighten and internationalize the US embargo on Cuba and on 12 March he signed into law the Cuban Freedom and Democratic Solidarity Act. The new legislation allows legal action against any company or individual benefiting from properties expropriated by the Cuban government after the Revolution. Claims on property nationalized by the Cuban state extended to persons who did not hold US citizenship at the time of the expropriation, thus including Batista supporters who fled at the start of the Revolution. It brought universal condemnation: Canada and Mexico (NAFTA partners), the EU, Russia, China, the Caribbean community and the Río Group of Latin American countries all protested that it was unacceptable to extend sanctions outside the USA to foreign companies and their employees who do business with Cuba. In 1997, the EU brought a formal complaint against the USA at the World Trade Organization (WTO), but suspended it when an EU/US agreement was reached under which Clinton was to ask the US Congress to amend Title IV of the law (concerning the denial of US entry visas to employees and shareholders of 'trafficking companies'). Clinton was also to carry on waiving Title III (authorizing court cases against 'trafficking' of expropriated assets).

In 1999, Human Rights Watch produced a report that strongly criticized the US embargo, arguing that it had helped Castro to develop and maintain his repressive regime, restricting freedom of speech, movement and association. It had also divided the international community, alienating Washington's potential allies who, it argued, should be working together to push for change in Cuba. The same year, the UN Human Rights Commission expressed concern about 'continued repression' in Cuba, following the trial and conviction of four Cubans for sedition. They were jailed for receiving funds and instructions from the USA aimed at obstructing foreign investment. A civil suit brought in Cuba claimed US$181 bn in damages from the US government for its aggressive policing over the previous 40 years, causing the deaths of 3478 Cubans. The case was seen partially as a retaliation for the Helms-Burton Law.

Recent events

A spate of bombings targeted at the tourist industry caused alarm in 1997. The first was in April at the hotels **Meliá Cohiba** in Havana, followed by one in July at the **Capri** and another at the **Nacional**. The **Meliá Cohiba** was hit again in August, while in September three hotels on the seafront were bombed and an Italian was killed by flying glass. In an extraordinarily successful piece of detective work, it only took about a week for the Interior Ministry to announce it was holding a former paratrooper from El Salvador, Raúl Ernesto Cruz León, who confessed publicly on TV to working as a mercenary and planting six bombs. He did not say who he was working for, but it was assumed in Cuba that the Miami-based Cuban American National Foundation (CANF) was behind the bombings. Two Salvadorians were sentenced to death in 1999 for their part in the 1997 bombing campaign.

1997 was the 30th anniversary of the death of Che Guevara in Bolivia, whose remains were returned to Cuba in July. The country held a week of official mourning for Che and his comrades in arms. Vast numbers filed past their remains in Havana and Santa Clara, where they were laid to rest on 17 October. In December 1998 the remains of the 10 more guerrillas killed in Bolivia in 1967 were also interred in the Che Guevara memorial in Santa Clara (see page 220). They included Haydée Tamara Bunke, known as Tania, who was believed to be Che's lover.

In January 1998, the Pope visited Cuba for the first time. During his four-day visit he held open-air masses around the country, attended by thousands of fascinated Cubans encouraged to attend by Castro. The world's press was represented in large numbers to record the Pope's preaching against Cuba's record on human rights and abortion while also condemning the US trade embargo preventing food and medicines reaching the needy. The visit was a public relations success for both Castro and the Pope. Shortly afterwards, 200 prisoners were pardoned and released.

In November 1999 a six-year-old boy, Elián González, was rescued from the sea off Florida, the only survivor from a boatload of illegal migrants which included his mother and her boyfriend. He was looked after by distant relatives in Miami and quickly became the centrepiece of a new row between Cuban émigrés, supported by right-wing Republicans, and Cuba. The US Attorney General, Janet Reno, supported the decision, by the US Immigration and Naturalization Service (INS) on 5 January 2000, that the boy should be repatriated and reunited with his father in Cuba by 14 January, but she postponed the deadline indefinitely to allow for legal challenges. Mass demonstrations were held in Havana in support of Elián's return but legal manoeuvres by US politicians stalled any progress and caused further disputes. Amid enormous controversy, the US authorities seized Elián on 22 April and reunited him with his father, who had travelled to the USA earlier in the month with his second wife and baby. The family finally took him home, amid celebrations in Cuba, where the boy had become a symbol of resistance to the USA.

The election of George W Bush to the US presidency was bad news for any prospects of a thaw in relations with the USA. A crackdown on spies was ordered and in June 2001, five Cubans (arrested in 1998) were convicted of conspiracy to commit espionage and murder in a US Federal Court in Miami. Castro referred to them as 'heroes', who he said had not been putting the USA in danger but had been infiltrating Cuban-American anti-Castro groups and defending Cuba. Their faces are on billboards across Cuba and their case is still part of the propaganda war between Cuba and the USA. The prisoners known as the 'Miami Five' are being held in separate prisons across the USA and are being denied access to their families because their wives have been denied US visas.

However, 2001 saw the first commercial export of food from the USA to Cuba, with a shipment of corn from Louisiana to Alimport, Cuba's food-buying agency. The debate on the lifting of sanctions was fuelled by the visit of former US President Jimmy Carter in 2002 and an ever-increasing number of Americans travelled to the island, legally or illegally. However, the thaw came to a grinding halt in 2003 when Castro had three ferry hijackers executed and imprisoned 75 journalists, rights activists and dissidents, many of whom had allegedly been encouraged by the head of the US Interests Section in Havana. Amid universal condemnation, the EU announced a review of its relations with Cuba and curtailed high-level governmental visits. In 2002, Osvaldo Paya, leader of the dissident Varela project (Félix Varela was an independence hero), delivered a petition with 11,020 signatures to the National Assembly demanding sweeping political reforms, but it was dismissed. Undeterred, Paya submitted a second petition in October 2003 with 14,384 signatures, calling for a referendum on freedom of speech and assembly and amnesty for political prisoners. At the same time, the US administration announced a clampdown on its citizens travelling to the island. Immigration and Customs officers were ordered to carry out the letter of the law, with thousands of baggage searches and the first prosecutions were announced. In January 2004, the USA cancelled semi-annual migration talks as relations deteriorated. With 2004 being another presidential election year in the USA, Cuba knew it was in for a rocky ride, but this time Bush hit out at ordinary Cubans as well as their government. Remittances were sharply curtailed and Cuban Americans were limited in their travel to the island, with only one trip permitted every three years to see a close relative, even if they were dying.

In August 2006 Fidel Castro had his 80th birthday. The occasion was to have been marked by national celebrations, parades and speeches, but shortly beforehand Castro made the surprise announcement that he was about to undergo major abdominal surgery and that he was handing over the reins of power temporarily to his brother, Raúl. The nature of his illness, operation and subsequent condition was shrouded in secrecy, with rumours of terminal illness and even his death circulating in Cuba and in Miami. Coinciding with Fidel dropping out of the limelight, in the USA the Democrats won control of both houses of Congress and there were moves towards closer relations. Raúl made conciliatory noises to the USA, which the Bush administration rebuffed. By mid-2007, Fidel was well enough to receive foreign dignitaries and write articles on world issues. Nevertheless, he was still not seen in public and in 2008 the temporary handover of power became permanent. Raúl initially made attempts to liberalize the economy, allowing certain materialistic freedoms for Cubans with access to foreign exchange (permission to own laptops, stay in hotels. etc) and introduced bonuses for workers who exceed their targets, but was stymied by the arrival of three devastating hurricanes, which between them caused US$10 bn in damage. This, together with the world financial crisis and a dramatic fall in the price of nickel, completely stalled the economy and seriously hampered the government's room for manoeuvre. The celebration of the 50th anniversary of the Cuban Revolution on 1 January 2009 was a low-key, no-frills, low-budget affair. Many factories had to close or cut output, energy was rationed, transport restricted and imports and budgets slashed as further austerity was required.

The succession to the Castro regime had long been thought to lie with the group of protegées groomed by Fidel, but in 2009 Raúl took Cuba and the world by surprise by replacing ten members of the Council of Ministers and other key personnel. Fidelista loyalists were removed while army and communist party officials were promoted to run the economy. Hopes were raised when US President Obama took office and lifted travel restrictions on Cuban Americans visiting the island. However, he kept the US trade embargo in place to press Cuba to improve human rights and political freedoms. Castro agreed to talks on migration and other issues, but refused to make concessions.

Economy

Following the 1959 Revolution, Cuba adopted a Marxist-Leninist system. Almost all sectors of the economy were state controlled and centrally planned, the only significant exception being agriculture, where some 12% of arable land was still privately owned. The country became heavily dependent on trade and aid from other Communist countries, principally the USSR (through its participation in the Council of Mutual Economic Aid), encouraged by the US trade embargo. It relied on sugar and, to a lesser extent, nickel for nearly all its exports. While times were good, Cuba used the Soviet protection to build up an impressive, but costly, social welfare system, with better housing, education and healthcare than anywhere else in Latin America and the Caribbean. The collapse of the Eastern European bloc, however, revealed the vulnerability of the island's economy and the desperate need for reform. A sharp fall in GDP of 35% in 1990-1993, accompanied by a decline in exports from US$8.1 billion (1989) to US$1.7 billion (1993), forced the government to take remedial action and the decision was made to start the complex process of transition to a mixed economy.

Transformation of the unwieldy and heavily centralized state apparatus has progressed in fits and starts. The government initially encouraged self-employment to enable it to reduce the public sector workforce, but Cuban workers are cautious about relinquishing their job security. Some small businesses sprang up, particularly in the tourism sector, but numbers of registered tax payers have subsequently fallen. Free farm produce markets were permitted in 1994 and these were followed by similar markets at deregulated prices for manufacturers, including goods produced by state enterprises and handicrafts. Cubans were allowed to hold US dollars and in 1995 a convertible peso at par with the US dollar was introduced, which is fully exchangeable for hard currencies. There was initial success in reducing the fiscal deficit, which was bloated by subsidies and inefficiencies.

Although commercial relations with market economies were poor in the late 1980s, because of lack of progress in debt rescheduling negotiations, Cuba made great efforts in the 1990s to improve its foreign relations. The US trade embargo and the associated inability to secure finance from multilateral sources led the government to encourage foreign investment, principally in joint ventures. All sectors of the economy, including sugar and real estate, are now open to foreign investment and in some areas majority foreign shareholdings are allowed. Some 400 foreign companies are now established in Cuba, with capital from 38 countries in 26 economic sectors, mostly in tourism, oil, mining and telecommunications. Under new legislation passed in 1996, free-trade zones were established, the first one at Havana with others at Cienfuegos, Mariel and Wajay, outside Havana. Some 75% of production must be exported but the rest can be sold in Cuba. The external accounts remain weak. Foreign debt is around US$11 billion (excluding debt to former members of COMECON – Russia claims Cuba owes it US$20 billion), and Cuba's dependence on high-interest, short-term trade finance is a burden. Cuba is ineligible for long-term development finance from multilateral lending agencies because of the US veto. Low sugar and nickel prices, high oil prices, a decline in tourism after the 11 September 2001 terrorist attack and massive hurricane damage in 2002 and 2008 all hindered recovery from the economic crisis of the 1990s.

There is a huge gap between those who have access to CUC$ and those who live in the CUP$ economy, which has encouraged highly skilled professionals, such as doctors, to give up their training and become waiters or tourist guides.

Health

Free healthcare is provided to all Cubans by the state as their right. In the 1960s the state took on the task of curing the population of many infectious diseases, despite having lost half of its 6000 doctors, who left the country after the Revolution. Mortality rates were high and attention was focused on eradicating specific diseases, improving ante-natal and post-natal care and training large numbers of doctors and other health care workers. Health facilities in operation before the Revolution were consolidated into a single state health system. In the 1970s, there was more emphasis on community healthcare, and polyclinics were set up with specialist services around the country. Positive results were soon evident as mortality rates fell and life expectancy rose. By the 1980s, policy had shifted again, this time towards preventive medicine rather than curative care. Mass immunization programmes were carried out and screening became regular practice. In 1985 the Family Doctor programme was started to take pressure off the hospitals and clinics and provide continuity of care. Each doctor cares for 120 families as well as collecting health and social information on all patients, providing the state with a database on the health of the nation.

The results of this attention to health care are staggering. Cubans may be poor and live in inadequate housing but their health is equal to that of industrialized countries. 95% of the population has been vaccinated against 12 diseases and several (such as polio, diphtheria, measles and mumps) have been eliminated from the island completely. Between 1986 and 1993, the entire population was tested for HIV and the 'sexually active' population is still tested annually. No cases of HIV-positive new-born babies have been recorded since 1998 as a result of ante-natal screening. The UN Population Report puts Cuba's infant mortality rate at 5.1 deaths per 1000 live births, ranking it

Sugar is an important crop and traditionally the leading foreign exchange earner. However, the industry has consistently failed to reach the targets set with output falling from eight million tonnes in 1990 to 3.2 million tonnes in 1998, the lowest for 50 years. World prices then fell to a 12-year low, while poor weather and shortages of fertilizers, oil and spare parts limited any great improvement in income. In 2003, 71 of the country's 156 sugar mills were closed and the land under production cut by 60%, with consequent severe job losses.

Citrus is now an important agricultural export with production of around 1,850,000 tonnes a year. Production is mostly in the centre and west of the island and in the Isla de la Juventud. Cuba became a member of the International Coffee Agreement in 1985 and produces about 22,000 tonnes of **coffee** a year but exports are minimal. Drought and disease have limited expansion. **Tobacco** is a traditional crop and Cuban cigars are world famous, but this too has suffered from lack of fuel, fertilizers and other inputs. Production is recovering with the help of Spanish credits and importers from France and Britain. A Spanish company has taken a shareholding in the cigar exporting company, Habanos SA, to boost sales abroad.

Diversification away from sugar is a major goal, with the emphasis on production of **food** for domestic use because of the shortage of foreign exchange for imports. The supply of food for the capital has greatly improved, partly with the introduction of city

28th in the world (UK and Canada 4.8, USA 6.3). Life expectancy is 76 years for men and 80 years for women although spending on health per person is one of the lowest in the world. As a result of the intensive training of doctors, there is now a better doctor/patient ratio than anywhere in the world except Israel.

Healthcare is now also an export item. Cuba's expertise is sought by developing countries worldwide. Cuban doctors work abroad in teams to provide specific services and foreign medical students come to Cuba to receive training. The Carlos J Finlay Medical Detachment was set up in the 1980s to prepare community doctors and in the first graduation year it included 147 graduates (out of a total of 3440 that year) from 45 different countries. The Detachment was named after the 19th-century Cuban physician who discovered the mosquito as vector of yellow fever. In 1996, South Africa requested the services of 600 English-speaking Cuban doctors under a three year contract to make up a shortfall caused by the emigration of South African doctors. Cuban emergency medical teams have helped overseas with hurricane relief and other natural disasters. Over 18,000 victims of the Chernobyl nuclear disaster, mostly children, have been treated at the Tarará medical facility outside Havana by Cuban medical staff since the programme was set up in 1990. Cuba has done more for the Chernobyl victims than all the rest of the world put together, paying for all accommodation and medical costs.

Exports of medicines and vaccines are also substantial: Brazil has bought the meningitis vaccine from Cuba; in 1996 it was proposed Cuba's debt to Venezuela, of around US$46 million, should be amortized with revenue earned from medicines exported to that country, while now the supply of oil is exchanged for medical staff and services; and an agreement with Vietnam involves the Cuban import of rice in exchange for sales of medical and pharmaceutical products. Exports of pharmaceuticals are now around US$350 million a year and rising, exceeding traditional products such as sugar or tobacco.

vegetable gardens, *agropónicos*, but the main staple, rice, is still imported to make up a shortfall in domestic production caused by inefficiencies. The beef herd declined in the first half of the 1990s because of the inability to pay for imports of grains, fertilizers and chemicals. Production is now less intensive, with smaller herds on pastures, and numbers are beginning to rise again. Similarly, milk production has also increased. The opening of farmers' markets in 1994 helped to stimulate diversification of crops and greater availability of foodstuffs, but shortages still remained. Drought in the east, hurricanes and flooding have all in recent years affected crops of beans, grains, vegetables and fruit. The area of cultivated land fell 33% from 1997 to 2008 and Cuba produced only a third of the food it needed. Some 250,000 small family farms and 1100 cooperatives worked about 25% of the land but still produced nearly 60% of crops and livestock, far more than the state farms. In 2009 the government began distributing idle state land to private farmers in an effort to boost food production and cut the US$11 bn trade deficit caused by rising food imports and falling exports. The policy marked a shift away from inefficient state farms and Raúl Castro has made raising food production a national security priority.

The sudden withdrawal of **oil** supplies, when trade agreements with Russia had to be renegotiated and denominated in convertible currencies, was a crucial factor in the collapse of the Cuban economy. Although trade agreements involving oil and sugar remain, Cuba had to purchase oil from other suppliers with extremely limited foreign exchange. As a result, Cuba stepped up its own production: foreign companies explore for oil on and off-shore and investment has borne fruit, with over 92% of electricity generated by domestic oil and gas and half of all consumption met by domestic production. Agreements with Venezuela for preferential oil supplies have eased the situation.

Mining was expected to attract foreign interest and in 1994 a new mining law was passed. Major foreign investors included Australian (nickel), Canadian (gold, silver and base metals) and South African (gold, copper and nickel) companies. Cuba's three nickel-processing plants make it one of the world's largest producers and it produces 10% of the world's cobalt, but while prices soared in 2006-2008, they fell from US$50,000 a tonne in 2008 to US$10,000 a tonne in 2009, putting huge pressure on already weak export earnings.

Tourism is now a major foreign exchange earner and has received massive investment from abroad. New hotel projects have come on stream and many more are planned. Most of the development has been along the Varadero coast, where large resort hotels attract package tourism, but the northern cays are undergoing major construction. Despite political crises, numbers of visitors rose steadily from 546,000 in 1993 to 2.3 million in 2008, generating revenues of US$2.5 billion. It is estimated that if the travel ban were lifted in the USA, some one million American tourists would immediately book holidays in Cuba. The sector is already benefiting from the relaxation of US restrictions on family visits for Cuban Americans and also from the lifting of the ban on Cubans visiting hotels. During the summer season of 2008, it was estimated that 10% of all guests at high-end, all-inclusive hotels were Cuban, many paid for by relatives visiting from Miami.

Culture

Art

Until the 19th century Cuban artists were mainly concerned with emulating the styles fashionable in Spain at the time, to gain favour with their colonial rulers. But then painters began to develop styles that were endemic to the island. Even at the end of the 19th century, when Impressionism was revolutionizing painting in France, the Cuban style still retained its roots in the academic tradition of landscape and portrait painting. One of the artists known for his major contribution to the emerging Cuban style of painting was **Leopoldo Romañach**, born near Coralillo in Villa Clara in 1862, although he spent most of his life abroad.

It was the 1920s that saw Cuban artists finally developing their own avant-garde movement and the art magazine *Avance* made its appearance in 1927. **Víctor Manuel**'s (1897-1969) 1924 painting *Gitana Tropical*, with its echoes of Cézanne and Gaugin, caused a sensation when the public first saw it. Now it has become the painting that symbolizes the beginning of modernism in Cuban art. US encroachment on the failing Cuban sugar industry in the 1920s led to a new nationalism among artists and intellectuals, with painters looking to Afro-Cuban images for inspiration. The generation of painters of 1927-1950 are known as La Vanguardia. They combined the modernism of post-Impressionist European artists with the vibrant landscapes and people found in Cuba. Today, their paintings are worth a small fortune and there is a ready market in forgeries.

Wifredo Lam (1902-1982) is still Cuba's most famous painter. He spent many years in France and Spain, becoming friends with Picasso and André Bréton, who introduced him to primitive art. Lam blended synthetic cubism, African masks and surrealism to create an essentially Cuban vision. Although he did most of his major work in Cuba, he always intended to show those outside Latin America the reality there.

Amelia Peláez (1896-1968) looked west for her inspiration, to the mural painting of Mexico, although her early work was influenced by Matisse, Braque and Picasso. Her brightly coloured murals can be seen in the Tribunal de Cuentas building and the Office of the Comptroller in Havana. It was this divergence of influences that characterized Cuban art during the 1940s.

Carlos Enríquez (1900-1957) lived in Cuba, New York, Paris and Madrid, while his style evolved through surrealism to expressionism.

René Portocarrero (1912-1985) was one of the few painters not to be influenced by the movements in Europe. His big colourful paintings incorporate Afro-Cuban imagery. He travelled to Haiti, Europe and the USA and worked with ceramics and murals.

Mariano Rodríguez (1912-1990) studied under Mexican muralists. His most popular work is his series 'Gallos' (roosters) produced in the 1940s and he exhibited widely in the USA.

Mario Carreño (1913-1999) was a nomad for the first half of his life, working as a graphic artist in Spain, a muralist in Mexico, a painter in Paris before the war and an abstract painter in New York after the war, with only visits to his homeland. In 1957, he took up permanent residence in Chile and lived there until his death.

The 1950s and 1960s saw a big influence on painting of imagery from the cinema; a major group of artists around this time were known as the *Grupo de los Once*, and included **Luis Martínez Pedro** (1910-1990), originally an architect who exhibited his paintings worldwide and designed theatre sets and costumes for contemporary dance, and **Raúl Milián** (1914-1986), who didn't start painting until 1952 and never worked in oils, preferring water-based inks.

The Revolution had a strong influence on developments in the art world: the first national art school was founded in the early 1960s; and in 1976 the Escuela Superior de Arte was founded. These institutions gave more people access to the serious study of applied art. **Raúl Martínez** (1927-1995) was the most well known of the Cuban Pop Artists. Unlike their North American contemporaries, the imagery of Cuban Pop Art came from the ubiquitous faces of revolutionaries, seen on murals all over Cuba.

The 1970s was the most difficult era for artists in Cuba, with many political restrictions on their work; of the few that made it past the censors, **Flavio Garciandia** (born 1954) was the most notable, producing paintings which mixed abstract and figurative styles together.

The 1980s saw the emergence of conceptual art in Cuba, as elsewhere, and many alternative groups were formed, such as *Artecalle* – street art. There was also the *Puré* group, the most important member being **José Angel Toirac** (born 1966) who famously put Castro's image on Marlboro cigarette advertisements and Calvin Klein's Eternity. Though most of the better-known artists were now abroad, the art scene still flourished. Some, like the sculptor **Alejandro Aguilera** (born 1964), distorted patriotic symbols in a confrontational way. In Cuba, as in other parts of the world, the 1980s was a decade in which everything was questioned and deconstructed.

The 1990s saw the rise of performance art as a means of expression. **Carlos Garaicoa** is one of the bigger names in this field, already having taken part in the *1997 Havana Biennal* along with **Tania Bruguera**, who had also exhibited in the *1996 Sao Paulo Biennal*. Many alternative galleries have sprung up, the best being 'El Espacio Aglutinador', founded in 1994 by two well-known artists from the 1980s, **Sandra Ceballos** and **Esequiel Suárez**. The gallery, which gave an exhibition space to many up-and-coming artists ignored by state cultural institutions is in Sandra's home in the Vedado area of Havana, Calle 6, 602 entre 25 y 27. The 1990s also saw a return to painting, after the vogue for installation of the 1980s. This reflects the economic need, during the special period (see History, page 415), for artists to make saleable objects again, although it also has its conceptual roots in post-modernism.

The **Museo Nacional Palacio de Bellas Artes** reopened in 2001 and is essential viewing for anyone interested in colonial and modern Cuban art (see page 80). The national collection is divided between two buildings in Old Havana, one for Cuban art and the other for world art, with many pieces having been in private collections before the Revolution. Other state-run galleries in Havana are the **Centro de Desarrollo de las Artes Visuales** and the **Wifredo Lam Centre**, which has shows by contemporary artists. You can also see some small exhibitions of avant-garde work at the **Casa de Las Américas**. Look out for the many small private galleries around Old Havana and Central Havana as well. In the provinces there are several places where you can see local artists exhibit their work, either in galleries or in provincial museums. Online you can keep up with what's going on at www.cubarte.cult.cu.

Architecture

The oldest house in Cuba still standing today is Diego Velázquez's residence in Santiago, built in 1522. However, the most important architectural works of the 16th century were the forts of Havana and Santiago, built in response to the many pirate attacks Cuba suffered. The original fort on the site of the **Castillo de la Real Fuerza** in Havana was burnt to the ground in 1555 by the French pirate Jacques de Sores. Felipe II commissioned a new fortress but the work was delayed when the architect was replaced in 1562 by Francisco de Calona, who completed the reconstruction in 1582. The building is a technological marvel, considering the primitive resources available when it was built: the walls are 6 m thick and 10 m high, with huge triangular bulwarks at each corner; a drawbridge leads over the wide moat to the vaulted interior. The early 17th century saw the construction of two castles in Havana and Santiago, by the Italian architect Juan Bautista Antonelli. They are both known as **Castillo del Morro**, and both still stand. Also built in the 17th century were the Havana city walls. One and a half metres thick and 10 m high, they ran for nearly 5000 m around the edge of the bay. A few fragments remain at Calle Egido y Avenida del Puerto.

Baroque

The most notable Baroque building in Havana is the **cathedral**; completed in 1777, it features an eccentric, undulating façade, asymmetrical towers, and wooden-ribbed vaulting over its three naves. The increased power enjoyed by the church in the 17th and 18th centuries led to bishops such as Diego Evelino de Compostela having a big say in city planning, with the result that many churches were built during this period. The gardens of Evelino's house in Calle Compostela, Havana, were the site of the first baroque church in Havana, **Iglesia de Nuestra Señora de Belén**, completed in 1718 and now a day-care centre for the elderly. The classic baroque façade features a nativity scene framed within a shell. Diego de Compostela also built the **Colegio de San Francisco de Sales** in Havana. A typical central patio, surrounded by thick columns and slatted doors, receives rainbows of light from the *mediopuntos* – semicircular windows with fan-shaped stained glass.

The **San Francisco de Asís** church in Old Havana was rebuilt in the baroque style in 1730. When a 40-m tower was added it became one of the highest religious buildings in Latin America. It is no longer a church and only the exterior, in particular the Escorial style of the façade, retains the baroque splendour of its day.

Colonial mansions

In a typical Spanish colonial house of some wealth, there was a series of large, airy rooms on the first floor surrounded the central patio, based on the Sevillian style; the ground floor was reserved for warehouses and shops, and the *entresol*, between the ground and first floors, was where the slaves lived. Ornate carved *rejas* adorned the windows, and half-doors set with coloured glass divided the rooms. A good example in Havana is **Casa de La Obra Pía**, on Obrapía and Mercaderes.

Neoclassical

The first neoclassical building in Havana was the **Templete**, a small doric temple on the Plaza de Armas. In the early 19th century, the cathedral in Havana had its baroque altars removed and replaced with neoclassical ones by Bishop Juan José de Espada. There are three fine neoclassical buildings in Matanzas: the cathedral, the **Iglesia de San Pedro Apóstol**, and the theatre. Many elaborate country houses were built around this time, for example **Quinta de Santovenia** near Havana, now an old people's home. Its inlaid marble floor, fountains and wrought-iron *rejas* are typical of the neoclassical period. The **Palacio de Aldama** (Amistad y Reina in central Havana) has a stunning neoclassical interior with fine decorated ceilings. It is now the **Instituto de Historia de Cuba**.

20th century

One of the most notable art nouveau buildings is the **Palacio Velasco**, on Capdevila esquina Agramonte in Central Havana. Built in 1912, it is now the Spanish Embassy. There are also many good examples of art deco in Havana; the best is the **Edificio Bacardí** on Avenida de las Misiones, Old Havana (now renovated and looking fabulous), built in 1929 by the founder of Bacardi rum, and the neo-Renaissance **Casino Español**, now the Palacio de Los Matrimonios, on Paseo de Martí (Prado). The **Capitolio** was the brainwave of former dictator Machado, who sought to demonstrate his allegiance to the USA by erecting a copy of the Capitol building in Washington DC. Built in 1932, it has a 62-m dome and a 120-m very ornate entrance hall.

More examples of 1930s architecture can be seen in Santiago, where there are some attractive art deco buildings on the Malecón, as well as the **Palacio Nacionalista**. The **Vista Alegre** neighbourhood, begun in 1906, contains some outstanding examples of art nouveau, notably the Palacio de Pioneros. This pink building on Manduley entre 9 y 11 was one of the Bacardí family residences.

Aquiles Capablanca was the most popular architect of the 1950s. His **Tribunal de Cuentas** in Havana is one of the most admired 20th-century buildings in Latin America. He also built the **Office of the Comptroller**, in Plaza de la República. Both buildings feature murals by well-known artist Amelia Peláez. Capablanca employed many elements inspired by Le Corbusier, whose influence can also be seen in residential work of the 1950s; conical designs called paraboloids were incorporated in the roof, whose purpose was to allow fresh air to circulate in the building. These avant-garde designs were combined with a revival of the colonial construction around a central patio, which hadn't been used for 70 years. The **Tropicana** nightclub, built by Max Borges Jr in 1952, was another work of stunning originality: exotic, sinuous curves on the shell-like structure are combined with tropical vegetation and the architect's own sculptures.

Korda and the making of an icon

Alberto Díaz Gutiérrez (1928-2001) was the son of a railway worker and tried a variety of jobs before turning to photography as a way of meeting beautiful women. The scheme worked; he established himself as a fashion photographer and married one of Cuba's most beautiful models. He took the name 'Korda' because he thought it sounded like Kodak and set up a studio in Havana where he lived the lifestyle of the successful and famous.

The 1959 Revolution changed his world completely and he became converted to the cause after a photographic expedition into the countryside that year. He saw at first hand the grinding poverty of the peasants and the inequality caused by the dictatorship. Instead of fashion pictures for *Vogue*, he took photos of the new leadership, which he sold to the newspaper, *Revolución*. He followed Castro, Che and their entourage around the country giving speeches and holding rallies or joining workers in the sugar harvest. On one of these occasions he took the photo of Che which was to make him world famous and convert the Argentine into an icon to inspire student revolutionaries for a generation. The occasion was the funeral in 1960 of 100 dock workers who were killed when a French freighter loaded with arms exploded in Havana harbour. Interpreted as a CIA-backed terrorist attack, the Cubans were furious and grief stricken at the funeral and Che's expression reflects the mix of emotions he felt as he surveyed the crowd before taking his leave. Korda's photo was rejected by *Revolución*, but it was precious enough to him to hang it on the wall of his studio for years.

In 1967, Korda received a visit from the Italian publisher, Giangiacomo Feltrinelli, to whom he gave a print of the photo as a present. The matter might have rested there if Che had not been killed in Bolivia a few weeks later. A Ministry of the Interior official discovered the photo and hung a huge version of it on the building overlooking the Plaza de la Revolución where it served as a backdrop for Castro when he paid homage to his friend and colleague. Images of the event were screened on televisions all round the world and Feltrinelli realised what could be done with such a powerful picture. Without permission and without paying Korda a cent, Feltrinelli printed millions of posters of the photo which later adorned student rooms and were carried in demonstrations in Europe and Mexico in the late 1960s. This single image of Che has been used on posters, T-shirts, hats, books, cards and any number of other items to reinforce revolutionary thought or just to sell goods with the aid of a beautiful young man with a stern but wistful gaze. In December 1999 an exhibition in Paris called '*100 Photographs of the Century*' had Korda's photo of Che on the cover of the catalogue, in recognition of its impact.

For 20 years Korda did nothing about his copyright and received no royalties. It was only in 1998 when Smirnoff advertised a vodka with the picture of Che and the slogan 'Hot and Fiery' that he decided to take action. Incensed that Che should be used to advertise alcohol when he didn't even drink, Korda took the advertising and picture agencies to court and won. When damages were paid in 2000 he donated them to the Cuban health service to buy medicines for Cuban children, as he believed Che would have done. He died of a heart attack in Paris while attending an exhibition of his work and was buried in Havana. Despite a huge photographic legacy including an underwater record of Cuba as well as fashion and news photos, it is for the single photo of Che Guevara that he will always be known.

Post-Revolution

The Revolution saw less construction of new buildings than the conversion of former emblems of the Batista dictatorship into more functional buildings for public benefit. This happened with the **Moncada Garrison** in Santiago, now a school and museum, and the **Capitolio** in Havana, now a library and museum. Some new structures did appear, such as the **School of Plastic Arts**: started in 1961 by Ricardo Porro, and completed after his defection by Vittorio Garatti in 1965, it has been described as resembling a stretched-out woman's body, with breast-like domes and curved walkways. Another good example of post-Revolution creativity is the **Coppelia** ice cream parlour, by Mario Girona, completed in 1966.

Soviet influence and materials after the Revolution saw the appearance of the grey monolithic buildings associated with the former USSR. However, the negative aura of such buildings in Eastern Europe has often much to do with the climate. Many similar buildings in Cuba, for example state-run hotels built during the 1960s and 1970s, have such wide, open-plan interiors and vast windows, often coloured with modernist stained glass, that the effect is entirely positive, allowing light and air to move freely through the building. The **Hotel Sierra Maestra** in Bayamo and the **Hotel Guacanayabo** in Manzanillo are good examples of this.

An excellent way to get an overall picture of the architecture of Havana is to visit the **Maqueta de La Habana**, on Calle 28 113 entre 1 y 3, Miramar. This is a detailed model of the city with a scale of 1 m:1 km, covering all its buildings dated by colour from the colonial period to the present.

Literature

The earliest known work of Cuban literature was a poem called *Espejos de paciencia*, published in 1605 by **Silvestre de Balboa**. An epic *canto* about the struggles between a Spanish bishop and a French pirate, it is an esteemed work for its time, though it now retains only historical value. Early schools of writers in Cuba were too influenced by Spanish literature to produce anything essentially Cuban and it was not until the first half of the 19th century that poets begin to formulate a voice of their own: the first collection of verse by a native Cuban was **Ignacio Valdés Machuca's** (1792-1851) *Ocios poéticos*, published in 1819.

José María Heredia y Heredia (1803-1839) is considered the turning point for Cuban letters. His *Meditación en el teocalli de Chobula* (1820) marked the beginning of Romanticism, not only in Cuba, but in the Spanish language. He was also the first of many Cuban writers to be involved in the struggle for independence. He was expelled from the country for his part in anti-colonial conspiracies, and wrote most of his work while in exile in Mexico and the USA.

Cuba's most prolific woman writer was **Gertrudis Gómez de Avellaneda** (1814-1873). Her anti-slavery novel *Sab* (1841) was the first of its kind to be published anywhere in Latin America, its theme predating *Uncle Tom's Cabin* by a decade. A qlut of abolitionist novels followed, the most notable being *Cecilia Valdés* (1882) by **Cirilio Villaverde** (1812-1894). The poet **Domingo Delmonte** (1804-1853) led a protest against Cuba's continued acceptance of slavery after its official abolition in 1815, and many writers had to publish their anti-slavery novels in New York.

The most influential figure in Cuba's struggle for independence was **José Martí** (1853-1895). He was deported to Spain in 1880 for his part in the independence movement. He later died in battle during the second War of Independence in 1895. He wrote *Versos Sencillos* (1891), based on the drama of his own life, while in exile in the USA. Martí also wrote highly acclaimed prose, which appeared in political journals published in Argentina and Venezuela. Many of his prophesies about Cuba's political future have been fulfilled.

Two poets associated with the transition from romanticism to modernism are **Enrique Hernández Miyarés** (1859-1914) and **Julián del Casal** (1863-1893). The latter, influenced by Baudelaire, praised the value of art over nature in *Hojas al Viento* (Leaves in the Wind, 1890). His posthumous *Bustos y Rimas* (Busts and Rhymes, 1893) has been compared with the great Nicaraguan poet Rubén Darío. Another important modernist poet was **Regina Eladio Boti y Barreiro**. Although she only published three collections of verse, she was responsible for taking Cuban poetry from modernism to post-modernism.

In the 1920s, the *negrismo* movement began, which created non-intellectual poetry based on African dance rhythms. The poet **Lydia Cabrera** (1899-1999) dedicated her life to research of Afro-Cuban culture. As well as numerous stories, in which she created a prose based on the magical-mythical beliefs passed orally through black folklore, she published many books on the ethnography and linguistics of Afro-Cubans. The *negrismo* group consisted of poets both black and white, although its most famous member, **Nicolás Guillén Batista** (1902-1989), was mulatto. *Motivos de son* (1930), in which he incorporated African rhythms in his *son* poetry, is considered his best work. He joined the Communist party and after the Revolution, was made president of the Union of Cuban Writers, and declared the National Poet by Castro.

Two of Guillén's former colleagues on the Communist newspaper *Hoy* were the writers **Lino Novás Calvo** (1905-1983) and **Carlos Montenegro** (1900-1981). Novas Calvo is recognized as one of the finest short story writers in Latin America. He used the narrative techniques of Hemingway and Faulkner to capture the feel of Havana slang. He was the first of many writers to go into voluntary exile with the instalment of Castro's régime. *La Luna Nona y Otros Cuentos* (The Ninth Moon, 1942) is his best collection. Carlos Montenegro's *Hombres Sin Mujer* (Life Without Women) has been compared to Céline and Genet. He was jailed for life aged 18 for killing a sailor who sexually assaulted him. The novel is based on the sexual exploits of his 15 years in prison.

The major writers at the time of the 1959 Revolution were the novelists **Virgilio Piñera** (1914-1979) and **Alejo Carpentier** (1904-1980) and the poet **José Lezama Lima**. All publishers were merged into the National Printing Press, with Alejo Carpentier as manager. The founder of magical realism, Carpentier's early novels are among the most highly rated in Latin American literature. Many are available in English, including *Los Pasos Perdidos* (The Lost Steps), the most accessible of his richly baroque tales.

José Lezama Lima (1910-1976) scandalized post-Revolution Cuba with his novel *Paradiso* (Paradise, 1966), a thinly disguised account of his homosexual experiences. Primarily a poet, Lezama was one of the driving forces behind the *criollismo* movement of the 1940s and 1950s. His rebellious, apolitical stance is an inspiration to the young Cuban poets of today, who seek to create a non-politicized poetry with a more spiritual dimension.

One of the most famous dissident novelists was **Reinaldo Arenas** (1943-1990). Dogged by state security for most of his youth, he was imprisoned several times as a dissident and a homosexual, and only managed to publish his novel *El Mundo Alucinado* (Hallucinations, 1971) by smuggling the manuscript out of the country through foreign friends. He finally escaped to Miami in the Mariel exodus, but, suffering from AIDS, he committed suicide in New York. His memoirs, *Antes Que Anochezca* (Before Night Falls) were published posthumously and have since been made into a film, see Cinema, page 439. This and his other works are available in translation. Also available in English are the works of **Guillermo Cabrera Infante** (born 1929). In 1959 he became editor of the literary weekly, *Lunes de la Revolución*, but it was closed after two years when he got into trouble with the government. In 1962, he went to Brussels as cultural attaché, but resigned in 1965 and began exile in London in 1966. His witty novel about Havana nightlife during Batista's dictatorship, *Tres Tristes Tigres*, first version 1964, second version 1967 (Three Trapped Tigers, 1971), brought him literary fame. The book won him the Premio Biblioteca Breve in Barcelona in 1964, but led to him being expelled from the Cuban Union of Writers in 1968. Conflict between artistic creativity and the Revolution exploded in the 1970s with the Padilla affair. Herberto Padilla, a poet, won a literary prize in 1971, but instead of guaranteed publication, his book of satirical and questioning poems was blocked. He was imprisoned as a counter-revolutionary and forced to make a public confession of crimes he had not committed, a humiliating act which caused an outcry among the intellectuals of Europe.

As a reaction to the political restrictions placed on writers after the Revolution, a movement of experimental literature sprang up in the 1960s, influenced by the French avant-garde and North American pop culture. **Severo Sarduy** (1937-1993), who left Cuba for Paris immediately after the Revolution, was the leading member; his *¿De dónde son los cantantes?* (From Cuba with a Song, 1967), with its complex layering of cultural history and linguistic puzzles, is still regarded as a classic by Cuban intellectuals. Sarduy became a citizen of France in 1967 and lived there until his death.

Nowadays Cuban writers find it easier to express their ideas in public. Havana has its first legally recognized literary group. At the centre of the group is **Reina María Rodríguez** (born 1952), a poet who has gained admiration outside Cuba. Many young poets and writers see themselves as carrying on where literature left off after the 1960s, when the repressive measures of the Revolution induced a state of creative inertia and self-censorship. Writers such as **Pedro Juan Gutiérrez** and **Leonardo Padura Fuentes** (see page 457) openly discuss the difficulties of life in Havana and question the ethics of state-imposed hardship with the toll it takes on friendship, work and sex. There is also a new generation of Cuban American writers, whose parents fled in the 1960s, who are now discovering their roots.

Music and dance

There are few countries in the world with so rich a musical heritage as Cuba. No visitor can fail to be moved by the variety of sounds that surround them, whether it be a street corner rumba or a *septeto* in the *Casa de la Trova*. Music is everywhere – it seems that nothing can happen without it.

The origins of Cuban music lie in the movement of numerous, primarily European, and African cultures. Through the inauspicious conditions of migration, enslavement, war and colonization, elements of these disparate identities have fused into a Cuban identity, forged in the villages and on plantations, in tenements and dockyards. African music and dance forms whose paths might never have crossed on their own vast continent did so in Cuba, enriching each other, and drawing also upon European forms. The mirror image is equally true with European dances finding new, African interpretations, while musicians have absorbed African harmony and chorus styles as well as rhythm. Most of today's popular genres are neither Yoruba nor French, Ekiti, Ashanti, nor Spanish, but fusions from this vast cultural gene pool.

José Martí (1853-1895)

Born into a poor family in Havana, José Martí dedicated his life from a young age to rebellion against the colonial Spanish rule. The head of his school, the poet and freedom fighter Rafael Mendive, was a strong influence on him, and it was his connection with Mendive that was used as evidence for Martí's sentence of forced labour for his part in the 1868 Independence Conspiracy while he was still a boy. The experience of gross injustice, slaving in the sun with old men and young boys chained at the ankles, implanted in the young Martí a lifelong commitment to the struggle for independence from Spanish rule.

Martí's sentence was commuted to exile. He was sent to Spain in 1871-1874, where aged 18 he wrote the first of many political essays, *El presidio político de Cuba*, in which he denounced the sufferings of his fellow Cubans at the hands of an authoritarian colonial rule. He completed his studies in Spain, and then went to Mexico to become editor of *Revista Universal*. From there he taught at the University of Guatemala in 1877. He then lived in Venezuela until 1881 and the last years of his exile were spent in the USA. He left in 1895 to join the liberation movement in Cuba, where he was welcomed as a political leader. Tragically, he was killed on 19 May that year while fighting in the War of Independence at Boca de Dos Ríos in the east, see also page 329.

José Martí's work was primarily concerned with the liberation of Cuba, but many of his poems focused on nature, with Man at the centre engaged in a continual process of betterment. He combined a love of poetry with a desire for his prose work to have some effect on the world; all his energies were directed towards securing a future in which justice and happiness could flourish. Although one of the greatest modernist poets, he did not share other modernists' views that the role of poetry was outside conventional society.

Martí also differed from his contemporaries in his rejection of contemporary European literature. He saw pre-Columbian culture as having far more importance to a Latin American poet. His views were expanded upon in his essay *Nuestra América*, in which he welcomed the contributing force of Amerindians and blacks in contemporary culture.

Martí set the tone for all his poetry with *Ismaelillo* (1882), demonstrating the simplicity and sincerity he felt was lacking in current Spanish poetry. He developed this style in 1878, with *Versos libres*, and later in his most admired collection *Versos sencillos* (1891), in which the upheavals of his own life were his biggest inspiration. Martí is perhaps best known in Europe by the song *Guantanamera* – an adaptation by Pete Seeger of Martí's verse, put to the melody of Joseíto Fernández. In Cuba, however, he is the figure head of Cuban liberation and has become an icon, deliberately exploited by Fidel Castro, of anti-colonialism, independence and freedom.

The Cuban music most universally accepted on the island is surely the **son**, which, in spite of its more urban variations and offspring, remains essentially rural. Played by Cuba's oldest and youngest musicians, it is a principal root of salsa, and, however unlikely it might at times seem, also *timba*. In its various forms *son* still thrives both in the countryside and cities throughout the island, pointing to the nascent character of urban culture. *Son* began its life in Oriente where old songs from Spain combined with African call-and-response choruses. The syncopated notes of the guitar and *tres* (a small guitar-like instrument) contributed to other genres such as *guaracha*, full of satire and humour, and soon evolved new ones such as the *guajira*, resulting in the famous '*guajira Guantanamera*', and *nengón*. With the addition of bongo, maracas and marimbula, *nengón* developed into the style known as **son changüí**. From Guantánamo (where *changüí* is still strong), the *son* reached Havana around 1909, along with elements of the new Permanent Army, and gained there the disdain of society, which disregarded and feared it as the music of the lower, particularly black, class. Persecuted by the authorities, *son* simmered in a few black neighbourhoods, existing there through illegal parties for some ten years. However, given Society's taste for expropriating the surplus value of the lower orders' uncouth labour, it was perhaps inevitable that they would eventually appropriate also their dynamic culture. By the early 1920s, and with tasteful modifications, small *son* combos were beginning to displace the cumbersome and expensive *danzón* orchestras from La Habana's exclusive dance salons. Capturing the most gifted writers and band leaders of the time this gentrification of *son* was not entirely without benefit to its continued evolution and precipitated its spread not just across social but also national boundaries. Although few if any recordings were made of *son* prior to this, a multitude followed, and whatever criticisms one might make, they remain a rich source of material for inspiration and re-interpretation.

As the 1930s approached, **Ignacio Piñero** formed his **Septeto Nacional**. (A *septeto* is a seven-piece band, including guitars, percussion, brass, vocals, playing traditional Cuban music.) Their *sones* not only featured his exceptional vocal improvisations (honed in the large choral societies called *Coros de Clave*), but added a hot trumpet to the central rhythm of the *clave*. **Nicolás Guillén** busied himself composing *sones* and *son* was now recognized as the sound of Cuba (to stand alonside such 'exotic' names as samba, conga and tango, in Europe and the USA it was marketed as the '*rhumba*'). The *septeto* style is still heard today in the popular music bars and *Casas de la Trova*. Piñero continued to innovate by mixing styles, creating *guajira son*, *bolero son* (also popularized by Santiago's *Miguel Matamoros*) and even *son pregón son* which used Havana street cries, including the famous *echalé salsita*.

A new development in the 1930s was Arsenio Rodriguez' *conjunto* style, which marked the beginning of modern **salsa**. To the traditional *septeto* came conga drums, *timbales* (or '*paila*' – optional), piano and more trumpets. This 'big band' *son* made much of the final, with call-and-response or *montuno* section of the song. The later *Descargas* were improvised jam sessions over strong *paila*, conga and bongo rhythms, which had major influences on US jazz. The *tumbao* played by the *tumbadoras* is derived from rumba, so salsa combines elements of the three most prominent musical traditions: *son*, *danzón* and rumba.

During the 1950s, Beny Moré emerged as *Sonero Mayor* (meaning greatest singer and lyric improviser more than interpreter of *son*) and he remains one of the most revered figures in Cuban music history. Beny and his *Banda Gigante* were as adept with the newer styles, mambo and cha cha cha, as with *son* and its variations. Of equal importance, the size of his orchestra allowed the introduction of American Big Band Jazz to the Cuban melting pot. The era also saw the arrival of such artists as **La Sonora Matancera** and **Celia Cruz**, both of whom found fame in exile. There, in the USA, Celia (died 2003) won world wide acclaim as the Queen of Salsa. Back in Cuba, **Miguel Cuní**, **Félix Chapottín** and **Lilí** forged a somewhat harder edged urban son to serenade the arrival of Castro's nationalist Revolution.

If Cuba of the sixties is remembered more in connection with Russian nuclear missiles than for earth-shattering music, the foundations were being laid for future musical revolutions. It's hard to find any virtue in the frankly awful experiments with pop music by **Elio Revé** and

Alicia Alonso and the Ballet Nacional de Cuba

Although there was dancing in Cuba during the Spanish colonial period, with occasional visiting companies from Spain, ballet was not seen until 1842, when the great Romantic ballerina Fanny Elssler appeared at the Teatro Tacón. Performances by touring companies followed, including a visit by Anna Pavlova in 1917. Home-bred ballet started with the ballet evenings of the Sociedad Pro-Arte Música in 1931, whose conservatory produced Alicia Alonso and the two Alonso brothers, Alberto and Fernando, among other outstanding dancers and choreographers of their generation.

Alicia Alonso has been the most influential Cuban dancer and ballet director ever, having made her name on the world stage before returning to Cuba to direct the development of ballet. Born Alicia Ernestina de la Caridad del Cobre Martínez Hoyo in Havana on 21 December 1921, she studied in Havana and at the School of American Ballet in New York. After working on Broadway, in 1940 she became a member of the Ballet Theatre and temporarily joined the Sociedad Pro-Arte Música in Havana. She suffered periods off work because of a detached retina but returned to the Ballet Theatre in 1943 as ballerina. In 1948, she set up her own company in Havana, the Ballet Alicia Alonso, followed by a school in 1950, but continued to dance abroad, both with the American Ballet Theatre and as a guest of many other companies.

Alonso is known for her classical style and flawless technique, but she has also successfully interpreted modern roles. In New York she worked a lot with the choreographer Anthony Tudor, who once said of her during a rehearsal, "Oh, this excitable, temperamental Cuban, very savage, very primitive, you should try to be more educated!" Knowing that his remarks were hurtful, he asked when she would start crying. "Never!" came the reply, and she kept her promise. In fact, Tudor loved her superb technique, her spirit and her combination of vulnerability and defiance, but believed that her natural expressiveness and her tendency to show all her emotion in her face was vulgar and needed to be restrained. He held that the movement itself should show the expression. A

Juan Formell, but both talents went on to lead bands of enormous importance and popularity through the 1970s and 1980s. Formell's band, **Los Van Van**, have undergone a number of reinventions and remain very much at the cutting edge of today's music.

No less than the development of a popular education system on the island following the Revolution, US policy towards Cuba has had a powerful effect on the subsequent unfolding of popular Latin music in both countries, actually creating something of a schism. Cut off from its source, the music of Cuban exile and Puerto Rican communities has tended to become bogged in old musical language in the way of ex-pats, at the same time absorbing the economic ethos of the host nation. Polished and manicured and formularised, salsa has become a multi-million dollar industry in the USA and its southern sphere of influence, its product as personal as any other factory-produced commodity. Cubans on the other hand have never ceased to import, fuse and re-fuse ideas from their rich musical larder and from elsewhere and, less driven by market trends, their bands tend to develop distinctive sounds. Through the 1970s and 1980s the distinctions between genres such as *son* and charanga blurred somewhat, however, while economic pressure forced the replacement of acoustic with electric bass guitar. The Baby Bass (a substitute compromise was reached. One of Alonso's most famous roles was, like Fanny Elssler, that of *Giselle*, but she has created roles in Tudor's *Undertow* (1945), Alberto Alonso's *Romeo and Juliet* (1946), Balanchine's *Theme and Variations* (1947), de Mille's *Fall River Legend* (1948), and the title role in Alberto Alonso's *Carmen* (1967).

Alicia married Fernando Alonso, a dancer and ballet director, and brother of dancer and choreographer, Alberto Alonso. The three of them worked to establish the company, Ballet Alicia Alonso, which in 1961 became the Ballet Nacional de Cuba. The company became a showpiece for the Revolutionary government, even touring to the USA in 1978. The school's young dancers have a reputation for technique and artistic interpretation, winning many medals at international competitions. In Havana they perform a repertory of classical ballets, folklore-based works and modern dance at the Teatro García Lorca. Several important ballets have been especially created for the company. The grande dame of Cuban ballet is now blind, but continues to work and to oversee the company. Aficionados should visit the Museo de la Danza in Havana.

The world-famous ballet star, Carlos Acosta, is a product of Alonso's school and although he currently dances with the Royal Ballet in London, he maintains close links with the Ballet Nacional de Cuba. In July 2009, he was instrumental in negotiating the visit by the Royal Ballet to Cuba, the first time for over 30 years that an international dance company had visited the island. The non-profit visit showcasing the company's classical and avant-garde repertoire was so popular that not only were all tickets for the performances sold out instantly, but thousands more watched on giant screens outside the Capitolio. The moment Acosta walked out on stage for the pas de deux of El Corsario, the knowledgeable audience rose to its feet with a standing ovation and cheers so rapturous that the dancers couldn't hear the music. Acosta grew up in a poor barrio and was in danger of going off the rails until his truck-driver father sent him to ballet classes to instil some discipline into him. Now frequently compared with Rudolf Nureyev and Mikhail Baryshnikov, he is known for his soaring leaps which have earned him the nicknames of 'the flying Cuban', or 'Air Acosta'.

electric upright electric bass) which is de rigueur in salsa bands was almost unheard of in Cuba. This reality alone sent Cuban music off on its own path. Some bands began to borrow heavily from funk and other urban black American styles, but overall the feel of music from this era is quite rustic. As well as the bands mentioned above, **Orquesta 440** (not to be confused with Juan Luis Guerra) stands out, as do **Son 14**, and **Adalberto Alvarez y su Son**, both the latter two being led by the same Adalberto.

Not for the first time, the new generation has continued the tradition of innovation to the point of creating a new music, **timba**. That a prominent pioneer such as Giraldo Piloto should protest his music to be merely *progressive son* alludes to the power of this revered tradition, the strength in Cuban culture of lineage principles as against individuation and, within this, the dependence of urban culture on its rural roots. Timba and Cuban rap were born not in the hills, but in the cities. They incorporate musical ideas from the outside urban world that resonate with city dwellers and certainly *timba* is the product of musicians who have enjoyed a technical training their predecessors could not have imagined. This is fundamentally urban music which perhaps has yet to become fully self aware, and you will hear little of it outside La Habana.

While *son* was appearing in Cuba's countryside, an African rhythm known as the **yuka**, which had survived on the sugar plantations, was joining forces with the Spanish *décima* and livening up the ports of Havana and Matanzas. This style soon came to be known as **rumba**. African rhythms were played on whatever came to hand: boxes used to pack fish or candles gave a good tone. Characters such as *Mama'buela* were created in mime and singers commented on current events or battled with each other for honours. This *rumba de cajón* also involved the stately *yambú* dance, where following the vocal section, a couple would mime courtship. Soon the rhythms passed onto drums, the large *tumba* providing a solid bass, the conga a repeated cross rhythm which was accompanied by brilliant improvisations on the small *quinto*. There are other terms like *llamador, trabajador, tres dos,* and *tres golpes* to describe the deeper-sounding drums, which seem to be named after their role in the rumba. To this was added a pair of *claves* and a struck length of bamboo known as the *guagua* or *cata*. The more sexual dance form known as *guaguancó* (still the main rumba style) demanded more rapid playing. Great rumberos emerged, such as **Florencio Calle, Chano Pozo, Estéban Latrí** and **Celeste Mendoza**, as well as groups who specialized in rumba, such as **Los Papines, Conjunto de Clave y Guaguancó** and the well-travelled **Muñequitos de Matanzas**, who used the rhythms of the Abakuá religion in their rumbas. The *Muñequitos* also play the Matanzas style known as *Columbia*. This rumba echoes African solo dancing, involving an element of danger such as the use of knives. Even faster playing underpins a singing style which makes use of Bantu phrases and ends in a call-and-response.

Rumba is a playfully competitive art form, although sometimes the competitiveness is not always so playful. The men, particularly the '*guapos*', or 'hard guys', take it very seriously and people do get hurt, sometimes even killed. The rhythms have got faster, break dancing and karate moves have been incorporated into the dance, *rumberos* sing about the special period; in this way, rumba survives as a true reflection of Cuban street life.

Matanzas is also the birthplace of the **danzón**. The popular *Típica* orchestras, influenced by the great cornettist **Miguel Faílde**, added subtle African rhythms to the European Contradanza, along with a call-and-response *montuno* section, creating a balance between formal dance and syncopated rhythm, almost a Cuban ragtime. The **Orquesta Típica** slowly changed, adding piano and further percussion, while the 1920s saw a new arrival, the *charanga francesa*. Of French Haitian descent, this was another development of the *típica*, featuring wooden flute and strings as well as *pailas*. It is in this format, so different from its origins, that *danzón* is generally remembered and occasionally interpreted. It was the beginning of the **Charanga** style developed by contemporary Cuban groups such as **Orquesta Aragón** and **Los Van Van**.

During the 1940s and 1950s, **Orestes López** (*Cachao*) and the violinist **Enrique Jorrín** created the new mambo and **cha cha cha** styles directly from *danzón*. These driving rhythms are still popular all over Cuba, and were fundamental to the explosion of Latin music and dance worldwide.

The **canción habanera** is regarded as the first truly Cuban vocal style. Emerging in the 1830s as a mixture of the so-called *tongo congo* rhythm and Spanish melodies, it had its greatest exponent in **Eduardo Sánchez**. *Habaneras* were also composed by **Eduardo Lecuona**, a pianist who was internationally feted during the 1930s and 1940s.

Another *canción* style, involving simply a singer and a guitar, was developed during the 19th century in Oriente by **Pepe Sánchez**. His simple, beautiful songs, such as *Rosa No 1* and *Rosa No 2*, inspired others such as **María Teresa Vera** and the remarkable **Sindo Garay**, who claimed to be the only man who had shaken the hand of both Jose Martí and Fidel Castro! The romantic style known as bolero soon developed from *canción*.

Realizing the potential for expression offered by *canción*, young musicians like **Silvio Rodríguez**, **Sara González** and **Pablo Milanés** created the **nueva trova**. Their songs reflect the path of the Revolution, **Silvio**'s '*Playa Girón*' telling its own story. '*Pablito*' is an exceptional composer and interpreter, especially of Guillén's poetry.

Cuban **jazz** is exceptionally healthy. **Orquesta Irakere** continue to renew themselves, inspired by the pianistic genius of Jesús 'Chucho' Valdéz, while **Grupo Afro-Cuba** fuse jazz with traditional Cuban rhythms, including the *bata* drums of *Santería*. Among the generation of the 1980s and 1990s the incredible pianist **Gonzalo Rubalcaba** is supreme, composing pieces using *danzón* rhythms amongst others. The annual Jazz Festival in Havana was for years attended by **Dizzy Gillespie**, whose influence is evident in the playing of Cubans such as **Arturo Sandóval** and has recently heard British jazzers giving their all. Less well known but of no less virtue as the above are **Los Terry**, a family-based band which plays an unusually rural form of Latin jazz. Lacking the polish of its New York equivalent that tends to struggle self-consciously to integrate Afro-Cuban elements, **Los Terry** have nothing to prove. If their jazz is elementally powerful, it is also totally absorbing in its complexity, dipping into Afro-Cuban folklore intuitively and naturally, rather than to make a point.

The rhythms and songs of **Santería** remain strong across the island. The three African *bata* drums are regarded as the most complex of all to master and the rhythms, each assigned to a particular deity, accompany the singing in old Yoruba. **Merceditas Valdés** is loved throughout Cuba for her interpretation of these songs. Meanwhile, '*bembe*' parties on Saints' days are accompanied by singing and drumming. The singer **Lázaro Ros** has developed a band, **Síntesis**, who combine traditional *Santería* music effectively with jazz rock.

The music of the Cuban **carnival**, recently revived following the debilitating effects of the special period, is truly exhilarating. Both Havana and Santiago have their own styles of **conga**, the thunderous music which drives on the parade. During August in Havana, the conga drums, bells and bass drums of groups such as **Los Dandy La Jardinera**, support brass players as they belt out popular melodies, the lanterns spinning in the dancers' hands. In Santiago, each *barrio* is represented by massed ranks of *bocué* drums, bass drums and brake drums. The cloaked and masked revellers of Los Hoyos and San Agustín sing in response to the wailing *corneta china*, a remnant of Cuba's Chinese communities. Other bands' *paseos* combine brass players with the usual barrage of percussion during the late July festivities. The carnival procession usually features the old *Cabildos*, whose drums keep alive the rhythms of Africa. In Oriente, the *Tumbas Francesas* parade the rhythms and dances developed by Africans in Haiti, before the 18th-century Revolution forced yet another move across the ocean.

All of this music can be heard in Cuba now: at the *Casas de La Trova*, at the *Focos Culturales*, in the theatres and the cafés, in the parks, the backyards and on the streets. From *changüí* to cha cha cha, from rumba to bolero, from *son* to *Santería*, the music of Cuba is gloriously, vibrantly alive.

The rise and decline of timba and salsa nueva

"*Que sabrosura viva, tremenda expresividad*," echoes the chorus, following an opening riff from '*los metales del terror*,' surely the scariest horn section ever. La Habana circa 1989 and like never before, a new band is rocking the city with a tribute to the neighbourhoods. This is not salsa as we've known or might expect it. The structure and feel are fresh and innovative, actually disconcerting. Isn't it jazz or some weird form of rock? You have to

Ten classic timba/salsa nueva CDs

1 **Azúcar Negra**, Andar Andando (Bis Music, 2000). After this first recording lead singer Haila from Bamboleo went her own way. Here you will find the most eloquent expression of timba at high tide.

2 **Bamboleo**, Yo No Me Parezco a Nadie (Ahí Na'Ma', 1998). Imagine two loud young women busting into a cabaret where a highly accomplished band is earning its daily bread. The girls bustle their way on stage, where, disarmed by decorum, nobody can prevent them from taking over the show. Undeniably lowering the tone, it nevertheless works out for the better as inspired by this raw energy, the band now realize their potential. Rough and smooth in perfect harmony, that was Bamboleo at their best.

3 **Conexión Salsera**, Muy Caliente Para Ti (EGREM, 1997). Featuring Danny Lozada en route for La Charanga Habanera, this is subtle in its use of contrasting chorus and lead vocal styles, beautifully focused percussion, and some of the greatest Cuban piano work on record. All quite understated, great for dancing Casino.

4 **Giraldo Piloto y Klimax**, Oye Como Va (Eurotropical, 2000). Piloto pilots his band through seamless changes of genre and style, a kind of aural painting. More a musician's than a popular band, the trajectory is towards jazz-rock-funk-timba fusion and in this field Piloto has no company let alone equals. Probably one of the greatest CDs released ever.

5 **Isaac Delgado**, El Malecón (La Formula) (Bis Music/Ahí Na'Ma', 2000). The king of salsa nueva when he pulls his finger out, you will find here a fistful of cracking dances, and a lot more besides. Songs tend to have long gentle intros, then the bass lets rip under a steaming rhythm section.

pay attention though because this band overflows with virtuosity, breaking tradition consciously, rather than from incompetence. Not a slow number but it feels laid back, grounding you with heavy *tumbadoras*, driving kit drums and bass, lifting you with blinding horn riffs, and there's a vocalist whose ease of delivery sends your head swimming. "¿Quién se come el calamar? La gente de Miramar" asks and answers the chorus. Then half the band cuts out leaving the bass booming and growling under syncopated thumps, to a rhythm section which has taken almost as much from jazz-rock and funk as its Afro-Cuban roots. Almost as much. The percussion breakdown or '*bomba*' in salsa makes its debut.

This was **NG La Banda**, as they said with characteristic modesty, '*la que manda*,' a talent concentrate from which some of Cuba's current leading artists emerged to form bands in their own right. The working title of '*bomba-son*' evolved through the 1990s and onwards with new bands and ideas taking shape from an unprecedented pool of talent. Each has added new ingredients to this urban fusion, lending diversity that defies homogenisation. Today the music has become known loosely as *timba*.

Not by chance, the pioneers of **NG** (new generation) **La Banda** were drawn largely from two other bands with histories in pushing forward the frontiers of traditional Cuban music. Though not necessarily for dance music, **Irakere** has been acclaimed internationally for its fusions of jazz with funk, disco, rock and Afro-Cuban rhythm. On the other hand **Los Van Van** had enjoyed 20 years or so as Cuba's number one dance band, combining elements of pop and pan-Caribbean rhythm within a modernized Charanga

6 **David Calzado y La Charanga Habanera**, Tremendo Delirio (Universal 1997). For many, the definitive timba CD, certainly none of the bands that formed from the CH's subsequent split have produced anything comparable. With the addition of Danny Calzado, it is phenomenal.

7 **Los Van Van**, Te Pone La Cabeza Mala (Caribe, 1997). Van Van's finest moment. Juan Formell and band had developed and ran parallel along with timba. They offer here the most complex crowd-pleasing music you could hope to find, music that seeks the highest common denominator while remaining truly popular. Singer Mayito shines through the frontline.

8 **Manolín** (El Médico de la Salsa), De Buena Fé (Caribe, 1997). Opportunist El Médico is a psychiatrist without a very good voice who turned to singing. Having attempted to straddle the Cuba/Miami divide, Manolín settled in the States after suffering power cuts during his gigs and other such 'accidents' on the island. Musically, this CD has enormous depth in its arrangements, a master class in timba percussion, keyboard, chorus and bass, so who cares if he can't sing?

9 **NG La Banda**, En La Calle (Qbadisc, 1989). The one that started it all. Here you will find the young Issac Delgado, Giraldo Piloto, El Tosco, and the 'terror brass'. Such explosions are rare and this one hasn't dated a second A million miles both from what preceded and what succeeded it.

10 **Paulo FG**, Una Vez Más…Por Amor (2000). Paulito runs the gamut between sublimely complex sophisticated timba, and slushy salsa romántica and ballads. This penultimate CD contains a good handful of ultra smooth timba tracks that almost slide in one ear and out the other.

band. When some of these two bands' strongest elements got together, then the result was bound to be explosive. Principal among the founders was the multi-talented director **José Luis Cortés** (El Tosco) who lays claim with equally gifted **Giraldo Piloto** (now with his own band, Klimax) to be the inventor of this new music.

The emergence of *timba* rested upon the state education system and changing conditions of life no less than upon Cuba's traditions and gifted musicians. These days a musician or arranger's innate talent is complemented with the discipline of a comprehensive academy training. Through the early and mid 1990s the dissemination and development of technique and style among musicians continued, each innovation tested in the street practices and rehearsals that maintain contact between the public and even the most prestigious bands. A shouted joke or taunt from the crowd is transformed in a moment to a chorus line and improvised around. It becomes the line that hooks you when you hear the record; the symbiotic relationship between the bands and their audience gives inspiration to musicians while elevating to the stage the lives, dreams and preoccupations of Havana's youth. As such, and along with more familiar subjects, songs abounded about prostitution, the virtues of soya mince, girlfriends disappearing with rich foreign men and just the struggle to survive. Presented with irony, and the facility of street wit, *timba* constituted an antidote to the escapism of ubiquitous *telenovelas* (soap operas). It is pop music in the truest sense of the word and it has shaken salsa to its foundations.

Lagging a little behind *timba*, **salsa nueva** emerged as a music to bridge the gap between old and new. Integrating with salsa elements of *timba* such as syncopated bass

Buying music

Obviously on your return from Cuba you will want to transform your little room into the local Casa de la Trova and invite all the neighbours round for a *traguito* of Havana Club rum. Luckily there is a large choice of music available. The state record company EGREM has shops alongside recording studios in the main towns. Every hotel should stock CDs at least of the major artists. Thanks to a distribution deal with a French company, much of the EGREM back catalogue is seeing the light of day again under the name of ARTEX, in a series of well-balanced compilations and major reissues. ARTEX is involved in all cultural marketing so they too have shops in every town centre, which stock posters, crafts and books alongside the sound and vision. Shops such as Cubalse also have a good range. The series *El son es lo más sublime* features an extensive history of the genre and there are excellent series on rumba, *danzón*, *bolero*, Cuban jazz, conga and folkloric styles, as well as the latest by Van Van, El Médico and the others. These should also be for sale, along with recordings by house bands, in the Casas de la Trova. Occasionally the booksellers on street corners and in the plaza will have old vinyl discs (probably unplayable) and you might even chance upon one of the newly emerging second-hand record stores for those rare '*descarga*' sessions. These are sometimes worth it for the sleeves alone. If you fancy a go yourself, EGREM shops stock a range of mass-produced Afro-Cuban instruments: conga drums, bongos, claves and suchlike, which are reasonably priced, especially compared with prices in Europe. You'll need to watch your baggage allowance though (and your back muscles as you stagger home). If you don't have time for music shopping, or you want to brush up on your *son* before you go, the Latin American music and craft shop Tumi (Tumi Music Ltd, Unit 2 Ashmead Business Center, Keynsham, Bristol BS31 1SX , T01225 852474, www.tumi.co.uk) are now distributing the best of EGREM's compilations in Britain. For people with a taste for the new generation of music from La Habana, Tumi can also satisfy all those desires, with an extensive list of contemporary artists, including cutting-edge urban music, hip hop, rock, jazz and compilations.

It's difficult to find a book purely about Cuban music in English. The best at the moment is the study of salsa *Havana Heat, Bronx Beat*, by Hernando Calvo Ospina. If your Spanish is up to it, you could try the short essays (and lovely pen sketches) *Música por El Caribe*, by Helio Orovio. María Teresa Linares' *La Música y El Pueblo* is a classic and the African roots are brilliantly explored in *Los Cabildos y la Fiesta Afrocubanos del Día de Reyes*, by Cuba's pioneering ethnologist Fernando Ortiz. All these should be adequate for the new lending library attached to your recently opened '*Casa de la Trova experience*'. The neighbours will be ecstatic.

lines and sparing use of a shouted chorus, it is more restrained and comprehensible to a traditional salsa ear. Eschewing the more nihilistic trends of incessant *bloques* (percussion breaks), structural shifts and breakdowns, it is also easier to dance to for anyone who needs something solid to hang on to. What culminated in a wave of inspired, original, infectious music around 1997, three years later had reached maturity, and was promising to extinguish in a final blast. Everything subsequently has been little more of an afterglow, although if you prefer sophistication and balance to youthful exuberance it is in this later period that you'll find a spattering of truly timeless gems. While bands of lesser originality begin to repeat themselves or go all out for the Latin pop market, some of the greatest band leaders are restrained by the confines of dance music, even for a musically sophisticated people like the Cubans. Each exploration by the likes of **Giraldo Piloto** might continue breaking musical boundaries, but ultimately estranges them from the mass audience upon which they once depended. Their music is just too complex and never settles into comforting recognizable formulas. In this context **Cuban rap** makes its appearance. First to make waves were **Orishas**. In spite of a hip hop parody stage act, their first CD fused rap to powerful effect with the morose nostalgia of the *guajira*. Another notable is **Clan 537** whose more recent hit '*¿Quién Tiró La Tisa?*' is stunning more in its social than musical content. Officially, racism and class prejudices do not exist in Cuba, although they are deeply ingrained in Cuba's people and culture. However restrained by American standards, **Clan 537** show their resentment of this reality as frankly as *timba* artists in their day dealt with the problems they could.

Timba will never disappear though. Many bands whose reputations are built on other genres have nodded *timba*'s way and, in doing so, have incorporated its innovations into the mainstream. This is where *timba* now lies, so don't be surprised to hear syncopated electric bass lines and percussion breakdowns from the younger generation of *son* bands. Neither has the standard of musicianship upon which *timba* depended disappeared. It has merely lost focus for its employment. Many now wait in anticipation of the next wave.

Cinema

One of the great success stories of the Cuban Revolution is the Cuban film industry. The Film Institute, known familiarly as **ICAIC** (Cuban Institute of Cinematographic Art and Industry), was set up by the new government in March 1959, only three months after the victory of the Revolution. Headed by **Alfredo Guevara**, it aimed to produce, distribute and show Cuban films to as wide a domestic audience as possible, to train film-makers and technicians, and to promote film culture generally. Open to anyone with an interest in film, excepting pro-Batista collaborationists, the institute built up an industry with an international reputation within 10 years, virtually from scratch.

Before the Revolution, films had been made in Cuba by foreign companies or amateurs. The staple diet of the Cuban filmgoer, even in 1959, was Hollywood movies. In the early 1960s, after the Bay of Pigs episode (1961) and the missile crisis (1962), several film directors (including **Néstor Almendros**), cinematographers and technicians, left the island, taking their precious equipment with them. Adequate government funding, which depended on the fluctuating Cuban economy, and state-of-the-art training and technology, became critical problems following the US trade embargo. The majority of the crew working on **Tomás Gutiérrez Alea**'s comedy *The Twelve Chairs*, for example (the assistant director, director of cinematography, camera operator, focus puller, camera assistant and continuity girls), were first-timers. Yet in learning to make the most of their scant resources, the Cuban film-makers introduced striking new techniques which, in addition to their youthful enthusiasm, improvisation and revolutionary focus, created a forceful impact on the world of film. Five Cuban films won international awards in 1960 alone. As Francis Ford Coppola remarked, "We don't have the advantage of their inconveniences". Measures such as the launch of the film journal *Cine cubano*, the inauguration of the **Havana Cinemateca** (1960), a national network of film clubs, and a travelling cinema (*cinemóvil*) showing films to peasants in remote rural districts, the

Films

If you know Spanish (and even if you don't) the following comedies are a must: *La Muerte de un Burócrata* (Death of a Bureaucrat, Gutiérrez Alea, 1966), in which a worker is mistakenly buried with his identity card. His widow needs it to claim her pension but when the family try to exhume the body officially they are caught up in a Kafkian tangle of bureaucracy forcing them to dig up the body themselves. When the body starts to smell, they try to bury it again, with hilarious results. This is a side-splitting, but no less serious, criticism of state officialism.

The social satire *¡Plaff!* (Splat!, Juan Carlos Tabio, 1988) picks up on the same theme. A woman dies of a heart attack when an egg is thrown at her. Who threw the egg and why? This parody of a detective film delves deep into social issues, such as the Cuban housing crisis and the scarcity of resources, while lampooning 'imperfect cinema'. The preference for foreign imports is ridiculed when a home-made polymer made from pig shit at the Institute of Excrement is proved to be far superior to a Canadian brand. The highlight of the film, however, is when the director of the Institute asks for a new filing cabinet, to store the letters he has written asking for a new filing cabinet.

Adorables Mentiras (Adorable Lies, Gerardo Chijona, 1991) is a much more poignant comedy. An unsuccessful scriptwriter tries to impress a young streetwalker by pretending to be a film director, while she in turn deceives him by pretending to be a professional actress. The complex web of sex, lies and audiotape unravels when the writer's wife, who thinks he's gay, is delighted to find out he is having an affair with a woman. But the objective of this apparently farcical charade is deadly serious. Cuban society of the 1980s is shown to be rife with petty corruption, resulting from self-delusion and material constraints. Young people are urged to face reality and get on with their lives, even if it means painful compromise.

nationalization of the film distribution companies, and the 1961 literacy campaign enabling 700,000 viewers to read the subtitles of undubbed foreign films for the first time, placed cinema at the forefront of revolutionary cultural innovation. Even the posters, designed under the auspices of ICAIC by individual artists, became world famous.

The types of films made during the 1960s were national, nonconformist and cheap. ICAIC aimed to keep as independent a criteria as possible over what constituted art, and encouraged imaginative, popular films, directly relevant to the Revolutionary process and challenging the mass culture of acquiescent consumption. The preferred format was the documentary shot on 8-mm or 16-mm film (40 were made in 1965), honed to perfection by **Santiago Alvarez**, but there were a good number of excellent features too: *Cuba Baila* (Cuba Dances), *Historias de la Revolución* (Stories of the Revolution), *El Joven Rebelde* (The Young Rebel, based on a script by Zavattini), *La Muerte de un Burócrata* (Death of a Bureaucrat) and *Aventuras de Juan Quinquin* (The Adventures of Juan Quinquin), the most popular feature in Cuba of all time, until the release of *Fresa y Chocolate* (Strawberry and Chocolate).

In 1967, the film director **Julio García Espinosa** published his seminal essay *For an Imperfect Cinema* which, with the work of **Octavio Getino** and **Fernando Solanas** in Argentina and **Glauber Rocha** in Brazil, laid the basis of the New Latin American cinema movement, also known as **Third Cinema**, a key concept in film culture today. Cuban cinema reached its high point in 1968, with groundbreaking films such as *Lucía* (Lucia) and *Memorias del Subdesarrollo* (Memories of Underdevelopment) and, in 1969, *La Primera Carga al Machete* (The First Charge of the Machete). Cuban film-makers, a number of whom had been trained in the **Centro Sperimentale** in Rome in the 1950s, were influenced predominantly by Italian Neorealism, French New Wave Cinema and *cinéma verité* – British Free Cinema (Tony Richardson and Lindsay Anderson), and the Soviet classics. Films shot on location, with hand-held cameras featuring ordinary people engaged in a revolutionary process, have remained the trademarks of classic Cuban cinema ever since.

By the 1970s, however, uncomfortable questions were being asked about the appropriateness of avant-garde art for the needs of the Cuban mass public. Tensions between creative artists and government bureaucrats exploded in the **Padilla affair** (1970), resulting in a five-year government clampdown. **ICAIC**'s production programme was reduced to three features a year, while young, often amateur film-makers (average age 36), were favoured over the more experienced. Nevertheless, important films were produced, tending to focus on women's issues, historical and/or multiracial themes (particularly slavery and African-Cuban culture), with a view to consolidating a strong, cohesive sense of national identity. The black film director **Sergio Giral**'s *El Otro Francisco* (The Other Francisco) and Gutierrez Alea's *La Ultima Cena* (The Last Supper), both depicting the courage and resistance of Cuban slaves, black director Sara Gómez's *De Cierta Manera* (One Way or Another), highlighting the problem of *machismo* among black men, and Pastor Vegas' *Retrato de Teresa* (Portrait of Teresa), denouncing sexist attitudes in post-revolutionary society, all date from this period.

In 1976, the **Ministry of Culture** was set up, ushering in yet another episode in Cuban film history. In 1982, **Julio García Espinosa** took over from Alfredo Guevara as the Head of **ICAIC**, and the organization was incorporated into the ministry. Until 1980 it had been self-financing. Nevertheless, despite the increasing influence of the Hollywood format (favouring sentimental melodrama and romance), perhaps indicative of a deeper crisis of belief, films still tended to be critical of Cuban social reality. Production figures increased to some six features a year during the 1980s, many of these co-productions with countries such as Mexico and Spain. By the end of the 1980s there were 60 million film goers, each Cuban visiting a cinema on average six times a year. The Cuban audiences, mostly young white-collar workers, technicians and specialists, tend to be educated and demanding. A network of video clubs and libraries were set up in the 1980s to meet their needs.

In the late 1980s, **ICAIC** recovered its independence and was restructured on the basis of three 'creation groups' each under an experienced film director in charge of encouraging and training young film makers. But, as Cuba moved into the special period (1990-1994) in response to the fall of the Eastern block and the intensified US trade embargo, **ICAIC** faced another crisis. After the release of a controversially critical film, *Alicia en el Pueblo de Maravillas* (Alice in Wonderworld), in a climate of political tension, moves were made to incorporate the Institute into Radio and Television, directly controlled by the **Central Committee of the Communist Party**. This strategy was actively resisted by leading filmmakers, such as Gutiérrez Alea, the plans were scrapped, and Alfredo Guevara was appointed director once more. Paradoxically, at a time when resources were scarcer than ever before, **ICAIC** produced its most successful film, *Fresa y Chocolate* (Strawberry and Chocolate, 1993), suggesting, perhaps, that the best Cuban films are made when circumstances are at their worst.

Daniel Díaz Torres followed his *Alicia* hit with *Kleines Tropikana* (Little Tropicana, Cuba/Germany/Spain, 1997), a hilarious pastiche of Gutiérrez Alea films and a fitting homage to the master. This satirical snapshot of Cuban xenophobia, played by the actors starring in *Alicia* and Vladimir Cruz *(Fresa y Chocolate)*, features a detective fiction writer, a dead German tourist and a British hippy girl, cleverly targetting European audiences. Music, laughter and social critique dominate the scene. Films of the late 1990s to watch out for are **Fernando Pérez**'s award-winning *La vida es silbar* (Life is to whistle, Cuba/Spain, 1998), **Manuel Herrera**'s *Zafiros locura azul* (Zafiros [Sapphires], Blue Madness, 1998) and **Juan Carlos Tabío**'s *El elefante y la bicicleta* (The Elephant and the Bicycle, 1998), all of which starred **Luis Alberto García** ('*Plaff!*' and '*Adorables mentiras*'). The first film is yet another sharp-edged comedy about life's illusions and disappointments, a bitter-sweet genre that the Cubans have made their own. As might be expected, the three protagonists (a dropout, a nurse and a ballet dancer) all have sexual hang-ups and are seen attempting to make sense of their chaotic lives in today's Havana. The second film is a musical biopic partly produced in the USA, again starring García. It tells the story of Miguel Cancio (the producer's father), founder of the 1960s quartet **Los Zafiros** who developed a unique blend of up-beat r&b and bolero music.

The international explosion of Cuban music, old and new, has led to a trend in Cuban musical documentaries. The film that has made the greatest impact in recent years is without doubt **Wim Wender**'s documentary *Buena Vista Social Club* (Cuba/Germany, 1998), a nostalgic reconstruction of the lives and times of the band of the same name, whose original members are now in their 80s and 90s. The late **Rubén González**'s piano playing, **Ibrahim Ferrer**'s crooning, accompanied by **Ry Cooder** on guitar (with his son, **Joaquín Cooder**, on drums) practising for two gigs in Amsterdam (April 1998) and New York (July 1998) and – above all – the stunning colour photography are quite unforgettable. Two Grammy Award-winning CDs are available: *Buena Vista Social Club* (WCD050) and *Buena Vista Social Club Presents Ibrahim Ferrer* (WCD055). The rhythmic soundtrack of *Tropicola* (Cuba 1998), directed by **Steve Fagin**, is exciting too, although this film is more concerned with today's problems in Cuba: the harmful effects of tourism and the dollar economy. Entirely different, but just as Cuban, is the wonderfully evocative short *Misa cubana* (Cuban Mass, Cuba, 1998), a collage of 16th- and 17th-century sacred music with a score written by maestro **José María Vitier**.

Cuba has once again hit the headlines in several films made about the island in the USA and elsewhere. First there was *Cosas que dejé en la Habana* (Things I left in Havana, 1998) by Spanish film director **Manuel Gutiérrez Aragón** starring Jorge Perugorría (of *Fresa y Chocolate* fame). The film, funny yet critical, tells the story of three Cuban sisters who come to Madrid in search of a better world but are exploited by their aunt who, among other things, tries to marry the youngest girl to her gay son. Then **Roger Donaldson**'s political thriller *Thirteen Days* starring Kevin Costner, released in 2000, presented yet another version of the 1962 Cuban Missile Crisis, when the world was pushed to the brink of nuclear war. Despite its length (over two hours), the film received favourable reviews and was screened in Cuba. Costner and the producers were invited to dinner with Fidel and then collaborated with **ICAIC** to get the film put on in the island. Costner is still a frequent visitor to the island.

The most controversial film about Cuba in recent years (when aren't films about Cuba controversial?) is **Julian Schabel**'s *Before Night Falls* (2001), which is loosely based on the autobiography of gay Cuban writer **Reinaldo Arenas**' *Antes que anochezca* (Barcelona, 1992) (Before Night Falls, London, 1993). Arenas was born near Holguín in 1943 and was self-taught. After the Revolution he was given posts in the National Library and as editor of

Tomás Gutiérrez Alea (1928-1996)

The two most famous Cuban films, *Memorias del Subdesarrollo* (Memories of Underdevelopment, 1968), on the role of the intellectual in society, and *Fresa y Chocolate* (Strawberry and Chocolate, 1993), about gay issues in Cuba, were made by the director who has contributed more than any other to Cuban cinema.

Tomás Gutiérrez Alea made over 12 features and 13 documentaries/ shorts. His films vary from the hilarious *La Muerte de un Burócrata* (Death of a Bureaucrat, 1966) to the sentimental romance *Hasta Cierto Punto* (Up to a Point, 1984). Except for *Cartas del Parque* (Letters from the Park, 1988), based on a screenplay by Gabriel García Márquez, they all have a sharp critical edge.

Gutiérrez Alea started filming in 1947, then studied at the *Centro Sperimentale* in Rome in 1953. His first serious work was a 1955 documentary on the charcoal workers, confiscated by the Batista police. During the Revolution he played a leading part organizing the cinema section of the Revolutionary army and made (with García Espinosa) the first post-victory documentary, *Esta Tierra Nuestra* (This Our Land). His first feature film, *Historias de la Revolución* (Stories of the Revolution) dates from 1960.

Since then, Gutiérrez Alea has won many international awards and retrospectives of his work have been shown across the world (including San Francisco, New York, Toronto and New Delhi).

Repeatedly, particularly in the late 1980s, he was refused entry into the USA. Yet in 1994, *Fresa y Chocolate* was nominated for an Oscar in the best foreign film category. Made primarily for a domestic market, it stages the dramatic encounter between a young Communist student and a gay intellectual. Both are patriotic Cubans but, while the student embraces the culture of Che and Fidel, the intellectual identifies with the refined artistic world of pre-Revolutionary Cuba. Each learns from the other, but the intellectual, hounded by the authorities, finally seeks political asylum in Europe. Gutiérrez Alea's last film, the road movie *Guantanamera* (1995), which returns to the macabre comedy format of *La Muerte de un Burócrata*, was completed shortly before his death. The leading actress in both films was his wife, Mirta Ibarra.

the famous *Gaceta de Cuba* (1968-1974). His first novel was published in Cuba in 1967, but in the early 1970s he ran into trouble with the authorities and was imprisoned for two years (1974-1976). He left Cuba in the Mariel exodus of 1980 and was employed in the USA as a literature professor. He contracted HIV and committed suicide in New York in 1990. His autobiography, although beautifully written, is hyperbolical (he boasts of having had 5000 gay sexual encounters before the age of 25) and especially hostile to Castro. It should not be read as documentary fact, as several of Arenas' Cuban friends and colleagues have since pointed out. The film represents events at an even further remove from historical reality, yet has been widely reviewed as the most recent indictment of Castro's apparently brutal government. In other words, the film is deliberately politically biased. This is not to say it is not a good film; it is, but it is fiction and should be viewed as such. The Spanish actor Javier Bardem, playing Arenas, is powerful and convincing; the film also features famous Hollywood actors (Sean Penn, Johnny Depp) in cameo roles. Although the camera work is excellent, if you don't know Arenas's story you may be confused by the complex plot.

At the 2002 International Film Festival, the largest crowds queued to see *Balseros* (Rafters), a film documentary about seven Cubans who set sail for Miami in 1994, a time of economic crisis when Castro allowed thousands to flee on any home-made craft for Florida. Their stories show the pain of leaving families behind and the culture shock of living and working long hours in the USA. Directors **Carles Bosch** and **Josep Domenech** presented a frank account of the poverty driving Cubans to leave, but also the harsh reality of life elsewhere. In 2003, one of the most talked about films was a silent movie directed by **Fernando Pérez**, *Suite Habana*, a documentary of a day in the life of the city and its inhabitants, with a sound track limited to music and city noises. It can be interpreted as either a subversive criticism of Castro's system, or as a tribute to the courage and resilience of Habaneros, struggling against all odds to survive without losing their revolutionary dreams.

The big foreign film of recent years is the monumental *Che* (Steven Soderbergh, 2008), which was so long that it was divided into two films, *Che Part 1: The Argentine*, and *Che Part 2: The Guerrilla*. This blockbuster biopic of Che Guevara, starring Benicio del Toro, who won the Best Actor Award at the 2008 Cannes Film Festival, was filmed mostly in Spanish for veracity. The first part covers the Cuban Revolution, but was filmed in Mexico and Puerto Rico because of the US embargo. The second part is about Guevara's attempt to export revolution to Bolivia, with disastrous consequences. The film was shown to huge acclaim in Havana as part of the 2008 Latin American Film Festival, although Benicio del Toro was understandably anxious about such a knowledgeable audience. The state newspaper, *Granma*, gave del Toro a glowing review, while the 2000-strong audience at the Yara cinema gave him a 10-minute standing ovation.

In Cuba, meanwhile, Cuba mourned the death from cancer of film-maker **Humberto Solás** (1941-2008). He had a prolific output but first came to international attention with his 1968 film, *Lucía*, charting the lives and fortunes of three women called Lucía in different stages of Cuban history. It was filmed in Gibara, north of Holguín, a small town with which he maintained a long association. Solás was the first Cuban director to be nominated for an Oscar, with his film *Un Hombre de Exito* (1985). In 2001 he brought out *Miel para Oshún* (Honey for the Goddess Oshun, 2001), the story of a Cuban, Roberto (played by Jorge Perugorría, yet again), who was taken to the USA as a child after the Revolution and returns 30 years later to find his mother. Like Alea's *Guantanamera*, this is a road movie, more notable for its outstanding photography of the Cuban landscape than for its penetrating character analyses. Some of this film was again shot in Gibara and in 2003 Solás founded a festival for 'poor' cinema to be held annually in the town. The festival is dedicated to movies made against seemingly overwhelming odds and no film shown there has cost more than US$300,000 to make. After Solás death the film festival was renamed in his honour as the Festival Internacional del Cine Pobre de Humberto Solás.

Lovers of wry humour at the expense of the Cuban predicament should seek out the films of **Juan Carlos Tabío**. His 2001 award-winning comedy, *Lista de Espera* (Waiting List) was scripted by Senel Paz and Arturo Arango and stars Vladimir Cruz (of *Fresa y Chocolate* fame) and Jorge Perugorría (now playing a blind man). The action takes place in a remote, dilapidated bus station. The passengers wait and wait for a bus but they are all full so they try and repair an old Soviet wreck in a collective effort to repair the broken dream. The bus is a metaphor for the better times that never materialize and the passengers' solidarity a comment on the resilience and blind optimism of those that try to make things work despite all odds. Tabío's more recent comedy, *El Cuerno de la Abundancia* (Horn of Plenty, Cuba/Spain 2008), again starring Jorge Perugorría, follows the hopes and aspirations of the extended Castiñeiras family from a small town in Cuba who hear they've inherited a fortune from the 17th century, left to them in a bank in London by three nuns. To escape the poverty and stagnation of their lives in Cuba they go through bureaucratic hoops to prove their parentage, squabbles between different factions of the family, love affairs driven by greed, but it all comes to nothing when they hear it has gone to a branch of the family in Miami. They are left with debts and broken marriages but at the end there is new hope of an inheritance and the cycle starts all over again.

In short, the Cuban film industry is progressing well in the 21st century and the International Film Festivals (Festival Internacional del Nuevo Cine Latinoamericano, www.habanafilmfestival.com, Festival Internacional del Cine Pobre de Humberto Solás, www.festivalcinepobre.org) are major events that should not be missed.

Religion

The major characteristic of Cuban culture is its combination of the African and European. Because slavery was not abolished until 1886 in Cuba, black African traditions were kept intact much later than elsewhere in the Caribbean. They persist now, inevitably mingled with Hispanic influence, in religion: in *Santería*, for instance, a cult which blends popular Catholicism with the Yoruba belief in the spirits that inhabit all plant life. This now has a greater hold in Cuba than orthodox Catholicism, which has traditionally been seen as the religion of the white, upper class: opposing independence from Spain in the 19th century and the Revolution in the 1950s.

The Roman Catholic Church

Church and State were separated at the beginning of the 20th century when Spain was defeated by the USA and a constituent assembly approved a new constitution. The domination of the USA after that time encouraged the spread of Protestantism, although Catholicism remained the religion of the majority. Nevertheless, Catholicism was not as well supported as in some other Latin American countries. Few villages had churches and most Cubans rarely went to mass. Even before the Revolution, the Church was seen as right wing, as most of the priests were Spanish and many of them were supporters of General Franco and his fascist regime in Spain.

After the Revolution, relations between the Catholic Church and Castro were frosty. Most priests left the country and some joined the émigrés in Miami, where connections are still strong. By the late 1970s, the Vatican's condemnation of the US embargo helped towards a gradual reconciliation. In 1979, the Pope was invited to visit Cuba on his way back from a trip to Mexico, but he also received an invitation from the Cuban émigrés in Miami. Caught between a rock and a hard place, the Pope opted to go to the Bahamas instead. In the 1980s, Castro issued visas to foreign priests and missionaries and allowed the import of bibles, as well as giving permission for new churches to be built.

In 1994, Cardinal Jaime Ortega was appointed by the Vatican to fill the position left vacant in Cuba since the last cardinal died in 1963. A ban on religious believers joining the Communist Party has been lifted and Protestant, Catholic and other church leaders have reported rising congregations. In the archdiocese of Havana, there were 7500 baptisms in 1979 but this figure shot up to 34,800 in 1994.

In 1996, Fidel visited Pope John Paul II at the Vatican and the Pope visited Cuba in January 1998. Castro has stated in the past that there is no conflict between Marxism and Christianity and has been sympathetic towards supporters of liberation theology in their

The Orishas

Every *toque de santo* begins and ends with the evocation of **Elegguá**, lord of the roads and crossroads and guardian of our destiny, dressed always in red and black. In the calendar of Christian saints he is equated with the Child of Prague. Most powerful *orisha* of all is red-clad **Changó**, lord of fire, thunder, war, drums and virility, who is syncretized with St Barbara. *Santeros* believe he was born of **Yemayá**, alter ego of the Virgin of Regla, Havana Bay's patron saint. Dressed in blue and white, she is mistress of the seas and goddess of motherhood.

Oggún (St Peter) is another war god and patron of blacksmiths. Brother to **Changó**, he is also his rival for the affection of **Yemayá**'s sensual dancing sister **Ochún**, the yellow-clad goddess of rivers and springs, beauty and sexual love. Christianized as the Virgin of Charity of El Cobre, she is Cuba's patron saint. Her shrine at the Basilica of El Cobre, outside Santiago de Cuba, is always filled with fragrant *mariposas*, the national flower, and the walls are hung with countless offerings from those whose prayers have been answered, including crutches, sachets of Angolan earth brought by returning veterans, a medallion left by Fidel Castro's mother after his safe return from the guerrilla struggle, and Hemingway's Nobel Prize.

Olofi or **Olorun**, syncretized as both the Eternal Father and the Holy Spirit, is the supreme creator of all things, but, say *santeros*, takes little interest in our world, and long ago handed over the care of it to **Obatalá** who, dressed all in white like his devotees or *hijos* (children), is god of peace, truth, wisdom and justice. In Christian guise he is Our Lady of Mercy. His son is **Orula** (colours: yellow and green), syncretized as St Francis of Assisi and others. Known also as **Ifá**, he is the ancient, implacable lord of divination. Unlike other **orishas**, who 'descend on' and possess their *hijos*, he communicates only with the *babalawo* or priest who interprets his predictions. Divination of what the future holds is a central feature of Regla de Ocha, and may be achieved through casting the *ékuele*, a set of eight pieces of turtle or coconut shell.

Other popular *orishas* include **Oyá** (St Teresa of Ávila), mistress of the winds and lightning, queen of the cemetery; and **Babalú Ayé**. Dressed in bishop's purple, covered in sores, limping along on crutches and followed by stray dogs, he is the deity of leprosy and venereal and skin diseases. Every 17 December thousands of his followers, make the pilgrimage to the chapel of St Lazarus, his Christian manifestation, at El Rincón on the southern outskirts of Havana.

quest for equality and a just distribution of social wealth. During the Pope's visit to Brazil in October 1997, he criticized free market ideology which promotes excessive individualism and undermines the role of society, which he further emphasized in his visit to Cuba. The two septuagenarians clearly share common ground on the need for social justice, although they are poles apart on the family, marriage, abortion and contraception, let alone totalitarianism and violent Revolution. At the Pope's request, Castro decreed 25 December 1997 a public holiday, initially for one year only, but it is now a regular event. Christmas Day was abolished in the 1960s because it interfered with the sugar harvest; a whole generation has grown up without it and many people were unsure of its religious significance when it was reinstated. Nevertheless, artificial Christmas trees sold out and tinsel and religious imagery were to be found in many homes.

Afro-Cuban religion

From the mid-16th century to the late 19th century, countless hundreds of thousands of African slaves were brought to Cuba. Torn from dozens of peoples between the Gulf of Guinea and southern Angola, speaking hundreds of languages and dialects, they brought from home only a memory of their customs and beliefs as a shred of comfort in their traumatic new existence on the sugar plantations. The most numerous and culturally most influential group were the Yoruba-speaking agriculturalists from the forests of southeast Nigeria, Dahomey and Togo, who became known collectively in Cuba as *lucumí*. It is their pantheon of deities or *orishas*, and the legends (*pwatakis*) and customs surrounding these, which form the basis of the syncretic Regla de Ocha cult, better known as **Santería.**

Although slaves were ostensibly obliged to become Christians, their owners, anxious to prevent different ethnic groups from uniting, turned a blind eye to their traditional rituals. The Catholic saints thus spontaneously merged or syncretized in the *lucumí* mind with the *orishas*, whose imagined attributes they shared.

While the Yoruba recognize 400 or more regional or tribal *orishas*, their Cuban descendants have forgotten, discarded or fused together most of these, so that today barely two dozen regularly receive tribute at the rites known as *toques de santo* (see box, page 446).

Santería, which claims to have at least as many believers as the Roman Catholic Church in Cuba, in all walks of life including Communist Party members, enshrines a rich cultural heritage. For every *orisha* there is a complex code of conduct, dress (including colour-coded necklaces) and diet to which his or her *hijos* must conform, and a series of chants and rhythms played on the sacred *batá* drums.

Santería is non-sectarian and non-proselytizing, co-existing peacefully with both Christianity and the **Regla Conga** or **Palo Monte** cult brought to Cuba by *congos*, slaves from various Bantu-speaking regions of the Congo basin. Indeed many people are practising believers in both or all three. Found mainly in Havana and Matanzas provinces, **Palo Monte** is a much more fragmented and impoverished belief system than **Regla de Ocha**, and has borrowed aspects from it and other sources. Divided into several sects, the most important being the *mayomberos*, *kisimberos* and *briyumberos*, it is basically animist, using the forces of nature to perform good or evil magic and predict the future in ceremonies involving rum, tobacco and at times gunpowder. The focus of its liturgy is the *nganga*, both a supernatural spirit and the earthenware or iron container in which it dwells along with the *mpungus* or saints. **Regla Conga** boasts a wealth of complex magic symbols or *firmas*, and has retained some exciting drum rhythms.

The **Abakuá Secret Society** is, as its name suggests, not a religion but a closed sect. Open to men only, and upholding traditional *macho* virtues, it has been described as an Afro-Cuban freemasonry, although it claims many non-black devotees. Found almost exclusively in Havana (particularly in the Guanabacoa, Regla and Marianao districts), and in the cities of Matanzas, Cárdenas and Cienfuegos, it has a strong following among dock-workers; indeed, outsiders often claim its members have *de facto* control over those ports. Also known as **ñañiguismo**, the sect originated among slaves brought from the Calabar region of southern Nigeria and Cameroon, whose Cuban descendants are called *carabalí*. Some **ñáñigos** claim the society was formally founded in 1836 in Regla, across the bay from Havana, but there is evidence that it already existed at the time of the 1812 anti-slavery conspiracy. **Abakuá** shares with freemasonry the fraternal aims of mutual assistance, as well as a series of seven secret commandments, secret signs and arcane ceremonies involving special vestments.

The Afro Trail

It is not so long since traditionalist believers were scandalized when the renowned jazz and salsa band **Irakere** started to use the sacred *cueros batá* (the three drums used in *Santería* rites) on stage. In these times, when all's fair in the scramble for tourist dollars, you may well find a more-or-less Disneyfied all-singing, all-dancing version of *lucumí* or congo ceremonies on offer as part of your hotel's entertainment. Enjoy the spectacle but season liberally with salt.

Alternatively you can witness expertly choreographed and largely genuine performances of Yoruba and Congo devotional and profane song and dance, as well as the intricacies of the *real rumba* in all its variants, at the Sábado de la Rumba sessions put on by the **Conjunto Folklórico Nacional** on Saturday afternoons at their Calle 4 headquarters in Vedado (see box, Music in Havana, page 117). Despite the colourful trappings, this is only incidentally a spectacle for tourists, who are regularly outnumbered by the Cubans fervidly chorusing the *santero* chants in Yoruba and swaying to the infectious *guaguancó*. The **Casa de África** (Obrapía 157, entre San Ignacio y Mercaderes, Old Havana, Tue-Sun 1300-2000) is an untaxing and pleasant way to get a glimpse of the wealth of African cultures, in Cuba and in Africa itself. As well as small collections from various African countries, it houses the Afro-Cuban devotional artifacts collected by the late Don Fernando Ortiz, the founding father of Afro-Cuban ethnographic studies.

Also worth a visit is the **Museo Municipal de Regla** (Martí 158, entre Facciolo y Piedra, Regla, Mon-Sat 0930-1830, Sun 0900-1300). The most atmospheric way to reach Regla is by *lanchita* (ferry) across the bay from the terminal near the Plaza de Armas. The collection of history of African religions in Cuba, formerly in the **Museo Histórico de Guanabacoa** (Martí 108, entre Versalles y San Antonio) in the district popularly regarded as the Mecca of Afro-Cuban cults, is now in the Casa de Africa. Any *habanero* afflicted by aches and pains or generally down in the mouth will sooner or later be advised, "What you need is a trip to Guanabacoa."

Land and environment

Geology and landscape

Geologically at least, Cuba is part of North America; the boundary between the North American and Caribbean plates runs east–west under the Caribbean Sea to the south of the island. Along the plate margin is a deep underwater rift valley, which runs between Cuba and Jamaica. This feature is quite close to the Cuban coast to the south of the Sierra Maestra, with water plunging to 6000 m only a few miles offshore. Earth movements along the plate boundary make the eastern region of Cuba the most earthquake-prone part of the country, with earthquakes in Bayamo in 1551 and Santiago de Cuba in 1932.

Current plate movements are pushing Cuba to the west and the Caribbean plate to the east. What is now the Sierra Maestra in southern Cuba was probably joined 40 million years ago to geologically similar areas on the north coast of Haiti and the Dominican Republic. Plate movements since then have caused a displacement of around 400 km.

Cuba is also being tilted gradually to the north. The northern coastline is gradually emerging from the sea. Old coral reefs have been brought to the surface, and now form much of the coastline, so that much of the northern coast consists of coral limestone cliffs and sandy beaches. A short way inland, old cliff lines marking stages of coastal emergence form a series of coral terraces, one of which runs just northeast of the **Hotel Nacional** in Havana. There are well-developed series of old cliff lines and coral terraces on the southeast tip of the island near Baracoa and to the west of Santiago near Cabo Cruz. By contrast the southern coastline is being gradually submerged, producing a series of wetlands and mangroves running from the Ensenada de Cortés in the west to the Gulf of Guacanayabo in the east, with fewer sandy beaches than the north of the island.

During the glacial periods of the last million years, sea levels worldwide fell by about 120 m; as much of the world's water was locked up in the northern ice sheets. The shallow seas which now form Cuba's continental shelf were dry land, and the coastline generally followed the line of Cuba's 4000-plus offshore islands: the Sabana island chain to the north and the Canarreos and Jardines de la Reina to the south. At this time, central Cuba was separated from the Bahamas by a narrow channel, about 32 km wide.

Cave systems which formed during glacial periods in what were then coastal limestone plains have since been flooded by the sea. In coastal areas such as the western Guanahacabibes peninsula and Playa Girón, there are small, deep lakes known to English-speaking geologists as Blue Holes where these submerged cave systems meet the surface.

There is no clear agreement about Cuba's more distant geological origins. The curve of the island follows the line of a collision in the Cretaceous period around 100 million years ago between an arc of volcanic islands and the stable Bahamas platform which then formed the southern edge of the North American plate. There is disagreement about whether this arc faced north or south, and about how the collision took place. But the powerful forces associated with the process produced a complex pattern of folding and faulting, while many rocks were greatly altered by heat and pressure. Many of Cuba's rocks predate this collision. These include the Caribbean's only pre-Cambrian rocks, metamorphics more than 900 million years old in the province of Santa Clara; and the Jurassic limestones, around 160 million years old, which form the Sierra de los Organos.

After the collision, what is now Cuba was submerged for long periods, and there were new deposits of limestone and other rocks. For most of the tertiary period, from 35 million years ago, Cuba was a series of large islands and shallow seas, emerging as a single land mass by the start of the Pliocene period five million years ago. Limestones of various types cover about two-thirds of the island. In most areas, there is a flat or gently rolling landscape. The most common soils, both formed on limestone, are terra rossa, stained bright red by iron oxides, and vertisols, black, fertile, and developing deep cracks during the dry season.

There are three main mountain areas in the island. In the west, the Cordillera de Guaniguanico is divided into the Sierra del los Organos in the west, with thick deposits of limestone which have developed a distinctive landscape of steep-sided flat-topped mountains; and the Sierra del Rosario in the east, made up partly of limestones and partly of lavas and other igneous rocks. Another mountainous area in central Cuba includes the Escambray mountains north of Trinidad, a double dome structure made up of igneous and metamorphic rocks, including marble.

The Sierra Maestra in the east has Cuba's highest mountains, rising to Pico Turquino (1974 m) and a different geological history, with some rocks formed in an arc of volcanic activity around 50 million years ago. Older rocks include marble, and other metamorphics. The country's most important mineral deposits are in this area; nickel mined near Moa is the third largest foreign currency earner, after tourism and sugar.

For those interested in further information on the physical and human geography of Cuba, the *Nuevo Atlas Nacional de Cuba* (Geocuba, Calle F y 13, Havana, T7-323494) provides a beautifully produced series of detailed thematic maps on every possible topic down to the distribution of ants and spiders, with informative commentaries.

Flora and fauna

When the Spanish arrived at the end of the 15th century, more than 90% of Cuba was covered with forest. When Fray Bartolomé de las Casas visited the island, he said *"La isla tiene de luengo cerca de 300 leguas y se puede andar toda por debajo de los árboles"* (the island is 300 leagues long and you can walk the length of it beneath the trees). However, clearance for cattle raising and sugar cane reduced this proportion to 54% by 1890 and 14% by 1959, although reafforestation since the Revolution has increased this figure. Some 75% of the land is now savannah or plains, 18% mountains and 4% swamps. The mesophytic semi-deciduous tropical woodland which covered most low-lying areas was hardest hit by forest clearance. Besides semi-deciduous woodland, vegetation types include rainforest, coastal and upland scrub, distinctive limestone vegetation found in the Sierra de los Organos and similar areas, savannah vegetation found on nutrient-deficient white silica sands, pine forests, xerophytic coastal limestone woodland, mangroves and other bird-rich coastal wetlands.

Cuba is characterized by extraordinarily high rates of biodiversity and endemism, particularly concentrated in four regions: the **Montañas de Moa-Nipe-Sagua-Baracoa**, which have the greatest diversity in all the Caribbean and are among the highest in the world, and 30% of the endemic species on the island; **Parque Nacional Sierra de los Organos** and the **Reserva de la Biósfera Sierra del Rosario** come a close second, with high rates of endemism, followed closely by the **Reserva Ecológica del Macizo de Guamuhaya**. There is a high proportion of endemic species, found only in Cuba, one region of Cuba, or in the extreme case of some snail species, only on one small mountain in the Sierra de los Organos. Around half the plant species, 90% of the insects and molluscs, 82% of the reptiles and 74 bird species are endemic.

Why the high proportion of endemics? Cuba has a five million-year history as an isolated land mass, with species following their own evolutionary path. There are also a number of specialized environments with geological or soil constraints such as chemical toxicity, poor water retention, low nutrient retention, on ultrabasic igneous rocks, silica sands and limestones. A catalogue is in preparation of all the flora and fauna found in Cuba's protected areas as well as a large percentage of those outside the reserves.

Flora

There are over 7000 plant species in Cuba, of which around 3000 are endemic, and 950 plant species that are endangered, rare, or have become extinct in the last 350 years. Oddities in the plant world include the **Pinguicola lignicola**, the world's only carniverous epiphytic plant; the **cork palm** (*Microcycas colocoma*), an endemic living fossil which is a threatened species; and the **Solandra grandiflora**, one of the world's largest flowers, 10 cm across at the calyx and 30 cm at the corolla.

There are around 100 different palm trees in Cuba, of which 90 are endemic. The Royal palm (*Roystonea regia*) is one of four species of *Roystonia*; it is the national tree and can be seen in the countryside throughout the island. Cubans use the small, purple fruits to feed pigs, as they are oily and nutritious. They develop in bunches below the crown shaft, which can weigh 20-25 kg. They would naturally drop one by one when ripe, but they are usually harvested before then by *trepadores*, men who skilfully climb the trunk of the palm by means of two slings, one supporting the thigh and another supporting a foot. You can also see many flowering trees: pines, oaks, cedars, etc, although original forest is confined to some of the highest points in the southeast mountains and the mangroves of the Zapata Peninsula.

There are a multitude of flowers and in the country even the smallest of houses has a flower garden at the front. The **orchid** family includes some 300 endemic species, but more are constantly being discovered. You can find orchids all over the island, especially in the mountainous regions, some of which live above 700 m. There is one tiny orchid, *Pleurothallis shaferi*, which is only 1 cm, with leaves measuring 5 mm and flowers of only 2 mm. The orchidarium at Soroa has over 700 examples of orchids and other flowers. To complement the wide variety of butterflies that can be found here, the butterfly flower, **mariposa**, a type of jasmine, has been named the national flower.

Fauna

Animal life is also varied, with nearly 14,000 species of fauna, of which 10% could be on the verge of extinction: 250 vertebrate species are endangered, rare or have become extinct in the last 350 years. The total number includes 54 mammals (40% endemic), 330 species of bird (8 genus, 22 species, 32 endemic sub-species), 106 reptile (81% endemic), 42 amphibian (93% endemic), over 1700 mollusc (87% endemic), 7000 insect and 1200 arachnid, as well as a variety of marine species.

There are no native large mammals but some genera and families have diversified into a large number of distinct island species. These include mammals such as the **hutia** (*Capromys*; 10 species, *jutía* in Spanish), a rodent, **bats** (26 species, Cuba has more species of bat per sq km than all North America) and the protected **manatee** with more than 20 breeding groups, mostly in the Ciénaga de Zapata and north of Villa Clara. Reptiles range from three types of crocodile including the **Cuban crocodile** (*Crocodylus rhombifer*) now found only in the Ciénaga de Zapata (there is a farm on the Zapata Peninsula) to iguanas to tiny salamanders. An **iguana**, *Cyclura nubila*, found only in Cuba and the Cayman Islands, is in danger of extinction. Cuba claims the smallest of a number of animals, for instance the **Cuban pygmy frog** (*Eleutherodactylus limbatus*, 12 mm long, one of some 30 small frogs), the **almiquí** (*Selenodon cubanus*, a shrew-like insectivore, the world's smallest mammal, found only in the Sierra de Nipe-Sagua-Baracoa), the **butterfly** or **moth bat** (*Natalus lepidus*, 186 mm, 2 g, often confused with moths at night, it eats mosquitoes) and the **bee hummingbird** (*mellisuga helenae*, 63 mm long, called locally the *zunzuncito*). The latter is an endangered species, like the **carpintero real woodpecker** (*Campephilus principalis*), the **cariara** or **caracara** (*Caracara plancus*, a hawk-like bird of the savannah), the **pygmy owl** (*Glaucidium siju*), the **Cuban green parrot** (*Amazona leucocephala*) and the **fermina**, or **Zapata wren** (*Ferminia cerverai*). Less attractively, there is also a **dwarf scorpion** (*Microtytus fundorai*, *alacrán* in Spanish, 10 mm long).

The best place for **birdwatching** on the island is the Zapata Peninsula, where 170 species of Cuban bird have been recorded, including the majority of endemic species. In winter the number increases as migratory waterbirds, swallows and others visit the marshes. The area around Santo Tomás contains rare birds such as the **Zapata rail**, the **Zapata wren** and the **Zapata sparrow** (*Torreornis inexpectata*, or *cabrerito de la Ciénaga*). The national bird is the forest-dwelling **Cuban trogon** (*Priotelus temnurus*, the *tocororo*), partly because of its blue head, white chest and red underbelly, the colours of the Cuban flag. Other good birdwatching places include La Güira and Soroa, west of Havana, Cayo Coco on the north coast and Najasa, southeast of Camagüey (contact local biologist Pedro Regalado), but there is no shortage of opportunities for spotting endemics anywhere on the island.

Protected areas

The first national park, the **Parque Nacional Pico Cristal**, was established in 1930, but with little regulation and less financing. Conservation only really got started in Cuba with the passing of Law 27 in 1980, which provided funds and legislation to set up more parks. They started in the **Sierra Maestra**, where there are now 13 parks, reserves and refuges. In 1985, UNESCO started working with Cuba in selecting first-class sites, collecting data on biodiversity and endemic species, highlighting the need to give priority to conservation and give total protection in some areas. Within a year a coordinating committee had set out financing needs and donations began to come in to develop the first international reserves in Cuba. Four biosphere reserves were established as pilot programmes and education programmes were offered to neighbouring communities on conservation and sustainable development. In 1991, a consultative group was formed which set up a new **Sistema Nacional de Areas Protegidas** (national system of protected areas) and proposed 73 reserves. Overnight, 12% of Cuba's territory was protected, taking in 96% of vegetation and 321 species of vertebrate. Cuba also ratified the Cartagena Agreement for the protection of the marine environment and certain UNESCO conventions on World Heritage sites and Biosphere Reserves. In 1995, a new strategy was adopted, reorganizing the national environmental plan with the formation of 12 institutions. The key agency is the Centro Nacional para las Areas Protegidas (CNAP), which, together with the Centro Nacional para la Administración Ambiental and the Centro Nacional para la Información, now has responsibility for the protection of the natural environment.

A new environmental law passed in 1997 strengthened the legal framework for wildlife conservation. There is now a comprehensive system of protected areas covering 30% of Cuba, including its marine platform, and incorporating examples of more than 96% of Cuba's vegetation types, 95% of plant species and almost all terrestrial vertebrates. There are 11 categories of protection: *reserva natural, parque nacional, reserva ecológica, elemento natural destacado, reserva florística manejada, refugio de fauna, parque natural, área natural turística, área protegida recursos manejados, área protegida de uso múltiple* and *área protegida sin categoría*. These areas include 14 national parks and four UNESCO biosphere reserves: **Guanahacabibes** in the extreme western tip of the island; the **Sierra del Rosario**, 60 km west of Havana; **Baconao** in the east and **Cuchillas del Toa**. However, not all legally established conservation areas have any infrastructure, personnel or administration in place.

In practice, Cuba's record on preservation of species is not perfect. Crocodiles, highly endangered at the time of the Revolution were subsequently protected and breeding programmes were set up. Now that numbers have been brought to a healthy level in captivity, crocodiles are farmed, killed for their meat, skin and teeth, which are exported. Black coral, protected by CITES, is openly sold as jewellery. Despite the SPAW agreement, to which Cuba is a signatory, dolphins are caught in the wild and kept in dolphinariums for tourists' amusement or allegedly exported to other Caribbean islands for the same purpose. No zoo in the world now takes animals caught in the wild, relying instead on breeding in captivity, but Cuba does not apply this rule to dolphinariums. ▸▸ *See page 22 for further details about dolphinariums in Cuba.*

National parks

Parque Nacional Alejandro de Humboldt 59,771 ha in the Montañas de Toa, near Moa, ranging in altitude from 20 m to 1168 m, and established with assistance from the German NGO, Green Gold. It is the nucleus of the **Cuchillas del Toa UNESCO Biosphere Reserve**, and basically the union of a group of reserves: Cupeyal del Norte, Ojito de Agua, Jaguaní, Alto de Iberia, Taco and Yamaniguey. This tropical woodland has examples of 16 of Cuba's 28 vegetation types and has the highest rate of endemism, with 150 species found only in this area. Of the 64 species of bird that have been recorded, 12 are endemic. Endangered species include the *Carpintero real*, the *almiquí*, the Cuban kite (*Chondrohierax wilsonii*, known in Spanish as the *gavilán caguarero*), the Cuban parakeet (*Aratinga euops*, or *catey* in Spanish), the Cuban parrot (*Amazona leucocephala*, or *cotorra* in Spanish) and the manatee.

Parque Nacional Turquino 17,450 ha national park in the Sierra Maestra, including Cuba's highest mountains: the Pico Turquino (1974 m), the Pico Suecia (1934 m) and the Pico Cuba (1872 m), it is managed in collaboration with WWF Canada. This park contains humid montane forest and has a high percentage of endemics, *Juniperus saxicola* trees, fruit-bearing *Rubus turquinensis*, and small frogs, *Eleutherodactylus albipes* and *Eleutherodactylus turquinensis*.

Parque Nacional Desembarco de Granma Includes the marine terraces of Cabo Cruz, 25,764 ha, which is managed in collaboration with WWF Canada. This is the world's second biggest series of marine coral terraces, a staircase-like formation of 22 old shorelines and sea cliffs formed on emerging coral coast, with dry tropical forest and mangrove. There have been 58 endemic plant species recorded here and the fauna includes species like the primitive lizard (*Cricosaura typica*) and a brightly coloured snail (*Ligus vittatus*), which only lives in a small area of the park. There is a network of interpretative paths, archaeological sites with petroglyghs and pictographs, manatees, and diving on the offshore reef.

Parque Nacional La Bayamesa 21,100 ha in the Sierra Maestra around Pico Bayamesa (1730 m), north of Uvero.

Parque Nacional La Mensura Pilotos (Pinares de Mayarí) 5340 ha in the Altiplanicie de Nipe of pine forests with traditional coffee and livestock farming, while also home to 460 endemic species. There are interpretative paths, some ecotourism and you can see parrots.

Parque Nacional Pico Cristal 16,010 ha in the Sierra de Cristal of pine forest and broadleaved humid tropical forest, where you can find parrots and nightingales (*Myadestes elizebeth*) and possibly the *almiquí*. There is no administration yet in place. This was the first protected area in Cuba, dating from 1930, although it was never managed as such until recently.

Parque Nacional Caguanes 22,690 ha (5387 on land and 17,303 under water) in the Cayería Caibarién Caguanes, a group of small islands just offshore. Cayo Caguanes, which gives its name to the park, has 25 caves on only 1.1 sq km and is joined to the mainland by mangroves. Some caves have endemic invertebrates and a rare fresh water sponge has been found in flooded caves. They are also sites of prehistoric interest, with cave drawings and 40 archaeological sites. The park is also home to one of the 10 colonies in Cuba of sandhill cranes, known locally as *grulla* (*Grus canadensis nesiotes*), a tall, long-legged bird with a long neck which it stretches out in front of it when flying. In 2009 more caves were discovered on Cayo Fábrica, with a colony of butterfly bats.

Parque Nacional Viñales 21,600 ha in the Sierra de los Organos, with the distinctive *mogotes*. There is no administration in place for these limestone uplands with extensive cave systems (Santo Tomás and Palmarito are thought to be the largest in the Caribbean) and distinctive xerophytic vegetation, where you can find sierra palm (*Gausio princeps*), ceibón (*Bombracopsis cubensis*) and cork palm (*Mycrocicas calocoma*). Several types of snails have become so isolated that they live only on one part of a *mogote*.

Parque Nacional Marino Punta Francés, Punta Pedernales 17,924 ha of marine platform going down to 200 m, with untouched coral formations and abundant flora and fauna. There is no park management as such, but it is looked after by the International Diving Centre at **Hotel Colony**, Isla de la Juventud.

Reserva Ecológica Los Indios-San Felipe A 3050-ha reserve on the white-sand plains of Isla de la Juventud, administered in collaboration with WWF Canada. As well as exceptional bird life, there is pine-covered savannah with 24 endemics and the carniverous plants of the genera *drosera*, *pinguicola* and *utricularia*. Many plants and trees have adapted to become resistant to fire. As a result of management and protection of the area, it is now the site of one of the largest nesting groups of Cuban parrot, and is another of the sites for the sandhill crane.

Reserva Ecológica El Naranjal 3,068-ha reserve in the Guamuhaya mountains at an altitude of 70-870 m, where you can find the Cuban parrot, the Cuban parakeet and the *jutía conga* (*Capromys pilorides*). Over 600 plant species have been recorded here, of which 22% are endemic and 12 are found nowhere else. An area of 12,494 ha in the Guamuhaya mountains (or Sierra del Escambray) is classified as **Paisaje Natural Protegido Topes de Collantes**, or protected natural landscape. Topes de Collantes is a popular hiking excursion from Trinidad. Abundant rainfall encourages mosses, lichens, ferns, orchids and other vegetation, home to many birds and invertebrates.

Reserva Ecológica Punta Negra-Punta de Quemados On the Maisí marine terraces are 3972 ha of the world's largest and best developed system of marine coral terraces, with 27 levels and the driest natural environment in Cuba, many endemic, and some unique plants. A substantial part of the first three levels is included in the reserve.

Refugio de Fauna Santo Tomás y Las Salinas These are two reserves which form the basis of the 70,277-ha **Parque Nacional Ciénaga de Zapata**. They are still being defined and established but there is rich bird life here, in what is the largest wetland in the Caribbean. More than 170 species of bird have been recorded. At Las Salinas there are huge populations of waterbirds and at Santo Tomás there are two species found nowhere else in the world, the Zapata rail, known as the *gallinuela de Santo Tomás* (*Cyanolimnas cerverai*), and the Zapata wren, known as ferminia (*Ferminia cerverai*). The Zapata rail is dark, with a mixture of olive brown on top, slate grey underneath and on its forehead and cheeks, without any spots or streaks, except for white tips to its flank feathers and conspicuously white under its tail. Its bill is green, with red at its base, it has red feet and very short wings, so it does not fly very well. The Zapata wren measures 16 cm, it has short wings and a long tail, has a spotted head, greyish brown back with black bars and whitish underparts. It lives in the dense bushes and hardly ever flies but it has a loud voice, with a varied, musical warbling. There are also crocodiles (*Crocodylus rhombifer*), which are endemic, and the manatee, or sea cow.

Refugio de Fauna Silvestre Río Máximo 12,500 ha of mangroves on the north Camagüey coast, with saline and freshwater lakes and semi-deciduous coastal woodlands. It is a major site for flamingos with two colonies of some 4000 birds and the world's largest nesting population. There is also a large population of the American crocodile (*Crocodylus acutus*). Largest of all, however, is the number of water fowl which migrate here in season, when tens of thousands of duck (*Anas*, 11 species), glossy ibis (*Plegadis falcinellus*), white ibis (*Eudocimus albus*) (both known locally as *cocos*), roseate spoonbill (*Ajaia ajaia*) and other birds can be seen.

Crocodiles

The endemic crocodile in Cuba, the *Rhombifer*, was facing extinction under the Batista dictatorship and it was only in 1959 after the Revolution that it gained a reprieve. A serious effort was made to set up farms and breed the species, with a programme to release some of the offspring into the wild.

There are now several crocodile farms around the island, but one of the most visited by tourists is at Guamá in the Zapata peninsula (see page 194). Here the animals are graded according to size and age and there are 25 sections containing a total of some 2000 crocodiles. A visitor will see only a small part of the farm, with a selection of crocs on display, from a group of 5-10 months old measuring less than a metre, to one of four years old with his mouth tied up so that he can be made to pose to be touched and photographed. The path circles some ponds in which you can see fully grown monsters which can

live up to 100 years. They often lounge on the banks with their mouths open to regulate their temperature, giving you a good view of their teeth.

A crocodile reaches maturity at six years, laying eggs in the spring. It eats only once a week and its diet in Cuba is enlivened by dead or sick and dying domestic animals brought by their owners for disposal. As farmed creatures, the crocodiles' skin, meat and teeth are used and exported.

According to CITES they are endangered in the wild, but by farming them Cuba now has thousands of crocodiles in captivity. These farmed animals are used for meat and their skins are used in leather goods, but there is a CITES ban on the export of crocodile products. You will find farmed crocodile on menus in a few places in Cuba, which you can try if you wish. Wild crocodile is not permitted.

Refugio de Fauna Silvestre Río Cauto Delta Just north of Manzanillo, 60,000 ha of mangroves, hypersaline and freshwater lakes and wetlands, which are rich in bird life as well as home to flamingos and the American crocodile.

Refugio de Fauna Silvestre Hatibonica 5220 ha refuge overlooking the US naval base at Guantánamo Bay, with sparsely vegetated hill country and varied fauna including iguanas (*Cyclura nubila nubila*) and endemic cacti. Strange wind-blown, variegated rock formations, called *Monitongos*, characterize this arid landscape. There is an interpretative path: Los Monitongos.

Area Protegida de Recursos Manejados Cayos del Norte de Villa Clara 17,500-ha protected area above and below water down to 20 m in the Sabana de Camagüey archipelago, part of **Parque Nacional Cayo Guillermo Santa María**. Wildlife includes the second largest colony of manatees in the country around the Cayos del Pajonal, hutia or *jutía rata* (*Capromys auritus*) on Cayo Fragoso, flamingos on Las Picuas, iguanas on Cayo Cobo and endemic birds and reptiles on Cayo Francés and Cayo Santa María.

Reserva de la Biósfera Guanahacabibes On the extreme western tip of the island, covering 101,500 ha of 'dogstooth' landscape of bare limestone, with scattered pockets of soil and dry coastal evergreen and semi-deciduous woodland. Terraces and beaches are interspersed along the coast. There are two well-established nuclei of the biosphere reserve, **Reserva Natural El Veral** and **Reserva Natural Cabo Corrientes**, where an ecological station carries out research.

Reserva de la Biósfera Sierra del Rosario 25,000 ha of the Sierra del Rosario mountain range, with the best example of evergreen forest in western Cuba. There are three nuclei in the reserve, El Salón, Las Peladas and Las Terrazas, where there is an ecological station and the local community is directly involved with protecting the environment. Birdwatching is rewarding and you may see the bee hummingbird. There are nearly 800 plant species, of which 34% are endemic.

Reserva de la Biósfera Baconao 80,000 ha along the foothills of the Sierra Maestra, stretching east from Santiago de Cuba to Laguna Baconao. The reserve includes many tourist facilities such as hotels, a dolphinarium, the Valle de la Prehistoria and others, but the fauna and flora in the park are varied, with many endemic species.

Books

Architecture
Guía de Arquitectura La Habana Colonial, La Habana (1995), Sevilla. Useful guide to Old Havana, with maps, ground plans and photos.

Culture
Calder, Simon and Hatchwell, Emily, *In Focus: Cuba, A Guide to the People, Politics and Culture*, Latin America Bureau (ISBN 0-906156 -95-5). One of an excellent series of books on Latin America and the Caribbean, covering history, economics, politics and culture.
Daniel, Yvonne, *Rumba, Dance and Social Change in Contemporary Cuba* (1995), Indiana University Press. Also in the series: *Blacks in the Diaspora* (ISBN 0-253-31605-7, paperback ISBN 0-253-20948-X). A good general book on Cuba as well as on music, portrait of life on the streets, the author is a professional dancer who completed her research in 1991.
Lumsden, Ian, *Machos, Maricones and Gays, Cuba and Homosexuality* (1996), Temple University Press, Philadelphia, also published in the UK by Latin American Bureau (ISBN 1-56639-371-X). Very readable account of the attitudes of Cubans towards gays since the days of slavery, with related treatment of blacks and women.
Pérez Sarduy, Pedro and Stubbs, Jean (Editors), *AfroCuba, an Anthology of Cuban Writing on Race, Politics and Culture* (1993), Ocean Press, Melbourne, Australia, also by the Latin American Bureau (ISBN 0-906156-75-0). Collection of fiction, theatre, poetry, history and political commentary, dealing with the relationship between Africa and Cuba.

Literature and fiction
Arenas, Reinaldo, *Antes que Anochezca* (Before Night Falls, 1994, Viking). Autobiography of a homosexual growing up in Cuba after the Revolution, facing persecution, censorship and imprisonment. Arenas left Cuba in the Mariel boat lift but never settled in the USA, finally committing suicide in 1990 aged 47, when dying of AIDS.
Cabrera Infante, Guillermo, *Tres Tristes Tigres* (1967) (Three Trapped Tigers, 1989, Faber & Faber). One of the funniest novels in Spanish, a tableau of Havana's nightlife in the time of Batista, written after the author emigrated.
Ferguson, James, *A Traveller's History of the Caribbean* (1998), Windrush Press. Concise and easy to dip into, from Columbus to Castro, with interesting asides on recent issues such as drugs trafficking, characters such as Fidel and the US influence and intervention throughout the Caribbean.
García, Cristina, *Dreaming in Cuban* (1992) Flamingo, London (1982) Knopf, New York. Cuba as seen by 3 generations of women, the grandmother who stayed behind, the daughter who emigrated to the USA and the granddaughter, who returns to visit.
Greene, Graham, *Our Man in Havana: An Entertainment* (1958), William Heinemann. Spy thriller set in Havana at the end of the Batista regime as the Revolutionaries close in.

Gutiérrez, Pedro Juan, *Dirty Havana Trilogy*, translated by Natasha Wimmer (2001), Faber and Faber. Pedro Juan gives up his job as a reporter to re-educate himself in his attitude to life and what makes him happy. This involves lots of sex, drugs, rum, music and other good things in life, highly explicit and with insights into what makes Havana tick.

Padura Fuentes, Leonardo, *Havana Quartet: Havana Red, Havana Black, Havana Blue, Havana Gold*, translated by Peter Bush (2005, 2006, 2007, 2008), Bitter Lemon Press, and *Adiós Hemingway*, translated by John King (2005). Prize-winning detective fiction, all featuring Lieutenant Mario Conde of Havana, whose musings on life in the city, sex, friendship and drinking are as important as the plots, eminently readable, hugely atmospheric, take them with you.

History and society

Collier, Simon, Skidmore, Thomas E and Blakemore, Harold (Editors), *The Encyclopaedia of Latin America and the Caribbean* (1992), Cambridge University Press, 2nd edition. Useful reference book which includes cultural, geographical and economic information on Cuba in the Latin American context.

Ferguson, James, *The Traveller's Literary Companion, The Caribbean* (1997), Windrush Press. A good introduction to Cuban literature and writings on Cuba, with chapters by Jason Wilson. Includes a good reading list.

Parry, JH, Sherlock, PM and Maingot, Anthony, *A Short History of the West Indies* (1987), Macmillan. Academic but very readable.

Stubbs, Jean, *Cuba, the Test of Time* (1989) Latin American Bureau, London (ISBN 0-906156-42-4). Short historical and economic analysis of the first 30 years of the Revolution, still useful even without the upheaval of the 1990s.

Thomas, Hugh, *Cuba, or the Pursuit of Freedom* (2002), Eyre and Spottiswoode, London. First published in 1971, this is the best history book specifically on Cuba.

Williamson, Edwin, *The History of Latin America* (1992), Penguin, London. Excellent general history of Cuba's colonial past and independence and revolutionary struggles, set in the context of the Spanish Empire and independent Latin American republics.

Music and dance

Calvo Ospina, Hernando, *Salsa! Havana Heat, Bronx Beat* (1995), Latin American Bureau. An avid salsa dancer traces the development of modern salsa from the slave ships to New York commercial cut-throat business, via *son*, jazz and cha cha cha. Other Latin styles are covered, including Colombian *cumbia* and Dominican Republic *merengue*.

Roy, Maya, *Cuban Music* (2002), Latin American Bureau. Comprehensive and accessible, all you wanted to know about the historical and ethnic roots of Cuban music, the political dimension and the artists involved. Rumba, *danzón, son, guaracha*, are all explained. It includes the Buena Vista Social Club phenomenon.

Travelogues

Miller, T, *Trading with the Enemy: a Yankee travels through Castro's Cuba* (1996). Set in the early 1990s this is a sharply observed travelogue. Detailing Miller's encounters with colourful Cubans from bartenders to baseball players, it steers away from political issues.

Smith, Stephen, *Land of Miracles* (1998), Abacus. A quirky travelogue set in the Special Period when times were hard and the Cubans had to be inventive to survive. Written by a British TV Channel 4 reporter, whose search for the real Cuba turns into a search for Castro.

Religion

There is a vast array of reading matter on Afro-Cuban religions, most of which is in Spanish. Those titles published in Cuba are available in dollars at large hotel bookstores (eg the Habana Libre), or at Librería Fernando Ortiz (opposite the Habana Libre, esq 23 y L), or possibly at La Moderna Poesía in Old Havana, esq Obispo y Bernaza. Ediciones Unión has its own bookshop at the UNEAC (Unión de Escritores y Artistas de Cuba) headquarters Calle 17 351, esq H, Vedado. Casa de las Américas is on Av 3 y G, Vedado. Letras Cubanas has its own bookshop in the Palacio del Segundo Cabo, O'Reilly 4 (Plaza de Armas, Old Havana).

Barnet, Miguel, *Cultos afrocubanos: la regla de Ocha, la regla de Palo Monte* (1995), Ediciones Unión, Havana.

Bolívar, Natalia, *Los orishas en Cuba,* Editorial Unión, Havana.

Bolívar, Natalia and **González Díaz de Villegas, Aróstegui & Carmen,** *Mitos y leyendas de la comida afrocubana* (1993), Colección Echú Bi, Editorial de Ciencias Sociales, Havana.

Cabrera, Lydia, *El Monte: Igbo, Finda, Ewe Orisha, Vititi Nfinda* (Colección del Chicherekú, Ediciones Universal, 3090 SW 8th Street, Miami, Florida, ediciones@kampung.net, 1992, first published in Havana 1954); *Reglas de Congo: Palo monte mayombe* (Ediciones CR, Miami, Florida, 1979).

Feijóo, Samuel, *Mitología cubana* (1985), Editorial Letras Cubanas, Havana.

González-Wippler, Migene, *Santería – the religion: a legacy of faith, rites and magic* (1994), Llewelyn Publications, St Paul, Minnesota, *Legends of Santería* (1994), Llewelyn Publications, St Paul, Minnesota.

Martí, Agenor, *Mis porfiados oráculos* (1992), Fuentetaja Ediciones, Madrid.

Núñez Cedeño, Rafael A, *The Abakuá secret society in Cuba: language and culture* (1988), Hispania, vol 71, No 1.

Ortiz, Fernando, *Los negros esclavos* (1987), Editorial de Ciencias Sociales, Havana. *Los bailes y el teatro de los negros en el folklore de Cuba* (1985), Letras Cubanas, Havana.

Sasa Rodríguez, Enrique, *Los ñáñigos* (1982), Casa de las Américas, Havana.

Wildlife

Flieg and Sander, *A Photo Guide to the Birds of the West Indies,* http://johnbirding.wolweb.nl. A report on a private birding trip to Cuba in 2001 with maps and photos of sites, GPS locations and species list.

Garrido and Kirkconnel, *Birds of Cuba* (2000) Helm/Black, London, or Cornell University Press. Essential if you are visiting only Cuba.

Raffaele et al, *A Guide to the Birds of the West Indies* (1998), Princeton University Press. Birdwatching in the wider Caribbean, thorough and heavy.

Contents

Footnotes

Basic Spanish for travellers

Learning Spanish is a useful part of the preparation for a trip to Cuba and no volumes of dictionaries, phrase books or word lists will provide the same enjoyment as being able to communicate directly with the people of the country you are visiting. It is a good idea to make an effort to grasp the basics before you go. As you travel you will pick up more of the language and the more you know, the more you will benefit from your stay.

General pronunciation

Whether you have been taught the 'Castilian' pronounciation (*z* and *c* followed by *i* or *e* are pronounced as the *th* in think) or the 'American' pronounciation (they are pronounced as *s*), you will encounter little difficulty in understanding either. Regional accents and usages vary, but the basic language is essentially the same everywhere.

Vowels

a	as in English *cat*
e	as in English *best*
i	as the *ee* in English *feet*
o	as in English *shop*
u	as the *oo* in English *food*
ai	as the *i* in English *ride*
ei	as *ey* in English *they*
oi	as *oy* in English *toy*

Consonants

Most consonants can be pronounced more or less as they are in English. The exceptions are:

g	before *e* or *i* is the same as *j*
h	is always silent (except in *ch* as in *chair*)
j	as the *ch* in Scottish *loch*
ll	as the *y* in *yellow*
ñ	as the *ni* in English *onion*
rr	trilled much more than in English
x	depending on its location, pronounced *x*, *s*, *sh* or *j*

Spanish words and phrases

Greetings, courtesies

hello	*hola*	I speak Spanish	*hablo español*
good morning	*buenos días*	I don't speak Spanish	*no hablo español*
good afternoon/	*buenas*	do you speak English?	*¿habla inglés?*
evening/night	*tardes/noches*	I don't understand	*no entiendo/*
goodbye	*adiós/chao*		*no comprendo*
pleased to meet you	*mucho gusto*	please speak slowly	*hable despacio por*
see you later	*hasta luego*		*favor*
how are you?	*¿cómo está?*	I am very sorry	*lo siento mucho/*
	¿cómo estás?		*disculpe*
I'm fine, thanks	*estoy muy bien, gracias*	what do you want?	*¿qué quiere?*
I'm called...	*me llamo...*		*¿qué quieres?*
what is your name?	*¿cómo se llama?*	I want	*quiero*
	¿cómo te llamas?	I don't want it	*no lo quiero*
yes/no	*sí/no*	leave me alone	*déjeme en paz/*
please	*por favor*		*no me moleste*
thank you (very much)	*(muchas) gracias*	good/bad	*bueno/malo*

Questions and requests

Have you got a room for two people?	¿Tiene una habitación para dos personas?
How do I get to_?	¿Cómo llego a_?
How much does it cost?	¿Cuánto cuesta? ¿cuánto es?
I'd like to make a long-distance phone call	Quisiera hacer una llamada de larga distancia
Is service included?	¿Está incluido el servicio?
Is tax included?	¿Están incluidos los impuestos?
When does the bus leave (arrive)?	¿A qué hora sale (llega) el autobús?
When?	¿Cuándo?
Where is_?	¿Dónde está_?
Where can I buy tickets?	¿Dónde puedo comprar boletos?
Where is the nearest petrol station?	¿Dónde está la gasolinera más cercana?
Why?	¿Por qué?

Basics

bank	el banco	market	el mercado
bathroom/toilet	el baño	note/coin	le billete/la moneda
bill	la factura/la cuenta	police (policeman)	la policía (el policía)
cash	el efectivo	post office	el correo
cheap	barato/a	public telephone	el teléfono público
credit card	la tarjeta de crédito	supermarket	el supermercado
exchange house	la casa de cambio	ticket office	la taquilla
exchange rate	el tipo de cambio	traveller's cheques	los cheques de viajero/
expensive	caro/a		los travelers

Getting around

aeroplane	el avión	insured person	el/la asegurado/a
airport	el aeropuerto	to insure yourself against	asegurarse contra
arrival/departure	la llegada/salida	luggage	el equipaje
avenue	la avenida	motorway, freeway	el autopista/la
block	la cuadra		carretera
border	la frontera	north, south, west, east	norte, sur, oeste
bus station	la terminal de		(occidente), este
	autobuses/camiones		(oriente)
bus	el bus/el autobús/	oil	el aceite
	el camión	to park	estacionarse
collective/	el colectivo	passport	el pasaporte
fixed-route taxi		petrol/gasoline	la gasolina
corner	la esquina	puncture	el pinchazo/
customs	la aduana		la ponchadura
first/second class	primera/segunda clase	street	la calle
left/right	izquierda/derecha	that way	por allí/por allá
ticket	el boleto	this way	por aquí/por acá
empty/full	vacío/lleno	tourist card/visa	la tarjeta de turista
highway, main road	la carretera	tyre	la llanta
immigration	la inmigración	unleaded	sin plomo
insurance	el seguro	to walk	caminar/andar

Accommodation

air conditioning	el aire acondicionado	power cut	el apagón/corte
all-inclusive	todo incluido	restaurant	el restaurante
bathroom, private	el baño privado	room/bedroom	el cuarto/la habitación
bed, double/single	la cama matrimonial/ sencilla	sheets	las sábanas
		shower	la ducha/regadera
blankets	las cobijas/mantas	soap	el jabón
to clean	limpiar	toilet	el sanitario/excusado
dining room	el comedor	toilet paper	el papel higiénico
guesthouse	la casa de huéspedes	towels, clean/dirty	las toallas limpias/ sucias
hotel	el hotel		
noisy	ruidoso	water, hot/cold	el agua caliente/fría
pillows	las almohadas		

Health

aspirin	la aspirina	diarrhoea	la diarrea
blood	la sangre	doctor	el médico
chemist	la farmacia	fever/sweat	la fiebre/el sudor
condoms	los preservativos, los condones	pain	el dolor
		head	la cabeza
contact lenses	los lentes de contacto	period	la regla
contraceptives	los anticonceptivos	sanitary towels	las toallas femeninas
contraceptive pill	la píldora anti- conceptiva	stomach	el estómago
		altitude sickness	el soroche

Family

family	la familia	boyfriend/girlfriend	el novio/la novia
brother/sister	el hermano/la hermana	friend	el amigo/la amiga
daughter/son	la hija/el hijo	married	casado/a
father/mother	el padre/la madre	single/unmarried	soltero/a
husband/wife	el esposo (marido)/ la esposa		

Months, days and time

January	enero	Monday	lunes
February	febrero	Tuesday	martes
March	marzo	Wednesday	miércoles
April	abril	Thursday	jueves
May	mayo	Friday	viernes
June	junio	Saturday	sábado
July	julio	Sunday	domingo
August	agosto		
September	septiembre	at one o'clock	a la una
October	octubre	at half past two	a las dos y media
November	noviembre	at a quarter to three	a cuarto para las tres/ a las tres menos quince
December	diciembre		
		it's one o'clock	es la una

it's seven o'clock	son las siete	in ten minutes	en diez minutos
it's six twenty	son las seis y veinte	five hours	cinco horas
it's five to nine	son las nueve menos cinco	does it take long?	¿tarda mucho?

Numbers

one	uno/una	sixteen	dieciséis
two	dos	seventeen	diecisiete
three	tres	eighteen	dieciocho
four	cuatro	nineteen	diecinueve
five	cinco	twenty	veinte
six	seis	twenty-one	veintiuno
seven	siete	thirty	treinta
eight	ocho	forty	cuarenta
nine	nueve	fifty	cincuenta
ten	diez	sixty	sesenta
eleven	once	seventy	setenta
twelve	doce	eighty	ochenta
thirteen	trece	ninety	noventa
fourteen	catorce	hundred	cien/ciento
fifteen	quince	thousand	mil

Food

avocado	el aguacate	goat	el chivo
baked	al horno	grapefruit	la toronja/el pomelo
bakery	la panadería	grill	la parrilla
banana	el plátano	grilled/griddled	a la plancha
beans	los frijoles/ las habichuelas	guava	la guayaba
beef	la carne de res	ham	el jamón
beef steak or pork fillet	el bistec	hamburger	la hamburguesa
boiled rice	el arroz blanco	hot, spicy	picante
bread	el pan	ice cream	el helado
breakfast	el desayuno	jam	la mermelada
butter	la mantequilla	knife	el cuchillo
cake	el pastel	lime	el limón
chewing gum	el chicle	lobster	la langosta
chicken	el pollo	lunch	el almuerzo/la comida
chilli or green pepper	el ají/pimiento	meal	la comida
clear soup, stock	el caldo	meat	la carne
cooked	cocido	minced meat	el picadillo
dining room	el comedor	onion	la cebolla
egg	el huevo	orange	la naranja
fish	el pescado	pepper	el pimiento
fork	el tenedor	pasty, turnover	la empanada/ el pastelito
fried	frito	pork	el cerdo
garlic	el ajo	potato	la papa

prawns	los camarones	spoon	la cuchara
raw	crudo	squash	la calabaza
restaurant	el restaurante	squid	los calamares
salad	la ensalada	supper	la cena
salt	la sal	sweet	dulce
sandwich	el bocadillo	to eat	comer
sauce	la salsa	toasted	tostado
sausage	la longaniza/el chorizo	turkey	el pavo
scrambled eggs	los huevos revueltos	vegetables	los legumbres/vegetales
seafood	los mariscos	without meat	sin carne
soup	la sopa	yam	el camote

Drink

beer	la cerveza	ice/without ice	el hielo/sin hielo
boiled	hervido/a	juice	el jugo
bottled	en botella	lemonade	la limonada
camomile tea	la manzanilla	milk	la leche
canned	en lata	mint	la menta
coffee	el café	rum	el ron
coffee, white	el café con leche	soft drink	el refresco
cold	frío	sugar	el azúcar
cup	la taza	tea	el té
drink	la bebida	to drink	beber/tomar
drunk	borracho/a	water	el agua
firewater	el aguardiente	water, carbonated	el agua mineral con gas
fruit milkshake	el batido/licuado	water, still mineral	el agua mineral sin gas
glass	el vaso	wine, red	el vino tinto
hot	caliente	wine, white	el vino blanco

Key verbs

to go	**ir**	there is/are	hay
I go	voy	there isn't/aren't	no hay
you go (familiar)	vas		
he, she, it goes,		**to be**	**ser**	**estar**
you (formal) go	va	I am	soy	estoy
we go	vamos	you are	eres	estás
they, you (plural) go	van	he, she, It is,		
		you (formal) are	es	está
to have (possess)	**tener**	we are	somos	estamos
I have	tengo	they, you (plural) are	son	están
you (familiar) have	tienes		
he, she, it,		
you (formal) have	tiene	This section has been assembled on the basis of glossaries
we have	tenemos	compiled by André de Mendonça and David Gilmour of
they, you (plural) have	tienen	South American Experience, London, and the Latin American
		Travel Advisor, No 9, March 1996

Index → Entries in bold refer to maps

Acknowledgements

This fifth edition was revised and updated with the welcome help of a team of researchers. Sarah Cameron and Claire Boobbyer travelled the length and breadth of the island between them but much of the hard labour was carried out by Sarah's long-standing friends in Cuba: Federico Llanes was of invaluable help in Havana, always on call to answer queries; Omelio Moreno and family in Santa Clara gave her the benefit of an experienced eye and thorough updating of the text; Julio Muñoz in Trinidad checked, revised and checked again; Juan Carlos Otaño in Pinar del Río kept his ear to the ground with frequent bulletins on what was going on. In addition, with the invaluable assistance of the Moreno address book, this year Sarah found a small army of helpers covering nearly every town and city in Cuba who were kind enough to research, check and update their patch in the book: Mayra Rodríguez Vera and family in Matanzas, María Caridad (Kuki) Alonso Maya in Cienfuegos, Waldo Rodríguez del Rey in Cienfuegos, Pedro Hernández Castro in Sancti Spíritus, Lisbeth Guevara Machado in Morón, Miriam Guerra de la Cruz in Camagüey, Santiago and Consuelo Andraca in Holguín, Arturo and Esmeralda Guerra in Bayamo, Gladys Domenech Castillo, her niece Keyla Díaz Hernández and Adela Acosta Vaillant (of Sol y Son) in Santiago de Cuba and Andrés Cruzata Rigores in Baracoa. Sarah is also grateful to the many *casa particular* owners who helped provide information and insight into the current state of affairs in Cuba and developments in tourism there, particularly María Teresa Lorento Orozco in Sancti Spíritus, Rafael Requejo in Camagüey and Maite Valor in Morón. The book has surely benefited from the knowledge and experience of so many Cubans, making it the most authoritative in its field.

Thanks are also due to all the readers who have sent in information since the last edition in 2004, to Philippa Farrant for being such an easy-going travelling companion to Sarah and last, but definitely not least, to Ben Box, for pulling out all the stops and helping her at home to get the book finished.

Claire Boobbyer would also like to thank the many Cubans who helped her across Cuba.

Specialist contributors Art, architecture and literature by **Gavin Clark**; Music by **Dave Willetts**, with additional material by **Rufus Boulting-Vaughan**; Cinema by **Catherine Davies**, with assistance from **Steve Wilkinson** and updated by Sarah Cameron; Che Guevara by **Patrick Symmes**. Afro-Cuban religion by **Meic Haines**. Geology and climate by **Mark Wilson**.

About the author

After a degree in Latin American Studies **Sarah Cameron** has been travelling and writing on the Americas ever since, both as an economist and as an author for Footprint Handbooks. Initially moonlighting for the South American Handbook while working for a British bank, in 1990 she parted company with the world of finance and has been contributing to the expansion of Footprint titles ever since. Sarah still dabbles in South America but concentrates on the Caribbean and is the author of Footprint Caribbean Islands as well as individual island titles such as Cuba, the Dominican Republic, Barbados, St Lucia, Antigua and the Leeward Islands. When she is not travelling around the Caribbean sampling beaches and rum cocktails, she retreats to her 17th-century farmhouse in rural Suffolk (England).

Credits

Footprint credits
Project editor: Felicity Laughton
Layout and production: Emma Bryers
Picture editors: Kassia Gawronski, Rob Lunn
Maps: Kevin Feeney
Series design: Mytton Williams
Proofreader: Ria Gane

Managing Director: Andy Riddle
Commercial Director: Patrick Dawson
Publisher: Alan Murphy
Publishing Managers: Jo Williams,
Felicity Laughton
Digital Editor: Alice Jell
Design: Rob Lunn
Picture research: Kassia Gawronski

Marketing: Liz Harper, Hannah Bonnell
Sales: Jeremy Parr
Advertising: Renu Sibal
Finance and administration:
Elizabeth Taylor

Photography credits
Front cover: David Norton Photography/
Alamy
Back cover: Imagebrokers/Alamy

Printed in India by Aegean Offset Printers,
New Delhi

Footprint feedback

We try as hard as we can to make each
Footprint guide as up to date as possible
but, of course, things always change. If you
want to let us know about your experiences –
good, bad or ugly – then don't delay, go to
www.footprintbooks.com and send in
your comments.

Publishing information
Footprint Cuba
5th edition
© Footprint Handbooks Ltd
February 2010

ISBN: 978 1 906098 88 9
CIP DATA: A catalogue record for this book
is available from the British Library

® Footprint Handbooks and the Footprint
mark are a registered trademark of Footprint
Handbooks Ltd

Published by Footprint
6 Riverside Court
Lower Bristol Road
Bath BA2 3DZ, UK
T +44 (0)1225 469141
F +44 (0)1225 469461
www.footprintbooks.com

Distributed in the USA by Globe Pequot Press,
Guilford, Connecticut

Every effort has been made to ensure that
the facts in this guidebook are accurate.
However, travellers should still obtain
advice from consulates, airlines, etc about
travel and visa requirements before travelling.
The authors and publishers cannot accept
responsibility for any loss, injury or
inconvenience however caused.

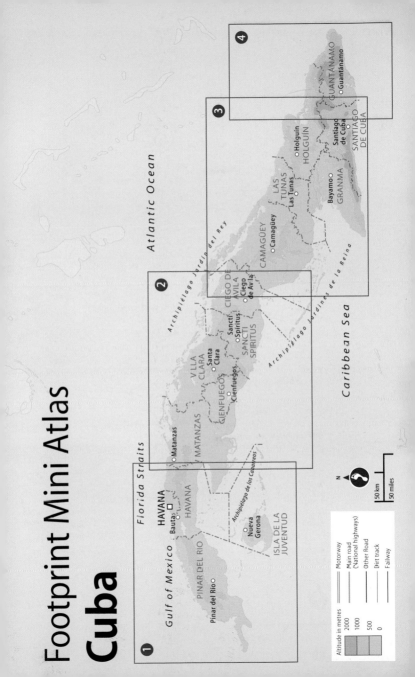

Footprint Mini Atlas
Cuba

Map 1

Gulf of Mexico

Cayo Levisa

Palma Rubia

Archipiélago de los Colorados y de Santa Isabel

Cayo Arenas

Cayo Inés de Soto

Manuel Sanguily

El Rosario

Parque Nacional La Güira

Cayo Jutías

Puerto Esperanza

La Palma

San Cayetano

Pico Grande (521m)

San Andrés

Santa Lucía

Parque Nacional Viñales

Viñales

Ancón

Pan de Azúcar (616m)

Punta Tabaco

Minas de Matahambre

El Moncada

Pilotos

Consolación del Sur

Dimas

Santa Rita

Sumidero

Cabeza

Aguas Claras

Herradura

Cayo Rapado Grande

Sierra de los Órganos

Llanura del Norte

Cayo de Buenavista

Arroyos de Mantua

Pinar del Río

PINAR DEL RÍO

Mazón

Las Ovas

Puerta de Golpe

Mantua

Alonso de Rojas

San Juan y Martínez

Llanura del Sur

El Corojo

La Coloma

Las Cañas

Playa el Guanal

Las Clavelinas

Guane

Isabel Rubio

Boca de Galafre

Punta de Cartas

Playa La Salina

Las Cañas

Golfo de Guanahacabibes

Bolívar

Sandino

Bailén

Cayos de San Felipe

Las Coloradas

La Fé

Cayo Real

Cayo En Coco

Punta El Cajón

Cayos de la Leña

Reserva de la Biósfera Guanahacabibes

Manuel Lazo

Cabo de San Antonio

Las Tumbas

La Bajada

Vallecito

Las Martinas

Caleta Larga

Bahía de Corrientes

María La Gorda

Cabo Corrientes

N

20 km

20 miles

A

B

C

1

2

3

Florida Straits

Santa María del Mar
Cojímar
Guanabo
Camilo Cienfuegos
Santa Cruz del Norte
Jibacoa

HAVANA
Barreras
Campo Florido
San Antonio de Río Blanco
Caraballo
Matanz

Santa Fé
Santa María del Rosario
Jarúco
Casigua
Aguacate

Marina Hemingway
La Boca
Mariel
Bauta
Caimito
Santiago de las Vegas
San José de las Lajas
Catalina de Güines
Ceiba Mocha

San Pedro
Cabañas
HAVANA
Madruga
Unió de Re

El Morrillo
Bahía Honda
San Diego de Núñez
Quiebra Hacha
Guanajay
San Antonio de los Baños
Quivicán
San Antonio de las Vegas
Güines
San Nicolás
Vegas
Cabezas

Luis Carrasco
Pan de Guajaibón (698m)
Reserva Biósfera Sierra del Rosario
Las Terrazas
Las Cañas
Güira de Melena
Melena del Sur
Osvaldo Sanchez
Héctor Molina
Palos
Alácranes
Nueva Paz

Soroa
Candelaria
Artemisa
Alquízar
Boca de Cajío
Batabanó
El Estant

Sierra del Rosario
San Cristóbal
José Martí
Playa Majana
Surgidero de Batabanó
Playa Mayabeque
Punta Mora
Playa Rosario
Playa de Caimito
Playa Tasajera

San Diego de los Baños
Santa Cruz de los Pinos
Los Palacios
Guanimar
Playa de Cajío
Punta Rosario

Paso Real de San Diego
Cantón
Cayería Las Cayamas
Ensenada de la Broa

Cubanacán
Cayos los Guzmanes
Cayería de Buenavista
Punta Gorda
Punta Sombrero

Maspotón
Cayo Manterrey
Ciénaga de Zapata
Maneadero
Ciénaga

Playa Dayaniguas
Punta Curujuyu
Cayos del Hambre
Parque Naci Ciénaga de Z

Punta del Gato
Cayo Las Gordas

Cayo de la Pipa
Cayo Juan Ruiz
Cayería de Diego Pérez

Cayos de Mangles
Cayos La Manteca
Cayo Grande

Cayos de Tirry
Nueva Gerona
Cayos de los Inglesitos
Cayo Rabihorcado

Cayos de los Barcos
Playa Bibijagua
Archipiélago de los Canarreos

Reserva Ecológica Los Indios-San Felipe
Presidio Modelo
Júcaro
Cayo San Juan
Cayo Tablones
Cayo Pasaje

Cayos Los Indios
Sierra de Casada
La Fé
La Reforma
Cayo Divisa de Piedra

Punta Buenavista
Siguanea
Julio Antonio Mella
Cayo Matías
Cayo del Rosario

Parque Nacional Punta Francés-Punta Pedernales
Cayo Piedra
Punta del Este
Cayo Campos
Cayo Cantiles

Cocodrilo
Ciénaga de Lanier

Playa Larga

ISLA DE LA JUVENTUD

Caribbean Sea

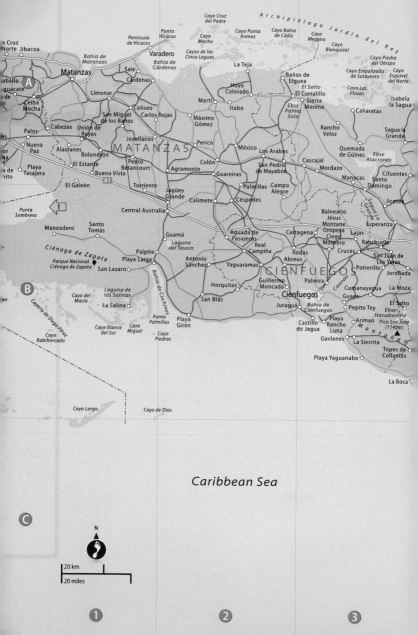

Map 2

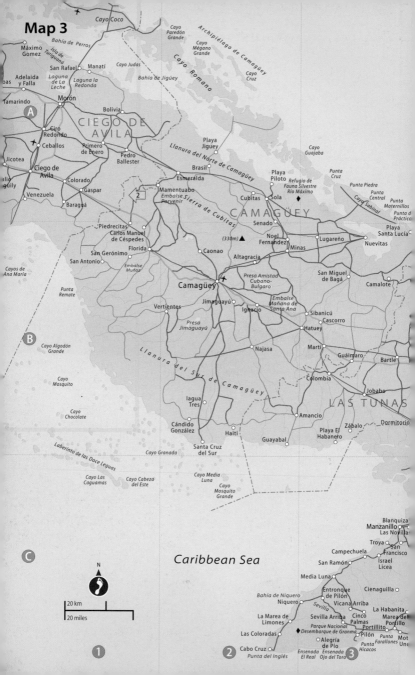

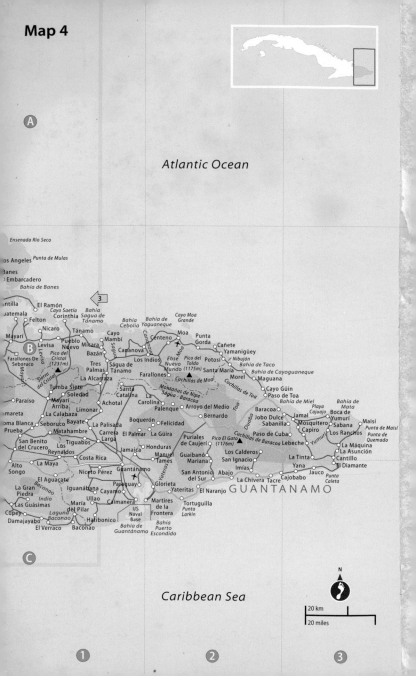

Index

Map symbols

- □ Capital city
- ○ Other city, town
- ⟝⟝ International border
- ⟝⟝ Regional border
- ⊖ Customs
- ⬭ Contours (approx)
- ▲ Mountain, volcano
- ⥴ Mountain pass
- ⤴ Escarpment
- ⬡ Glacier
- ▨▨ Salt flat
- ▨ Rocks
- ▨▨ Seasonal marshland
- ▨ Beach, sandbank
- ⟋ Waterfall
- ⌁ Reef
- ═ Motorway
- ━ Main road
- ─ Minor road
- ┅ Track
- ⋯ Footpath
- ── Railway
- ⊢▪ Railway with station
- ✈ Airport
- ⊟ Bus station
- Ⓜ Metro station

- ---- Cable car
- ╫╫╫ Funicular
- ⛴ Ferry
- ⊏⊐ Pedestrianized street
- Σ ⊂ Tunnel
- → One way-street
- ⫿⫿⫿ Steps
- ⤫ Bridge
- ▃▃ Fortified wall
- ▨▨ Park, garden, stadium
- ⊜ Sleeping
- ⦿ Eating
- ⦿ Bars & clubs
- ▬ Building
- ▪ Sight
- ✝✝ Cathedral, church
- ⛩ Chinese temple
- ⛩ Hindu temple
- ▲ Meru
- ⛩ Mosque
- ⌂ Stupa
- ✡ Synagogue
- ▪ Tourist office
- ⏚ Museum
- ✉ Post office
- ⓟ Police

- Ⓢ Bank
- @ Internet
- ♪ Telephone
- ⓜ Market
- ⊞ Medical services
- Ⓟ Parking
- ⛽ Petrol
- ⛳ Golf
- ⛏ Archaeological site
- ◆ National park, wildlife reserve
- ✿ Viewing point
- ▲ Campsite
- ⌂ Refuge, lodge
- ⛫ Castle, fort
- ⟍ Diving
- ♈♈♈ Deciduous, coniferous, palm trees
- ⇧ Hide
- ⚘ Vineyard, winery
- ⚗ Distillery
- ⟆ Shipwreck
- ✕ Historic battlefield
- ▧ Detail map
- ◁ Related map